HANDBOOK OF

Water Use
AND Conservation

HANDBOOK OF

Water Use
AND Conservation

AMY VICKERS

WATERPLOW PRESS™

Amherst, Massachusetts

WaterPlow Press
P.O. Box 2475
Amherst, MA 01004-2475
Tel. (413) 253-1520 • Fax (413) 253-1521
www.waterplowpress.com • sales@waterplowpress.com

The registered trademark for WaterPlow Press and the registered copyright for the WaterPlow Press colophon are owned by Amy Vickers & Associates, Inc., Amherst, MA.

Cover photo © 2012, 2010, 2001 by Amy Vickers & Associates, Inc.

First edition
ISBN-13: 978-1-931579-09-4 (Paperback-*this copy*)
ISBN-13: 978-1-931579-07-0 & ISBN-10: 1-931579-07-5 (Hard cover-previous printings)
Fourth printing June 2012

Printed in the United States of America on recycled paper

9 8 7 6 5 4

Library of Congress Cataloging-in-Publication Data

Vickers, Amy
    Handbook of water use and conservation: homes, landscapes,
businesses, industries, farms / by Amy Vickers.
    p. cm.
    Includes index.
    ISBN 1-931579-07-5 (alk. paper)
1. Water conservation—Handbooks, manuals, etc.
2. Water efficiency—Handbooks, manuals, etc.
3. Water consumption—United States—Handbooks, manuals, etc.
4. Water use—United States—Handbooks, manuals, etc.
5. Water conservation projects—Planning—Handbooks, manuals, etc.
I. Vickers, Amy II. Title.
  TD388.V53 2001
  333.91'16 21
                                                            99-025179

WaterPlow Press books are available at special quantity discounts for use in academic, corporate, government, and utility training programs and to use as premiums and sales promotions. For more information, please contact the Director of Special Sales, WaterPlow Press, P.O. Box 2475, Amherst, MA 01004-2475.

With my deepest gratitude and affection,
I dedicate this book
to my mother

J U D I T H

dis manibus sacris

whose enduring love, wit, and courage
have inspired my life immeasurably

Contents

1 Planning a Successful Water Conservation Program, 1

2 Residential and Domestic Water Use and Efficiency Measures, 11

3 Landscape Water Use and Efficiency Measures, 139

      *Select Native, Drought-Resistant, or Low-Water-Use Turf Grasses • Select
      Native or Low-Water-Use Plants • Avoid Invasive Plants • Verify Growing
      Conditions Before Purchasing Plants • Consider Microclimates • Group
      Plants by Similar Water Needs (Hydrozones) • Establish Plants Properly*

4 Industrial, Commercial, and Institutional Water Use and Efficiency Measures, 229

5 Agricultural Water Use and Efficiency Measures, 329

6 The Water Conservation Network, 395

ABOUT THE AUTHOR

AMY VICKERS is an engineer with an independent consulting practice that specializes in water conservation and integrated resources management. President of Amy Vickers & Associates, Inc., based in Amherst, Massachusetts, for more than a decade, Vickers has worked with water utilities, private companies, government agencies, and other organizations throughout the United States, Canada, and overseas. She is also a frequent speaker at national and international conferences related to innovative water and environmental technologies, policies, and programs.

In addition to publishing numerous professional papers and articles on water conservation measures, trends, and policy, Vickers was author of the federal water efficiency standards for plumbing fixtures adopted by the U.S. Energy Policy Act of 1992. Prior to that, in 1988 she wrote an amendment to the Massachusetts Plumbing Code requiring 1.6 gallon per flush toilets, an initiative that 16 other states followed. Vickers has also contributed to the development of several educational and commercial software programs, including the "Greening of the White House CD-ROM" and the "Green Home CD-ROM."

Before starting her own consulting practice, Vickers worked in Boston with the engineering firm of Brown and Caldwell Consultants and the Massachusetts Water Resources Authority's Capital Engineering Department. Prior to her move to Boston, she served as director of the New York City Council's Environmental Protection Committee, where she directed a wide range of city legislative and budgetary matters pertaining to the environment, including water supply and water quality, watershed protection, hazardous materials management, solid waste, recycling, and air pollution. During her tenure with the city council, Vickers directed the drafting of several bills on hazardous materials emergency management and asbestos removal that were passed into law.

Vickers holds an M.S. in engineering from Dartmouth College and a B.A. in philosophy from New York University. A member of the American Water Works Association (AWWA) and its Water Conservation Division, she also serves on the association's Water Accountability Committee. For six years she served as an appointed member of the Editorial Advisory Board of *Journal AWWA*. In addition to her work in the water field, Vickers is a member of the National Writers Union and a lifetime member of the International Dark Sky Association, an organization dedicated to preservation of the natural dark sky.

To contact the author, please direct correspondence to:
ava-inc@amyvickers.com

ACKNOWLEDGMENTS

OVER THE SEVERAL YEARS of researching and writing this book, I was fortunate to receive support and encouragement from many kind and generous people. I am enormously grateful to all of them.

My thanks go first to the American Water Works Association and the members of AWWA's Conservation Division. For more than a decade, the Conservation Division has been the "Central Station" for the U.S. water conservation community, and it has nurtured my work and introduced me to many colleagues and friends. Without the members of the AWWA Conservation Division, this book would probably never have been written. In particular, I would like to thank those who have served as division chair: Mary Ann Dickinson, executive director of the California Urban Water Conservation Council, Sacramento, California; Jeff Featherstone, deputy executive director, Delaware River Basin Commission, West Trenton, New Jersey; Tony Gregg, manager of water conservation, City of Austin, Texas; and John Olaf Nelson, John Olaf Nelson Water Resources Management, Petaluma, California. Thanks also to Liz Gardener, manager of conservation at Denver Water, Denver, Colorado, a long-time member of the division and an unwavering supporter of its mission.

Access to good research and information on water use and conservation was key to writing this book, and AWWA's staff was very helpful in this regard. In particular, my thanks to Rick Harmon, technical and educational programs manager. On many occasions, I also utilized WaterWiser®, the Water Efficiency Clearinghouse, located at AWWA's Denver headquarters, and found it to be invaluable.

Nancy Zeilig, an independent editor based in Denver, Colorado, took on the task of honing my manuscript for publication, and I am deeply grateful to her. She applied her editorial expertise with great insight and worked long hours to ensure that this book met the editorial standards expected by water professionals and academicians. To many in the water industry, Nancy is well known as the former editor of *Journal AWWA*, a position she held for 19 years. During her tenure, Nancy helped make the *Journal* one of the most respected professional publications in the drinking water field. It was a privilege to have her edit this book.

Warm and special thanks to Maripat Murphy, a Denver-based independent editor and writer who stepped in with her expert editor's eye during the book's final prepublication proofing stages. Maripat, who also serves as an editorial consultant to *Journal AWWA*, made a number of keen observations and suggestions, and I very much appreciate her contributions.

The dynamic transformation of my manuscript and hundreds of reference tables and illustrations into a book was crafted by Potter Publishing Studio in Shelburne Falls, Massachusetts. I owe special thanks to Jeff Potter, editorial and creative director, for bringing his fresh ideas about book design and production to this project. Given the complexities of producing a technical book, Jeff's thoughtful and patient approach was a real asset that helped keep the project moving forward. My thanks also to designers Soren Johnson and Ben Shippee who lent their creativity and helped fine-tune the many details that went into production.

This book was enhanced by the thoughtful comments and suggestions of twelve reviewers who read the draft manuscript and shared their particular areas of water conservation expertise. Many thanks to Janice Beecher, Ph.D, president of Beecher Policy Research, Inc., Indianapolis, Indiana; Baryohay Davidoff, Ph.D., chief, Agricultural Water Conservation Unit, California Department of Water Resources, Sacramento, California; Sandi Douglas Edgemon, former research engineer, Pacific Northwest National Laboratory, Richland, Washington; John Flowers, Water Efficiency Program director, Office of Wastewater Management, U.S. Environmental Protection Agency, Washington, D.C; Warren Liebold, director of technical services/conservation, New York City Department of Environmental Protection, Corona, New York; Fox McCarthy, Water Sourcebook coordinator, Georgia Water Wise Council, Conyers, Georgia; Sandra Postel, director, Global Water Policy Project, Amherst, Massachusetts; Marsha Prillwitz, environmental specialist, California Department of Water Resources, Sacramento, California; Tracy Slavin, water conservation specialist, U.S. Bureau of Reclamation, Sacramento, California; John T. Sutton, manager, Water Conservation, Texas Water Development Board, Austin, Texas; Jon Sweeten, P.E., engineer, Conservation Programs, Metropolitan Water District of Southern California, Los Angeles; and John Wright, consultant and former manager, Water Wiser.

I owe many thanks to the individuals and organizations who provided a number of the photographs and illustrations that are included in this book. Some images were not easy to capture and others required special efforts to prepare. In particular, my thanks to Liz Gardener and Cris Call, Denver Water; Joe Keyser, Montgomery County (Maryland) Department of Environmental Protection; Peter Mayer, Aquacraft, Inc., Boulder, Colorado; Carmon McCain, High Plains Underground Water Conservation District No. 1, Lubbock, Texas; Jim Patchett, Conservation Design Forum, Inc., Elmhurst, Illinois; Jane Ploeser, Phoenix Water Services Department, Arizona; Bret Rappaport, Wild Ones–Natural Landscapers, Ltd., Chicago, Illinois; James B. Smith, JBS Associates, Inc., Houston, Texas; and Frederik van Bolhuis, Financial Resource Mobilization Department, World Bank, Washington, D.C.

Sincere thanks to George Raftelis, president of Raftelis Financial Consulting, PA, Charlotte, North Carolina. I have had the opportunity to know and collaborate with George for more than a decade, and it has always been enjoyable, interesting, and inspiring. George encouraged me to write this book, and his positive thinking and support helped me to get started and keep going to the finish.

I owe many thanks to my clients—water and wastewater utilities, businesses, organizations, government agencies, and others—who have afforded me the opportunity to work with them on a wide variety of interesting and exciting conservation-related projects over the years. I have learned a tremendous amount from my clients, and several projects that we collaborated on are cited in these pages. I also thank my former employers—the Massachusetts Water Resources Authority, Boston, Massachusetts; Brown and Caldwell Consultants, Walnut Creek, California; the New York City Council; and the New York City Department of Environmental Protection—for providing me with challenging and engaging work in the formative years of my water career.

The work and accomplishments of the Water Supply Citizens Advisory Committee of the Massachusetts Water Resources Authority have long been a source of inspiration to me. If more water systems had groups as committed as WSCAC working beside them, I believe that the future of our drinking water supplies would be much brighter. I am very grateful to WSCAC for their many contributions as well as the ways they have supported my work over the years. In particular, I give warm thanks to WSCAC members Bill Elliott, Robie Hubley, and Eileen Simonson.

At key points in this book's development, I was blessed by guidance and assistance from several individuals, especially Eric Linter, Ellen Tadd, and Kathrin Unger. Their sharp insights and practical suggestions were often right on target.

My life has been graced by loving friends who have stayed with me in the long writing of this book. For their attentiveness and understanding, I give heartfelt thanks to Jean Hamerman, Seth Hollander, Stephanie Cooper Schoen, and Caralyn Shapiro. I am particularly grateful to Jean because she opened the door to my water career and our lifetime friendship.

In a place all her own, I owe extra special thanks and appreciation to Sandra Postel. Sandra generously shared her expert knowledge and insights about global water issues and also remained an enthusiastic and steadfast supporter throughout the years that it took me to complete this book. To her I am deeply grateful.

Invisible to my sight but always in my heart, I close these acknowledgments by paying homage to loved ones now passed who shaped my life profoundly and continue to guide me: my mother, Judith; my grandmother, Renee; and my great-grandparents, Anna and Wilbert.

PREFACE

For the Love of Water

"We conserve what we love."

A MIDST THE WORLD'S GROWING POPULATION and increasing demand for more water, many regions around the globe are facing the hard realities of groundwater depletion, chronic drought, dried-up rivers, poor water quality, mounting infrastructure costs, and diminishing alternatives for additional supplies. These constraints are placing limits on how much water will be available—and affordable—in the future. As we peer into the twenty-first century, water conservation is looking far more like an imperative than an option.

"Water is our most precious natural resource" is a refrain expressed by many—from engineers and poets to politicians—yet humanity's actions have too often belied those words. If we truly seek to ensure that the world has enough safe water in the future, then we must act more aggressively to preserve what we claim to hold dear.

I offer this book as a constructive response to the challenge of meeting the water needs of an expanding global population in an economically and environmentally sustainable manner. By understanding *where* and *how* water is used and then applying *effective efficiency technologies and practices*, we can achieve substantial water savings and other benefits in our homes, on lawns and landscapes, at businesses, institutions, factories, and on farms. The water-efficiency measures described in this book constitute the nuts and bolts of water conservation. Collectively, they complement or present sound alternatives to conventional water supply strategies. They represent a new frontier in water engineering and management, territory whose potential has just begun to be explored.

Conservation: The Great Untapped Water Supply

Water conservation has historically been viewed by the mainstream water industry as a standby or temporary source of supply that is typically invoked only during times of drought or other emergency water shortage. This limited view of conservation's role is both outdated and rapidly changing: utilities that have pioneered the use of conservation as a viable long-term supply option have achieved remarkable results, which in some cases have downsized or averted planned water and wastewater system expansions. This approach has saved considerable capital and operating costs for utilities and consumers, avoided environmental degradation, and built political bridges instead of walls.

Consider the outcomes of these successful water conservation programs: Since the late 1980s, the Massachusetts Water Resources Authority (MWRA) has reduced systemwide water requirements in the greater metropolitan Boston area by 25% as a result of implementing a comprehensive demand-reduction program. This feat allowed the cancellation of a plan to dam the Connecticut River—a politically controversial proposal—and saved MWRA's 2.1 million customers more than half a billion dollars in capital expenditures alone. The city of Albuquerque, New Mexico, has reduced per capita demand by 20% since the mid-1990s and has established the goal of a 30% reduction. Since the early 1990s, New York City has saved more than 250 million gallons per day in water and sewer flows through a conservation program that included an aggressive low-volume toilet rebate program involving more than 1 million fixture replacements. These savings allowed the city to avoid spending more than $1 billion to expand a wastewater treatment plant and have indefinitely postponed development of new water supply sources. Seattle, Washington, has reduced its per capita water demand by 20% over the past decade and has a goal of continuing to reduce demand by 1% annually until 2010.

How were these impressive water savings, wastewater flow reductions, avoided costs, and other accomplishments achieved? Through a combination of factors: leadership, political will, commitment to more sustainable water supply and wastewater systems, concern about long-term costs to consumers, and, most important, an understanding of and strategic investment in large-scale, innovative yet dependable water-efficiency technologies and practices.

What I find so intriguing and exciting about these and other examples of successful conservation programs is that no water or wastewater utility has yet exploited its full potential for water conservation or optimized the use of its existing system. Although there are stellar examples of individual homeowners, businesses, government facilities, and farms that have boosted their productive use of water through conservation, most utilities have only scratched the surface of what is possible in their service areas. Systemwide demand reductions of *at least* 25% from conservation may be a reasonable goal for many North American water utilities. As innovations in water conservation continue to progress, I expect the potential savings to rise even higher in the decade ahead.

Proven Measures to Save Water

This handbook describes the water-use characteristics of each major customer category and presents more than 100 state-of-the-art water-efficiency measures or practical "tools" that can be used to reduce and control water demand in each use sector. Factors affecting the efficiency of water use are presented for each category of user—residential and domestic; landscape; industrial, commercial, and institutional; and agricultural. The book discusses sources of water waste and the latest advances in conservation. It also provides water audit steps for assessing water use and opportunities for conservation among user groups. Each chapter contains case studies demonstrating the results achieved through a variety of measures and programs.

Two types of water-efficiency measures are presented: *technologies* and *practices.* Technology or hardware measures can be used to retrofit or replace inefficient water appliances, equipment, devices, fixtures, and processes.

Water-efficiency practices are behavior patterns or management steps and design changes that can modify and lower water use.

Water conservation measures were selected for inclusion in the handbook based on the existence of reliable data to support them as credible water-saving technologies or practices when used appropriately. Baseline performance data, potential water savings and related benefits, estimated costs, applicable codes and standards, implementation considerations, and relevant case studies are provided for nearly every measure. Each measure was carefully researched, and all sources consulted are referenced, both to give due credit to other contributors to the water conservation literature and to direct readers to other information they might find useful.

Chapter 1, *Planning a Successful Water Conservation Program,* outlines ten key planning steps to guide water and wastewater utilities in putting their conservation goals into action. Chapter 2, *Residential and Domestic Water Use and Efficiency Measures,* presents water-efficiency measures that are applicable to residential use and to domestic use in nonresidential settings. Chapter 3, *Landscape Water Use and Efficiency Measures,* describes conservation measures for landscaping and related irrigation practices. Chapter 4, *Industrial, Commercial, and Institutional Water Use and Efficiency Measures,* presents water-saving measures applicable to industrial, commercial, and institutional (e.g., municipal and public) buildings and facilities. Chapter 5, *Agricultural Water Use and Efficiency Measures,* describes on-farm water conservation measures for agricultural irrigation water users. Chapter 6, *The Water Conservation Network,* identifies some of the organizations, government agencies, publications, directories of manufacturers, and Internet resources related to water conservation.

The handbook includes eight appendices to aid in water conservation research and planning, program implementation, and policy activities. The standard unit of water measurement used in the handbook is usually gallons. A list of conversion factors for other units and related technical measurements, plus a glossary of terms, appears at the end of the book.

Conservation: Building a Water Trust

Given the Earth's limited water budget, conservation is essential if we are to build a water trust, an endowment that generations to come can rely on for their own security and prosperity. By exercising greater stewardship to preserve our water supplies for the future, may we honor and revel in the glorious power of water.

—*Amy Vickers*
Amherst, Massachusetts

Planning a Successful Water Conservation Program

"You must be the change you wish to see in the world."
—Mohandas Gandhi

A CAREFULLY DESIGNED PLAN is the blueprint for a successful water conservation program for water and wastewater systems seeking to implement water-efficiency measures that will reduce water demand and wastewater flows—and thereby achieve a range of economic, environmental, and regulatory benefits. Developing a sound conservation plan is an important activity. This chapter outlines ten key planning steps for putting conservation goals into action.

Water Conservation Planning Approaches

Preparing and implementing a conservation plan can involve a level of commitment and resource allocation comparable to that required for conventional water supply planning efforts. Although supply-side approaches to amplifying water system capacity are different from demand-side methods, both result in increased system capacity so commensurate investments are justifiable. Key steps in developing a comprehensive water conservation plan are outlined in the box "Ten Key Planning Steps to a Successful Water Conservation Program" below. Similar conservation planning approaches include those described in the U.S. Environmental Protection Agency's (USEPA's) *Water Conservation Plan Guidelines* and those incorporated into integrated resource planning for water systems, as described later in this chapter.

Ten Key Planning Steps to a Successful Water Conservation Program

1. Identify Conservation Goals
- Establish water reduction goals (e.g., percent or volume per day)
- Determine the time frame of the program (e.g., short-term drought response, reduction of peak demand, or long-term demand reduction plan) and the planning horizon.
- Avoid or defer capital facility expansion plans and costs for water and wastewater facilities.
- Reduce marginal operating costs (treatment chemicals and energy for pumping, treatment and distribution of water and wastewater).
- Reduce energy combustion by-products (carbon dioxide, nitrogen oxides, and sulfur dioxide) that contribute to air pollution and global warming.
- Reduce environmental impact (e.g., instream flows, groundwater overpumping, effects on wetlands).
- Comply with regulations.
- Increase community involvement in conservation program implementation.
- Boost the utility's credibility as a resource steward.

2. Develop a Water-Use Profile and Forecast
- Identify existing water supply sources and production capacities (average and peak demand).
- Determine the impact of prior conservation efforts and regulatory requirements (e.g., plumbing codes, sprinkling ordinances) on water demand.

- Evaluate forecast(s) of anticipated future water demand, including potential adjustments (e.g., changes in population growth, land use rezoning, conservation effects, regulatory requirements for water-efficient plumbing fixtures and appliances, and other uncertainties).
- Develop a water-use profile by analyzing the current and historical water-use characteristics of each customer category (residential, commercial, landscape irrigation, industrial, public/institutional, agricultural, and other), numbers of customers, indoor use versus outdoor use, and total, annual average, and peak demand.
- Evaluate system unaccounted-for water—system leaks and losses, meter inaccuracies, unmetered uses, theft, and lost revenues resulting from unaccounted-for water.
- Revise future demand forecasts, taking into account conservation efforts (see the guidelines in step 6, "Analyze Benefits and Costs").

3. Evaluate Planned Facilities
- Forecast total system capacity over the planning horizon (years).
- Project total, annualized, and unit costs of planned expanded or new water supply and wastewater facilities.
- Break down cost projections according to requirements for quantity (e.g., water demand and wastewater flows) versus quality (e.g., regulatory standards for water and wastewater treatment).

4. Identify and Evaluate Conservation Measures
- Identify all conservation measures that save water—"hardware" devices and technologies as well as behavior and management practices.
- Develop a matrix of measures that can be considered options for each customer group, including system unaccounted-for water.
- Evaluate measures in terms of their potential water savings, benefits and costs, implementation considerations, and applicable laws, codes, and standards.
- Assess market saturation for previously implemented measures (the number of customers who have installed and continue to use a conservation device or who continue to follow a specific conservation practice).
- Identify any short-term or long-term socioeconomic, aesthetic, and legal obstacles to implementation of the measures.

5. Identify and Assess Conservation Incentives
- Identify incentives that would motivate water users to accept and install conservation devices or implement conservation measures.
- Assess factors that might be causing customer apathy toward conservation, such as low water and wastewater costs, declining rate structures, customer affluence, a prevailing "perfect green lawn" aesthetic, weak en-

A sound water conservation plan is goal-oriented, cost-effective, and practical in design and implementation. Common goals for conservation programs include reducing water waste, optimizing system capacity, containing customer costs, and minimizing environmental burdens associated with water supply and wastewater management. Because the characteristics and needs of each water system are unique, the goals of water conservation plans differ from one system to another.

Ideally, development of a conservation plan involves the participation of all stakeholders—water managers, planners, engineers, financial administrators, information specialists, the public, businesses, environmental interests, and policymakers. The stakeholders should be involved throughout the planning process, not just at the end during the public hearing or approval stage.

Developing a water-use profile for each customer category—residential, landscape, industrial, commercial, institutional, and agricultural—can require a sig-

The beginning is the most important part of the work."
—Plato

forcement of conservation policies, and customer reluctance to try measures that have no local precedence.

6. Analyze Benefits and Costs
- Estimate the short-term, long-term, average-day, and peak-day water savings that can be achieved by each measure, considering such factors as number of eligible customers, desired participation rate (number of customers needed to accept and adopt a measure), market saturation rate, potential removal of the conservation device or long-term noncompliance rate, and expected life of the measure.
- Estimate conservation program benefits, including utility cost savings (reduced need for additional water supplies; reduced operation and maintenance costs; deferred, downsized or eliminated new facilities; program cost-sharing), customer benefits (lower water, sewer, and energy bills; reduced landscape and property maintenance costs and services), environmental preservation, and utility credibility as a responsible resource steward.
- Estimate conservation program costs, including implementation costs (administration and consultants, hardware and materials, training, field labor, marketing and education efforts, financial incentives, program monitoring and evaluation), initial fluctuations in utility revenues and rate adjustments, and short-term program participant costs (adjustment to new water-use practices, acceptance of new design aesthetics, changes in operation and maintenance of equipment).

- Determine cost-effectiveness of measures based on benefits and costs over the life of the program.
- Compare net implementation costs for conservation with avoided supply-side costs.

7. Select Conservation Measures and Incentives
- Identify quantitative (e.g., water savings, cost-effectiveness of measures, avoidance of capital costs) and qualitative (e.g., ease of implementation, water rights and permits, regulatory approvals) criteria for selecting measures and associated program incentives.
- Evaluate and rank measures using quantitative and qualitative selection criteria.
- Justify why each measure should be selected or rejected.

8. Prepare and Implement the Conservation Plan
- Prepare a conservation plan that describes conservation needs and goals, the water-use profile, conservation incentives and disincentives, the conservation measures selected, benefits and costs of conservation, measures' cost-effectiveness, effects on revenues and rates, program budget and schedule, program marketing and outreach strategies, and processes for monitoring and reporting progress.
- Anticipate and plan necessary (usually short-term) rate adjustments for fluctuations in utility revenues as a result of demand reductions from conservation.
- Present plan to and secure approval from

stakeholders, including utility managers, elected officials, ratepayers, business and community leaders, and regulators.
- Solicit public involvement to secure community "buy-in" and boost customer participation in conservation program efforts.
- Transform the conservation plan into a program by implementing the plan's measures.

9. Integrate Conservation and Supply Plans, Modify Forecasts
- Modify plans for water and wastewater capital facilities, incorporating adjustments necessitated by projected effects of conservation on future demand.
- Evaluate and adjust future contracts for water purchases and related water and wastewater services that are volume-based.
- If appropriate, incorporate the conservation plan into an integrated resource plan that incorporates both supply-side and demand-side issues and needs.

10. Monitor, Evaluate, and Revise Program as Needed
- Monitor and evaluate each measure's effectiveness by assessing actual water savings, customer participation, device retention rates, and program costs and benefits.
- If necessary, adjust the conservation program, based on findings from the monitoring and evaluation process, to ensure that water-saving goals are met.
- Report program results and successes to the public regularly.

It is one thing to find fault with an existing system. It is another thing altogether, a more difficult task, to replace it with an approach that is better."

—Nelson Mandela

nificant amount of data analysis or "crunching." For example, understanding average annual demand versus monthly and daily demand, quantifying outdoor use versus indoor use, ascertaining peak flows, ferreting out top users and inefficient users, and determining other characteristics of water demand are time-consuming and complex tasks. Identifying where, when, and how water is used is a critical pathway to determining which conservation measures will yield the most reliable water savings.

An important component of conservation planning is an analysis of all measures and incentives that could be applied to reduce water demand. Evaluating each option for cost-effectiveness, public acceptance, and impact on water and wastewater capital facility plans, rates and revenues, and the environment is crucial to developing the best mix of program incentives and measures for a particular system. Finally, other key ingredients of a well-planned conservation program are a unifying implementation strategy and ongoing monitoring and evaluation activities that allow the program to be adjusted as needed to realize goals.

Federal Conservation Planning Guidelines for Water Utilities

Water-use efficiency in the United States may be furthered in coming years by federal water conservation planning guidelines that USEPA established for water utilities in 1998. Development of these guidelines was required by the 1996 amendments to the Safe Drinking Water Act[1] to help integrate conservation into water utility capital facility planning.[2]

Given the substantial infrastructure needs of U.S. water systems, USEPA promotes the development of conservation programs to help extend the economic value and life of water and wastewater utility infrastructure assets, thereby ensuring more cost-effective use of ratepayer dollars and public funds allocated to the Drinking Water State Revolving Loan Fund (SRF) and other programs. States can require water systems to prepare a water conservation plan that is consistent with the federal guidelines in order to qualify for a loan under the SRF, but such plans are not required of utilities by federal law or regulation.

USEPA's water conservation plan guidelines set forth three levels of planning based on the size of the population served by a water utility:

• Basic guidelines (for water systems serving 10,000 or fewer people),
• Intermediate guidelines (for water systems serving 10,000 to 100,000 people), and
• Advanced guidelines (for water systems serving more than 100,000 people).

The basic guidelines offer a simplified planning approach that is appropriate for many small water systems. The intermediate and advanced guidelines are designed to lead to development of a comprehensive conservation plan,[3] as outlined in Appendix A, *Contents of a Comprehensive Water Conservation Plan According to the USEPA's Water Conservation Plan Guidelines.*

Integrated Resource Planning for Water

In recent years, conventional approaches to water supply master planning that considered only supply-side options (e.g., new source development or expansion) to meet increasing water demand have been superseded by a more comprehensive model—integrated resource planning (IRP). Endorsed by the American Water Works Association (AWWA),[4] the IRP process encourages water utilities to consider both supply-side as well as demand-side options.[5] IRP emphasizes conservation and demand management as potential alternatives for meeting future water needs because they are often more cost-effective and pose little or no adverse environmental effects compared with conventional strategies. The IRP approach recognizes that the added "capacity" (water savings) achieved through conservation programs is just as tangible and valid as the same unit of supply that would otherwise be produced by conventional supply-side projects.

With the IRP approach, water utilities engage in a dynamic and more open process than that practiced in traditional water supply planning. IRP includes community participation and consideration of social and environmental factors related to water supply management. IRP expert Janice A. Beecher, president of Beecher Policy Research, Inc. in Indianapolis, Indiana, defines water IRP as "a comprehensive form of water utility planning that encompasses least-cost analysis of demand-management and supply-management options, as well as an open and participatory decision-making process, the construction of alternative planning scenarios, and recognition of the multiple institutions concerned with water resources and the competing policy goals among them."[6]

The basic elements of a comprehensive approach to water IRP are outlined in Appendix B, *Basic Elements of a Water Integrated Resource Plan.*

What Constitutes a Conservation Measure?

In my work as an engineer and consultant helping utilities, businesses, and government agencies to develop water conservation plans and programs, I've found it helpful to discuss and define what constitutes a conservation "measure," a conservation "incentive," and a conservation "program," because these terms are often confused. Through the process of identifying specific tools (technologies) and practices (behavior changes)—*measures*—that result in more efficient water use, the strategies required to achieve a particular system's conservation goals become clearer. Without a shared understanding of what constitutes a conservation measure, good intentions often go astray and water savings goals aren't reached.[7, 8]

Most people recognize that a conservation measure saves water or involves using water more efficiently. In practice, however, these definitions often become blurred with conservation *incentives*—public education campaigns, rate strategies, and policies and regulations—that promote conservation and motivate consumers to adopt specific measures. For example, mailing consumers a brochure on water-saving tips can be effective at raising public awareness about the value of conservation, but such an incentive by itself doesn't save a drop of water. Conservation programs that rely on incentive-only approaches may send a conservation message but fail to accomplish the next step, which is getting people to do something practical that saves water directly.

Never doubt that a small group of thoughtful, committed citizens can change the world. Indeed, it's the only thing that ever has."
—Margaret Mead

In summary, a conservation *incentive* increases customer awareness about the value of reducing water use. A conservation *measure* is the device or practice that actually reduces demand. A utility conservation *program* includes a strategic combination of measures and incentives.

Conservation Measures

Conservation or efficiency measures such as those described in subsequent chapters of this book can be grouped into two general categories: (1) "hardware" devices or equipment and (2) behavior or management practices. The "Examples of Conservation Measures" sidebar to the left provides a simple illustration of these points. (Throughout this book, the terms "conservation measure" and "efficiency measure" are used interchangeably.)

Hardware measures are generally more reliable in achieving long-term water savings because they typically need to be installed only once and require no ongoing effort to maintain water savings. For example, a low-volume 1.6 gallon per flush (gpf) toilet installed to replace a leaking 3.5 gpf fixture will have an operational life of at least 20 years, saving considerable amounts of water without any additional effort beyond normal maintenance. In contrast, educating people to adopt low-water-use or native landscaping and irrigation practices, though essential to reducing outdoor water use, requires considerable time, and ongoing reminders are necessary if water-efficient landscape practices are to be maintained.

Comprehensive conservation programs that achieve long-term reductions in water demand typically include both hardware- and behavior-driven measures. Even though the two types of measures require different levels of effort, both are needed to realize conservation goals. For example, outdoor water conservation programs usually emphasize ongoing, efficient landscape management practices (such as shorter lawn watering times) as well as one-time or infrequent hardware measures (such as sprinkler system repairs or upgrades, turf replacement, and improved irrigation system controllers).

Conservation Incentives

Incentives that motivate water users to implement conservation or efficiency measures can be classified into three categories: educational, financial, and regulatory. Examples of these three types of incentives are given in the "Examples of Conservation Incentives" sidebar to the right.

Educational incentives and related outreach activities are usually the first (and sometimes the only) component of utility conservation efforts. Education is essential to any conservation program to make the public aware of the program's goals, benefits, and opportunities to adopt specific water-saving measures. To be effective, incentives should not only increase public awareness about conservation but should also motivate consumers to implement specific measures that yield water savings. Financial and regulatory incentives often garner public attention because they can result in adverse consequences if not heeded. For example, penalties or higher rates for excessive lawn watering have proved to be a strong inducement for many people to guard against outdoor water waste.

Public Education: Conservation for Young and Old

Education programs to raise public awareness about the need for conservation are critical to the success of a comprehensive conservation program (Figure 1.1). Young people, water and sewer ratepayers of the future, are often the focus of public education programs, and numerous materials have been created for them (e.g., the *Water Sourcebook* series, for grades K–2, 3–5, 6–8, and 9–12, distributed to schools by organizations such as the Georgia Water Wise Council and developed by the Tennessee Valley Authority in cooperation with teachers and USEPA).[9] Although school programs to educate youth about water issues and conservation are important, it is also critical that adults be fully informed participants in practical conservation efforts. For example, educating homeowners about water-wise sprinkling practices and providing technical workshops to train industrial and commercial facility managers in water-efficiency technologies and practices are valuable conservation education programs.

Survey research and focus groups on water use often glean information on consumer attitudes that can be used in the design of conservation programs to elicit public attention and participation. For example, a market survey conducted by Seattle Public Utilities found that single-family residential water users were aware of the importance of conservation and often practiced water-wise behavior inside their homes. However, consumer patterns of outdoor water use indicated some inconsistencies with their stated beliefs; some people underestimated their outdoor use and overestimated the effectiveness of their conservation practices (e.g., the amount of time allowed for lawn watering was too long). Survey participants provided several insights that helped define the types of messages to be sent to the public, including the suggestion that educational efforts focus on simple and practical tips to conserve. The study found that among single-family households in the Seattle area, radio advertising was an effective communication tool but that posters and bus signs had less impact (in contrast to cities with large populations who depend on public transportation). The study also found that printed material would be positively received if it was colorful and of high quality and included photos.[10]

Examples of Conservation Incentives

- **Educational**—direct-mail literature, bill inserts, redesigned bills that include historical water consumption information, television and radio advertisements, media coverage, demonstration gardens and projects, school curriculums, conservation checklists developed for specific industries, local workshops and training programs for specialized users (e.g., efficient landscape-irrigation systems and water-efficient turf and plants for homeowners and managers of industrial facilities with cooling towers).

- **Financial**—bill credits, rebates, conservation rate structures, incentive or surcharge fees, cost-sharing with other utilities and businesses, and performance contracting (contractor compensation based on water savings achieved).

- **Regulatory**—water-efficiency policies and ordinances, laws and plumbing codes for water-efficient fixtures and appliances, standards for landscape design (including water-efficient turf, plants, and irrigation systems), irrigation scheduling (allowable days per week and times of day), penalties for outdoor water waste, pollution prevention requirements, and water demand offset requirements for builders.

Figure 1.1
Educational poster to promote water conservation, Massachusetts Water Resources Authority (Photo courtesy of Amy Vickers & Associates, Inc.)

Conservation Pricing Techniques

Increasingly, water utilities are using conservation rates or conservation pricing strategies to promote more efficient water use among residential and non-residential customers. Conservation rate structures can incorporate cost-of-service principles as well as set pricing signals that motivate customers to reduce waste. Conservation rates can be defined as "rates that encourage efficient use of water resources" according to George A. Raftelis, president of Raftelis Financial Consulting, PA in Charlotte, North Carolina, and author of *2000 Water and Wastewater Rate Survey*[11] and *Comprehensive Guide to Water and Wastewater Finance and Pricing.*[12] Conservation rate structures, if properly designed and implemented by a utility, can promote efficient water use and allow the utility to meet essential revenue requirements.

There are four generally accepted conservation rate structures: uniform rates, inverted block rates, seasonal rates, and marginal cost rates.[13] Uniform rates assign the same charge for all customer groups at all levels of consumption (e.g., $2 per 1,000 gallons); uniform rates can be used as an interim step for utilities that are discontinuing use of a declining or decreasing block rate structure (which discourages conservation). Inverted (inclining) block rates increase with water consumption, in contrast to declining block rates, which charge lower rates per incremental volume of water used. Seasonal rates vary during different periods of the year and are typically higher during the summer to discourage inefficient outdoor water use (e.g., excessive lawn sprinkling). Marginal cost rates are based on the cost of providing the next incremental volume (unit of service); marginal cost rates are a step higher than the average cost-of-service rate and thus a deterrent to excessive water use. Excess use rates, not commonly used because of their complexity, are based on customized water budgets or allotments for customers; water demand above acceptable levels triggers an "abusive use" rate that sends a strong price signal to discourage excessive use, particularly during peak lawn-watering periods. A year 2000 survey of water and wastewater service charges assessed by more than 200 utilities in the United States and Canada found that 36 percent of the utilities had a uniform pricing structure, 35 percent had a declining block structure, and 29 percent had an inclining block structure.[14]

A schedule of representative water and sewer utility rates in the United States and their associated marginal cost savings according to a range of reduced volumes is provided in Appendix D, *Water and Sewer Rates, Costs, and Savings by Volume of Use.*

Regulatory Approaches to Conservation

In recent years, regulatory approaches have become powerful tools at the local, state, and national levels in establishing water conservation requirements for virtually every customer sector. For example, local outdoor watering restrictions have helped to limit excessive lawn watering and street runoff; state plumbing code amendments requiring water-efficiency standards for plumbing fixtures have profoundly influenced product designs and markets; and federal laws and regulations have set forth national water-efficiency standards for plumbing fixtures as well as clothes washers and dishwashers (through energy-efficiency standards for hot water). Numerous examples of conservation laws and policies are included in this book; for more information, see the sections on specific conservation measures throughout this book.

~

1. Safe Drinking Water Act Amendments of 1996, U.S. Code 42, Section 300f, Aug. 6, 1996.

2. U.S. Environmental Protection Agency, *Water Conservation Plan Guidelines*, US EPA (EPA-832-D-98-001), Washington, D.C., August 1998, p. xi.

3. U.S. Environmental Protection Agency, *Water Conservation Plan Guidelines*, pp. 12–13.

4. American Water Works Association, *White Paper on Integrated Resource Planning in the Water Industry*, AWWA, Washington, D.C., Dec. 21, 1993.

5. Office of Consumer Advocate, Advance Notice of Proposed Rulemaking: Integrated Resource Planning for Water Utilities (Docket No. L-00930077), Comments of the Office of Consumer Advocate, Harrisburg, Pa., May 24, 1993, p. 2.

6. Janice A. Beecher, "Integrated Resource Planning Fundamentals," *Journal AWWA*, vol. 87, no. 6, 1995, p. 34.

7. Amy Vickers, "So You Think You're Conserving Water?" *Fine Homebuilding*, Fall/Winter 2000, no. 135, pp. 6–8.

8. Amy Vickers, "What Makes a True Conservation Measure?" *Opflow*, vol. 22, no. 6, 1996, pp. 8–9.

9. *Water Sourcebook*, Tennessee Valley Authority, Environmental Education Section, Knoxville, Tenn., May 1994.

10. Preeti Shridhar, "The Right Research: Measuring the Success and Effectiveness of Public Information Programs," *Proc. Conserv96*, AWWA, Denver, Colo., 1996, pp. 597–605.

11. Raftelis Financial Consulting, *2000 Water and Wastewater Rate Survey*, Raftelis Financial Consulting, PA, Charlotte, N.C., 2000.

12. George A. Raftelis, *Comprehensive Guide to Water and Waste Water Finance and Pricing*, second edition, Lewis Publishers, Boca Raton, Fla., 1993.

13. Raftelis, *Comprehensive Guide to Water and Waste Water Finance and Pricing*, p. 212.

14. Raftelis Financial Consulting, *2000 Water and Wastewater Rate Survey*, pp. 1–6.

15. Memorandum of Understanding Regarding Urban Water Conservation in California, California Urban Water Conservation Council, Sacramento, Calif., amended Sept. 16, 1999.

Residential and Domestic Water Use and Efficiency Measures

"Nothing so needs reforming as other people's habits."
—Mark Twain

THIS CHAPTER DESCRIBES residential water use and presents water-efficiency measures that can be applied in the home and in many nonresidential settings where domestic plumbing fixtures and appliances are used. Descriptions of the water-efficiency measures include potential water savings as well as related benefits and costs.

Average indoor and outdoor use—101 gallons per capita per day (gpcd)

Outdoor Use
(31.7 gpcd), 31%

Indoor Use
(69.3 gpcd), 69%

Sources: Indoor use data—Reference 12; outdoor use data—Reference 2

Figure 2.1 Average indoor and outdoor water use in a typical U.S. single-family home

Residential Water Use

Total residential water use in the United States for indoor and outdoor purposes is estimated to average 26,100 million gallons per day (mgd). Consumptive use of water for residential purposes constitutes about 26% of total use, according to the most recently reported survey of national water use by the U.S. Geological Survey.[1] Of total U.S. residential water use, 87% is provided from public water supply sources; the balance is drawn from self-supplied groundwater and surface-water sources.[2]

For public water supply systems in the United States, residential water use in single-family and multifamily dwellings typically represents 50 to 80% of billed urban water demand. Combined indoor and outdoor water use in a single-family American household is estimated to average 101 gallons per capita per day (gpcd),[2] as shown in Figure 2.1. Per capita water use in multifamily dwellings tends to be less, ranging from 45 to 70 gpcd, because these households usually use little or no water outdoors and have fewer fixtures and appliances.

Residential water use varies considerably by region, climate and weather conditions (especially temperature and rainfall), socioeconomic factors, and other customer characteristics. Thus, the 101 gpcd average for single-family users will not be found in all water systems and service areas. For example, a survey of per-capita residential (single-family and multifamily accounts) water use in 13 cities and the United Kingdom[3-11] reflects a broad range in demand, as shown in Figure 2.2. In the United States, regional differences in average per-capita residential demand are primarily attributable to variations in outdoor water use. (See Chapter 3, *Landscape Water Use and Efficiency Measures*, for a more detailed description of outdoor water use in the United States).

Several factors affect the amount of water used in homes, especially single-family detached houses: efficiency of plumbing fixtures and appliances, household income, cost of water and wastewater service, occupancy rates, age and lifestyle of residents, climate, local landscape aesthetic, lawn watering and outdoor water-use practices, and awareness of the need to conserve water. For example, in hot, dry climates, affluent homeowners with large areas of turf tend to have high outdoor water use, whereas low-income households in multifamily buildings use little or no water for landscape irrigation.

Residential Water Users and Customer Classifications

Residential water users include single-family and multifamily customers. Single-family customers typically live in a single detached house with a meter sized at 5/8 or 3/4 inches. Multifamily customers live in buildings containing multiple dwelling units (e.g., apartments, townhouses, garden-style properties, condominiums, and other private-household living spaces). The number of dwelling units included in each multifamily account varies considerably, and thus total water use per account also varies. Without knowing the number of tenants served by multifamily accounts, it is difficult to determine per-capita use for this customer group. Some multifamily dwelling units, particularly those in newly constructed, owner-occupied buildings, are submetered, meaning that each tenant pays directly for water (instead of the cost of water being included in the rent).

Classification of residential customers is not uniform among water utilities. Single-family and multifamily accounts may be classified separately or combined under one residential grouping. Multifamily customers may be listed under single-family or commercial billing categories. Some commercial and multifamily accounts may include mixed-use buildings, such as those with a retail business on the street level and residential apartments on the upper floors.

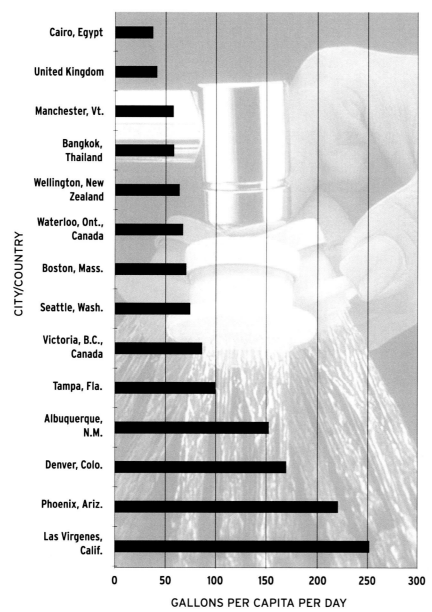

Figure 2.2 Survey of average combined indoor and outdoor residential water reported for 13 cities and the United Kingdom

Sources: References 3–11

Indoor Residential Water Use

Indoor single-family residential water use in North America is reported to average 69.3 gpcd, based on a 1999 empirical study of water use in more than 1,100 homes in 12 cities in the United States and Canada,[12] as shown in Figure 2.3. In most regions of North America, water is used inside the home primarily for two functions: cleaning and sanitation. Indoor residential use typically ranges from 60 to 80 gpcd in households with older (pre-1980) high-volume plumbing fixtures and appliances.

Multifamily water-use characteristics have not been studied as widely as single-family use. In general, people living in apartments and other multifamily dwelling units use less water indoors than people living in houses. Combined indoor and outdoor residential water use for a person living in an apartment or similar multiunit building often ranges from 45 to 70 gpcd, because such users are likely to have fewer appliances (e.g., dishwashers and clothes washers). Exceptions sometimes occur in multifamily buildings occupied by many low-income, unemployed, or elderly people because these populations tend to be at home more during the day and live in buildings with a greater incidence of leakage as well as older, high-volume fixtures and appliances. For example, a study of water use in nearly 2,000 apartments that are managed by the New York City Housing Authority and are occupied primarily by low-income residents and people on public assistance found water use to average 128 gpcd, a figure that is actually lower than averages for many other low-rent apartment buildings in New York City. In some cases, water-use figures for multifamily dwellers can be deceptive because occupancy rates do not count renters who are doubling up with unauthorized relatives and friends.[13]

Affluent Homes Typically Use More Water

Affluent households often have higher-than-average indoor (as well as outdoor) water use because these customers generally consume more goods and services than nonaffluent customers. For example, luxury appliances such as hot tubs and whirlpool baths, multiple-head showers, fish tanks, and fountains demand water not only for operation but also for maintenance and cleaning.

Evaporative Water Coolers Increase Residential Use in Arid Regions

Evaporative water coolers are common residential water-using appliances in hot, arid sections of the western and southwestern United States; these appliances are usually not found in other regions of North America. There are two types of evaporative coolers: nonrecirculating (very water inefficient) and recirculating. A field study in Phoenix found that approximately 46% of that city's single-family customers operate recirculating evaporative coolers, sometimes in conjunction with electric air-conditioning. Water use by the evaporative coolers averaged 66 gallons per household per day (gphd) during the 214-day cooling season, or 15% of total average single-family household demand.[14] (For more information on evaporative coolers, see Chapter 4, *Industrial, Commercial, and Institutional Water Use and Efficiency Measures,* "Evaporative Coolers," under Section 4.7.)

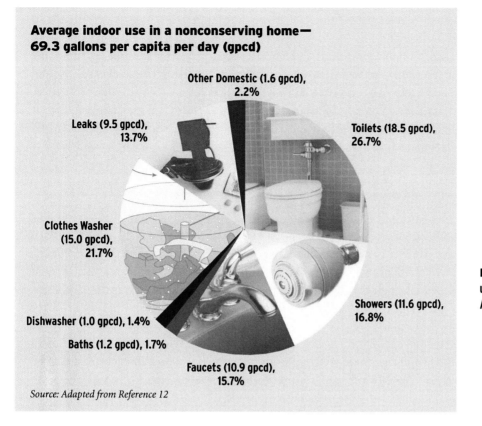

**Average indoor use in a nonconserving home—
69.3 gallons per capita per day (gpcd)**

Other Domestic (1.6 gpcd),
2.2%

Leaks (9.5 gpcd),
13.7%

Toilets (18.5 gpcd),
26.7%

Clothes Washer
(15.0 gpcd),
21.7%

Dishwasher (1.0 gpcd), 1.4%

Baths (1.2 gpcd), 1.7%

Showers (11.6 gpcd),
16.8%

Faucets (10.9 gpcd),
15.7%

Source: Adapted from Reference 12

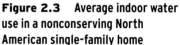

Figure 2.3 Average indoor water use in a nonconserving North American single-family home

Nonrecirculating coolers, which are no longer manufactured in the United States but are still in use from installations that continued until the 1960s, circulate water through the system only once and then dump it into the sewer line attachment. A field survey by the city of Fresno, California, found that some of the 550 nonrecirculating evaporative coolers still in use there may be responsible for as much as 328 million gallons of water use per year. The water use of each cooler varied with its capacity. The 5-ton units were measured to use 14.1 gallons per minute (gpm), 3-ton units use 9.4 gpm, 2-ton units use 6.4 gpm, and 1-ton units use 3.1 gpm. The estimate of total use assumes the units run 8 hours a day, 150 days per summer season (May through September). In an effort to eliminate the inefficient water coolers, Fresno initiated a pilot program to offer residents no-interest loans of up to $3,000 to purchase and install energy-efficient replacements.[15]

Outdoor Single-Family Water Use

Outdoor single-family residential water use for turf and landscape irrigation and other purposes (e.g., car washing, cleaning, and swimming pools) in the United States is estimated to average 31.7 gpcd. This figure, adapted from a U.S. average of 101 gpcd for combined indoor and outdoor residential water use, is based on a national U.S. Geological Survey database of water use reported by public water supply systems.[2] In a separate study, indoor single-family use was reported to average 69.3 gpcd,[16] leaving a balance of 31.7 gpcd attributable to outdoor demand.

Local climatic conditions and landscape design aesthetics often result in outdoor residential water demand that differs from the national average. Actual outdoor water use can range from a few gallons a day to more than 100 gpcd. Hot, dry areas typically use significantly more water than wet, cool regions. A more detailed discussion of residential irrigation characteristics and related efficiency measures is provided in Chapter 3, *Landscape Water Use and Efficiency Measures*.

Climate and Other Factors Influence Outdoor Water Use

The amount of outdoor water use in a given region or within a particular customer group is usually correlated with four key factors: climate, amount of rainfall, water rates and the total cost of water, and household income. For example, a study of five western U.S. cities found that outdoor water use averaged 65% of total single-family residential water demand during the spring and summer growing season.[17] Such averages would typically not apply to other U.S. regions, particularly New England and the Pacific Northwest, because these areas have more rainfall and cooler climates. Findings from water-use studies in Vermont and the metropolitan Boston[18] area reported outdoor water use to be less than 10% of total, year-round residential water demand, and outdoor use was not significantly greater in warm months.

Outdoor Water Use by Multifamily Dwellings Is Often Low

On a per-capita basis, outdoor water use by apartment dwellers in multifamily units tends to be low or even negligible and is typically much lower than that of residents of single-family homes in a given area when measured by household unit. Exceptions can include customers living in affluent multifamily complexes featuring large irrigated landscaped areas, swimming pools, fountains, and maintenance practices involving water, such as sidewalk cleaning.

Sources of Residential Water Waste

Water waste inside the home can result from old, inefficient plumbing fixtures and appliances, leaking toilets and faucets, and wasteful water-use habits. Common water-wasting behavior includes letting faucets run when they are not being used (e.g., while brushing teeth, when washing but not directly rinsing dishes, or when filling a container) and washing less than full loads of clothes or dishes. Excessive outdoor water use and irrigation are also common sources of unnecessary use, particularly in hot, dry regions and in water service areas with many affluent customers and automatic irrigation systems.

To some extent, advances in water-efficient plumbing fixtures and appliances, which reduce indoor use, can be counteracted by the installation of new products that increase water demand, particularly in affluent households. More homeowners are installing water-intensive whirlpool baths and hot tubs than in years past. Approximately four out of ten renovated bathrooms in the United States now include whirlpool bathtubs, which use 21 to 61 gallons of water, according to a 1998 survey;[19] conventional bathtubs hold 30 to 50 gallons.[20]

Similarly, the concept of what constitutes a shower has been expanded beyond its basic personal hygiene function to create a market for integrated shower–whirlpool systems whose multihead water jets provide full-body coverage that use large volumes of water. For example, the Kohler Company's BodySpa™ Hydro-Massage Systems product line offers consumers a "water revolution in bathing and personal care." The 10-Jet BodySpa™ System, a showerlike enclosure, includes a showerhead (for body washing) plus a separate "tower" featuring a cascading waterfall above 10 water jets that can deliver up to 80 gpm of recirculating water for "hydro-massage" purposes.[21] Similar products are offered by other manufacturers. Collectively, they negate a portion of the water savings resulting from recent improvements in basic plumbing fixture efficiencies.

Changes are occurring in outdoor water use as well. Although some homeowners are adopting water-efficient landscaping (e.g., native and Xeriscape) and irrigation practices, installation of automatic irrigation systems appears to be a trend in the construction of new single-family homes. Automatic irrigation systems were less common in years past. Perhaps their increase reflects greater affluence as well as the reality that working adults are willing to devote less time to such tasks as dragging a hose to water their lawn and garden. Further, home gardening and the desire for perfect-looking lawns are becoming more popular, particularly among the baby-boomer generation of homeowners.

Advances in Indoor Residential Water-Use Efficiency

Indoor residential water demand has been declining in many U.S. households since the mid-1980s. A 1999 study of residential water use conducted for the American Water Works Association (AWWA) Research Foundation found that single-family indoor water use in more than 1,100 homes averaged 69.3 gpcd,[22] 10% less than the indoor use of 77.3 gpcd reported in 1984 for the average nonconserving home. The 1984 data were based on a study of residential water use conducted for the U.S. Department of Housing and Urban Development.[23]

Increased Water Efficiency of Plumbing Fixtures and Appliances

Reductions in indoor U.S. household water use since the mid-1980s stem primarily from steady improvements in the efficiency of plumbing fixtures and appliances. These improvements have resulted from state and national legislative initiatives and voluntary industry standards. In 1989, Massachusetts became the first state to require 1.6 gallon per flush (gpf) toilets.[24] Sixteen more states followed suit over the new few years, as the benefits of water-efficient plumbing fixtures became more widely known.[25] In 1992, the U.S. Energy Policy Act (EPAct) was passed by Congress and signed by President George H. W. Bush.[26] The EPAct established for the first time national maximum allowable water-flow rates for toilets, urinals, showerheads, and faucets. Maximum allowable water-use rates for plumbing fixtures in the United States are provided in Table 2.1. More recently, the water and energy efficiency of clothes washers and dishwashers has also improved.

According to the U.S. General Accounting Office, "Substantial evidence shows that the use of water-efficient plumbing fixtures conserves water."[27] Improvements

*W*ater, taken in moderation, cannot hurt anybody."
—Mark Twain

TABLE 2.1

Federal maximum water-use requirements for toilets, urinals, showerheads, and faucets*

Fixture†	Maximum Water Use Allowed‡	Date Standard Became Effective§
Toilets (Water Closets)		
Gravity-tank	1.6 gpf	1/1/94
Gravity-tank, white, two-piece, labeled "Commercial Use Only"	3.5 gpf	1/1/94 to 12/31/96
	1.6 gpf	1/1/97
Flushometer-tank	1.6 gpf	1/1/94
Flushometer-valve (except blowout-valve)	1.6 gpf	1/1/97
Blowout-valve	3.5 gpf	1/1/94
Electromechanical hydraulic	1.6 gpf	1/1/94
Urinals		
Any type	1.0 gpf	1/1/94
Showerheads		
Any type (except those used for safety reasons)	2.5 gpm (at 80 psi) or 2.2 gpm (at 60 psi)	1/1/94
Faucets and Replacement Aerators		
Lavatory faucets	2.5 gpm (at 80 psi) or 2.2 gpm (at 60 psi)	1/1/94
Lavatory replacement aerators		
Kitchen faucets		
Kitchen replacement aerators		
Metering faucets	0.25 gpc**	

* Established by the U.S. Energy Policy Act (EPAct). EPAct allows certain exceptions to the standards shown, e.g., when they are not consistent with public health or safety. The actual language of the law should be consulted for full details about exceptions.

† For fixtures manufactured or imported in the United States

‡ Standards shown apply to fixtures that must also meet the requirements of ASME/ANSI A112.19.6 (for toilets and urinals) and A112.18.1 (for showerheads and faucets).

§ Some states changed their plumbing codes and laws prior to enactment of EPAct to require water-efficiency standards for the fixtures shown.

** Measured at a flowing water pressure of 80 pounds per square inch (psi)

gpf = gallons per flush

gpm = gallons per minute

psi = pounds per square inch

gpc = gallons per cycle

Source: Reference 26

in the water-use efficiency of plumbing fixtures and appliances will continue to reduce indoor household water use for many customers. For homes with old, high-volume, or leaking fixtures and appliances, installation of more efficient replacements can result in significant water savings and a much lower per-capita use rate, as illustrated in Figure 2.4. For a typical single-family home that uses an average of 69.3 gpcd indoors, most of it in the bathroom (Figure 2.5), installation of water-efficient fixtures and appliances would reduce average use to an estimated 45.2 gpcd, an 24.1 gpcd savings or a 35% reduction in demand for indoor use.

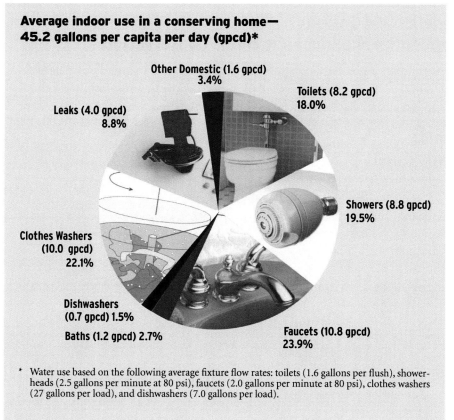

**Average indoor use in a conserving home—
45.2 gallons per capita per day (gpcd)***

Other Domestic (1.6 gpcd) 3.4%

Toilets (8.2 gpcd) 18.0%

Leaks (4.0 gpcd) 8.8%

Showers (8.8 gpcd) 19.5%

Clothes Washers (10.0 gpcd) 22.1%

Dishwashers (0.7 gpcd) 1.5%

Baths (1.2 gpcd) 2.7%

Faucets (10.8 gpcd) 23.9%

* Water use based on the following average fixture flow rates: toilets (1.6 gallons per flush), shower-heads (2.5 gallons per minute at 80 psi), faucets (2.0 gallons per minute at 80 psi), clothes washers (27 gallons per load), and dishwashers (7.0 gallons per load).

Source: Amy Vickers & Associates, Inc.

Figure 2.4 Average indoor water use in a conserving North American single-family home

On-Site Graywater Systems for Homes: Wave of the Future?

Several states now have standards and laws that allow for the installation and use of on-site graywater systems in some residential and nonresidential settings. Jurisdictions differ in their definition of graywater, but graywater is typically defined as untreated used household water that does not contain human wastes; examples include wash or rinse water from a sink, shower, bathtub, or other household fixture, except a toilet. By some definitions, graywater does not include waste water from sinks, dishwashers, or laundry water because it may have come into contact with human wastes (e.g., a soiled diaper). Where permitted, graywater that does not contain human wastes or pose a health hazard may be reused for toilet flushing and other nonpotable applications, including outdoor irrigation of nonfood crops.

Graywater systems can reduce potable water use, but as household plumbing fixtures and appliances become more water-efficient, graywater systems for residential applications may have limited benefits in terms of indoor water-use savings. Further, the less water used indoors, the less graywater available for outdoor irrigation purposes. Given these facts, as well as the system's installation costs, energy requirements, and maintenance needed for proper operation, a graywater system offers few practical benefits for most single-family homeowners. However, some homes and many types of buildings and facilities with large water demands that can benefit from on-site graywater systems.

Figure 2.5 Federal standards for water-efficient toilets, urinals, showerheads, and faucets are reducing indoor residential water demand. (Photo courtesy of Amy Vickers & Associates, Inc.)

Benefits and Costs of Residential and Domestic Water Conservation

A number of benefits accrue to utilities, residential customers, and nonresidential property-owners who conserve water. Likewise, some costs and behavior modifications may be associated with water efficiency.

Benefits

- Water savings
- Reduced wastewater flows
- Reduced costs for energy and chemicals
- Reduced costs for water, sewer, and associated electric and gas utility services
- Reduced costs for clothes-washing and dishwashing detergents
- Reduced size and extended septic system life
- Improved safe yield and pumping reliability in wells
- Improved local environment (instream flows, wetlands protection, topsoil preservation)
- Pollution prevention (reduced energy combustion by-products and chemical use)

Costs

- Price of conservation device (hardware)
- Cost to install device
- Cost of any necessary renovation of existing plumbing, appliances, or related connections
- Changes in water-use habits

AUDIT

Basic Steps in a Residential Water Audit

Water audits are a common component of residential (and nonresidential) conservation programs. Water utilities that provide audits often offer them to all customers, although customers with high-volume water use are typically contacted first. Target customers may be contacted via letter, postcard, phone call, or door-to-door solicitation (Figure 2.6). Studies have shown that home water audits can result in water savings when plumbing retrofit devices are installed and customers are given practical guidance about more efficient outdoor water-use practices, particularly with respect to lawn irrigation. Though the design of residential water audits varies, those that involve installing some efficiency devices and spending time with customers to educate them about reduced outdoor water use have reported savings for combined indoor and outdoor use ranging from 20 to 30 gallons per day (gpd) per single-family household[32] (Figure 2.7).

A water audit for a single-family household takes a trained technician 45 to 60 minutes to perform on site (15 to 20 minutes for indoor water use, 30 to 45 minutes for outdoor use), excluding follow-up analysis and paperwork. The cost of a contracted water auditor ranges from $40 to $75 per home, depending on

Residential Submetering: Pros and Cons

Submetering—the installation of meters to measure water use in individual apartments or small dwelling units—is increasing in certain areas, particularly among newly built condominiums, apartment buildings, multifamily homes, mobile home parks, and certain types of commercial sites. Some utilities endorse submetering because they believe it can help reduce water use. However, a study by the San Francisco Water Department found little difference in water use in apartments that were submetered compared with that of apartments in buildings with master meters (one meter for the building), according to Kimberley Knox, the water department's water conservation administrator.[30]

Many apartment building owners favor submetering because it allows them to pass on directly to tenants water and sewer costs that would otherwise be charged indirectly through the rent bill. Some tenants like the equitability of submetering because they pay only for the water they use instead of subsidizing (through rent) other tenants who use more water, such as those with large families or many occupants. However, tenants and consumer advocates who oppose submetering argue that submetering is not cost-effective, particularly for tenants who use small amounts of water, because the cost of submetering (installation, maintenance, meter reading) can outweigh its benefits. Unlike outdoor use, most indoor water use is nondiscretionary—for essential purposes such as sanitation, cooking, and cleaning; thus, having tenants pay directly for water used indoors may not have much influence on use. When a few tenants use excess water (e.g., a tenant who runs a small household business such as photo processing), a more effective solution may be found between the parties involved or in landlord-tenant court. Another argument against submetering is that it removes the financial incentive for landlords to install conservation devices and perform related maintenance work, such as installing low-volume toilets and retrofit devices and repairing leaks. Tenants may be unwilling to make such improvements themselves since they don't own the property and such investments are "sunk costs" (i.e., they are not reimbursed by the landlord and are not tax-deductible). The cost of installing a submeter ranges from $200 to $400 per apartment, depending on the amount of retrofitting that is necessary. Meter reading and billing service fees cost an additional $2 to $4 per month per submetered dwelling unit.[31]

the services provided and whether it is a single-family or multifamily dwelling. If retrofit devices or other materials are provided to the customer, these also increase the cost of the audit.

The basic steps for conducting a residential water audit are listed here. A sample residential audit data collection form is provided in Appendix E, *Sample Worksheet: Residential (Indoor) Water Audit*.

1. **Explain purpose of audit.** Explain the purpose of conducting the water audit to the customer (e.g., to identify ways to save water and energy, implement simple water-efficiency measures and repairs, reduce environmental burdens, and help control water and sewer costs). Provide information about additional conservation programs the consumer may be eligible for (e.g., toilet and clothes washer rebates, landscape water audits, and leak repairs).

2. **Determine water use.** Based on water billing data or actual meter readings, estimate the water use and efficiency of toilets, showerheads, faucets, clothes washers, dishwashers, and other indoor and outdoor water-use activities.

3. **Test and repair leaks.** Test toilets for leakage using leak detection dye tablets; repair or recommend repairs for leaking toilets (e.g., adjust or re-

Figure 2.6 Door-to-door outreach to residential customers increases acceptance of household water audits. (Illustration courtesy of City of Albuquerque, New Mexico)

place the flapper valve and float arm). Conduct a visual inspection to detect dripping faucets and other leaking connections.

4. **Provide retrofit devices.** Install or provide the following low-volume plumbing retrofit and outdoor hose devices, as needed:
   - Toilet displacement devices
   - Low-volume showerhead (2.2 gpm or less at 60 pounds per square inch [psi] of pressure or 2.5 gpm or less at 80 psi)
   - Faucet aerators for lavatory faucets and control flow aerators for kitchen faucets (2.2 gpm or less at 60 psi or 2.5 gpm or less at 80 psi). Faucet aerators that reduce flows to 1.5 gpm are often sufficient for lavatory uses.
   - Automatic hose shutoff nozzle

   The contents of a typical indoor residential retrofit kit are shown in Figure 2.8.

5. **Evaluate lawn and irrigation characteristics and recommend design modifications.** Note the species of grass as well as the condition of the lawn (e.g., thatch buildup, soil compaction, green and brown spots), the rate of water application and uniformity of distribution, and other relevant features to assess irrigation efficiency and effectiveness. A more detailed discussion of landscape water-use and efficiency measures, including steps for conducting an outdoor water-use audit, is provided in Chapter 3, *Landscape Water Use and Efficiency Measures.*

6. **Evaluate other outdoor water uses.** Evaluate the efficiency of outdoor water-use features such as hoses and pools. Check to see if outdoor hoses have automatic shutoff valves or are leaking. For homes with pools, check for leaks, water temperature (to assess evaporative losses), and whether a pool cover is used.

7. **Customize home irrigation schedule if needed.** Provide advice on water-efficient practices for lawn and landscape irrigation; offer to reprogram the schedule for automatic irrigation systems.

8. **Identify all water conservation opportunities.** Give the homeowner a checklist of findings from the audit plus a list of recommended conservation measures that apply to toilets, showerheads, faucets, clothes washers, dishwashers, garbage disposers, and other indoor and outdoor water-use practices.

9. **Evaluate water-efficiency measures.** Based on an analysis of water use and potential reductions from each water-efficiency measure, determine the capital (one-time) costs and related expenses associated with the measure. Estimate avoided costs (benefits) associated with the measure (e.g., reduced water and sewer bills, reduced energy and chemical treatment costs). Using these data, calculate a simple payback period—the amount of time required for the projected cost savings to equal the investment costs. The payback period can be calculated as follows:

$$Simple\ Payback\ Period\ (years) = \frac{Capital\ Costs\ (\$)}{Net\ Annual\ Savings\ (\$/year)}$$

For long-term estimates of paybacks, interest rates should also be considered.

Figure 2.7 Household water audits can result in water savings of 20 to 30 gallons per day, sometimes more. (Photo courtesy of Amy Vickers & Associates, Inc.)

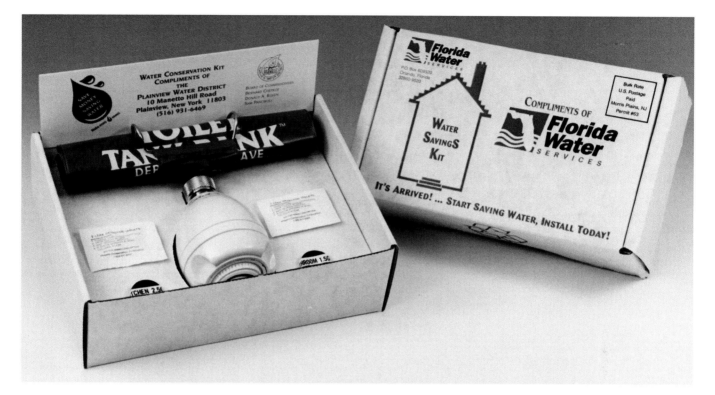

10. **Educate customers.** As part of the on-site audit, encourage customers to think about their water-use habits and to practice conservation in their daily activities (e.g., turning off the faucet during teeth-brushing). Review and discuss the customer's water-use history over the past three years, particularly during maximum irrigation periods. Show customers how to read their water meter, detect leaks, and estimate the volume of any leaks discovered. Provide brochures on additional conservation measures and application forms for rebates on purchases of low-volume toilets, clothes washers, and dishwashers.

Figure 2.8 Plumbing fixture retrofit kit: toilet displacement device (bag), low-volume showerhead, faucet aerators, and leak-detection dye tablets (Photo courtesy of Niagara Conservation, Inc.)

Indoor Residential and Domestic Water-Efficiency Measures

This section describes water-efficient plumbing fixtures, appliances, and related technologies and efficient-use practices that are applicable to indoor water use in homes as well as in nonresidential settings where domestic fixtures and appliances are used. (In this book, "domestic" water use refers to water used for domestic purposes in nonresidential settings—for example, hand-washing and toilet-flushing in office restrooms.)

The following types of information are included for each water-efficiency measure:

- *Water use.* The measure's water-use characteristics are described.
- *Operation and performance.* The measure's design and operation are discussed along with performance considerations.

- *Water savings and related benefits.* The measure's potential water savings, estimated water and sewer cost savings, estimated energy savings, and related benefits are outlined.
- *Costs.* Estimated costs are presented, including the price of devices or hardware, labor and installation, and related costs.
- *Applicable laws, codes, and standards.* Laws, regulations, and industry codes and standards that apply to the measure are discussed.
- *Implementation.* Targeted water users for the measure are identified, along with selection and design options. Planning for a large-scale; installation program is discussed, along with customer program participation, incentives, number of fixtures or appliances installed, installation and technical considerations, and maintenance needs.

When applicable, case studies are provided to illustrate potential water savings, benefits and costs, and program implementation considerations.

2.1 TOILETS

This section describes four measures to reduce water use by toilets: low-volume toilets, waterless and composting toilets, toilet displacement and flushing devices, and toilet leak repair. These measures apply to toilets installed in residential and nonresidential properties (e.g., office buildings, schools, commercial facilities, hotels, hospitals, and many types of institutional facilities).

Low-volume toilets use 1.6 gallons per flush (gpf) or less. Waterless and composting toilets require no water to flush. There are a variety of retrofit devices to reduce flush volumes for conventional, high-volume (3.5 gpf or more) toilets, and there are several leak repair measures that can be applied to low- and high-volume toilets.

Improvements in the water efficiency of toilets began in the early 1980s as a result of refinements in the design of conventional gravity toilets, the introduction of new technologies and fixture designs, and local, state, and federal initiatives to promote water conservation. Although some of the early "low-flow" fixtures in the United States in the late 1980s received mixed reviews in terms of performance, manufacturers have improved the design and performance of low-volume toilets so that consumers can now choose from a large number of reliable products.

"Toilets flush in E flat."
—www.uselessfacts.net

According to EPAct requirements, all toilets sold, installed, or imported in the United States must be low-volume fixtures that use no more than 1.6 gpf, or 6 liters, as shown in Table 2.1. Other countries, such as Australia, Denmark, Finland, Norway, and Singapore, allow low-volume toilets that use no more than 0.8 to 1.2 gpf (3.0 to 4.5 liters).[33] Technological improvements along with federal requirements have spurred a number of U.S. water utilities to realize significant water savings not only through new installations and renovations but also by offering direct rebates to customers who replace high-volume toilets with low-volume fixtures.

TABLE 2.2

Estimated water use and savings by low-volume toilets in households

Years Manufactured or Installed*	Toilet Water-Use Rate	Frequency of Toilet Use Daily Per Person	Estimated Water Use Daily		Estimated Water Savings With a 1.6 gpf Toilet[†] Daily		Yearly	
			Per Capita	Per Household[‡]	Per Capita	Per Household[‡]	Per Capita	Per Household[‡]
	gpf	number of uses	gal	gal	gal	gal	gal	gal
1994-present	1.0	5.1	5.1	13.5				
1997-present[§]	**1.6**	5.1	8.2	21.5				
1994-present**	**1.6**	5.1	8.2	21.5				
1980-1994	3.5	5.1	17.9	47.1	9.7	25.6	3,537	9,337
	4.0	5.1	20.4	53.9	12.2	32.3	4,468	11,794
	4.5	5.1	23.0	60.6	14.8	39.0	5,398	14,252
1950s-1980	5.0	5.1	25.5	67.3	17.3	45.8	6,329	16,709
	5.5	5.1	28.1	74.1	19.9	52.5	7,260	19,166
Pre-1950s	7.0	5.1	35.7	94.2	27.5	72.7	10,052	26,538

* Time periods are approximate. Dates in state and local jurisdictions may vary somewhat from dates shown except when they are superseded by the Jan. 1, 1994, federal requirement (shown in bold) allowing a maximum of 1.6 gpf for most toilets installed after that date, per the Energy Policy Act.

† Excludes water used for cleaning and losses attributable to leaks

‡ Based on the average of 2.64 persons per occupied U.S. household

§ Flushometer-valve fixtures and gravity-tank, white, two-piece fixtures labeled "Commercial Use Only" (most common in nonresidential settings)

** Gravity-tank, flushometer-tank, and electromechanical hydraulic fixtures (most common in residential and small office and commercial settings)

gpf = gallons per flush

number of uses = average number of times per day toilet is flushed

gal = gallon

Sources: Amy Vickers & Associates, Inc.; References 26, 29, 37, and 52

Water Use by Toilets

Average water use by low-volume and high-volume toilets (estimated according to their flush volume) is shown in Table 2.2. Low-volume toilets designed to use 1.5 gpf, 1.1 gpf, and 1.0 gpf are available, but fixtures that use less than 1.0 gpf are uncommon in the United States. Moderate- to high-volume toilets have flush rates of 3.5 gpf (referred to as "water-saver toilets" when introduced in the late 1970s), 4.0 gpf, 4.5 gpf, 5.0 gpf, 5.5 gpf, and up to 7.0 gpf for pre-1950 fixtures. In addition to the 1.6 gpf fixture, there are some fixtures in this classification that use about 2.0 gpf, but these are not common. The actual volume of water used by flush toilets sometimes varies from the manufacturer's reported flow rate for reasons that include improper mechanical adjustments to fixture components at the time of installation (e.g., not properly setting the water used by a gravity-flush fixture to the factory-marked water level inside the tank); manufacturing defects; low or high supply line pressure, particularly for nongravity-flush fixtures; previous adjustments to the fixture flow rate; and - leakage.

Exceptions allowed by EPAct and local and state authorities may be granted for special uses and circumstances that require higher flow volumes, although such conditions are uncommon. Toilets designed for prisons are allowed to use up to 3.5 gpf, but most manufacturers of these specialty fixtures also offer 1.6 gpf models.

Residential Water Use by Toilets

Water use by toilets is typically the largest source of indoor residential water demand, averaging 18.5 gallons per capita per day (gpcd), or 26.7% of indoor use in a typical nonconserving single-family home.[34] The average flush volume of a residential toilet is 3.48 gpf.[35] A 1984 study conducted for the U.S. Department of Housing and Urban Development found average water use by toilets in a non-conserving home to be 22.0 gpcd, an average of 5.5 gpf.[36] Thus, the water efficiency of toilets has been increasing. Depending on the approximate year that a toilet was installed, its residential water-use characteristics can be estimated, as shown in Table 2.2.

The frequency of toilet flushing in homes averages 5.1 flushes per person per day,[37] although it was previously assumed to be 4.0.[36] The use of restrooms in office buildings is estimated to be about three times per workday for women and men; women use toilets about three times per workday, whereas men typically use a toilet once and a urinal twice during a workday.[38–40]

Nonresidential Water Use by Toilets

The range of water use by toilets in nonresidential sites (e.g., industrial, commercial, and institutional) has been estimated from water audit data, as shown in Table 2.3. For example, water use by toilets in office buildings is estimated to be about 4.8 gpcd for females when 1.6 gpf fixtures are installed and 10.5 to 13.5 gpcd when high-volume fixtures installed after 1980 are in use, as shown in Table 2.4. For males in office buildings, water use by toilets is estimated to be about 1.6 gpcd when a 1.6 gpf fixture is installed and 3.5 to 5.5 gpcd if a high-volume toilet is in use; water use by urinals is also a factor in office restrooms for males.

There are several ways to determine how much water a particular toilet uses if its flush rate is unknown: (1) read the water meter before and after flushing the toilet while keeping all other fixtures and water-using appliances turned off (this method is more reliable for single-family homes and small facilities with small meters than big buildings with large meters, because large meters may not record

TABLE 2.3

Types of toilets installed at nonresidential sites*—estimates†

Toilet Water-Use Rate	Range of Use Observed	Toilet Type	
		Flushometer-Valve	Gravity-Tank
gpf	gpf	Percent	
1.6	Up to 2.0	7	5
3.5	2.0 to 4.0	59	51
5.0	More than 4.0	34	44
	Total	100	100

* Industrial, commercial, and institutional (ICI) facilities

† Based on audit information collected for 38,517 toilets at 818 ICI sites located within the service territory of the Metropolitan Water District of Southern California

gpf = gallons per flush

Source: Adapted from Reference 58

TABLE 2.4

Estimated water use and savings by low-volume toilets in office buildings

Years Manufactured or Installed *	Toilet Water-Use Rate	Frequency of Toilet Use[†] Daily		Estimated Water Use Daily		Estimated Water Savings With a 1.6 gpf Toilet[‡] Daily		Yearly (260 workdays)	
		Per Male	Per Female	Per Male	Per Female	Per Male	Per Female	Per Male	Per Female
	gpf	number of uses	number of uses	gal	gal	gal	gal	gal	gal
1994-present	1.0	1.0	3.0	1.0	3.0				
1997-present [§]	**1.6**	1.0	3.0	1.6	4.8				
1994-present **	**1.6**	1.0	3.0	1.6	4.8				
1980-1994	3.5	1.0	3.0	3.5	10.5	1.9	5.7	494	1,482
	4.0	1.0	3.0	4.0	12.0	2.4	7.2	624	1,872
	4.5	1.0	3.0	4.5	13.5	2.9	8.7	754	2,262
1950s-1980	5.0	1.0	3.0	5.0	15.0	3.4	10.2	884	2,652
	5.5	1.0	3.0	5.5	16.5	3.9	11.7	1,014	3,042
Pre-1950s	7.0	1.0	3.0	7.0	21.0	5.4	16.2	1,404	4,212

* Time periods are approximate. Dates in state and local jurisdictions may vary somewhat from dates shown except when they are superseded by the Jan. 1, 1994 federal requirement (shown in bold) allowing a maximum of 1.6 gpf for most toilets installed after that date, per the U.S. Energy Policy Act of 1992.

† Females and males use office building restrooms in about equal numbers but not by fixture type. Women use toilets approximately three times per workday; men use toilets about one time per workday and urinals about two times per workday. (See Table 2.10 for water use and potential savings by urinals in office buildings.) For facilities without urinals, water use and savings should be based on frequency of use per female.

‡ Excludes water used for cleaning and losses attributable to leaks.

§ Flushometer-valve fixtures and gravity-tank, white, two-piece fixtures labeled "Commercial Use Only" (most common in nonresidential settings)

** Gravity-tank, flushometer-tank, and electromechanical hydraulic fixtures (most common in residential and small office and commercial settings)

gpf = gallons per flush

number of uses = average number of times per day toilet is flushed

gal = gallon

Sources: Amy Vickers & Associates, Inc.; References 26, 29, 38, and 39

small flows reliably); (2) note the fixture's year of manufacture (which may be imprinted inside the tank or on a label affixed to the tank, back of the bowl, or flush valve), and check its probable flow rate as shown in Table 2.2; (3) determine the most recent date of fixture installation or building renovation or the age of the building (if the fixture appears to be the original installed during construction) to find its probable flow rate as shown in Table 2.4; or (4) contact the manufacturer.

2.1.1 Low-Volume Toilets

Low-volume toilets, also referred to by the terms *low-flow, low-flush, low-consumption, ultralow-flush,* and *ultralow-volume,* typically use 1.6 gpf (6 liters) or less. Low-volume toilets are available in the same operating designs as high-volume fixtures. Similarly, low-volume toilets can be either floor- or wall-mounted and are available in a range of styles, sizes, and colors. Low-volume toilets can be installed to replace high-volume toilets in residential and nonresidential settings (including prisons), with a few exceptions. Three basic types of low-volume toilets are commonly available, along with several alternative ultra-efficient designs.

Although 3.5 gpf toilets are sometimes referred to as "water-saving" or "water-saver" toilets, they are less water-efficient than 1.6 gpf toilets. The 3.5 gpf fixtures received conservation status around 1980 when they were developed in response to several major U.S. droughts and to more stringent plumbing codes. Planners who are specifying toilets for large-scale replacement programs need to keep this distinction in mind to avoid selecting the wrong fixtures.

2.1.1.1 Low-Volume Gravity-Tank Toilets

The gravity-tank or gravity-flush toilet, as shown in Figure 2.9, is the most common type of toilet in use, particularly in homes. Gravity-tank fixtures account for more than 80% of toilets sold in the United States. Most low-volume, gravity-tank toilets use 1.6 gpf, but some fixtures are designed to operate at 1.5 gpf, 1.0 gpf, 0.8 gpf (e.g., those used in Denmark and Sweden), and even lower. Gravity-tank toilets are installed primarily in residences and in low-use commercial and office facilities.[40]

The 1.6 gpf gravity-tank toilets work on the same principles and typically have the same parts as the 3.5 and 5.0 gpf fixtures, as illustrated in Figure 2.10. A gravity-tank toilet operates when the handle is pulled, causing the flush (flapper) valve at the bottom of the tank to open and start releasing water from the tank into the bowl. The weight of this water—pressured by gravity because the tank is positioned above the bowl—causes the water to rush out of the tank and into the bowl, either through rim holes at the top of the bowl, a siphon hole, or both. The rushing water creates a vacuum or siphon that pulls solid and liquid wastes from the bowl, into the trapway (or outlet), and on to the sewer drain below. Meanwhile, as the bowl is being emptied, the flapper valve inside the tank is closing (to lie flat against the bottom of the tank), and the ballcock (or automatic fill valve) is tripped to allow water to refill the tank.[41] Gravity-tank toilets

The flush toilet was patented in England in 1775.

Figure 2.9 Gravity-tank toilets are commonly installed in households and small offices. Low-volume toilets use a maximum of 1.6 gallons per flush, but many older toilets use as much as 5.5 gallons per flush. (Photo courtesy of TOTO USA)

What makes a gravity toilet flush?

Old 5 gallon toilets and new 1.6 gallon gravity toilets work the same way. The tank holds the water above the bowl. The lever opens the flush valve, which lets the water rush out of the tank into the bowl, either through rim holes, a siphon hole, or both. In the bowl, the pressure of the water rushing down the drain creates a vacuum or siphon effect that draws the waste with it. Meanwhile, an automatic valve refills the emptied tank.

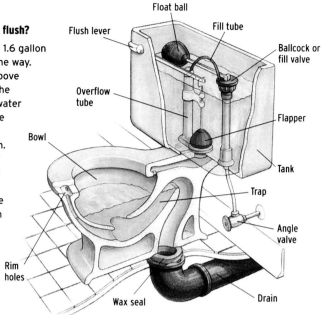

Float ball · Flush lever · Fill tube · Ballcock or fill valve · Overflow tube · Flapper · Bowl · Tank · Trap · Angle valve · Rim holes · Wax seal · Drain

Figure 2.10 Low-volume and high-volume gravity-tank toilets operate on the same principles. (Drawing by Bob LaPointe, courtesy of *Fine Homebuilding* Magazine)

usually require a minimum water pressure of 10 to 15 pounds per square inch (psi) to work properly.

Several differences characterize the design of low-volume, gravity-tank toilets compared with older, high-volume fixtures. Low-volume gravity fixtures typically have smaller tanks, steeper bowls, and redesigned ballcocks and flapper valves. Unfortunately, like the high-volume models, some low-volume, gravity-tank fixtures are prone to leakage, particularly when operated with corrosive water, poor quality mechanical parts inside the tank, or both.

Nearly all gravity-tank toilets have a two-piece design with a tank that sits on top of the bowl. There are also one-piece toilets with the tank and bowl combined; they work on the same principle as the two-piece fixtures. One-piece gravity toilets are usually found in more expensive, designer product lines and have a sleek, low profile—the tank is smaller and closer to the floor compared with that of the two-piece fixture.

DUAL-FLUSH TOILETS Dual-flush toilets have been in use in many parts of the world for a number of years, and several types provide reliable service when used properly. Dual-flush toilets are designed with either one or two flush handles (or levers). Flushes for liquid-only wastes are activated by depressing the handle in the direction for a minimal flush (1.0 gpf or less), and flushes for solid wastes are activated by depressing the handle in another direction for a full flush (1.6 gpf or less), as shown in Figure 2.11. If not flushed properly (e.g., flushing for liquid-only waste when solids are present), dual-flush toilets can clog or require double-flushing. Signs or arrows are sometimes posted near the handles of dual-flush toilets to instruct people, particularly children, on how to flush them correctly.

Figure 2.11 The handle of a dual-flush toilet offers users the choice of a 1.6 gallon flush for solid wastes or a 1.0 gallon flush for liquid-only wastes. (Photo courtesy of Kohler Co.)

Figure 2.12 A 1.6 gallon per flush, pressure-assisted flushometer-tank toilet (Photo courtesy of Sloan Valve Co.)

2.1.1.2 Low-Volume Flushometer-Tank (Pressurized) Toilets

Flushometer-tank (pressurized or pressure-assisted) toilets, introduced in the late 1980s for residential, office, and light commercial applications, operate on the same principles as the flushometer-valve toilet. The exterior appearance of flushometer-tank toilets is usually identical to that of gravity-tank toilets (i.e., bowl, tank, flush handle or button), as shown in Figure 2.12. The difference between the two types is on the inside of the flushometer tank, which contains a pressurized plastic vessel that holds the water used for flushing, as illustrated in Figure 2.13. When a flushometer-tank toilet is flushed, compressed air forces the water out of the tank and into the bowl, inducing syphonic action that pushes the contents of the bowl down the drain. Flushometer-tank toilets clear the bowl in less than 10 seconds (compared with about 45 seconds for gravity toilets), although they need 60 to 90 seconds to complete the flushing cycle and refill the plastic tank before being flushed again. The flushometer-tank toilet is virtually leak-proof because of the design of the pressurized vessel inside its tank, an important consideration when total water savings and costs over the life of a fixture are evaluated.

2.1.1.3 Low-Volume Flushometer-Valve Toilets

Flushometer-valve toilets are tankless fixtures consisting of a wall- or floor-mounted bowl and a flushometer valve with a hand lever, as shown in Figure 2.14. This type of fixture is often found in office, commercial, and institutional settings, high-traffic facilities (e.g., airports, sports arenas, shopping malls), and some older apartment buildings (less than 10% of toilets installed in multiunit facilities are the flushometer-valve type).[43] Flushometer-valve toilets operate on the same principle as flushometer-tank toilets: pressure from the water supply line creates a strong flushing action.

AUTOMATIC FLUSHING SENSORS Some flushometer-valve toilets and urinals in public restrooms are operated with an infrared or fiber-optic sensor that flushes the fixture automatically. The sensor is usually located on the wall behind the toilet and trips the flushing mechanism once the user begins to move away from the fixture. Automatic flushing control devices are used primarily to reduce the spread of germs. Automatic flushing sensors do not save water and sometimes waste water when the sensor is set incorrectly or is hyper-alert and causes multiple flushing. (Some sensors are smarter than others.) To prevent unnecessary flushing caused by inadvertent motion in front of the sensor, the sensor should contain a time-delay circuit.

2.1.1.4 Alternative Low-Volume Toilet Designs

In addition to the more common gravity-tank and flushometer toilets, there are several alternative designs and operating systems for low-volume toilets, some of which use less than 1.6 gpf and require electricity to operate. Toilets with alternative flushing systems may be preferred in situations with low water pressure or scarce water supplies. Some drawbacks to toilets with electrically generated flushing systems are that they won't work during a power failure and they typically cost more than conventional toilets.

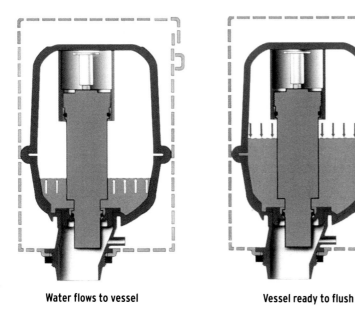

Water flows to vessel   Vessel ready to flush   Air pressure empties vessel

FLAPPERLESS TOILETS Several types of flapperless gravity-tank toilets are now available, although some of the designs are new and untested by large numbers of consumers. Flapperless toilets have several advantages over gravity fixtures: they are less prone to leakage, provide reliable flow rates (because they are more difficult to adjust), and require less maintenance. Disadvantages include uncertainties about their durability (because of their recent introduction on the market), noisier operation, and potential backflow problems with some models. Flapperless fixtures include *siphonic* toilets, commonly used in the United Kingdom, and a "bucket" fixture equipped with a tray inside the tank that empties water to the bowl inlet.[44]

VACUUM-ASSISTED TOILETS Similar to a gravity-tank fixture, a vacuum-assisted toilet uses 1.6 gpf and is equipped with two plastic vessels inside the tank that create a vacuum when the toilet is flushed. The vacuum pulls water and waste from the toilet bowl.[45]

ELECTROMECHANICAL HYDRAULIC TOILETS Electromechanical toilets use electrically operated devices, such as air compressors, pumps, solenoids, motors, or macerators, in place of or to assist gravity in evacuating waste from the bowl. Some of the most common electromechanical hydraulic toilets use less than 1.0 gpf and rely on electrically generated compressed air. For example, the Microflush toilet, manufactured by the Microphor Company, uses less than 1.0 gpf and operates like a gravity-tank toilet except that the flushing action is assisted by compressed air generated by an electrical compressor. The compressor releases pressurized water into the bowl rim, simultaneously opening the flapper valve and releasing a small amount of water, which forces waste out of the bowl and into a lower chamber. As the waste enters the lower chamber, air is bled off a sequence valve, which causes pressure in the lower chamber to increase rapidly, breaking down the waste and discharging it into the drainpipe.[42]

Figure 2.13 Schematic of operating system for a 1.6 gallon per flush, pressure-assisted flushometer-tank toilet (Illustration courtesy of Sloan Valve Co.)

Figure 2.14 Floor-mounted, flushometer-valve toilet (Photo courtesy of Amy Vickers & Associates, Inc.)

PUMP-ASSISTED TOILETS This type of toilet is a combination gravity-tank and pressure-assisted fixture. The flushing action on this toilet is powered by an electric water pump (located under the tank), which sends a high-velocity blast of water into the bowl.[45]

Performance of Low-Volume Toilets

Numerous studies have documented the performance of low-volume toilets to equal or exceed that of high-volume fixtures in terms of flushing reliability, sewer drainline carriage, bowl cleaning, and other attributes, despite some exaggerated media reports to the contrary. Incidents of double-flushing, clogging, and poor bowl cleaning have occurred with some 1.6 gpf toilets, but these problems can usually be traced to certain models only.

PROBLEM 1.6 GPF TOILETS Not every 1.6 gpf fixture provides adequate performance. Poor performance can result from flaws such as a badly designed bowl, trapway, or mechanical parts or from improper adjustments to the fixture or interior tank components (e.g., the flapper valve, float arm, fill valve, dam, or overflow tube) at the time of installation. A well-designed toilet with flushing problems can also result from a rotted or incorrectly installed wax ring at the toilet's base, water pressure irregularities, or inadequate sewer trapway or drainpipe design.

SUCCESS STORIES The most extensive reports of consumer experience with 1.6 gpf toilets can be found in customer satisfaction studies conducted by water systems and cities with large-scale toilet rebate and replacement programs, efforts that have resulted in the installation of several million low-volume toilets on an accelerated basis. Findings from several major studies of customer satisfaction with low-volume toilets follow.

| Case Study | *New York City Program Installs 1.3 Million Low-Volume Toilets.* The New York City Department of Environmental Protection sponsored a $297-million rebate program for residential and commercial customers from 1994 to 1997, resulting in the installation of 1.3 million 1.6 gpf toilets (Figure 2.15). The program achieved estimated water savings of 70 million gallons per day (mgd) and saved an estimated 53.8 gallons per day (gpd) per low-volume toilet installed (Figure 2.16).[46] (This large amount of savings per toilet is likely due to the replacement of a large number of 5 to 7 gpf toilets in high-density neighborhoods.) A 29% reduction in water use was achieved among 67 apartment buildings surveyed. In a random survey of 60,000 program participants, approximately three quarters of homeowners reported double-flushing the 1.6 gpf fixture less often or about the same as the high-volume toilet it replaced. Customer satisfaction with the ten most commonly installed 1.6 gpf models differed, underscoring the differences among models and the importance of careful selection of a 1.6 gpf toilet.[47]

Low-Volume Toilets in Los Angeles Save Almost 32 Gallons Per Day Per Fixture. Since 1990 the Los Angeles Department of Water and Power has helped fund the installation of more than 900,000 1.6 gpf toilets

> "A lie can travel halfway around the world while the truth is putting on its shoes."
> —Mark Twain

Figure 2.15 Educational poster promoting low-volume toilets, New York City Department of Environmental Protection (Photo courtesy of Amy Vickers & Associates, Inc.)

Figure 2.16 More than 1.3 million low-volume toilets were installed through New York City's conservation program in the mid-1990s. Overall, the program reduced water and sewer flows by more than 70 million gallons per day and saved $1 billion in avoided costs for sewer infrastructure upgrades. (Photo courtesy of Amy Vickers & Associates, Inc.)

through customer rebate and community-based funding programs. The program has achieved estimated water savings of 28.7 mgd, with estimated savings of 31.7 gpd per low-volume toilet.[46] Program costs from 1990 through 2000 totaled about $107 million, minus a small portion used for showerhead and clothes washer rebates.[46] In a customer satisfaction survey with more than 7,000 respondents, more than 80% said that they would be very likely or somewhat likely to participate in the program again. Respondents also reported less sewer line clogging, fewer mechanical problems, equivalent bowl cleaning and plunger use, and somewhat higher incidences of double-flushing with the 1.6 gpf fixtures. As with the customer satisfaction findings in New York, fixture performance and overall customer satisfaction with 1.6 gpf toilets correlated with those models that have the highest performance ratings.[48]

Case Study *Tampa Water Department Sponsors Successful Toilet Rebate Program.* The Tampa Water Department's 1.6 gpf toilet rebate program helped sponsor the installation of 15,300 fixtures in homes from 1993 to 1999. The program achieved estimated water savings of 0.44 mgd, with estimated savings of 29.1 gpd per low-volume toilet.[46] Program costs from 1993 through 1999 totaled $1.7 million.[46] Between 84 and 95% of the people surveyed said the 1.6 gpf fixture performed as well as or better than the high-volume toilet it replaced. Further, they were more satisfied with the performance of the

1.6 gpf fixture (in terms of double-flushing, bowl clogging, bowl cleanliness, and mechanical problems) than were residents in a control group who did not install low-volume toilets. At the same time, residents who installed 1.6 gpf fixtures reported more frequent incidences of sewer line clogging (0.16 clogs per home per year) compared with those in the control group (0.08 clogs per home per year). This did not seem to be a significant concern, however, because 91% of the respondents with 1.6 gpf fixtures said they would be very likely or somewhat likely to purchase a 1.6 gpf fixture again.[49]

Case Study *Consumers in Austin, Texas, Express Satisfaction With New Low-Volume Toilets.* Since the early 1990s, the city of Austin, Texas, has sponsored a 1.6 gpf toilet rebate program as well as a free toilet replacement program for low-income residents. The program has achieved estimated water savings of 1.4 mgd, with estimated savings of 29.3 gpd per low-volume toilet.[46] Program costs from 1992 through 1999 totaled $2 million.[46] Surveys of both groups of customers found that about 95% of respondents were either satisfied or very satisfied with their new low-volume toilet.[50]

The performance of 1.6 gpf toilets has improved significantly since the early 1980s when they were first introduced in the United States. Although 6-liter-per-flush fixtures were already in use in Scandinavia, Japan, and parts of Europe and Central and South America by the early 1970s,[25] they met considerable resistance from some U.S. plumbers and related groups in the mid- to late-1980s when Glendale, Arizona, and Massachusetts became the first city and state, respectively, to require them. Although the concerns at that time were never substantiated, they focused on the potential for an increase in drainline-carriage problems—the ability of toilet wastes to flow down a lateral sewer line—and bowl markings from feces deposited into smaller water surface areas. What is often not mentioned in discussions about the performance of low-volume toilets is that prior to the large-scale introduction of the 1.6 gpf fixture, not all high-volume conventional toilets operated well, as plumbers will attest. Today, because of innovative bowl and flushing designs, the operating and cleaning performance of many models of low-volume fixtures is better than that of the conventional fixtures they replaced.[51]

Specific findings about the performance of gravity-tank and pressure-assisted toilets, the types most commonly installed in homes, are presented in the following paragraphs.

GRAVITY-TANK TOILETS Many of the currently available 1.6 gpf low-volume, gravity-tank models have been reported to provide very good to excellent performance, despite some problems associated with earlier versions.[45] In most situations, removing a high-volume, gravity-tank toilet and replacing it with a new 1.6 gpf gravity fixture should result in equal if not improved performance, and the consumer will save water. Nonetheless, anecdotal evidence suggests that if consumers and plumbers are not careful in selecting and installing a good-quality gravity-tank fixture, there are circumstances under which some products will use additional water and cause performance problems that will have to be rectified:

- Larger than normal volumes of waste and toilet tissue flushed by gravity toilets can result in temporary clogging problems and double-flushing. Double-flushing is sometimes necessary no matter what flush volume a toilet uses, but if it is excessive, the fixture may require repair, adjustment, or both (but this should not involve replacing the tank with a larger one to increase the flush volume over its rated capacity). If the problem persists, the fixture may have inherent design flaws, and a different type of fixture could be a solution.

- All gravity-tank toilets, particularly inexpensive fixtures and those subject to corrosive water conditions (including those caused by chemicals released from toilet bowl cleaners), should be checked regularly for leaks and repaired to minimize water waste (see Section 2.1.4, "Toilet Leak Repair," later in this chapter).

- Poor-quality mechanical parts (ballcock assembly, fill valve, flapper valve, and related components) are sometimes used in otherwise well-designed gravity-tank toilets, soon causing leaks and unnecessary water waste. The actual flush volume of a fixture should be measured regularly after it is installed. If it is not meeting its designated flush volume, installation of high-quality replacement parts may improve its performance.

FLUSHOMETER-TANK (PRESSURIZED) TOILETS   Only about 5% of toilets sold are 1.6 gpf pressure-assisted fixtures,[41] but these toilets are gaining acceptance and market share in the residential and commercial (particularly hotel and motel) sector because they provide higher-velocity flushes and better bowl cleaning than some gravity fixtures, reducing the chance of double-flushing, extra cleaning, and clogs in the bowl or in long lateral sewer lines. These fixtures are also less likely to leak than gravity-tank toilets because of the encapsulated vessel in the tank that holds the pressurized water, a feature that minimizes water waste and associated repair costs. Some considerations for customers who are not familiar with these fixtures include:

- Flushometer-tank toilets tend to be noisier than gravity toilets when flushed, although the loud "whooshing" sound lasts only a few seconds. The loudness of the flush varies by model, and some are less noisy than others.

- Although pressure-assisted toilets require a minimum water pressure to perform reliably, this should not be a problem in most settings. *Consumer Reports* magazine reported that these fixtures require at least 25 psi to run well and thus may not be suited for homes with low water pressure.[45] Household water pressure usually ranges from 40 to 60 psi, though this can fluctuate, particularly in areas with high peak water demands (e.g., during summer months). If adequate pressure is not available, the tank may require additional time to fully recharge, slowing down the flushing action considerably. Successive use may slow or stall the flushing action, causing the bowl to clog with wastes if flushing is attempted before the tank is repressurized enough to complete the flush cycle. This may not be a problem in homes or other places where users know to allow the tank enough time to recharge fully, but it may be troublesome in restrooms that must accommodate many users in rapid succession.

- Replacement parts for these fixtures may not be readily available from all home and plumbing supply sources, resulting in repair delays. The flush button on some pressure-assisted toilets can be difficult for people with limited strength to push; models with lighter levers may be preferred.

FLUSHOMETER-VALVE TOILETS USED IN INSTITUTIONS   Stainless steel 1.6 gpf flushometer-valve toilets (including blowout-jet and siphon-jet types), which are typically used in hospitals and prisons, have been anecdotally reported to deliver excellent bowl flushing and cleaning. This good performance is the result of the bowl being precision-cut to its optimal design, an expensive process not used with conventional vitreous china bowls.

Water Savings and Related Benefits From Low-Volume Toilets

WATER SAVINGS   Estimated water use and water savings from replacing a high-volume toilet with a 1.6 gpf fixture in homes and office buildings are shown in Tables 2.2 and 2.4, respectively.[52] For example, installing a 1.6 gpf toilet to replace a 3.5 gpf model in a home will save an estimated 9.7 gpcd or 25.6 gallons per household per day (gphd). This is equivalent to annual water savings of 3,537 gallons per capita per year (gpcy) or 9,337 gallons per household per year (gphy).

TABLE 2.5

Survey of actual household water savings from low-volume toilets

City/Water System	Water Savings by Program Participants	Basis for Reported Water Savings
Metropolitan Water District of Southern California	Average net savings per single-family household—41.2 gphd; mean savings—29.9 gphd with one 1.6 gpf toilet, 20.6 gphd with two 1.6 gpf toilets, and 19.1 gphd with three 1.6 gpf toilets; estimated net savings per 1.6 gpf toilet installed—21.6 gpd	Estimated net mean household water savings achieved by 1.6 gpf toilet rebate programs in Los Angeles and Santa Monica, Calif., using statistical models of billed water use in participating and nonparticipating households during a drought emergency
	Average net savings per multifamily household—44.0 gphd; mean savings—44 gphd with one 1.6 gpf toilet and 34 gphd with two 1.6 gpf toilets; estimated net savings per 1.6 gpf toilet installed—40.3 gpd	
Tampa (Florida) Water Department	Average savings per single-family household—38 gphd	Measured from water-use records of 395 houses equipped with 1.6 gpf toilets compared with 375 control houses; figure represents a statistically significant savings at a 95 percent confidence level using a Student's t-Test.
New York, New York	Average water savings of 9.3 gpcd citywide in household units with 1.6 gpf toilet	Data records for 72,359 residential units in New York City
	Average savings in apartment buildings—29% reduction in total use (savings include replacement of some showerheads and faucets as well)	Survey findings for 67 apartment buildings that participated in New York City's toilet rebate program
El Paso, Texas	18.8% reduction in monthly residential water consumption	Water consumption records of 268 residential customer accounts 12 months before and 12 months after installation of 1.6 gpf fixtures (adjusted for outdoor use)
City of Barrie, Ontario, Canada	Mean savings per single-family household—16.38 gpcd	Analysis of billing records for 310 metered single-family accounts

gpf = gallons per flush
gphd = gallons per household per day
gpcd = gallons per capita per day
gpd = gallons per day

Sources: Amy Vickers & Associates, Inc.; References 49, 54–57, and 60

TABLE 2.6

Estimated water savings by low-volume toilets in nonresidential* market segments

Market Segment	Water Savings Per 1.6 gpf Toilet Installed–gpd[†‡]
Wholesale Establishment	57 (19–94)
Grocery Store	48 (37–59)
Restaurant	47 (36–58)
Retail Establishment	37 (33–42)
Automotive Business	36 (22–50)
Multiple-Use Facility	29 (14–45)
Religious Institution	28 (20–37)
Manufacturing Site	23 (15–32)
Health-Care Facility	21 (13–28)
Office	20 (17–23)
Miscellaneous	17 (11–23)
Hotel/Motel	16 (11–20)

* Industrial, commercial, and institutional buildings and facilities

† Estimates based on analysis of water billing records for nonresidential sites in the service territory of the Metropolitan Water District of Southern California

‡ 90% confidence interval shown in parentheses

gpd = gallons per day

Source: Adapted from Reference 58

In an office, replacing a 3.5 gpf toilet with a 1.6 gpf fixture will save an estimated 1.9 gpcd for males and 5.7 gpcd for females, the equivalent of annual water savings of 494 gpcy and 1,482 gpcy, respectively. A study of more than 200 1.6 gpf pressurized-tank toilets that replaced high-volume (2.5 gpf and higher) fixtures in a variety of commercial properties in two California communities, the city of Petaluma and Rohnert Park, found that the average savings *per toilet* was 26 gpd.[53]

Examples of actual measured savings from household-oriented 1.6 gpf toilet replacement programs are reported in Table 2.5.[54–57] The estimated residential water savings provided in Table 2.2 for replacing 3.5 to 5.5 gpf toilets with 1.6 gpf fixtures (9.7 to 19.9 gpcd or 25.6 to 52.5 gphd) are close to the measured household water savings given in Table 2.5.

A study sponsored by the California Urban Water Conservation Council researched potential water savings at industrial, commercial, and institutional facilities. The study indicated that some of the greatest water savings can be achieved in grocery stores, restaurants, and retail and wholesale sites. Among 12 broad market segments, the estimated water savings per 1.6 gpf toilet ranged from a low of 16 gpd at hotels and motels to 57 gpd at retail and wholesale establishments,[58] as shown in Table 2.6.

Case Study *Athletic Center Achieves Payback Six Months After Retrofitting Flushometer-Valve Toilets.* A college athletic center in the metropolitan Boston area reduced its annual water demand by 164,000 gallons by retrofitting 18 wall-mounted flushometer-valve toilets that saved 1.0 gpf. Hardware and

Differences in Estimated Versus Actual Water Savings From Efficiency Measures

Differences between estimated and actual water savings achieved from replacing high-volume fixtures and appliances with low-volume models or other retrofit devices or adjustments can result from various factors.

- Occupancy rates, lifestyle characteristics, frequency of fixture or appliance use per person, and water use per fixture or appliance vary by household and water-use environment.

- No two homes or nonresidential facilities are exactly alike in terms of actual flow rate of the fixture or appliance being replaced, particularly where leaks exist.

- The water savings achieved per water-efficiency measure installed in a home or non-residential property typically decreases, because the most frequently used fixture is often replaced first. For example, in homes and other sites with more than one toilet, each fixture is not used with equal frequency; thus a declining marginal effectiveness of water savings can be expected for each additional toilet replaced, particularly in single-

family households, according to a study by Chesnutt, et al. In a study of water savings from rebate programs in Los Angeles and Santa Monica, Calif., the mean savings per toilet installed was 24.2 gpd per 1.6 gpf toilet in single-family homes with only one toilet. In houses with two toilets, the first 1.6 gpf fixture installed saved 33.7 gpd, but the second saved only 20.8. In houses with three toilets, the first replacement fixture saved 45.9 gpd, the second saved 36.1 gpd, and the third saved 20.1 gpd.[60]

- Not all water-efficiency measures and devices achieve the same performance standards or water savings. For example, poorly designed 1.6 gpf toilets that have been adjusted to use more water will not save as much water as toilets that operate well at 1.6 gpf. The same is true of low-volume showerheads. Consumers will accept high-quality low-flow showerheads but can be expected to remove inferior ones. In large-scale fixture replacement programs that have not achieved projected water savings, the source of the shortfall may be traced to poorly performing fixtures.

- Inaccurate meter readings do not reflect actual customer use and thus prevent accurate calculations of potential water savings expected from conservation measures.

- Leakage, which commonly occurs with gravity-flush toilets, may represent part of measured water savings if the pre-replacement fixture leaked. However, because new gravity-tank 1.6 gpf fixtures can also be expected to leak over time, a small portion of the water savings from fixture replacement may eventually be lost if future leaks are not controlled through regular maintenance and repair.

- Many showers are connected to tub-spout diverters that release a small amount of water when the shower is turned off and sometimes while the shower is running. Similarly, showerheads with shutoff valves, which should continue to dribble to maintain water temperature and help prevent scalding, also cause some wasted water. These small water losses may slightly reduce the savings expected from showerheads with these features.

installation costs for the valve retrofits totaled $400. With the saved water valued at $750 a year, the simple payback period for this measure was just over six months.[59]

WATER AND SEWER COST SAVINGS   Avoided water and sewer costs associated with the installation of low-volume toilets can be calculated by multiplying the volume of water (and wastewater) reductions expected in homes and offices (see Tables 2.2 and 2.4) times the local utility rates for water and sewer use (excluding fixed charges). A schedule of representative water and sewer utility rates in the United States and their associated marginal cost savings according to a range of reduced water and wastewater volumes is provided in Appendix D, *Water and Sewer Rates, Costs, and Savings by Volume of Use.*

ENERGY SAVINGS   No direct energy savings are associated with installation of the most common types of low-volume toilets (gravity-tank, flushometer-valve, and pressurized-tank), but water and wastewater utilities reap indirect energy savings from the reduced volumes of water and wastewater pumped and processed for treatment and distribution. Toilets that require electricity for operation increase energy costs for consumers.

TOILET CLEANING AND CHEMICALS   Some low-volume toilets with a steep bowl and a small "water spot" (the surface area of the water in the bowl) may require additional brush cleaning. At the same time, smaller concentrations of chemical toilet-bowl cleaner may be needed with low-volume toilets because smaller amounts of water create less dilution.

Costs Associated With Low-Volume Toilets

HARDWARE COSTS   The purchase price of a low-volume toilet is comparable to that of a conventional high-volume toilet in most instances, although fixtures with innovative designs and operating systems usually cost more. Local market conditions and other factors influence the price of toilets significantly, particularly when they are purchased wholesale. Approximate retail costs for water-efficient toilets (bowl and tank) include:

- Gravity-tank (two-piece): $75 to $225 (one-piece models often cost more)
- Flushometer-valve: $150 and up for bowl; $50 to $125 for valve
- Flushometer-tank (pressure-assisted): $150 to $650
- Stainless steel flushometer-valve, blowout-valve, blowout-jet, and siphon-jet toilets for high-security facilities (prisons) and other institutions (hospitals and schools): $600 to $850
- Compressed air: $500 to $950

LABOR AND MATERIAL COSTS   The cost of hiring a plumber to install a typical low-volume, gravity-tank toilet in a home should not be any more than that for a conventional fixture unless the replacement fixture requires reconfiguration of the plumbing and electrical systems or related aesthetic and building renovations (e.g., floor tile or wall remodeling). Depending on local market conditions, the cost of hiring a plumber to install a gravity-tank toilet ranges from $50 to $125; this fee usually includes replacement of the wax ring on the floor at the base of the bowl and disposal of the old toilet.

In multifamily and large utility or municipal toilet replacement programs, the costs of fixtures and installation usually decline because of economies of scale and competitive bidding. Installation fees for commercial and institutional facilities vary depending on the number of fixtures installed. In some instances, maintenance staff may be able to install replacement fixtures at no direct cost.

For residential and nearly all commercial applications, toilet bowls and tanks are made of china; only a small number are made of plastic or other materials. In the past, prisons, hospitals, schools, and other large institutional facilities typically used vitreous china or ceramic bowls and tanks, but stainless steel (1.6 gpf and 3.5 gpf) toilets may be preferred in these facilities because of their excellent flushing performance (achieved by precision-cutting of the bowl), near indestructibility, and ease of cleaning. However, stainless steel toilets are more expensive (excluding the cost of the valve, a stainless steel bowl costs about $400 compared with about $150 for a china bowl), and in facilities other than prisons, their appearance may be considered unattractive. In such instances, stainless steel fixtures can be covered with white epoxy to give them the appearance of conventional china fixtures along with the durability and performance of stainless steel.

PRODUCT MANUFACTURERS   Manufacturers of low-volume toilets and related products are listed in Chapter 6, *The Water Conservation Network.*

Laws, Codes, and Standards Applicable to Low-Volume Toilets

All applicable laws, codes, standards, and health and safety requirements associated with toilets and related devices should be observed when any fixture, appliance, or related plumbing or water system connection is installed or adjusted. These include but are not limited to the federal, state, and local requirements described in the following paragraphs.

FEDERAL WATER-EFFICIENCY REQUIREMENTS   Water-use efficiency requirements for toilets installed, manufactured, or imported in the United States were established by the federal EPAct of 1992 and are regulated by the U.S. Department of Energy (DOE). State and local authorities may set stricter water-use standards for toilets only if granted approval by DOE. EPAct mandates that all gravity-tank, flushometer-valve, flushometer-tank, and electromechanical hydraulic toilets shall use a maximum of 1.6 gpf, as shown in Table 2.1. Exceptions to this requirement include fixtures designed for installation in prisons and blowout toilets (typically used in hospitals and incarceration facilities), which may use a maximum of 3.5 gpf.[26] Some manufacturers of these products now offer 1.6 gpf models for these applications as well. EPAct also requires that toilets (including the flushometer valve that may be connected to the fixture) bear a permanent marking indicating the fixture's maximum flow rate in gallons per flush, as specified by the product marking and labeling requirements established by the American Society of Mechanical Engineers (ASME) in ASME Standard A119.2).[26] EPAct establishes maximum water-use requirements, thereby allowing for fixtures that use less water than the amount established by the legislation.

Performance Test Standards The maximum water-use requirements established by EPAct for toilets incorporate minimum-performance tests and related product requirements for toilets, which are established by ASME and the American National Standards Institute (ANSI), nonprofit standard-setting organizations. The standards applicable to toilets are ASME Standard A112.19.2 *(Vitreous China Plumbing Fixtures)*, ASME Standard A112.19.5 *(Trim for Water Closet Bowls, Tanks and Urinals)*, and ASME Standard A112.19.6 *(Hydraulic Requirements for Water Closets and Urinals)*. The ASME/ANSI standards establish minimum-performance testing protocols that toilets must meet in order to be in compliance with EPAct. The ASME/ANSI standards for toilets used in residences include: the "ball test," which involves flushing 100 ¾-inch-diameter plastic balls; the "granule test," which requires that 2,500 tiny plastic granules be flushed away adequately; the "ink test," in which an ink line drawn inside the upper rim of the bowl must be washed away; and the "dye test" and "drainline transport test," which measure how well solid wastes are flushed down a sewer line. A toilet should be able to easily pass the ASME/ANSI tests; if it cannot, it may be more likely to have performance and reliability problems. In addition to complying with the ASME/ANSI performance tests, manufacturers of toilets have created their own more stringent tests to make sure their products work acceptably.

LOCAL AND STATE AUTHORITIES   Historically, state and local plumbing authorities set water-use standards for toilets, but federal EPAct requirements now supersede these authorities in most instances. Although in practice some state and local authorities may continue to amend their water-use requirements for toilets, according to EPAct only DOE (through passage of a rule) can grant states the power to establish exemptions for water-efficiency requirements that are more stringent than those stipulated by EPAct.

Some states and municipalities require permits that allow toilets to be installed, adjusted, or retrofitted only by a licensed plumber, but these requirements are sometimes waived for large-scale rebate and replacement programs in which trained technicians are used. Installation of composting toilets may also require the approval of health officials. Similarly, adjustments to an electrical system connected to a plumbing fixture typically require a licensed electrician, and modifications to building structures may also have to be completed by a licensed contractor with a permit.

Implementing a Low-Volume Toilet Program

Several considerations should be taken into account in planning a program to replace high-volume toilets with low-volume fixtures.

SELECTING A LOW-VOLUME TOILET   Purchasing agents and consumers can choose from a variety of excellent low-volume toilet designs and price options. In selecting a particular type of operating design (e.g., gravity-tank or pressurized-tank), a number of owners and managers of nonresidential facilities have been pleased with pressurized-tank and pressurized-valve toilets because of their powerful flushing capabilities. Fixtures with performance problems can be avoided by checking consumer surveys and product reviews. Several sources of information may need to be consulted for this task because there is currently no consumer-oriented authority that conducts extensive tests and issues a "seal of approval" rating for low-volume toilets. The ASME/ANSI tests and standards for toilets and other plumbing fixtures are more industry- and code-oriented and primarily serve manufacturers; some toilets that passed the ASME/ANSI tests have received poor ratings in consumer satisfaction surveys and product studies.[45]

A useful guide in selecting a dependable 1.6 gpf toilet is to check survey findings on participants in toilet replacement programs sponsored by cities and water utilities; the most satisfied customers are typically those who purchase fixtures with the best performance ratings. Internet searches may also help uncover this information, either through direct links to program sponsors or articles covering this topic. Because many toilet models are regularly redesigned, it may be useful to consider only those survey data that are recent and based on a significant sample size. Consumer-oriented magazines and buying guides may also be good sources of information about the cost and performance of specific toilet models; again, the most current data should be used because manufacturers sometimes redesign models without changing their names or product numbers.

Those involved in selecting low-volume toilets to be installed in older homes and buildings with large-diameter sewer lines (e.g., 4 to 6 inches) may want to consider a pressurized fixture or some other type of 1.6 gpf toilet with a strong flushing velocity. A fixture with a strong flushing velocity may be preferable if

By installing low-flow water fixtures and taking other steps to conserve water, consumers do a favor for themselves."

—Jack Hoffbuhr,
executive director of AWWA

there is concern about adequate transport of solid wastes down a long sewer lateral, because wide pipes can slow waste movement. Also, gravity-tank fixtures with round bowls may have a faster flushing velocity than those with elongated bowls. Although cost is not always an indicator of quality, toilets sold at cut-rate prices on the retail market should be considered with caution; they may be prone to performance problems (as well as leaks and repair bills) because of cheap materials or imperfect designs or because they are rejects.

PLANNING A TOILET REBATE OR REPLACEMENT PROGRAM

Many water utilities have sponsored toilet replacement programs, often offering a rebate as an incentive to boost customer participation. Successful toilet rebate and replacement programs must be well planned and include these basic components:

- Identification of potential participants (residential and nonresidential), potential water savings, program benefits and costs, schedule, and program budget and human resource requirements.
- Program outreach and marketing strategies targeted to specific customer groups and subgroups.
- Attractive financial incentives—typically a rebate, water bill credit, or fixture giveaway.
- Installation guidance (e.g., printed instructions, call-in technical assistance, referrals to certified plumbers) or assistance (e.g., direct installation service, particularly for the elderly and disabled).
- Purchasing information about 1.6 gpf toilets, such as a description of types available for various applications, along with the names and model numbers of fixtures reported to be reliable in consumer surveys and technical studies.
- Rebate application forms.
- A convenient inspection process.
- Timely rebate processing and payment.
- Evaluation and reporting of program results.

Targeted Water Users and Fixtures   Low-volume 1.6 gpf toilets can be installed to replace nearly all high-volume fixtures typically found in homes and nonresidential properties. Because toilets are significant water users in homes, public buildings, and many commercial and institutional facilities, conservation programs that promote the installation of low-volume toilets have many potential customers.

Number of Toilets Installed   There are several ways to estimate the number of toilets currently installed in a given service area or among a group of customers. In residential customer groups that include both single-family and multifamily dwellings, there is usually one toilet for every 1.5 persons, although this ratio varies by size and age of housing (new homes tend to have more lavatories and bathrooms) and among single-family and multifamily dwellings. An average of 2.27 toilets per home was reported in the Residential End Uses of Water Study (REUS), a report on mail-survey responses from more than 1,100 single-family homes;[61] this number is likely smaller for multifamily dwellings. The number of toilets in nonresidential properties varies widely and is often based on a build-

*W*hen purchasing toilets for distribution, regardless of the brand, demand to know what flapper is installed on those units and, if it is not one of the latest durable materials... insist that the flapper of your choosing be in the unit...."
—John Koeller,
Koeller and Company

ing's type and rated occupancy load. Many buildings have more fixtures than the minimum specified by codes.

In nonresidential facilities, a minimum of one to four toilets for females and one to three toilets for males per 100 occupants (including employees) is usually specified for restrooms in offices, restaurants, and places of assembly; a higher ratio of toilets per occupants is often specified for schools, dormitories, hospitals, prisons, and special uses (see also "Number of Urinals Installed" under Section 2.2 for additional fixtures provided for men). The number of fixtures (toilets and urinals) in restrooms for females and males is often not equal, particularly in older buildings, because previous codes and practices frequently provided more fixtures for males when urinals are counted. As a result of newer codes, modern facilities are more likely to have equal numbers of fixtures. However, the lack of "potty parity" in older buildings, such as theaters, airports, and sports arenas, that have not been renovated in recent years may contribute to waiting lines in women's restrooms.

The *Uniform Plumbing Code* (UPC), adopted by many state and local plumbing and building codes and authorities, specifies the minimum number of fixtures required for male and female restrooms in a range of building types (offices, schools, auditoriums, hospitals, factories, and so on). In addition, the *Uniform Building Code* (UBC) specifies the number of occupants that should be assumed in buildings based on exiting requirements, square footage, and other features (e.g., fixed seating in sports arenas). Together, the UPC and UBC can be used to estimate the number of fixtures expected in a nonresidential building, with a few caveats: (1) some state and local authorities amend the UPC and UBC in their jurisdictions, or they may use a different code (e.g., the *National Standard Plumbing Code*); (2) the number of toilets installed in a facility is usually based on the code requirements at the time of construction or renovation, whichever is most recent; and (3) in some restrooms the number of fixtures installed has been reduced in order to accommodate the requirements of the U.S. Americans with Disabilities Act of 1992.

Life Cycle of Toilets   It is useful to know the life cycle of both old and new toilets because this information can be used in estimating potential water savings as well as the benefits and costs that could be expected from a fixture replacement program.

The useful life of a toilet depends on several factors, including the frequency and type of use, quality of mechanical parts, and water quality. Gravity-flush toilets made of porcelain can have a life span of 25 to 50 years with normal maintenance (replacement of flapper valves and ballcocks and related leak repair as needed). However, in many households, gravity-tank fixtures are replaced more frequently (about every 15 to 20 years) as part of remodeling. Flushometer-valve toilets can last 30 to 50 years, although they deteriorate faster in nonresidential facilities and high-traffic public areas where they are subject to heavy use, abuse, and vandalism. Well-maintained and high-end facilities tend to undergo more frequent remodeling and may have newer fixtures. Generally, toilets installed in office, commercial, and public facilities will be in use for 10 to 15 years before being replaced. The life cycle of pressure-assisted flushometer-tank toilets is less well known because they were not installed in large numbers until the late 1980s.

Pay toilets captured as much as $45,000 a year at Denver's Stapleton airport until 1974, when the Women's Coalition to End Pay Toilets sued the city. Women protested that men had free urinals. After pondering how to meter urinals, Mayor William H. 'King Solomon' McNichols, Jr., had half the locks removed on the women's stalls."
—Thomas J. Noel, *Mile High City*

Nevertheless, it is likely that the exterior vitreous china tank and bowl of flushome-ter-tank fixtures will have durability similar to that of gravity fixtures.

Based on historical plumbing-industry sales figures and fixture installation patterns, the estimated replacement rate for toilets in existing homes is 2 to 6% per year. Additional installations should be expected for new home and building construction, including building conversions (e.g., alteration of old factory buildings for office or condominium use).

Incentives   Large-scale toilet replacement programs sponsored by water utilities and agencies typically involve payment of a financial incentive, or rebate, to qualified customers whose installation of a 1.6 gpf toilet has been verified. In some cases, the program sponsor will pay the customer in other ways, such as a voucher or credit to the water bill. Financial incentives such as rebates are sometimes linked with other strategies designed to motivate people to install low-volume toilets. For example, the Santa Monica, California, "Bay Saver Program," one of the earliest toilet-rebate programs in the United States, added an "incentive fee" ($2 per month for single-family homes and $1.35 for multifamily units) to the bills of customers who had not participated in the toilet rebate program; the incentive fee was removed if they did. This strategy helped the program replace almost 60% of the toilets in Santa Monica.[62, 63]

The rebate amount is usually based on several factors, including: the economic value of the water expected to be saved, based on avoided marginal and capital water and wastewater facility costs (these costs vary by water and sewer service provider); the cost of administering the program; and the minimum rebate amount considered necessary to attract participants. Some sponsoring utilities establish tiered rebate structures, through which customers are offered different rebate amounts depending on the number of toilets installed. A recent survey of numerous toilet-rebate programs cited significantly variable rebate values across the United States.[63] For example, the water authority serving Asheville, North Carolina, offered rebates of $25 or $50 depending on the number of fixtures installed, whereas New York City offered up to $240. Examples of rebate amounts that have been offered include:

- Single-family homeowners: $25, $50, $75, $100, or $240 per toilet
- Multifamily building owners: $25, $50, $75, or $100 per toilet
- Commercial property owners: $150 per toilet
- Installation: not offered (customer pays cost), $25 to $35, or free
- Toilet-rebate programs sometimes include distribution of free low-volume 2.5 gpm showerheads and faucet aerators. A few programs also offer small rebates (usually less than $10) for installation of a 2.5 gpm showerhead, but most do not.

CUSTOMER PARTICIPATION IN TOILET REPLACEMENT PROGRAMS   A high rate of consumer participation and satisfaction with low-volume toilet replacement programs is usually achieved by well-designed programs that offer attractive rebates and are adequately staffed to assist customers, oversee inspections, and process rebates in a timely manner. The number of customer participants in 1.6 gpf toilet rebate programs can vary widely depending on the program's goals, budget, and schedule.

Case Study *Los Angeles Replaces One Third of City's Residential Toilets Through Rebate Program.* The Los Angeles Department of Water and Power has helped to fund the installation of more than 750,000 1.6 gpf toilets in Los Angeles, about 33% of residential toilets installed citywide. The utility has accomplished this through a combination of direct rebates to customers and the involvement of community-based organizations. Residential customers are offered rebates of $100 per low-volume toilet installed, and $75 rebates are available for other installations. Community organizations such as the Mothers of East LA and the Korean Youth Community Center have received $25 for each free toilet they have installed in low-income homes.[48, 63]

Case Study *Santa Monica's Toilet-Rebate Program Reduces Wastewater System Costs.* Santa Monica's "Bay Saver" toilet-rebate program, one of the first in the United States, resulted in the replacement of almost 60% (more than 23,000 fixtures) of that city's toilets with 1.6 gpf models by 1993 and has lowered water use and sewage flows by about 15% each. Offering rebates first of $100 and then $75 (increased sales of the fixtures brought local prices down), the program also offered installation services for $35. Projections indicate that this largely residential community of more than 85,000 people will save $6 million from the program by 2002. Estimates also indicate that for every dollar invested in the program, $2 will be returned in avoided water and wastewater system capacity and treatment costs.[64]

Some utilities view rebate programs as primarily an educational endeavor to raise awareness about the need for conservation; they may designate only a small budget and short schedule to sponsor a limited number of fixture replacements. Others have embarked on aggressive replacement efforts as major capital programs because they generate high, reliable water savings. Collectively, the toilet replacement programs sponsored by New York City's Department of Environmental Protection, the Metropolitan Water District of Southern California, and the U.S. Department of Energy's Federal Energy Management Program's water conservation program (which assists federal agencies in installing low-volume toilets and other water-efficient technologies) have spent hundreds of millions of dollars and installed well over a million 1.6 gpf toilets in the United States in less than five years. These efforts have resulted in the avoidance of significant capital facility costs for new water supplies and sewage treatment facilities, plus other benefits. A number of other programs, although smaller, continue to accelerate the installation of low-volume fixtures to reduce water demand and associated costs.[63]

*A*lways do right. This will gratify some people and astonish the rest."
—Mark Twain

INSTALLATION OF LOW-VOLUME TOILETS Installation of low-volume toilets should be done by properly trained technicians or plumbers and should be based on applicable rules and practices. In a jurisdiction that allows consumers to install toilets themselves, consumers should be fully advised about proper procedures, tools, and precautions to ensure competent, safe installation. Installers should be careful to avoid damaging a customer's property.

Low-volume toilets can be installed in the same "rough-in" dimensions as existing conventional toilets if the fixtures are of the same type (e.g., installing a floor-mounted 1.6 gpf gravity-tank fixture to replace a floor-mounted 3.5 gpf gravity-tank fixture). The rough-in dimension is the distance between the wall and the sewer drainline for the toilet. The standard rough-in dimension is 12 inches, although some toilets are available in rough-in sizes of 10 inches, 14 inches, and other specialty sizes. The rough-in size of an existing toilet should be measured before a new fixture is purchased and installed.

Older flushometer-valve toilets with floor outlets require minor plumbing reconfigurations if the replacement fixture has a wall outlet.

Water Pressure Adequate water pressure (25 to 40 psi) is required for flushometer-valve and flushometer-tank toilets to operate properly. This is particularly important for single-family and small multifamily homes and other dwellings that previously relied on a gravity-tank toilet operated under lower pressures than those required for flushometer fixtures. In some cases, changing flushometer-activated toilets from 3.5 gpf to 1.6 gpf may require higher pressure (e.g., 30 to 35 psi) for optimal performance. When line pressure is inadequate, flushometers will not operate or shut off as designed. For older buildings in which scale buildup has reduced the diameter of the water pipes, flushing may be a problem.[43]

Troubleshooting Performance Problems When performance problems such as bowl clogging, trapway clogging, and drainline stoppages occur with low-volume toilets (as they do with 3.5 gpf and higher-volume fixtures), these may be due to one or multiple sources. The first step in preventing problems is selecting a well-designed low-volume toilet that is known to have good performance. The late Wendy L. Corpening, president of W.L. Corpening & Associates in Avery, California, an expert on water-efficient plumbing products, identified solutions to potential problems with the performance of low-volume and retrofitted toilets. Her suggestions are summarized here:[65]

- The sewer laterals should be cleaned before a low-volume toilet is installed. Where drainline problems exist, installing a pressure-assisted (flushometer-valve or -tank) toilet or leaving a high-volume fixture at the end of a lateral may help waste transport.
- Proper installation of the toilet is imperative; the trap outlet should fit as exactly as possible over the toilet flange and pipe in the floor or wall. Any offset can cause clogs as waste exits the trapway into the drainline.
- Only toilet paper and human waste should be deposited in a toilet; paper towels, sanitary and contraceptive products, and other items should be discarded in trash bins (signs to this effect may be advised in public restrooms).
- Flushometer fixtures depend on a "marriage" of the valve and bowl for proper flushing, i.e., each valve and bowl should be designed by the manufacturer to work together as a unit.

- The interior of the toilet trapway should be inspected for porcelain nodules that may remain from the manufacturing process. These lumps of claylike material should be cleared to avoid clogs.
- The pressure of flowing water *at the connection to the toilet* should be at least 25 psi to operate properly.

RECYCLING USED TOILETS   In large-scale fixture replacement programs, collecting and disposing of old toilets can be a significant expense and environmental burden that can be lessened by recycling. Some rebate programs collect and crush porcelain from the bowls and tanks of old toilets so they can be recycled for other purposes, such as road aggregate, building-material mix, artificial reefs, and other items.[66] Similarly, the metal, rubber, and plastic parts of old tanks and flushometer fixtures may be recycled as scrap or reused for other purposes.

MAINTENANCE OF LOW-VOLUME TOILETS   All toilets should be checked regularly for leaks and to ensure they are properly adjusted to operate within their design flush volume. Gravity-tank toilets in particular should be inspected at least twice a year and require ongoing maintenance to minimize water losses from leakage. This is especially important for fixtures that have inferior-quality mechanical parts or operate in corrosive water conditions. A study of flapper valves installed in low-volume toilets indicates that 1.6 gpf toilets in particular may be prone to higher leakage as a result of poorly designed or adjusted flush-valve closure devices[67] (see Section 2.1.4, "Toilet Leak Repair").

Sensor-activated toilets should be checked periodically to ensure they are set properly and are not causing unnecessary flushing. Used batteries from sensor-controlled toilets should be properly disposed of to comply with applicable waste disposal laws and to minimize adverse environmental effects or safety hazards.

2.1.2 Waterless Toilets

The types of waterless toilets typically in use are composting or incinerator units that require no water for flushing. Oil-flush, chemical, and vacuum toilets are also waterless alternatives although they are used less frequently.

Waterless toilets use no water for flushing and require only small amounts for periodic cleaning and maintenance. Some waterless toilets are cleaned with chemicals instead of water. Some toilets that are described as waterless but that regularly require small amounts of water for flushing may be more appropriately classified as ultralow-volume fixtures.

Composting toilet systems, which have been in use for more than 50 years, and incinerator toilets represent a very small percentage of toilets installed.[68] Waterless toilet systems are unconventional in their installation requirements as well as their operation and maintenance, but they are gaining acceptance by users and code authorities because they represent a viable method of human waste management when they are properly maintained. Composting and incinerating toilets are available in a variety of designs to accommodate a number of site conditions and needs.

The driest places on Earth are a series of valleys near Ross Island in Antarctica where for the past two million years at least, no rain has fallen."
—www.uselessfacts.net

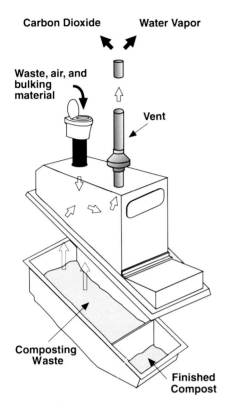

Carbon Dioxide   Water Vapor

Waste, air, and bulking material

Vent

Composting Waste

Finished Compost

Figure 2.17   **Composting toilets do not need water or sewer connections, but they require regular maintenance. (Illustration courtesy of Clivus Multrum, Inc.)**

2.1.2.1 Composting Toilets

Composting (or "biological") toilets are not flushed and need virtually no water to convert human waste into humus; thus they require no connections to a plumbing system. Composting toilets rely on microorganisms that are naturally present in human waste and added bulk materials to decompose, or compost, the waste. Because they have their own waste treatment system, they also don't need sewer or septic system hookups.

There are two types of composting toilets—self-contained units and central composting systems. Self-contained units are usually small and portable, although they are available in a number of capacities. Some require electricity to operate, but others do not. Central composting systems are larger and collect waste from one or multiple toilets and urinals that are connected to a collection and decomposition tank, or composter (usually located in the basement or adjacent to a building), as shown in Figure 2.17. The Clivus Multrum® composting toilet has been the model for many types of composting systems, but other designs are also available.[69] Centralized composting units are available in electric and nonelectric models, including solar-powered systems. An illustration of a composting toilet system is shown in Figure 2.18.

Composting toilets operate by collecting wastes (feces, urine, and toilet paper) that fall from the toilet bowl into a compost tank either directly under the toilet or connected to it by a chute. There is no flushing with water, although liquid chemicals are sometimes used to move solid wastes to the tank. Once inside the tank, wastes are mixed with organic bulk material (wood shavings, mulches, sawdust, grass clippings, or leaves) and fresh air (oxygen). The mixing process involves turning over the wastes inside the chamber either manually or automatically, depending on the composter's design. Organic carbon in the mixing material and solid waste along with nitrogen from the urine promote the growth of aerobic (oxygen-hungry) bacteria, which facilitate the decomposition of wastes in the tank. This process creates two gases, carbon dioxide and water vapor, which are vented.

Adequate warmth and air circulation are required to evaporate water from the waste and promote decomposition; 65°F or higher is preferred. The process also needs adequate moisture, usually 40 to 75% within the composting pile, to mix with sufficient air to maintain aerobic conditions. Temperatures below 50°F will slow decomposition but won't stop it indefinitely; waste breakdown resumes as soon as the chamber is warmed up. A small heater is often installed in the tank for operation in cold climates and winter months to ensure that the intake air is adequately warm. Composting systems require periodic mixing to aerate and blend the compost, and some systems have a motor and fan inside the composter for this purpose. Adding a small amount of water can keep the compost moist and facilitate decomposition. The composting process reduces the original waste material by up to 90% after venting carbon dioxide and water vapor, rendering the remaining material a form of humus.[68, 70]

The end product of the composting process, usually removable by a clean-out tray, should be odor-free and safe if the process has been correctly managed. For example, the manufacturer of the Clivus Multrum system explains that the Clivus process "involves oxidation of ammonia to nitrite and nitrate (portions of a process known as nitrification). Both nitrite and nitrate are very toxic to human pathogens and this part of the process is responsible for rendering the end-product safe. Safe end-products do not require a complete nitrification but enough to perform the 'sterilization.'"[71] Composting systems require careful management to operate properly and safely, but they need no water or sewer lines or septic systems and leach fields.[70, 72]

2.1.2.2 Incinerator Toilets

Incinerator toilets use high-temperature electric or propane heat to burn wastes, leaving a fine ash by-product. Incinerator toilets are typically used on boats and in remote locations where plumbed and composting toilets are not practical, such as cabins, arctic environments, and oil rigs, but they can also be used in homes and other types of buildings.

A basic incinerator toilet consists of a boxlike unit with a fan to control temperatures and to vent gases and moisture outside through a polyvinyl chloride or metal pipe, as shown in Figure 2.19. Waste is deposited onto a plastic liner inside the unit, and a button or switch is activated to begin the incineration process after each use. For example, the Incinolet, an incinerator toilet produced by Research Products/Blankenship, USA, is reported by its manufacturer to incinerate waste at a temperature of about 1,400°F. After the waste is destroyed, a fan cools the toilet and vents the heated exhaust.[73]

PERFORMANCE OF WATERLESS TOILETS The performance of composting, incinerator, and other waterless toilets has not been studied to the extent that the performance of low-volume flush toilets has, although many composting toilets meet NSF International's Standard 41 design requirements for these types of toilets (see "Laws, Codes, and Standards Applicable to Waterless Toilets" later in this section).[68] NSF International, formerly the National Sanitation Foundation, is an independent, nonprofit organization that has established voluntary testing and performance standards for certain sanitation and other environmental products.

Case studies about the performance of waterless toilets often report that users are very satisfied with these products. A review of product information from several manufacturers of composting systems indicates that more than 50,000 units have been installed worldwide since these toilets were first installed in Sweden in the 1930s.[71] At least one incinerator toilet manufactured since the 1960s is reported by its manufacturer to be used extensively in Japan, Norway, and other countries.[73]

Water Savings and Related Benefits From Waterless Toilets

WATER SAVINGS The use of waterless toilets will reduce water use and leakage from toilets by virtually 100% (excluding the small amount required for cleaning), as shown for households in Table 2.7 and for office buildings in Table 2.8. Households with 3.5 gpf "water-saver" toilets will save an estimated 17.9 gpcd or 47.1 gphd, equivalent to an annual water savings of 6,515 gpcy or 17,200 gphy, as shown in Table 2.7. Nonresidential facilities with conventional toilets and urinals that have high water demand can reap substantial water savings. For example, an office that replaces a 3.5 gpf toilet with a waterless fixture will save an estimated 3.5 gpcd per male and 10.5 gpcd per female, or 910 gpcy for

Figure 2.18 Generic composting toilet system for toilet and urinal connections (Photo courtesy of Ecos, Inc.)

Figure 2.19 Incinerator toilets use electricity to incinerate human waste, leaving an odor-free ash that can be disposed of in the trash. (Photo courtesy of Research Products/Blankenship)

TABLE 2.7

Estimated water savings by waterless toilets in households

Years Manufactured or Installed *	Toilet Water-Use Rate	Frequency of Toilet Use Daily Per Person	Estimated Water Savings With a Waterless Toilet†			
			Daily		Yearly	
			Per Capita	Per Household‡	Per Capita	Per Household‡
	gpf	number of uses	gal	gal	gal	gal
1994-present	1.0	5.1	5.1	13.5	1,862	4,914
1997-present §	**1.6**	5.1	8.2	21.5	2,978	7,863
1994-present **	**1.6**	5.1	8.2	21.5	2,978	7,863
1980-1994	3.5	5.1	17.9	47.1	6,515	17,200
	4.0	5.1	20.4	53.9	7,446	19,657
	4.5	5.1	23.0	60.6	8,377	22,115
1950s-1980	5.0	5.1	25.5	67.3	9,308	24,572
	5.5	5.1	28.1	74.1	10,238	27,029
Pre-1950s	7.0	5.1	35.7	94.2	13,031	34,401

* Time periods are approximate. Dates in state and local jurisdictions may vary somewhat from dates shown except when they are superseded by the Jan. 1, 1994 federal requirement (shown in bold) allowing a maximum of 1.6 gpf for most toilets installed after that date, per the U.S. Energy Policy Act of 1992.

† Excludes water used for cleaning and attributable to leaks

‡ Based on the average of 2.64 persons per occupied U.S. household

§ Flushometer-valve fixtures and gravity-tank, white, two-piece fixtures labeled "Commercial Use Only" (most common in nonresidential settings)

** Gravity-tank, flushometer-tank, and electromechanical hydraulic fixtures (most common in residential and small office and commercial settings)

gpf = gallons per flush

number of uses = average number of times per day toilet is flushed

gal = gallon

Sources: Amy Vickers & Associates, Inc.; References 26, 37, and 52

males and 2,730 gpcy for females, as shown in Table 2.8. These water reductions will also yield a corresponding reduction in outflows to sewer and septic systems.

A composting toilet system installed at Salisbury Beach in Massachusetts was designed to accommodate 10,000 users daily and is saving an estimated 1 million gallons of water (and equivalent sewer loads) annually. A similar but smaller composting system is used by visitors to Walden Pond, the inspiration for Henry David Thoreau's classic, *Walden*, and now a state park in Concord, Massachusetts.[74]

WATER AND SEWER COST SAVINGS Avoided water and sewer costs associated with installation of a waterless toilet can be calculated by multiplying the expected volume of water (and wastewater) reductions (see Tables 2.7 and 2.8 for estimates for residential and office buildings, respectively) times the local utility rates for water and sewer use (excluding fixed charges). A schedule of representative water and sewer utility rates in the United States and their associated marginal cost savings according to a range of reduced water and wastewater vol-

TABLE 2.8

Estimated water savings by waterless toilets in office buildings*

Years Manufactured or Installed†	Toilet Water-Use Rate gpf	Frequency of Toilet Use‡ Daily Per Male number of uses	Per Female number of uses	Estimated Water Savings With a Waterless Toilet§ Daily Per Male gal	Per Female gal	Yearly (260 workdays) Per Male gal	Per Female gal
1994-present	1.0	1.0	3.0	1.0	3.0	260	780
1997-present **	**1.6**	1.0	3.0	1.6	4.8	416	1,248
1994-present ††	**1.6**	1.0	3.0	1.6	4.8	416	1,248
1980-1994	3.5	1.0	3.0	3.5	10.5	910	2,730
	4.0	1.0	3.0	4.0	12.0	1,040	3,120
	4.5	1.0	3.0	4.5	13.5	1,170	3,510
1950s-1980	5.0	1.0	3.0	5.0	15.0	1,300	3,900
	5.5	1.0	3.0	5.5	16.5	1,430	4,290
Pre-1950s	7.0	1.0	3.0	7.0	21.0	1,820	5,460

* Applies to office buildings with men's restrooms that include urinals; if facilities do not include urinals, water use and savings should be based on the frequency of use per female.

† Time periods are approximate. Dates in state and local jurisdictions may vary somewhat from dates shown except when they are superseded by the Jan. 1, 1994 federal requirement (shown in bold) allowing a maximum of 1.6 gpf for most toilets installed after that date, per the U.S. Energy Policy Act of 1992.

‡ Females and males use office restrooms in about equal numbers but not by fixture type. Women use toilets approximately 3 times per workday; men use toilets about 1 time per workday and urinals about 2 times per workday. (See Table 2.10 for water use and potential savings by urinals in office buildings.)

§ Excludes water used for cleaning and attributable to leaks

** Flushometer-valve fixtures and gravity-tank, white, two-piece fixtures labeled "Commercial Use Only" (most common in nonresidential settings)

†† Gravity-tank, flushometer-tank, and electromechanical hydraulic fixtures (most common in residential and small office and commercial settings)

gpf = gallons per flush

number of uses = average number of times per day fixture is used

gal = gallon

Sources: Amy Vickers & Associates, Inc.; References 26, 38, and 39

umes is provided in Appendix D, *Water and Sewer Rates, Costs, and Savings by Volume of Use.*

REDUCED SEWER AND SEPTIC SYSTEM NEEDS   Waterless composting and incinerator toilets (and urinals) require no plumbing and no sewer or septic system hookups. For new houses and facilities built with waterless toilet systems, capital and operating costs can be saved as a result of smaller septic tanks and leaching fields.

For existing homes and facilities served by septic systems, installation of composting and incinerator toilets can often extend the useful life of the system. Similarly, the cost-effectiveness of installing and maintaining a waterless toilet might increase significantly in situations where continued use of flush toilets would necessitate expansion or replacement of an existing system to comply with sanitary or environmental codes (e.g., Title V of the Massachusetts Environmental Code requirements for septic systems).

ENERGY SAVINGS   Most waterless toilet systems require energy to operate (see "Costs Associated With Waterless Toilets" later in this section). However, these systems also account for some indirect energy savings at water and wastewater treatment plants because they are not hooked up to those systems.

TREATED COMPOSTER WASTE FOR NONCROP REUSE   Waste from composting systems that is properly treated according to all applicable laws and codes can sometimes be redirected for noncrop applications. For example, the treated waste from a composter serving the Massachusetts Audubon's Wellfleet Bay (Cape Cod) visitor center is used to amend the soil in a 300-foot-long raised planter bed for noncrop species.[74]

Costs Associated With Waterless Toilets

HARDWARE COSTS   Composting systems and incinerator toilets cost considerably more than conventional flush toilets, although some of this cost is offset by avoided or reduced plumbing and sewage costs. Purchase and installation costs for composting and incinerator toilets vary by size and design and can be found in these approximate ranges:

- Composting toilet system for a single-family home: $2,000 to $16,000
- Composting toilet system for a small commercial building: $5,000 to $20,000
- Portable composting toilet: $700 to $1,700
- Incinerator toilet: $900 to $1,800

LABOR AND MATERIAL COSTS   Costs associated with installation of a composting toilet system in an existing building include those for the toilet(s), composting storage container (including electric variable-speed fan to provide oxygen to the composting waste and to prevent odors from exiting through the toilet or urinal instead of the vent stack), vent system, and building alterations.

In most cases, simple incinerator toilets that are permanently installed in restrooms require removal of the old flush toilet (and related plumbing disconnections), minor floor and wall remodeling, installation of a vent stack, and connection to an electrical outlet.

OPERATING COSTS   Operating costs for composting toilets include electricity or other power source to operate the fan in the waste container, foam or other material to facilitate decomposition and to aid the movement of wastes down pipe bends, filter replacements, and (sometimes) worms to enhance decomposition in the composter. Some portable composting toilets do not have separate composting containers and require some accommodation for venting and removal of decomposed waste.

Operating costs for incinerator toilets include electricity (see "Energy Costs" later in this section) and plastic liners for waste collection.

REMOVAL OF DECOMPOSED WASTE   Depending on the amount of waste generated, removal and off-site disposal costs may be incurred for waste material collected in composters. Some composting systems, particularly larger ones, are maintained through service contracts.

ENERGY COSTS   Use of electricity or other energy source to operate a composting or incinerating system adds to the toilet's operating cost, but this cost can be minimized when renewable energy sources such as solar or wind are used or when composting systems can be heated by nearby passive sources such as chimney flues or hot water pipes. Solar heating of decomposing waste may improve a composting system's evaporation rate and increase digestion, helping to reduce the volume of compost and the frequency of its removal.[68] The energy requirements of specific models vary.

- Composting toilets that are dependent on electricity for operation show a wide range of energy use.
- The Incinolet toilet is offered in several models with different capacities and energy requirements. For example, one model uses about 2 kilowatt-hours (kWh) of energy during each incineration cycle; one cycle can incinerate up to four urine deposits (an average of 0.5 kWh), according to the product's manufacturer. The manufacturer estimates that four persons using the toilet will consume an average of 8 kWh per day, based on a 120-volt unit with an 1,800-watt heater.[73]

PRODUCT MANUFACTURERS   Manufacturers of composting systems and incinerator toilets and related products are provided in Chapter 6, *The Water Conservation Network.*

Laws, Codes, and Standards Applicable to Waterless Toilets

All applicable laws, codes, standards, and health and safety requirements associated with waterless toilets and related devices should be observed when any fixture, appliance, or related plumbing or water system connection is installed or adjusted.

Approval to use a composting toilet varies by state and local authorities, which may have rules affecting installation and use. Acceptance of alternative toilet waste disposal technologies seems to be increasing in states such as Massachusetts, where more stringent septic system requirements have been imposed. (In addition to composting systems, a number of innovative, alternative waste-removal technologies have been approved for general use by the Massachusetts Department of Environmental Protection.)[75]

Some regulators may easily approve the installation of a composting toilet but may have requirements for managing waste collection, treatment, and disposal. Because human waste is regulated for the purpose of protecting public health, improper or careless management of stored human waste can create health hazards. Depending on local and state laws, the waste product (humus) from composting systems may be required to be either buried or removed by a licensed septage dealer. For example, Massachusetts state regulations require that compost be buried a minimum of 6 inches below the ground's surface. In addition, central composting systems that accommodate more than one toilet may also need an NSF International–approved facility where unevaporated liquid can be collected or drained.[68]

NSF International grants an "NSF mark of approval" for centralized composting toilet systems that meet the requirements of ANSI/NSF Standard 41 (*Non-Liquid Saturated Treatment Systems*). Some jurisdictions require that centralized composting models comply with NSF Standard 41 to be approved for installation. Tests for this standard include waste-loading, routine operation at the

Nature never breaks her own laws."

—Leonardo da Vinci

design-rated capacity, stress-testing, liquid containment, and odor control (at the toilet bowl and ground-level composter chamber).[70]

Some states and municipalities require permits that allow waterless toilets to be installed, adjusted, or retrofitted only by a licensed plumber, but these requirements are sometimes waived for large-scale rebate and replacement programs in which trained technicians are used.

Implementing a Waterless Toilet Program

Waterless toilets can be a viable measure to reduce water use for human waste removal, but they are significantly different from conventional flush toilets and require careful selection, installation, and ongoing maintenance to operate reliably and safely. For these reasons, the costs and benefits of a waterless toilet system should be evaluated thoroughly before one is installed. Further, all technical requirements as well as applicable health, building, and plumbing codes and laws should be carefully reviewed to ensure that the waste system will be properly installed and maintained.

SELECTING A WATERLESS TOILET   Selection of a waterless toilet is usually site-specific and is determined by such factors as cost, applicable codes and laws, installation requirements, ease of use, and maintenance requirements.

TARGETED WATER USERS   Waterless toilet systems can be used to replace water-using toilets in homes, offices, and other facilities that have been modified for their operation, but they are most commonly found in highway rest areas, national and state parks, ski resorts, seasonal homes, nature centers, camps, temporary work sites, and remote locations where water is scarce or conventional sewage and septic systems are unavailable. Small portable waterless toilets are sometimes used in places that are infrequently visited, such as cabins, boats, and isolated workplaces.

Customers participating in toilet-rebate programs rarely install waterless toilets, probably because of their higher cost and more complicated installation requirements. For facilities with large numbers of users, however, they may yield superior water savings and long-term cost savings compared with flush toilets.

NUMBER AND LIFE CYCLE OF WATERLESS TOILETS INSTALLED   The number of waterless toilets in operation in the United States is not well established, and little literature on the longevity of composting and incinerator toilets exists other than manufacturer claims. Anecdotal reports indicate that composting toilet systems can have a long life (20 years or more) if they are properly maintained.

INSTALLATION OF WATERLESS TOILETS   Installation of waterless toilets should be done only by properly trained technicians or plumbers and electricians (in the case of fixtures that rely on electricity) and should be based on applicable rules and practices. In a jurisdiction that allows consumers to install such products themselves, consumers should be fully advised about proper procedures, tools, and precautions to ensure competent, safe installation.

Except for self-contained and portable composting toilets, installation and operation of a composting toilet may involve several steps: structural alterations to create a space to accommodate decomposition, wiring for electricity to operate a vent system, reconfiguration of existing floor and wall areas near the fixture to ensure correct fit and aesthetic appearance, and applicable permits.

Electrical Requirements   Most composting systems and incinerator toilets require electricity to run compressors, heaters, and air vents, but some solar-heated systems are available. Both electrical and solar-heated systems typically require design and construction modifications of existing buildings to accommodate vents and electrical requirements. Nonelectric composting systems rely on the natural heat output from the compost itself and the draft induced by the chimney on the vent stack to release odors above the ridge of a building's roof. Extra moisture can remain with this method, necessitating a leach field or other removal system.[76]

MANAGEMENT OF HUMAN WASTE MATERIAL FROM WATERLESS TOILETS   Human waste collected in a composter requires four to six years to fully biodegrade into the humus material that remains after the decomposition process.[75] For the Clivus composting system, approximately 5% of the original amount of solid waste remains at the end of the process.[74]

Reusability of human waste by-products from composting and incinerator toilets is limited, and disposal is subject to regulation in some if not all states and locales. Costs may be incurred if the waste material requires special handling or must be removed off site. Some authorities consider the liquid remaining in the composter to be septage and require it to be pumped by a septage contractor.[74] The ash by-product from incinerator toilets has no organic value and can usually be discarded as garbage, but this should be verified with appropriate authorities in a given locale.[68]

Claims that untreated decomposed waste material from composting toilet systems is "organic," "natural," or otherwise "safe" for reuse in a garden, as potting soil for houseplants, or for other uses that could involve human or animal contact may be unrealistic and, as noted, may be prohibited for several reasons. First, waste decomposition in composting systems is dependent on sufficient oxygen, temperature control, and proper management. If necessary conditions are not met due to technical failure or human error, seemingly decomposed waste may still contain pathogens and other hazardous substances that present health risks. Second, the layers of waste material in a composting tank are not at equal stages of decomposition, so ascertaining when the material is safe may be difficult. Third, people who are on medication, receive radioactive pharmacological treatment, or consume or are exposed to chemical substances may produce hazardous human waste products that do not easily break down and that persist in the environment. Thus, handling and disposal of human waste material from composting and incinerator toilets should be carried out strictly according to manufacturer directions as well as applicable health and related regulations.

Cologne, also called EAU DE COLOGNE, *in perfumery, is a scented solution usually consisting of alcohol and about 2-6 percent perfume concentrate. The two terms, cologne and toilet water, however, have come to be used interchangeably."*
—Encyclopædia Brittanica

MAINTENANCE OF WATERLESS TOILETS Composting toilets require periodic if not daily maintenance (particularly systems serving many users) to ensure that waste is decomposing properly, adequate carbon materials are added and mixed, the liquid chamber is drained, and insect and odor control are adequate. Some systems are enhanced with composting worms that accelerate the rate of decomposition through improved aeration and mixing of the compost pile. Regular inspection of the composting system by a trained professional may be advisable to ensure proper, safe operation.[69]

Incinerator toilets require cleaning primarily on the seat and exterior of the fixture; the incineration process destroys wastes inside the unit. The unit can hold incinerated wastes from a number of uses before the ash pan requires emptying.

2.1.3 Toilet Retrofit Devices

Toilet retrofit devices are used in residential and nonresidential water conservation programs to reduce the amount of water needed to flush high-volume toilets that use 3.5 gpf or more. Toilet retrofit devices are often included in retrofit kits that contain other water-saving devices such as low-volume 2.5 gpm showerheads, 2.0 to 2.5 gpm faucet aerators, and dye tablets for diagnosing toilet leaks.

High-volume gravity-tank and flushometer-valve toilets that use 3.5 gpf or more can be retrofitted with a variety of devices to reduce their water use, sometimes by more than a gallon per flush. Identifying the right device for a particular toilet is the key to achieving reliable water savings and avoiding disruption to the flushing mechanism. Low-volume 1.6 gpf toilets as a rule cannot accommodate retrofit devices to reduce water use and still flush reliably; however, in some instances they can be adjusted with dual-flush devices designed specifically for low-volume fixtures.

A variety of alternative flushing and retrofit devices and adjustments can be used to reduce the water requirements of toilets designed to use 3.5 to 7.0 gpf. The most common devices and adjustments include:

- Displacement devices (bottles and bags or "bladders")
- Toilet dams (plastic or metal)
- Early closure devices
- Dual-flush adapters
- Diaphragm retrofit kits (for flush-valve fixtures only)
- Efficiency adjustments for flush valves

2.1.3.1 Displacement Devices

Toilet displacement devices such as bags, as shown in Figure 2.20 (A), and bottles are commonly used in gravity-tank toilets because they are easy to install, generally reliable, and inexpensive. Displacement devices save water by occupying a part of the toilet tank that would otherwise be filled with water, thereby reducing the amount held in the tank and released for each flush.

Displacement bags come in a range of materials and styles. The more durable products are made with high-strength plastic and rubber materials and with

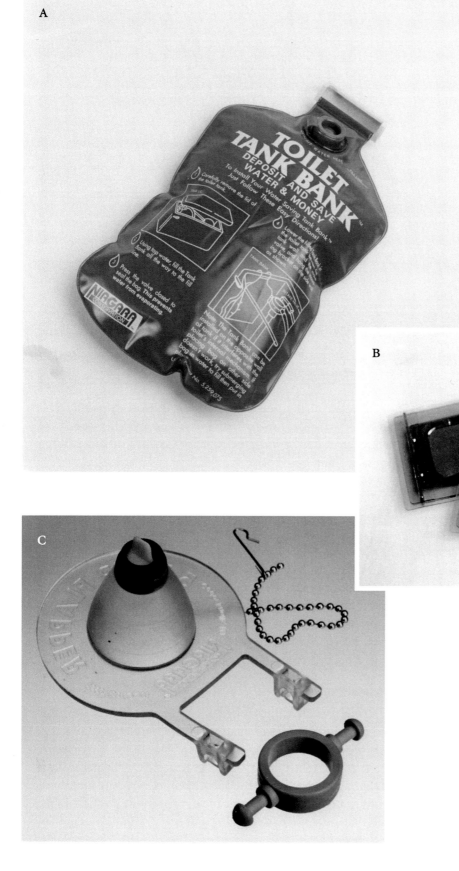

Figure 2.20 Retrofit devices for high-volume, gravity-tank toilets can save 0.5 to 1.5 gallons per flush: (A) toilet displacement bag, (B) toilet dams, and (C) adjustable flapper valve and flapper connection adapter. (Photos A and C courtesy of Niagara Conservation, Inc.; Photo B courtesy of Amy Vickers & Associates, Inc.)

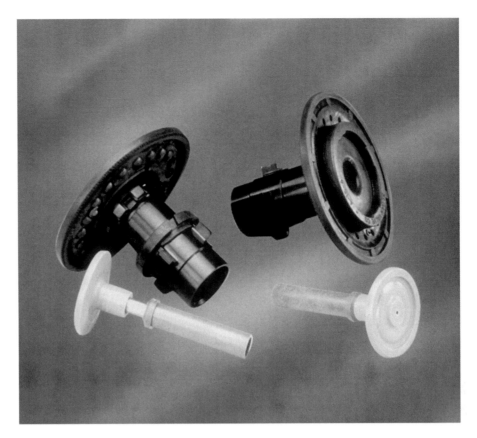

Figure 2.21 Diaphragm retrofit kits installed in high-volume, flushometer-valve toilets and urinals can save about 1.0 gallon per flush per fixture. (Photo courtesy of Sloan Valve Co.)

easy closures and tank attachments. Bottle displacement devices are usually plastic containers that are filled with gravel or water and placed on the side of the intake valve or below the bottom level of the ballcock—a location that will not disrupt the flushing mechanism.

2.1.3.2 Toilet Dams

Toilet dams save water by maintaining the head pressure of a full tank of water to provide adequate flushing velocity but with a smaller amount of water. The dams, as shown in Figure 2.20 (B), are flexible panels, about 5.0 by 8.5 inches, and are usually made of plastic, rubber, and metal reinforcements. Dams are inserted across the bottom of the tank of a gravity toilet. The edge of the dam is flared slightly so it can fit tightly against the bottom and walls of the tank on either side of the flush valve (it should fit as closely as possible without interfering with the flushing mechanism). One or two dams are installed, depending on the toilet's size and tank configuration.

2.1.3.3 Early Closure Devices

Early closure devices, usually adjustable flappers, as shown in Figure 2.20 (C), can be installed in most high-volume, gravity-tank toilets to replace or amend the original flapper valve. When the toilet is flushed, the early closure device uses the pressure from the full tank of water to force the flapper to close early, releasing a reduced amount of water but with enough velocity for a complete flush. Some adjustable flappers are available in high-grade plastic, rubber, and metal materials that are resistant to the effects of chlorine and chloramines, ensuring a longer flapper life and minimal leakage.[77]

Early closure devices are available in various styles. Some use a regular flapper valve that bleeds air from below the valve, causing a shorter flush. Another type fits over the overflow tube and forces the flapper to close early.[77]

2.1.3.4 Dual-Flush Adapters

Dual-flush adapters can be installed in many gravity-tank fixtures to provide alternative low- and high-volume flush controls. Although most dual-flush adapters are used to retrofit high-volume fixtures, dual-flush adapters for 1.6 gpf toilets are now available as well. These devices provide reduced water flows for liquid-only (with paper) flushes, accomplished by holding the handle down for a short length of time or by pulling it in a designated direction. The handle can be depressed for a longer time or in another direction to provide a higher volume of water for flushing solids from the bowl.

Like dual-flush toilets, conventional toilets that have dual-flush adapters may cause confusion for some users, particularly children and the elderly. When the handle is pulled in the wrong direction (e.g., for a short flush when the bowl contains solid wastes), clogging or the need to double-flush may result and water savings will be lost. Confusion can be minimized by teaching users how the flush handle adapter is operated and, in public restrooms, by installing a directional decal or sign near the toilet handle.

2.1.3.5 Diaphragm Retrofit Kits for Flushometer-Valve Toilets and Urinals

The flush volumes of some older 3.5 to 5.0 gpf flushometer-valve toilets (as well as flush-valve urinals) can be reduced by about 1.0 gpf by installing a valve replacement kit inside the flush valve. A retrofit kit for a flushometer-valve toilet or urinal is shown in Figure 2.21. As noted, a "marriage" of the valve and the bowl is required so that a bowl designed for a high-volume fixture can accommodate reduced flows without creating clogging problems; many flush-valve fixtures can do this successfully, but some cannot. Existing 3.5 to 7.0 gpf flushometer-valve toilets cannot be retrofitted to the 1.6 gpf level simply by installing a 1.6 gpf flush valve because bowls for 1.6 gpf flushometer-valve toilets are designed differently from those for higher-volume fixtures.

Disassembling and retrofitting older flushometer valves may be problematic because they can be corroded. For example, retrofitting 30- to 50-year-old flush valves in New York City apartments sometimes resulted in the old valves having to be rebuilt or replaced. According to Warren C. Liebold, director of conservation and technical services for the New York City Department of Environmental Protection, "Once you take the thing apart, you're on your own."[78]

2.1.3.6 Efficiency Adjustments for Flush Valves

Water use by high-volume, flush-valve toilets and urinals can sometimes be lowered by turning the screw under the cap located on the horizontal portion of the valve. This adjustment can save 0.5 to 1.0 gpf and should not adversely affect flushing performance. In some flush valves, this adjustment screw is located externally on the top of the diaphragm flush valve. These types of adjustments may require some experimentation to determine the minimum acceptable volume per fixture, and they should be made only by qualified technicians or plumbers.

Performance of Toilet Retrofit Devices

The performance of toilet retrofit devices is often very good, although their reliability depends on good design, durable materials, and correct installation. The newer displacement bags or pouches made of high-quality plastics are considered by many to be an improvement over older dams and bottles in terms of ease of installation and longevity. Early closure and dual-flush devices can definitely save water, but they require installation and adjustment by a plumber or trained technician to ensure proper operation. Toilets with dual-flush adapters also require proper flushing if they are to save water. The effectiveness of dual-flush adapters has been reported to range from 45 to 80%, indicating a high potential for misuse compared with other toilet retrofit devices.[79] Diaphragm replacement kits for toilet and urinal flush valves are generally considered to provide reliable performance and water savings in fixtures with bowls that can accommodate reduced flows.

Water Savings and Related Benefits From Toilet Retrofit Devices

WATER SAVINGS The water savings achieved by most toilet retrofit devices vary from 0.5 to 1.5 gpf, depending on the type of device installed and the adaptability of a particular toilet to operate at reduced flows. In a household, the savings range from 2 to 4 gpcd.[80]

In general, greater savings can be expected when retrofit devices are installed in older, higher-volume fixtures because they have more generous design tolerances.[81] The number of toilets retrofitted and the frequency of fixture use also influence water savings. Over time, however, the water savings may decline if the retrofit device starts to deteriorate, is out of adjustment, or is removed.

Potential water savings from retrofit devices that are properly installed in high-volume toilets, based on engineering estimates and reported savings,[80, 81] can be estimated as follows:

- Displacement devices (bags and bottles): 0.5 to 1.5 gpf
- Toilet dams: 0.5 to 1.0 gpf per dam installed
- Early closure devices: 1.0 to 1.5 gpf
- Dual-flush adapters: 0.6 to 1.2 gpf
- Water-saving valve replacement kits (for high-volume flushometer toilets and urinals only): 1.0 gpf
- Flush-valve adjustment: 0.5 to 1.0 gpf

A 1992 study of five toilets (3.5, 5.0, and 7.0 gpf models), laboratory-tested with more than 30 alternative toilet flushing and retrofit devices, found that water savings for the devices tested ranged from 0.60 to 1.40 gpf, as reported by the Stevens Institute of Technology in Hoboken, New Jersey.[81]

Case Study *Hospital Saves 3 Million Gallons of Water in First Year After Retrofitting Toilet and Urinal Flush Valves and Installing Faucet Aerators.* The Norwood Hospital in Massachusetts installed water-efficient flush valves on toilets and urinals as well as low-volume aerators on all lavatory faucets. These efficiency measures resulted in a combined annual water savings of 3 million gallons. With a cost of $8,092 for purchase and installation of the devices and annual water and sewer cost savings of $19,679 (not including heat energy savings), the payback on these measures was less than six months.[82]

WATER AND SEWER COST SAVINGS   Avoided water and sewer costs associated with the installation of toilet retrofit devices can be calculated by multiplying expected reductions in water (and wastewater) times the local utility rates for water and sewer use (excluding fixed charges). A schedule of representative water and sewer utility rates in the United States and their associated marginal cost savings according to a range of reduced water and wastewater volumes is provided in Appendix D, *Water and Sewer Rates, Costs, and Savings by Volume of Use.*

ENERGY SAVINGS   Customers reap no direct energy savings from toilet retrofit devices, but indirect energy savings accrue to utilities from reduced pumping and treatment associated with reduced flows at water and wastewater facilities.

Costs Associated With Toilet Retrofit Devices

HARDWARE COSTS   The price of toilet retrofit devices varies considerably depending on whether they are purchased individually on the retail market or in bulk from wholesale vendors. Approximate retail costs for these devices are:

- Displacement devices (bags and bottles): $0.59 to $1.50
- Toilet dams: $3 to $4 (set of two)
- Early closure devices: $2.50 to $4 (with adapter)
- Dual-flush adapters: $8 to $20
- Flush-valve replacement kits: $20 to $25

Laboratory tests conducted by the Stevens Institute of Technology on more than 30 alternative toilet flushing and retrofit devices indicated that the price of a retrofit device did not always correlate with performance or water-savings potential.[81]

INSTALLATION COSTS   Generally, no costs are incurred for installing toilet displacement dams, bottles, and bags in single-family homes because many retrofit programs encourage customers to install these devices themselves. On the other hand, programs that provide installation service may achieve higher installation rates. Retrofit devices in multifamily rental units are usually installed by maintenance staff or paid installers; residents of these buildings are typically not motivated to install a retrofit device because it gives them no direct cost benefit.

Depending on local market conditions and the amount of time required to install a particular retrofit device (15 to 45 minutes), a trained technician may charge $8 to $15 per installation, and a plumber's fee may range from $20 to $40 (though some plumbers charge a minimum fee). Dual-flush adapters, early closure flappers, and flush-valve replacements are typically installed by trained technicians or plumbers to ensure correct operation. Early closure and dual-flush adapters may require replacement of other parts in the toilet tank to accommodate the device, thereby increasing hardware and installation costs somewhat (see "Installation of Toilet Retrofit Devices" later in this section).

Bathroom grafitti has been found in the baths of ancient Crete, Greece, and Rome."
—Robinson Research
World of Knowledge,
"The Evolution of the Privy"

PRODUCT MANUFACTURERS Manufacturers of toilet retrofit devices are listed in Chapter 6, *The Water Conservation Network*.

Well done is better than well said."

—Benjamin Franklin

Laws, Codes, and Standards Applicable to Toilet Retrofit Devices

All applicable laws, codes, standards, and health and safety requirements associated with toilets and urinal retrofit flush valves and related devices should be observed when any fixture, appliance, or related plumbing or water system connection is installed or adjusted.

Toilet and urinal retrofit devices have not been subject to the same performance standards as other plumbing products. Some toilet retrofit devices are certified by product testing organizations, but certification is not a guarantee that a retrofit product will operate satisfactorily on every toilet because many toilet design features (e.g., the size and configuration of tanks and bowls, flapper-valve seats, rim-hole and jet-hole diameters, and other features) affect the volume of water required for adequate flushing. There is a testing and performance standard for dual-flush devices for gravity-tank toilets that use 3.5 gpf or more, ASME A112.19.10 *(Dual-Flush Devices for Water Closets)*.

Some states and municipalities require permits that allow toilets and urinals to be installed, adjusted, or retrofitted only by a licensed plumber, but these requirements are sometimes waived for large-scale retrofit programs in which trained technicians are used.

Implementing a Toilet Retrofit Program

SELECTING A TOILET RETROFIT DEVICE Selection of a toilet retrofit device is based primarily on the type of toilet to be retrofitted, i.e., whether it is a gravity-tank or flushometer-valve fixture. Next, the flushing volume of the fixture to be retrofitted should be considered, because a 5.0 gpf tank may more readily adapt to two bags or dams (and achieve greater water savings) than some 3.5 gpf fixtures that can only accommodate one displacement device.

Most large-scale utility-sponsored retrofit programs include displacement bags or "bladders" (high-grade versions of a simple plastic bag) in the retrofit kit given to or installed for residential customers. Displacement bags and bladders are inexpensive and easy to install with the help of simple diagrams. Some utilities provide early closure and other devices as part of their retrofit programs, often with installation assistance to ensure proper operation.

Flushometer-valve toilets and urinals in which retrofit kits have been installed, like devices installed to reduce flows in gravity-tank fixtures, should be tested at the time of installation to ensure that the particular bowl connected to the valve can accommodate reduced flows without the occurrence of clogging or other problems.

PLANNING A TOILET RETROFIT DEVICE INSTALLATION PROGRAM
Successful toilet retrofit device installation programs are well planned and include these basic components:

TABLE 2.9

Effective date of state requirements for 1.6 gpf low-volume toilets

State	Year 1.6 gpf Toilet Requirement Became Effective
Massachusetts *	1989
Rhode Island †	1990
Delaware, New Jersey, Utah	1991
California, Connecticut, Georgia, Maryland, New York, Texas	1992
Arizona, Minnesota, Nevada, North Carolina, Oregon, Washington	1993
All states (per U.S. Energy Policy Act of 1992) ‡	1994

* 1989 for new two-piece toilets; 1991 for all others

† 1990 for new two-piece toilets; 1991 for all others

‡ See Table 2.1 for later effective dates for certain fixtures and some exceptions.

Source: Amy Vickers & Associates, Inc.

- Identification of potential program participants, potential water savings, program benefits and costs, schedule, and program budget and human resource requirements.
- Identification of the types and condition of toilets used by the target population so that a variety of retrofit devices can be offered and a high rate of installation can be achieved.
- Program outreach and marketing.
- Distribution of retrofit devices or kits.
- Installation guidance for retrofit devices (e.g., printed directions, call-in technical assistance, referrals to certified plumbers) or assistance (direct installation service, particularly for the elderly and disabled).
- Evaluation and reporting of program results.

Targeted Water Users   Toilet retrofit programs are typically targeted to single-family and multifamily customers, particularly in residential areas known to have older or deteriorated fixtures that would benefit from a tune-up—both in terms of water savings and performance. Toilet retrofit efforts have also targeted the industrial, commercial, and institutional sectors, although installation strategies in these programs may differ. Toilet retrofit programs sometimes include leak detection and repair work by trained technicians or plumbers. In the short term, toilet retrofit devices are more cost-effective than replacement of high-volume fixtures with 1.6 gpf fixtures, but they save significantly less water and have a shorter life expectancy than a low-volume toilet.

Toilet retrofit devices can be installed in high-volume, gravity-tank toilets, fixtures that were widely installed up to 1994 in most states. States that enacted requirements for 1.6 gpf toilets in all new installations prior to passage of the EPAct of 1992 are shown in Table 2.9. Many retrofit programs have targeted homes with fixtures installed before 1980, in most cases toilets that use 5.0 gpf or more, but retrofitting 3.5 gpf toilets can also yield water savings.

High-volume, flushometer-valve toilets and urinals can also be retrofitted to reduce water requirements in many instances, but not all. Some flushometer toilet bowls can adjust better than others to reduced flows after a valve retrofit kit has been installed. If a bowl designed for flush volumes of 3.5 gpf or higher cannot accommodate reduced flows, it may be more prudent to replace the entire toilet (valve and bowl) with a 1.6 gpf fixture than to risk increased clogging and repair problems—and minimal or no water savings. Low-volume 1.6 gpf gravity-tank, flushometer-tank, and flushometer-valve toilets in general cannot be retrofitted to use less water, although some low-volume, gravity-tank toilets may be adapted with dual-flush devices.

Number of Toilet Retrofit Devices Installed Just as the number of toilets in homes and nonresidential facilities varies, so does the need for retrofit devices and the ability of fixtures to be retrofitted successfully. Single-family homes have an average of one toilet for every 1.5 persons, although newer, larger, and more affluent homes have more bathrooms than older, smaller homes and multifamily buildings. See "Number of Toilets Installed" under Section 2.1.1 of this chapter for more details on toilet installations in residential and nonresidential properties.

Life Cycle of Toilet Retrofit Devices The useful life of a toilet retrofit device is determined by the quality of its construction and materials, the precision of its installation, the frequency of the toilet's use, and the quality of the water. The length of time a particular device is expected to save water should be estimated to determine whether it will help meet the water-savings goals and budget of a particular conservation program. Several of the product designs and materials used for toilet retrofit devices have improved since the early 1990s, factors that enhance the value of these products.

In general, toilet displacement bags and pouches should last at least five years and probably longer, although their durability has not been well evaluated by long-term tests. Older plastic bags lasted two to five years, but this shorter lifespan may be partly due to customers removing the devices. The product life for high-quality dams is two to five years. The life span of dams made with inferior materials can be as little as six months, particularly if they are immersed in corrosive water. The useful life and water-saving ability of dams can quickly be shortened if they become dislodged.[77] Even fewer data exist on the life cycle of replacement flapper valves. Those made of high-quality rubber and plastic are expected to have a long life (five to ten years) if they are properly fitted and used in a tank with noncorrosive water. Little information is available on the longevity of dual-flush adapters; again, quality of materials, installation accuracy, and frequency of use influence a device's life cycle. Replacement kits for toilet and urinal flush valves should last at least ten years.

Manufacturers and distributors of toilet (and urinal) retrofit devices may be able to provide warranty, case study, and test information on the life cycle of specific products.

Incentives See the sidebar "Installation Strategies for Large-Scale Fixture Retrofit Programs" in this chapter.

CUSTOMER PARTICIPATION IN TOILET RETROFIT PROGRAMS
Consumer acceptance of retrofit kits is usually high (as many as 60 to 85% of targeted program participants), provided the device is easy to install, does not mar the appearance of the toilet, and causes no flushing problems. Most customers who accept a kit will install it, but a small number of program participants can be expected to remove the device later. Thus, the program's "penetration" of the targeted customer group may be somewhat lower than the overall program participation rate.

INSTALLATION OF TOILET RETROFIT DEVICES   Installation of toilet retrofit devices can often be handled by consumers but in some cases requires a trained technician or plumber. In a jurisdiction that allows consumers to install toilet retrofit devices themselves, consumers should be fully advised about proper procedures, tools, and precautions to ensure proper installation and operation. User-friendly installation instructions and diagrams should always be provided in retrofit kits to be installed by customers.

Displacement devices and dams are easy to install, but they sometimes require trial-and-error adjustments to ensure proper fit inside the tank and an adequate amount of water for flushing. Other toilet retrofit devices, such as early closure flappers, diverters, dual-flush adapters, and flush-valve kits, are more difficult for laypersons to install; installation by a trained technician or plumber is the surest route to success with these devices.

Regardless of which toilet retrofit device is selected, in most cases the manufacturer's recommended water level should be maintained inside a gravity-tank toilet, usually about 1 inch below the overflow tube (early closure devices are an exception). The water level is sometimes marked inside the tank with a line or water-level identifier.[81] If no such marking is provided, the water level may be evident by a line of discoloration around the inside perimeter of the tank.

Installation guidelines for the most common toilet retrofit devices follow.

Displacement Devices (Bags and Bottles) Displacement bags and bottles may be the most user-friendly toilet retrofit device to install. Customers can easily slip these devices into the tank by following simple diagrams. One or two bags or bottles can be installed depending on the size of the tank and the flushing requirements of the bowl.

Toilet Dams One or two dams can be installed depending on the size of the tank, although placing two dams can be difficult or impossible with smaller tanks or fixtures whose valve-and-flapper mechanism is located tightly against the wall of the tank. Customers may be more reluctant to install toilet dams than bag or bottle displacement devices; thus dams have a lower installation rate. Some customers have difficulty understanding the directions for installing dams correctly. Also, some people are reluctant to place their hands in the toilet tank because they consider it unsanitary, even though the tank contains no wastewater.[83]

Early Closure Devices Assistance is often required for correct installation of early closure devices. Operation of an early closure device is usually optimized

Installation Strategies for Large-Scale Fixture Retrofit Programs

Plumbing fixture retrofit programs are a common conservation strategy implemented by water and energy utilities. Plumbing retrofit programs typically involve the distribution of retrofit kits containing devices for toilets, showerheads, faucets, and toilet leak detection. The percentage of participants in a retrofit program—those customers who accept receipt or installation of a kit—is always greater than the percentage of "penetration"—the program's rate of success at gaining the cooperation of targeted water users—because not all customers who receive a kit can be expected to install the devices provided or to keep them installed. The contents of a typical retrofit kit are shown in Figure 2.8.

The results of plumbing fixture retrofit programs vary because each program is designed and managed differently for a population of customers with unique characteristics (i.e., number and age of fixtures installed, perceived need for conservation, attitude toward the utility, and so on). Nevertheless, according to the AWWA manual *The Manager's Guide to Residential Retrofit*,[77] four basic distribution strategies are used for large-scale toilet retrofit device programs.

- *Direct installation.* Direct installation programs can be particularly effective in multifamily housing where facility managers have easy access to residents' units. This is

particularly true for rental units, because residents who do not pay directly for water may have no incentive to install water conservation devices.

- *Door-to-door drop-off.* This method may be particularly suited for single-family neighborhoods where someone is likely to be home to accept a free retrofit kit. Programs that use the drop-off method often offer free installation assistance to customers who request it.

- *Mass mailings.* Mass-mailing programs mail retrofit kits primarily to residential customers within a target area. This method may be effective for households where people are not at home during the day or are otherwise difficult to reach in person. Though some customers receiving a kit in the mail may consider it a gift, this does not guarantee that they will be as motivated to install it as if the kit were delivered to their door with the offer of installation assistance.

  Mail-out programs often have low participation rates compared with other kit distribution strategies, but participation in these programs can be boosted with aggressive marketing and telephone follow-up. For example, a mail-out program in Bridgeport, Connecticut, targeted 33,400 residential customers served by the

Bridgeport Hydraulic Company in the first year of a three-year program. A customer survey conducted after kits had been distributed indicated that the utility had achieved a program participation rate of 61% (about 20,270 customers ordered kits by mail after they were sent a request card) and that 38% (about 12,800) of the targeted customers actually installed at least one of the devices in the kit.[84]

- *Depot pickup.* Depot programs rely on designated locations, such as water utility offices, libraries, schools, and shopping malls to distribute kits to customers. This method generally elicits the lowest rate of customer participation and device installation because only the most motivated customers go out of their way to pick up a kit.

Some large-scale retrofit programs use a combination of installation strategies to reach as many customers as possible. It is also common practice for the utility or sponsoring organization to offer direct installation assistance to people who request it, particularly elderly or disabled customers or others who are unsure of their ability to install the devices without damaging the flushing mechanism.

if the pressure on the device is increased. This can often be accomplished by raising the water column in the tank to the highest level possible, usually about 0.5 inches below the top of the overflow tub. If the water level is lowered too much, the pressure will be inadequate for flushing, resulting in clogged bowls, double-flushing, and minimal water savings.[77] Sometimes the entire flush assembly needs to be changed or a new seating surface installed so that the new flapper valve will seal properly. The interior parts of older toilets in particular may need to be rebuilt to operate successfully with an early closure device. Many types of early closure devices are available; care should be taken in selecting a proven, reliable device.

Installation of early closure and dual-flush devices may also require that the toilet's ballcock be replaced or adjusted. Because these devices refill the tank before the bowl during flushing, an improper trap seal can occur during the refill cycle and allow sewage gases to escape. An inadequate trap seal may also prevent the removal of all solids in the bowl. A properly sized ballcock that increases the fill-rate ratio of water filling the bowl versus the tank should cause the tank to refill more slowly, putting the bowl and trap seal at their correct levels.[77]

Dual-Flush Adapters Assistance is often required for correct installation of dual-flush adapters. Installation of dual-flush adapters may also necessitate replacing a toilet's flush handle, handle arm, and ballcock.

Flushometer-Valve Replacement Kits and Adjustments Assistance is also often required for correct installation of flushometer-valve replacement kits and adjustments. Flush-valve retrofit devices and adjustments should be carefully tested at the time of installation to ensure that the high-volume bowl can adapt effectively to reduced flows from the retrofitted valve.

RECYCLING USED TOILET PARTS See "Recycling Used Toilets" under Section 2.1.1 of this chapter.

MAINTENANCE OF TOILET RETROFIT DEVICES Toilet retrofit devices should be checked regularly (at least once a year) to see if they require cleaning or readjustment. Over time, bottles and dams may become deformed, migrate inside the tank, collect mold and scum, and possibly interrupt the flush valve or ballcock mechanism, causing leaks and other problems. Bags, particularly thin, flimsy types, also deteriorate over time and may need to be refilled with water, reanchored to the tank wall, or replaced if they are leaking or have worn seams.[77] As they age, the interiors of gravity tanks and flushometer valves can also collect grit that interferes with flushing; simple cleaning and correct replacement of parts may extend the life of these retrofit devices and fixtures. Low pressure can cause flushing problems; most flushometer-valve fixtures need a minimum flow pressure of 25 psi.[65]

2.1.4 Toilet Leak Repair

Toilet leaks are a common but potentially large source of water losses that can often be recovered through simple repairs. Whether a toilet is a high- or low-volume model, the quality of mechanical parts in most gravity-tank toilets and the water environment in which they reside are such that leaks need to be monitored and repaired regularly if water losses are to be minimized.[85]

Water Losses From Toilet Leaks

The amount of water lost through leakage is 9.5 gpcd in the average non-conserving single-family home, according to the 1999 REUS study.[86] Most of this loss is attributable to toilet leakage. Water losses from toilet leaks can vary from several gallons to more than 100 gpd per leaking fixture. In general, the incidence of toilet leakage and the volume of losses increase over time, particularly with gravity-tank toilets. Up to 25% of toilets in U.S. homes are estimated to leak,[77] although surveys conducted by individual water supply systems indicate a wide range of leakage incidence and associated water loss. For example, a

> *A leaky ball-cock may easily permit 1,000 gallons per day to pass it. Unless this leakage inconveniences the householder, he will seldom repair the defective fixtures if not compelled to."*
> —A. Prescott Folwell,
> *Water-Supply Engineering, 1899*

survey of three types of toilets installed in more than 80,000 residential units in New York City found the following leakage rates:[87]

- 1.5% of 1.6 gpf toilets leaked an average of 200 gpd.
- 4.8% of 3.5 gpf toilets leaked an average of 180 gpd.
- 6.0% of 5.0+ gpf toilets leaked an average of more than 200 gpd.

Similar percentages of leaking toilets (4.0% of 3.5 gpf fixtures and 5.6% of 5.0 to 7.0 gpf fixtures) were reported in an evaluation of an audit program of approximately 2,500 single-family households in San Diego. The study found no leaks among 1.6 gpf toilets, although they made up less than 8% of the toilets in the survey sample.[88]

Comparative estimates of the frequency and amount of leakage among toilets (and urinals) in nonresidential facilities are not well established, although jammed or malfunctioning flush-valve toilets and urinals lose about 35 gpm (2,100 gallons per hour) when they lock in an open position (the default setting on most flush valves). Most toilet leaks are assumed to occur in gravity fixtures rather than flushometer-valve fixtures, primarily because leaks in gravity-tank toilets are usually silent and unseen. Malfunctioning flush valves, on the other hand, cannot easily be ignored because they are often loud and release large amounts of water.

Sources of Toilet Leaks

Toilet leaks can be caused by a number of problems, most of which apply to gravity-tank fixtures.

AGING AND DETERIORATED FLAPPER VALVES AND VALVE SEALS Deteriorated flapper valves and seals are the most common cause of leaks in gravity-tank toilets. A normal flapper valve, as shown in Figure 2.22, prevents water in the tank from seeping into the bowl. A deteriorated flapper valve, as shown in Figure 2.23, or an improperly sized flapper inhibits the valve from sealing correctly against the drain seat (the hole in the bottom of the tank through which water is released to the bowl during flushing). Failing flapper valves typically cause slow but constant seepage of water.

WORN AND BROKEN BALLCOCKS, REFILL VALVES, LIFT CHAINS, AND HANDLE RODS Malfunctioning parts prevent proper closure of the flapper and complete flushing in gravity-tank toilets. Weakened or broken ballcocks often fail to shut off after the tank has refilled, causing water to pour over the top of the overflow tube. The flapper's lift chain and the handle rod it is connected to can also break.

POORLY SIZED REPLACEMENT PARTS Most toilets can be repaired with replacement parts available at hardware and plumbing supply stores, but these parts are usually one-size-fits-all and cannot match the exact specifications of the original equipment manufacturer. Similarly, improperly installed tank components, such as easily twistable or poorly designed metal and plastic chains connected to the flapper valve, inhibit proper seating of the valve.

Figure 2.22 New toilet flapper valve (Photo courtesy of Metropolitan Water District of Southern California)

Figure 2.23 Deteriorated toilet flapper valve (Photo courtesy of Metropolitan Water District of Southern California)

ACCELERATED DETERIORATION FROM CHLORAMINES AND AUTOMATIC TOILET BOWL CLEANERS Deterioration of the rubber and thermoplastic materials used in flapper valves and other toilet parts is accelerated by chloramine-treated or "aggressive" (low pH) water and the use of caustic toilet bowl cleaners. To the extent that advanced elastomer materials are available for replacement parts, they should be able to withstand these two common causes of breakdown:

• *Chloramine-treated water.* An AWWA Research Foundation–sponsored study found that the increasing use of chloramines by water treatment plants (particularly in Florida and Southern California) as an alternative disinfectant to reduce the formation of disinfection by-products appears to correspond with "substantially higher rates of elastomer gasket failure." The most commonly reported failures are related to rubber parts in toilet tanks and aerator washers in residential and nonresidential properties. "The single largest source of complaint appears to be failure of toilet tank components, particularly tank balls, flapper valves, and diaphragms associated with automatic flow control devices," reported the study. The failure is usually characterized by swelling (water absorption), which grossly distorts shape and prevents the part from performing its function.[89]

- *Automatic toilet bowl cleaners.* These products may be particularly aggressive in degrading flapper valves and other toilet parts because they are often time-released rather than flush-released. This causes high concentrations of chemicals (primarily chlorine and halogenating solutions) to build up in the tank and bowl during periods of infrequent use, such as when people are away at work or on vacation. Acidity in some bowls has been reported to equal the pH of car battery acid.[85, 90]

- *Poor-quality materials used in fixture components.* The durability of materials used in the mechanical components of gravity-tank toilets depends on the water quality conditions in which the materials must function. Nevertheless, toilet parts that are made of high-grade materials and are sold separately as water-saving devices have a longer service life than others. Thus, higher-grade, better-designed materials are correlated with reduced leakage.

- *Flushometer valves locked in an open position.* Flushometer valves that are damaged or malfunctioning because of rust or debris can become locked in an open position, causing water to flow between flushes.

Detecting Toilet Leaks

Leaks in gravity-tank toilets are often silent, allowing losses to go undetected for long periods of time. However, large toilet leaks and malfunctions often produce a running-water sound that is easy to hear. Some leaks are visible as a small trickle running continuously from the rim into the water-surface area of the bowl, causing small ripples. Conversely, leaks and malfunctions in flushometer-valve fixtures are usually obvious because they often cause high-pressure sprays or continuous flushing.

DYE TESTS FOR LEAKS Leaks in gravity-tank toilets are commonly detected with dye tablets (Figure 2.24) or leak detector fluid. A nontoxic dye tablet can be placed inside the toilet tank; after it has dissolved (usually within 10 to 15 minutes), colored water will appear in the bowl if the fixture has a leak. One commercial liquid dye product, which works on gravity and flushometer toilets and urinals, detects leaks by applying the dye as a line inside the rim of the bowl; if there's a leak, it will quickly become evident by the dye running down the inside of the bowl. A similar but potentially messier method is to place several drops of food coloring inside the tank.

Types of Toilet Leak Repairs

Once the source of a toilet leak has been determined, several types of repairs can be made. Leak repairs needed for gravity-tank toilets typically involve one or a combination of the following measures:

- *Flapper valve.* Replacement flappers should close tightly against the valve seal. If water can be seen or heard flowing into the bowl (i.e., if the toilet sounds like it is "running" or flushing when no one is using it), the flapper valve is not fitting correctly into the seal. This can be checked by flushing the toilet several times and adjusting the flapper and chain so that the flapper rests evenly against the seal on the bottom of the tank and the chain does not catch under the flapper. (It is usually helpful to shut off the water to the tank before undertaking this task.) If the flapper is still leaking after the adjustment, it probably needs to be replaced. If the existing or new flapper is sealed properly but is still leaking, rust or grit may have built up around the valve seal; this can be cleaned with a plastic cleaning pad or sandpaper (for rubber valve seals) or fine steel wool (for metal valve seals). If there is still leakage after cleaning, the valve seal may also need to be replaced. A glue-on valve may be needed to create a new surface over an uneven or old one.[91]

- *Ballcock and float ball.* The ballcock shuts off the flow of water to the tank once the float ball reaches a set height; if it doesn't shut off, water continues to rise and escape out the overflow tube. (Some newer toilets have "float-cup" ballcocks instead of a traditional float ball, but they perform the same function.) If water continues to run into the bowl after flushing and the running water can be stopped temporarily by pulling up the float arm, the ballcock, float ball, or both may be corroded or worn out and need to be replaced.

- *Fill tube.* The small fill tube connected to the overflow tube should be checked to make sure it is slightly above the water level of the filled tank. If it is not, the small fill tube can be adjusted by pulling it upward to empty into the overflow tube. Sometimes the float arm can be bent so that the fill valve shuts off before water spills into the overflow tube; if this doesn't work, the valve probably needs to be replaced.

- *Broken handle rod or flush lever.* The flush lever inside the tank should be connected to the flush handle and chain pull for the flapper. If these connections are broken, the flush lever should be replaced.

- *High-water-level leaks.* The water level in a toilet tank should be 1 inch to 0.5 inches below the overflow pipe. If the level is less than half an inch below the overflow pipe, water can seep into the overflow tube during periods of high pressure. This causes water to trickle into the bowl, creating a silent leak. The refill valve then fills the tank up again, a cycle that can occur repeatedly. Leaks from high water levels can waste as much as 100 gpd per fixture.[91]

- *Loose connections.* Some toilet leaks are caused by loose nuts and bolts that can be fixed by tightening connections. Bolts inside the tank should be checked, as well as connections between wall-mounted tanks and pipe connections to the toilet.

Product Life Cycle

Toilet tank parts should last several years before they malfunction and start to cause leaks. However, for the reasons described—corrosive water conditions, poor-quality materials, and improper sizing—the life expectancy of a toilet's mechanical components can be as little as several months or as long as five to ten years.

The society which scorns excellence in plumbing because plumbing is a humble activity, and tolerates shoddiness in philosophy because philosophy is an exalted activity, will have neither good plumbing nor good philosophy. Neither its pipes nor its theories will hold water."

—John W. Gardner

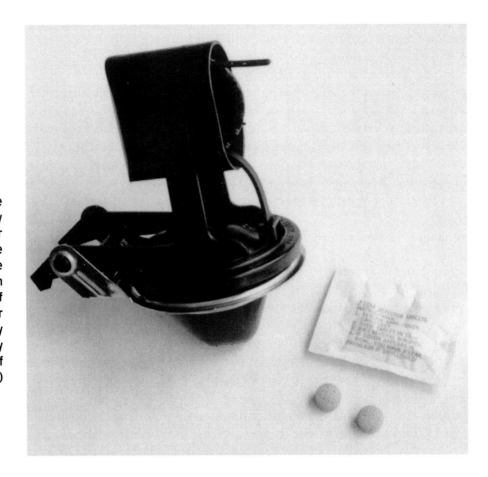

Figure 2.24 Leaks can be detected in gravity toilets by dropping a dye tablet (right) or drops of food coloring in the tank; if there is a leak, the dye will enter the bowl in about ten minutes. A common source of leakage is a deteriorated flapper valve, which can be fixed by installing a new high-quality flapper (left). (Photo courtesy of Amy Vickers & Associates, Inc.)

Water Savings and Related Benefits From Toilet Leak Repairs

WATER SAVINGS Because toilet leaks are often undetected by meters, it can be difficult to measure how much water will be saved from a particular repair. Leaks that occur on customer property but that are not detected by a meter represent part of the water system's unaccounted-for water, which is measured by the water supplier.

The amount of toilet leakage in households that is recoverable from repairs is probably somewhat less than the average 9.5 gpcd leakage level reported in the 1999 REUS study of residential water use in the United States and Canada, although some leaks can be considerably higher. The REUS study also found 5.5% of homes with leaks averaging more than 100 gpd.[92] On a daily basis, small leaks from a running toilet or malfunctioning ballcock may not appear to cause large water losses, but on an annual basis such leaks can add up. For example, a toilet that leaks 5 gpd wastes 1,825 gallons of water a year. A fixture losing 25 gpd wastes more than 9,000 gallons annually.

WATER AND SEWER COST SAVINGS Depending on the sensitivity of a customer's water meter, recovered water losses from leak repairs may or may not be reflected in water and wastewater bills. When the losses can be measured, the avoided water and sewer costs associated with toilet leak repair can be calculated by multiplying the expected volume of water (and wastewater) reductions times the local utility rates for water and sewer use (excluding fixed charges). A schedule of representative water and sewer utility rates in the United States and their associated marginal cost savings according to a range of reduced water and wastewater volumes is provided in Appendix D, *Water and Sewer Rates, Costs, and Savings by Volume of Use.*

ENERGY SAVINGS   Energy savings from toilet leak repairs are indirect and are accrued by utilities from the reduced volumes of water and wastewater pumped and treated.

PREVENTION OF PROPERTY DAMAGE   Unchecked toilet leaks can result in damage not only to the toilet but also to flooring, ceilings, tile, rugs, wood, and other items near the fixture.

Costs Associated With Toilet Leak Repairs

HARDWARE COSTS Estimated costs for hardware to repair leaking toilets include:

- Leak dye tablets: $0.10 to $0.25 (package of two)
- Flapper valve: $2 to $10
- Ballcock assembly: $5 to $18
- Overflow pipe and refill tube: $8 to $20
- Handle rod: $3 to $5

LABOR COSTS   Labor costs for toilet repairs vary regionally but are $15 to $20 an hour for a trained technician and $35 or more per hour for a licensed plumber. Simple repairs involving the changeout of one or two parts can usually be accomplished within an hour; additional adjustments can increase the time and labor charges.

PRODUCT MANUFACTURERS   The manufacturers and brands of replacement and repair parts for toilets are best determined by recommendations provided by the fixture's original manufacturer. If another manufacturer's replacement parts are used, care should be taken to ensure that the replacement devices fit properly and do not increase flush volumes. Manufacturers of toilet replacement and repair parts are listed in Chapter 6, *The Water Conservation Network.*

Laws, Codes, and Standards Applicable to Toilet Leak Repairs

All applicable laws, codes, standards, and health and safety requirements associated with toilet repairs and related devices should be observed when any fixture, appliance, or related plumbing or water system connection is installed or adjusted.

Some states and municipalities require permits that allow toilets to be installed, adjusted, or retrofitted only by a licensed plumber, but these requirements are sometimes waived for large-scale rebate and retrofit programs in which trained technicians are used.

Requirements for fill valves (ballcocks) are defined in a standard established by ANSI and the American Society of Sanitary Engineers (ASSE), ANSI/ASSE Standard 1002.

Remote Sensors for Toilet and Urinal Flushing

Automatic-sensor (infrared or fiber-optic) flushing devices are activated by motion or high-frequency sound waves. These devices are sometimes attached to fixtures at highway rest areas, airports, and similar locations. The purpose of these devices is usually twofold: to prevent underflushing or overflushing by users and to minimize user contact with germs. Although these sensors are designed to make double-flushing difficult, they sometimes cause multiple flushing if they are not positioned properly.

Implementing a Toilet Leak Detection and Repair Program

Several considerations should be taken into account in planning a program to repair leaking and broken toilets.

SELECTING REPLACEMENT PARTS FOR TOILETS Replacement parts for toilets should be selected carefully for correct fit based on manufacturer specifications. Finding and properly installing the correct replacement flapper is often not easy. Typically, the best replacement flapper is the one designed by the manufacturer, but it might not be available at most retail hardware stores. A study of 50 replacement flappers obtained from several major retail chains in Southern California found that many off-the-shelf flappers would not fit correctly in existing toilets, a situation that can cause flushing problems, leaks, and increased flushing volumes. The study also found that replacement flappers that can maintain the flush volume characteristics of most 1.6 gpf toilets are "rarely available" to the average consumer.[67] Given these disadvantages, two guidelines may be helpful in selecting a replacement flapper:

- Contact the manufacturer for guidance about how to obtain a suitable replacement flapper for a particular toilet model.
- When purchasing replacement flappers on the retail market, take the old flapper to the hardware or plumbing supply store to identify acceptable replacements. For example, flappers are either adjustable or nonadjustable. Adjustable flappers can cause toilets to use more or less water during flushing, depending on how much slack is allowed on the chain connecting the flapper and handle rod. Too much slack can increase the volume of water used in flushing, and too little may provide insufficient water to complete a flush. Nonadjustable replacement flappers come in a fixed size and may be more prone to increase the flush volumes of 1.6 gpf toilets than adjustable, correctly sized replacement flappers.[67]

PLANNING THE PROGRAM A key part of planning a toilet leak detection and repair program is determining the extent of toilet leakage in the targeted service area or facility and the potential water savings and associated benefits and costs that could be expected from reducing the leaks. Factors to evaluate include age and condition of toilets, water quality, types of toilets installed (e.g., gravity versus flushometer), and types of repairs and replacement parts required. As for toilet rebate and retrofit programs, these data could be collected by means of several methods: analysis of customer water-use data, field surveys, and telephone surveys of building managers and plumbing contractors.

Targeted Water Users Toilet leak repair programs should be targeted toward customer properties where leaks are most prevalent—typically among gravity-tank toilets in homes and small office and commercial buildings. Older and low-income housing units tend to have higher rates of toilet leakage. Large leaks are sometimes detected by sudden increases in customer water bills or by meter readers who notice turning dials when a home has no occupants.

Flush-valve toilets and urinals, typically found in nonresidential facilities, can also have leaks, but they are less common and more easily noticed than leaks in gravity fixtures.

Life Cycle of Toilet Replacement Parts   Corrosive water conditions or poor-quality parts can cause some gravity-tank toilets to develop leaks within just six months of installation or replacement of flapper valves and ballcocks. Thus, in estimating the life span of toilet repairs, it is useful to know the environment in which the toilet is operating and the reliability of the products used as replacement parts.

Incentives   Because many toilet leaks are silent and not measured by meters, customers are often unaware of a leak until it becomes obvious, is detected during a water audit, or causes an increase in their water bill. One way to remind customers to check regularly for leaks is to print a reminder on the water bill, along with information about how to detect and repair leaks and how to get assistance with such tasks.

CUSTOMER PARTICIPATION IN TOILET REPAIR PROGRAMS   Repairing large numbers of leaking toilets in order to conserve water appears to be accomplished more effectively when the utility provides the service rather than relying on the voluntary efforts of customers. Evaluations of programs that rely on customers to install retrofit devices often report that customers were less willing to use the leak detection tablets provided than to install a low-volume showerhead, toilet displacement device, or faucet aerator. An even smaller number of customers who find leaks will make repairs. For example, a study of the mail-out program in Bridgeport, Connecticut, showed that only 23% of the customers surveyed used the toilet leak detection tablets provided in the kit, but 43 to 50% installed the showerhead, toilet dam, and faucet aerator.[84]

INSTALLATION AND MAINTENANCE OF TOILET LEAK REPAIRS   In most cases, installation of toilet replacement parts should be done by properly trained technicians or plumbers and should be based on applicable rules and practices. In a jurisdiction that allows consumers to install and repair fixtures themselves, consumers should be fully advised about proper procedures, tools, and precautions to ensure proper installation and operation. Particular attention should be paid to ensuring that new parts fit correctly. The installer should test the toilet several times to make sure it has been adjusted for optimum flushing performance. Also, the customer should measure the flush volume of the fixture after the repairs have been made (by reading the water meter before and after the repair) to ensure that additional water is not being used.

Toilet maintenance checks should be made at least every six months or more frequently if the water is corrosive or leakage problems have occurred in the past.

RECYCLING USED TOILET PARTS   See "Recycling Used Toilets" under Section 2.1.1 of this chapter.

2.2 URINALS

This section describes four water-efficiency measures to reduce water use by urinals: low-volume urinals, waterless urinals, composting urinals, and urinal repair. These measures apply to urinals installed in nonresidential lavatories for males—office buildings, schools, dormitories, factories, sports arenas, airports, hospitals, and many types of institutional facilities. (There are urinals designed for residential use, but these are uncommon.)

Low-volume urinals use 1.0 gallon per flush (gpf) or less. Waterless and composting urinals require no water to flush. The water efficiency of urinals in the United States has improved considerably since the mid-1980s with the introduction of improved flushing systems as well as waterless fixtures.

Many existing urinals are flush-valve types, which work like flushometer-valve toilets. These valves have a metal or plastic diaphragm inside that opens when the fixture is flushed, releasing a quick stream of water at full pressure. Another kind of urinal is the trough type, in which water runs intermittently or continuously to flush the fixture. Several types of low-volume, waterless, and composting urinals are available, in addition to several retrofit options to reduce flows for high-volume urinals.

According to EPAct, urinals that are sold, installed, or imported in the United States must be low-volume fixtures that use no more than 1.0 gpf, or 3.8 liters.[26] Because of the water savings that can be achieved by replacing high-volume fixtures with waterless or 1.0 gpf urinals, the U.S. government and the private sector have sponsored a number of large-scale urinal replacement programs in recent years.

Water Use by Urinals

Average water use and savings for waterless, low-volume, and high-volume urinals (estimated according to flush volume) are shown in Table 2.10. Although low-volume urinals generally require only 1.0 gpf or less, urinals that use 1.5 gpf are also sometimes referred to as low-volume. Moderate- to high-volume urinals have flush rates of 1.5, 2.0, 3.0, 4.5, and 5.0 gpf; continuous- and intermittent-flow urinals use even higher volumes of water. Actual water use by flush urinals can vary from the manufacturer's reported flow rate for several reasons, including previous adjustments to the flush valve to alter flow rates, improper mechanical adjustments to the flush valve, low or high pressure in the supply line, and leaks.

Water use by urinals in office restrooms for males is estimated to be about 2.0 gallons per capita per day (gpcd) when a 1.0 gpf fixture is installed and 3.0 to 9.0 gpcd when high-volume fixtures are in use. Water use by toilets is also a factor in office restrooms for males. The frequency of urinal flushing by males in office lavatories is estimated to be about two times per workday.[38, 39]

There are several ways to determine how much water a particular urinal uses if its flush or flow rate is unknown: (1) for continuous-flow urinals, read the water meter while all other water-using fixtures are inactive, and for intermittent-flow urinals, read the meter before and after flows while other water-using fixtures are inactive; (2) note the urinal's year of manufacture, which may be imprinted on the

TABLE 2.10

Estimated water use and savings by waterless and low-volume urinals in office buildings

Years Manufactured or Installed*	Urinal Water-Use Rate	Frequency of Urinal Use† Daily Per Male	Estimated Water Use Daily Per Male	Estimated Water Savings With Waterless Urinal‡ Daily Per Male	Estimated Water Savings With Waterless Urinal‡ Yearly (260 workdays) Per Male	Estimated Water Savings With 1.0 gpf Urinal‡ Daily Per Male	Estimated Water Savings With 1.0 gpf Urinal‡ Yearly (260 workdays) Per Male
	gpf	number of uses	gal	gal	gal	gal	gal
1990-present (waterless urinals)	0.0	2.0	0.0				
1994-present (flush urinals)	**1.0**	2.0	2.0	2.0	520		
1980-1994 (flush urinals)	1.5	2.0	3.0	3.0	780	1.0	260
	2.0	2.0	4.0	4.0	1,040	2.0	520
	3.0	2.0	6.0	6.0	1,560	4.0	1,040
	4.5	2.0	9.0	9.0	2,340	7.0	1,820
Pre-1980s (flush urinals)	5.0	2.0	10.0	10.0	2,600	8.0	2,080
	Continuous-flow, trough-style	2.0	§	§	§	§	§

* Time periods are approximate. Dates in state and local jurisdictions may vary somewhat from dates shown except when they are superseded by the Jan. 1, 1994 federal requirement (shown in bold) allowing a maximum of 1.0 gpf for most urinals installed after that date, per the U.S. Energy Policy Act of 1992.

† Applies to urinals used in office buildings; urinals in other settings may have different frequencies of use.

‡ Excludes water used for cleaning and attributable to leaks

§ Water use and potential water savings are site-specific.

gpf = gallons per flush

number of uses = average number of times per day urinal is flushed

gal = gallon

Sources: Amy Vickers & Associates, Inc.; References 26, 38, and 39

bowl or flush valve, and check its probable flow rate as shown in Table 2.10; (3) determine the most recent date of fixture installation or the age of the building (if the urinal appears to be the original installed during construction) to find its probable flow rate as shown in Table 2.10; or (4) contact the manufacturer.

Low-volume and waterless urinals are either wall-mounted or floor-mounted and are available in a number of designs and sizes. There are several styles of low-volume flushometer-valve urinals, two types of waterless urinals, and several urinal repair and adjustment options to increase water efficiency.

2.2.1 Low-Volume Urinals

Low-volume, flushometer-valve urinals that use 1.0 gpf or less can be installed to replace high-volume, flush-valve fixtures, often with no modifications to the bowl or to wall or floor connections. In some cases only the flush valve needs to be replaced to lower the flow rate to 1.0 gpf. Low-volume, flush-valve urinals operate the same way as high-volume, flush-valve urinals and toilets, except that the diaphragm orifice in the valve has a smaller diameter. Installation of low-volume, flush-valve urinals to replace other types of high-volume urinals (such as siphonic, washout, washdown, and trough urinals) requires removal of the old fixture and flushing apparatus and installation of an entirely new fixture and valve.

Figure 2.25
No-Flush®
waterless urinal
(Photo courtesy
of Waterless
Co. LLC)

2.2.2 Waterless Urinals

Waterless urinals, which are different from composting urinals (see Section 2.2.2.1, "Composting Urinals") require no water for flushing and can often replace conventional fixtures connected to standard 2-inch drainlines. The waterless urinal system is reported to have originated in Switzerland in the 1890s, and various designs have been in use in parts of Europe since the mid-1960s.[93] Since the early 1990s,[93] the waterless urinal has been gaining acceptance and is being installed more frequently in the United States and other countries.

One type of waterless urinal is the Waterless Company's No-Flush® urinal, as shown in Figure 2.25. The No-Flush urinal is designed to have no odor and to minimize bacterial growth on dry surfaces. The No-Flush uses a special drain insert (the Eco Trap®) containing a 3-ounce layer of a biodegradable liquid (BlueSeal®), which floats in the urinal trap and forms a barrier barring the escape of sewer vapors, as illustrated in Figure 2.26. The BlueSeal layer also prevents urine odors and lasts for about 1,500 uses. These chemical products are reported by the manufacturer to be biodegradable.[94]

Waterless urinals require different, though not necessarily more, maintenance than flush urinals. When a waterless urinal is first installed, maintenance personnel need to be instructed on how to replace the trap seal when necessary and how to wash the fixture because flushing without water will leave more of the bowl's surface area covered with urine residue. In certain facilities, such as schools, bars, and high-traffic areas where urinals may become receptacles for cigarette butts, paper, and other trash, flush urinals and waterless urinals require different cleaning tasks. Some flush urinals may easily clear small pieces of trash, but large items (e.g., towels, shoes, tennis balls) may cause clogs either at the top of the trap or inside the trapway if they are pushed down or carried by the force of flushing; in this situation, the fixture may have to be dismantled to dislodge the items. With a waterless urinal, material dumped on top of the trap should be easy to remove because the trap is covered by a screen. Items that have been forced into the trapway of a waterless urinal have to be cleared in the same way required for flush urinals (although lack of a flushing mechanism may result in fewer trapway clogs).

Some early waterless urinals had problems with staining and splash-back, but these inadequacies have largely been corrected. First-time users are sometimes confused by the absence of a flush valve and the fact that the fixture is not connected to a water pipe; notices are sometimes posted to let users know

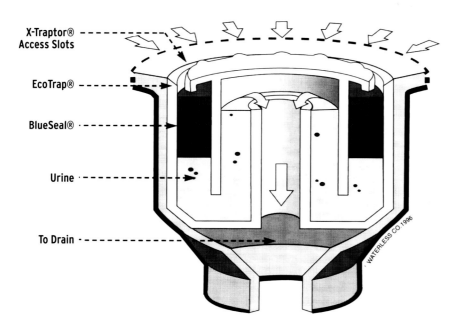

Figure 2.26 Cross section of Eco Trap® design for waterless urinal (Illustration courtesy of Waterless Co. LLC)

why replacement fixtures are different from the old ones. Waterless urinals have been installed in more than 200 locations in the United States, including facilities as diverse as Kirtland Air Force Base in Albuquerque, New Mexico; Mt. Sinai Medical Center in New York City; and the Hard Rock Cafe in La Jolla, California.[94] An evaluation of 20 No-Flush urinals installed since 1993 at various schools in the San Diego Union High School District found annual water savings of 45,000 gallons per urinal (about 900,000 gallons for the district), yearly cost savings of $122 per fixture in parts and labor for repairs, and $144 per fixture in reduced water costs. With annual maintenance costs totaling about $460, the district's net savings is about $4,900 a year for all 20 fixtures.[93]

2.2.2.1 Composting Urinals

Composting urinals require no water and are connected to composting toilet systems (see Section 2.1.2.1, "Composting Toilets"). Urine deposited in a composting urinal is conveyed by gravity through a vertical drain directly to the composter. The fan used to vent the composter creates a negative pressure that continually draws air from the urinal drain, preventing the escape of odor and gases through the fixture. Decomposition of the urinal waste occurs in the composter.

2.2.3 Urinal Retrofit Devices

2.2.3.1 Flush-Valve Replacement and Retrofit

For high-volume, flush-valve urinals, three retrofit options are available to reduce flush volumes: (1) install a new 1.0 gpf flush valve, although this may be possible only with 1.5 to 3.0 gpf fixtures; (2) install a valve-diaphragm replacement kit; (3) if feasible, install a new orifice insert inside the existing flush valve (this typically works in newer flush valves only; older or corroded valves usually require replacement).[59, 95] A flush-valve retrofit kit for flushometer urinals and toilets is shown in Figure 2.21.

Installation of a 1.0 gpf flush valve on a high-volume fixture may require some modifications to the connection and, in some cases, replacement of the urinal bowl. Perforated (usually plastic) orifice inserts can be placed inside high-volume urinal flush valves to reduce water use by about 1.0 gpf, just as they can for many high-volume toilet flush valves. For flush valves that cannot accommodate an orifice insert, a flush-valve replacement kit can be installed in most instances. Some flush valves are already equipped with reversible diaphragm rings, which can be flipped over to reduce the flush volume, precluding the need to install an orifice insert or valve replacement kit.[59]

2.2.3.2 Flush-Valve Efficiency Adjustments

Water use by conventional, high-volume flush valves in urinals can sometimes be reduced by turning the adjusting screw under the cap located on the horizontal portion of the valve; this adjustment will save 0.5 to 1.0 gpf and should not adversely affect the fixture's flushing performance. These adjustments may require some experimentation to determine the minimum acceptable volume per fixture.

2.2.3.3 Timers for Siphonic-Jet and Blowout-Valve Urinals

Timers or time clocks to control the frequency of flushing or water flow can be installed on urinals that flush periodically or continuously, such as siphonic-jet and blowout-valve urinals. The timer can be set to operate only when a building or facility is in use.[95]

Siphonic-jet urinals have no flushing mechanism but are equipped with elevated flush tanks that cause water to discharge automatically when water in the tank reaches a certain level. Siphonic-jet urinals can remove solid materials that most other urinals cannot (e.g., cigarette butts and gum wrappers) and thus may be effective in high-use public facilities. Though they are more self-maintaining than other types of urinals because they are flushed regularly, siphonic-jet urinals demand high volumes of water and operate continuously—24 hours a day, 365 days a year. Blowout-valve urinals operate similarly, except that they rely on a hydraulic flushing mechanism to regularly empty the tank's contents and flush waste out of the urinal. Thus, installation of a timer or sensor to flush the fixture only when necessary and with small volumes of water can reduce demand.[95]

2.2.3.4 Infrared and Ultrasound Sensor-Activated Flush Controls

Infrared and ultrasound sensor-activated controls may be used to reduce double-flushing on washout, washdown, and blowout-valve urinals,[95] although the primary value of these controls may be reducing exposure to germs. Unless double-flushing is a problem, the water conservation benefits of these devices are uncertain, particularly if they are prone to malfunction and *cause* double-flushing.

2.2.4 Urinal Leak Repair

Urinals should be checked for leakage at least every six months. Water losses from flush-valve urinals are more likely due to malfunctions than leaks (e.g., the valve gets stuck in the open position and flushes continuously until it is unlocked), but seepage should be checked at the valve and all connections. Siphonic-jet and blowout-valve urinals should be checked for leaks at their elevated water tanks and other connections. Washout and washdown urinals should be checked for leaks at all pipe and handle connections.[95]

Performance of Water-Efficient Urinals

Low-volume, waterless, and composting urinals and retrofit devices generally render excellent performance. This is probably because liquid wastes are easier to transport and dispose of than solid wastes.

Waterless urinals are operated with positive performance reports in a growing number of government facilities, such as military installations, national park facilities, offices, sports arenas, airports, and other local, state, and federal buildings. A number of commercial and institutional facilities have also installed them, including McDonalds and the San Diego Zoo.[96]

Water Savings and Related Benefits
From Water-Efficient Urinals and Retrofit Devices

WATER SAVINGS Estimated water use and water savings from replacing a high-volume urinal with a waterless or 1.0 gpf fixture in an office building are shown in Table 2.10. For example, installing a waterless urinal to replace a 3.0 gpf model will save an estimated 6.0 gallons per capita per day (gcpd) per male occupant, equivalent to 1,560 gpcy for an average 260-workday year. Installing a 1.0 gpf urinal to replace a 3.0 gpf fixture will save about 4.0 gpcd per male occupant, equivalent to 1,040 gpcy for an average 260-workday year.

Water savings from adjustments to urinal flush valves are estimated to range from 0.5 gpf to 2.0 gpf; actual savings vary depending on the original flush rate of the fixture and its ability to operate at reduced flows. The amount of water saved by installing time clock–activated controls on trough urinals depends on the pressure and flow rate controlled by the new time clock.

WATER AND SEWER COST SAVINGS Avoided water and sewer costs associated with the installation of waterless and low-volume urinals can be calculated by multiplying the expected volume of water (and wastewater) reductions (see Table 2.10) times the local utility rates for water and sewer use (excluding fixed charges). A schedule of representative water and sewer utility rates in the United States and their associated marginal cost savings according to a range of reduced water and wastewater volumes is provided in Appendix D, *Water and Sewer Rates, Costs, and Savings by Volume of Use.* Waterless and low-volume urinals installed in high-use facilities often yield excellent paybacks. For example, the National Aeronautics and Space Administration's Jet Propulsion Laboratory in Pasadena, California, installed 335 waterless urinals and is reported to have achieved a payback on its investment in 2.2 years.[97]

ENERGY SAVINGS No direct energy savings accrue from the use of waterless and low-volume urinals, but utilities glean indirect energy savings from the reduced volumes of water and wastewater pumped and processed for treatment.

REDUCED SEWER AND SEPTIC SYSTEM NEEDS New water and sewer connections may be downsized when waterless or low-volume urinals are installed in newly constructed facilities, particularly when other water-efficient fixtures and appliances are also installed. For existing facilities served by wastewater and septic systems, installation of waterless, composting, and low-volume urinals can often extend the useful life of the system. For example, the U.S. Bureau of Reclamation expects to save more than $600,000 by avoiding an expansion of the sewage treatment system at the Glen Canyon Dam Visitor Center in Arizona as a result of installing waterless urinals and other water-efficient plumbing fixtures. The three waterless urinals installed there are projected to lower water demand by 675,000 gallons per year, saving $830 annually from reduced water, sewer, and maintenance costs and yielding a three-year payback period. The Visitor Center receives more than one million tourists a year.[98]

SAVINGS ON MAINTENANCE AND REPAIRS In terms of maintenance, waterless urinals have several advantages compared with flush urinals. Waterless urinals do not require valve repairs or flange exchanges, and there is no risk of overflow. The surfaces of waterless and composting urinals may have lower concentrations of germs, according to one manufacturer, because studies of restrooms have shown that bacteria are more prevalent on moist surfaces such as washbasins and flush urinals and toilets.[99]

Costs Associated With Water-Efficient Urinals

HARDWARE COSTS The cost of a low-volume urinal is comparable to that of a conventional high-volume urinal in most instances; waterless and composting urinals require a somewhat higher initial cost outlay. Local market conditions and other factors significantly influence the price of urinals, particularly when they are purchased wholesale. Approximate retail costs for waterless and low-volume urinals and retrofit devices include:

- Waterless urinal: $350 to $600
- Composting urinal: $250 per fixture (excluding cost of composting system)
- Low-volume 1.0 gpf urinals: $200 to $450 (fixture and flush valve)
- 1.0 gpf urinal flush valve: $100 to $150
- Urinal flush-valve replacement kit: $20 to $25
- Infrared control device: $250 to $400

LABOR AND MATERIAL COSTS The cost of hiring a plumber to install a waterless or low-volume urinal should not be any higher than that for a conventional fixture unless the replacement fixture requires reconfiguration of the plumbing and electrical systems or related aesthetic renovations (e.g., floor tile or wall remodeling). Depending on local market conditions, a plumber can install a simple urinal for $45 to $125.

OPERATING COSTS Waterless urinals use no water, but at least one manufacturer's products require a trap seal liquid that must be replenished (at a cost of about $20) after approximately 1,500 uses. Operating costs for composting urinals are similar to those for composting toilets (see Section 2.1.2.1, "Composting Toilets"). Automatic flush sensors for urinals rely on batteries or are connected to an electrical system for operation; thus, installation of these devices may require hardware as well as installation and maintenance costs.

ENERGY COSTS Composting urinals and automatic flushing devices connected to systems that rely on electricity for venting and other purposes incur some energy costs.

PRODUCT MANUFACTURERS Manufacturers of waterless and low-volume urinals and related products are listed in Chapter 6, *The Water Conservation Network.*

Laws, Codes, and Standards Applicable to Urinals

All applicable laws, codes, standards, and health and safety requirements associated with urinals and related devices should be observed when any urinal or related plumbing or water system connection is installed or adjusted. These include but are not limited to the following federal, state, and local requirements:

FEDERAL WATER-EFFICIENCY REQUIREMENTS Water-efficiency requirements for urinals in the United States were established by EPAct and are regulated by the DOE. State and local authorities may set stricter water-use standards for urinals only if granted approval by DOE. EPAct mandates that all flush urinals shall use a maximum of 1.0 gpf, as shown in Table 2.1, with few exceptions. The maximum water use allowed for trough urinals is the product of (a) the maximum flow rate for a urinal and (b) the length of the urinal in inches (or meters) divided by 16 inches (0.406 meters). EPAct also requires that urinals (including the flushometer valve that may be connected to the fixture) bear a permanent marking indicating the maximum flow rate of the fixture expressed in gallons per flush, as specified by the product marking and labeling requirements established by ASME Standard A119.2.[26] As with other plumbing fixtures regulated by this legislation, EPAct establishes *maximum* water-use requirements, thereby allowing for urinals that use *less* than 1.0 gpf.

Performance Test Standards EPAct's maximum water-use provisions for flush urinals incorporate minimum-performance tests and related product requirements for urinals established by ASME and ANSI. The standards applicable to urinals are ASME/ANSI Standard A112.19.2 *(Vitreous China Plumbing Fixtures)*, ASME Standard A112.19.5 *(Trim for Water Closets, Bowls, Tanks and Urinals)*, and ASME Standard A112.19.6 *(Hydraulic Requirements for Water Closets and Urinals)*. In addition to complying with the ASME/ANSI performance tests, many manufacturers of urinals have created their own more stringent tests to make sure their products work acceptably.

Waterless urinals are allowed as alternative systems under all plumbing codes, and in 1996 the National Standard Plumbing Code specifically permitted their use. Waterless urinals comply with ANSI Z124.9-9 *(Plastic Urinals)*.[100]

LOCAL AND STATE AUTHORITIES Historically, state and local plumbing authorities set water-use standards for urinals and allowed exceptions under special circumstances, but EPAct requirements now supersede such authorities. Although in practice some state and local authorities may continue to amend their water-use requirements for urinals or allow exemptions, according to EPAct only DOE (through passage of a rule) can grant states the power to establish exemptions for water-efficiency requirements that are more stringent than those stipulated by EPAct.

Some state and local plumbing and building codes require permits and allow urinals to be installed, adjusted, or retrofitted only by a licensed plumber, but these requirements are sometimes waived for large-scale rebate and replacement programs. Installation of composting urinals may also require the approval of health officials. Similarly, adjustments to an electrical system connected to a plumbing fixture typically require a licensed electrician, and modifications to building structures may also have to be completed by a licensed contractor with a permit.

*T*HE URINALS, *a five-piece parody of punk rock, came together at a UCLA dorm-wide party on Halloween Eve in 1978. Their performance was a four-song set, including "This is the Modern World" and "The Jetsons" theme song. The acclaim was immediate, and the jazz band that followed them was thoroughly outraged.*

Implementing a Urinal Replacement Program

Several considerations should be taken into account in planning a program to install waterless and low-volume urinals.

SELECTING LOW-VOLUME AND WATERLESS URINALS A number of low-volume and waterless urinals are available, and most of them can easily be installed to replace existing high-volume fixtures. Composting urinals are typically connected to a larger composting system that includes toilets; selecting these fixtures involves additional installation and maintenance considerations.

PLANNING THE PROGRAM Components of a urinal replacement program are similar to those of toilet replacement programs, except that urinal programs are targeted toward nonresidential customers and large-volume users who could reap appreciable water savings. More than 40 U.S. government facilities have installed waterless urinals through large-scale urinal replacement programs.[98] Programs that promote waterless urinals need to familiarize building managers and owners with the maintenance needs of these fixtures.

Targeted Water Users and Fixtures Waterless and low-volume 1.0 gpf urinals can be installed to replace high-volume flush urinals as well as trough urinals that are flushed by a washdown-pipe assembly connected above the fixture to provide intermittently or continuously flowing water. Exceptions may be granted for special uses and circumstances that require higher flow volumes, although such conditions are uncommon because urinals in most facilities contain only liquid wastes.

Urinal retrofit devices can also be installed on many high-volume urinals to reduce flows. Waterless composting urinals can be installed to replace water-using urinals, but they usually require building and plumbing alterations and different maintenance procedures.

Number of Urinals Installed There are several ways to estimate the number of urinals currently installed in a given service area or nonresidential facility. As with toilets, the number of urinals in nonresidential properties varies widely and is often based on a building's type and rated occupancy load; however, many buildings have more fixtures than the minimum specified by codes. A minimum of one to two urinals per 100 occupants (including employees) is usually specified for male restrooms in offices, restaurants, and places of assembly, and a minimum of three to four urinals per 100 occupants (including employees) can be expected in institutions such as schools, dormitories, and hospitals.

The UPC, adopted by many state and local plumbing and building code authorities, specifies the minimum number of fixtures required for male restrooms in a range of facilities (offices, schools, dormitories, auditoriums, hospitals, factories, sports arenas, and so on). In addition, the UBC specifies the number of occupants that should be assumed based on exiting requirements, square footage, and other features (e.g., fixed seating in sports arenas). Together, the UPC and UBC can be consulted to estimate the number of urinals and other fixtures expected in a nonresidential building, with a few caveats: (1) some state and local authorities amend the UPC and UBC in their jurisdictions, so differences among states can occur; (2)

the number of urinals installed in a building is usually based on code requirements at the time of construction or renovation, whichever is most recent; and (3) in some restrooms, the number of fixtures has been reduced in order to accommodate the requirements of the U.S. Americans with Disabilities Act of 1992.

In 1996, THE URINALS performed at west L.A.'s Alligator Lounge for their debut CD release party.

Life Cycle of Low-Volume Urinals   The useful life of china or plastic urinals should be a minimum of 20 years if the fixture is not subject to vandalism or other damage. The longevity of valves and related retrofit devices for flush-valve urinals depends on the frequency with which they are used and the wear they receive, but they should have a useful life of about ten years. Aggressive water can accelerate the corrosion of urinal valves, connections, and tanks and can hasten deterioration that leads to leaks and the need for parts replacement and repairs.

Incentives   In addition to letting consumers know about the reduced water and sewer costs associated with waterless and low-volume urinals, large-scale replacement programs often offer rebates as a financial incentive to promote installation of these fixtures. Seattle Public Utilities offers building owners a rebate of $150 per waterless urinal installed to replace an existing fixture using 2.0 gpf or more. Rebates are not given for fixtures in newly constructed buildings because EPAct requires that newly installed urinals use no more than 1.0 gpf.[101]

INSTALLATION OF WATER-EFFICIENT URINALS AND RETROFIT DEVICES   Installation of waterless and low-volume urinals and related retrofit devices should be done by properly trained technicians or plumbers and should be based on applicable rules and practices. In a jurisdiction that allows consumers, such as building managers, to install fixtures themselves, installers should be fully advised about proper procedures, tools, and precautions to ensure competent, safe installation. Installing waterless urinals is different from installing water-using urinals. For example, at least one type of waterless urinal requires a vented plumbing system and cannot be connected to copper drainlines.

Fixture Rough-In   The rough-in size of existing urinals should be measured before a water-efficient replacement fixture is purchased and installed. Replacement of older urinals and installation of urinals with a different operating system may require floor, wall, and plumbing alterations.

Water Pressure   Adequate water pressure, 25 to 40 psi, is required for flushometer-valve urinals to operate properly.

RECYCLING USED URINALS   See "Recycling Used Toilets" under Section 2.1.1 of this chapter.

MAINTENANCE   No additional maintenance should be required for low-volume, 1.0 gpf flush-valve urinals compared with the high-volume fixtures they replace. Waterless and composting urinals do require different maintenance tasks than flush urinals.

Waterless Urinals A U.S. military facilities manager has offered some advice based on lessons learned at facilities that installed waterless urinals for the first time: (1) Be sure drain is clear before installation; snake it, if necessary. (2) Be sure urinal and trap seal are installed properly. (3) Be sure custodial staff are trained to clean urinals thoroughly and routinely. Whenever the trap is removed or replaced, it's a good idea to first clean the pipes by pouring down a few gallons of hot water. (4) Expect a learning curve before personnel become accustomed to using a waterless urinal.[102] If odor is a problem with waterless urinals, it probably means that the trap seal is due for replacement or the fixture needs to be cleaned.

Composting Urinals See Section 2.1.2.1, "Composting Toilets," for installation and maintenance requirements for composting urinals.

Urinal Flush Timers and Motion Sensors These devices should be checked periodically to ensure that they are set properly and are not causing double-flushing. Used batteries from sensor-controlled urinals should be properly disposed of to comply with applicable hazardous waste disposal laws and to minimize adverse environmental effects and safety hazards.

2.3 SHOWERHEADS

This section describes three measures for reducing water use by showerheads: low-volume showerheads, showerhead retrofit devices, and showerhead adjustments. These measures apply to showerheads in residential and nonresidential properties (e.g., office buildings, schools, public and commercial facilities, hotels, hospitals, and many types of institutional facilities); they are not applicable to safety showers or other special-use showering devices.

Low-volume showerheads use a maximum of 2.5 gallons per minutes (gpm) at a pressure of 80 pounds per square inch (psi), or 2.2 gpm at 60 psi. Showerhead retrofit devices are usually low-volume showerhead replacement fixtures. (Flow-restricting devices can be inserted into existing showerheads to reduce flows, but they are not considered a viable, long-term conservation measure because of their low rate of acceptance by consumers.)

The quality and water efficiency of showerheads in the United States have improved significantly since the early 1980s, as a result of state and national legislation and conservation programs initiated by a number of energy and water utilities. Today, a number of high-quality, efficient showerheads and related devices are easily accepted by consumers, despite some residual skepticism among those who previously installed (and typically removed) poor-quality showerhead restrictors with meager flows or uncomfortable sprays. Improved low-volume showerheads include devices that increase the mix of air with water to create the effect of wetness over more surface area, devices with increased flow velocity to offset the reduced volume, and devices with narrower spray areas. EPAct requires that showerheads sold, installed, or imported in the United States be low-volume fixtures that use no more than 2.5 gpm at 80 psi.[26]

C onserve water. Shower with a friend."
—Bumper Sticker

TABLE 2.11

Estimated water use and savings by low-volume showerheads in households

Years Manufactured or Installed [*†]	Showerhead Water-Use Rate[‡]		Frequency of Shower-head Use[§]	Estimated Water Use		Estimated Water Savings With 2.5 gpm Showerhead			
	Rated Flow (MFC)	Actual Flow (MFR)	Per Person	Per Capita	Per House-hold[**]	Per Capita	Per House-hold[**]	Per Capita	Per House-hold[**]
	gpm	gpm	min/day	gpd	gpd	gpd	gpd	gpy	gpy
1994–present	**2.5**	1.7	5.3	8.8	23.3				
1980–1994	2.75	1.8	5.3	9.7	25.7	0.9	2.3	322	851
	3.0	2.0	5.3	10.6	28.0	1.8	4.7	645	1,702
	4.0	2.7	5.3	14.1	37.3	5.3	14.0	1,935	5,107
Pre-1980 [††]	5.0–8.0	4.3	5.3	23.0	60.6	14.1	37.3	5,159	13,619

* Time periods are approximate. Dates for state and local jurisdictions may vary somewhat from dates shown except when they are superseded by the Jan.1, 1994 federal requirement (shown in bold) allowing a maximum of 2.5 gpm for most showerheads installed after that date, per the U.S. Energy Policy Act.

† Excludes safety showers

‡ Flow rates at 80 pounds per square inch (psi); a showerhead with a flow rate of 2.5 gpm at 80 psi is equivalent to a showerhead with a flow rate of 2.2 gpm at 60 psi.

§ The average residential indoor water-use rate for showering has been reported to be 8.2 minutes per shower; however, on a daily basis, a total of 11.6 gallons per capita is used for showering at an average flow rate of 2.2 gpm, or 5.3 minutes per capita per day for showering.

** Based on the average of 2.64 persons per occupied U.S. household

†† Showerhead MFR for pre-1980 fixtures is averaged for range shown.

MFC = maximum fixture capacity (rated flow)

MFR = measured fixture rate is actual flow rate (equal to about two thirds the MFC)

gpm = gallons per minute

min/day = average number of minutes per day showerhead is used

gpd = gallons per day

gpy = gallons per year

Sources: Amy Vickers & Associates, Inc.; References 12, 26, 29, 37, and 52

Water Use by Showerheads

Average water use and water savings for low-volume and high-volume showerheads, estimated according to their flow rates, are shown in Table 2.11. Low-volume showerheads use a maximum of 2.5 gpm or less and include 2.2 and 1.5 gpm fixtures with flows rated at 80 psi; showerheads with pressures of 60 psi have lower rated flows. (Although EPAct originally required low-volume showerheads to use no more than 2.5 gpm at 80 psi, a March 1998 amendment to EPAct revised the maximum flow for showerheads to 2.2 gpm when measured at 60 psi.) Moderate- to high-volume showerheads use 2.75, 3.0, 4.0, and up to 8.0 gpm. Manufacturers usually show full-throttle flow rates (maximum fixture capacity, or MFC) for showerheads at 80 psi, as shown in Table 2.11, but actual flows (measured fixture rate, or MFR) are usually about two thirds (67%) of rated flows because most people prefer less than a full blast of water for showering.[36] For example, a person showering with a fixture rated at 3.0 gpm with the handle two-thirds open would be using about 2.0 gpm.

Water use by showerheads is typically the third largest source of indoor residential water demand, averaging 11.6 gallons per capita per day (gpcd); this represents 16.8% of indoor use in a typical single-family home. Actual average flow through a residential showerhead is 2.2 gpm.[103] An earlier (1984) study found average water use by showerheads in a nonconserving home to be 16.3 gpcd, an actual average flow of 3.4 gpm.[36] These figures reflect the increasing water efficiency of showerheads since the mid-1980s. Depending on the approximate year in which a showerhead was installed, residential water use by showerheads can be estimated, as shown in Table 2.11.

The 1999 REUS study reported that the frequency of shower and bath use in a single-family home averaged 0.75 uses per person per day. The study also reported an average shower water-use rate of 11.6 gpcd and an average flow rate of 2.2 gpm, making the average showering rate 5.3 minutes per person per day. Based on the average showering rate (not the average daily use), the average shower lasts 8.2 minutes and uses 17.2 gallons of water.[104] A 1984 study found the average showering rate to be 4.8 minutes per person per day.[36] The frequency of showering in nonresidential facilities and the amount of water used are not well established.

Studies of water use by showerheads have found that *actual* flow rates often differ from *rated* flows.[88, 105] There are several ways to determine more precisely how much water a particular showerhead uses if its flow rate is unknown: (1) run the shower, collecting the water in a premeasured bag or bucket, and record the flow rate; (2) read the water meter before and after running the shower (keeping all other fixtures and water-using appliances turned off); (3) look for markings on the showerhead showing its rated flow (this is a federal requirement that became effective in 1994 under EPAct); (4) determine the most recent date of showerhead installation (this may have occurred during a renovation or retrofit program) or the age of the building (if the showerhead appears to be the original installed during construction) to find its probable flow rate as shown in Table 2.11; or (5) contact the manufacturer.

The terms *low-volume, low-flow, low-consumption,* and *high-efficiency* are used interchangeably to refer to fixtures that use less than 2.5 gpm (at 80 psi), although before 1994 these terms also referred to showerheads that used 2.75 gpm to 3.0 gpm, based on previous energy-efficiency standards. Low-volume showerheads can fit into the same connections as high-volume showerheads without any special adapters (except those needed to reverse male or female threads). The low-volume showerheads, showerhead retrofit devices, and related modifications that are available to reduce water use by showers are described in the following three sections.

2.3.1 Low-Volume Showerheads

Low-volume showerheads improve water-use efficiency compared with high-volume showerheads through such features as improved spray patterns, better mixing of air with water, and narrower spray areas to give the user the "feel" of water without high-volume flows. Flow restrictors are sometimes embedded in low-volume showerheads; these should not be confused with customer-installed showerhead restrictors or "disk inserts" (see Section 2.3.2). Some flow restrictors are permanent and cannot be removed; others can be removed for cleaning and then reinstalled. Showerheads that have a flow restrictor often cost less than fixtures that have a flow-control device. A showerhead flow-control device is a disk containing an elastic O-ring that is controlled by pressure. Under high

The optimum depth of water in a birdbath, says the Audubon Society of America, is two and a half inches. Less water makes it difficult for birds to take a bath; more makes them afraid."
—www.absolutetrivia.com

TABLE 2.12

Survey of actual water savings from low-volume showerheads and retrofit kits

City/Water System	Water Savings Reported for Program Participants	Basis for Reported Water Savings
Metropolitan Water District of Southern California	Estimated net water savings of 5.5 gpd per single-family household and 5.2 gpd per multifamily household; estimated net savings of 5.2 gpd for every 2.5 gpm showerhead installed in a multifamily household	Fixture rebate programs in Los Angeles and Santa Monica, Calif.; estimated savings calculated by using statistical models of billed water use in participating and nonparticipating households during a drought emergency
Tampa (Florida) Water Department	Estimated water savings of 3.6 gpcd in households with showerheads used at actual flow rates of 1.5 gpm (about 60% of the showerhead's rated capacity of 2.5 gpm)	Water-use monitoring network installed in 25 single family residences in Tampa
New York, New York	Estimated average water savings of 12.4 gpcd in household units with 2.5 gpm showerhead; based on an estimated average showering time of 7.5 minutes (actual time may be shorter)	Data records for 72,359 residential units in New York City
Massachusetts Water Resources Authority	Estimated net reductions in water demand of 5.7% for single-family households and 10% for multifamily units; estimated systemwide water savings of approximately 5.0 mgd	"Operation Watersense," a direct-install fixture retrofit program implemented 1990–1993 in 348,871 of more than 647,800 targeted households (54% participation rate, excluding 13,300 households receiving kits from depots) in 44 communities in metropolitan Boston
Pinellas-Aclote River Basin Board, Pinellas and Pasco counties, Florida	Water savings of 6 gpd per occupied hotel/motel room	Hotel/motel retrofit program retrofitted 1,905 rooms with toilet displacement devices, low-flow showerheads, and faucet aerators

gpm = gallons per minute

gphd = gallons per household per day

mgd = million gallons per day

Sources: Amy Vickers & Associates, Inc.; References 54, 60, 109–111

water pressure, the O-ring flattens and reduces water flow; under low pressure, the O-ring relaxes and allows a higher flow (within specifications), providing smoother changes in spray patterns compared with flow restrictors.[106]

Optional Features in Low-Volume Showerheads

Low-volume showerheads designed for fixture retrofit programs are available in the screw-on, fixed-position (wall-mounted) style and the screw-on, hand-held style (with regular, pulsating, and massaging sprays). Utility-sponsored retrofit programs typically provide screw-on fixtures, as shown in Figure 2.27, because they are more economical. A variety of spray and other design options are available for low-volume showerheads used in retrofit programs:

- *Aerating-spray showerheads* use an aerator to mix air with fine water droplets, enabling the spray to wet more surface area with less water than conventional showerheads.[95]
- *Atomizing showerheads* create many small, misty water droplets to wet large surface areas.[95]
- *Pulsating showerheads* have variable spray and flow patterns, pausing the flow and releasing water in spurts to create a massaging effect.[95]
- *Temporary shutoff buttons* on showerheads slow water flow to a trickle and allow the user to save additional water while shampooing and washing. A good shutoff valve maintains the same mix of hot and cold water before and after it

is switched on to prevent scalding. Shutoff valves that don't reactivate at the same temperature can give users an unexpected blast of hot water when turned on, creating a safety hazard. The extent to which people actually use shutoff valves is not well established, and thus their potential for saving water is unknown.[77] If used properly, shutoff valves can increase water savings, but some people may use them as permanent shutoff valves and thus create problems. Because shutoff valves are designed to trickle (to prevent backflow and scalding), water can be wasted if the shower handle is not turned off after use. Properties that have shutoff valves but do not have pressure-balancing valves risk causing cross-connection problems between the hot and cold water lines because the two are usually at different pressures.[107]

- *Vandal- and tamper-proof showerheads* have flow restrictors that cannot be removed.

2.3.2 Showerhead Retrofit Devices

Two devices are commonly used to restrict flows on high-volume showerheads: temporary cutoff valves and flow restrictors. Cutoff valves, like temporary shutoff buttons, can be attached to existing showerheads to reduce water

A

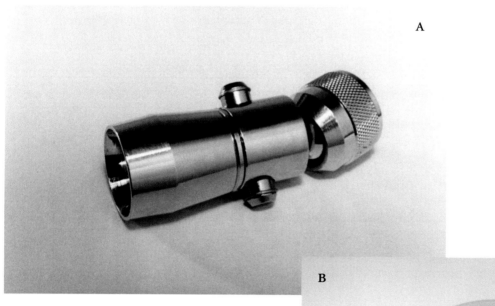

B

Figure 2.27 Low-volume showerheads are available with a variety of features, such as models with (A) shutoff valves and (B) massage-spray patterns. (Photos courtesy of Niagara Conservation, Inc.)

use, but these devices should be used only if they are designed and installed properly because they can cause scalding.

Showerhead Flow Restrictors (Disk Inserts)

Not to be confused with the higher-quality flow restrictors embedded into the body of some low-volume showerheads, these devices are typically inexpensive plastic or metal disks with a small hole in the center. They reduce the flow of water and can be fitted into the coupling of some older, high-volume showerheads where the shower arm is connected.

For several reasons, disk inserts have a poor rate of acceptance by consumers and are typically *not* used by experienced conservation managers. Some of the earliest water utility conservation programs, such as those developed during droughts in the 1960s through the mid-1980s, were based on mass mailings of home retrofit kits that included a showerhead disk. Because of their crude design, many disk inserts are not compatible with the varied flow and spray characteristics of existing showerheads. Squeezing less than 2 gallons of water per minute (gpm) through a spray nozzle designed for a flow rate of 5.0 gpm or more results in weak or sometimes piercing and irregular sprays. Although millions of disk inserts have been distributed, few have stayed installed. Because so many people had negative experiences with disk inserts, remaining negative associations may inhibit the public's acceptance of the much-improved, contemporary, low-volume showerheads. Disk inserts are generally no longer considered an acceptable long-term conservation measure,[77] except perhaps during extreme water shortages when quality of shower spray and user satisfaction are not priorities.

Adjustments to Reduce Showerhead Flow Rates

In addition to replacing or retrofitting inefficient showerheads, several adjustments can be made to reduce their water use: (1) reducing the water pressure will reduce water flow to showers, but this adjustment may cause users with long hair to take extended showers to remove shampoo; and (2) lowering the hot water temperature setting can save some *hot* water, but it won't necessarily cause users to use less water overall. Adjustments such as these should be made only by qualified plumbers and technicians to ensure that proper safety and minimum operating standards are maintained.

Performance of Low-Volume Showerheads and Retrofit Devices

User satisfaction with the performance of low-volume showerheads (e.g., wetness, spray intensity, spray pattern, ability to remove shampoo) is usually very good; when it isn't, the problem often stems from a poor-quality fixture. The amount of water a showerhead uses often does not correlate with the quality of the showering experience; sometimes a showerhead that uses 2.5 gpm or less can provide a better spray than a high-volume fixture.[108]

As noted, showerhead disk inserts often deliver unreliable and unsatisfactory performance. Inserting a disk insert into a 3.0 gpm showerhead will produce a much skimpier shower than inserting it into a 5.0 or 7.0 gpm fixture. Many disk inserts have such a small orifice that they produce unpleasant, hard, or high-pressure sprays.

Water Savings and Related Benefits
From Low-Volume Showerheads and Retrofit Devices

WATER SAVINGS   Estimated water use and water savings from replacing a high-volume residential showerhead with a low-volume showerhead are shown in Table 2.11. For example, installing a 2.5 gpm showerhead to replace a 3.0 gpm model will save an estimated 1.8 gpcd or 4.7 gallons per household per day (gphd), equivalent to an annual water savings of 645 gallons per capita per year (gpcy) or 1,702 gallons per household per year (gphy). Replacing a 4.0 gpm showerhead with a 2.5 gpm model will save an estimated 5.3 gpcd or 14.0 gphd, equivalent to 1,935 gpcy or 5,107 gphy. Actual savings from specific showerhead replacement programs are shown in Table 2.12.[109–111]

AWWA's handbook *The Water Conservation Manager's Guide to Residential Retrofit* identifies the following formula for calculating potential water savings from showerhead replacement for a targeted group of residential customers:

$$(S_a - S_b) \times M \times C = D$$

in which S_a = the average flow rate of existing showerheads at average psi, S_b = the average flow rate of retrofitted showers at average psi, M = the average number of minutes per shower, C = the total number of showers per year taken by the target group, and D = the potential number of gallons saved per year.[77]

This formula is useful for estimating the *potential* water savings that could be achieved from a showerhead replacement program before it is initiated. To determine *actual* water savings, the formula must be adjusted to factor in actual program participation (the number of customers who install a showerhead), installation retention rates (the number of devices installed minus those later removed), and other relevant variables.

Case Study *Athletic Facility Achieves Payback One Month After Retrofitting Showerheads.* Thirty-five low-volume 2.5 gpm (80 psi) showerheads were installed to replace 4.0 gpm models in an athletic facility in Massachusetts. Water savings totaled 328,000 gallons a year. With an initial cost of $300 and an annual savings of $3,330 from reduced water, sewer, and hot water energy costs, the payback on this measure was achieved in approximately one month.[112]

WATER AND SEWER COST SAVINGS   Avoided water and sewer costs associated with installation of a low-volume showerhead can be calculated by multiplying the expected volume of water (and wastewater) reductions (see Table 2.11) times the local utility rates for water and sewer use (excluding fixed charges). A schedule of representative water and sewer utility rates in the United States and their associated marginal cost savings according to a range of reduced water and wastewater volumes is provided in Appendix D, *Water and Sewer Rates, Costs, and Savings by Volume of Use.*

ENERGY SAVINGS   Estimated energy savings from reduced hot water use associated with low-volume showerheads is shown in Table 2.13. For example, installing a 2.5 gpm showerhead to replace a fixture rated to use 4.0 gpm will save an estimated 0.7 kilowatt-hours (kWh) per day per person, or about 1.8 kWh

What difference does it make how much you have? What you do not have amounts to much more."
—Seneca

per day per 2.64-person household. Even greater savings would be achieved by installing a showerhead that uses less than 2.5 gpm, particularly if it replaces a pre-1980 showerhead that uses 5.0 to 8.0 gpm. Utilities also glean indirect energy savings from the reduced volumes of water and wastewater pumped and processed for treatment.

Avoided energy costs from reduced hot water use by a low-volume showerhead can be calculated by multiplying the expected reductions in kilowatt-hours or therms (see Table 2.13) times the local electric or gas utility rates per kilowatt-hour or therm (excluding fixed charges).

Costs Associated With Low-Volume Showerheads and Retrofit Devices

HARDWARE COSTS   The cost of low-volume showerheads rated at 1.5 to 2.5 gpm, particularly if they are purchased in bulk quantities, is estimated to be $4 to $8.

Showerheads to be used in a retrofit program should not be selected based on the lowest price available or the lowest water-use rate that can be achieved. Cost can be a factor in product quality and durability, but showerhead hardware will

TABLE 2.13

Estimated energy use and savings from low-volume showerheads in households

	Showerhead Water-Use Rate[‡]		Frequency of Showerhead Use[§]	Estimated Energy Use for Showerheads[**]		Estimated Energy Savings With 2.5 gpm Showerhead			
	Rated Flow (MFC)	Actual Flow (MFR)	Per Person	Per Capita	Per House-hold[††]	Per Capita	Per House-hold[††]	Per Capita	Per House-hold[††]
Years Manufactured or Installed [*†]	gpm	gpm	min/day	kWh/d	kWh/d	kWh/d	kWh/d	kWh/y	kWh/y
1994-present	2.5	1.7	5.3	1.1	3.0				
1980-1994	2.75	1.8	5.3	1.3	3.3	0.1	0.3	42	111
	3.0	2.0	5.3	1.4	3.6	0.2	0.6	84	221
	4.0	2.7	5.3	1.8	4.9	0.7	1.8	251	664
Pre-1980 [‡‡]	5.0–8.0	4.3	5.3	3.0	7.9	1.8	4.9	671	1,770

* Time periods are approximate. Dates for state and local jurisdictions may vary somewhat from dates shown except when they are superseded by the Jan.1, 1994 federal requirement (shown in bold) allowing a maximum of 2.5 gpm for most showerheads installed after that date, per the U.S. Energy Policy Act.

† Excludes safety showers with a flow rate of 2.2 gpm at 60 psi

§ The average residential indoor water-use rate for showering has been reported to be 8.2 minutes per shower; however, on a daily basis, a total of 11.6 gallons per capita is used for showering at an average flow rate of 2.2 gpm, or 5.3 minutes per capita per day for showering.

** Estimates based on 0.13 kilowatt-hour (kWh) of electricity per 1.0 gallon of water at 106°F; actual energy use may vary because of user temperature preferences, pressure, energy efficiency of water heater, and related factors. For gas water-heating systems, convert figures for electric energy use and savings to therms (1 kWh = 0.034 therm, or 1 therm = 29.3 kWh).

†† Based on the average of 2.64 persons per occupied U.S. household

‡‡ For pre-1980 showerheads, MFR is averaged.

MFC = maximum fixture capacity (rated flow)

MFR = measured fixture rate is actual flow rate (equal to about two thirds the MFC)

gpm = gallons per minute

min/day = average number of minutes showerhead is used a day

kWh/d = kilowatt-hours per day

kWh/y = kilowatt-hours per year

Sources: Amy Vickers & Associates, Inc.; References 26, 29, 37, 52, and 178

play an important role in determining the success of a retrofit program in terms of customer satisfaction and device retention. A poor-quality showerhead with an unsatisfactory spray or flow rate may be removed by a large percentage of customers, defeating the purpose of the program. Further, because the appearance of a product can also affect customer acceptance, attention should be paid to the showerhead's size, shape, and color. Many people prefer showerheads with massage and spray options; a number of low-volume showerheads designed for large-scale distribution in retrofit programs offer these features at reasonable prices.

LABOR AND MATERIAL COSTS   The cost of installing a low-volume showerhead in a utility-sponsored direct installation or audit program ranges from $12 to $30 per installation and often includes a toilet displacement device, faucet aerators, and a toilet leak-detection test with dye tablets. The time needed to install a retrofit kit is 30 to 45 minutes per household, excluding travel and related administrative time. Programs that use drop-off and bulk-mailing distribution methods cost less because they provide little installation assistance (e.g., only for the elderly and the disabled).

A small strip of Teflon® tape is usually placed around the thread of the new showerhead neck to ensure a tight fit, reduce leakage, and allow easy removal for cleaning.

PRODUCT MANUFACTURERS   Manufacturers of low-volume showerheads and related products are provided in Chapter 6, *The Water Conservation Network.*

Laws, Codes, and Standards Applicable to Showerheads

All applicable laws, codes, standards, and health and safety requirements associated with showerheads and related devices should be observed when any fixture, appliance, or related plumbing or water system connection is installed or adjusted. These include but are not limited to the following federal, state, and local requirements:

FEDERAL WATER-EFFICIENCY REQUIREMENTS   Water-use efficiency requirements for showerheads installed, manufactured, or imported in the United States were established by EPAct and are regulated by DOE. State and local authorities may set stricter water-use standards for showerheads only if granted approval by DOE. EPAct mandates that showerheads shall use a maximum of 2.5 gpm at 80 psi (or 2.2 gpm at 60 psi), as shown in Table 2.1. Exceptions include showerheads used for safety purposes. EPAct also requires that showerheads bear a permanent marking indicating the fixture's maximum flow rate expressed in gallons per minute or gallons per cycle at a specific psi, as specified by the product marking and labeling requirements of ASME Standard A112.18.1 *(Plumbing Fixture Fittings).*[26] EPAct establishes *maximum* water-use requirements, thereby allowing for showerheads that use *less* water than that established by the legislation.

Performance Test Standards   The maximum water-use requirements for showerheads established by EPAct incorporate the minimum-performance tests and related product requirements for showerheads established by ASME Standard

A112.18.1 *(Plumbing Fixture Fittings)*. In addition to complying with the ASME/ANSI performance tests, many manufacturers of showerheads have created their own more stringent tests to make sure their products work acceptably.

LOCAL AND STATE AUTHORITIES   Historically, state and local plumbing authorities set water-use standards for showerheads, but now the federal EPAct requirements supersede such authorities in most instances. Although in practice some state and local authorities may continue to amend their water-use requirements for showerheads, EPAct specifies that only DOE (through passage of a rule) can grant states the power to establish water-efficiency requirements more stringent than those established by EPAct.

Some states and municipalities allow showerheads to be installed, adjusted, or retrofitted only by a licensed plumber, but these requirements are sometimes waived for large-scale retrofit and replacement programs in which trained technicians are used.

Implementing a Showerhead Retrofit or Replacement Program

SELECTING A LOW-VOLUME SHOWERHEAD OR RETROFIT DEVICE
Low-volume showerheads selected for large-scale retrofit programs are often designed to include one or several of the following features:

- *Fixed showerheads*. Fixed showerhead devices are usually selected for retrofit programs because they cost less to purchase and install than the detachable, flexible showerhead assembly. Exceptions may include showerheads for people with disabilities and for other special uses.
- *Massage and variable-spray options.* Low-volume showerheads with massage features and alternative spray patterns (e.g., atomizing, sharp, and misted sprays) may enhance user satisfaction and thereby increase device retention rates in retrofit programs.
- *Temporary shutoff valves.* Showerheads embedded with a temporary shutoff button or cutoff valve are sometimes purchased for retrofit programs. It is not clear to what extent consumers actually use this feature or whether it saves an appreciable amount of water. Showerheads with shutoff valves should be carefully selected to ensure that they do not cause scalding.

PLANNING A SHOWERHEAD OR RETROFIT KIT INSTALLATION PROGRAM   The following steps for creating an ideal retrofit program were adapted from a study by the Rocky Mountain Institute in Snowmass, Colorado:[113]

1. Select and customize a program installation method(s) to maximize participation by targeted customers and customer subgroups in each neighborhood (Figure 2.28).
2. Select high-quality retrofit devices. Obtain sample showerheads and other devices from manufacturers whose products are under consideration for use in the program. Evaluate these products for acceptability by means of a focus group or other representative groups from the service area.
3. Promote the program heavily (e.g., bill inserts; newspaper, television, and radio ads).
4. Finance the program with other utilities (water, wastewater, electric, and gas)

Figure 2.28 Planning for the distribution of retrofit kits in a neighborhood

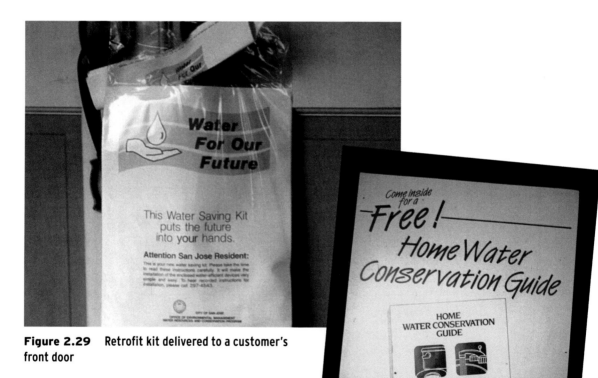

Figure 2.29 Retrofit kit delivered to a customer's front door

Figure 2.30 *Home Water Conservation Guide,* Massachusetts Water Resources Authority

(Photos 2.28 through 2.30 courtesy of Amy Vickers & Associates, Inc.)

to spread costs and boost customer participation.

5. Target customers with high indoor water use in the early phase of the program (e.g., low-income housing facilities and other residential and institutional customers).

6. Deliver or offer retrofit kits to all customers in the service area to ensure that everyone has an opportunity to participate in the program, and make sure there are sufficient numbers of devices for customers who need them (Figure 2.29). The retrofit package should include a simple installation guide and tips on additional water conservation measures (Figure 2.30).

7. Recycle old plumbing fixtures.

8. Monitor water savings, and report on overall program effectiveness.

Choosing a Delivery Method   There are six commonly used methods of delivering low-volume showerheads and plumbing fixture retrofit kits to customers: door-to-door canvass, direct installation, mass mailing, depot pickup, rebate, and kit request. These methods are summarized in Table 2.14.[114]

TARGETED WATER USERS AND FIXTURES   Showerheads that use 2.5 gpm or less can be installed to replace high-volume showerheads in homes and nonresidential facilities (excluding safety showers and those for special uses).

Customers should be targeted for participation in showerhead retrofit programs according to priority. Households and facilities known to have showerheads with the highest flow rates should be targeted first. Nonresidential facilities with frequent and sometimes heavy water use by showers include hotels, motels, schools, dormitories, hospitals, gymnasiums, sports arenas, and health clubs. As shown in Table 2.11, the year that the showerhead was installed is often a good clue about its approximate flow rate. An exception would be showerheads that have already been retrofitted as part of an electric, gas, or water conservation program that installed 3.0 gpm fixtures. Unless reliable documentation is available about when and where such efforts were undertaken, it may be advantageous to determine the types of fixtures in use before embarking on a retrofit program. One way to accomplish this is to test a number of existing showerheads within subsections of the service area. Compliance with fixture and appliance efficiency codes should not be assumed; some field-testing is usually recommended.[77]

A low-volume showerhead is probably the most common piece of hardware provided to residential customers by water and energy utility conservation programs. The showerheads are often packed in a retrofit kit and are usually given to customers free of charge. Low-volume showerheads are also frequently installed through home water and energy audit programs. Because low-volume showerheads are inexpensive and simple to install, relative to other conservation measures, many homes and nonresidential facilities with showers have already been retrofitted with water-efficient showerheads, although some older retrofit devices may not save as much water as newer models. Studies of households that have installed low-volume showerheads typically report high retention rates for programs that provided only high-quality devices.

TABLE 2.14

Distribution methods, potential participation rates, and approximate costs for plumbing fixture retrofit kit programs

Kit Distribution Method*	Description	Pros	Cons	Potential Customer Participation Rates†	Approximate Cost of Program Per Household‡
Door-to-Door Canvass	Retrofit kits are delivered directly to households for installation by residents. Follow-up canvassing by trained technicians encourages or assists residents with installation.	High participation rates reported by targeted customers who respond to telephone surveys	Discrepancy between customer-reported installation rates and actual installation rates; not all customers who receive a kit can be certain to install it.	50–75%	$13–$20
Direct Installation	Trained technicians are hired to install fixtures directly in homes, helping to ensure that the devices are installed correctly and not wasted. This method is often combined with an indoor and outdoor water-use audit.	Perhaps the most reliable installation technique for achieving water savings with retrofit devices because it is verified by installers; particularly effective for multifamily dwellings where users may not be motivated to install devices themselves	Usually the most expensive installation method	40–60%	$17–$30
Mass Mailing	Kits are mailed directly to all customers or targeted customers for installation by residents.	Low-cost delivery method gets kit directly to customers who return cards requesting mail-out kit.	No direct contact with customer to encourage installation unless they request help or information; not all customers who receive a kit can be certain to install it.	15–60%	$10–$15
Depot Pickup	Customers are notified of depot locations, such as public buildings, libraries, and schools, where they can pick up free kits.	Low administrative costs and responsibility	May attract only customers who are motivated to pick up a kit; it cannot be assumed that all customers who pick up kits will install the devices.	5–40%	$8–$13
Rebate	Utility provides rebates to customers who install a low-volume showerhead (and possibly other devices or fixtures).	Reward for customers who install conservation devices	May attract only customers who are motivated to install devices; rebate application process may be time-consuming and expensive for both program sponsor and customer without significant water savings if participation rate is low.	5–30%	$15–$20
Kit Requests	Water utility or sponsoring agency offers kits to customers who request them. Kits can be customized for residents' needs.	Minimal program design, management, and administrative responsibilities for program sponsor	Not all customers who request a kit can be certain to install it. Verifying installation is difficult.	Poor	$7–$12

* Assumes each delivery method provides the same type of kit: two toilet displacement devices, two 2.5 gpm showerheads, two faucet aerators, toilet leak-detection tablets, and water conservation information booklet.

† Range shown is possible but not certain depending on a particular program's design, implementation, and targeted customer base.

‡ Includes approximate cost of kit and delivery method; actual costs vary according to unit price per kit and program-specific costs for promotion, contracted labor, postage, printing, surveys, and other program expenses.

Sources: Amy Vickers & Associates, Inc.; References 23, 77, 113–115

Number of Showerheads Installed　In residential customer groups that include both single-family and multifamily dwellings, there are approximately 1.6 showerheads per household,[36, 116] although this number varies according to size and age of housing (new homes have more bathrooms) and among single-family and multifamily dwellings. The 1999 REUS study[117] reported an average of 2.0 showers per home (specifically, 1.2 bathtubs with showers plus 0.74 showers with no tub); this number is likely smaller for multifamily dwellings. Most retrofit kits include two showerheads for single-family households and one to two for multifamily dwellings.

Life Cycle of Low-Volume Showerheads and Retrofit Devices　The life cycle for a showerhead is 10 to 15 years, sometimes longer, regardless of its flow rate (although poor-quality fixtures are often removed shortly after installation). The useful life of a showerhead may be shortened if it is clogged by grit, sand, mildew, or other material. A clogged showerhead can usually be cleared by periodically removing it and flushing it under a faucet.

Disk inserts, if accepted by the customer, last five to ten years, depending on the quality of the material and the extent of particle buildup. Most customers can be expected to remove disk inserts that deliver poor-quality sprays.

CUSTOMER PARTICIPATION IN SHOWERHEAD RETROFIT AND REPLACEMENT PROGRAMS
Acceptance of low-volume showerheads is usually excellent when program participants are given a high-quality showerhead and a choice about the fixture's spray pattern (e.g., a variable-spray setting, such as aerating or massaging). More than 50% of consumers targeted in a retrofit program are usually willing to install a low-volume showerhead if it is of high quality. On the other hand, prior experience with a showerhead disk insert or other poor-quality retrofit device may cause some customers to be reluctant to try another water-saving product. Skeptical customers can be won over by helping them understand that the new device will deliver the same performance as their existing high-volume showerhead, if not better.

INSTALLATION OF LOW-VOLUME SHOWERHEADS OR RETROFIT DEVICES
Installation of low-volume showerheads and other retrofit devices should be based on applicable rules and practices and in some instances should be carried out by properly trained technicians or plumbers. When a jurisdiction allows consumers themselves to install showerheads and related retrofit devices, consumers should be fully advised about proper procedures, tools, and precautions to ensure proper installation and operation. Particular attention should be paid to removing existing showerheads and aerators from the showerneck or showerarm, because these fittings can become calcified and break if they are not handled carefully. For example, if too much pressure or leverage is used in removing the old showerhead, the threads on the showerneck can be stripped or the showerneck can snap. Similarly, installing a threaded arm to replace a ball-joint showerneck requires care to ensure that the water supply pipe does not fall to one side in the wall; if the pipe does slip to one side, it may be difficult to retrieve without opening up the wall (a clothes hanger or other device is sometimes used to anchor the pipe). If a showerneck breaks inside a wall or the supply

line is somehow damaged when the old showerhead is removed, the wall will likely have to be opened up—a costly project. Though such events are uncommon, sponsors of retrofit programs should allocate a budget for contingency funds to handle necessary repairs.[77]

Showerhead installation usually includes the following steps:

1. ***Wrap showerneck threads.*** A small strip of Teflon tape is often wrapped around the threads of the showerneck to create a tight seal, limit leakage, and facilitate removal of the showerhead for cleaning.

2. ***Provide showerhead adapters.*** Because showerheads are made with different types of connections and threads, some installations require a male or female adapter between the showerneck or showerarm and the new showerhead. About 18% of showernecks are made with a ball joint that requires an adapter to fit a new showerhead not designed with that particular connector. According to the AWWA handbook *The Manager's Guide to Residential Retrofit,* three major manufacturers' adapters are needed for showernecks: about 10% need Price Pfister™, about 4% need American Standard™, and another 4% need Gerber™ adapters. Because customers may find it inconvenient to obtain an adapter (they're not sure what to ask for, or they don't want to spend the time or money), organizations that sponsor retrofit programs usually make adapters easily available to ensure higher installation rates. Literature for showerhead replacement and retrofit programs should inform customers about the possible need for adapters and provide instructions on how they can be obtained and installed.[107]

3. ***Check safety from scalding.*** The risk of scalding should not increase with the use of a low-volume showerhead, but this possibility should be checked prior to a new showerhead's installation. The problem of scalding during showering usually results from an improperly plumbed bathroom that allows a sudden drop in cold water pressure and flow (often from a nearby toilet being flushed), causing a rapid influx of hot water to compensate for the pressure reduction. This is a problem in some old homes and buildings that do not have pressure- or temperature-compensating valves. Some showerheads are equipped with antiscald devices, and others can sometimes be retrofitted with them if scalding is a problem. Showerheads with temporary shutoff valves should dribble some water when in the "off" position to help maintain a safe water temperature. According to *Consumer Reports,* the risk of scalding can be prevented by setting the water heater temperature to a maximum of 120°F (this will also reduce energy costs).[105] However, applicable codes and laws should be checked before water temperature or pressure conditions are adjusted, because some building codes may include specific requirements or prohibitions.[107]

4. ***Remove old showerheads.*** Old showerheads that are replaced should be removed from the premises to discourage reinstallation.

RECYCLING USED SHOWERHEADS Old showerheads can often be recycled for their scrap metal, plastic, and rubber materials. Collecting old showerheads for this purpose can be easy for showerhead retrofit programs that provide direct installation of the new showerhead because the old one is usually taken away by the installer.

MAINTENANCE OF LOW-VOLUME SHOWERHEADS AND RETROFIT DEVICES Showerheads and showerhead retrofit devices should be checked about once a year to remove sand and grit that may accumulate and inhibit the flow of the shower spray. Cleaning can be accomplished by (1) unscrewing the showerhead and placing it upside down under a running faucet or (2) removing, cleaning, and reinstalling the flow restrictor or aerator screen.

When you drink from the stream, remember the spring."
—*Chinese Proverb*

2.4 FAUCETS

This section describes four measures to reduce water use by faucets: low-volume faucets, faucet retrofit devices, faucet leak repair, and faucet-related food disposer options. These measures apply to faucets installed in residential and nonresidential properties (e.g., office buildings, schools, restaurants, public and commercial facilities, and many types of institutional facilities).

Low-volume faucets use a maximum of 2.5 gallons per minute (gpm) at 80 pounds per square inch (psi) or 2.2 gpm at 60 psi. Water-efficient kitchen faucets are often designed to flow at the maximum 2.5 gpm, whereas low-volume lavatory faucets are also available at maximum flows of 2.0 and even 1.5 gpm. (Higher flows are needed in kitchens for filling pots and containers, but lavatory faucets, used mostly for hand-washing, require smaller volumes of water.) Some existing high-volume faucets can be retrofitted with aerators, restrictors, and other retrofit devices that lower flow rates. Faucet aerators or restrictors are often included in plumbing fixture retrofit kits and water audit programs targeted to the residential sector.

The design and water-use efficiency of faucets used in kitchens and lavatories have improved since the early 1980s. These improvements stem from better designs for faucet spray and flow patterns as well as new aerating and restricting devices that provide good wetting characteristics with reduced flow rates. EPAct requires that lavatory and kitchen faucets (and their replacement aerators) sold, installed, or imported in the United States use no more than 2.5 gpm at 80 psi (2.2 gpm at 60 psi) and that metering faucets use a maximum of 0.25 gallons per cycle (gpc).[26]

Water Use by Faucets

Average water-use rates and savings for low-volume and high-volume faucets, estimated according to their flow rates, are shown in Table 2.15. Low-volume kitchen and lavatory faucets use a maximum of 2.5 gpm at 80 psi, or 2.2 gpm at 60 psi. (Although EPAct originally required low-volume faucets to use no more than 2.5 gpm at 80 psi, a March 1998 amendment of EPAct revised the maximum flow for kitchen and lavatory faucets to 2.2 gpm when measured at 60 psi.) Moderate- to high-volume faucets use 2.75, 3.0, and up to 7.0 gpm at 80 psi. As with showerheads, manufacturers usually show flow rates for kitchen and lavatory faucets at full throttle (maximum fixture capacity, or MFC), as shown in

TABLE 2.15

Estimated water use and savings by low-volume faucets in households

Years Manufactured or Installed *†	Faucet Water-Use Rate†		Frequency of Faucet Use	Estimated Water Use		Estimated Water Savings With a 2.5 gpm Faucet or Aerator				Estimated Water Savings With a 1.5 gpm Faucet or Aerator			
	Rated Flow (MFC)	Actual Flow (MFR)	Per Person	Per Capita	Per House-hold§	Per Capita	Per House-hold§	Per Capita	Per House-hold§	Per Capita	Per House-hold§	Per Capita	Per House-hold§
	gpm	gpm	min/day	gpd	gpd	gpd	gpd	gpy	gpy	gpd	gpd	gpy	gpy
1994-present	1.5	1.0	8.1	8.1	21.4								
	2.5	1.7	8.1	13.5	35.6					5.4	14.3	1,971	5,203
1980-1994	2.75	1.8	8.1	14.9	39.2	1.4	3.6	493	1,301	6.8	17.8	2,464	6,504
	3.0	2.0	8.1	16.2	42.8	2.7	7.1	986	2,602	8.1	21.4	2,957	7,805
Pre-1980 **	3.0–7.0	3.3	8.1	27.0	71.3	13.5	35.6	4,928	13,009	18.9	49.9	6,899	18,212

* Time periods are approximate. Dates for state and local jurisdictions may vary somewhat from dates shown except when they are superseded by the Jan. 1, 1994 federal requirement (shown in bold) allowing a maximum of 2.5 gpm for most faucets (and 0.25 gpc for self-closing faucets) installed after that date, per the U.S. Energy Policy Act of 1992.

† For use in kitchens and bathrooms

‡ Flow rates at 80 pounds per square inch (psi); a faucet with a flow rate of 2.5 gpm at 80 psi is equivalent to a faucet with a flow rate of 2.2 gpm at 60 psi. Kitchen faucets often have higher flow rates than faucets in bathrooms and lavatories.

§ Based on the average of 2.64 persons per occupied U.S. household

** MFR for pre-1980 faucets is averaged for range shown.

MFC = maximum fixture capacity (rated flow)

MFR = measured fixture rate is actual flow rate (equal to about two thirds the MFC); does not apply to self-closing or metering faucets

gpm = gallons per minute; does not apply to self-closing or metering faucets

min/day = average total number of minutes per day faucet is used

gpd = gallons per day

gpy = gallons per year

gpc = gallons per cycle

Sources: Amy Vickers & Associates, Inc.; References 26, 29, 37, 52, and 176

Table 2.15, but actual flow is usually about two thirds (67%) of the rated flow (measured fixture rate, or MFR) because most people don't fully open a faucet except when filling a container.[36] For example, a person filling a pot or bucket at a kitchen sink with a completely opened (at full throttle) faucet rated at 2.5 gpm at 80 psi would be using 2.5 gpm. Likewise, a faucet rated at 3.0 gpm at 80 psi with the handle two-thirds open for rinsing or cleaning would be using about 2.0 gpm.

Combined water use by kitchen and lavatory faucets is typically the fourth largest source of indoor residential water demand, averaging 10.9 gallons per capita per day (gpcd); this represents 15.7% of indoor use in an average single-family nonconserving home, according to the 1999 REUS study.[118] The actual average volume of water used by a residential faucet is 1.34 gpm.[119] An earlier (1984) study found average water use by faucets in a nonconserving home to be 10.3 gpcd, an average volume of 2.6 gpm.[36] These figures reflect the increasing water efficiency of faucets since the mid-1980s. Depending on the approximate year a faucet was installed, its residential water use can be estimated, as shown in Table 2.15.

Residential kitchen and lavatory faucets are used an average of 8.1 minutes per person per day in single-family nonconserving homes, according to the 1999

REUS study,[120] though this figure was previously assumed to be 4.0 minutes per person per day.[36] The frequency of faucet use in nonresidential facilities is not well established, and neither is the amount of water used. Metering faucets used in public restrooms and lavatories are often set to run for about 10 seconds, whereas self-closing faucets shut off as soon as the user releases the tap. Lavatory and bathroom faucets tend to have lower-volume flows than kitchen and utility sink faucets in commercial and institutional facilities.

Water losses caused by leaking faucets can amount to several gallons to hundreds of gallons of water a day. Faucets left in the open running position waste several hundred to several thousand gallons of water a day.

There are several ways to determine how much water a faucet uses if its flow rate is unknown: (1) run the faucet (at the fully open position to measure its rated flow and at about half or two-thirds open to measure actual flow) using a premeasured bag or bucket, and record the flow rate; (2) read the water meter before and after running the faucet (keeping all other fixtures and water-using appliances turned off); (3) look for markings on the faucet that may show its rated flow (this is a federal requirement that became effective in 1994 under EPAct); (4) determine the most recent date of faucet or aerator installation (which may have occurred during a renovation or retrofit program) or the age of the building (if the faucet appears to have been installed during construction) to find its probable flow rate, as shown in Table 2.15; or (5) contact the manufacturer.

The terms *low-volume, low-flow, low-consumption,* and *high-efficiency* are used interchangeably to refer to faucets that use a maximum of 2.5 gpm at 80 psi (or 2.2 gpm at 60 psi), as well as 1.5 gpm and 2.0 gpm faucets and 0.25 gpc metering faucets. Before 1994 these terms sometimes referred to faucets that used 2.75 to 3.0 gpm based on previous energy-efficiency standards. Low-volume faucets can fit into the same connections as high-volume faucets without any special adapters, except those needed to reverse male or female threads. Further, many high-volume kitchen and lavatory faucets can be retrofitted with aerators or flow-control devices to reduce flows. The types of low-volume faucets, faucet retrofit devices, and leak repairs that are available to reduce water use by kitchen and lavatory faucets are discussed in the next four sections.

2.4.1 Low-Volume Faucets

Low-volume kitchen and lavatory faucets look the same as conventional, high-volume fixtures, as shown in Figures 2.31 and 2.32. Reduced flows can be achieved with aeration or flow-control devices, spray features, or a combination of these options. Aerators and flow-control devices are usually located at the end of the faucet head or incorporated into the tee that connects the hot and cold services at the base of the faucet. Some faucets are designed so that the flow-control devices cannot be removed; others are removable so they can be cleaned periodically.

Several design features in low-volume faucets allow for reduced flows without sacrificing performance. Some faucets have an embedded flow restrictor located at the tee of the faucet. The restrictor may be a narrowed opening or an elastic O-ring that restricts flow based on water pressure. Under low pressure, the O-ring provides a higher flow; under high pressure, the O-ring reduces flow.

Figure 2.31 Low-volume kitchen faucets use a maximum of 2.5 gallons per minute at 80 pounds per square inch (or 2.2 gallons per minute at 60 pounds per square inch).

Figure 2.32 Low-volume lavatory and bath faucets use a maximum of 2.5 gallons per minute at 80 pounds per square inch (or 2.2 gallons per minute at 60 pounds per square inch).

(Figures 2.32 and 2.33 courtesy of Moen Incorporated)

Some faucets have laminar flow attachments that create many thin parallel streams of water, producing a clear flow that is not mixed with air. Laminar flow attachments provide good wetting characteristics that please users but with less noise and splashing than some aerators.

2.4.2 Faucet Retrofit Devices

The flow-control devices found in low-volume faucets are also available as retrofit devices to reduce flows in most high-volume faucets. In most cases, retrofitting a high-volume faucet is much less expensive than replacing the entire unit, and retrofitting can usually achieve equivalent or nearly equivalent water savings. Faucet retrofit devices include aerators, metered-valve and self-closing faucets, and sensor-activated faucets.

2.4.2.1 Aerators

Faucet aerators are circular screen disks, usually made of metal as shown in Figure 2.33, that are screwed onto the head of the faucet to lower flows. Aerators reduce flows by mixing air with water, giving the sensation of ample water yet at reduced volumes. An aerator is a simple, economical, and effective device for reducing water use by faucets.

Most faucet aerators can be screwed off and replaced with a low-flow one; retrofitting faucets without aerators may or may not be possible. If the aerator is missing but the faucet spout has aerator threads, the previous aerator has been removed and a new one can be installed. Some faucets, particularly older ones, have the flow-control feature embedded in the stem of the faucet and may not require or be able to accommodate an aerator.

Lavatory faucets can be retrofitted with aerators that limit flows to 1.5 to 2.5 gpm (and even lower) at 80 psi. Installing aerators that are too restrictive may simply cause consumers to remove them, particularly in the case of kitchen and utility faucets where volume is needed to fill containers. Aerators for kitchen faucets are available with a variety of spray patterns (for cleaning) and flow-control features. Faucets used as hookups for portable washing machines or dishwashers may not be easily retrofitted with aerators; the faucet and appliance connections should be checked before an aerator is installed.

Aerators are often removable so that they can be cleaned periodically; aerators that are missing should be replaced to ensure that flow volumes do not exceed 2.5 gpm.

Figure 2.33 Inexpensive and easy-to-install aerators and flow restrictors can reduce faucet flows to 1.5 gallons per minute (at 80 pounds per square inch) or less. (Photo courtesy of Amy Vickers & Associates, Inc.)

- *Fingertip control valves for on–off aerators.* Some low-volume kitchen faucets are designed with on–off aerators, which allow a reduced volume of water ("on") for cleaning or rinsing and a full stream of water ("off") for filling containers, as shown in Figure 2.34. High-volume faucets retrofitted with aerators that have fingertip control valves are more likely to be retained by consumers than other aerators. Users can easily adjust faucets that have fingertip control valves by means of a simple flip handle attached to the faucet; flows cannot exceed 2.5 gpm at 80 psi in either position. Fingertip control valves can maintain the desired temperature mix of hot and cold water when the aerator is flipped open or closed.
- *Vandal- and tamper-proof aerators.* Vandal-resistant aerators, which require a special tool for installation and removal, may be a good choice for lavatories in nonresidential buildings such as schools and public facilities, where they might be subject to tampering.

2.4.2.2 Metered-Valve, Self-Closing, and Sensor-Activated Faucets

Metered-valve faucets, self-closing (spring-loaded) faucets, and sensor-activated (e.g., infrared or fiber-optic) automatic-shutoff faucets limit flows according to a preset amount of water or a specified period of time. Metering faucets installed after 1994 must use no more than 0.25 gpc and usually have a 10-second operating cycle. The water-use efficiency of these faucets varies, depending on two factors: the flow rate and the length of time they are set to run. Generally, these faucets tend to be more water-efficient than other types because they operate only as long as they are needed (sometimes less in the case of me-

tered-valve and self-closing faucets). Older, high-volume metered-valve, self-closing, and sensor-activated faucets can often be retrofitted or adjusted to reduce flows without replacing the entire fixture.

- Metered-valve faucets deliver a preset amount of water before shutting off.
- Self-closing faucets feature a spring-loaded knob that automatically shuts off the water when the user releases the knob. For example, one style of self-closing faucet that operates on a 10-second cycle delivers about 0.1 gpc (based on a flow rate of 0.5 gpm).
- Sensor-activated faucets contain light- or motion-sensing devices that cause water to flow once they detect hands or other objects directly in front of them. When the user steps away, the faucet should turn off readily, although like any device it can malfunction and keep running. Periodic cleaning of these types of faucets may minimize malfunctions caused by sediment obstructions.[59]

Figure 2.34 This low-volume, spray-style aerator for kitchen faucets has both spray (for cleaning and rinsing) and full-flow options (for filling containers). (Photo courtesy of Moen Incorporated)

2.4.3 Faucet Leak Repair and Adjustments

Faucet leaks are a common source of water waste. Faucets should be checked regularly for leaks at the faucet head and for seepage at the base and its connections. Faucet leak repairs and adjustments include the following measures:

- *Replace worn washers.* Dripping faucets or those losing a steady stream (five drips per second) of water are most often caused by a worn "seat," and sometimes the packing washer located under the handle also needs to be replaced. Most two-handle household faucets are compression-type, or "stem," faucets. Stem faucets have a hard rubber washer that is often the source of leaks. In some cases, the stem that opens and closes the valve seat may be a source of leakage. Leaks from a diaphragm-stem faucet can often be repaired by replacing the seat washer(s) or diaphragm. Washerless, single-lever faucets, common in many new homes, come in four basic types (disc, valve, cartridge, and ball-and-cam) and are usually best repaired with a repair kit designed for the particular model that is leaking.[121]
- *Tighten or repack faucet.* Leaks at the faucet stem (just below the handle) or base usually indicate that the fixture needs to be tightened or that new packing needs to be placed in the packing nut.
- *Adjust flows.* Several types of adjustments can reduce flows from existing high-volume faucets. Reduction of water pressure in a building—within flow requirements for each floor and water supply connection—can reduce flows to faucets and other fixtures, appliances, and equipment. Similarly, flow valves to faucet controls are sometimes adjustable to allow for increases or decreases in flow volumes at the tap.

   CAUTION: Because incorrectly executed adjustments to a water supply system could potentially harm people and property, any adjustments to a water system or its connections should be made only by qualified individuals (e.g., licensed plumbers or engineers) whose work complies strictly with applicable codes and regulations and does not compromise the flow requirements for fire protection, essential operations, and other existing water uses.

2.4.4 Food Disposer Retrofit Options

Water use by faucets includes that used by food or garbage disposers. Approximately 48% of U.S. households have a food disposer connected to the kitchen sink, according to a national survey;[122] 68% of the single-family homes in the fourteen-city REUS study were reported to have disposers.[123]

Water use by food disposers can be reduced in several ways. First, removing the disposer will save water and electricity and will also eliminate future repair bills for the appliance. In general, food disposers are not needed; food wastes can easily be collected in a small container placed in or near the kitchen sink for later composting or disposal. Most food (except for animal and dairy) wastes can be disposed of in outdoor composters and subsequently reused as garden or potting soil, practices that also reduce household solid waste loads. Further, houses that have food disposers and that rely on septic systems sometimes require larger-capacity systems; not installing a disposer at the time of construction may downsize the septic system, and removing an existing one may allow for less frequent cleanouts. Second, water use by food disposers can be minimized by operating the kitchen faucet at the lowest flow necessary (see Section 2.4.2, "Faucet Retrofit Devices").

Performance of Low-Volume Faucets and Retrofit Devices

The performance of low-volume faucets and related retrofit devices has improved in recent years, as more sophisticated flow- and spray-control technologies have been developed. The water-use efficiency of sensor-activated faucets compared with that of conventional manual and metering faucets in public facilities is not well established.

Water Savings and Related Benefits From
Low-Volume Faucets, Retrofit Devices, and Leak Repairs

WATER SAVINGS   Estimated water use and water savings from replacing a high-volume faucet with a low-volume one in a home are shown in Table 2.15. For example, installing a 2.5 gpm faucet to replace a 3.0 gpm model will save an estimated 2.7 gpcd or 7.1 gallons per household per day (gphd), equivalent to an annual water savings of 986 gallons per capita per year (gpcy) or 2,602 gallons per household per year (gphy). Replacing a pre-1980 3.0 to 7.0 gpm faucet will save an estimated 13.5 gpcd or 35.6 gphd, equivalent to an annual water savings

Point-of-Use Hot Water Demand Units Can Save Water and Energy

Hot water supplied to faucets, showerheads, and tubs in certain homes and other facilities (e.g., remote living quarters, mobile homes, offices, service stations, and boats) is sometimes used inefficiently because of heat losses that occur when hot water pipes are poorly insulated or when water from the heater must travel through long lateral lines to the end user. In such situations, hot water starts to cool before it gets to the fixture, causing the user to keep the faucet or shower running while waiting for hot water to arrive. This problem may be addressed by installing a point-of-use, instantaneous hot water demand unit or heater. These units use a valve and a pump to divert the cold water sitting in the hot water line to a heater that quickly warms it and returns it to the hot water tap. These simple, compact water heaters can fit under a sink, as shown in Figure 2.35. Small water heater tanks placed in a nearby storage area are also an option. Compact, under-sink, point-of-use heaters retail for about $200 to $250, and small water heater tanks retail for about $150 to $400. Both types of heaters require an electrical outlet for operation.

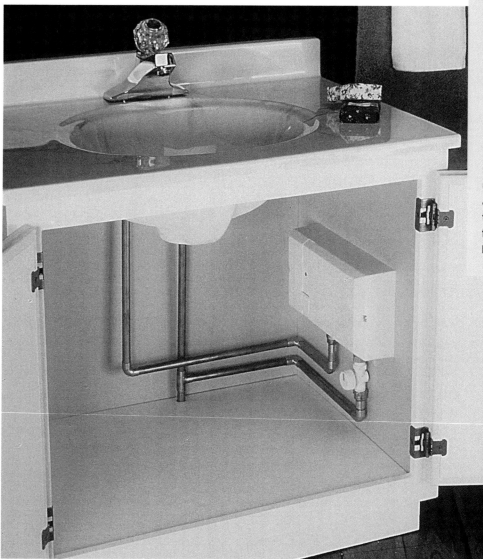

Figure 2.35 Under-sink, point-of-use, instantaneous water heater (Photo courtesy of Controlled Energy Corporation)

of 4,928 gpcy or 13,009 gphy. Similarly, installing faucets rated at 1.5 gpm to re-place 3.0 gpm models will save an estimated 8.1 gpcd or 21.4 gphd, equivalent to 2,957 gpcy or 7,805 gphy; however, it is unlikely that many homes would have all pre-1980 faucets.

Water savings associated with faucet flow-control devices, repairs, and faucet shutoffs vary somewhat, depending on water pressure conditions at the faucet as well as the size and frequency of leaks or drips. Estimates of potential savings from low-volume faucets, aerators and other retrofit devices, and leak repairs include:

- Installation of faucet aerator: 0.5 to 2.0 gpm
- Installation of faucet flow restrictor: limits flows to 0.5 to 2.5 gpm
- Repair of slow drip: 5 to10 gallons per day (gpd)
- Repair of fast drip: 20 to 30 gpd
- Repair of steady-stream drip: 40 to 55 gpd
- Repair of faucet stuck at one-quarter open: 550 to 1,800 gpd*
- Repair of faucet stuck at one-half open: 1,100 to 3,600 gpd*
- Repair of faucet stuck at the fully open position: 2,150 to 7,200 gpd*

Case Study *Faucet Flow Controls in Hospital Rooms Save 32,000 Gallons Annually.* The Carney Hospital in Dorchester, Massachusetts, in-stalled 1.5 gpm flow-control devices on all patient and examination room faucets that were using 5.0 gpm, reducing flow by 3.5 gpm for each faucet. Average wa-ter use per sink is estimated to be 25 minutes per day, resulting in water savings per sink of about 88 gpd, or 32,000 gallons per year. With an estimated cost of $12 for retrofitting each sink and annual w ater and hot water energy savings of $280 per sink, the payback period for this retrofit effort was less than one month.[124]

WATER AND SEWER COST SAVINGS Avoided water and sewer costs asso-ciated with the installation of low-volume faucets and related devices can be cal-culated by multiplying the expected water (and wastewater) reductions (see Table 2.15) times the local utility rates for water and sewer use (excluding fixed charges). A schedule of representative water and sewer utility rates in the United States and their associated marginal cost savings according to a range of reduced water and wastewater volumes is provided in Appendix D, *Water and Sewer Rates, Costs, and Savings by Volume of Use.*

ENERGY SAVINGS Estimated energy savings from reduced hot water use as-sociated with low-volume faucets is shown in Table 2.16. For example, installing a 2.5 gpm (80 psi) faucet to replace a fixture rated to use 3.0 gpm will save an estimated 0.2 kilowatt-hours (kWh) per person per day, or about 0.4 kWh per 2.64-person household per day. Even higher savings would be achieved by in-stalling a faucet that uses less than 2.2 gpm (60 psi) or 2.5 gpm (80 psi), partic-ularly if it replaced a pre-1980 faucet that used more than 3.0 gpm. Water and

It takes 11 gallons of water to produce 1 slice of white bread, and 7 gallons for 1 slice of whole wheat bread.
—Water Education Foundation

---

* Based on the manufacturer's maximum fixture capacity (rated flow), or MFC, for faucets listed in Table 2.15.

TABLE 2.16

Estimated energy use and savings by low-volume faucets in households

Years Manufactured or Installed *†	Faucet Water-Use Rate‡ Rated Flow (MFC) gpm	Faucet Water-Use Rate‡ Actual Flow (MFR) gpm	Frequency of Faucet Use Per Person min/day	Estimated Energy Use for Faucets§ Per Capita kWh/d	Estimated Energy Use for Faucets§ Per House-hold** kWh/d	Estimated Energy Savings With a 2.5 gpm Faucet or Aerator Per Capita kWh/d	Estimated Energy Savings With a 2.5 gpm Faucet or Aerator Per House-hold** kWh/d	Estimated Energy Savings With a 2.5 gpm Faucet or Aerator Per Capita kWh/y	Estimated Energy Savings With a 2.5 gpm Faucet or Aerator Per House-hold** kWh/y	Estimated Energy Savings With a 1.5 gpm Faucet or Aerator Per Capita kWh/d	Estimated Energy Savings With a 1.5 gpm Faucet or Aerator Per House-hold** kWh/d	Estimated Energy Savings With a 1.5 gpm Faucet or Aerator Per Capita kWh/y	Estimated Energy Savings With a 1.5 gpm Faucet or Aerator Per House-hold** kWh/y
1994–present	1.5	1.0	8.1	0.5	1.2								
	2.5	1.7	8.1	0.8	2.0					0.3	0.8	112	297
1980–1994	2.75	1.8	8.1	0.8	2.2	0.1	0.2	28	74	0.4	1.0	140	371
	3.0	2.0	8.1	0.9	2.4	0.2	0.4	56	148	0.5	1.2	169	445
Pre-1980 ††	3.0–7.0	3.3	8.1	1.5	4.1	0.8	2.0	281	741	1.1	2.8	393	1,038

* Time periods are approximate. Dates for state and local jurisdictions may vary somewhat from dates shown except when they are superseded by the Jan. 1, 1994 federal requirement (shown in bold) allowing a maximum of 2.5 gpm for most faucets (and 0.25 gpc for self-closing faucets) installed after that date, per the U.S. Energy Policy Act of 1992.

† For use in kitchens and bathrooms

‡ Flow rates at 80 pounds per square inch (psi); a faucet with a flow rate of 2.5 gpm at 80 psi is equivalent to a faucet with a flow rate of 2.2 gpm at 60 psi. Kitchen faucets often have higher flow rates than faucets in bathrooms and lavatories.

§ Based on 0.057 kilowatt-hour (kWh) of electricity per 1.0 gallon of water at 80° F; actual energy use may vary according to user temperature preferences, pressure, energy efficiency of water heater, and related factors. For gas water-heating systems, convert figures for electric energy use and savings to therms (1 kWh = 0.034 therm, or 1 therm = 29.3 kWh).

** Based on the average of 2.64 persons per occupied U.S. household

†† MFR for pre-1980 faucets is averaged for range shown.

MFC = maximum fixture capacity (rated flow)

MFR = measured fixture capacity (equal to about two thirds the MFC)

gpm = gallons per minute

min/day = average number of minutes per day faucet is used

gpc = gallons per cycle

kWh/d = kilowatt-hours per day

kWh/y = kilowatt-hours per year

Sources: Amy Vickers & Associates, Inc.; References 26, 29, 37, 52, and 178

wastewater utilities also glean indirect energy savings from the reduced volumes of water and wastewater pumped and processed for treatment.

Avoided energy costs resulting from reduced hot water use by a low-volume faucet can be calculated by multiplying the expected savings in kilowatt-hours or therms (see Table 2.16) times the local electric or gas utility rates per kilowatt-hour or therm (excluding fixed charges).

Costs of Low-Volume Faucets and Retrofit Devices

HARDWARE COSTS Estimated costs of low-volume (i.e., 2.5, 2.2, and 2.0 gpm and lower) faucets, aerators, and related devices are:

- Kitchen faucet: $50 to $250
- Lavatory faucet: $40 to $150
- Lavatory faucet (metering): $80 to $170
- Faucet aerator: $0.50 to $3
- Sensor-activated (touchless) faucets (battery or wired): $100 to $600

LABOR AND MATERIAL COSTS Direct labor costs for installing a faucet retrofit device are not well established because they are usually included in the total cost of installing a home retrofit kit (see "Labor and Material Costs" under Section 2.3, "Showerheads"). For simple faucets that can easily accept a screw-on aerator or related device, installation time is just a few minutes. If an existing faucet requires an adapter or has encrustation that must be removed, additional time is required. A small strip of Teflon tape is usually provided with aerators and other flow-control devices to be wrapped around the thread of the faucet to ensure a tight fit, reduce leakage, and facilitate removal for cleaning.

PRODUCT MANUFACTURERS Manufacturers of low-volume faucets and related retrofit devices are listed in Chapter 6, *The Water Conservation Network*.

Laws, Codes, and Standards Applicable to Faucets and Food Disposers

All applicable laws, codes, standards, and health and safety requirements associated with faucets and related devices should be observed when any fixture, appliance, or related plumbing or water system connection is installed or adjusted. These include but are not limited to the following federal, state, and local requirements:

FEDERAL WATER-EFFICIENCY REQUIREMENTS Water-use efficiency requirements for faucets installed, manufactured, or imported in the United States were established by EPAct and are regulated by DOE. State and local authorities may set stricter water-use standards for faucets only if granted approval by DOE. EPAct mandates that kitchen and lavatory faucets and replacement aerators shall use a maximum of 2.5 gpm at 80 psi (which is equivalent to 2.2 gpm at 60 psi)[125] and that metering faucets shall use a maximum of 0.25 gpc, as shown in Table 2.1. EPAct also requires that kitchen and lavatory faucets and replacement aerators bear a permanent marking indicating the maximum flow rate of the fixture, expressed in gallons per minute or gallons per cycle at a specific psi, as specified in the product marking and labeling requirements established by ASME Standard A112.18.1 *(Plumbing Fixture Fittings)*.[26] EPAct establishes *maximum* water use requirements, thereby allowing for faucets that use *less* than the amount established by the legislation.

Performance Test Standards The maximum water-use requirements for faucets established by EPAct incorporate minimum-performance tests and related product requirements for faucets, which are established by ASME Standard A112.18.1 *(Plumbing Fixture Fittings)*. The ASME/ANSI standards establish the minimum-performance testing protocols that kitchen and lavatory faucets, metering faucets, and replacement aerators must meet in order to be in compliance with EPAct. In addition to complying with the ASME/ANSI performance tests, many manufacturers of faucets have created their own more stringent tests to make sure their products work acceptably.

Food Disposers Appliance industry standards for the performance and plumbing requirements of household food waste disposers connected to kitchen sinks have been established by ANSI, the Association of Home Appliance Manufacturers

(AHAM), and the American Society of Sanitary Engineers (ASSE). They include ANSI/AHAM FWD-1 *(Performance Evaluation Procedure for Household Food Waste Disposers)* and ANSI/ASSE 1008/AHAM FWD-2PR *(Plumbing Requirements for Household Food Waste Disposer Units)*.

LOCAL AND STATE AUTHORITIES   Historically, state and local plumbing authorities set water-use standards for faucets, but now the federal EPAct requirements supersede such authorities in most instances. Although in practice some state and local authorities may continue to amend their water-use requirements for faucets, according to EPAct only DOE (through passage of a rule) can grant states the power to establish exemptions for water-efficiency requirements that are more stringent than those provided by EPAct.

Some states and municipalities allow faucets and related retrofit products to be installed, adjusted, or retrofitted only by a licensed plumber, but these requirements are sometimes waived for large-scale retrofit and replacement programs in which trained technicians are used.

Faucets in public lavatories are required to be self-closing in some communities, including Austin, Texas, and Tucson, Arizona.[126]

Some municipalities ban food disposers, but more than 90 communities actually require them in new construction, including Detroit, Los Angeles, and Denver.[127]

Implementing a Faucet Retrofit or Replacement Program

SELECTING LOW-VOLUME FAUCETS AND FLOW-CONTROL DEVICES
The quality and characteristics of faucet flows produced by water-saving retrofit devices are just as varied as those produced by low-volume showerheads. Consumers often judge the quality of a faucet by the characteristics of its flow, which is most often controlled by the aerator. Aerators create differences in the straightness and width of the flow and generate different amounts of splash, clog resistance, and noise. When an aerator or other flow-control device is selected for a retrofit program, each device under consideration should be tested for these qualities as well as for its performance under different pressures. Several types of aerators or flow-control devices may be needed to meet varied conditions in the homes and buildings to be retrofitted.[43]

Experience suggests that the maximum flows at 80 psi for residential kitchen and lavatory faucets targeted for retrofitting include:

* Lavatory and bath faucets in homes and residential facilities: 1.5 to 2.5 gpm
* Lavatory and bath faucets in commercial and public facilities: 0.5 to 1.5 gpm
* Kitchen faucets: retrofit aerators should have a fingertip control valve or dual-spray control that restricts flows to no more than 2.5 gpm

Aerator Threads   Aerators are threaded one of two ways: "female" aerators have threads on the inside; "male" threads are on the outside of the aerator.

Aerator Sizes   Aerators are sized one of two ways. Standard-size aerators can fit a nickel snugly into the threaded end; they are sized at $^{55}/_{64}$-inch for female and $^{15}/_{16}$-inch for male threads. Small aerators can fit a dime (but not a nickel) into

*I*t takes 88 gallons of water to produce 1 cup of plain yogurt and 40 gallons for a serving of cantaloupe.
—Water Education Foundation

the threaded end; they are sized at ¾ inch for female and ¹³/₁₆ inch for male threads.[121]

Attachments Most faucets, particularly lavatory faucets, are threaded at the head so that aerators, disk inserts, or other retrofit devices can be attached. Some faucets may require specific flow rates for attachments (e.g., portable washing machines, dishwashers, and other equipment installed in laboratories); these requirements should be verified prior to installation of any retrofit device.[128]

PLANNING THE PROGRAM For a discussion of common methods of delivering low-volume faucet aerators and restrictors included in plumbing fixture retrofit kits, see "Planning a Showerhead or Retrofit Kit Installation Program" in Section 2.3 of this chapter. These methods are summarized in Table 2.14.

Targeted Water Users and Fixtures High-volume and leaking faucets in residential and nonresidential properties should be targeted first for faucet retrofitting, repair, or replacement. Typically, the older the faucet, the more likely it is to use high volumes of water and have leaks. Nonresidential facilities where water use by kitchen and lavatory faucets can be frequent and high-volume include office buildings, restaurants, hotels, motels, dormitories, schools, laboratories, hospitals, and many commercial and industrial properties.

A faucet aerator or related device is often given to residential customers as part of a plumbing fixture retrofit program sponsored by a water or energy utility. The faucet itself is rarely replaced in such programs because installing an aerator can often save as much water as replacing the entire faucet, which would be much more expensive. Faucets that have previously been retrofitted with aerators and other flow-restricting devices, particularly in nonresidential properties, may be targets for future replacement because such devices are sometimes removed by property owners or vandals.

Number of Faucets Installed The number of kitchen and lavatory faucets in residential dwellings varies. The REUS study reported an average of 2.5 bathroom sinks, 1.1 kitchen sinks, and 0.4 indoor utility room or garage sinks per home;[129] these numbers are likely smaller for multifamily dwellings. Most retrofit kits include two faucet aerators for single-family and multifamily households.

Life Cycle of Faucets Depending on its use and maintenance, a faucet should last at least 15 years. Faucet retrofit devices such as aerators and restrictors can provide reliable service for 5 to 15 years, although factors such as the quality of installation and materials, water quality, and whether the device has been cleaned periodically affect longevity.

Incentives Financial incentives to promote the installation of low-volume faucets or retrofit devices may be cost-effective only in situations in which sufficient water savings and avoided costs can be expected. Some toilet rebate programs have required customers to also retrofit their faucets and showerheads in order to qualify for a rebate.

*I*t takes 49 gallons of water to produce 1 cup of orange juice and 48 gallons for an 8-ounce cup of milk.
—Water Education Foundation

CUSTOMER PARTICIPATION IN FAUCET RETROFIT PROGRAMS   User acceptance of faucet retrofit devices is often very good when a high-quality device is provided. This may be attributable to improved faucet designs and spray styles introduced in recent years because people generally care less about the volume of water used for a specific task than the quality of service delivered by a particular fixture. Some customers may remove aerators and flow restrictors installed on high-volume kitchen and utility faucets because they become impatient with the extra time needed to fill containers. In such instances, a fingertip control valve might solve the problem.

INSTALLATION OF LOW-VOLUME FAUCETS AND FLOW-CONTROL DEVICES   Installation of low-volume faucets, flow-control devices, and related repairs should be done by properly trained technicians or plumbers and should be based on applicable rules and practices. When a jurisdiction allows consumers to install fixtures themselves, consumers should be fully advised about proper procedures, tools, and precautions to ensure proper installation and operation. Particular attention should be paid to removing existing faucets and aerators from their connections because they can become calcified and break if not handled carefully. For example, if too much pressure or leverage is used in removing an old faucet, aerator, or other flow-control device, the threads can be stripped or the faucet and possibly the supply line could snap. For these reasons, sponsors of retrofit and audit programs should budget for contingency funds to handle unexpected repairs.[77]

RECYCLING USED FAUCETS   Old faucets removed for replacement can often be recycled for their scrap metal, plastic, and rubber materials.

MAINTENANCE OF LOW-VOLUME FAUCETS AND FLOW-CONTROL DEVICES   Faucet aerators and restrictors require periodic cleaning of grit and scale buildup that may inhibit flow. In some cases, aerators and restrictors have been removed because of unsatisfactory flows when all that was required was a simple rinse to clean out the material causing the clog. Sensor-activated faucets should be checked periodically to ensure they are set properly and are not causing unwanted flows. Faucets with battery-operated sensors need to have the batteries replaced periodically. Used batteries from sensor-controlled faucets should be disposed of properly to comply with applicable waste disposal laws and to minimize adverse environmental effects and safety hazards.

2.5 CLOTHES WASHERS

This section describes two measures for reducing water use by clothes washers: high-efficiency clothes washers and efficient water-use practices for clothes washers. The water-efficient washers described in this section can be installed in residences and in nonresidential properties where family-size commercial washers are used (e.g., coin-operated machines installed in multifamily dwellings, laundromats, dormitories, and military barracks). Likewise, the efficient-use practices for clothes washers apply to both household-size washers and many larger machines used in nonresidential and institutional facilities. (In the U.S., household-size washers usually have a 14-pound load capacity, whereas family-size commercial washers used in nonresidential facilities have a capacity of 16 pounds or more.)

High-efficiency residential clothes washers use a maximum of 27 gallons of hot and cold water per load (gpl) for a normal-size, 8-pound wash load in a standard washer with a 14-pound capacity. Some washers that use more than 27 gpl are described as "efficient" by their manufacturers because they use less energy than conventional washers, but these models are not considered high-efficiency here.

The design of residential clothes washers sold in the United States has been changing since the mid-1990s, and consumers can now choose between conventional, high-volume, top-loading, vertical-axis washers and more water- and energy-efficient, "high-efficiency" or "tumble" washers. These newer resource-efficient washers, as shown in Figure 2.36, are also sometimes referred to as high-performance or front-loading, horizontal-axis machines, although some top-loading, vertical-axis models are also resource-efficient now.

Improvements in the resource efficiency of clothes washers in the United States were prompted, in part, by the DOE's ENERGY STAR®* Partnerships Program.[130] This program has facilitated the introduction of new water- and energy-efficient washers into the market through coordinated efforts between appliance manufacturers and incentive-based programs sponsored by water and energy utilities. In addition, the prospect of more stringent energy-efficiency standards for washers, expected from DOE in 2004 and 2007, has prompted many manufacturers to improve the resource efficiency of their appliances beforehand.

More than 10% of the clothes washers installed in the United States meet DOE's ENERGY STAR designation,[131] whereas 90% of the washers used in Europe are considered high-efficiency. However, European-designed washers usually have smaller capacities and require longer wash cycles than those designed for North America, so the two styles are not directly comparable.[132]

Water Use by Clothes Washers

High-efficiency residential clothes washers use an average of 27 gpl for a normal-size, 8-pound load of laundry washed in a standard washer with a 14-pound capacity.[132] Some high-efficiency washers use as little as 16 gpl, but these machines typically have less than a 14-pound capacity and their water use for large loads cannot be compared.[133] Conventional washers installed since about 1990 are estimated to use 39 to 43 gpl.[134–141] Washers installed from 1980 to 1990 use 48 to 55 gpl,[142, 143] with the typical washer using about of 51 gpl, as shown in Table 2.17. Washers installed before 1980 used roughly 56 gpl, although few of these are likely to be still in use.[144, 145]

Although there are federal energy-efficiency requirements for the hot water used by clothes washers, there are no maximum water-use standards for combined hot and cold water used by clothes washers in the United States. Thus, assump-

---

* ENERGY STAR is a USEPA-registered trademark that has been licensed to DOE.

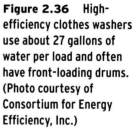

Figure 2.36 High-efficiency clothes washers use about 27 gallons of water per load and often have front-loading drums. (Photo courtesy of Consortium for Energy Efficiency, Inc.)

tions about water use for washers, as shown in Table 2.17, have been adapted from several reported tests and studies. A 1998 DOE study of 103 clothes washers in Bern, Kansas (population approximately 200), found that conventional, high-volume, vertical-axis washers used an average of 41.5 gpl for an 8-pound load of laundry. Replacement of these washers with high-efficiency machines reduced consumption to an average of 25.8 gpl, yielding a water savings of 38%.[136] The Bern study confirmed similar water-use findings reported by *Consumer Reports:* a year 2000 test of models from major manufacturers found that high-efficiency, front-loading washers used 25 to 31 gpl for an 8-pound load of laundry; high-volume, top-loading models were measured to use 30 to 41 gpl, [132] a range covering DOE's baseline assumption of 39 gpl for conventional washers.[146] Similar *Consumer Reports* tests conducted in 1997 through 1999 found comparable results (25 and 28 gpl for two high-efficiency models compared with an average of 43 gpl for 16 top-loading models).[133, 135, 137]

Water use by clothes washers is typically the second largest source of indoor residential water demand, averaging 15.0 gallons per capita per day (gpcd). This represents 21.7% of indoor use in a typical single-family nonconserving home, according to the 1999 REUS study.[147] Residential clothes washer use averages 0.37 loads per person per day,[148] or the equivalent of about 41 gpl. Depending on the efficiency of the particular washer, average residential water use by clothes washers installed between 1980 and the late 1990s is estimated to range from 10.0 gpcd (27 gpl) to 18.9 gpcd (51 gpl), as shown in Table 2.17. (High-volume washers were still being manufactured and installed through the late 1990s.) These figures indicate the increasing water efficiency of clothes washers.

In most cases, high-efficiency clothes washers can be installed to replace existing high-volume washers without special connections or considerations, although the purchase price of resource-efficient washers is usually higher than that of conventional high-volume machines. In addition to installing a high-efficiency washer, consumers can follow several water-efficient practices to reduce water use by clothes washers. These conservation practices are discussed in Section 2.5.2 of this chapter.

2.5.1 High-Efficiency Clothes Washers

The widespread availability of water-efficient clothes washers in the United States and Canada is relatively recent. By 2000, more than 14 brands and 25 models of resource-efficient washers were available,[149] some of which use 27 gpl or less. Many high-efficiency washers are front-loading, horizontal-axis machines, but some are not. Currently, about 90% of the clothes washers in residential use (and nearly as many in commercial applications) in North America are top-loading units.[131]

The new water- and energy-efficient clothes washers in the U.S. market were developed primarily by switching the operating design of washer tubs from top-

TABLE 2.17

Estimated water use and savings by high-efficiency clothes washers in households

Years Manufactured or Installed *	Clothes Washer Water-Use Rate[†] Per Load gal	Frequency of Clothes Washer Use[‡] Per Person loads/day[††]	Estimated Water Use[§] Daily Per Capita gal	Estimated Water Use[§] Daily Per House-hold** gal	Estimated Water Savings With a 27 gpl Clothes Washer Daily Per Capita gal	Estimated Water Savings With a 27 gpl Clothes Washer Daily Per House-hold** gal	Estimated Water Savings With a 27 gpl Clothes Washer Yearly Per Capita gal	Estimated Water Savings With a 27 gpl Clothes Washer Yearly Per House-hold** gal
1998-present	**27**	0.37	10.0	26.4				
1990-present	39	0.37	14.4	38.1	4.4	11.7	1,621	4,278
	43	0.37	15.9	42.0	5.9	15.6	2,161	5,705
1980-1990	51	0.37	18.9	49.8	8.9	23.4	3,241	8,557
Pre-1980s	56	0.37	20.7	54.7	10.7	28.3	3,916	10,339

* Time periods are approximate.

† Figures show typical water-use rates for normal-size loads of laundry. Figure in bold (27 gpl) represents water-efficient clothes washers made by several major appliance manufacturers and reported to deliver reliable performance; some manufacturers also produce clothes washers that use less than 27 gpl, and these may also provide reliable performance.

‡ U.S. Department of Energy assumptions vary from this slightly and are based on 392 wash loads per household per year and apply only to homes with washers.

§ Based on a normal-size, 8-pound load of laundry washed for a full cycle in a machine with a tub capacity of 2.7 to 2.9 cubic feet (enough space for about 14 pounds of laundry)

** Based on the average of 2.64 persons per occupied U.S. household

†† Levelized over all households—with and without clothes washers

  gpl = gallons per load

  gal = gallons

Sources: Amy Vickers & Associates, Inc.; References 37, 52, 132, 133, 135–141, 143–146, 151, 170, 175, and 178

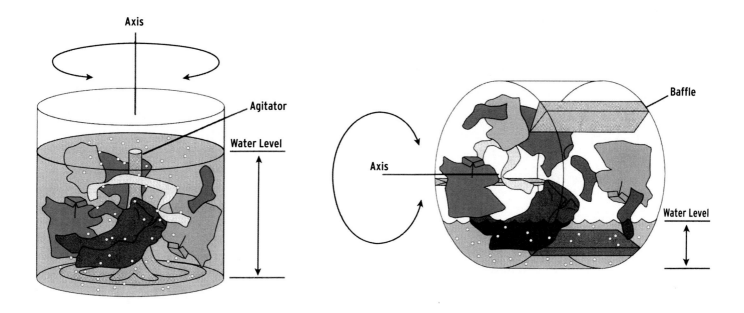

loading, vertical-axis models to horizontal-axis tubs, often with front-loading doors. Vertical-axis machines clean laundry by immersing it in a full tub of water and agitating it on a vertical axis during wash and rinse cycles. High-efficiency machines tumble laundry repeatedly at fast cycles, much like a clothes dryer does, through a shallow pool of water; this tumbling motion produces the agitation for cleaning and rinsing, using less water and energy in the process. Because they have faster spin cycles, the newer washers are also better at extracting water from washed and rinsed laundry, helping to reduce the time and energy needed for drying.[136] The method of operation and the relative water levels of a high-efficiency, horizontal-axis clothes washer and a vertical-axis machine are illustrated in Figure 2.37.

The technology for high-efficiency residential and commercial washers in the United States is almost identical, with just a few minor differences. Washers installed in laundromats, multifamily dwellings, and institutional facilities have a larger load capacity (16 pounds or more) than typical residential washers (which have a maximum capacity of 14 pounds), as well as faster spin speeds, shorter cycles, and a coin box.

Figure 2.37 Relative water levels required by a conventional, top-loading, vertical-axis clothes washer (left) and a high-efficiency washer (right) (Illustration courtesy of *EPRI Journal)*

2.5.2 Clothes Washer Water-Efficiency Practices

Several conservation practices can reduce water use by low- or high-volume clothes washers:

- Operate the washer with full loads only.
- For washers with variable settings for water volume, select the minimum amount required per load.
- Pretreat stains to avoid rewashing.

- Use the shortest wash cycle for lightly soiled loads because this uses less water than most "normal" and permanent-press wash cycles.
- Check hoses regularly for cracks that could result in water leaks or bursts.

Performance of Water-Efficient Clothes Washers

High-efficiency washers have been shown to provide equal if not improved performance compared with high-volume washers in several performance criteria. First, many high-efficiency washers have a faster spin speed than conventional vertical-axis machines, resulting in improved moisture extraction and drier clothes at the end of the wash cycle, a feature that shortens drying time and saves energy. Second, high-efficiency machines may use detergent and bleach more efficiently; because these products are concentrated in a smaller volume of water, smaller amounts can be used. Third, because high-efficiency machines do not have a central agitator, it has been claimed that they clean more gently than vertical-axis washers. Anecdotal reports seem to confirm this; however, one evaluation found this claim was not supported.[137]

Consumer acceptance of high-efficiency washers appears to be mostly favorable, based on initial product sales and market studies, although these appliances are relatively new to the U.S. market. However, at least one consumer study indicated that North American consumers may be somewhat reluctant to purchase a high-efficiency machine that is front-loading because it would require more bending and could pose child safety concerns. On the other hand, the Electric Power Research Institute's THELMA study (The High-Efficiency Laundry Metering and Marketing Analysis) found that consumers would consider high-efficiency machines if convinced that these models are at least as good as their old washers in terms of purchase price, reliability, ease of use, and cleaning ability.[150] Even though consumers already have to bend to load clothes dryers, acceptance of front-loading washers may require touting their resource efficiency and long-term financial benefits.[150]

Water Savings and Related Benefits From High-Efficiency Clothes Washers

The water- and energy-saving benefits of high-efficiency washers may not be directly comparable. Because American and European models typically differ in tub capacity, resource-efficiency comparisons should be based on equivalent-size loads—small (less than 8 pounds), normal (8 pounds), and large (up to 14 pounds). In general, larger loads and loads washed on a permanent-press setting demand more water than normal-size loads. High-efficiency models typically provide automatic water-level adjustments that help ensure efficient use; conventional high-volume washers do not always have this feature, and the amount of water they use is determined by the wash setting selected by the user. Some high-efficiency washers are better at saving water than energy, and vice versa. Furthermore, some washers are more efficient at water extraction, saving drying time and energy.[133]

WATER SAVINGS Estimated water use and water savings from replacing a conventional, high-volume clothes washer with a 27 gpl model in a home are shown in Table 2.17. For example, installing a 27 gpl washer to replace a model

TABLE 2.18

Estimated energy use and savings by high-efficiency clothes washers in households

Years Manufactured or Installed *	Clothes Washer Water-Use Rate[†] Per Load	Frequency of Clothes Washer Use[‡] Per Person	Estimated Energy Use for Clothes Washers[§][**]			Estimated Energy Savings With a 27 gpl Clothes Washer			
			Per Load	Per Capita	Per House-hold[††]	Per Capita	Per House-hold[††]	Per Capita	Per House-hold[††]
	gal	loads/day[‡‡]	kWh	kWh/d	kWh/d	kWh/d	kWh/d	kWh/y	kWh/y
1998–present	27	0.37	1.6	0.58	1.52				
1990–present	39	0.37	3.0	1.10	2.91	0.5	1.4	192	506
	43	0.37	3.3	1.22	3.21	0.6	1.7	233	615
1980–1990	51	0.37	3.9	1.44	3.81	0.9	2.3	316	833
Pre-1980s	56	0.37	4.3	1.58	4.18	1.0	2.7	367	969

* Time periods are approximate.

† Figures show typical water-use rates for normal-size loads of laundry. Figure in bold (27 gpl) represents water-efficient clothes washers made by several major appliance manufacturers and reported to deliver reliable performance; some manufacturers also produce clothes washers that use less than 27 gpl, and these may also provide reliable performance.

‡ U.S. Department of Energy assumptions vary from this slightly and are based on 392 wash loads per household per year and apply only to homes with washers.

§ Energy use rates shown for washers are based on an estimated average energy requirement (combined water heater, washer, and dryer) for normal-size loads. Energy used to heat the water in the washer is roughly three-quarters of the total energy use shown. Actual energy use and savings vary depending on model design, appliance settings, water heater temperature, and other product design features. Energy use and water use by clothes washers are not always directly correlated. See the specific energy ratings for a particular model to determine its actual use and potential savings.

** For a normal-size, 8-pound load of laundry washed for a full cycle in a machine with a tub capacity of 2.7 to 2.9 cubic feet (enough space for about 14 pounds of laundry). For gas water heating and dryer systems, convert figures for electric energy use and savings to therms.

†† Based on the average of 2.64 persons per occupied U.S. household

‡‡ Levelized over all households—with and without dishwashers

gpl = gallons per load

kWh = kilowatt-hours

kWh/d = kilowatt-hours per day

kWh/y = kilowatt-hours per year

Sources: Amy Vickers & Associates, Inc.; References 37, 52, 132, 133, 135–141, 143–146, 151, 170, 175, and 178

using an average of 39 gpl is estimated to save an average of 4.4 gpcd or 11.7 gallons per household per day (gphd), equivalent to an annual water savings of 1,621 gallons per capita per year (gpcy) or 4,278 gallons per household per year (gphy). Households with even higher-volume conventional washers, such as those that were installed between 1980 and the late 1990s and whose water use averages 43 to 51 gpl, will save an estimated 5,705 to 8,557 gphy.

WATER AND SEWER COST SAVINGS Avoided water and sewer costs associated with the installation of water-efficient clothes washers can be calculated by multiplying the expected volume of water (and wastewater) reductions (see Table 2.17) times the local utility rates for water and sewer use (excluding fixed charges). A schedule of representative water and sewer utility rates in the United States and their associated marginal cost savings according to a range of reduced water and wastewater volumes is provided in Appendix D, *Water and Sewer Rates, Costs, and Savings by Volume of Use.*

In 1915, the American Washing Machine Manufacturers' Association was formed by 60 clothes washer manufacturers to educate consumers on the need for, and use of, the clothes washer.

ENERGY SAVINGS   Energy savings from water-efficient clothes washers, as estimated in Table 2.18, result from reduced use of water heaters, more efficient motors, and reduced drying time. Actual energy savings vary (sometimes considerably) by brand, model, and consumer patterns of use (e.g., load size, water temperature, and frequency of operation). For example, installing a 27 gpl clothes washer to replace a machine that uses an average of 39 gpl will save an estimated 192 kilowatt-hours (kWh) per person per year and about 506 kWh per 2.64-person household per year. This represents an annual energy savings of more than 40%. Similar projections of savings by the Pacific Northwest National Laboratory for replacing a standard washer that uses 15,300 gallons of water a year (based on 392 normal-size wash loads with average water use of 39 gpl) estimate that a high-efficiency washer will reduce annual energy use (for the washer, water heater, and dryer) from about 1,250 kWh of electricity or 47 therms of natural gas to 725 to 775 kWh or 24 to 27 therms, yielding annual household savings of 475 to 525 kWh or 20 to 23 therms (for 5,600 to 10,800 gallons of water saved annually). This represents average annual energy savings of 40% or greater.[151]

The water temperature selected by the user affects energy use by both high-efficiency and high-volume clothes washers. Consumers who wash with cold water use less energy than those who wash with warm and hot water. A survey of consumer clothes-washing habits found that wash-water temperatures averaged 63.8°F for cold settings, 92.3°F for warm settings, and 120.1°F for hot settings.[139]

Avoided energy costs associated with the installation of a high-efficiency clothes washer can be calculated by multiplying the expected savings in kilowatt-hours or therms (see Table 2.18) times the local electric or gas utility rates per kilowatt-hour or therm (excluding fixed charges).

ADDITIONAL BENEFITS   Additional benefits associated with high-efficiency washers compared with conventional models include better handling of unbalanced loads (which results in less wear and tear on clothes), better moisture extraction and thus shorter drying times, and reduced detergent needs resulting from smaller volumes of water and better use of wash water through tumbling action. Some clothes washer manufacturers recommend using a low-sudsing detergent with high-efficiency washers, but simply reducing the amount of detergent per load may solve oversudsing problems. Another practical benefit of high-efficiency washers is that many of them are front-loading and thus can be stacked with a dryer or used as a workspace.[152]

Costs Associated With High-Efficiency Clothes Washers

HARDWARE COSTS   High-efficiency and front-loading washers retail for $600 to $1,100, somewhat more than the $300 to $700 price of many conventional high-volume, vertical-axis, top-loading washers.[132] Nevertheless, the higher initial cost of these washers may be offset in several ways, as described under "Incentives" later in this section. For example, residential customers served by a water, electric, or gas utility that offers rebates on the price of new tumble washers can receive incentives ranging from $75 to $230 per washer; commercial customers such as laundromats are usually offered higher rebates and tax credits by utility-sponsored washer replacement programs.[131]

Average residential savings on water and energy costs as well as detergent costs from operating high-efficiency washers instead of conventional machines have been estimated to range from $80 to $100 per household per year, yielding a payback period of two to four years, depending on local utility rates and frequency of household washer use. A faster payback period can be achieved with a rebate or other financial incentive such as a tax or utility bill credit.[135]

LABOR AND MATERIAL COSTS   No additional labor or material costs are involved in installing a water-efficient clothes washer compared with higher-volume models.

PRODUCT MANUFACTURERS   Manufacturers of high-efficiency clothes washers are listed in Chapter 6, *The Water Conservation Network.*

Laws, Codes, and Standards Applicable to Clothes Washers

All applicable laws, codes, standards, and health and safety requirements associated with clothes washers should be observed when any fixture, appliance, or related plumbing or water system connection is installed or adjusted.

Many local and state codes require clothes washers to be installed by licensed plumbers. In 2004 and 2007, DOE is expected to mandate more stringent water- and energy-use requirements for washers; these requirements could establish high-efficiency machines as the new standard.

Appliance industry standards for the performance and plumbing requirements of household clothes washers include ANSI/AHAM Standard HLW-1 *(Performance Evaluation Procedure for Household Washers)* and ANSI/ASSE 1007/AHAM HLW-2PR *(Plumbing Requirements for Home Laundry Equipment).*

Implementing a Clothes Washer Rebate or Replacement Program

Several considerations should be taken into account in planning a program to replace high-volume clothes washers with high-efficiency washers. These are discussed in the following paragraphs.

SELECTING A WATER-EFFICIENT CLOTHES WASHER   High-efficiency washers for residential use differ in tub size or wash-load capacity. The U.S. standard-size tub is about 2.9 cubic feet (about 27 to 29 inches wide) and can clean up to 14 pounds of laundry. The European-size tub is smaller and has a maximum capacity of 8 to 11 pounds. High-efficiency washers with a conventional 14-pound capacity are designed as comparable-size washers to replace high-volume machines in North American households. Water use by these high-efficiency washers averages about 27 gallons per normal-size 8-pound load of wash. The European washers are not only smaller but also are often slower in completing a wash load. Consumers who expect the convenience of washing large loads of laundry (including bulky items such as comforters and blankets) in less than an hour at home will likely prefer high-efficiency washers with the conventional 14-pound capacity. Consumers who have limited space, typically wash small loads (8 pounds or less), and are not bothered by long wash times may favor the smaller machines.[133]

PLANNING THE PROGRAM   More than 200 water and energy utilities in 19 states are now implementing programs to accelerate the installation of high-efficiency washers.[149] For example, DOE's ENERGY STAR Partnerships Program promotes sales of high-performance washing machines through local initiatives with utilities and organizations that include large-volume purchases and appliance rebate programs.

The city of Austin, Texas, with its WashWise Program was DOE's first local partner. Since 1997, the city has been assisting local appliance distributors with news releases, advertisements, and other promotional activities to encourage consumers to purchase high-efficiency washers. For each qualified purchase of a high-efficiency washer, the city offers a $100 rebate, plus the consumer can collect an additional $50 rebate from the local energy utility. Owners of multi-family housing receive rebates of $150 for each qualifying washer that is coin-operated and located in a common-use area.[153] During the first two months of the program, approximately 150 customers purchased a high-efficiency washer, giving the city a projected annual savings of 0.84 million gallons of water, 25.2 megawatt-hours of electricity, and 2,310 natural gas therms. Annual water and energy cost savings for consumers were projected to average $42 (for a gas water heater and dryer) or $82 (for an electric water heater and dryer); measured over an estimated 13-year life of the appliance, these savings equate to $624 for gas systems or $1,066 for electric systems.[130]

Targeted Water Users   High-efficiency clothes washers can be installed to replace household (14-pound capacity) and many family-size commercial (16-pound capacity) high-volume washers used in multifamily dwellings, laundromats, and similar facilities.

Number of Clothes Washers Installed   Approximately 81 million U.S. households (about 77%) have a clothes washer, and about 10.5 million washers are sold annually in the U.S. market.[149]

Households with washers complete about 7.4 loads of wash a week, or 385 loads a year, according to a survey of 1,522 households.[139] This figure is higher than the 7.0 loads per week per single-family household, based on 0.37 loads per capita per day, that can be interpolated from data collected in the 1999 REUS study (although these data are levelized across all households surveyed, including a small number that did not have washers).[154] DOE also assumes a slightly higher figure for clothes washer use—an average of 7.5 loads a week, or 392 loads a year.[155]

About 14% of residential laundry is done in family-size commercial washers in laundromats, multifamily housing, and institutions. An estimated two to three million family-size commercial machines are installed in the United States.[156] Approximately 250,000 of them are replaced annually, and most have a useful life of seven to ten years. About 17% of commercial family-size washers are used in laundromats.[156] The Coin Laundry Association estimates that there are about 35,000 laundromats in the United States, with an average of 12 machines per laundromat.[156]

Life Cycle of Clothes Washers   The useful life of a conventional vertical-axis clothes washer used under normal household conditions (more than 300 wash loads a year) is 10 to 16 years,[157] typically about 13 years. Greater or lesser frequency of use influences the life of a washer. The longevity of the recently introduced high-efficiency washers designed for the U.S. market is not yet known, although some engineers expect them to have a longer operating life because of their design improvements.

Incentives   Financial incentives such as rebates, bill credits, and tax incentives to accelerate purchases of water-efficient clothes washers are offered by a number of utilities, organizations, and jurisdictions. For example, the Consortium for Energy Efficiency, a Boston-based utility-related organization, has a high-efficiency clothes washer initiative designed to promote the development and widespread use of high-efficiency washers through various rebate programs. By 2000, water, electric, and gas utilities serving roughly 20% of U.S. households were participating in the consortium's clothes washer initiative. Residential customer rebates offered by more than 200 participating utilities in 19 states have ranged from $50 to $500. Many utilities also offer rebates of $50 and higher to nonresidential customers (e.g., businesses, multifamily dwellings, and laundromats); other utilities and agencies offer bill credits and tax credits based on eligible product costs. Some utilities even offer incentives to appliance retailers, such as the $50 sales incentive San Diego Gas and Electric offers retailers for each high-efficiency clothes washer sold. Water, electric, and gas utilities that have sponsored rebate programs for high-efficiency washers represent a number of states, including California, Colorado, Florida, Iowa, Massachusetts, New Jersey, New York, Oregon, Texas, Vermont, Washington, and Wisconsin.[138, 153, 158]

Oregon's Office of Energy offers qualifying residential consumers tax credits for a portion of the net purchase price of water- and energy-efficient appliances such as clothes washers; qualifying businesses are offered tax credits of up to 35% of the purchase price.[156] These tax credits amount to $120 to $230 for residents.[153, 159] The Posh Wash, a laundromat in Portland, Oregon, which participates in the program, installed 50 high-efficiency washing machines and expects to save about 20 gallons of water per load. Annual water and energy cost savings from the new washers are projected to average $5,500 a year, not including the one-time $5,740 state tax credit the laundromat received for purchasing resource-efficient washers.[160]

Installation and Maintenance of High-Efficiency Clothes Washers

Installation and maintenance requirements for water-efficient clothes washers are no different from those for high-volume machines. At least one manufacturer of high-efficiency washers recommends using a low-sudsing detergent, but oversudsing problems may be solved simply by using less detergent.

RECYCLING USED CLOTHES WASHERS   Nearly every state in the United States either bans the disposal or requires the separation of home appliance "white goods," such as clothes washers, for recycling purposes.[161] A number of states have white goods collection and recycling programs that facilitate the recycling of scrap steel from old appliances to make new products. The average

After World War II, the demand for washers grew quickly. By the early 1950s, automatic washers were outselling wringer washers ten to one.

steel content of a clothes washer is 45 pounds. According to USEPA, six major benefits are achieved by using scrap instead of virgin materials (iron ore and coal) in manufacturing new steel: a 97% reduction in mining wastes, 90% savings in use of virgin materials, 86% reduction in air pollution, 76% reduction in water pollution, 74% savings in energy, and 40% reduction in water use.[157]

2.6 DISHWASHERS

This section describes two measures to reduce water use by residential dishwashers: water-efficient dishwashers and efficient water-use practices for dishwashers. The water-efficient dishwashers discussed here are built-in (not portable) units that can be used in residences and in other facilities that use residential-size dishwashers. The efficient-use practices described apply to both residential-size dishwashers and larger machines used in some nonresidential and institutional facilities.

Residential water-efficient dishwashers use a maximum of 7.0 gallons per load (gpl), as shown in Figure 2.38. Some super-efficient machines use as little as 4.5 gpl, but they are not yet widely available and tend to be more expensive than the more commonly available 7.0 gpl models. In some cases, super-efficient dishwashers have smaller capacities than the typical built-in dishwasher sold in U.S. appliance markets and are not always comparable in terms of water use and performance.

The water and energy efficiency of dishwashers installed in the United States has improved considerably since the mid-1990s. These changes have also resulted in less noise during operation and better cleaning performance compared with older high-volume dishwashers.[162]

The relatively recent water- and energy-efficiency improvements to dishwashers are largely the result of energy-efficiency requirements established by the National Appliance Energy Conservation Act of 1987. This legislation helped prompt manufacturers to reduce the hot water use and associated energy needs of dishwashers. Additional incentives for efficiency improvements can be attributed to ENERGY STAR programs such as the Super-Efficient Home Appliance Initiative. Sponsored by the Consortium for Energy Efficiency in Boston, this initiative promotes energy-efficient dishwashers that use 26% less electricity than many conventional dishwashers.[163]

In 1886, Josephine Cochrane invented the first practical dishwasher after proclaiming "If nobody else is going to invent a dishwashing machine, I'll do it myself."

Water Use by Dishwashers

Estimated average water-use rates and savings for water-efficient dishwashers are shown in Table 2.19. Water-efficient dishwashers use a maximum of 7.0 gpl for a normal wash setting, and some models use as little as 4.5 gpl. Some European models that use 4.5 to 5.5 gpl have been reported to require one to two additional gallons of water for pre-rinsing, which reduces net water savings.[164]

Conventional moderate- to high-volume dishwashers, which use 7.0 to 14.0 gpl, likely represent most of the dishwashers currently installed in U.S. households, given an average 13-year life per machine. For both conventional and water-ef-

Figure 2.38 Water-efficient dishwashers use about 7.0 gallons of water per load. (Photo courtesy of KitchenAid Home Appliances.)

ficient dishwashers, actual water use per load varies depending on the setting selected by the user.[139, 162, 165–167] Estimates of average water use during a typical wash cycle (pre-wash through rinse) in water-efficient and high-volume dishwashers designed for residential use are shown in Table 2.19.

Water requirements for dishwashers vary among models and according to the setting selected by the user or the level of soiling detected by a particular machine. Thus, a water-efficient dishwasher measured to use 7.0 gpl for a normal load may use several gallons more than that when set for heavily soiled loads, such as pots and pans, or less than that when set for lightly soiled loads.

Water use by dishwashers typically comprises one of the smallest portions of indoor residential water demand, averaging 1.0 gallon per capita per day (gpcd). This represents just 1.4% of indoor use in the average single-family non-conserving home, according to the 1999 REUS study.[168] Household dishwasher use, levelized for all households (not just those with dishwashers), averages 0.10

TABLE 2.19

Estimated water use and savings by water-efficient dishwashers in households

Years Manufactured or Installed*	Dishwasher Water-Use Rate[†] Per Load gal	Frequency of Dish washer Use[‡] Per Person loads/day**	Estimated Water Use Daily Per Capita gal	Per House-hold§ gal	Estimated Water Savings With a 7.0 gpl Dishwasher Daily Per Capita gal	Per House-hold§ gal	Yearly Per Capita gal	Per House-hold§ gal
1997-present	4.5	0.10	0.5	1.2				
1995-present	**7.0**	0.10	0.7	1.8				
	7.0–10.5	0.10	0.9	2.3	0.2	0.5	64	169
1990-1995	9.5–12.0	0.10	1.1	2.8	0.4	1.0	137	361
1980-1990	14.0	0.10	1.4	3.7	0.7	1.8	256	675

* Time periods are approximate.

† Figures show range of water-use rates (with the average of the range used to estimate water use and savings) or typical rates for normal full-cycle operation of a fully loaded dishwasher (not applicable to compact models). Figure in bold (7.0 gpl) represents water-efficient dishwashers made by several major appliance manufacturers and reported to deliver reliable performance; some manufacturers also produce dishwashers that use less than 7.0 gpl, and these may also provide reliable performance.

‡ U.S. Department of Energy assumptions are higher (322 wash loads per household per year) and apply only to homes with dishwashers.

§ Based on the average of 2.64 persons per occupied U.S. household

** Levelized over all households—with and without dishwashers

gal = gallons

Sources: Amy Vickers & Associates, Inc.; References 37, 52, 139, 162, 164–167, 170, 172–175, and 178

loads per person per day,[169] equivalent to average daily water use of about 10.0 gpl. Depending on the water efficiency of the particular dishwasher used, average daily residential water use by dishwashers installed between 1980 and the late 1990s is estimated to range from 0.7 gpcd (7.0 gpl) to 1.4 gpcd (14.0 gpl), as shown in Table 2.19. These figures reflect not only the increased water efficiency of dishwashers but also a shift in consumer habits. For example, a 1984 water-use study conducted by the U.S. Department of Housing and Urban Development reported that dishwasher use averaged 1.6 gpcd based on 0.17 loads per capita per day.[36] The differences between dishwasher use data reported in 1984 and 1999 indicate that dishwasher use is declining, perhaps because of smaller households and more meals eaten away from home. Take-out food brought home requires less dishwashing (but it increases solid waste and recycling needs).

Water-efficient dishwashers can be installed to replace existing high-volume machines without special connections or considerations. In addition to installing a water-efficient dishwasher, consumers can save water used by dishwashers by following several water conservation practices, which are outlined in Section 2.6.2.

2.6.1 Water-Efficient Dishwashers

Water-efficient household dishwashers use a maximum of 7.0 gpl. This latest water-efficiency threshold has been achieved by several leading dishwasher brands for which reliable, positive performance data have been reported for several years. A few models for which good performance data have been reported use less than 7.0 gpl (e.g., 4.5, 5.5, and 6.0 gpl), but these data have not always been consistent.[162, 166, 167]

Recent improvements in the water and energy efficiency of dishwashers have been accomplished through several design and operating innovations, principally: improved electronic components that can program wash cycles to reduce water consumption; better integrated pump, filter, and grinder systems, which reduce the volume of water required to break down and remove particles; and "smart" electronic controls that can figure out minimum water requirements based on the amount of soiling detected (e.g., by how readily light travels through the initial wash water).[165]

2.6.2 Dishwasher Water-Efficiency Practices

Washing and rinsing dishes by hand is often less water-efficient than running a dishwasher that uses 7.0 gpl or less, with several qualifications. First, people who keep the faucet running while not using the water directly for scrubbing or rinsing waste several gallons of water per minute. Second, studies have shown that most people pre-rinse dishes more than is needed before loading a dishwasher, resulting in wasted water at the faucet. One survey reported that 83% of respondents claimed to routinely pre-rinse most items.[170]

Water use for dishwashing can be reduced in several ways:

- Operate the dishwasher with full loads only.
- Install an aerator or other flow-control device on the kitchen faucet to reduce flows while rinsing and cleaning dishes and cooking vessels. An exception to this measure would be dishwashers that must be hooked up directly to a faucet to operate, because a flow-control device could prevent sufficient water from being supplied to this type of dishwasher.
- When hand-washing dishes and cooking vessels, wash them in a filled sink or container and let the water run only while rinsing items under the faucet.
- Scrape off food with a utensil or used paper napkin, not water.
- Do not pre-rinse dishes except in cases of sticky or burned-on food.
- For best results, load the dishwasher so that water can reach all surfaces of the items to be washed; incorrect loading may cause all or part of the load to need rewashing.
- Use the shortest wash cycle for lightly soiled loads. With most dishwashers, running normal and lightly soiled loads at the setting for heavily soiled loads will *not* clean the dishes any better, and it will waste water.

Performance of Water-Efficient Dishwashers

The performance of water-efficient dishwashers appears to be comparable to that of higher-volume machines, according to recently reported evaluations of a number of brands and models. For example, *Consumer Reports* studies in 1999 and 2000 examined the performance of more than 30 dishwasher models with water use ranging from 4.5 to 11.5 gpl; the studies found that more than half of the models provided "very good" washing and cleaning performance (which included consideration of the appliances' energy efficiency, noise, and convenience). *Consumer Reports* added, "Even the dumbest dishwashers can be made

In 1920 the first freestanding dishwasher with permanent plumbing is introduced. In 1935, portable dishwashers enter the marketplace. Water spots are no longer a problem after 1940 when the first fully-automatic dishwasher with heated drying debuts."

—www.whirlpool.com

*M*ost energy use by dishwashers is for controlling hot water temperatures and drying cycles.

to use less water—simply run them at their lightest cycle. Those cycles [that] use as little as half the water of a normal cycle may well suffice for many loads."[162, 167] An earlier (1997) *Consumer Reports* study of 16 dishwasher models drawn from the five brands comprising more than 80% of the market reported that dishwashers have realized water-efficiency improvements "without sacrificing cleaning performance."[166] This indicates that both the water efficiency and operating performance of dishwashers have improved and that reliable products are available.

Water Savings and Related Benefits From Water-Efficient Dishwashers

WATER SAVINGS Estimated water use and water savings achieved by replacing a high-volume dishwasher with a 7.0 gpl model in a home is shown in Table 2.19. For example, installing a 7.0 gpl dishwasher to replace a model using 9.5 to 12.0 gpl is estimated to save an average of 0.4 gpcd or 1.0 gallon per household per day, equivalent to an annual water savings of 137 gallons per capita per year or 361 gallons per household per year.

WATER AND SEWER COST SAVINGS Avoided water and sewer costs associated with installation of a water-efficient dishwasher can be calculated by multiplying the expected volume of water (and wastewater) reductions (see Table 2.19) times the local utility rates for water and sewer use (excluding fixed charges). A schedule of representative water and sewer utility rates in the United States and their associated marginal cost savings according to a range of reduced water and wastewater volumes is provided in Appendix D, *Water and Sewer Rates, Costs, and Savings by Volume of Use.*

ENERGY SAVINGS Estimated energy savings from reduced operational costs and hot water use associated with water-efficient dishwashers are shown in Table 2.20. Actual energy savings vary by brand, model, and consumer patterns of use (e.g., load size, dirt load, water temperature, and frequency of operation). For example, installing a 7.0 gpl dishwasher to replace a model rated to use 9.5 to 12.0 gpl will save an estimated 1.0 kilowatt-hour (kWh) per capita per day or 2.6 kWh per 2.64-person household per day. On an annual basis, this amounts to an estimated energy savings of 356 kWh per capita per year or 940 kWh per 2.64-person household per year.

A dishwasher requires energy for several functions—to heat water sufficiently to clean and sanitize dishes, run the motor, and operate the heater or fan that dries the dishes. The largest energy-related cost of operating a dishwasher is usually running the water heater; if a water heater delivers water that is not sufficiently hot, the dishwasher usually boosts the temperature and may run its wash cycle longer because fatty soils and detergents need 140°F to liquefy adequately. [171, 172] Dishwasher models that offer temperature settings above 140°F for "anti-bacterial" washes increase energy demand and kill more germs—until the dishes are touched by a human hand.[167]

Avoided energy costs associated with installation of a water-efficient dishwasher can be calculated by multiplying the expected savings in kilowatt-hours or therms (see Table 2.20) times the local electric or gas utility rates charged per kilowatt-hour or therm (excluding fixed charges).

TABLE 2.20

Estimated energy use and savings by water-efficient dishwashers in households

Years Manufactured or Installed *	Dishwasher Water-Use Rate[†] Per Load gal	Frequency of Dishwasher Use[†] Per Capita loads/day[‡‡]	Estimated Energy-Use Rate[§] Per Load kWh	Estimated Energy Use for Electric Water Heating** Per Capita kWh/d	Per Household[††] kWh/d	Estimated Energy Savings With a 7.0 gpl Dishwasher Per Capita kWh/d	Per Household[††] kWh/d	Per Capita kWh/y	Per Household[††] kWh/y
1997-present	4.5	0.10	0.90	0.09	0.24				
1995-present	7.0	0.10	1.40	0.14	0.37				
	7.0–10.5	0.10	1.83	0.18	0.48	0.4	1.1	155	410
1990-1995	9.5–12.0	0.10	2.38	0.24	0.63	1.0	2.6	356	940
1980-1990	14.0	0.10	2.76	0.28	0.73	1.4	3.6	496	1,310

* Time periods are approximate.

† Figures show range of water-use rates (with the average of the range used to estimate water use and savings) or typical rates for normal full-cycle operation of a fully loaded dishwasher (not applicable to compact models). Figure in bold (7.0 gpl) represents water-efficient dishwashers made by several major appliance manufacturers and reported to deliver reliable performance; some manufacturers also produce dishwashers that use less than 7.0 gpl, and these may also provide reliable performance.

‡ U.S. Department of Energy assumptions are higher (322 wash loads per household per year) and apply only to homes with dishwashers.

§ Based on an estimated average energy requirement (combined cycles of washing, rinsing, and drying) for a normal load of dishes, cookware, and utensils. Actual energy use and savings vary depending on model design, appliance settings, dirt load, water temperature, and other product design features. Energy use and water use by dishwashers are not always directly correlated; see the specific energy ratings for a particular model to determine its actual use and potential savings.

** For gas water-heating systems, convert figures for electric energy use and savings to therms.

†† Based on the average size of 2.64 persons for occupied U.S. households

‡‡ Levelized over all households—with and without dishwashers

gpl = gallons per load

gal = gallons

kWh = kilowatt-hours

kWh/d = kilowatt-hours per day

kWh/y = kilowatt-hours per year

Sources: Amy Vickers & Associates, Inc.; References 37, 52, 139, 162, 164–167, 170–175, and 178

For several years, *Consumer Reports* studies of dishwashers have found that differences in water-use efficiency significantly affect operating costs. For example, the difference in energy costs for operating a 4.5 gpl dishwasher compared with a 10.5 gpl machine is about $300 (for a water heater powered by gas costing $0.619 per therm) to $450 (for a water heater powered by electricity costing $0.084 per kWh); these estimates are based on a 10-year machine life and normal cycles using water at a temperature of 140°F.[162, 165]

Costs Associated With Water-Efficient Dishwashers

HARDWARE COSTS   Dishwashers whose water use averages 6.0 to 7.0 gpl retail for $300 to $690 and are cost-competitive with models that are less water-efficient. A few exceptions are some ultra-water-efficient (4.5 to 5.5 gpl) models, which cost up to $1,400.[162, 167]

LABOR AND MATERIAL COSTS   No additional labor or material costs are involved in installing a water-efficient dishwasher compared with installing higher-volume models.

PRODUCT MANUFACTURERS   Manufacturers of water-efficient dishwashers are listed in Chapter 6, *The Water Conservation Network.*

Laws, Codes, and Standards Applicable to Dishwashers

All applicable laws, codes, standards, and health and safety requirements associated with dishwashers should be observed when any fixture, appliance, or related plumbing or water system connection is installed or adjusted.

Many local and state codes require dishwashers to be installed by licensed plumbers. Appliance industry standards for the plumbing requirements and performance of household dishwashers include ANSI/AHAM DW-1 (*Household Dishwashers*) and ANSI/ASSE 1006/AHAM DW-2PR (*Plumbing Requirements for Household Dishwashers*).

Implementing a Dishwasher Rebate or Replacement Program

SELECTING A WATER-EFFICIENT DISHWASHER   The "smart" controls incorporated into most new dishwashers economize on energy and water use and can help reduce operating costs if they work properly, but some models are not always reliable. Electronic dirt-detector technology is generally improving, but when it doesn't work, dishwashers may use more water than necessary for heavily soiled loads.[162]

PLANNING THE PROGRAM   Large-scale dishwasher rebate or replacement programs, similar to those for low-volume toilets and clothes washers, are beginning to be implemented. Consumer acceptance of water-efficient dishwashers should be very good because reliable products are available from a growing number of appliance manufacturers. For example, Consumers Union, an independent product-testing organization, found "many good-cleaning machines" that are water- and energy-efficient.[173]

Targeted Water Users   Water-efficient dishwashers that use 7.0 gpl or less can be installed to replace conventional high-volume dishwashers in residences and in other facilities in which residential dishwashers are used.

Number of Dishwashers Installed   Approximately 50.2% of U.S. households have a dishwasher.[174, 139] In the U.S. market, approximately 5,791,000 dishwashers were sold in 2000, and 5,844,000 were projected to be sold in 2001 (including domestically produced and imported shipments). Of those dishwashers sold, about 97% were built-in and 3% were portable units.[175]

In the 45 to 55% of U.S. households that do not have a dishwasher,[176] dishes must be washed by hand. These households use about 2.5 gallons of water each time dishes are washed and clean the equivalent of 10.03 dishwasher loads a week (522 loads a year). This represents water use of 25.1 gallons a week, or about 1,300 gallons a year. The average temperature of water used to hand-wash dishes is 115°F.[139]

Figures reported for the frequency of dishwasher use *by households that have them* (in contrast to the average frequency of dishwasher use, 0.10 times per person per day, for all households[177]) vary somewhat. A national survey of consumer appliance use found that households with dishwashers use 9.5 to 12.0 gpl and operate them an average of 4.7 times a week (242 loads a year). This represents water use of 44.3 to 55.9 gallons a week, or 2,300 to 2,900 gallons a year.[170] However, DOE assumes that households with dishwashers operate them 6.2 times a week, or 322 times a year,[178] an assumption that dates back to at least 1987.[171]

Life Cycle of Dishwashers   The life cycle of a residential dishwasher is 10 to 16 years,[157] about 13 years in a typical household that operates the appliance four to six times per week (200 to 300 loads per year). More or less frequent use influences a dishwasher's useful life.[165, 178]

Incentives   Financial incentives such as rebates, bill credits, and tax incentives for water-efficient dishwashers are not as common as for high-efficiency clothes washers because the potential water savings from dishwashers is generally not as significant. Nevertheless, at least one jurisdiction offers a financial incentive to promote the installation of water-efficient dishwashers. Oregon's Office of Energy offers qualifying residential consumers tax credits for up to 25% of the net purchase price of water- and energy-efficient appliances including dishwashers; qualifying businesses are offered tax credits for up to 35% for similar purchases.[179]

Installation and Maintenance of Water-Efficient Dishwashers

Installation and maintenance requirements of water-efficient dishwashers are no different from those of high-volume machines.

Recycling Used Dishwashers

Nearly every state in the United States either bans the disposal or requires the separation of home appliance "white goods," such as dishwashers, for recycling purposes.[161] A number of states have white goods collection and recycling programs to allow the scrap steel from old appliances, such as dishwashers, to be recycled to make new products. The average steel content of a dishwasher is 22 pounds for built-in units and 36 pounds for portable models. According to USEPA, six major benefits are achieved by using scrap instead of virgin materials (iron ore and coal) in manufacturing new steel: a 97% reduction in mining wastes, 90% savings in use of virgin materials, 86% reduction in air pollution, 76% reduction in water pollution, 74% savings in energy, and 40% reduction in water use.[157]

~

1. Wayne B. Solley, Robert R. Pierce, and Howard A. Perlman, *Estimated Use of Water in the United States in 1995*, U.S. Geological Survey Circular 1200, U.S. Dept. of the Interior, U.S. Geological Survey, Reston, Va., 1998.
2. Wayne B. Solley, Robert R. Pierce, and Howard A. Perlman, *Estimated Use of Water in the United States in 1995*, p. 24.
3. Peter W. Mayer et al, *Residential End Uses of Water*, American Water Works Assoc. (AWWA) Research Foundation and AWWA, Denver, Colo., 1999, p. 114.
4. Personal communication, Jean Witherspoon, Water Conservation Officer, City of Albuquerque, N.M., July 15, 1998.
5. Water Conservation Potential Costs in the Greater Vancouver Regional District, prepared by Kerr Wood Leidal Associates Ltd., North Vancouver, B.C., and Amy Vickers & Associates, Inc., Amherst, Mass., for the Greater Vancouver Regional District, Burnaby, B.C., Canada, 2000.
6. Massachusetts Water Resources Authority, Boston, Mass., 1996.

The best time to plan a book is while you're doing the dishes."
—Agatha Christie

7. Water Supply Conservation and Demand Management, Final Report to Wellington, N.Z., City Council, prepared by Montgomery Watson, Sydney, Australia, November 1994.

8. John Darmoody et al, "Water Use Surveys—An Essential Component of Effective Demand Management," *Proc. AWWA Annual Conf.*, Toronto, Ont., Canada, 1996.

9. Vermont Water Conservation Study, prepared by Amy Vickers & Associates, Inc., Amherst, Mass., for the Vermont Dept. of Environmental Conservation, July 1997.

10. David Howarth and Amy Vickers, "Water Conservation in the U.K.: Why We Don't Have Toilet Rebate Programs," *Proc. AWWA Annual Conf.*, Atlanta, Ga., 1997.

11. Jack A. Weber and Fraser M. Parsons, "Water Conservation Planning and Evaluation in Cairo, Egypt," *Proc. AWWA Annual Conf.*, Atlanta, Ga., 1997.

12. Mayer et al, *Residential End Uses of Water*, p. 86.

13. Peter H. Judd, *How Much Is Enough? Controlling Water Demand in Apartment Buildings*, AWWA, Denver, Colo., 1993, pp. 70–71.

14. Martin M. Karpiscak et al, "Evaporative Cooler Water Use in Phoenix," *Journal AWWA*, vol. 90, no. 4, 1998, p. 121.

15. Personal communication, Dave D. Todd, Supervisor of Water Conservation, City of Fresno, Calif., June 9, 1998.

16. Mayer et al, *Residential End Uses of Water*, p. 86.

17. 1997 Residential Water Use Summary, prepared by John Olaf Nelson, Water Resources Management, for AWWA's "WaterWiser" web site, www.waterwiser.org, 1997.

18. Final Report: Water Conservation Planning USA Case Studies Project, prepared by Amy Vickers & Associates, Amherst, Mass., for the Environment Agency, Demand Management Centre, Worthing, West Sussex, U.K., June 1996.

19. "Bubble, Bubble . . . or Toil and Trouble?" *Consumer Reports*, vol. 63, May 1998, p. 46.

20. Duane D. Baumann, John J. Boland, and Michael W. Hanemann, *Urban Water Demand Management and Planning*, McGraw-Hill, New York, 1998.

21. Kohler Co., *Bodies of Water: Kohler K-600 Design Manual*, Section 7 (Performance Showering), Kohler, Wis., 2000.

22. Mayer et al, *Residential End Uses of Water*, p. 86.

23. William O. Maddaus, *Water Conservation*, AWWA, Denver, Colo., 1987.

24. Amy Vickers, "New Massachusetts Toilet Standard Sets Water Conservation Precedent," *Journal AWWA*, vol. 81, no. 3, 1989, p. 48.

25. Amy Vickers, "Water-Use Efficiency Standards for Plumbing Fixtures: Benefits of National Legislation," *Journal AWWA*, vol. 82, no. 5, 1990, pp. 51–54.

26. *Energy Policy Act of 1992*, Public Law 102-486, 106 Stat. 2776, 102d Congress, Oct. 24, 1992.

27. U.S. General Accounting Office, Water Infrastructure: Water-Efficient Plumbing Fixtures Reduce Water Consumption and Wastewater Flows, document GAO/CED-00-232, U.S. General Accounting Office, Washington, D.C., August 2000, p. 7.

28. U.S. General Accounting Office, Water Infrastructure, p. 4.

29. Amy Vickers, "Implementing the U.S. Energy Policy Act," *Journal AWWA*, vol. 87, no. 1, 1996, p. 18.

30. Kimberley M. Knox, "Water Consumption Difference With Apartment Buildings With Master Meters Versus Individual Unit Meters," presented at the AWWA Annual Conf., Dallas, Texas, June 23, 1998.

31. Richard Bennett, "Water Submetering Questions and Answers: With a California Perspective," presented at the AWWA Annual Conf., Dallas, Texas, June 23, 1998.

32. William H. Bruvold and Patrick R. Mitchell, "Evaluating the Effect of Residential Water Audits, *Journal AWWA*, vol. 85, no. 8, 1993, p. 79.

33. J.C. Griggs et al, Water Conservation: Design, Installation and Maintenance Requirements for the Use of Low Flush WCs Flushed Siphonically or by Valves, Building Research Establishment, Watford, Hertfordshire, England, 1997, p. 36.

34. Mayer et al, *Residential End Uses of Water*, pp. 107–108.

35. Mayer et al, *Residential End Uses of Water*, p. 98.

36. Residential Water Conservation Projects—Summary Report, prepared by Brown & Caldwell Consulting Engineers for the U.S. Dept. of Housing and Urban Development. Rept. No. HUD-PDR-903, June 1984.

37. Mayer et al, *Residential End Uses of Water*, p. 95.

38. Thomas P. Konen, "Water Use in Office Buildings," *Plumbing Engineer*, July 1986.

39. Patrick J. Behling and Nicholas J. Bartilucci, "Potential Impact of Water-Efficient Plumbing Fixtures on Office Water Consumption," *Journal AWWA*, vol. 84, no. 10, 1992, pp. 74–78.

40. Amy Vickers, "So You Think You're Conserving Water?" *Fine Homebuilding*, Fall/Winter 2000, no. 135, pp. 6–8.

41. Steve Culpepper, "Choosing a Toilet," *Fine Homebuilding*, October/November 1997.

42. Nhora Cortes-Comerer, "In Search of the Perfect Flush," *Mechanical Engineering*, February 1988, pp. 40–47.

43. Thomas Horner, "Water Efficiency For Multi-Unit Properties," presented at Savewater96—A Symposium on Water Conservation, Westchester, N.Y., Mar. 12, 1996.

44. Allan J. Dietemann, "Flapperless Technology for the New Millennium," presented at the AWWA Annual Conf., Denver, Colo., June 13, 2000.

45. "In Search of a Better Toilet," *Consumer Reports*, vol. 63, May 1998, pp. 44–46.

46. U.S. General Accounting Office, Water Infrastructure, p. 31.

47. Evaluation of New York City's Toilet Rebate Program: Customer Satisfaction Survey Final Report, prepared by Westat, Inc., Rockville, Md., for the New York City Dept. of Environmental Protection, Dec. 16, 1996.

48. A Survey of Ultra-Low-Flush Toilet Users, prepared by The Wirthlin Group, Irvine, Calif., for the Los Angeles Dept. of Water and Power, October 1995.

49. Diane M. Mullville-Friel, Damann L. Anderson, and Wendy L. Nero, "Water Savings and Participant Satisfaction Realized: City of Tampa Toilet Rebate Program Evaluation," *Proc. Conserv96: Responsible Water Stewardship*, AWWA, Denver, Colo., 1996, pp. 371–375.

50. Dan Strub, "ULF Toilet Outreach Program Customer Feedback: First Quarter Report, FY 1998," Planning, Environmental and Conservation Services Dept., City of Austin, Texas, 1998.

51. Jim Olysztynski, "Jim Olysztynski on the Record: Study Shows Low-Flow Plumbing Has Paid Off," *PMEngineer*, vol. 4, no. 4, May 1998, pp. 10–12.

52. Statistical Abstract of the United States: 1998, U.S. Bureau of the Census, Sept. 29, 1998, Table 71.

53. Personal communication, John Olaf Nelson, Water Resources Management, June 2, 1998.

54. William S. Nechamen, Steven Pacenka, and Warren Liebold, "Assessment of New York City Residential Water Conservation Potential," *Proc. Conserv96: Responsible Water Stewardship*, AWWA, Denver, Colo., 1996, pp. 523-527.

55. New York City Water Conservation Programs: A Summary, New York City Dept. of Environmental Protection, New York, 1997.

56. Anthony J. Tarquin et al, "Effectiveness of an Ultra-Low-Flush Toilet Program," *Proc. Conserv93: The New Water Agenda*, AWWA, Denver, Colo., 1993, pp. 885-893.

57. Chris Gates, Judith Ramsay, and Ken Brown, "An Evaluation of the Effectiveness of a Municipal Toilet Replacement Program," presented at the AWWA Annual Conf., Toronto, Ont., Canada, June 26, 1996.

58. The CII ULFT Savings Study: Final Report, prepared by Hagler Bailly Services, Inc., San Francisco, Calif., for the California Urban Water Conservation Council, Aug. 5, 1997.

59. A Guide To Water Management: The MWRA Program for Industrial, Commercial and Institutional Water Use, prepared in collaboration with Douglas Kobrick of Black & Veatch Engineers, Massachusetts Water Resources Authority, Boston, Mass., June 1995.

60. Thomas W. Chesnutt, Casey N. McSpadden, and Anil Bamezai, Ultra Low Flush Toilet Programs: Evaluation of Program Outcomes and Water Savings, prepared for the Metropolitan Water District of Southern California, Los Angeles, Calif., November 1994.

61. Mayer et al, *Residential End Uses of Water*, p. 96.

62. Atossa Soltani et al, "Low-Volume Toilet Replacement: The Santa Monica Bay Saver Program," presented at the American Water Resources Assoc. Annual Symposium on Water Supply and Reuse: 1991 and Beyond, San Diego, Calif., June 1991.

63. Edward R. Osann and John E. Young, *Saving Water, Saving Dollars: Efficient Plumbing Products and the Protection of America's Waters*, Potomac Resources, Inc., Washington, D.C., April 1998.

64. International Council for Local Environmental Initiatives, Water Conservation, Santa Monica, USA, ICLEI Case Study 12, Toronto, Ont., Canada, 1993.

65. Wendy L. Corpening, "Commercial ULF Toilets—First the Good News," *Proc. AWWA Annual Conf.*, Anaheim, Calif., 1995, pp. 217–223.

66. Carolyn Seiler, "Flushing Out A Trend: Toilets as Street Material," *Proc. AWWA Annual Conf.*, Anaheim, Calif., 1995.

67. John M. Koeller, William P. McDonnell, and Harvey O. Webster, "After-Market Replacement of Flush Valve Flappers in Ultra-Low-Flush Toilets: A Study of Compatibility and Flush Volumes," presented at the AWWA Annual Conf., Dallas, Texas, June 23, 1998.

68. Ken Wilcox, "Alternative Toilets: To Flush, or Not To Flush," *Small Flows*, vol. 10, no. 1, Winter 1996 (April 1993 reprint).

69. Scott Whittier Chaplin, "Alternative Supplies: Rainwater Collection Systems, Graywater Systems, and Composting Toilets," *Proc. Conserv93: The New Water Agenda*, AWWA, Denver, Colo., 1993, pp. 1807–1816.

70. Clement Solomon et al, Fact Sheet: Composting Toilet Systems, National Small Flows Clearinghouse, Morgantown, W. Va., 1998.

71. Clivus Multrum, http://clivusmultrum.com, May 2, 1998.

72. Amy Vickers, "Low-Flow Toilets," *Fine Homebuilding*, June/July 1990, p. 62.

73. Incinolet: That Electric Toilet, product brochure prepared by Research Products /Blankenship, U.S.A., Dallas, Texas, provided to author May 1998.

74. Marty Carlock, "No Flush, No Fuss, No Odor: Clivus Waste-Composting System Could Help Solve Some Title 5 Problems," *The Boston Sunday Globe*, Apr. 21, 1996.

75. Elizabeth Atkinson, "Alternative Septic Systems: You May Have a Choice," *West Newbury (Mass.) News*, Jan. 29, 1997, p. 8.

76. The Ecos Catalog: Tools for Low-Water and Waterless Living, product catalog prepared by Ecos, Inc., Concord, Mass., 1997.

77. *The Water Conservation Manager's Guide to Residential Retrofit*, AWWA, Denver, Colo., 1993.

78. E-mail message to WaterWiser Discussion List, http://waterwiser-list@listserv.waterwiser.org, from Warren C. Liebold, Director of Conservation, New York City Dept. of Environmental Protection, November 1997.

79. Richard J. Scholze, "Investigation of Water Conserving Toilet Retrofit Devices," *Proc. Conserv93: The New Water Agenda*, AWWA, Denver, Colo., 1993, pp. 1435-1438.

80. U.S. Environmental Protection Agency, *Water Conservation Plan Guidelines* (EPA-832-D-98-001), August 1998, p.166.

81. Thomas P. Konen et al, *Alternative Flushing and Retrofit Devices For the Toilet*, prepared by the Stevens Institute of Technology, Hoboken, N.J., for the Metropolitan Water District of Southern California, Los Angeles, Calif., June 1992.

82. Reducing Costs in Hospitals: A Case Study of Norwood Hospital, Massachusetts Water Resources Authority, Boston, Mass., February 1996.

83. Frank Gradilone and Michael S. Bennettt, "A Water Conservation Program for the Spring Valley Water Company," *Proc. Conserv93: The New Water Agenda*, AWWA, Denver, Colo., 1993, pp. 1671-1685.

84. Amy Vickers, "Achieving A High Customer Participation Rate With A Bulk Mail-Out Retrofit Program," *Proc. Conserv93: The New Water Agenda*, AWWA, Denver, Colo., 1993, pp. 1649–1659.

85. Technical Issues and Recommendations on the Implementation of the U.S. Energy Policy Act, prepared by Amy Vickers & Associates, Inc., Boston, Mass., for AWWA, Washington, D.C., Oct. 25, 1995.

86. Mayer et al, *Residential End Uses of Water*, pp. 107-108.

87. Warren C. Liebold, Director of Technical Services/Conservation, New York City Dept. of Environmental Protection, data cited at Plumbing Fixtures/Water Conservation Workshop, June 9, 1995.

88. The 1992 City of San Diego Residential Water Audit Program: Evaluation of Program Outcomes and Water Savings, prepared by Anil Bamezai and Thomas W. Chesnutt, A&N Technical Services, Inc., Encinitas, Calif., for the Metropolitan Water District of Southern California, December 1994.

89. Steve Reiber, "Investigating the Effects of Chloramines on Elastomer Degradation," *Journal AWWA*, vol. 85, no. 8, 1993, pp. 101–111.

90. Harvey O. Webster, William P. McConnell, and John M. Koeller, *Toilet Flappers: Materials Integrity Tests*, Metropolitan Water District of Southern California, Los Angeles, Calif., January 2000, pp. 7–13.

91. *Toilets 101: The Basics of Repairing Your Toilet*, Conservation Section, San Francisco Water Department, San Francisco, Calif., 1996.

92. Mayer et al, *Residential End Uses of Water*, pp. 90–94.

93. Sharon Whitley, "Water-Saving, No-Flush Urinal Seems Promising," *The San Diego Union-Tribune*, Dec. 8, 1996.

94. The Waterless Advantage,™ promotional literature prepared by The Waterless Co., Del Mar, Calif., 1997.

95. Water Management: A Comprehensive Approach For Facility Managers, prepared by Enviro-Management & Research, Inc., Washington, D.C., for the U.S. General Services Administration, Office of Real Property, Management and Safety, Washington, D.C., 1994.

96. Partial Reference List for Waterless No-Flush™ Urinals, promotional literature prepared by The Waterless Company, Del Mar, Calif., Nov. 11, 1996.

97. Sample Project Details, promotional literature provided by The Waterless Company, Del Mar, Calif., Nov. 11, 1996.

98. "Waterless Urinals Reduce Water and Maintenance Costs for Government Agencies," *FEMP Focus*, Federal Energy Management Program, U.S. Dept. of Energy, Washington, D.C., August/September 1997, p. 4.

99. No-Flush™ Urinals and Restroom Hygiene, product information prepared by The Waterless Company, Del Mar, Calif., 1996.

100. Patrick J. Higgins, More About Permitted Use of Waterless Urinals, e-mail message to WaterWiser Discussion List, http://waterwiser-list@listserv.waterwiser.org, June 17, 1996.

101. Personal communication, Allan J. Dietemann, Seattle Public Utilities, Feb. 4, 1997.

102. Waterless Urinals, memo prepared by Joseph W. Dooley, U.S. Office of the Deputy Under-Secretary of Defense, Energy and Engineering, Arlington, Va., Dec. 4, 1996.

103. Mayer et al, *Residential End Uses of Water*, p. 102.

104. Mayer et al, *Residential End Uses of Water*, pp. 94–101.

105. "Low-Flow Shower Heads: Which Give You the Best Shower for the Least Water?" *Consumer Reports*, vol. 60, February 1995, pp. 118–120.

106. Amy Vickers, "Water-Saving Showerheads and Faucets," *Fine Homebuilding*, October/November 1993, p. 82.

107. Personal communication, Warren C. Liebold, Director of Technical Services /Conservation, New York City Dept. of Environmental Protection, July 13, 1998.

108. "Improved Low-Flow Showerheads Make Retrofit Program a Success," *U.S. Water News*, December 1996, p.15.

109. Damann L. Anderson and Wendy L. Nero, "The Impact of Water Conserving Fixtures on Residential Water Use Characteristics in Tampa, Florida," *Proc. Conserv93: The New Water Agenda,* AWWA, Denver, Colo., 1993, pp. 611-628.

110. Operation Watersense, Massachusetts Water Resources Authority, Boston, Mass., 1996.

111. William Miller and Kathy Foley, "Regional Plumbing Retrofit Initiative Targeting West Central Florida Residents and Visitors," *Proc. Conserv96: Responsible Water Stewardship,* AWWA, Denver, Colo., 1996, pp. 263-267.

112. A Guide To Water Management: The MWRA Program for Industrial, Commercial and Institutional Water Use, p. 23.

113. Andrew P. Jones, High-Efficiency Showerheads and Faucets: Water Efficiency Technology Report #2, Rocky Mountain Institute, Snowmass, Colo., 1993.

114. D. Morgan et al, "Evaluation of Nine Residential Retrofit Methods," *Proc. Conserv96: Responsible Water Stewardship,* AWWA, Denver, Colo., 1996, pp. 251-256.

115. Denise Ruzicka, Thomas E. Reed, and Deborah Ducoff-Barone, "Retrofitting A Wet State," *Proc. Conserv96: Responsible Water Stewardship,* AWWA, Denver, Colo., 1996, pp. 256–261.

116. Efficient Showerhead Consumer Preference Study, prepared by Pacific Rim Resources, Inc., for Seattle City Light, Seattle, Wash., February 1992.

117. Mayer et al, *Residential End Uses of Water,* Table A .1, pp. 202–246.

118. Mayer et al, *Residential End Uses of Water,* pp. 107–108.

119. Mayer et al, *Residential End Uses of Water,* p. 94.

120. Mayer et al, *Residential End Uses of Water,* p. 94.

121. *How To Save Water At Home: A Step-By-Step Manual for the Do-It-Yourselfer,* Water Conservation Office, City of Albuquerque, N.M., undated, pp. 30–32.

122. Good Housekeeping Appliance Survey: Consumer Use Patterns, April 1997, Assoc. of Home Appliance Manufacturers and *Good Housekeeping,* Chicago, 1997.

123. Mayer et al, *Residential End Uses of Water,* Table A.1, pp. 202–246.

124. *Water Efficiency & Management for Hospitals* (bulletin), Masschusetts Water Resources Authority, Boston, Mass., Apr. 8, 1994.

125. U.S. Dept. of Energy, Final Rule: "Energy Conservation Programs for Consumer Products: Test Procedures and Certification and Enforcement Requirements for Plumbing Products; and Certification and Enforcement Requirements for Residential Appliances," *Federal Register* (63 FR 13308), Mar. 18, 1998.

126. Local Ordinances For Water Efficiency, prepared by The Bruce Company for the U.S. Environmental Protection Agency, Office of Policy Analysis, EPA Contract No. 68-W2-0018, Subcontract No. EPA 353-2, Work Assignment 24, Mar. 31, 1993, Appendix B (unnumbered).

127. William Pressman, *Kitchen Garbage Grinders in New York City,* prepared for the Emerson Electric Co., February 1991, p. 10.

128. Judd, *How Much Is Enough,* p. 8.

129. Mayer et al, *Residential End Uses of Water,* Table A.1, pp. 202–246.

130. Sandi D. Edgemon, Tony T. Gregg, and Michael C. Baechler, "ENERGY STAR® Partnerships Clothes Washer Volume Purchase: Partnering With the City of Austin," presented at the AWWA Annual Conf., Dallas, Texas, June 23, 1998.

131. Consortium for Energy Efficiency, "Market Penetration of Energy Star Washers is Encouraging," *CEE Update: Residential Clothes Washers,* May 2000, p. 3.

132. "Product Updates: Top Loaders Meet the Front-Loader Challenge," *Consumer Reports,* vol. 66, January 2001, pp. 45–47.

133. "A New Spin on Clothes Washers: Is It Time to Switch to a Front-Loader?" *Consumer Reports,* vol. 63, July 1998, pp. 50–54.

134. Allan J. Dietemann, "Department of Energy Clothes Washer Standards Update," presented at the AWWA Annual Conf., Denver, Colo., June 14, 2000.

135. "Spin City: Ratings of Washing Machines and Clothes Dryers," *Consumer Reports,* vol. 64, July 1999, pp. 30–33.

136. J. J. Tomlinson and D. T. Rizy, *Bern Clothes Washer Study Final Report,* prepared by the Energy Division, Oak Ridge National Laboratory, for the U.S. Dept. of Energy, Rept. ORNL/M-6382, March 1998, p. ix.

137. "A Move to the Front: Front-Loading Washers Are Better for the Environment, But Are They Worth the Extra Cost?" *Consumer Reports,* vol. 62, July 1997, pp. 48–97.

138. "Washing Machines," *Consumer Reports Buying Guide 1998,* Consumers Union of the United States, Inc., Yonkers, N.Y., 1997, pp. 83–85.

139. John T. Erikson, excerpts from the *National Habits and Appliance Tracking Study,* Procter & Gamble Company, Cincinnati, Ohio, in a memorandum to James E. McMahon, Lawrence Berkeley National Laboratory, May 4, 1995.

140. "Washing Machines: What's Ahead? What's In Stores Now?" *Consumer Reports,* vol. 60, February 1995, pp. 96–101.

141. Clothes Washers: Energy Efficiency and Consumption Trends, Assoc. of Home Appliance Manufacturers, Chicago, Ill., 1993.

142. Energy Conservation Standards for Consumer Products—Dishwashers, Clothes Washers, and Clothes Dryers, technical support document, U.S. Dept. of Energy, Washington, D.C., December 1990.

143. "Washing Machines," *Consumer Reports*, vol. 50, June 1985, pp. 359–363.

144. "Washing Machines," *Consumer Reports*, vol. 47, October 1982, pp. 508–512.

145. "Washing Machines," *Consumer Reports*, vol. 43, October 1978, pp. 572–577.

146. ENERGY STAR® Partnerships: Volume Purchase of High-Performance Clothes Washers, program brochure, U.S. Dept. of Energy, Washington, D.C., June 1997.

147. Mayer et al, *Residential End Uses of Water*, pp.107–108.

148. Mayer et al, *Residential End Uses of Water*, p. 95.

149. Consortium for Energy Efficiency, "Residential Clothes Washer Initiative," *CEE Fact Sheet*, January 2000.

150. John Kesselring and Richard Gillman, "Horizontal-Axis Washing Machines," *EPRI Journal*, vol. 22, no. 1, January/February, 1997, pp. 38–41.

151. Sandi Douglas Edgemon, U.S. Department of Energy Clothes Washer Volume Purchase, Pacific Northwest National Laboratory (U.S. Department of Energy), Richland, Wash., 1997.

152. "Horizontal Axis Technology May Improve Clothes Washer Efficiency," *The Cross Section* (published by High Plains Underground Water Conservation District No. 1, Lubbock, Texas), September 1997, p. 2.

153. "Program Summaries," *CEE Update: Residential Clothes Washers*, Consortium for Energy Efficiency, Boston, Mass., May 2000, pp. 6–11.

154. Mayer et al, *Residential End Uses of Water*, Table A.1, pp. 202–246.

155. Lawrence Berkeley National Laboratory, *Buying Energy-Efficient Products*, "How to Buy Energy-Efficient Family-Sized Commercial Clothes Washers," prepared for the U.S. Dept. of Energy's Federal Energy Management Program, Washington, D.C., November 2000, p. CA-5.

156. Commercial, Family-Sized Washers: An Initiative Description of the Consortium for Energy Efficiency, Consortium for Energy Efficiency, Boston, Mass., 1998, pp. 4–7.

157. InfoBulletin 1: Recycling Major Home Appliances, Appliance Recycling Information Center, Washington, D.C., June 1998.

158. Consortium for Energy Efficiency, *CEE Update: Commercial Clothes Washer Program Summary* (draft), June 2000.

159. Personal communication, Curt Nichols, City of Portland Energy Office, Portland, Ore., July 22, 1998.

160. "Oregon Laundromat Gets a Make Over," *Water Conservation News*, Water Conservation Office, California Dept. of Water Resources, Sacramento, Calif., October 1997, p. 8.

161. InfoBulletin 3: State White Goods Disposal Laws (August 1996), Appliance Recycling Information Center, Washington, D.C., June 1998.

162. "Dishing It Out: We Put 27 Dishwashers, Including Expensive European Models, to Very Tough Tests," *Consumer Reports*, vol. 64, March 1999, pp. 50–53.

163. Super-Efficient Home Appliance Initiative: Dishwashers, Consortium for Energy Efficiency, Boston, Mass., www.ceeformt.org/resid/seha/dishw/dishw-main.php3, Sept. 26, 2000.

164. "Dishwashers," *Consumer Reports*, vol. 66, May 2001, pp. 40–43.

165. "Dishing Out Dollars: Many Pricey Dishwashers Offer Surprisingly Few Pluses," *Consumer Reports*, vol. 63, March 1998, p. 37.

166. "Less Noisy, Less Thirsty: New Dishwashers Continue to Become Quieter and More Water Efficient," *Consumer Reports*, vol. 62, January 1997, p. 42.

167. "Clean Enough for You? The Best Dishwashers Do the Job on 'Normal,' Even If You Don't Rinse First," *Consumer Reports*, vol. 65, March 2000, pp. 47–50.

168. Mayer et al, *Residential End Uses of Water*, pp. 107–108.

169. Mayer et al, *Residential End Uses of Water*, p. 95.

170. Dishwashers and Clothes Washers: Water Consumption and Conservation Facts, Assoc. of Home Appliance Manufacturers, Chicago, Ill., 1991.

171. Dishwashers: Energy Efficiency and Consumption Trends, Assoc. Home Appliance Manufacturers, Chicago, Ill., Oct. 30, 1997.

172. "Dishwashers," *Consumer Reports*, vol. 52, June 1987, pp. 384–391.

173. "Dishwashers," *Consumer Reports 2000 Buying Guide*, Consumers Union of the United States, Yonkers, N.Y., 1999, pp. 90–92.

174. Statistical Abstract of the United States: 1998, Table 1223—Appliances and Office Equipment Used by Households, By Region and Family Income (1997), U.S. Bureau of the Census, Oct. 13, 1998.

175. Assoc. of Home Appliance Manufacturers, *Trends and Forecasts: Industry Shipments of Major Appliances*, Assoc. of Home Appliance Manufacturers, Washington, D.C., May 2000.

176. J. D. Lutz et al, Modeling Patterns of Hot Water Use in Households, Lawrence Berkeley National Laboratory, LBL-37805, UC-1600, November 1996, p. 5.

177. Mayer et al, *Residential End Uses of Water*, p. 95.

178. Lawrence Berkeley National Laboratory, *Buying Energy-Efficient Products*, "How to Buy an Energy-Efficient Residential Dishwasher," prepared for the U.S. Dept. of Energy's Federal Energy Management Program, Washington, D.C., October 1998, pp. RA-3 to RA-4.

179. Oregon Residential Energy Tax Credit, program brochure prepared by the Oregon Office of Energy, Portland, Ore., January 1998.

3

Landscape Water Use and Efficiency Measures

"Plants don't waste water; people do."

THIS CHAPTER describes water use for irrigating landscaped areas, including lawns, and presents water-efficiency measures for conserving water on residential and nonresidential landscapes. Descriptions of the water-efficiency measures include potential water savings plus related benefits and costs. Specific water-efficiency measures are presented.

PHOTO COURTESY OF JANE HELLER PLOESER

Figure 3.1 This natural landscaped yard relies only on rainwater that is more than sufficient to maintain its lush appearance. In contrast, a typical American single-family home uses about 10,000 gallons of water a year for lawn irrigation. (Photo courtesy of Andy Wasowski)

Landscape Water Use

The volume of water used for lawn and landscape (nonagricultural) irrigation in the United States is not well documented but is estimated to be significant. Residential water demand in the United States averages more than 26 billion gallons per day (bgd), according to the U.S. Geological Survey (USGS),[1] and an estimated 7.8 bgd (about 30%) is devoted to outdoor use, primarily lawn irrigation. A typical suburban lawn in America soaks up about 10,000 gallons of supplemental (nonrainwater) water a year.[2]

In the summer months, particularly during hot or dry weather, many U.S. water supply systems experience peak demands 1.5 to 3.0 times higher than average demand on a winter day. Most water utilities have the capacity to meet peak demands within limits, although when peak use is particularly high or lasts for a sustained period of time, the public is often asked or required to limit water use, particularly for lawn irrigation. A chief concern of water suppliers during peak-use periods is the system's ability to maintain adequate water pressure for basic functions such as consumption and toilet flushing, to supply tall buildings (e.g., hospitals and office towers), and, especially important, to provide water for firefighting.

Although design and irrigation practices for many landscaped areas in the United States do not use water efficiently and no longer represent the native environment, the extent to which irrigated landscaping is discretionary is debatable. From one perspective, excessive irrigation increases water costs, depletes water supply sources and other natural systems, adds to pollution from lawn and other landscape chemicals, and requires considerable time, labor, and energy for maintenance. From another viewpoint, irrigated landscapes support important functional, recreational, aesthetic, and economic interests for society, including erosion control, temperature modification, and the creation of recreational areas such as playing fields, parks, and golf courses. Such irrigated areas not only enhance the functional and aesthetic value of land but also expand the economic value of residential and commercial real estate as well as the public outdoor spaces around which communities are sustained (Figure 3.1).[3]

Conventional notions of what affects water use on landscaped areas are changing as more daring communities, water suppliers, and individuals make commitments to stop wasting water. Historically, the amount of water used for landscape irrigation and other factors that drive peak water demands were assumed to be immutable givens necessitating the construction of large water supply and treatment facilities. Now, water supply systems such as that managed by the city of Albuquerque, New Mexico, are challenging such assumptions with innovative conservation strategies. Since 1995, when Albuquerque launched a comprehensive, long-term conservation program with the goal of reducing per capita water demand by 30% by 2004, the city has reduced its per capita demand by about 20%. Before the program, outdoor water demand accounted for 50% of water use; now it comprises about 40%. These savings have been achieved despite a growing population. The water savings have been attributed to several program measures, including conservation-oriented landscaping, ordinances restricting water waste, and a rebate of up to $250 for homeowners who reduce turf, according to Jean Witherspoon, Albuquerque's water conservation officer.[4]

Outdoor Residential Water Use

In the United States, outdoor residential water use for turf and landscape irrigation and other purposes (e.g., car washing, cleaning, swimming pools) is estimated to average 31.7 gallons per capita per day (gpcd). This figure is adapted from a USGS national database of water use reported by public water supply systems indicating that combined indoor and outdoor residential water use in the United States averages 101 gpcd.[5] A separate study reports that indoor single-family use averages 69.3 gpcd,[6] leaving a balance of 31.7 gpcd that can be attributed to outdoor use. On average, 80 to 90% of the outdoor component of residential water use (25 to 29 gpcd) goes to watering lawns, plants, and gardens.

Local variations from estimates of national average single-family outdoor water use can be extreme, depending on the region. The amount of water used outdoors in the United States and Canada can range from a few gallons per capita per day to hundreds of gallons, or from 10 to 75% of total residential water demand,[7] as shown in Figure 3.2. Hot, dry areas of the United States, such as Texas, California, and the Southwest, typically have the highest per capita outdoor water use. Such high-volume use often grossly exceeds natural rainfall levels.

High estimates of outdoor water demand typically do not apply to other U.S. regions, particularly New England and the Pacific Northwest, because these areas have more rainfall and cooler climates. Outdoor water use in cool, wet climates

We talk [water] scarcity, yet we have set [some of] our largest cities in deserts, and then have insisted on surrounding ourselves with Kentucky bluegrass. Our words are those of the Sahara Desert; our policies are those of the Amazon River."
—Richard Lamm, Governor of Colorado, 1975-1987

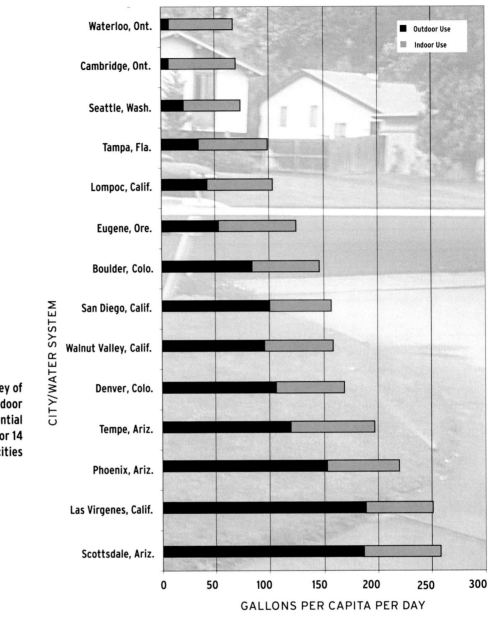

Figure 3.2 Survey of average outdoor and indoor single-family residential water use reported for 14 North American cities

CITY/WATER SYSTEM

Waterloo, Ont.
Cambridge, Ont.
Seattle, Wash.
Tampa, Fla.
Lompoc, Calif.
Eugene, Ore.
Boulder, Colo.
San Diego, Calif.
Walnut Valley, Calif.
Denver, Colo.
Tempe, Ariz.
Phoenix, Ariz.
Las Virgenes, Calif.
Scottsdale, Ariz.

■ Outdoor Use
■ Indoor Use

0   50   100   150   200   250   300

GALLONS PER CAPITA PER DAY

Source: Adapted from Reference 7

usually constitutes 10 to 30% of average residential water demand. For example, water-use studies in Vermont[8] and the metropolitan Boston[9] area reported outdoor water use to be less than 10% of total, year-round, residential water demand, and the percentage was not significantly higher in warm months. On the other hand, this pattern may be changing because summertime peak demand in the Northeast has been increasing in recent years. Growing affluence, more new homes with in-ground irrigation systems, and hotter summers appear to be responsible.

In the southeastern United States, which has a warm climate and generally receives high levels of rainfall, native and water-efficient landscapes can thrive easily. Still, as in other regions of the United States, excessive outdoor water use in the Southeast is not uncommon.

Principal factors that influence residential water use for landscape irrigation are climate, amount of natural rainfall, the price of water, household income, and, perhaps most influential of all, the prevailing landscape aesthetic. Today, a lush green lawn is established as the standard groundcover for the ideal American home.

High-volume outdoor water use for lawn and landscape watering is often associated with single-family residential accounts. "These customers tend to be well-educated, affluent, professional people who desire large, lush, well-maintained turf areas," notes Nancy G. Scott, conservation manager for Water District No. 1 of Johnson County, Kansas. Other customer characteristics associated with high-volume outdoor use include new homes, large areas of turf, automatic irrigation systems, and high-water-use grasses.[10]

Outdoor Water Use by Multifamily Dwellings Is Often Low

On a per capita basis, outdoor water use by apartment dwellers in multiple-family units tends to be low or even negligible; on a per household basis, it is typically much lower than that of single-family homes in a given area. Exceptions include customers in affluent multifamily complexes featuring large irrigated landscaped areas, swimming pools, fountains, and maintenance practices that use water (for example, sidewalk cleaning).

Nonresidential Outdoor Water Use

Outdoor water use by nonresidential customers such as commercial and publicly owned landscaped areas is largely devoted to turf irrigation. Demand for irrigation water among nonresidential customers varies considerably and is difficult to generalize about because of variations in size of landscaped area, plant materials, climate, rainfall, water costs, and other factors. Overall, irrigated turf for recreational areas, including the more than 16,000 golf courses in the United States,[11] demands some 2.7 bgd,[12] about twice the amount consumed by New York City. In Pima County, Arizona, a typical 18-hole golf course uses 185 million gallons a year, an average of about 500,000 gallons per day (gpd), according to state officials.[13]

Increasing Water Rates Can Encourage Conservation

Increased water rates can be a strong incentive for water users to reduce excessive outdoor use. Low- and middle-income residential customers in particular tend to be sensitive to the price of water. Affluent homeowners are sometimes indifferent to the cost of water and may curb waste only if they are required to by law or if they are convinced through education that conservation is the right thing to do. Increasing block rate structures, seasonal rate charges, and other pricing strategies may be used to help reduce demand. Depending on how water rates are structured, reductions in consumer demand may be short- or long-term. Increased rates are sometimes implemented only during summer months to reduce peak use. An increasing rate structure charges more per unit of de-

Figure 3.3 Street runoff from overwatered lawns is one of the most common signs of outdoor water waste. (Photo courtesy of Denver Water)

mand, e.g., $3 for the first 10,000 gallons of water used, $5 for the next 10,000 gallons, and so on.

The Irvine Ranch Water District (IRWD) in Irvine, California, has used pricing strategies successfully to discourage excessive outdoor water use. By implementing an increasing block rate structure, the IRWD has reduced outdoor watering among customers by nearly 50%. Each customer group in the IRWD service area receives a designated water allocation that sets the upper limit of efficient use for watering their particular property. IRWD determines the residential allocation based on the assumption that indoor use is about 80 gpcd, with outdoor watering a function of weather, evapotranspiration estimates, and the size of the landscaped area to be irrigated.[14] Customers who exceed their target allocation pay a higher rate.

Sources of Landscape Water Waste

Poor irrigation scheduling— watering too often and for too long—is the primary source of water waste associated with landscape irrigation. Inefficient irrigation systems and practices can be observed frequently during warm weather. A common example is wet sidewalks, pavement, and highway areas that have received the overspray and runoff from irrigation systems that are not accurately directed to adjacent turf areas, as shown in Figure 3.3. In addition to improper scheduling, other causes of water waste by irrigation include poor irrigation system design, inefficient equipment, and poor maintenance. Fixed cultural notions about what constitutes an attractive and functional landscape are also an underlying cause of water waste. Only in recent years has awareness of the need for landscape water efficiency become a concern for the public and for members of the "green industry" (e.g., horticulturists, landscape architects, retail and wholesale nurseries, irrigation system designers, contractors, and landscape maintenance managers).

Lawn Crazy?

The American obsession with lawns and lawn care products has come under scrutiny in recent years because of concerns about wasted water and the burdens of time, cost, and pollution that a well-manicured green lawn exacts from its owner and the larger environment. Turf grass, planted on residential lawns as well as corporate, government, and roadside areas, covers an estimated 30 million[15] to 50 million acres in the United States,[16] an area larger than Pennsylvania and greater than the acreage used to grow any single U.S. agricultural crop.[17] Members of approximately 60 million U.S. households regularly spend time engaged in lawn care.[18] Americans spend more than $750 million annually just to seed this grass, plus an additional $25 billion for mowers, hoses, clippers, gardening gloves, and related tools.[19] An estimated nearly 600 million gallons of gasoline are used annually for lawn mowing equipment in the United States.[20] Also significant is the amount of lawn chemicals applied on residential properties; homeowners apply nearly 10 times more pesticide per acre of turf than farmers use on crops.[21]

Origins of the Lawn Aesthetic in the United States

In *The Lawn: A History of an American Obsession*, author Virginia Scott Jenkins traces America's current multibillion-dollar turf grass industry back to cultural influences associated with the gardens of early European immigrants and to economic links with the post–Civil War period.[21] As the United States began to rebuild and grow after the Civil War, so did home and landscape development. The first U.S. patents for lawn mowers were granted in 1868,[22] followed by the first sprinkler patent in 1871.[23] Frank J. Scott's publication "The Art of Beautifying Suburban Home Grounds," which appeared in 1870, exhorted homeowners to "let your lawn be your home's velvet robe." At a time when detached housing was emerging as the preferred American habitat,[24] Scott, the founder of a lawn care company with the same name, extolled the virtues of the lawn. "A smooth, closely shaven surface of grass is by far the most essential element of beauty of the grounds of a suburban house," he opined.[25]

By the beginning of the twentieth century, U.S. turf grass expansion was accelerating, spurred by seed, lawn care, and irrigation equipment suppliers and by the golf industry. By 1902, more than a thousand golf clubs had been established in the United States.[26] Now, a century later, lawns are deeply rooted in American culture. The word "lawn" is included in the name of 155 U.S. communities, and innumerable products related to the lawn image or lifestyle have been marketed and sold.[27] Jenkins posits that America's front lawns symbolize human control—superiority—over the environment: "Americans have moved from regional landscapes

We made too many wrong mistakes."

—Yogi Berra

based on local vegetation and climate to a national landscape based on an aesthetic that considers grassy front yards necessary to domestic happiness." However, she adds, such attempts at dominance over nature have not completely succeeded, and the perfect green carpet is more a constant challenge than a fixed reality.

Advances in Landscape Water-Use Efficiency

New approaches to landscape design, better choices in turf and plant selection, and improvements in irrigation technology are key steps in boosting landscape irrigation efficiency. The current American lawn aesthetic, which prizes a fine-bladed green mat, may be changing. In her book, *Planting Noah's Garden: Further Adventures in Backyard Ecology*, author Sara Stein declares that lawns are the ecological equivalent of asphalt—"ridiculously expensive, ecologically arid, an area in which nothing can live but their own pests."[28] Increasing water shortages and costs, climate change and variability (including more frequent droughts), less discretionary time for lawn care, and the desire for more natural landscapes that do not rely on chemicals may contribute to more sustainable landscapes in the future.[29]

Water-Wise Landscaping Principles

Several landscape design and management approaches that emphasize low-water-use and native plants and other water-saving practices have been introduced in recent years and are starting to take hold. Terms such as *water-wise*, *Xeriscape*, and *natural landscaping* describe somewhat different conceptual approaches to landscape design and management, but the approaches have similar goals—reduced water demand, less maintenance time and lower maintenance costs, and little or no reliance on lawn or garden chemicals.

Xeriscape,™ a trademarked term pronounced "zera-scape" (not "zero"), is derived from the Greek word "xeros" (dry) and "scape" from landscape. The Xeriscape concept incorporates seven principles that promote quality landscapes as well as conserving water and protecting the environment:

- Proper planning and design
- Soil analysis
- Appropriate plant selection
- Practical turf areas
- Efficient irrigation
- Use of mulches
- Appropriate maintenance

The Xeriscape principles—and the term itself—were conceived by a water conservation task force formed by Denver Water, then called the Denver Water Department, in 1981. Since that time, the principles have inspired many water-efficient demonstration gardens, programs, and ordinances, particularly in hot, dry regions of the United States. A number of water utilities have incorporated these principles into "water-wise" outdoor water conservation programs promoting the use of native or low-water-use plants, turf reduction (sometimes facilitated by "cash for grass" rebate programs), and improved watering schedules

Hudson River School. (First American school of Landscape painting active from 1825-1870): "Adapting the European ideas about nature to a growing pride in the beauty of their homeland, for the first time a number of American artists began to devote themselves to landscape painting instead of portraiture…. The works of these artists reflected a new concept of wilderness—one in which man was an insignificant intrusion in a landscape more beautiful than fearsome."
— *The Columbia Encyclopedia: Sixth Edition, 2000*

(e.g., changing the frequency of watering or the time of day). Often, local members of the green industry have championed and facilitated these initiatives. Program participants—homeowners, businesses, and managers of public properties—have, to varying extents, transformed their landscapes into more water-efficient yet lush, attractive areas.[30] Studies have shown that implementing water-wise or Xeriscape landscaping practices can achieve at least a 50% reduction in water use compared with conventional landscaping practices, savings that are typically accompanied by reduced landscape maintenance and chemical costs as well.[31]

The terms *water-wise, Xeriscape,* and similar expressions that promote water-efficient landscaping are often used interchangeably, but they do not always have quite the same meaning. Some conservation managers prefer to use *Xeriscape* when educating the public about low-water-use landscaping practices because the term prompts the question, "What's that?" More than a few water conservation programs incorporate the Xeriscape principles but use terms such as *water-wise, water-smart,* or *low-water* to refer to their programs, avoiding *Xeriscape* because it can be misunderstood to advocate desertlike conditions—only rocks and sand. Realistically, people in cool, wet climates have difficulty relating to a water-efficient landscaping approach that includes "dry" in its definition, despite the fact that the Xeriscape principles can easily be adapted to areas such as New England and the Pacific Northwest. Furthermore, there are those who now consider Xeriscape to be outdated or not ecologically sustainable, in part because its principles accept a reliance on supplemental irrigation, the use of landscape chemicals, and the establishment of non-native plants. It may make sense to use the term *Xeriscape* for water-efficient landscaping programs in hot, dry regions, but terms such as *water-wise landscaping* may have greater acceptance in wet or cooler regions.

Beyond Xeriscape: The Natural Landscaping Movement

A natural landscaping movement is burgeoning in the United States and Canada. In many ways, the natural landscaping approach surpasses Xeriscape and similar water-wise principles by advocating design and management concepts that rely on native plants and minimal, if any, irrigation other than rainwater. The purpose of natural landscaping is to preserve and reintroduce indigenous plants, a practice that can virtually eliminate the need for supplemental watering after the plants are established, barring extreme drought. This naturalistic approach embodies the philosophy of seeking a more harmonious and restorative relationship with nature.[32]

Restoration of native landscapes is occurring in an increasing number of areas, including homeowners' yards, community properties, golf courses, roadways, and corporate landscapes. In the midwestern United States, numerous residential and corporate properties have been converted to native turf and plants. For example, Prairie Crossing, as shown in Figure 3.4, is a 667-acre residential subdivision located 40 miles north of Chicago. Prairie Crossing has defined its landscape by reconstructing the native prairie vegetation that once flourished on the site. Native grasses such as prairie brome, fescue, and Virginia wild rye and wildflowers such as purple prairie clover are a few of the indigenous plants that have been reestablished. As this vegetation has returned, so have

The landscape of the United States will shift drastically in the next few decades. Western states are running out of water. Baby boomers everywhere are worried about chemicals on the lawns where their kids play. And a traditional lawn sometimes just takes too much time to care for."

—Margaret Roach, garden editor of *Martha Stewart Living*

Figure 3.4 Natural landscaping practices rely on native plants and turf grasses, such as those used in this housing subdivision in Prairie Crossing, Illinois. (Photo courtesy of Michael Sands, Prairie Crossing, Illinois)

the leopard frogs and other wildlife that were once driven away. In addition to reinstating the region's natural beauty, the native prairie grasses are helping to control erosion and have reduced runoff by 50% compared with conventional lawns. Further, the grasses also provide a natural filter for storm water that drains into a lake used for community swimming and fishing. "The beauty of the prairie comes from the power of what we've lost by our own hand," says Vicky Ranney, a historian who helped develop Prairie Crossing. To further reestablish cultural connections to the prairie era, Margaret McCurry and other Chicago architects who designed many of the homes in Prairie Crossing often added eaves and porches and situated residences on wide streets built around groves of old trees. The community helps pay for maintaining its prairies and wetlands by charging a 0.5% levy on home sales (an average of $1,500). Houses in Prairie Crossing are clustered on about 200 acres of land in order to preserve more than 450 acres of open space.[33]

In a similar initiative to restore the native landscape, Sears, Roebuck & Company's headquarters outside Chicago was designed to eschew the conventional corporate lawn, as shown in Figure 3.5. In place of a lawn are extensive open areas of prairie grasses and wildflowers. The company's director of facility resources, Richard Kotarba, describes the site as "a less stressful landscape than manicured lawns."[33]

Dewees Island, a 1,206-acre barrier island off the coast of Charleston, South Carolina, allows *only* indigenous plants on the entire island. When the island began to be developed in 1991, its master plan set aside 65% of the land for permanent conservation. Formal lawns are not allowed on Dewees; according to the development's subdivision policy, all plants used for landscaping must be native to the coastal plain barrier island.[34]

Several organizations are also advancing the ideas and practices of natural landscaping. The Wild Ones–Natural Landscapers, Ltd., a nonprofit organization based in Appleton, Wisconsin, has about 3,000 members.[32] The Wild Ones promotes the use of native species to encourage biodiversity and environmentally sound landscaping practices. In recent years, several publications on natural landscaping practices have emerged—*Wild Ones® Journal*,[35] *Source Book on Natural Landscaping for Local Officials*,[36] and others.

Reuse: Pros and Cons

The practice of reusing treated municipal wastewater for irrigation purposes is becoming more accepted, particularly for large turf areas such as golf courses, playing fields, and municipal parks. In some instances, reuse is a logical, cost-effective method for irrigating areas that would otherwise require more valuable potable water. In fact, there are more areas with abundant supplies of wastewater that could be reclaimed for nonpotable uses than there are communities with excess freshwater supplies. At the same time, some conservationists view reclaimed water as aiding and abetting excessive water use for landscape

Figure 3.5   The corporate office site for Sears' Prairie Stone Campus in Hoffman Estates, Illinois, includes approximately 200 acres of native prairie grasses and woodlands. (Photo courtesy of Conservation Design Forum, Inc.)

irrigation without addressing the basic problems—poor choices in landscape design, nonadaptive and nonnative plants with high water demands, overbuilt and improperly controlled irrigation systems, and inadequate consumer awareness about the environmental consequences of outdoor water waste.

The notion that using reclaimed water, particularly for residential irrigation, is a "sustainable" resource practice is debatable. Because *indoor* residential water use per household is decreasing in the United States as a result of the installation of low-volume plumbing fixtures and appliances since the early 1990s, the amount of wastewater available for reuse *outdoors* is also decreasing on a per capita basis. For the typical homeowner who uses hundreds of gallons of water for a single irrigation cycle, an amount exceeding daily water use indoors, augmenting irrigation supplies with utility-supplied reclaimed water or household graywater is not a truly sustainable system. From a resource-management perspective, reclaimed water can help recharge aquifers in some areas, whereas in others it may rob streams and rivers of vital returns needed to preserve natural habitat and instream flows, particularly during summer when water levels are low.

Like other water "supply-side" options, a reclaimed water system requires considerable resources—materials, energy, chemicals, and money—to construct, operate, and maintain its treatment, storage, and distribution facilities. Some communities may find it more cost-effective to invest in reusing their wastewater than to tap new potable supplies. Others may question the significant economic and resource investments needed to satisfy high-volume demand for lawn irrigation because they do not consider such demand an *essential* need and are concerned about the consequences of excessive irrigation, no matter what source it relies on. In addition, large-scale reuse of wastewater is still relatively new in North America, and the true costs of such reuse systems may not yet be fully understood. For example, the town of Cary, North Carolina, has invested $10 million in a reclaimed water system to supply irrigation water to its residential and commercial customers beginning in 2001.[37] Bulk water customers such as landscapers and construction companies will be offered reclaimed water free of charge. From another perspective, David Davis, an irrigation consultant in Rancho Cucamonga, California, notes that using reclaimed water for irrigation can be expensive when the reclaimed water must be stored underground. According to Davis, "Many water districts will say that reclaimed water costs 20 to 25 percent less money than potable water. The reality is that 10 to 15 percent more water is needed, because it is continually leached through soil."[38]

Automatic Irrigation Systems on the Rise: A Step Backward?

Despite increasing public awareness in some regions of the value of conservation, water-efficient landscape practices, and native plants, there is a growing trend to include automatic irrigation systems in the construction of new single-family homes. Automatic irrigation systems can be quite water-efficient if used properly. Unfortunately, for convenience, most homeowners operate them with a "set it and forget it" approach, which results in a landscape that is watered whether it needs to be or not. Automatic irrigation systems were less common in years past. Perhaps their current popularity is a reflection of affluence as well as the reality that many working adults are unwilling to devote time to such tasks as dragging a hose around to water the lawn. Further, the popularity of home gardening and perfect-looking green lawns—along with the water required to sustain them—appears to be increasing, particularly among the baby-boom generation of homeowners.

Benefits and Costs of Landscape Water Conservation

Numerous economic and environmental costs are associated with inefficient irrigation practices, particularly during periods of peak water demand. In order to satisfy consumer demand for landscape irrigation water during peak-use periods, a water supply system must have additional pumping and treatment capacity. Such enhanced infrastructure increases the water system's capital and operating costs as well as the ratepayers' water bills. Excess water use for landscape irrigation contributes to the adverse environmental impact of unsustainable water use, causing overdrafted groundwater sources, reduced stream flows, and degradation of water quality as well as concomitant disruptions to the ecosystems that depend on these water sources.

A number of benefits can accrue to utilities and residential customers who conserve water used for landscape irrigation. Similarly, some costs and behavior modification requirements are associated with water-efficient landscaping practices.

Benefits

- Reduced peak water demand
- Reduced groundwater overdraft and contamination
- Reduced water costs
- Improved long-term water utility revenue stability and less frequent rate adjustments
- Smaller water supply facilities (reservoirs, storage tanks, wells, pumps, motors)
- Reduced runoff, soil erosion, and costs for stormwater management
- Creation of distinctive, attractive properties
- Reduced use of lawn chemicals (fertilizers, pesticides, and herbicides)
- Reduced energy costs for landscape maintenance (electric and gasoline mowers, blowers, and edgers)
- Reduced air pollution and noise from gasoline-powered mowers and landscape equipment
- Extended life for lawn-mowing equipment and irrigation systems
- Reduced labor costs for mowing and landscape maintenance
- Increased native plant diversity
- Preservation of wildlife habitat and instream flows
- Reduced plant disease, rot, and mortality caused by overwatering
- Reduced need for construction and operation of alternative supply systems (e.g., reuse or desalinated water)

Water conservation and resource efficiency do not mean an end to business for green industry companies—just the opposite. A water-efficient landscape offers tremendous opportunities to sell higher valued services, introduce new plants and new technologies, make site upgrades, and attract new business."
—Tom Ash, *Landscape Management for Water Savings: How to Profit From a Water Efficient Future*

Costs

- Resistance to changing outdoor water-use habits, despite long-term benefits
- Increased time and care for maintenance during the transition from a conventional to a water-efficient landscape
- Difficulty in accepting the look of low-water-use and native plants compared with water-intensive turf and exotic imported plants
- Potential reductions in business among conventional green industry product and service providers who do not offer water-wise and natural landscaping services
- Potential short-term water utility revenue instability and more frequent rate adjustments during the years when outdoor demand drops as a result of conservation

AUDIT

Basic Steps in a Landscape Water Audit

The first step toward increasing landscape water-use efficiency typically involves conducting a water audit and preparing a site water conservation plan.

A landscape water audit for a residential property takes about an hour, depending on the number of steps performed and the amount of time spent with the customer. Water audits of large landscaped areas, such as public parks and golf courses, can take four to eight hours or even longer for sites with extensive irrigation systems. Additional time will be required for follow-up analysis and paperwork back at the office.

Landscape water audits usually yield the largest water savings for residential and nonresidential customers who rely on irrigation controllers that are incorrectly programmed or who have malfunctioning or poorly designed irrigation systems. Residential and large water audit programs vary greatly in design, but those that educate customers one-on-one about water-wise concepts, recommend site-specific conservation measures, and provide or install an efficiency device along with back-up technical support should result in at least a 10 to 15% reduction in landscape water demand.[39]

The basic steps for conducting a residential or small landscape water audit are listed here, along with recommended conservation measures. A sample residential or small landscape audit data collection form is provided in Appendix F, *Worksheet: Landscape and IrrigationWater Audit*. Basic steps for completing the audit are as follows:

1. **Explain purpose of audit.** Explain to the customer the purpose of the outdoor water audit (e.g., to identify ways to save water that will benefit the customer and the larger community). The customer may also be interested in indirect benefits of conservation, such as avoidance or reduced use of fertilizers, herbicides, and pesticides or reduced requirements for energy and labor.

2. **Review outdoor water use.** Based on water billing data or actual meter readings, review with the customer his/her water use, particularly the amount used for landscape watering and other outdoor purposes. Subtracting average winter or indoor use from total water demand yields a simple estimate of outdoor water demand for customers whose winter

use includes no irrigation (exceptions include homes in warm regions with year-round landscapes). If the customer's average indoor use is unknown, subtract an estimate of 70 gpcd from the total water demand for each household occupant to extract the outdoor component of that customer's water use. (Other methods can determine landscape water use more precisely, but this simple technique should suffice for customer education.)

3. **Evaluate lawn, landscape, and irrigation features.** Evaluate the water efficiency of the customer's landscape and irrigation features. Record the total irrigated area (this can be determined with a measuring wheel), including the square footage of each irrigated zone and the type of plant material being irrigated, particularly turf grass. Note the condition of the turf in terms of excess thatch, soil compaction, or brown spots. Some government agencies (local, county, and state) and private businesses have collected detailed information on property features such as landscaping and impervious areas in geographic information system (GIS) files. These data can be valuable to conservation managers because they can preclude the need for on-site measurements, can help prioritize audits, and can be used to prepare water budgets.

4. **Measure water use of irrigation equipment.** Measure the amount of water used for a typical irrigation cycle by running the customer's manual or automatic irrigation system for a full cycle. Measure water use in gallons per minute for each zone irrigated as well as total watering time. To keep the audit under an hour, it may be necessary to run only a part of the customer's typical irrigation program; adjust for this and make a best estimate based on the data collected. For automatic irrigation systems, locate the irrigation controller and record the following data: amount of time required for a full irrigation cycle, number of days per week watering occurs, number of zones irrigated, duration of watering for each zone, and presence of a rain sensor, moisture sensor, or a "cycle and soak" feature. Run the irrigation controller for each zone, returning to the meter after each run to measure the amount of water used per minute and in total. During each run, check sprinkler heads, microirrigation emitters, and bubblers for leaks, and check for breaks or malfunctions such as tilted heads, missing heads, and overspray. Complete this process for each zone, making notes of all findings. Perform a similar measurement of water use for manually operated sprinklers and hoses.

Conduct a "catch-can" test. A sprinkler system's distribution uniformity (DU) is sometimes measured as part of a landscape audit using the "catch-can" test, as shown in Figure 3.6. The catch-can test measures how evenly and how much water is applied by collecting water in graduated containers or small cans (e.g., tuna cans) placed at evenly spaced intervals throughout an irrigated area. A DU of 65 to 75% is acceptable, assuming no overspray or runoff occurs.[40] Some water conservation managers use the catch-can test only when auditing large landscapes. For residential and small commercial properties, it is often more useful for customers to know how long (in minutes) and how often (how many days per week) to water than to understand the DU percentage. Also, the catch-can test requires more of the auditor's time (at least an additional 30 minutes), and accurate

According to one study, 24% of lawns have some sort of lawn ornament."
—www.uselessfacts.net

results depend on the cans being placed correctly. In lieu of performing the catch-can test, an auditor can point out obvious areas of overspray or underspray to help the customer improve DU.

5. Provide landscape water-efficiency recommendations.

- *Suggest water-wise, natural landscaping principles and plants.* Give the customer basic information about water-wise and natural landscaping design and management practices, including a list of recommended native and location-appropriate, low-water-use (but not invasive) plants. (For an explanation of invasive plants, see the sidebar entitled "Selecting Native Plants Helps Thwart Damage From Invasive Plants.")

- *Recommend the amount of water to apply per week.* Review the water demand recorded for each irrigation run, and suggest how the customer might modify irrigation cycles to save water. Advise the customer about how many days per week to water and how many minutes to water each zone. Depending on climate, conventional irrigated lawns typically need a maximum of 1 inch, sometimes 2 inches, of water per week, some of which may be provided by rainfall. The frequency of irrigation is generally once, or sometimes twice, a week, often for no more than 15 to 30 minutes, and it should occur only during early morning or evening hours to avoid the heat—and evaporation—of the day. This rule of thumb may vary somewhat by region, climate, and season, but a water audit should result in the customer using less water in the future than in the past. It is sometimes helpful for customers to know that 1 inch of water applied over a 1,000-square-foot area equals 624 gallons.

  Customers who use irrigation system controllers should also be advised about the recommended frequency and length of irrigation cycles per week, the amount of water needed for each irrigation zone, the amount of water needed to replace moisture lost to evapotranspiration, and adjustment of controllers when rainfall temporarily precludes the need for irrigation. A healthy, green lawn can often be maintained with irrigation volumes of 50 to 80% of reference evapotranspiration values.[41, 42]

- *Specify "hardware" conservation measures.* As needed, recommend or provide conservation devices (e.g., an automatic shutoff valve for hoses or an automatic rain-sensing device or switch that shuts off an automatic irrigation system during or after rainfall) and repairs or adjustments to sprinklers, hoses, and irrigation system controllers. Advise the customer about how often to reprogram the irrigation controller (usually at least once a month to accommodate seasonal changes). For homes with swimming pools, provide recommendations about pool covers, leaks, and water temperature (to control evaporative losses).

6. Leave information and install conservation devices. In addition to checking the efficiency of the irrigation system, give the customer a rain gauge, install rain sensors on automatic irrigation systems and shutoff valves on manual hoses, provide suggestions on turf and landscape design as well as low-water-use plants and grasses, and advise the customer about how to reduce environmental burdens and help control water costs. Provide published information about additional conservation measures

and programs for which the customer may be eligible (e.g., irrigation system retrofits and rebates) and a list of vendors who sell local native and low-water-use plants.

7. **Conduct post-audit follow-up.** Follow up water audits with a phone call, visit, or letter to review the results with customers and remind them to implement the measures recommended. Some utilities track customers' water use before and after the audit to evaluate the audit's effectiveness. Utilities with customized billing capabilities can provide before-and-after water-use data directly on the customer's water bill.

Figure 3.6 The catch-can irrigation test is used to measure the distribution uniformity and efficiency of a sprinkler irrigation system. (Photo courtesy of Denver Water)

Landscape Water-Efficiency Measures

This section describes water-efficient landscape irrigation practices and technologies that are applicable to residential and nonresidential properties. The following types of information are provided for each measure:

- *Purpose.* The general purpose of the measure is described, and background information is provided.

- *Conservation policies and regulations.* Examples of water conservation ordinances, regulations, and policies that apply to landscape practices and irrigation equipment are given.
- *Water-efficiency measures.* Potential water-efficiency measures are identified for each type of landscape practice or irrigation system.
- *Water savings, benefits, and costs.* Potential water savings and related benefits and costs associated with the measure are described.
- *Implementation.* Ideas and considerations for large-scale implementation of the measure are discussed.

When applicable, case studies are provided to illustrate potential water savings, benefits and costs, and program implementation considerations.

3.1 WATER-WISE LANDSCAPE PLANNING AND DESIGN

Water-wise and natural landscape planning, design, and implementation are much like conventional approaches in that they can be applied anywhere in the world. The key difference is that they take into account water-efficiency considerations, native and adaptive plants, natural features, and rainfall and climate characteristics for every aspect of the site.

Key considerations such as plant selection, turf areas, watering requirements, soil conditions, the use of mulches, and maintenance practices are carefully evaluated and incorporated into the design of a water-efficient landscape (Figure 3.7). It is a common misconception that water-wise or Xeriscape designs are merely recreations of desert environments and are appropriate only in limited areas such as the southwestern United States. On the contrary, water-wise and Xeriscape principles are universal and naturally adaptive. For example, a low-water-use landscape in the Southwest might emphasize cacti, succulents, and sandstone, whereas a water-wise landscape in the Central Plains would likely feature prairie grasses and other native and adaptive plants.

A residential yard, public park, or commercial or institutional landscape with a water-wise design can be just as lush, colorful, and attractive as a traditional landscaped area, as shown in Figure 3.8. The need for functional play and walk areas can easily be accommodated in low-water-use landscape designs as sections that add aesthetic character. A water-wise or Xeriscape landscape promotes restoration of the natural environment, because it invites the return of native or adaptive plants, shrubs, and trees that naturally flourish in the area. This approach is "gaining a foothold in areas never suited for turf grass," asserts Joseph M. Keyser, public education coordinator for the Montgomery County (Maryland) Department of Environmental Protection. "Habitat plantings and chemical-free garden management practices are bringing wildlife back to our homes and lives."[43]

The planning and design of a water-wise landscape take into account at least six basic site conditions:

- Existing soil, vegetation, and topography
- Local climate and microclimates

Fundamentals of Water-Wise Landscaping

The basic blueprint for designing and maintaining a water-efficient landscape can be summed up in eight steps.

1. **Group plants according to their water needs.** Place native and drought-tolerant plants together, separating them from thirsty ones. This makes irrigation easier and more water-efficient.

2. **Use native and low-water-use plants.** Nature offers an abundance of turf grasses, shrubs, perennials, ornamentals, trees, and other plants that can thrive in their native or adaptive environments with little or no water other than rainfall, once they have become established.

3. **Limit turf areas to those needed for practical uses.** Lawns claim the lion's share of landscape irrigation water. By limiting turf to areas used for recreation and other functional purposes, customers can reserve the rest of the landscaped area for alternative plants that are beautiful but less water-needy and easier to maintain.

4. **Use efficient irrigation systems.** If a landscape requires watering, at least be sure the irrigation system is as efficient as possible. Well-designed and -installed irrigation systems, drip rain sensors, automatic shutoff valves, properly programmed controllers, and regular maintenance of hoses and sprinkler heads are essential components of an efficient irrigation system.

5. **Schedule irrigation wisely.** Even the most water-efficient irrigation system can waste water because the amount of water it uses depends on how often and how long it is allowed to run. Watering once, possibly twice, a week for 15 to 30 minutes is adequate for most residential landscapes, particularly those that are not accustomed to being waterlogged. Lawns and plants that have been overwatered often need to make the transition to receiving less water slowly to avoid shock. Once they've been properly "water-stressed" and have deeper roots, they should be able to get along with less water.

6. **Make sure soil is healthy.** Healthy soil is like a great pair of shoes for plants—it will anchor and support them so they can thrive. Healthy soil amended with organic matter such as compost and other nutrients helps plants to retain moisture and resist evaporation. Soil that gets compacted, like that under turf or in other areas used for walking, should be aerated occasionally with a pitchfork or other equipment.

7. **Remember to mulch.** Place mulch over the soil around plants (leaving some space around the trunk) to reduce evaporation, limit heat stress, and inhibit weed growth. Organic mulches include compost, shredded bark, leaves, and sawdust.

8. **Provide regular maintenance.** All landscaped areas need maintenance to look good and stay healthy, plus maintenance helps to minimize water use. Control weeds so they won't steal water from cultivated plants. Minimize the use of fertilizer to avoid plant overgrowth and increased water needs. Repair hose and sprinkler head leaks. Make sure your irrigation system is programmed properly and is adjusted in response to changing temperatures and rainfall over the seasons.

Figure 3.7 Water-wise landscape planning and design involve careful consideration of site characteristics and native and low-water-use plant resource guides, among other factors. (Photo courtesy of Amy Vickers & Associates, Inc.)

Figure 3.8   An award-winning Xeriscape landscape in Denver (Photo courtesy of Denver Water)

- Sunny and shady areas
- Plant water-use zones (low-, medium-, and high-volume)
- Property uses and preferences (functional, aesthetic)
- The customer's landscape maintenance preferences

Conservation Policies and Regulations Related to Water-Efficient Landscape Planning and Design

- *Ordinances aimed at reducing water waste related to landscaping.* Some U.S. communities have established ordinances to reduce water waste caused by landscape overwatering, poor landscape design, and excess runoff. For example, the city of Albuquerque, New Mexico, instituted a Water Conservation Landscaping and Water Waste Ordinance to help reduce per capita water use by 30%. To reduce lawn irrigation and irrigation-related water waste, the city established local requirements for low-water-use plants and improved irrigation system design, scheduling, and maintenance practices. In new developments, at least 80% of the plants must be low- or medium-water-use; otherwise, the landscape can be subject to a water budget.[44] The California Model Water Efficient Landscape Ordinance, created by the state's Department of Water Resources, contains similar types of provisions.[45]
- *Sustainable landscape practices on federal properties.* In 2000, the U.S. government established a requirement for all federal agency landscaping programs, policies, and practices to promote the use of environmentally and economi-

cally beneficial landscape practices, including water conservation, on managed federal lands and in federally funded projects. The purpose of the requirements is to promote "sustainable landscape design and management," recognizing the interconnection of natural and human resources, site design, building design, water supply, energy management, waste prevention, and facility maintenance and operation.[46, 47] The requirements are based on five underlying principles: (1) use regionally native plants for landscaping; (2) design, use, and promote construction practices that minimize adverse effects on natural habitat; (3) prevent pollution wherever possible; (4) implement water- and energy-efficient landscaping practices, such as the use of efficient irrigation technologies, judicious watering, and mulches; and (5) create outdoor demonstration projects, such as native and wildlife gardens.

- *Requirements for submission of landscape plans with water-wise or Xeriscape design elements.* In several U.S. communities, plans for new and modified landscapes must be submitted for approval to ensure they meet water-efficiency requirements. Approval criteria often include such features as limiting irrigated areas, water budgeting, and efficient irrigation design and maintenance requirements. For example, the city of North Miami Beach, Florida, requires submission and approval of a landscape plan incorporating water-efficiency principles and practices before a building permit can be issued. Requirements include that plants be grouped and irrigated according to hydrozones and that no more than 40% of the total landscaped area be a high-water-use zone. The ordinance mandates that "the use of Xeriscape techniques shall be an integral component of the landscape design and plan. No building permit shall be issued unless such landscape plan complies with the provisions herein."[48] Similar provisions are included in the California Landscaping Act,[49] the Florida model landscape code,[50] and a landscaping regulation in North Marin Municipal Water District, California.[51]

- *Site preparation requirements for new landscaping.* To increase soil water retention and plant uptake, some communities require site preparation for new and renovated landscapes (e.g., aeration, scarification, amendment with organic material, and mulching). These requirements help newly established turf and plants to develop deep, healthy root systems that allow plants to thrive with less water. Examples of ordinances with provisions such as these include the California Model Water Efficient Landscape Ordinance,[45] the Florida model landscape code,[50] and policies established by the cities of Aurora and Boulder, Colorado.[50]

Water-Efficiency Measures for Landscape Planning and Design

Water-efficiency measures related to landscape planning and design include:[52–56]

Evaluate the Existing Landscape

Starting with a base map of the property, draw in basic site features such as a house or other structures, site orientation, natural stone outcroppings, and existing vegetation. Native or adaptive plants that flourish with little or no ir-

We shall never produce an art of landscaping worthwhile until we have learned to love the soil and the beauty of our homeland."
—Jans Jensen, landscape architect and conservationist (1860–1951)

rigation can be used as the foundation of a redesigned landscape. (If weeds or other invasive plants are present, this redesign phase is a good opportunity to remove them.) Next, use a sheet of tracing paper over the base map to do a property site analysis.[53, 54] Indicate the site's existing plant materials and topographical features—including rainfall, soil conditions, wind, slope and grade, sunny and shady areas, and established plantings—as well as aesthetic preferences.

Develop a Master Landscape Plan

After evaluating the existing landscape, prepare a master plan for the water-efficient or Xeriscape landscape. The master plan should address a number of design issues.

FUNCTIONAL TURF AREAS   The largest water savings from water-wise landscapes are often achieved by reducing turf areas. The amount of turf needed for walking, sitting, picnicking, and other recreational activities should be clearly defined. Nonfunctional areas can be covered with drought-tolerant turf grasses, alternative groundcovers, and "hardscapes" (landscaped areas covered with nonliving material) that are just as aesthetically pleasing as water-intensive turf grass. [53,57] For more information on designing practical turf areas, see Section 3.3, "Practical Turf Areas," later in this chapter.

NONFUNCTIONAL PLANT AND HARDSCAPE AREAS   Landscape areas that are not needed for functional purposes can be filled with native and adaptive (noninvasive) plants, trees, and shrubs as well as various hardscapes such as patios, decks, gravel areas, and rock gardens. Nonpermeable surfaces, such as concrete or pavement, contribute to runoff, whereas permeable areas, such as gravel and other porous paving materials, can help prevent water from accumulating on walkways, driveways, and parking areas.[53]

LANDSCAPE FORM   The form of a landscape can influence water efficiency if supplemental irrigation is required. For example, irregular designs, narrow strips of turf or plants, and small areas may be difficult to irrigate efficiently with automatic systems that deliver water in rectangular spray patterns or cause overspray to nearby walkways and roads; however, these design elements may be well suited to drip, watering can, or hand-held hose irrigation.[53]

GRADING AND DRAINAGE   Landscape grading and drainage also influence a site's water efficiency. The type of soil and the slope affect soil water infiltration and runoff rates. To boost detention of rainwater or irrigation water, create shallow basins in areas with plants that have high-volume water requirements. This simple water-harvesting technique increases infiltration and ensures better root saturation. Conversely, little or no grading may be preferable in areas that will not receive much water. For example, minimizing irrigated slopes will help reduce runoff and preserve topsoil. For this reason, turf grass that requires irrigation may not be a good choice for steep grades, particularly those encompassing large areas, because they are difficult to irrigate uniformly, require more time to mow,

As daunting as the prospects may seem as we search for ways to protect and make room for nature, we must remember that there are success stories in all of this. Although we may not be able to save every single species, we can each do our part to protect them. Some of the answers lie as close as our own backyards, and as far as the highways that transverse this nation to its outermost reaches."
—Lady Bird Johnson, Lady Bird Johnson Wildflower Center

and are more prone to brown spots during hot, dry periods.[53] For additional information on rain-harvesting techniques through drainage, see Section 3.4, "Efficient Irrigation Systems and Devices," later in this chapter.

SUN AND SHADE   Note areas that receive sun and shade during particular times of the day. Landscape areas that receive hot, afternoon sun require different types of plants from areas that are consistently shady. Shady areas can be as much as 20°F cooler than sunny spots.[53]

WATER-USE ZONES   The vegetation in a water-wise or Xeriscape landscape can be divided into three water-use zones: *low* (fed solely by rainfall), *moderate* (needs occasional watering), and *high* (requires regular watering). A water-thrifty landscape does not have to incorporate plants representing each of these categories; it could include only low-water-use plants. Low-water-use zones rely on natural rainfall and require no supplemental irrigation. Moderate-water-use zones generally require watering only during hot, dry periods. High-water-use zones are usually limited in a water-wise landscape because they include plants that need regular watering. These zones are often called high-impact areas because they are highly visible, e.g., near home or commercial building entrances.[30,58] For more information on water-efficient plant and turf selection, see Section 3.2, "Native and Low-Water-Use Turf and Plants," later in this chapter. Mulches, which can be attractive groundcovers, also hold in moisture, as described in Section 3.7, "Mulches."

TOPSOIL PRESERVATION   Preserve good-quality topsoil because it has better growing and moisture-holding capacity than subsoil. Topsoil can be stockpiled and then returned after the site has been regraded. Soil that is damaged or deficient in nutrients may need amendment.[53] For more information on amending soil, see Section 3.6, "Soil Improvements."

Consider Maintenance Preferences

The amount of time and money the owner or manager of a landscape is willing to devote to maintenance should be taken into account when the landscape is designed and plants are selected.[54] For more information on maintenance practices for Xeriscape landscapes, see Section 3.8, "Maintenance of Water-Efficient Landscapes."

Take Budget Into Account

Low-water-use landscapes do not necessarily cost more than conventional landscapes; in many cases they cost less. For example, downsizing or eliminating an irrigation system will reduce capital costs as well as future water bills. Smaller turf areas, particularly those that are not heavily irrigated, will incur lower mowing, fertilizer, and related maintenance costs. Keeping some existing plants, trees, and shrubs—particularly those that provide shade and require minimal or no irrigation—may yield financial, aesthetic, and water-efficiency benefits.[53,54]

Sydney's "Green" Olympic Village Integrates With Nature

The design and operation of the 1900-acre Olympic Park built near Homebush Bay in Sydney, Australia, for the 2000 Summer Olympic Games incorporated a multitude of water-efficiency and environmentally friendly features. Roads and buildings were designed to channel stormwater for collection and filtration at a $10 million treatment plant for reuse by flush toilets accommodating 500,000 people and for irrigating athletic playing fields and landscapes. Rainwater was collected in cisterns for reuse as cooling water for buildings. Four worm farms helped to reduce food waste and created reusable compost material. The site, once an industrial wasteland, was also subject to other water and energy conservation measures, waste and pollution avoidance, and restoration of wetlands and other natural features.[59]

Water Savings, Benefits, and Costs
From Water-Wise Landscape Planning and Design

Studies of residential properties that have been partially or fully converted to water-wise landscapes have for several years reported actual water savings of 20 to 50%,[60–62] but savings can be even higher. The amount of water that can be saved by changing a conventional, high-water-use landscape to a water-efficient one varies considerably because of differences in landscape and irrigation conditions before and after the conversion. Properties converted from conventional irrigated landscaping to pure water-wise landscaping with no supplemental irrigation can potentially save as much as 100%, excluding the water initially required for plant establishment. Savings of this magnitude are not frequently reported, however, because many owners of water-wise properties provide some supplemental irrigation.

The cost of redesigning a landscape depends on several factors: fees for a professional landscape designer (if any), size of the area to be redesigned, quantity and types of plants to be purchased and installed, planting materials to be used (soil, fertilizer, and mulches), labor, and irrigation system retrofit or replacement costs. Most of the costs associated with installing low-water-use landscaping are for new plants and related materials. Depending on the size of the area to be redesigned and the types of plants and groundcover selected, costs can range from several hundred to several thousand dollars. Over the long term, these investments will be offset by avoided costs from reduced volumes of irrigation water, smaller amounts of lawn and landscape chemicals (e.g., fertilizers, herbicides, and pesticides), energy savings (gasoline or electricity) from decreased lawn-mowing time, reduced mower maintenance requirements (e.g., blade sharpening), and reduced use of landscape maintenance personnel (e.g., for lawn mowing).

An ancillary benefit of water-wise landscapes is that they also help reduce the cost of lawn maintenance and chemicals. Smaller turf areas, which require less time for mowing, result in less use of gasoline or electricity for power mowers. Similarly, because plants, trees, and shrubs selected for a water-wise landscape are naturally suited to the site or can easily adapt to it, they often don't need fertilizer to encourage them to grow.

Case Study *Residential Xeriscapes Use 43% Less Water Than Conventional Landscapes in Austin, Texas.* Residential properties designed and maintained according to Xeriscape principles on lots smaller than 9,000 square feet in Austin used an average of 43% less water than conventional landscapes, according to a water-use study of more than 6,000 single-family residential landscapes conducted by Austin's Environmental and Conservation Services Department. The study also demonstrated that several factors influence outdoor water use. Drought-tolerant turf grass species, such as buffalo and Bermuda grass, used an average of 31% less water per landscape than traditional water-intensive species such as St. Augustine grass (which also requires more frequent applications of lawn chemicals to stay healthy). Average water-use reductions reported in the study were about 175 gallons per day (gpd). The Austin study also found that high-income properties used significantly more water for landscaping than low- and middle-income properties. Further, the study showed a correlation between outdoor water use and landscape maintenance: the more water applied, the more time and money needed for maintenance.[61]

Case Study *Water-Conserving Landscapes Use 42% Less Water in California Single-Family Homes.* In the East Bay Municipal Utility District in Oakland, a study of more than 1,000 single-family homes found that those with water-conserving landscapes used 42% less water than those with traditional landscaping. The traditionally landscaped homes had well-maintained turf areas comprising 70% or more of the front yard. The study also showed that the amount of water saved by water-efficient landscapes increased proportionally as lot size increased.[62]

Case Study *Austin's "Xeriscape It!" Rebate Program Reduces Outdoor Water Use.* From 1993 to 1997, the Environmental and Conservation Services Department of the city of Austin, Texas, implemented its "Xeriscape It!" outdoor conservation program, offering single-family homeowners rebates of up to $240 ($0.08 per square foot for a maximum of 3,000 square feet) to replace high-water-use landscapes with low-water-use turf and other plants. During the four-year program, 469 projects received rebates totaling $77,621. In an evaluation survey, about 89% of program participants reported watering their Xeriscape landscapes less than their conventional ones. Along with data from water bills, the study showed that residential landscapes with Xeriscape features saved an average of 214 gpd in the summer compared with conventional landscapes. About 75% of program participants felt that the visual appeal of Xeriscape landscaping was "excellent" and that it required less maintenance. More than 60% of participants also reported using less fertilizer.[63]

Case Study *Some Xeriscape Landscapes Are Overwatered.* Some homeowners overwater even when their landscapes consist of native and drought-resistant plants. A field study of 18 residential properties in Phoenix found that homeowners with Xeriscapes used 30% more water than those with conventional landscapes; all the properties had automatic irrigation systems. "This is a behavioral issue, not a plant issue," said Chris Martin, a professor of urban horticulture at Arizona State University in Tempe. "People are not applying water based on how much the plants need," he observed. A related study of 40 sites in Phoenix found overwatering of low-water-use plants, even with drip irrigation. Irrigation efficiency for these plants was around 35%, whereas drip irrigation efficiency for agricultural applications averages more than 80%.[64]

The landscapes of homes can be complemented by, if not completely replanted in, native species. Is there a park in your neighborhood? Every kind of park—from a vest-pocket-sized park to a city, state, or industrial park—is a natural candidate for indigenous species. Median strips and roadsides filled with a bounty of regional native plants—perhaps the biggest 'gardens' in the world—increasingly capture the interest and applause of the driving public."

—Lady Bird Johnson, Lady Bird Johnson Wildflower Center

Implementation of Programs that Promote Water-Wise Landscape Planning and Design

Programs that promote water-wise landscape design and planning can be facilitated by the following actions on the part of the water utility or other sponsoring agency:

Establish a Water-Wise Ethic or Customized
Landscape Standards That Incorporate Ecologically Sustainable Practices

*N*o plot of ground is too small...
to sow the seeds of change."
—Evergreen Foundation

For many water supply systems and communities, following water-wise principles is a simple, proven, direct way to establish local landscape water-efficiency standards. Some communities may want to establish their own water-wise landscape standards that incorporate native landscaping or Xeriscape principles as well as related environmental goals. Concerns about the management of lawns and landscapes are not limited to the need for improved water efficiency. Public, environmental, and governmental attention is increasingly focused on related issues, such as controlling stormwater runoff, decreasing or eliminating the use of lawn chemicals to reduce pollution of drinking water supplies, and controlling weeds and other invasive plants that threaten indigenous plant species and ecosystems. In some communities, horticultural, environmental, and educational interests concerned about ecologically sustainable landscape issues are joining forces. They are launching dynamic, practical projects that incorporate both native plants and water-wise concepts into their own properties, such as the Wilmot Elementary School in Deerfield, Illinois, as shown in Figure 3.9 (A) and (B).

Ecological Restoration Projects Transform Communities, Businesses, and Schools

In his book *Cultures of Habitat: On Nature, Culture, and Story,* Gary Paul Nabhan writes of a growing movement among teachers, parents, and children who are initiating projects to "naturalize" schoolyard habitats. Such projects often incorporate natural landscaping concepts in that they include the use of native plants, trees, and shrubs. The "learning grounds" habitats created by these projects not only bring back the natural vegetative environment, but in so doing they also often invite the return of some insects, birds, and animals that had previously disappeared from the area. [65]

More than 50 federal, state, and international organizations now assist with or sponsor programs to promote native plants and natural landscaping, to help restore ecologically degraded areas, or to develop play areas and nature study guides that include native plants. Some of these groups and programs are described here.

- The Wild Ones–Natural Landscapers, Ltd., based in Appleton, Wisconsin, is a nonprofit national organization dedicated to promoting native plants and natural landscaping. The group educates and shares information with members and the community at the "plant-roots" level to promote biodiversity and environmentally sound practices.

- The Lady Bird Johnson Wildflower Center (formerly the National Wildflower Research Center) is a nonprofit educational organization that educates people about the environmental necessity, economic value, and natural beauty of native plants. The Wildflower Center is headquartered in Austin, Texas, with links to native plant societies and environmental organizations across the United States and around the world.

- A number of regional and local organizations are devoted to native plant identification and demonstration gardens. For example, the Native Plant Conservation Initiative (NPCI) is a national collaborative program that supports on-the-ground conservation projects that protect, enhance, and/or restore native plant communities on U.S. public and private lands. The projects typically fall into one of three categories: protection and restoration, information and education, and inventory and assessment. NPCI is a partner of the Plant Conservation Alliance (PCA), a cooperative program created in partnership with several federal agencies and more than 150 nongovernmental organizations. Federal agencies include the Bureau of Land Management, U.S. Department of Agriculture-Forest Service, Fish and Wildlife Service, and the National Park Service. PCA

links resources and expertise in developing a coordinated national approach to the conservation of native plants.

- The Evergreen Foundation in Toronto works with schools, communities, governments, and businesses to transform ill-planned asphalt, concrete, and turf areas into healthier, more vibrant, and educational environments. The Evergreen Foundation's mission is to bring communities and nature together across Canada by creating and sustaining healthy, dynamic outdoor spaces – on school grounds, on community public lands, and on the home landscape. The organization believes that local stewardship of the landscape creates vibrant neighborhoods, a healthy natural environment, and a sustainable society for all.

- The New England Wildflower Society, based in Framingham, Massachusetts, is one of the oldest organizations in the United States dedicated to the conservation of temperate North American plants. Programs include various education, horticulture, and conservation initiatives.

A more comprehensive list of these and similar organizations, along with contact information, can be found in Chapter 6, *The Water Conservation Network.*

Figure 3.9   (A) Before installation of a natural landscape at the Wilmot Elementary School in Deerfield, Illinois, the property hosted a conventional lawn with some weedy trees that had grown up on the site. (Photo courtesy of Donald Vorpahl)
(B) Wilmot's landscape was transformed, courtesy of 50 parents and children who installed 1,500 plantings on the 0.5 acre site. The area was overseeded with native grasses, forbs, and five native oak trees (a red oak, a bur oak, and three white oaks). (Landscape design by Donald Vorpahl, photo courtesy of Bret Rappaport)

Prepare a List of Local Native and Adaptive
Low-Water-Use Turf Grasses, Plants, Flowers, Shrubs, and Trees

This undertaking is discussed in detail in Section 3.2, "Native and Low-Water-Use Turf and Plants."

Offer Rebates or Other Incentives for Water-Wise Landscapes

Some water suppliers offer rebates and bill credits to customers who install water-wise landscapes. For example, the San Antonio (Texas) Water System offers a rebate in the form of a water bill credit to homeowners who install a "Watersaver Landscape." Qualifying sites are inspected, and a master gardener must approve rebate applications. Rebates are set at 10 cents a square foot, and converted landscapes must comprise a minimum of 1,000 square feet ($100); the maximum rebate is $500 for 5,000 square feet of converted landscape.[66]

Develop Partnerships With the Local Green Industry

Educating and engaging the local green industry is essential to developing successful community programs to reduce outdoor water use. Builders and developers also must be educated because they influence the specifications set by landscape architects and other green industry professionals who construct and renovate landscapes. Workshops, seminars, and other events focusing on water-wise landscaping practices among green industry professionals, garden clubs, and the public constitute a good beginning. Water-wise nurseries and plant stores often provide tags indicating native and low-water-use plants, a strategy that can increase plant sales to customers who want to replace high-water-use plants.

Establish Water-Wise Demonstration Gardens

Many conservation-minded communities and water systems initiate water-wise and natural landscaping programs by creating local demonstration gardens. Demonstration gardens are typically planted in highly visible public locations, such as parks, libraries, schools, or the water utility headquarters (Figures 3.10 and 3.11). Prominently located businesses, industries, and institutions can also be desirable sites for demonstration gardens, setting good examples of resource stewardship and serving as role models for owners and managers of similar properties. Xeriscape demonstration gardens typically provide literature and signage explaining the Xeriscape principles and how they were applied at the site; plant names, irrigation practices, and maintenance requirements are often included as well. The process of designing, building, and maintaining a local water-wise demonstration site in itself can play a significant role in a community's transition from conventional, water-intensive landscapes to more sustainable, water-wise environments. For example, local green industry professionals and workers assigned to a demonstration garden will become knowledgeable about the project's purpose and maintenance needs, helping them see the benefits and potential marketability of water-wise landscaping practices. Likewise, local residents who visit the site and learn about its advantages may become motivated to seek out similar services and products to create their own low-water-use landscapes.

Figure 3.10 A guidepost describes the natural landscape at the Wilmot Elementary School in Deerfield, Illinois. The plant selection and installation plan was created by Jina Rappaport and Patricia Glicksberg, both mothers of children who attend the school. Their goal was to maximize the early season and late season flowers to have as much in bloom in May and September, when the kids are in school. (Photo courtesy of Bret Rappaport)

Figure 3.11 Student Jeremy Rappaport enjoys the fall flowers in the natural landscape at the Wilmot Elementary School. (Photo courtesy of Bret Rappaport)

3.2 NATIVE AND LOW-WATER-USE TURF AND PLANTS

Selecting native and low-water-use turf grasses and plants is key to reducing or eliminating the need for supplemental irrigation.

Landscapes that depend on indigenous and low-water-use plants can be beautiful and functional as well as water-efficient, as shown in Figure 3.12. In a given locale, there can be hundreds of native or adaptive grasses, groundcovers, plants, shrubs, trees, and flowers that will require little or no watering once they have become established. Plants that are native to an area are "all about location and genetic purity," according to Andy Wasowski and Sally Wasowski, authors of *The Landscaping Revolution: Garden With Nature, Not Against Her.* These authors say native plants have three distinguishing characteristics:

*W*elcome to our perfectly wild world!"
—Lady Bird Johnson
Wildflower Center

Figure 3.12 Lawns planted with water-thrifty grasses (blue grama and buffalo grass) use 90% less water than conventional turf grasses. (Photo courtesy of Denver Water)

1. The plant arrived by means of flooding, wind, the fur of migrating mammals, or bird or animal droppings.
2. The plant evolved over a "very long period of time" and now thrives in the area.
3. The plant has not been subject to genetic tampering by humans.[67]

Provenance, or place of origin, is another important factor in identifying native plants. Plants that evolve in one specific spot are *endemic*; an endemic plant raised under local growing conditions is more suitable for that locale than the same kind of plant that is also indigenous to another part of the country with different growing conditions. "It's the provenance of a plant that truly determines whether or not it's native or indigenous to your region," according to the Wasowskis.[68]

Plants and turf grasses selected for their ability to survive drought are referred to as *drought-tolerant* or *drought-resistant*. The drought tolerance of plants varies considerably. Some plants have little ability to withstand drought conditions; others have great tolerance. Plants that are stressed as a result of low-water or drought conditions will wilt and exhibit other symptoms such as dull, rolling, folding, or shedding leaves.[69]

Designers of water-efficient landscapes should consult lists of native and adaptive species of vegetation suitable for the region to identify options for a particular site, recognizing that microclimates may add or subtract some choices.

For example, the University of California Cooperative Extension Service publishes a guide to the water-use needs of landscape plants for that state's six major growing regions; the guide is entitled "WUCOLS: Water Use Classification of Landscape Species (A Guide to the Water Needs of Landscape Plants)".[70] Similar guidance documents are available from many other state and county agencies and universities.

Care should be used in preparing or consulting lists of native and low-water-use plants to avoid the creeping problem of invasive plants, a serious concern in many areas of the United States and other parts of the world. Horticulturists and ecologists have begun to warn of invasive plants that literally choke out indigenous vegetation and overtake wetlands, grasslands, and ecosystems. Nonnative invasive plants can grow and propagate at surprising rates when they are planted in environments that do not include their natural enemies—the native diseases, pests, and parasites that control their growth in their indigenous habitats. Invasive plants not only threaten native vegetation but also destroy food sources for wildlife, disrupt drainage patterns, and encroach on water navigation and recreation. (For example, water hyacinths introduced into Florida after an exposition in New Orleans in 1884 have caused multiple ecological, economic, and aesthetic problems. Water hyacinths have taken over some lakes and waterways, forming thick floating mats that block sunlight needed for the survival of other aquatic plants and threatening fish that rely on these plants for food and habitat. The water hyacinths also entangle boat propellers and swimmers, creating safety and navigational problems.) Once established, invasive plants are difficult to control without the aggressive use of costly herbicides; biological controls, such as insects, have yet to be identified for most invasive plants. The best way to avoid invasive plants may be to "go natural" and select only plants that are naturally acclimatized to the region.[71]

Conservation Policies and Regulations Related to Native and Low-Water-Use Turf and Plants

- *Limits on portions of new landscaping devoted to turf and high-water-use plants.* Establishing limits on the amount of landscaped area devoted to turf and high-water-use plants, based on a percentage of total landscaped area, can help reduce overall irrigation demand. For example, the Marin Municipal Water District in California allows a maximum of 35% of the total landscaped area to be planted with high-water-use turf and plants.[73] Similar ordinances limiting the amount of landscaping devoted to turf and high-water-use plants have been adopted in Florida (the Florida model landscape code), Boulder, Colorado, and Tucson, Arizona.[50]
- *Restrictions on high-water-use plants in new developments.* Stipulations that only native and low-water-use grasses and plants can be used for newly established or renovated landscapes help avoid excessive water use for landscape irrigation over the long term. For example, Albuquerque, New Mexico, requires new developments to devote no more than 20% of landscaped areas to high-water-use plants or to establish a water budget that, if exceeded, triggers a rate surcharge of $0.21 per additional unit of water (1 unit = 100 cubic feet = 748 gallons) used on an annual basis.[44] Albuquerque requires city-owned

Native Plants Thwart Damage From Invasive Plants

Nonindigenous "alien" plants are nonnative plants that originated somewhere else—a region with a different ecosystem and climate and different soil, moisture, and light conditions. Not all nonnative plants are invasive, but because many are, sentiment to cultivate only native plants is growing. Nonnative plant species can be introduced into new environments for a variety of reasons, including being planted as "exotics" or as drought-tolerant species. Many nonnative, drought-tolerant species are particularly hardy (which is why they are preferred for low-water conditions), but in certain conditions they can grow aggressively, forming exotic monocultures in which they literally take over preexisting plants, lawns, wetlands, grasslands, and forests that had been thriving naturally. Invasive plants alter and often reduce the amount of space, water, light, and nutrients available to native flora and fauna. They also disrupt native plant-pollination and seed-dispersal relationships, increase erosion, and compete with rare and endangered plant species on which many animal and aquatic habitats depend. According to a study conducted for the U.S. Park Service, nonnative plants and organisms pose a significant threat to the natural ecosystems of the United States and are destroying parts of America's natural history and identity. For example, purple loosestrife, an invasive plant species, is taking over wetlands and choking out native plant species in many regions of the eastern United States. Approximately 4,000 nonnative plant species have established free-living populations in the United States, and about 20% of them have been documented to be causing billions of dollars worth of damage to agriculture each year. For these reasons, property owners and managers should exercise care in selecting nonnative, low-water-use turf grasses, plants, shrubs, and trees to avoid introducing invasive species that could do more harm than good.[72]

properties to use 100% low- and medium-water-use plants in all new landscapes; parks and golf courses are allowed water budgets of 40 and 44 inches per acre per year, respectively. City-owned properties that exceed their water budgets are also subject to the $0.21 per unit surcharge.[74]

- *Requirements for low-water-use plants in medians and rights of way.* Irrigated turf that is planted in narrow strips such as road medians and parking lot "islands" cannot be watered efficiently and is often the site of runoff. Prohibiting strips of high-water-use turf or other plants that require irrigation in narrow planting beds not only saves water but also helps reduce road hazards. Restrictions on plants that can be used in these areas have been established in the Arizona cities of Mesa, Chandler, Gilbert, Goodyear, and Phoenix.[50]

- *"Weed" ordinances.* Some communities have passed weed ordinances that require grass to be mowed once it reaches a certain height, often between 8 and 12 inches. Though these laws are designed to ensure the satisfactory appearance of neighborhoods, aesthetic "standards" for homeowners may be different from those of property managers who are concerned about landscape water use and costs and may prefer native landscapes and natural habitats. For example, a Chicago weed law prohibits "weeds in excess of an average height of 10 inches."[75] Bret Rappaport, president of Wild Ones–Natural Landscapers, Ltd., and a Chicago-based attorney who has defended natural landscapers in challenges to weed laws, has addressed these issues in a report entitled, "As Natural Landscaping Takes Root We Must Weed Out The Bad Laws—How Natural Landscaping and Leopold's Land Ethic Collide With Unenlightened Weed Laws and What Must Be Done About It."[76]

Water-Efficiency Measures for Native and Low-Water-Use Turf and Plants

Water-efficiency measures related to selecting native and low-water-use turf and plants include:[53, 77, 78]

Select Native, Drought-Resistant, or Low-Water-Use Turf Grasses

Select a native, drought-resistant, or low-water-use turf grass for nonfunctional turf areas. If a mowed, functional turf area is needed, some traditional turf may be necessary. Turf grass selection should be based on local rainfall ranges and the grass's ability to survive in drought or low-water conditions. Every grass is somewhat individual in how it adapts to the conditions in which it lives, so how well a specific type will fare at a given site cannot be predicted with total certainty. A grass that requires more water than is provided by natural rainfall can be trained to require less water by encouraging deep root growth; otherwise, it will need supplemental irrigation to maintain a green appearance and possibly even to survive. Regardless of which grass is planted, it will need some irrigation initially to establish it in the ground.[77] In some cases, aerating and amending the soil can improve a lawn's ability to retain moisture, helping to reduce excessive irrigation and runoff. Making these improvements before planting native or low-water-use turf grass will enhance its chances of adapting successfully.

More than 10,000 species of grasses exist worldwide, but only a few are used for lawn grass in the United States.[25] Turf grasses can be characterized as either warm-season or cool-season, and these categories are significant factors in the selection of a native or adaptive turf grass for a particular site. Five zones have been identified for cool- and warm-season grasses in the United States:[77]

- *Northeast*—cool, humid
- *Southeast*—warm, humid
- *Great Plains*—cool, dry
- *Southwest*—warm, dry
- *Northwest*—cool, humid

COOL-SEASON GRASSES   The most common grasses grown in the northern and central regions of the United States are Kentucky bluegrass, fescues, bent grasses, and rye grasses—cool-season varieties that grow best and are greenest in cool temperatures (e.g., spring and fall) but naturally turn brown during summer's heat. Kentucky bluegrass, a fine-bladed cool-season grass, is probably the most popular grass for lawns in Canada and the United States (even in arid regions), yet from a water-use standpoint it may be the least desirable because it requires a minimum of 35 inches of rainfall a year just to survive.[77] A considerable amount of water use and abuse, particularly in hot, dry climates, occurs as a result of trying to keep Kentucky bluegrass green during hot summer months and droughts because it quickly turns brown under such conditions.[77]

Cool-season grasses prefer cool, shady habitats and grow optimally in northern climates where spring and fall temperatures range from 60 to 75°F. They may turn brown during hot weather, especially when exposed to midday sun, but they hold their green color during the cool days of fall and winter much more than warm-season grasses, which lose their chlorophyll when temperatures drop below 50°F.[77] At their peak, cool-season grasses are greener than warm-season grasses, but they require intensive watering to maintain their appearance during hot weather. As a rule, warm-season grasses are considered more drought-resistant than cool-season grasses,[79] but both types of turf grass can usually withstand drought or high heat once they have established deep roots.

WARM-SEASON GRASSES   Warm-season grasses grow best and stay greenest during the warm summer months. In the southern states, warm-season Bermuda grasses and zoysia grasses are common choices for lawns; St. Augustine grass, Bahia grass, centipede grass, and carpet grass are also used. Warm-season grasses are best suited for southern climates because they come out of dormancy when temperatures climb above 50°F and grow until temperatures reach 80 to 95°F. In warm climates, buffalo grass, for example, may turn tan or brown by midsummer without supplemental irrigation but will "green up" shortly after receiving rainfall or irrigation water. Warm-season grasses stay green only during the growing season; they start to turn tan as temperatures drop below 50°F and get brown as temperatures dip below freezing.[77] Warm-season grasses grow best in sunny areas and require less water than cool-season grasses.[79]

Regardless of what type of turf grass a homeowner or property manager selects, it is worth recognizing that lawn grasses naturally thrive (i.e., grow and

And what is a weed? A plant whose virtues have not been discovered."

—Ralph Waldo Emerson

stay green) in cool, wet climates such as that in the United Kingdom. Lawns in other types of climates—including most of North America—require additional water and work if they are to stay green during dormancy periods when they would naturally turn brown. Not surprisingly, America's most popular and heavily irrigated lawn grass, Kentucky bluegrass, is originally from England.[25] The British colonists, upon arriving in America, are believed to have planted open areas with grass to remind them of home.[80]

NATIVE GRASSES Native grasses are a ubiquitous but typically overlooked feature of natural landscapes, such as unmowed roadsides, wooded areas, and some water-smart landscapes. Native American grasses called bunchgrasses grow naturally in clumps, although they can give the appearance of turf if maintained as lawn grasses (e.g., tall fescue). Fertilizing, watering, and mowing grass essentially keeps it from doing what it does naturally—grow several feet tall, produce seeds, and turn brown. Native grasses grow primarily during the hottest parts of the year, not the wettest.[25, 77]

Native prairie grasses and bunchgrasses may be particularly good choices as ornamentals for nonfunctional lawn areas, roadsides, landfill reclamation sites, corporate and institutional properties, parks, and out-of-play areas on golf courses. Some common grasses that are native to North America include blue grama (*Boutelous gracilis*), switchgrass (*Panicum virgatum*), and buffalo grass (*Buchloe dactyloides*), among others. Prairie buffalo grass and other buffalo grass cultivars may be preferred because they don't produce a seed head.[81]

Caution: When native grass used as an ornamental is allowed to grow to its full natural height, it can pose a fire hazard, particularly during hot, dry periods. To protect people and property, a swath of the grass can be mowed adjacent to a building or a path of egress, such as the perimeter of the house or property.[82]

DROUGHT-TOLERANT AND LOW-WATER-USE TURF GRASSES A number of drought-tolerant and native varieties of turf grass can be used to replace water-thirsty grasses throughout North America,[83] as shown in Table 3.1. Native grasses and other plants are not always drought-tolerant if they are planted in a hostile microclimate.[84] In general, the longer the roots of the turf grass, the more drought-tolerant it will be. Root depth is determined by the grass species as well as how the turf is watered. Naturally deep-rooting grasses, with roots as deep as 5 feet, include Bermuda grass, tall fescue, zoysia grass, and crown vetch,[85] although if these grasses are overwatered, they may have shallow root structures. Lawn grasses such as Bermuda, tall fescue, and zoysia usually "green up" when watered again after a drought or stress from low-water conditions.[86] Tall fescues can be a good low-water-use replacement for Kentucky bluegrass because they can maintain the appearance of a traditional lawn. In regions where rainfall is abundant and temperatures are almost always warm, such as the Gulf states and Hawaii, the more water-thrifty Bahia grasses, buffalo grass, Bermuda grasses, and zoysia grasses can be good low-water-use alternatives. Warm, dry regions are the most difficult places to grow lawn grasses without supplemental irrigation.[77] Climate also has some influence on the drought tolerance of plants and grasses. For example, tall fescues have a higher drought tolerance in hot, humid

TABLE 3.1

Drought tolerances of common turf grasses*

Poor-to-Fair Drought Tolerance	Species	Good-to-Excellent Drought Tolerance		Suitability to North America
		Warm-Season[†]	Cool-Season[‡]	
Bahia grass	Little Bluestem	•		Native to most of the United States and Canada (Quebec to Alberta, south to Florida and Arizona)
Bent grass (creeping, velvet, colonial)	Bermuda grass	•		Not native; adaptive to Pacific Northwest coast, southern and mid-Atlantic United States
Bluegrass (Kentucky, Canada, annual)	Blue grama	•		High desert landcapes in the United States
Centipede grass	Buffalo grass	•		U.S. Great Plains
Rye grass (perennial, annual)	Red fescue		•	Western Canada south to Mexico
St. Augustine grass	Fine fescues		•	Mid-Atlantic region and high-altitude regions of the middle to lower southern United States
	Pennsylvania sedge	•		Eastern and central United States
	California meadow sedge	•		California; durable in Colorado and Texas
	Zoysia grass	•		Not native; adaptive to southern regions of the United States

* Drought tolerances of turf grasses may vary from those shown because of microclimates, climate variability, soil and shade conditions, and other factors. There are many grass cultivars, each with somewhat different characteristics and growth needs. Lawn grass seed is often sold as a mix of several varieties.

† Warm-season grasses prefer temperatures of 80 to 95°F and do most of their growing in the summer. They become dormant during cool weather, when it is natural for their blades to turn brown.

‡ Cool-season grasses prefer temperatures of 60 to 75°F, grow best in the spring and fall, and often stay green in the winter. Cool-season grasses are dormant and grow slowly in the summer, when it is natural for their blades to turn brown.

Sources: References 82, 83, and 85

environments than in hot, arid climates with high light intensity (e.g., Albuquerque, New Mexico, or San Antonio, Texas).

Select Native or Low-Water-Use Plants

Choose indigenous or low-water-use plants to reduce or eliminate the need for supplemental water. In general, native vegetation has the best chance of surviving in landscapes that rely on natural rainfall only (after plant establishment). Adaptive low-water-use or drought-tolerant plants often require at least some supplemental watering, but some do not if they are carefully selected for the particular soil, sunlight, shade, and temperature characteristics of a site.

Evaluate microclimates and nonnative soil conditions at a given site before selecting plants and turf grasses, because they can radically alter what is suitable for the site. It is not uncommon for existing vegetation and topsoil to be stripped away during construction of new commercial and residential properties. In such instances, the original topsoil may not have been replaced, and the replacement soil used may sometimes be compacted. Added hardscapes such as new walkways, driveways, and parking lots—plus the heat from buildings and solar reflection from glass—can increase heat and light intensity.

Consult a variety of sources to compile a list of local low-water-use or native plants—horticulturists, garden clubs, cooperative extension offices, nurseries, municipal park and recreation departments, water utilities, and landscape architects, designers, and related professionals. In selecting native and low-water-use vegetation, use plant lists compiled specifically for the region and for the characteristics of the site where the plants will be established. Generally, avoid us-

The inescapable fact that the decline of wildlife is linked with human destinies is being driven home by conservation the nation over. Wildlife, it is pointed out, is dwindling because its home is being destroyed. But the home of wildlife is also our home."

—Rachel Carson

To learn that more than four thousand native plant species are in danger of extinction in this country gives us a wake-up call and brings close to home the Wildflower Center's mission. Will these plants be lost to all but memory, with succeeding generations losing even that fragile connection? Are there sources of food, fiber, or medicine that might perish with them? How do we save these species in the face of an ever-expanding human population and its impact on the land?"

—Lady Bird Johnson, Lady Bird Johnson Wildflower Center

ing lists of Xeriscape plants from other regions because choosing ill-adapted plants could result in costly failures and because such lists might include plants that have invasive characteristics in other locales.

Select plants for their visual appeal, drought tolerance, water requirements, and adaptability to local soils and climate. Screen selected plants for invasiveness (see "Avoid Invasive Plants" later in this section). Lists of local native and adaptive (but noninvasive) turf grass species and plants are often available from several local sources.

NATIVE PLANTS   A list of native plants will identify trees, shrubs, plants, flowers, and groundcovers that are indigenous to a particular region. Native vegetation is naturally adapted to survive the temperature and weather extremes of its place of origin and is most likely a "sure bet" in terms of water efficiency. (This "assured" success of native vegetation can be thwarted by such factors as poor soil quality, such as highly compacted and nutrient-deficient topsoil sometimes used in new developments, and unusual microclimate conditions.) Indigenous plants typically have deep root systems and leaves whose top surfaces retard evaporation. Native plants thrive particularly well when grouped with other native plants in the conditions they prefer. Because native plants are naturally adapted to the general soil profile of an area, they need little or no fertilizer if the native soil is still present. In addition to saving water, planting native vegetation helps restore the natural environment and invites the return of native birds, butterflies, insects, and animals.[82]

Native wildflowers are gaining popularity because of their beauty and other natural attributes, including the fact that they require minimal water and maintenance. An area planted with a careful mix of wildflowers can provide peak flowering from spring to fall. These types of landscapes are usually cut once a year in the fall and require reseeding every three to four years.

There is some debate as to what constitutes a native plant. As with a person, it is difficult to determine at what point a plant should be designated "native" when it has thrived in a place for a long time but is originally from somewhere else. For example, the crape myrtle, a deciduous shrub that is popular from Virginia to Texas, was imported to North America from China in 1747.[82]

DROUGHT-RESISTANT AND LOW-WATER-USE PLANTS   Slow-growing, drought-resistant perennials or shrubs can be good choices for water-efficient landscapes because they have low maintenance requirements. Plants described as "hard to establish," "susceptible to disease or pests," or "needs frequent attention" could be nonnative species or native species that cannot adapt to hostile microclimates. Some common characteristics of drought-tolerant plants, according to Ellefson et al, include:[82]

• Grayish, fuzzy, or finely divided foliage
• Low-growing plants that hug the ground
• Herbs and some scented plants that produce aromatic oils

Avoid Invasive Plants

Crosscheck lists of water-wise plants that include nonnative species with current lists of invasive plants and weeds. Use caution in consulting plants lists from other regions; for example, a plant that is drought-tolerant in California could be extremely invasive in a different climate such as that of Hawaii or southern Florida.[87] It is estimated that more than 100 million acres of U.S. land are already infested with nonnative plants.[88]

Verify Growing Conditions Before Purchasing Plants

Before purchasing new grass species, plants, shrubs, or trees, try to determine the conditions under which they were established, because these conditions influence how well the plants will adapt to their permanent environment, particularly in terms of water-use requirements. Previous overwatering may make it more difficult for plants to become established in their new environment—even if it is their natural or adaptive habitat. For example, indigenous and low-water-use plants can normally be expected to require little or no supplemental irrigation once they are established, but if they were initially grown under conditions in which they were overwatered (e.g., in a commercial greenhouse not attuned to water-efficiency practices), they may have difficulty adapting to a landscape that is watered sparingly. Likewise, many plants and cool-season grasses that thrive best under cool, moist conditions but that have been trained through "water stressing" techniques can survive quite well in hot, dry environments (although they may not appear as lush and green as other species that naturally thrive under such conditions).

Consider Microclimates

Another factor than should influence plant selection is the existence of microclimates, small climates in a specific area of the landscaping site (for example, a "heat island" created by black asphalt, which increases temperatures above normal, particularly at ground level). Microclimates can alter normal climatic conditions enough that the temperature, humidity, and sunlight characteristics of a particular site may be more hospitable to nonnative plants than to indigenous species.

Group Plants by Similar Water Needs (Hydrozones)

To avoid overwatering or underwatering, group plants in hydrozones according to their water requirements (for example, lush, transition, and arid zones). The zone closest to a house might contain the most lush, shade-producing vegetation, such as large shrubs and trees. This zone might also be good for water-thirsty plants and turf that requires some watering because it probably receives more rainfall runoff from roof areas and downspouts than other zones. Other hydrozones on the property may be better suited for drought-tolerant and low- and moderate-water-use vegetation that can survive on rainfall or infrequent irrigation (once a week or less).[89]

In Colorado, we crosscheck our lists of Xeriscape plants with the state's list of invasive weeds. We also check with various counties, because plants can be a problem in one county and not in another. I encourage everyone who promotes low-water-use plants to do this crosschecking and to keep lists current as new invasive plants are identified. For example, in Colorado, St. John's wort is on the list of invasive weeds, but many folks are growing it for sale because of its health benefits. We need constant vigilance about whatever plants we are promoting."
— Liz Gardener, manager of water conservation, Denver Water

Establish Plants Properly

Plants selected for native and low-water-use landscapes should be established carefully to give them the best chance to flourish.

- Place the plant in the right spot, based on its requirements for water, sun, or shade.
- Dig the right size hole to encourage proper root establishment and growth.
- Amend the soil, if needed.
- Carefully remove the plant from its container and separate matted roots, taking care not to damage the roots or leaves.
- Soak the plant and its entire root zone.
- Add a layer of mulch (2 to 4 inches deep, depending on the plant) to cool the soil, hold in moisture, and minimize weed growth.[89]

Conventional installation of sodded turf grasses may exceed $12,000 per acre. Planting turf grass seeds may cost in the range of $4,000 to $8,000 per acre. This contrasts with installation costs of $2,000 to $4,000 per acre for seeding native prairie grasses and forbs [any herbaceous plant that is not a grass].”
— *Source Book on Natural Landscaping for Public Officials*

Water Savings, Benefits, and Costs From Native and Low-Water-Use Turf and Plants

The water savings that can be achieved from installing native and adaptive plants and turf vary, depending on what was replaced and to what extent the previous plants were irrigated, but at least a 20% reduction in water use can probably be expected. For example, the city of Albuquerque, New Mexico, passed an ordinance requiring that all landscaping associated with new residential construction include no more than 20% high-water-use plants or be subject to a water budget that limits landscape irrigation. An analysis of preordinance water use at single-family properties during January through June 1996 (129,524 gallons) indicated that postordinance single-family customers used 28% less water (93,440 gallons).[90]

In addition to saving water, numerous other benefits result from planting native vegetation. Reestablishing indigenous plant species and varieties is essentially a step toward restoration of the natural environment, which in some communities has been virtually eliminated by the introduction of nonnative, high-water-use exotic vegetation. Because native plants are naturally well adapted to the environment, they often require little if any fertilizer, pesticides, or water, factors that reduce a landscape's maintenance needs and costs. Such practices encourage birds and other wildlife to flourish and support natural pest control.[91]

Implementation of Programs that Promote Native and Low-Water-Use Turf and Plants

Programs that promote the selection of native and low-water-use turf and plants can be facilitated by the following actions on the part of the water utility or other sponsoring agency:

Tag Plants

Encourage garden centers and plant shops to tag native and low-water-use plants to help potential buyers identify them. As incentives to these businesses, the utility or local government could offer help with arranging publicity in the gardening section of local newspapers and Web pages and could sponsor or participate in a fair where these garden centers and plant shops could display and sell their tagged plants.

Prepare Lists of Local, Low-Water-Use Native and Adaptive Turf Grasses, Plants, Flowers, Shrubs, and Trees

The public and the green industry need carefully prepared lists of low-water-use native and adaptive (but noninvasive) plants, shrubs, and trees that are appropriate for a particular region or locality. The utility or local government could expand and update plant lists and make them easily available to consumers and the green industry by including them in bill stuffers, program participant information kits, and local Web sites.

Avoid Invasive Plants and Weeds

Lists of invasive plants are available from numerous sources. One example is the Nature Conservancy's Wildland Weeds Management & Research Program, which lists invasive plants across North America (see Chapter 6, *The Water Conservation Network*).

Case Study *Xeriscape Rebates.* Several water systems offer rebates to water customers who replace existing high-water-use turf and plants with native and low-water-use plants or similar natural landscaping approaches. Examples include the Southern Nevada Water Authority in Las Vegas, Nevada, and the cities of Albuquerque, New Mexico, and Austin, Texas (discussed earlier in this chapter). Albuquerque's Xeriscape Retrofit Incentive Program offers qualifying customers a rebate, in the form of a water bill credit, of up to

Figure 3.13 This front yard in Prairie Crossing, Illinois, is planted with native meadow grass instead of turf grass. (Photo courtesy of Michael Sands, Prairie Crossing, Illinois)

Figure 3.14 A turf-free backyard (Photo courtesy of Denver Water)

$250 (up to 1,667 square feet of qualifying landscape at $0.15 per square foot). Participants in Albuquerque's program must convert their high-water-use landscapes to water-efficient Xeriscapes that meet the city's guidelines. The guidelines require at least 50% of a qualifying landscape to be covered by low-water-use plants that are on the city's list of approved plants. Landscaped areas that qualify for the rebate cannot use spray irrigation systems; only watering by drip, soaker, or bubbler systems is allowed. A minimum of 2 inches of mulch is required on open soil between and beneath plants; certain organic mulch materials such as gravel and bark are allowed, but impervious plastic is not permitted unless it is connected to a water-harvesting system. Customers submit their landscape retrofit proposals on an application form that is reviewed on site by a city inspector prior to approval of the rebate.[92]

3.3 PRACTICAL TURF AREAS

Limiting lawns to functional spaces devoted only to practical uses—for example, recreational and sitting areas—can significantly reduce landscape irrigation needs.

Lawns dominate the urban, residential, and corporate park landscape in many parts of the world, particularly North America, but keeping them green and lush can require considerable water and maintenance. In traditional irrigated landscapes, turf grass is typically the largest user of water. The water savings achieved by converting residential properties from conventionally irrigated to low-water-use or native landscapes often result primarily from reductions in turf areas, as shown in Figure 3.13. Reducing lawn areas to save water is particularly appropriate in hot, arid climates that require copious amounts of water to keep turf healthy and green. However, limiting turf areas on lawns that are located in cool, wet climates, are mostly rainfed, and receive little or no supplemental irrigation will not produce appreciable water savings. The amount of water a landscape needs to stay healthy and attractive is influenced not only by the amount of turf area but also by the type of grass planted and its placement and maintenance needs. "An inflexible limit on turf grass does not address the real problem of inefficient management, nor does it preserve the benefits turf grass provides," note Richard Bennett and Michael Hazinski in *Water-Efficient Landscape Guidelines*.[93]

Like other water-wise and natural landscaping practices, limiting turf to functional areas creates new possibilities for redefining the landscape, as shown in Figure 3.14. "Lawns will always be a part of our culture—a ready and handy environment for outdoor recreation. How those lawns are maintained—and how much land is dedicated to them—[are] the central question[s] to this part of our environmental future," suggests Joseph M. Keyser, public education coordinator for the Montgomery County (Maryland) Department of Environmental Protection. Keyser adds, "Do we continue to cultivate intensively a sterile (though green) desert, or relax a bit and give way to the natural systems around us?"[43]

I'm optimistic that the world of native plants will not only survive, but will thrive for environmental and economic reasons, and for reasons of the heart. Beauty in nature nourishes us and brings joy to the human spirit; it also is one of the deep needs of people everywhere."
—Lady Bird Johnson, Lady Bird Johnson Wildflower Center

Conservation Policies and Regulations Related to Practical Turf Areas

Ordinances Prohibiting Sod

The planning code for Seaside, Florida, a neotraditional development with small lots, does not permit sod, a measure that has encouraged natural landscaping approaches. Homeowners in this community have largely eschewed lawns, lawn mowers, watering, leaf blowers, edgers, fertilizers, and pesticides and instead have preserved much of the scrub forest along with other native plants and groundcovers such as pine-needle mulch.[94]

Limits on the Amount of Turf and High-Water-Use Plants in New Landscaping

The Marin Municipal Water District in California requires that the combined size of turf areas and swimming pools not exceed 25% of the total developed landscape area for new and modified landscaped properties irrigated with potable water. Properties irrigated with reclaimed water are limited to a maximum of 40% for the combined turf and pool area.[73] The nearby North Marin Water District has a similar ordinance.[51]

Policies Prohibiting Turf in Narrow Strips (e.g., Along Sidewalks and Highway Medians)

Irrigated turf planted in narrow strips such as roadway and parking lot medians is often the site of overspray and runoff, which can cause slippery pavement. Low-water-use plants are more suitable for these areas because they require no or little (e.g., drip) irrigation; they also require less maintenance.[51, 73]

Water-Efficiency Measures for Turf Areas

Water-efficiency measures related to appropriate and limited turf areas include:[53,77,78]

Limit Turf to Functional Areas

There are more goats than cows in mountainous countries since goats can survive well by eating grass and other brush.”

—www.absolutetrivia.com

Locate turf only in areas where it will serve practical uses, such as for recreation, pets, or minor foot traffic. Although turf areas should be large enough to be functional, it is best to keep them as small as practical. Plant turf in easy-to-irrigate sections that will not cause runoff or overspray. Avoid narrow or odd-shaped strips that are difficult to mow or water efficiently, and eliminate turf from steep slopes, around rock outcroppings, and under densely shaded areas.[77,95]

In selecting appropriate turf areas, also consider the environmental benefits that grass provides, such as climate control, soil erosion control, fire retardation, noise absorption, and oxygen generation.[96] Alternative groundcovers can often be used instead of turf for dust and noise abatement, glare reduction, and temperature mitigation.

Golf courses can save considerable amounts of money on turf irrigation, chemicals, and mowing by using native landscaping outside the course's actual playing surface. For example, the Prairie Dunes Country Club in Hutchinson, Kansas, has 30- to 40-foot-tall native sand dunes around its 18-hole layout.[97]

Select Appropriate Grass Species

When selecting native or low-water-use grass species and varieties, consider additional factors such as shade, temperature, soil quality, drought tolerance, and, of course, watering requirements. For example, a cool-season grass, such as Kentucky bluegrass, that requires ample amounts of water to stay green and lush would not be appropriate in the hot, dry American Southwest. Drought-tolerant grasses such as buffalo grass and blue grama would be better alternatives.

Use Alternative Groundcovers

Replace nonfunctional turf areas with low-water-use alternative groundcovers, plants, shrubs, and shredded organic and inorganic mulches. Ornaments that do not use water, such as lawn furniture and animal feeding stations, and natural groundcover materials, such as rocks, stones, and pebbles, can also be attractive replacements for turf areas, and they have the added advantage of reducing landscape maintenance time and costs. Numerous sources of design ideas for alternative lawns and suggested lawn replacement materials are available. For example, *The Wild Lawn Handbook: Alternatives to the Traditional Front Lawn*[98] by Stevie Daniels identifies a number of plant alternatives to turf grasses—e.g., heather and sedum, moss for shady areas, and wildflowers for sunny spots.

Use Separate Irrigation Systems for Different Hydrozones

Integrate lawn areas into landscape irrigation zones according to their water requirements. Because turf is likely to be the most water-intensive component of the landscape, it should be watered by a separate irrigation system to avoid overwatering other plants.

Practice Water-Efficient Turf Grass Maintenance

For more information on this topic, see Section 3.8, "Maintenance of Water-Efficient Landscapes."

Water Savings, Benefits, and Costs From Practical Turf Areas

Water savings that can be gleaned from limiting turf areas range from 15 to 50% for landscapes that continue to receive some supplemental irrigation. Discontinuing irrigation and switching to a native or rainfed-only landscape would result in water savings of 100%.

The costs of maintaining a heavily irrigated, manicured green lawn are high, both economically and environmentally. The U.S. Environmental Protection Agency has estimated that about 70 million pounds of lawn chemicals are applied in the United States annually, an amount that increases by 5 to 8% a year.[99] These lawn chemicals eventually end up in the rivers, wetlands, aquifers, and reservoirs that supply drinking water for consumers. Furthermore, the California Air Resources Board claims that a 3 1/2-horsepower gasoline lawn mower running for 30 minutes emits the same amount of hyrdocarbon pollution by-products as a 1997 automobile that has taken an 85-mile trip.[29]

Case Study *Water and Cost Savings Associated With Native Prairie or Wetland Seeding Versus Nonnative Turf Grasses.* A study by Applied Ecological Services, Inc. (Brodhead, Wisconsin) estimates that the 20-year cost of maintaining a landscape with native prairie grasses or wetland vegetation is about $3,000 per acre, compared with more than $20,000 per acre for nonnative turf grass landscapes started from seed or sod. The capital and maintenance costs saved with the native prairie landscape would be achieved primarily by avoiding installation of an underground automatic irrigation system, along with avoided costs for water, fertilizer, topsoil, and mowing. The estimated $168 in annual upkeep costs for the native turf grass landscape would be incurred by annual burns and occasional mowing and related expenses.

Implementation of Programs that Promote Practical Turf Areas

Programs that promote limited or practical turf areas can be facilitated by the following actions on the part of the water utility or other sponsoring agency:

Establish a Community Lawn-Minimization Campaign

Several communities, organizations, and individuals have initiated lawn-minimization efforts in the United States in recent years. One of these is the Smaller American Lawns Today (SALT) initiative, which originated at Connecticut College in New London, Connecticut. SALT promotes the transition of American lawns toward more ecologically sound landscapes by advocating the benefits of smaller lawns: reduced water and energy use. [100]

The major savings of natural landscaping is the lost cost of landscape maintenance. The combined costs of installation and maintenance for a natural landscape over a ten-year period may be one fifth of the costs for conventional landscape maintenance."
—Source Book on Natural Landscaping for Public Officials

Figure 3.15 Landscape overwatering can easily result in street runoff. (Photo courtesy of Jane Heller Ploeser)

3.4 LANDSCAPE IRRIGATION SYSTEMS AND DEVICES

Water-efficient irrigation equipment and practices ensure that water is applied only when and where it is needed. This not only conserves water but also avoids street runoff and safety hazards posed by slippery road and walking conditions (Figure 3.15).

Although many turf grasses and plants can survive long dry periods with little or no supplemental watering, irrigation systems and devices used to provide supplemental watering can be tailored to use water efficiently. Measures that can improve water efficiency include automatic hose-shutoff nozzles, sensors that shut off irrigation systems after rain, soil moisture sensors, soaker hoses, improved irrigation system design, weather-driven irrigation system programming, drip irrigation, improved sprinkler heads, rainwater harvesting, cisterns, leak repair, and other simple adjustments and repairs.

Irrigated lawns and landscaped areas are watered either manually or with an automatic irrigation system. Manual watering is usually done with a hand-held hose or a sprinkler that is placed on the lawn (a "hose dragger"). Automatic irrigation systems, whose hoses and sprinkler heads are typically buried in the ground, are operated by a programmed controller (also referred to as a timer or clock). Used properly, either irrigation method can be water-efficient. However, people who water manually using a portable sprinkler or a hand-held hose fitted with an automatic shutoff valve generally use less water than those who rely on automatic irrigation systems. (During droughts, water restrictions are usually placed on automatic irrigation systems first, with only manual watering allowed.) One of the reasons for this difference is that irrigation system controllers are not usually programmed to schedule irrigation runs efficiently. The saying "convenience breeds waste" applies to many users of automatic irrigation systems.[101]

Automatic irrigation systems often waste water because users or landscape service providers don't understand how or don't bother to set the frequency and duration of irrigation runs correctly. Poor irrigation system design, such as unwise placement of sprinkler heads (e.g., so that spray patterns overlap sidewalks and roadways), can also build in inefficiencies that are difficult to overcome even with proper scheduling. A well-designed automatic system can be extremely water-efficient, but proper use requires not only correct programming of the controller but also regular inspection and maintenance of the system to ensure that water is delivered efficiently and that malfunctions are repaired. Hand-held hoses are typically directed when and where water is needed. Manual sprinklers, which the user turns on and off at the tap, can also be more efficient because they tend to be used when needed instead of being programmed to run automatically.

To err is human, to repent divine; to persist devilish."
—Benjamin Franklin

Conservation Policies and Regulations Related to Landscape Irrigation Systems and Devices

Ordinances Requiring Efficient Irrigation Systems for New Landscaping

Some states and communities require drip irrigation, microsprays, and other types of efficient irrigation system and controllers (e.g., rain sensor/shutoff devices). The requirements can be enforced though landscape-plan review processes. Ordinances of this type can be found in California and Florida and in the cities of Boulder, Colorado, and Tucson, Arizona.[50]

Ordinances Requiring all Irrigation Systems to Have "Rain Shutoff Devices"

Some U.S. communities require the use of sensors and valves that shut off hoses and irrigation system controllers during and after rainfall. Communities with ordinances of this type include Hillsborough County, Florida,[102, 103] and Cary, North Carolina.[104]

Ordinances Requiring the Use of Soaker Hoses Rather Than Sprinklers to Irrigate Curbside Turf Areas and Other Narrow Strips of Vegetation

Soaker hoses can be an efficient way to irrigate rights of way and narrow strips of vegetation where conventional sprinkler systems often cause overspray and runoff. Corpus Christi, Texas, has an ordinance regulating irrigation of these areas.[105]

Ordinances Requiring Nonpotable Water, Efficient Irrigation Systems, or both for Irrigation of Commercial Turf-related Facilities Such as Golf Courses

An increasing number of communities with intensive irrigation demands are requiring new and, in some cases, existing customers to use only treated municipal wastewater for irrigation. Such ordinances have been established in Collier County, Florida,[106] and in Phoenix, Mesa, and Scottsdale, Arizona.[50]

Prohibitions on Wasteful Use

Many communities have established restrictions that prohibit wasteful water-use practices such as runoff of potable water into gutters, sidewalks, streets, and other nonlandscaped areas. Ordinances prohibiting wasteful outdoor water use are in place in Albuquerque, New Mexico;[44] Phoenix, Arizona; and Fresno, California.[50]

Policies Allowing Graywater to Be Used for Landscape Irrigation

The state of California allows reuse of graywater from residential buildings for landscape irrigation purposes.[107] Graywater is defined there to include untreated wastewater from bathtubs, showers, bathroom washbasins, clothes washers, and laundry tubs; it does not include wastewater from toilets, sinks, or dishwashers. The cost to install a graywater system, including pipes, valves, and tanks, at a single-family residential property is several hundred to several thousand dollars, depending on the size of the system and whether a professional is hired to do the installation.[108]

Water-Efficiency Measures for Landscape Irrigation

Water-efficiency measures related to landscape irrigation include:

"No Watering" Option

Although this is a controversial idea to some people, simply not watering and relying on rainwater to irrigate a landscape is an option.[110] Having a rain-fed-only versus an irrigated lawn has several pros and cons, as outlined in Table 3.2, but some homeowners and property managers are quite satisfied with lawns and landscapes that are only rainfed. Motivations for this approach are multiple: water conservation and reduced water bills, smaller quantities of lawn chemicals or none at all, reduced labor and costs for landscape maintenance, and reduced adverse environmental effects.

To rely strictly on rainwater for irrigation is to accept the fact that lawn grass naturally turns brown during hot, dry periods. The reason that many lawns, particularly those with cool-season grass species, look bright green under a broiling sun is that they are kept that way artificially with supplemental irrigation. Dormancy is nature's mechanism to help grass survive heat and drought; a lawn will "recover" with the return of rain and cooler temperatures. In some regions, such as portions of California and the Southwest that receive little or no rain during the hottest months of the year, nonnative or adaptive rainfed lawns will become dormant and, in some cases, die. In such instances, the lawn could be replaced with drought-tolerant or other native or adaptive turf grasses or groundcovers. Once the replacement vegetation is established, it should be able to survive on limited natural rainfall but, depending on what plant materials are

TABLE 3.2

Pros and cons of rainfed-only lawns versus irrigated lawns

Rainfed-Only Lawn

Pros	Cons
A more natural appearance	A "natural lawn" may conflict with conventional lawn aesthetics and contrast with neighbors' irrigated, perfectly manicured green landscapes.
Green appearance mostly during growing season (spring and fall) and after rain	Grass blades will turn tan and brown during hot, dry summer periods. Weed growth may increase.
No supplemental watering required	In some regions, turf grass that is not native or drought-tolerant may not survive if minimal or no rain falls during the growing season.
Reduced mowing requirements; time saved	May negatively influence real estate value for potential buyers who want a perfect green lawn all season
Deeper roots, enabling lawn to survive drought	
Reduced or eliminated lawn chemical requirements; a better balance with nature	

Irrigated Lawn

Pros	Cons
More consistent green and lush appearance	Requires high volumes of water to be applied frequently; increases water bills
Conforms to conventional notions of what an attractive lawn looks like	Manicured appearance requires excessive amounts of water, chemicals, and labor.
May maintain or boost real estate value for potential buyers who want a perfect green lawn all season	May conflict with local water conservation goals or environmental preservation values
	Increased runoff to storm drains, adding lawn chemicals to local rivers, watersheds, and aquifer recharge areas
	Increased maintenance costs
	Fertilizer and lawn chemical costs; adverse environmental impact
	Increased susceptibility to plant diseases and pests
	Shallower roots are more likely to turn brown or die during a drought when outdoor watering is banned.
	Increased mowing requirements

selected, might not have the look of a conventional lawn. For guidance in selecting native and low-water-use turf and plants, see Section 3.2, "Native and Low-Water-Use Turf and Plants," earlier in this chapter.

Success in converting a lawn, garden, or landscaped area to rainfed-only irrigation may be more likely to succeed if the process occurs gradually. Creating several test areas to gauge plant response may be helpful before applying the practice to the entire landscape. Newly planted turf and other vegetation (particularly nonnative and nonadaptive plants) as well as preestablished gardens,

Figure 3.16 Watering containers used for indoor plants can help save water when used outdoors. (Photo courtesy of Amy Vickers & Associates, Inc.)

crop-bearing plants, and fruit trees may not respond well or survive if supplemental water is stopped suddenly or discontinued altogether. For example, lawns that have received regular and large amounts of supplemental irrigation to keep them green should receive less-frequent applications of water in stages before irrigation is stopped completely. This will allow the turf grass to develop deeper roots and increase its chances of survival. Increasing the mowing height slightly can also help retain moisture. Properly established rainfed-only turf grass and vegetation typically grow deeper roots than overirrigated turf and plants. Turf and plants that receive infrequent but deep soakings develop deeper roots, boosting their chances of survival when droughts occur. However, extreme conditions caused by drought, microclimates, and other weather patterns can threaten the survival of any plant, even native and drought-tolerant vegetation.

Check for and Repair Leaks

Whatever landscape irrigation equipment is used—manual, sprinkler, or drip—it should be checked regularly for leakage. When leaks are found, they should be repaired promptly to save water and to avoid property damage or personal safety risks. Because not all leaks and water losses are obvious, irrigation systems should be checked at least annually for signs of leakage and malfunction. Overly green and soggy areas may indicate sources of leaks, but leaks from buried hoses or drip lines in sandy, porous soils will not be apparent. Unexplained increases in water use, as recorded on a water bill, may be traced to leakage. Automatic sprinkler and drip irrigation systems that are leaking sometimes generate a hissing sound near the hose or tubing, an indication that water is moving through the system. Potential causes and sources of leakage vary according to the type of irrigation equipment used.

HOSE LEAKS   Check hoses, nozzles, and manually operated sprinklers regularly for leaks and cracks. A hand-held hose may have thin, leaking cracks if it is old or subject to repeated pressure, such as that caused by a car driving over it. Hose leaks may be easily repaired with waterproof tape. Spray nozzles sometimes dribble or spray water at the hose connection. This problem can be fixed by cleaning grit from the connection and applying a strip of Teflon® tape around the hose threads for a more secure fit.

SPRINKLER SYSTEM LEAKS   Leaking hoses, broken spray heads, bubblers, and rotor heads, and low-level seepage are common sources of water waste from sprinkler systems. Obvious signs of leakage include overgrown or particularly green areas of turf, soggy areas around spray heads and aboveground hoses, jammed spray heads, and torn hoses.

DRIP SYSTEM LEAKS   Drip systems may have leakage problems from tubing or tape that has been damaged by foot traffic or gnawing and chewing animals. Drip systems are also vulnerable to vandalism. Water losses from drip system leaks are not as significant as those from sprinkler system leaks because drip irrigation systems are operated at lower pressures. However, drip system leaks may damage plants if they cause the plants to receive insufficient water.

Many of our [residential] audits are for residents who believe they may have a leak in their water system due to sharply increasing water bills. Our staff verify that a leak exists at the site by watching the water meter for a few minutes and informing the resident of how to determine if a leak exists. If one does exist, then we use a combination of our knowledge of leaks and causes, our visual senses, and usually—most importantly—we use a soil probe! We determine the most probable main water line path to the house and we use the soil probe (terrain permitting). Usually with a bit of effort we can insert the soil probe from 3" to 6" into the turf soil. When we are able to insert the probe easily in a foot or more then we know we have found an unusually wet area. I recently found a leak at a residence of about 185,000 gallons per month using this simple tool.

—Richard Chapman,
CTSI Corporation

Avoid Oscillating Sprinklers and Sprinkler Heads That Produce Mists or Fine Sprays

Oscillating sprinklers produce sprays that reach high into the air and cause water losses from evaporation and wind, robbing the plants targeted for irrigation of significant amounts of water. Similarly, sprinkler heads and hose nozzles that produce mist and fine sprays are often inefficient, especially when placed at some distance from the area to be irrigated.

Use Containers for Small Areas and Individual Plants

Using buckets and other containers (Figure 3.16) is an efficient way to water small gardens, flowers, plants, and shrubs compared with using automatic sprinklers or manual hoses and sprinklers.

Harvest Rainwater and Use Cisterns

Rainwater harvesting is the capture, diversion, and storage of rainwater for landscape irrigation and, in some cases, for use as a potable water supply. Rainwater harvesting for landscape irrigation purposes may be practical only in locations where rainwater can be collected in sufficient quantities during the time that it is needed. Rainwater is typically collected in cisterns, barrels, or large storage tanks, but it can also be detained in collection basins and ponds. In addition to being used for irrigation and potable purposes, rainwater cisterns are also sometimes used for firefighting. Rainwater harvesting, a common practice on islands and in many other parts of the world, is gaining in acceptance for multiple uses in the United States, particularly in Hawaii, the Southwest, and Texas. For example, construction of cisterns in Texas has increased significantly in recent years, and thousands are already in use, according to H.W. (Bill) Hoffman, a water conservation program coordinator for the city of Austin, Texas.[111] Several government publications on how to design and construct rainwater-harvesting systems for residential use are available, including *Rainwater Harvesting: Supply From the Sky,* prepared by the Water Conservation Office of the city of Albuquerque, New Mexico,[112] and the *Texas Guide to Rainwater Harvesting*, published by the Texas Water Development Board.[113]

Cisterns can be constructed for a specific site or purchased "as is," depending on the capacity needed. In hot, tropical climates, particularly on islands where freshwater supplies are limited, cisterns are often found on rooftops, but they can also be designed as holding tanks or barrels for installation adjacent to a house or building to collect water from downspouts connected to roof gutters. In Hawaii County, Hawaii, more than 8,000 homes have rainwater-catchment systems. The amount of water collected from a roof can be sizable; a 1,000-square-foot roof can collect 150 gallons of water during a quarter-inch rain.[114] Once rain has been harvested through the use of cisterns, other large catchment devices, or downspout collection systems, the water can then be applied to the landscape or directed into collection basins or ponds. Solid surfaces such as driveways, parking lots, patios, and even sidewalks can be graded or fitted with drainpipes to collect runoff and redirect it into a cistern, pond, or collection basin. Landscape grading techniques include creating small depressions at the base

D on't be a slave to your lawn. Spend money on good soil and drought-resistant grass seed, not irrigation. Let rainfall do your work."
—Jane Ceraso, environmental manager, Acton Water District, Acton, Massachusetts

of hills or slopes to catch runoff and building terraces into steep slopes to collect runoff or redirect it to lawn and garden areas.[115]

A typical homeowner who uses a cistern for landscape irrigation might place one or multiple rain barrels adjacent to the house to collect runoff from the roof, as shown in Figure 3.17. Commercial rain barrels are usually made of plastic and hold about 75 gallons, as shown in Figure 3.18. Water can be drawn from the rain barrel by attaching a simple spigot, as shown in Figure 3.19. Used but clean 55-gallon drums can also be remade as cisterns. Cisterns designed for rooftops can hold several thousand gallons of water, and above- or below-ground water tanks can hold up to 30,000 gallons. A cover, such as a debris screen or tank safety grid, should be secured over a cistern or tank to prevent children and animals from getting into it. If rainwater is to be used for potable purposes, water filtration and treatment systems can be added.

Use Manual Irrigation (Hand-Held Hoses and Portable Sprinklers)

AUTOMATIC SHUTOFF NOZZLES   Installing an automatic shutoff nozzle or self-closing spray attachment on a hand-held hose can provide an efficient form of supplemental irrigation for a typical lawn and garden. Most soil becomes saturated after being watered 10 to 15 minutes, about as long as someone would want to stand and water one area. Shutoff nozzles are available with multiple spray patterns, such as shower, mist, soaker, cone, and jet. An example of a hose with an automatic shutoff nozzle is shown in Figure 3.20.

FLOW-CONTROL DEVICES   A flow-control device can be used to set the run time and flow (in gallons) for manually operated, portable sprinklers, eliminating the need for sprinkler watching. Unlike automatic irrigation system controllers, which require electricity or batteries, a wind-up control device (similar to kitchen timers) can be attached to manual irrigation equipment at the hose bib and can be reset for each use. An example of a control device for a manual sprinkler is shown in Figure 3.21.

SPRINKLERS WITH VARIABLE SPRAY PATTERNS AND LOW PRECIPITATION RATES   Use sprinklers that emit large drops of water close to the ground. Portable sprinklers (e.g., fixed, rotor, or oscillating spray heads) often have circular spray patterns that are inefficient when used on lawns and landscapes because the design of landscaped areas seldom conforms to these circular shapes. In order to irrigate hard-to-reach areas, homeowners often place manually operated sprinklers on sites where the spray pattern overlaps sidewalks, driveways, and streets. This causes runoff and water waste. To avoid this problem, select a sprinkler that has variable spray patterns. Variable sprinkler heads have multiple spray patterns that are appropriate for such shapes as circles, squares, rectangles, half-moons, and thin median strips. An example of a variable sprinkler is shown in Figure 3.22. Sprinklers with low precipitation rates minimize runoff from clay soil, although sprinklers with higher precipitation rates may be better suited for use with sandy soils.[116]

SOAKER HOSES   Soaker hoses, an inexpensive and flexible alternative to drip irrigation systems, have thousands of tiny pores that drip water slowly and evenly

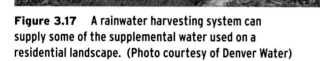

Figure 3.17   A rainwater harvesting system can supply some of the supplemental water used on a residential landscape. (Photo courtesy of Denver Water)

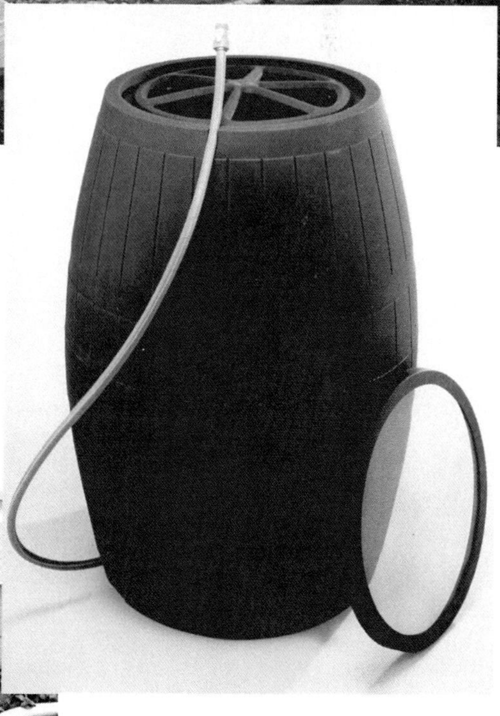

Figure 3.18   A rain barrel can collect and store about 75 gallons of rainwater. Rain barrel accessories may include a safety grid to prevent children and animals from falling in; a debris screen to keep leaves, bugs, and sticks out; an overflow hose; and an on/off hose valve. (Photo courtesy of Gardener's Supply Company)

Figure 3.19   A spigot and garden hose provide easy access to water collected in a rain barrel. (Photo courtesy of Christy Huddle)

Figure 3.20 Hose with an automatic shutoff nozzle. (Photo courtesy of Amy Vickers & Associates, Inc.)

at low pressure. The distribution range of soaker hose pores is about 3 inches, broader than most drip emitters (fittings that deliver water from drip irrigation systems). Soaker hoses are particularly effective for watering gardens, shrubs, perennial borders, and areas surrounding shrubs and trees because they deliver water at a slow but steady rate; the key to using them efficiently is turning them off when the targeted plants have received sufficient water. Soaker hoses are easy to use, can be moved around just like garden hoses, and can usually be adjusted to the desired length. They typically need a pressure-regulating device to reduce water pressure to 10 pounds per square inch (psi) or less. An example of a soaker hose is shown in Figure 3.23.

Maximize Automatic Irrigation System Efficiency

IRRIGATION SYSTEM DESIGN The design of an automatic irrigation system influences its water efficiency. An irrigation system should be designed or retrofitted to give the user maximum control over water applications to turf and other landscaped areas. The system should not apply water or create runoff on any hardscapes or other nonirrigated areas. A well-designed irrigation system will place spray heads or drip lines according to plant hydrozones; for example, a pop-up spray head may be needed for turf grass, but a slow drip emitter may be more appropriate for a vegetable garden or an area planted with shrubs.

MONTHLY ADJUSTMENT OF IRRIGATION SYSTEM CONTROLLERS Irrigation system controllers, also referred to as clocks or timers, are electrical or battery-operated devices that control the frequency and timing of wa-

Figure 3.21 Flow-control devices such as wind-up timers for manual sprinkler systems can be preset to irrigate lawns and other landscaped areas for only as long as needed. (Photo courtesy of Amy Vickers & Associates, Inc.)

Figure 3.22 Manual sprinklers with multiple spray patterns can help avoid runoff when irregularly shaped areas are watered (e.g., circles, half-moons, oblongs, and squares). (Photo courtesy of Gardener's Supply Company)

Figure 3.23 A soaker hose releases water to plants slowly, helping them develop deep roots that can survive on less water. (Photo courtesy of Gardener's Supply Company)

tering cycles for automatic irrigation systems. (Controllers for automatic irrigation systems are different from nonelectrical automatic timers and similar devices that are used with manual hoses and sprinklers and that must be reset for each use. See "Manual Irrigation" earlier in this section.) Controllers are usually mounted on outside walls or freestanding pedestals near the hose bib.

For maximum water efficiency, irrigation system controllers should be reprogrammed at least monthly to respond to changing rainfall and temperature conditions. In reality, however, few homeowners or landscape managers make such adjustments either because they don't know how or because they simply neglect to operate the controller properly. Some controllers are purposely set to use high volumes of water to ensure that grass stays green, no matter how hot or dry the weather. The most common—and most inefficient—practice with an irrigation system controller is to "set it and forget it" once a season. Unfortunately, relying on the same watering cycle for an entire irrigation season ignores the fact that turf has different watering requirements in spring than in summer, when most grasses are dormant. Similarly, the water needs of newly planted turf and other vegetation are high at first but diminish considerably once the plants are established.[53, 77] An example of an irrigation system controller is shown in Figure 3.24.

Once a controller is programmed, it will be activated at the preset time and will initiate irrigation at each watering zone (a group of sprinkler heads or drip emitters adjusted for a collection of plants with similar irrigation needs). A controller with multiple-programming capability allows the user to establish watering cycles for each hydrozone so that each group of plants with similar water requirements receives exactly the amount it needs. This helps to avoid overwatering some plants and underwatering others.[53]

RAIN SHUTOFF DEVICES Rain shutoff devices prevent automatic irrigation systems from being activated during and after rainfall. Available in several designs, these devices are typically wired to an irrigation system controller and override a scheduled irrigation when the water collection cup or sensor on the shutoff device detects water. Once the rainwater has evaporated from the device, scheduled irrigations resume. Rain shutoff devices are simple, economical, and useful tools for preventing irrigations that would be wasteful.[53] A rain shutoff device and its installation are shown in Figures 3.25 and 3.26, respectively.

MAINTENANCE OF SPRINKLER COMPONENTS Check sprinkler system heads and other components several times a season to ensure proper operation and to minimize outdoor water waste. The most common types of sprinkler heads are pop-up spray heads (Figure 3.27), gear-driven rotors, impact heads, and stream rotors. Broken, misdirected, or leaking heads and other components should be repaired or replaced. Sprinkler system adjustments and repairs can address a number of problems.

Runoff. The precipitation rate of a sprinkler head—the rate at which it delivers water—should be lower than the soil infiltration rate to minimize runoff.

Figure 3.24 Electronic irrigation system controllers ("timers") can schedule water-efficient irrigations if they are properly programmed and regularly adjusted to adapt to a landscape's changing water needs throughout the growing season. (Photo courtesy of Gardener's Supply Company)

A sprinkler system's precipitation rate is usually expressed in inches per hour. The flow rate—the amount of water distributed by a sprinkler head—is usually measured in gallons per minute. Shortening the irrigation cycle can reduce the amount of precipitation a sprinkler system delivers.[53]

Misdirected spray. Misdirected sprays or water streams that flow onto sidewalks, driveways, streets, and other hard surfaces are common sources of outdoor water waste. Misdirected pop-up spray heads can usually be adjusted by turning the nozzle in the desired direction. Misdirected impact rotors can often be reset by moving the trip collar to the correct position. Adjustments for misdirected gear-driven and stream rotors vary by product manufacturer and may require using a special tool or pushing down on the top of the head.[118]

Blocked spray. If possible, clear overgrown shrubs or other objects that are blocking the path of a spray or water stream. If the objects cannot be moved out of the way, other options include narrowing the spray pattern and relocating or capping the head. However, capping the spray head (replacing the existing nozzle with one that has no opening) may increase the pressure to remaining heads.[118]

Broken heads, seals, pipes, and valves. Replace broken or cracked irrigation heads, nozzles, risers, and seals (in caps). Repair pipes that are cracked or leaking, and repair or replace broken or leaking valves.[118]

Clogged or stuck heads. Remove any dirt or debris that is clogging the nozzle or riser in a spray head. In most spray heads, a screen placed before the nozzle or assembly can be taken out and cleaned with a brush. Gear-driven, impact, and stream rotors can get stuck in one position. Buildup of calcium deposits around the rotating mechanism is often the cause of stuck impact rotors; an irrigation professional can clean these deposits with a wire brush. Gear-driven and stream rotors usually cannot be repaired and must be replaced.[118]

Elevated, low, and tilted heads. Elevated spray heads can easily be damaged or knocked out of alignment by lawn mowers, foot traffic, or other forces. To make them less vulnerable, dig a hole around the head and lower the body or replace the nipple (the plastic piece that connects the head to the pipe) with a shorter one. Replace soil around the hole, making sure it is compacted. Spray heads positioned too low in the ground or overtaken by excess thatch cause poor water distribution. To reset elevated heads, follow similar steps except *raise* the head. Likewise, tilted heads should be redug, straightened, and recompacted.[118]

Long or short spray radius. If the sprinkler extends the spray too far (causing a spray radius that is too long) or fails to extend the spray far enough (causing a radius that is too short), adjust the radius with a screwdriver, allen wrench, or other tool provided by the product's supplier.[118]

Low head drainage. Low head drainage occurs when one irrigation system station shuts off and the next station begins watering, but water continues to be emitted from the heads in the low part of the zone that was just turned off. This situation can cause wet spots and discoloration of concrete. Installing a check valve at the base of the head usually corrects this problem, which commonly occurs in sloping areas.[118] Check valves must be drained during freezing weather conditions to prevent burst lines and damage to the irrigation system.[53]

SPRINKLER DISTRIBUTION UNIFORMITY As discussed earlier, distribution uniformity, or DU, is a measure of how evenly and efficiently a sprinkler applies water to the landscape. If the DU is low, water is probably being wasted because some turf and plant areas are not receiving enough water and other areas may be overwatered. The DU can vary even during the course of a day as a result of variable wind conditions or fluctuations in water pressure (pressure

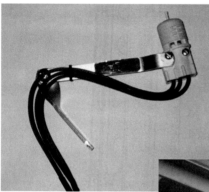

Figure 3.25 A shutoff device that responds to rainfall stops automatic irrigation systems from watering during and after rain. (Photo courtesy of Glen-Hilton Products, Inc.)

Figure 3.26 Installing a rain shutoff device connected to an automatic irrigation system (Photo courtesy of Denver Water)

tends to drop on hot days when irrigation system use is high). A simple method for measuring DU is the "catch-can" test (see "Basic Steps for Auditing Landscape Water-Use Efficiency and Preparing a Site Conservation Plan" earlier in this chapter).

The ideal DU is 100%, but achieving a perfect DU is impossible in practice because of such factors as wind and landscape grading. The minimum acceptable DU is 60 to 70% for turf and somewhat less for groundcover areas, shrubs and trees;[53] some jurisdictions set specific DU percentage goals. According to Marsha Prillwitz, water conservation specialist with the California Department of Water Resources in Sacramento, California, most water audits of residential landscapes find a DU of 50% or less.[119] Good uniformity can be achieved through proper irrigation system design and regular maintenance practices such as repairing broken, crooked, and plugged heads and maintaining correct operating pressures, adequate spacing of heads (overlapping sprinkler patterns to compensate for uneven distribution), and matched precipitation rates (uniform delivery of water when different arc patterns are used for a specific area, particularly turf areas). The DU for irrigated lawn grass is usually more important than that for shrubs or groundcovers because turf requires uniform moisture to maintain a green appearance. Also, shrubs and trees can often access other sources of water besides supplemental irrigation because they have deeper and broader root structures than grass.[53]

Figure 3.27 Automatic pop-up sprinkler head (Photo courtesy of Jane Heller Ploeser)

OPERATING PRESSURE Check the sprinkler system's required operating pressure and compare it with actual water pressure; differences can affect the system's operation and water efficiency. Residential sprinkler systems are usually designed to operate at 30 to 50 psi. Homes or properties in newly developed areas are especially likely to experience water pressures that exceed the operating limits of an irrigation system, and in such cases a pressure reduction valve may be needed. Pressure reduction is needed with drip systems more frequently than with sprinkler systems. The local water service provider should be able to identify water pressures in the main leading to a specific property, but a gauge at the hose bib can measure the actual pressure received by the sprinkler system. The maximum flow from the hose bib (measured in gallons per minute) can be determined by turning on the faucet full force and measuring how much water is collected in a container in one minute.[116]

The chief vice in gardens... is to be merely pretty."
—Fletcher Steele, landscape designer (1885–1971)

CENTRAL IRRIGATION CONTROLLERS FOR MULTIPLE SITES Irrigation systems for large landscaped areas, such as golf courses, playing fields, recreation sites, public parks, office complexes, and road medians, are often run by multiple controllers coordinated by a computerized central controller that is monitored by an irrigation specialist in an office. Central irrigation controllers are typically linked to evapotranspiration data that are regularly updated by readings from weather stations. Central controllers can enhance irrigation system efficiency because irrigation specialists can quickly adjust them in response to weather conditions, system pressure changes, and leaks.[53] The city of Aurora, Colorado, has spent more than $1 million to computerize its park irrigation system through a central controller that schedules irrigations at 90 parks. Thanks to the central controller, park personnel no longer need to turn sprinklers on and off manually. The computerized controller system is also helping the city to more readily identify broken and leaking pipes.[120]

SOIL MOISTURE SENSORS A practiced gardener can gauge soil moisture by look and feel, but those who are less experienced may find a soil moisture sensor useful in planning irrigations. Moisture sensors are most effective when used with uniform soil, but this means they may be impractical for many lawns and landscapes. Because landscaped areas commonly have a mixture of soil types, moisture levels can vary depending on where a measurement is taken. In such instances, moisture readings would probably be useful only if irrigation could be controlled for individual areas according to their moisture level. Collecting accurate data would necessitate taking several readings with a hand-held sensor or installing multiple in-place sensors, either of which might be too time-consuming and costly for residential and small commercially irrigated sites.

Two types of soil moisture sensors are common — tensiometers and electrical resistance blocks. Hand-held tensiometers and moisture sensors are relatively inexpensive, are available at lawn and garden stores, and give a moisture reading when the probe is pushed into the soil. Hand-held sensors are useful for people who irrigate manually, either with a hose or a sprinkler that they turn on and off. In-place moisture monitors are used with automatic irrigation systems. They also have a probe that is inserted into the ground, plus a wire connecting them to an irrigation system controller. The controller adjusts irrigation schedules in response to moisture readings from the sensor. Used properly, moisture sensors can boost irrigation water efficiency and save water. Wired, in-place moisture sensors require proper installation and regular maintenance (e.g., replacing gypsum blocks, removing corrosion from wires) to provide accurate readings.[53]

ALTERNATIVE WATERING SYSTEMS For some landscaped areas, alternative watering methods may be more efficient than automatic irrigation systems. Drip systems, soaker hoses, and manual watering practices are potential alternatives. Drip irrigation is especially effective for nonturf areas, but it is generally not practical for lawn grass because drip emitters have a short distribution range. Soaker hoses can be a better choice than sprinkler systems for gardens, shrubs, and trees because they operate like drip systems in delivering slow, steady, low-volume applications of water. Manual irrigation, particularly with a hand-held hose, is often more efficient than an automatic system because people tend to use a hose only when they perceive it is needed. For more details, see the subheading "Manual Irrigation" earlier in this section and the following subheading on "Drip Irrigation Systems."

Figure 3.28   **Drip irrigation (Photo courtesy of Denver Water)**

Figure 3.29   **Aboveground drip system for annual beds (Photo courtesy of Denver Water)**

Install Drip Irrigation Systems

DRIP IRRIGATION BASICS Drip irrigation, a form of "microirrigation," is generally considered the most water-efficient type of automatic irrigation system for nonturf areas. (Microirrigation encompasses a number of methods including drip, subsurface, bubbler, low-trajectory, and low-volume spray irrigation.) Drip systems can save up to 75% of the amount of water used by sprinkler systems; this saves money and also reduces soil erosion, which damages landscapes and streams. Drip irrigation uses narrow tubing or plastic tape to emit water directly to plant roots at low pressure using small drops; other types of microirrigation emitters use tiny streams or miniature sprays. Although drip systems may require a higher initial purchase cost, in many cases the extra expense will be paid back over time from reduced use of water, energy (for properties with a well pump), and landscape chemicals. Drip irrigation may be the best choice for gardens, plants, shrubs, flowers, and trees, but it is generally less effective for lawns because adequate coverage of large areas would require extensive (and expensive) drip lines.

Complete do-it-yourself drip installation kits are available for simple installations at homes and small properties. Drip irrigation kits designed for installation by homeowners are often sold at home centers, nurseries, and hardware stores. Some manufacturers and distributors of drip irrigation products offer installation assistance over the telephone; others can prepare a customized landscape plan. Large drip irrigation systems may require design and installation by a landscape professional. Drip systems can be buried underground or can lie on the surface. A layer of mulch is usually placed over underground drip lines to minimize emitter clogging and to reduce evaporation. Because drip systems apply water only where it is needed, they impede weed growth and help prevent many of the diseases caused by over- or underwatering (wetting leaf surfaces, scalding foliage by watering at midday, or encouraging fungal diseases and spotting on fruits and vegetables).[121]

Drip irrigation systems, as shown in Figures 3.28 and 3.29, consist of these basic components:

Microtubing. Microtubing or plastic tape installed near plants delivers water through emitters that are placed directly beside plant roots (see Figure 3.30).

Filter. Filters prevent sand and silt from clogging drip lines and emitters (a problem with earlier equipment).

Pressure regulator. Because drip systems operate best at lower water pressures (20 to 30 psi), they often require pressure regulators to reduce high-pressure systems to desired levels. Small pressure-compensating emitters can be used to adjust pressures directly where water is applied instead of installing a pressure-reduction valve, as shown in Figure 3.31, for the entire system.

Drip emitters. Drip emitters (see Figure 3.32) connected to microtubing or plastic tape are placed directly on or next to plant roots to deliver water at slow, consistent rates. Flow rates from drip emitters are measured in gallons per hour.

There are more stars in the sky then grains of sand on earth."
—www.uselessfacts.net

Figure 3.30 The microtubing used with drip irrigation systems is smaller and easier to handle than conventional irrigation lines.

Figure 3.31 A pressure regulator lowers the water pressure in a drip system to 10 to 30 pounds per square inch.

Figure 3.32 Drip emitters are connected to drip irrigation tubes to deliver water to plant roots slowly and directly.

(Photos 3.30 through 3.32 courtesy of Amy Vickers & Associates, Inc.)

Microsprays. Microsprays are the miniature equivalent of overhead sprinklers, except that they use far less water. A microspray, as shown in Figure 3.33, delivers water from a single riser pipe to multiple plant locations. Flow rates for each microspray emitter can be controlled by the emitter type and size, by setting the controller, or both.

Bubbler emitters. Bubbler emitters are placed aboveground to deliver water to targeted locations, such as shrubs, trees, and densely planted flower beds. Bubblers are typically operated at a higher flow rate than drip emitters.

Backflow preventer/antisiphon valve. Installing a backflow preventer can prevent irrigation water from siphoning back into the community water supply. Many water systems and communities require drip and other types of irrigation systems to have these safety devices to prevent contamination of the water supply.

DRIP IRRIGATION SYSTEM RETROFITS Replacing and upgrading system equipment can increase the water efficiency of drip irrigation systems.

DRIP SYSTEM PROTECTION Drip systems can be vulnerable to damage and vandalism when they are close to foot traffic. Mulch is usually a good protective cover for drip systems, and it also reduces evaporation. Using rigid polyvinyl chloride tubing and protected emitters may also help reduce damage.[53]

DRIP SYSTEM MAINTENANCE   Drip irrigation systems should be inspected regularly for damage and leaks. Because microtubing is thin, pliable, and located on the ground, it may be gnawed or eaten by animals. Damaged tubing results in leaks, which may or may not be obvious aboveground, depending on the porosity of the soil and the type of cover over the tubing. Tubes and emitters become clogged over time and need to be cleaned or replaced, depending on the frequency of use, soil conditions, and emitter design (some emitter designs prevent clogging better than others). Likewise, filters should be checked and cleaned regularly to make sure they are operating properly.

Water Savings, Benefits, and Costs From Efficient Landscape Irrigation Systems and Devices

This section discusses the estimated water savings that can be achieved by using specific types of water-efficient irrigation equipment. Estimated costs of these irrigation system components are given, and additional benefits are described.

Automatic Shutoff Nozzles

Using an automatic shutoff nozzle on a hand-held hose can be expected to save an estimated 5 to 10% of water used outdoors. The cost of these nozzles is about $7 to $15.

Flow-Control Devices (Manual Sprinklers and Hoses)

The amount of water that can be saved by installing a flow-control device on a manual sprinkler or hose is not well established. The cost of these devices is $15 to $25.

Figure 3.33 Microspray heads are closer to the ground and use less water than conventional sprinkler heads. (Photo courtesy of Denver Water)

Sprinklers With Variable Spray Patterns

The amount of water that can be saved by replacing a conventional (e.g., fixed-rotor) sprinkler head with a sprinkler head that has variable spray patterns is not well established, but most of the savings would result from reduced runoff. The cost of a sprinkler head with variable spray patterns is $20 to $35.

Soaker Hoses

The amount of water that can be saved by using a soaker hose instead of a sprinkler or hand-held hose is not well established. The cost of a soaker hose is $20 to $40, depending on the length, plus $6 to $10 for a pressure regulator.

Shutoff Devices Activated by Rainfall

Installing a device that shuts off an automatic irrigation system in response to rain can save an estimated 5 to 10% of water used outdoors. Rain sensors cost $15 to $45.

Irrigation System Controllers (for Automatic in-Ground sprinkler and Drip Systems)

The amount of water that can be saved through improved programming of an irrigation system controller varies but is estimated to be at least 10 to 15%. The cost of automatic irrigation system controllers for residential use ranges from about $50 to $250, depending on the features provided. Commercial-use controllers and central controllers can cost up to several thousand dollars.

Soil Moisture Probes and Sensors

Using a soil moisture probe or sensor can save an estimated 5 to 10% of water used outdoors, provided the moisture data are used to adjust irrigation schedules. Simple hand-held probes and soil moisture detectors cost $15 to $20. Moisture sensors and tensiometers cost $35 to $125. Gypsum blocks, which must be replaced at least every two years, cost $5 to $10, but the meter to read them costs $150 to $250. Simple moisture sensor devices such as tensiometers may be better choices for residential applications because they are portable and easy to read.

Sprinkler System Repairs

The cost of replacing broken sprinkler components ranges from $1 to $50. Replacement pop-up heads cost $7 to $11, impact heads and gear-driven rotors cost $15 to $20, and stream rotors cost $20 to $25. Replacement nozzles for heads cost $1 to $5. Spray head caps that have broken or loose seals cost about $1 each. A broken 1-inch valve can be replaced for about $50, but it might be repairable for less.

Drip Irrigation

Estimated water savings from using a drip irrigation system to replace a conventional sprinkler system for nonturf areas can range from 25 to 75%. A simple do-it-yourself, residential drip irrigation kit containing 50 feet of hose costs about $50 to $100; custom drip systems can cost hundreds or thousands of dollars, depending on the size of the area to be irrigated and the type of system installed. Installation of a drip irrigation system by a licensed installer costs $1 to $1.50 per square foot.

Rainwater Harvesting (Cisterns)

The amount of rainwater that can be harvested with a cistern or garden pond depends on the capacity of the cistern or pond, the frequency and volume of rainfall, and the rate at which the rainwater is used. For example, during a thunderstorm that delivers about one inch of rain, a custom home with 3,000 square feet of roof could receive as much as 1,800 gallons of water that could be diverted into a cistern or pond for reuse.[123] This is a considerable amount of water, given that homeowners use an average of 10,000 gallons per season for lawn irrigation.

In addition to saving tap water, rainwater harvesting has several environmental and financial benefits. For example, the city of Toronto sponsored a rain barrel installation program involving 150 single-family homes. Of the program participants who responded to a follow-up survey, 56% reported that they had emptied the barrel more than once a week to water their yards, saving 55 to 65 gallons per barrel (three different sizes of barrels were used in the trial program). However, 63% of respondents reported that the barrels were not large enough to meet all of their outdoor watering needs.[124] Water harvesting saves energy and chemical costs because the rainwater is used directly instead of first being treated, pumped, and distributed through a water system. Another advantage of rainwater harvesting is that it reduces stormwater runoff as well erosion and flooding caused by runoff. Rainwater is also cleaner than water taken from rivers and lakes because surface water sources often contain dissolved salts and minerals as well as industrial pollutants.[114]

In addition to collecting rainwater, roof cisterns provide a cover that can help extend the life of the roof. The presence of a large rainwater collection tank may also lower homeowner and fire insurance costs. Commercial rain barrels, which are made of plastic and have a capacity of about 75 gallons, retail for about $85 to $125. Larger downspout cisterns that hold several hundred gallons of water cost $250 to $350. Small household cistern systems cost $800 to $2,000. Prices for larger cisterns range from about $2,500 for a 2,000-gallon tank to about $15,000 for a 30,000-gallon tank. Large above- and below-ground cisterns, usually made of cement and other reinforcing materials, are typically lined and covered to inhibit algal and bacterial growth and to keep out insects, animals, and debris. Sand filters and purifiers that use ultraviolet light can be added for water treatment purposes. Large ground-level cisterns may need a pump, which will cost at least $50 plus electricity costs. Some communities have ordinance restrictions that prohibit cisterns or require permits for their use.

Garden ponds can be low-cost rainwater-catchment systems. For example, assuming the pond is dug by hand, a 16-foot by 26-foot pond that is 2 feet deep costs $100 to $175 for a plastic tarpaulin, tarp stakes, a 50-foot garden hose, and a submersible 110-volt sump pump.[125]

The average raindrop reaches a top speed of 22 miles per hour."
—www.uselessfacts.net

Case Study *Florida Nursery Saves Water With On-Site Rain and Irrigation Water Recapture and Reuse System.* Jon's Nursery, a 150-acre commercial nursery in Eustis, Florida, has reduced its groundwater pumping for irrigation by 75% (150,000 gpd) through a simple runoff and recovery system that reuses rain and irrigation water. Lined plant beds, paved lanes, roadways, and swales collect rain and irrigation water that is stored in two lined retention ponds. The recaptured water is later pumped through an overhead sprinkler system for reuse. In addition to reducing water use and pumping costs, nursery owner Jon Rackley now uses less fertilizer because the recycled water contains fertilizer from plant bed runoff. The first stage of the system covered 17 acres and cost $100,000; the second stage covers 25 acres and cost $168,000, half of which was reimbursed by the St. Johns Water District as part of its alternative water supplies program.[126]

Cost of Overwatering

In addition to paying for unneeded water, owners of landscaped property can incur multiple expenses as a result of damage caused by overwatering. For example, water that runs off of rooftops, lawns, and other areas onto sidewalks, driveways, and roads slowly eats away at concrete and asphalt. Runoff can also increase health risks caused by slippery conditions. Deteriorated asphalt contributes to potholes, which cost $150 to $300 to repair.[105]

Implementation of Programs that Promote Efficient Irrigation Systems and Devices

Programs that promote the use of water-efficient irrigation systems and devices can be facilitated by the following actions on the part of the utility or other sponsoring agency:

Perform Landscape Water Audits

Many water utilities offer their residential and nonresidential customers free landscape water audits to measure outdoor water-use efficiency and to help put water-efficiency measures in place. Typical audit tasks include measuring outdoor water use; analyzing soil, turf, and vegetation; helping to reset automatic irrigation system controllers; and providing information about water-efficient landscape practices and related conservation programs. Procedures for a landscape water audit are described earlier in this chapter under "Basic Steps for Auditing Landscape Water-Use Efficiency and Preparing a Site Conservation Plan."

Offer Rebates or Other Incentives for Efficient Irrigation Systems and Cisterns

The water conservation program of the city of Austin, Texas, offers a rebate up to $150 to customers who accept an irrigation audit and install recommended water-efficient equipment or improvements.[127] In addition, a 30% rebate up to $500 is available to homeowners and businesses that install permanent rainwater harvesting systems.[128]

Provide Irrigation-Efficiency Devices

Distribution of outdoor water-saving devices such as shutoff devices that are activated by rainfall, automatic shutoff nozzles for hoses, and simple rain gauges are often provided as part of a landscape water audit.

Offer Technical Assistance and Rebate Programs to Upgrade Landscape Water-Use Efficiency

Technical assistance and rebate programs, such as those designed to help water customers retrofit inefficient irrigation systems and replace high-water-use turf grasses, can accelerate the implementation of water-efficient landscape practices.

Establish Conservation-training Criteria for Irrigation Professionals and Landscape Managers

As consumer demand for more water-wise landscaping increases, irrigation professionals and landscape managers need to be educated about water-efficient landscaping concepts and practices to help ensure that new and existing irrigation systems are more efficient in the future. "Consumers are becoming more aware of irrigation. As economic and environmental conditions have allowed for more investment in landscaped areas, the reality is that efficient irrigation is critical for protection of that investment. Consumers, in turn, are making wiser choices when deciding on a contractor," according to Christopher Pine of the Rain Bird irrigation company.[129] Various training and certification programs for irrigation designers, contractors, auditors, and managers are offered by such organizations as the Irrigation Association (Falls Church, Virginia) and the Irrigation Training and Research Center at the California Polytechnic State University (San Luis Obispo, California), among others.

3.5 LANDSCAPE IRRIGATION SCHEDULING

Efficient irrigation scheduling involves understanding lawn and plant water needs and setting the *frequency* and *duration* of irrigations accordingly. Knowing *when* and *how much water is needed* and adjusting irrigation schedules in response to changing plant and weather characteristics is critical to efficient water use and optimal plant health. Determining how much and how often water is needed is site-specific. There is no single right way to schedule irrigations efficiently because several site-specific factors influence plant water needs and water availability—particularly as weather and seasonal changes occur. For example, new plants and lawn grasses require more water when first placed in the ground than after their root systems are established. Lawns also have different water needs during growth periods (usually in the spring) than during dormant and cool seasons, and rainfall patterns obviously influence irrigation scheduling.

Lawns and landscapes are typically watered too often and too long. Many irrigated lawns and landscaped areas can thrive on a watering schedule of once or twice a week for periods of no more than 15 to 30 minutes. Less time is usually better than more. People sometimes overwater when they see brown spots that they assume were caused by insufficient water. This is not always the case. Brown spots can be caused by multiple sources, including high salinity levels in the soil, overapplication of lawn chemicals, nematodes, and animals. In addition, overwatering can increase lawn and plant viruses, fungi, and insects—conditions that also create brown areas.[130] During hot summer months or periods

*T*he water needs of a lawn for peak color and appearance are scandalous. The best bet is to let the grass go dormant for a month or two. . . . Dormancy is normal for most cool-weather fescues and mixed varieties; color will return with late summer rains and cooler temperatures."
—Joseph M. Keyser, public education coordinator, Montgomery County (Maryland) Department of Environmental Protection

I have never let my schooling interfere with my education."
—Mark Twain

Hawaii's Mount Waialeale is the wettest place in the world — it rains about 90% of the time, about 480 inches per annum.

of drought, many homeowners and landscape managers believe that the only way to keep lawns and plants alive is to deluge them with water. Such practices not only raise water bills but also increase runoff, plant diseases, root rot, brown spots, and mowing and maintenance costs.

Overwatering seems to be more common with single-family properties and other lawns and landscapes that rely on automatic irrigation systems. Automatic irrigation systems are run by controllers programmed to set the days (start days), time of day (start times), and length of time (station run times) that each irrigation valve or station will operate. When programmed properly, the controller can boost water efficiency by giving turf and plants just the right amount of water, in just the right places, for the minimum amount of time needed. In reality, however, the average water-use efficiency of automatic irrigation systems is about 50%. In other words, for every two gallons of water applied, one is wasted. Automatic irrigation system controllers that are used correctly and are regularly adjusted and maintained can achieve water efficiencies as high as 85 to 90%.[131] However, such efficiencies are uncommon because most people don't know how or don't bother to program their controllers properly. Efficiencies in the range of 60 to 70% may be a more practical goal—as well as an improvement—for most systems.

Large, sophisticated automatic irrigation systems, such as those used for golf courses and professional playing fields, increasingly rely on the use of evapotranspiration (ET) data and other information from remote weather stations to schedule irrigations and improve water efficiency. ET, the amount of water lost from plant foliage and soil over a period of time, is usually expressed as a depth of water (in inches or feet) lost per day. ET is affected by several factors—temperature, sun, humidity, wind speed and direction, and other environmental influences. The reference ET (ET_0) is a standard estimate of the ET for a field of 4- to 6-inch-tall, well-watered, cool-season grass. Expressed in inches per year, month, week, or day, the ET_0 is used as the basis for determining water needs for specific plants, including turf. With necessary adjustments for factors such as plant species (e.g., type of vegetation), density of planted vegetation (e.g., leaf surface area), and microclimates (e.g., amount of heat-absorbing and heat-reflecting surfaces), the ET_0 is a helpful reference point for planning the amount of irrigation water needed by landscape plants and turf because it represents a specific rate of water use in response to local weather conditions.[132] Water use for a specific grass species, plant, or crop can be calculated by using ET_0 and adjusting for the specific crop coefficient (K_c), in which $ET_c = ET_0 \times K_c$. The ET_c estimates can be used to determine daily water losses, indicating when irrigation should occur and how much water should be applied. For residents of California, the publication *Water Use Classification of Landscape Plants* (WU-COLS) lists estimated plant coefficients to adjust weather station ET_0 data from the California Irrigation Management Information System (CIMIS) for these factors.[133] A note of caution is in order, however. Several studies suggest, and some water conservation managers have found, that using ET (even when adjusted with specific crop coefficients) may overestimate the actual water needs of plants and lead to overwatering.[134]

Basic Lawn-Watering Do's and Don'ts

Watering in the early morning hours (e.g., 3 a.m. to 7 a.m.) is generally better than watering during the day or evening. Daytime irrigations are subject to high rates of evaporation caused by higher temperatures and winds. Watering at night is usually discouraged because residual dampness can lead to plant fungal diseases and pest infestations, especially on hot evenings (85°F and warmer). Avoid watering on windy days, particularly with spray irrigation. Driveways, sidewalks, and roadways should not be irrigated or allowed to receive runoff because this wastes water, increases runoff to storm drains, causes soil erosion, and can cause accidents resulting from slippery conditions. Lawns should be watered only when they need it, typically when grass blades begin to look dull and bluish-gray. Most soils underlying turf grass can hold water for 10 to 15 min-

utes and then they become saturated; longer irrigation periods on lawns that have any slope will cause runoff as soon as soil saturation has been reached. Most lawns need a maximum of 1 inch of water per week (including rainwater) during the spring growing season and less during the summer months, provided the grass has been allowed to develop deep roots (Figure 3.34). Conventional irrigated lawns with water-thirsty turf grasses (e.g., bluegrass) in hot, dry areas with little or no rainfall may need up to 2 inches a week. The amount of water a lawn receives from rainfall can be monitored with a simple rain gauge, as shown in Figure 3.35. To estimate how long it takes a hose, sprinkler, or automatic irrigation system to deliver 1 inch of water, place several tuna fish cans on the lawn and determine how much time is required for water in the containers to reach a depth of 1 inch by calculating the average amount collected in the containers. Healthy soil should be moist to a depth of 4 to 6 inches (this does *not* mean that 4 to 6 inches of water should be applied—merely that rainwater and irrigation water should percolate that far beneath the ground). Soil moisture can be estimated by inserting a soil moisture probe or screwdriver into the ground and checking to what depth the soil is moist. In determining the frequency of landscape watering, remember that keeping a lawn green with no brown spots during midsummer is often a costly, losing battle, even with regular irrigation. Mow grass no lower than 2 to 3 inches; taller grass shades the soil, reducing surface heat and evap-

oration. Practice grass-cycling—let grass clippings remain on the lawn after it has been mowed. Clippings contain more than 90 percent water. Leaving them on the lawn allows them to filter to the soil surface, creating a temporary layer of mulch that conserves soil moisture and reduces supplemental irrigation needs.[101]

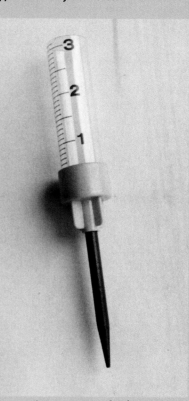

Figure 3.35 A rain gauge can be used to measure the amount of rain that has fallen.

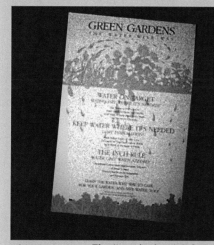

Figure 3.34 The "one inch rule" for weekly watering applies to many irrigated landscapes. (Figures 3.34 and 3.35 courtesy of Amy Vickers & Associates, Inc.)

Conservation Policies and Regulations Related to Landscape Irrigation Scheduling

Recommended or Mandated Watering Schedules

During normal (adequate system capacity and nondrought) conditions, the city of Austin, Texas, promotes a once-every-five-days watering schedule to all its customers between May 1 and September 30. Although the program is voluntary for customers, all city departments are required to follow the schedule. Austin discourages watering between 10 a.m. and 7 p.m. According to Tony Gregg, water conservation manager for the city of Austin, 50% of the city's water "customers have taken this [schedule] seriously" and on a voluntary basis are watering only once every five days.[135] Under a local ordinance, the same schedule and hours become mandatory when demand exceeds a preset Stage 2 trigger level.[136, 137] The mandatory five-day watering schedule also applies to washing vehicles. The Stage 2 trigger level is set below the maximum capacity of the water system to ensure adequate firefighting capacity. Watering schedules, based on whether the last number of a customer's street address is odd or even, are mailed out with utility bills in May and July of each year. First-time offenders of the mandatory restrictions are subject to a warning issued in person or by certified mail; second-time offenders receive a citation. Violations of the five-day schedule under mandatory Stage 2 conditions are subject to fines of a maximum of $2,000.[136, 137]

Recommended or Mandated Times of Day for Watering

Some communities have ordinances limiting lawn and landscape watering to late evening and early morning hours only, e.g., no watering is allowed between 9 a.m. and 5 p.m. Miami-Dade County, Florida, has such an ordinance.[138]

Watering Restrictions During Emergencies

Water suppliers or municipal ordinances often prohibit outdoor watering (including irrigating landscapes, filling pools, washing vehicles, and washing sidewalks or streets) during droughts or emergency water supply conditions.

Water-Efficiency Measures for Landscape Irrigation Scheduling

Water-efficiency measures related to irrigation scheduling include:

Water Every Five to Seven Days in Most Regions, up to Twice a Week in Hot, Dry Climates

Many conventional lawns can stay healthy if watered once every five to seven days; lawns in hot, dry regions may need to be watered about twice a week. With adequate rainfall, supplemental irrigation may be avoided altogether. Watering requirements vary by region, soil, and weather, but many conventional lawns and plants need *at most* 1 inch of water a week (including rainwater) during the growing season. Overwatered turf should be slowly transitioned to receive less water to avoid plant shock. The less grass is watered, the less it will need watering because appropriately stressed lawns develop deep roots that allow them to survive on less water, even during droughts. If the turf has been allowed to develop deep roots and receives adequate irrigation, the soil should contain enough moisture to maintain it. Deep, infrequent watering is better for lawn grass than frequent short irrigations, which reach only shallow roots.

Limit Watering Cycles to a Maximum of 15 to 30 Minutes

Watering cycles for lawn grass and landscaped areas should often last no more than 15 to 30 minutes, depending on such factors as plant water needs, landscape slope, sprinkler application rate, and the water infiltration rate of the soil, as shown in Table 3.3. In general, the flow rate of the water applied from a sprinkler or hose should be less than the soil infiltration rate. The slower the soil's infiltration rate, the more slowly water should be applied if it is to be absorbed. Once the soil's capacity for holding water has been reached, it is saturated; if irrigation continues, runoff begins. Some heavily compacted soils reach their infiltration rates in as little as 5 minutes. Most lawns with any gradient will have runoff about 15 minutes after sprinkler irrigation begins. Level surfaces and soils with high infiltration rates (sandy soils and loam) may need weekly sprinklings of about 30 minutes to give the grass a sufficient soaking. Extremely impermeable soils, such as clay or clay loam, may require two 15-minute irrigation cycles a week instead of one 30-minute cycle to avoid runoff.[140–142] For turf areas that have been overwatered for some time, a decrease in the frequency and duration of irrigation to improve water efficiency should be implemented in stages to allow the grass's roots to adjust and to avoid severe lawn stress. Incremental reductions in irrigation water will force the shallow roots of overwatered lawns to go deeper so they can live on a more thrifty water diet.

The amount of water delivered by a garden hose varies depending on the hose's diameter and operating pressure, as shown in Table 3.4. The estimated total volume of water used to irrigate landscaped areas varies considerably by region and by the number of inches applied weekly, with each additional inch of water applied increasing the total volume, as shown in Table 3.5.

Water During Early Morning Hours

Lawn and landscape watering should generally be carried out only during the cool hours of early morning. In most regions, the hours between 3 a.m. and 7 a.m. typically have the lowest temperatures and the least wind. Watering during the day is extremely inefficient because hot sun and wind maximize evaporative losses at this time.[143] Avoid spray irrigation during windy conditions (day or night); as much as 40% of the water applied by a sprinkler on a windy, sunny day can be lost to evaporation. Some locales suggest avoiding evening irrigation because excess dampness during hot evenings (85°F and warmer) can make lawns and plants more susceptible to disease, but this has not been documented to be a significant problem, particularly if people are judicious about the amount of water they apply.

Preferred hours for watering vary among specific locales because of local climate conditions and the local water supply system's capacity to handle peak water demand. Some water systems designate specific hours for watering to better manage peak demand. In some cases, water utilities may suggest a range of hours for outdoor watering to lower peak hourly demands or during periods of drought. Guidelines advising no midday watering or no midday outdoor water use are common in many water-wise communities, even during normal conditions. The nonwatering period usually covers 8 to 12 hours—e.g., no watering between 9 a.m. and 5 p.m. or no watering between 7 a.m. and 7 p.m.

These rules may be in effect only during irrigation months—e.g., year-round in hot desert areas and parts of Florida or April to October in other North American regions. During drought conditions or in areas with water supply constraints, bans on midday irrigation may be in effect permanently. For example, during droughts, Hillsborough County, Florida, has an ordinance that allows established lawns and landscapes to be watered only one day a week (even-num-

Avoid the trap of the odd/even watering schedule, and select an every four- or five-day schedule based on street addresses or [some] other method. Texas cities that implemented the odd/even schedule found no reductions and, in some cases, increases in water use."

—Tony Gregg, water conservation manager, Austin, Texas

TABLE 3.3

Water infiltration rates of common soils

Soil	Water Infiltration Rate Before Saturation–*inches per hour**	
	Sloped Area	Level Area
Light sandy soils or sandy loam	½	1
Loam	⅕	½
Clay or clay loam	¹⁄₁₀	¼

* Water applied faster than the infiltration rate will result in runoff. Rates do not include influence of thatch or soil compaction.

Sources: Adapted from References 141 and 142

TABLE 3.4

Estimated water use by garden hoses*

Hose Diameter–*inches*	Volume of Water Used During Each Watering–*gallons*			
	15 Minutes	30 Minutes	45 Minutes	60 Minutes
½	75	150	225	300
⅝	96	192	288	384
¾	132	264	396	528

* Based on an open (unobstructed) 50-foot hose operated at 40 pounds per square inch of pressure. Flow reduction nozzles, variable spray nozzles, and higher or lower pressures will change flow rates from those shown.

Source: Adapted from Reference 157

TABLE 3.5

Estimated volume of water applied to irrigated landscapes*

Volume of Water Applied to Irrigated Area Per Week–*inches*	Volume of Water Applied to Irrigated Area Per Week–*gallons*				
	1,000 Square Feet	2,000 Square Feet	3,000 Square Feet	4,000 Square Feet	5,000 Square Feet
0.5	312	624	936	1,248	1,560
1	624	1,248	1,872	2,496	3,120
2	1,248	2,496	3,744	4,992	6,240
3	1,872	3,744	5,616	7,488	9,360
4	2,496	4,992	7,488	9,984	12,480

* Assumes uniform coverage (in inches) of irrigated area, though actual uniformity and water volume often vary.

bered addresses on Tuesdays and odd-numbered addresses on Sundays) and prohibits watering between the hours of 8 a.m. and 6 p.m. on permitted days.[144]

Adjust Automatic Irrigation Schedules at Least Monthly

Irrigation controllers should be adjusted at least monthly. Controllers can be set for the days the system should operate (start days), the time of day each irrigation cycle will begin (start time), and the length of time each station or valve operates (station run times).[131] In theory, controllers should help landscape owners and managers achieve greater water efficiency, but actual water efficiencies of automatic irrigation systems average about 50%, meaning that one of every two gallons of water applied is wasted.[131] Although irrigation system efficiencies can never reach 100%, they should be able to approach 85 to 90%.[131] Used correctly, automatic irrigation system controllers can be programmed to give plants and turf the right amount of water, in the right places, for the minimum amount of time needed.

A study of residential and commercial properties in Tampa found that the way to achieve the greatest water savings with irrigation systems is to change the irrigation schedule—reduce run times for individual hydrozones, reduce irrigation frequency to once or twice a week, and adjust irrigation cycles as the weather and seasons change.[78] Similarly, water-use surveys of 902 commercial, industrial, and institutional facilities served by the Metropolitan Water District of Southern California indicated that reducing irrigation frequency may be one of the most cost-effective efficiency measures at the sites surveyed.[145]

Base Irrigation Schedules on Adjusted ET Data

An irrigation controller that schedules irrigations based on ET data from a weather station can achieve marked improvements in water-use efficiency, particularly if the controller also measures soil moisture. ET-based schedules are more common with irrigation systems for large commercial and public properties, but their use in the residential sector is increasing. ET-based irrigation schedules are predicated on ET rates determined by local daily weather data as well as site-specific data (e.g., grass and plant types, soil type, precipitation rates, DU, root depth, coverage zone area, slopes, and microclimates).

ET-based irrigation schedules are often adjusted to use less water than the ET factor, because many turf grasses do not need 100% of the ET factor to stay green and healthy. For example, when Water District No. 1 in Johnson County, Kansas, conducted landscape irrigation audits at more than 1,000 single-family homes, it found that more than one third of the properties were receiving significantly less water than the ET factor. These landscapes were deemed just as visually attractive as those receiving water in amounts equal to or greater than the ET factor.[146]

Adjust Irrigation Schedules by Hydrozones

Irrigated lawns, gardens, and landscaped areas typically have different watering needs, both in terms of volume and frequency of applications. When plants with similar water needs and growing conditions are grouped according to hydrozones, they are easier to irrigate appropriately than plants with differ-

Total Rainfall and Effective Rainfall

Property owners and managers who want to factor in the amount of rainfall that can contribute to a landscape's irrigation needs may find it useful to measure the *net usable effective precipitation.* In many regions, rain can fall in short, intense bursts, particularly during the summer months. This kind of rain results in a net usable effective rainfall that is less than total rainfall. As a result, average monthly rainfall and ET data alone can be somewhat misleading for determining the amount of supplemental irrigation needed in these regions unless this factor is taken into account.[10]

ent needs that are mixed together. A common mistake made by homeowners is to treat all elements of a landscaped area—grass, plants, shrubs, trees, and gardens—as if they have the same watering requirements. For example, some homeowners set up 360° oscillating sprinklers so that the arc of the spray reaches as many plants as possible. A basic irrigation schedule should take into account the water needs of individual hydrozones, e.g., low, moderate, and high.[121]

Lawn-watering requirements vary depending on grass type and species, rainfall, climate, and, most significantly, consumer choice about what constitutes an acceptable-looking lawn. Heavily irrigated grass will stay green but will demand large volumes of water as well as more frequent mowing and higher maintenance costs. Rainfed-only grasses, which have a more natural appearance, will be green during growth stages but brown during dormant periods. Warm-season grasses need less water than cool-season grasses to stay green during the summer, but warm-season grasses do not grow as well in shady areas. Cool-season grasses generally green-up in the spring and fall but turn brown during hot, dry summer months unless they are irrigated regularly. Without supplemental irrigation, warm-season grasses will flourish in sunny areas, and cool-season grasses will dominate shady areas. Planting a lawn with both kinds of grasses can create a somewhat patchy look, but the grasses will require little or no supplemental watering once they are established.[79]

Except for newly planted trees that must become established, trees usually have deep roots that can access underground water and should not need additional watering. In cases of extreme drought, trees that are showing distress may need supplemental watering. When supplemental watering is necessary, a soaker hose can be placed around the circumference of the tree (not the trunk but the tree's drip line—the ground perimeter of the tree's canopy) so that root hairs can access the moisture. Placing soil or mulch around the trunk of an established tree usually has no beneficial effect because most trees have deep root structures.[121]

Establish a Site-Specific Water Budget

A landscape water budget is a site-specific irrigation allowance based on a formula that can quantify the amount of water needed for a particular landscape. Some water utilities use water budgets to project or set guidelines for customers' outdoor water use, often for the purpose of setting peak-demand rates and charges. Factors that determine a site's water budget include: area (square footage of irrigated and nonirrigated areas); the water requirements—including the ET factor—of turf grass, plants, and water features (e.g., fountains or ponds); irrigation system efficiency; and effective precipitation (beneficial rainfall, excluding that lost to runoff or deep percolation).[40]

Water budgets can overestimate the amount of water a landscape needs if they aren't adjusted for the fact that many plants, including turf grass, can thrive on less water than their specified ET factor. (This is because the reference ET is for well-watered, cool-season turf grass; in many cases, cool-season turf grass with deep roots can thrive even when it is not so well watered.) For example, many lawns can hold up with supplemental water amounting to only 70 to 80% of their ET factors—and sometimes less—as evidenced by lawns that remain green despite not receiving supplemental water. Several conceptual approaches and formulas can be used to establish landscape water budgets on annual, monthly, weekly, and daily bases. These approaches and formulas are described by various sources, including publications and training manuals developed by the Irrigation Training and Research Center at California Polytechnic State University (San Luis Obispo) and the Irrigation Association (Falls Church, Virginia), among other sources.

Water Savings, Benefits, and Costs From Efficient Landscape Irrigation Scheduling

Case Study *ET-Based Irrigation Schedules Save Water.* Irrigation schedules for golf courses, playing fields, recreational sites, and large lawns are increasingly based on ET data in an effort to save water and control costs, often with very good results. For example, four Southern California commercial sites that switched from conventionally programmed irrigation (e.g., fixed volumes of water regardless of ET factors) to ET data–based forecasting programs achieved impressive water and cost savings. The four sites averaged 35,000 square feet of irrigated area and historically used an average of 68 inches of water a season, although water requirements according to ET data were 45 inches per season. Once the irrigation schedules were based on ET data, water used at the four sites averaged about 44 inches for the season. The water saved equaled 1,550 to 4,600 gallons per day per acre, or $1,500 to $4,500 per year per acre.[149]

Case Study *Improved Irrigation Controls Projected to Save School District 7.5 Million Gallons Per Season.* The Shoreline Public School District near Seattle received a $27,000 (50%) rebate from the Seattle Public Utilities' Water Efficient Irrigation Program toward the purchase price of a central irrigation control system for 14 playing fields and office landscapes scattered over a 15-square mile area. Before the central control system was installed, the irrigation systems at each site were operated manually with separate timers. About 130 person-hours were required each irrigation season just to adjust the timers. The new central controller uses an ET tracking system to communicate via radio (antennae and other hardware were installed at each irrigation site), improving the accuracy and speed of relaying ET data to the irrigation systems at each site.[150]

Implementation of Programs That Promote Efficient Landscape Irrigation Scheduling

Programs that promote water-efficient irrigation scheduling can be facilitated by the following actions on the part of the utility or other sponsoring agency:

Utilize Software and Training Programs

A number of software programs on water-efficient landscape irrigation practices are available from commercial sources and irrigation organizations, such as the Irrigation Association (Falls Church, Virginia) and the Irrigation Training and Research Center at California Polytechnic State University (San Luis Obispo), among others.

Weather Stations and Networks Provide ET Data to Program Irrigation Controllers

Weather stations and networks are used to access localized ET data that can directly program irrigation system controllers. Once used primarily by farmers and farm agencies to plan agricultural irrigations, weather station-based ET data and related information are now being used by water agencies, irrigation specialists, golf course and park managers, and other water users who need to optimize landscape irrigation schedules. For example, the California Irrigation Management Information System (CIMIS), one of the largest weather networks in the United States, is accessed daily by thousands of irrigation controllers in California for its real-time local ET data and other localized information. The CIMIS system collects weather data from more than 100 computer weather stations in California. Although CIMIS was originally developed to help farmers schedule irrigations, almost 50% of the data requests the system currently receives are for scheduling urban landscape irrigations.[148]

3.6 SOIL IMPROVEMENTS

Soil quality influences a plant's ability to absorb and hold water effectively, thereby influencing landscape water-use efficiency. Good quality soil, which may be naturally present at a site or may need to be imported, is critical to creating the growth environment necessary for a water-wise or native landscape to become established and thrive. High-quality soil retains water easily and thus helps to reduce irrigation needs. Given the amount of time and money that can be required to purchase and maintain lawns and plants, providing optimal soil conditions is a worthwhile investment.

The key to ensuring good soil is first to determine its quality by conducting a soil test and then to amend or loosen it sufficiently to create the best environment for seeds to grow and plants to become established. As plants mature, occasional soil amendment and nutrients may be needed, depending on the plant and its growing conditions. Some horticulturists automatically recommend that soil be improved prior to planting, but others do not. More is not always better; overfertilizing soil can cause excessive plant and weed growth and can create more demand for water than would normally be needed. Unless the soil is damaged or depleted, native and well-adapted plants may require nothing more than occasional reduced soil compaction.[53]

Conservation Policies and Regulations Related to Soil Improvements

Policies Requiring Soil Infiltration Rates to Be Factored Into Irrigation Schedules

Because the infiltration rates of soil and slopes influence plant selection and irrigation needs, some landscape policies and ordinances require irrigation application rates to be below infiltration rates. Such a practice may be more difficult than it appears because other factors besides soil and slopes also affect infiltration rates (e.g., plant material, sunlight, and temperature). At the least, the infiltration rate of soil, slopes, and other landscape features should be factored into plant selection and placement as well as irrigation requirements.[53]

Water-Efficiency Measures for Soil Improvements

Water-efficiency measures related to soil improvements include:

Perform a Simple "Look and Feel" Soil Test

Conduct a quick, easy soil test by digging a few inches below the soil surface using a screwdriver or other probe. Alternatively, use a soil probe, as shown in Figure 3.36, to reveal the look and feel of the soil and disclose root and moisture depth. The probe should go into the soil easily; if it does not, the soil is too dry or compacted. In general, soil underneath turf grass should be moist 4 to 6 inches below the ground. Soil underneath other groundcovers should be moist 6 to 12 inches belowground.[151] A soil probe can be an effective tool to teach people what's happening underground so they can make better decisions about wa-

Many landscape maintenance contracts specify regular applications of fertilizer regardless of the condition of the soil, turf, or plants. A visual examination of plant conditions or a soil test should determine a landscape's nutrient needs, not a contract."
—Tom Ash, *Landscape Management for Water Savings: How to Profit From a Water Efficient Future*

tering. Many people assume that if the surface of the soil is dry, the root zone is too—an incorrect assumption that can easily lead to overwatering. Studies of Orange County, California, residences where soil probes were used found that water use at these homes decreased by 15% during July–September.[152]

Analyze Soil

Soil quality influences how well plants survive or thrive. Before selecting plants, test the soil to decide which types of plants are best suited for its conditions and to determine whether it needs improvements to better support plants and retain water. Collecting several samples might be necessary because soil conditions at the site to be landscaped may vary. Avoid making assumptions about soil characteristics or quality without a test; even soil on adjacent properties may not represent the conditions of soil on the site to be landscaped. For instance, soil may have been damaged as a result of chemical dumping or overapplication, trash disposal, or topsoil removal and compaction (particularly in the case of newer properties). Such conditions may not be readily apparent or may be unknown to neighbors who claim to have excellent soil conditions.[53, 78]

Soil tests are usually simple and inexpensive and may be provided by regional agricultural or cooperative extension offices. Some plant nurseries and local farmers markets offer simple tests. A basic soil test will show the pH level and indicate whether lime applications are needed to change the pH for better plant uptake of nutrients (e.g., nitrogen, phosphorus, potassium, and other minerals).

Figure 3.36 A simple hand-held soil probe can reveal how wet or dry soil is at the turf or plant root zone. (Photo courtesy of Amy Vickers & Associates, Inc.)

Preserve Existing Topsoil

Unless it is damaged, existing topsoil is usually preferable to subsoil. Stockpiling the original topsoil is often advisable when construction or grading activities occur on a site to be landscaped; return the original topsoil to the site during the final grading process.[53]

Reduce Soil Compaction

Before planting, turn and loosen soil to a depth of at least 6 inches. This is particularly important for soil that has been compressed as a result of surface activity by construction, trucks, or machinery, a common problem at new and renovated sites. Similarly, the compacted roots of new plants, shrubs, and trees should be loosened prior to planting.[53]

Prepare Soil

When soil improvement would benefit plants, the addition of organic material, such as compost or manure, or inorganic materials is usually recommended. For example, sandy soil retains water and nutrients better if it is amended with organic matter. Clay soil absorbs water faster if it is loosened with organic matter, helping to reduce runoff and erosion. A general rule for soil amendment is to add 2 to 3 inches of compost, shredded leaves, or other fine organic material annually, although this rule varies somewhat depending on soil type and climate. Soil around established trees and shrubs can be amended with a 2- to 3-inch layer of organic mulch (e.g., coarse leaves, shredded bark, pine needles, or wood chips); decomposition of this material facilitates the leaching of humic acid into the ground.[55] In areas where a significant portion of the soil is damaged

Figure 3.37 Improving soil by rototilling amendments into dirt and reducing compaction is sometimes necessary to allow plants and turf grass to grow and stay water-efficient. (Photo courtesy of Denver Water)

or compacted, it may be necessary to rototill soil amendments into the dirt, as shown in Figure 3.37.

Avoid Overdosing Lawns With Fertilizers

Overapplying lawn chemicals such as fertilizer sets up a vicious cycle of excessive growth, overwatering, and increased labor requirements for mowing. Adverse environmental effects also result from excessive use of landscaping chemicals, including groundwater pollution and other potential hazards to human health, wildlife, and aquatic habitats. A study of Cape Cod, Massachusetts, communities conducted by the Woods Hole Oceanographic Institute identified elimination of landscape fertilizers as the easiest, least expensive way for a town to decrease excessive nutrients in its groundwater.[153]

Water Savings, Benefits, and Costs From Soil Improvements

Potential water savings associated with soil improvements for low-water-use landscapes have not been well established. When soil has not been depleted or damaged, however, cost savings can also be achieved, because many indigenous and adaptive plants prefer natural soil conditions and thus do not need enrichment.

Implementation of Programs That Promote Soil Improvements

Programs that promote good soil quality to support water-wise landscapes can be facilitated by the following actions on the part of the utility of sponsoring agency:

Identify Local Soil Analysis Services for Consumers

Cooperative extension services and some nurseries often offer free or low-cost soil analyses that can help consumers with decisions about soil improvements.

Promote Composting, Aerating, and Mulches

A number of communities have initiated household composting and grass-cycling programs to reduce solid waste and to promote the reuse of natural materials (e.g., leaves, grass) as mulches or compost for lawns and gardens. In some suburban and urban areas, the municipal department in charge of parks sponsors composting programs that enable residents to pick up compost materials at central collection places, such as parks and community gardens. See Section 3.7, "Mulches," for further discussion of the use of compost materials.

3.7 MULCHES

The use of mulches helps save water by reducing evaporative losses, cooling soil, and controlling weeds, which compete with desirable plants for available water. Proper use of mulches also slows soil erosion and compaction. *Top-dressing*, the practice of applying a thin layer of compost to the surface of a lawn, increases the soil's organic content, enhances earthworm activity, and serves as a mulch to protect grass's shallow roots.[101]

Organic mulches, such as the type shown in Figure 3.38, are often preferred because they are readily available, provide nutrients to soil, and do not add chemicals to the environment. They are often free or inexpensive and readily available to homeowners with landscapes that produce common mulch material— grass cuttings and leaves. Rock, gravel, pebbles, and marble "mulches" can be an option in cool climates but are generally avoided in hot, sunny regions because they radiate heat from the sun, increasing temperatures and water losses from plants and soil.[154]

Water-Efficiency Measures for Mulches

Water-efficiency measures related to mulches include:

Select Mulch

Organic and inorganic mulch materials, as well as nonwoven fabrics, can be used to boost the water efficiency and aesthetic characteristics of landscaped areas.

ORGANIC MULCHES Organic mulches include grass clippings, shredded leaves, wood chips, bark mulches, pine needles, and salt hay. Peat moss is not effective for water-efficiency purposes because peat draws water from the

Figure 3.38 Mulches: wood peelings, compost, bark, and humus (Photo courtesy of Denver Water)

soil as it dries. Fine-textured mulches hold moisture better than coarse-textured mulches, but they decompose more quickly than coarse-textured mulches.[154, 155]

GRASS-CYCLING Grass-cycling, the use of grass clippings as mulch, restores soil nitrogen and reduces evaporation. According to horticulturist Tom Ash, "Contrary to conventional wisdom, mulched grass clippings *do not* cause thatch buildup in turf. Thatch is caused by a buildup of plant shoots, stems, and rhizomes. Mulched grass clippings break down fast and do not build thatch in turf."[156]

INORGANIC MULCHES Inorganic but natural "mulch" groundcovers include rocks, pea gravel, pebbles, cobbles, beach stones, and boulders. Use caution in placing these mulches around plants and in areas where people or animals congregate because they can act as a heat sump, causing temperatures to soar if exposed to the sun. Marble chips are often avoided because they can damage plants and reflect sun glare, which hurts eyes and can scorch leaves. As marble chips weather, they can also increase soil pH, a condition that leads to iron deficiency and yellow leaves.[157]

NONWOVEN FABRICS Nonwoven landscape fabrics and newspapers can be used as mulch materials to hold in soil moisture and allow nutrients and air to penetrate soil freely. Landscape fabrics are cut to fit on the soil areas around plants and are usually covered with organic mulch. Newspapers can be used in much the same way but should be limited to two sheets to avoid creating a barrier too thick for water and nutrients.[154] Nonwoven fabrics can also serve as barriers to root growth along sidewalks and driveways, which can help prevent silting and clogging.[155]

Apply Mulch

For plants, shrubs, and garden beds, apply 2 to 3 inches of organic mulch, and spread it evenly. To control weed growth, apply up to 4 inches of mulch, but note that too much mulch can encourage shallow roots. Keep mulch away from the base of plants to avoid trunk rot. Top-dress the surface of a lawn, if it needs this, with about half an inch of composted mulch. At the end of the season, the mulch can usually be incorporated into the soil. Water both the mulch and plants thoroughly after the mulch has been spread because dry mulch can prevent moisture from getting into the soil. Fine-textured mulches (grass clippings, compost, shredded leaves, and leaf mold) may be preferred for more delicate annual or perennial flowers and vegetables. Wood mulches are often preferred for permanent plantings such as trees and shrubs.[101, 154, 158]

Water Savings, Benefits, and Costs From Mulches

Mulches have been reported to help prevent fluctuations in soil moisture compared with areas that have bare soil,[154] but the extent to which mulches reduce irrigation requirements is not well measured. When mulches are used to cover areas that were previously planted with irrigated turf or plants, the amount of water saved will equal that previously applied to the area.

In addition to improving moisture retention, mulches can also provide a barrier to some soilborne diseases that stress plants and increase water requirements. When mulches are used instead of turf or plants, the use of landscape chemicals (herbicides, fertilizers, and pesticides) is also reduced, which in turn saves money and reduces pollution loads and degradation of groundwater and surface water.[159]

Implementation of Programs That Promote Use of Mulches

Water conservation programs that promote the use of mulches on landscaped areas can be facilitated by the following actions on the part of the utility of other sponsoring agency:

PROMOTE HOUSEHOLD COMPOSTING AND GRASS-CYCLING Top-dressing the surface of a lawn with a thin layer of compost increases the soil's organic content, enhances earthworm activity, and serves as a mulch to protect grass's shallow roots.

PUBLICIZE THE AVAILABILITY OF FREE AND LOW-COST MULCHES Wood chips and shredded leaves are often available for free or for a nominal cost from municipal sanitation and parks departments. Include information about these services in water bills and community newspapers and on local Web sites.

3.8 MAINTENANCE OF WATER-EFFICIENT LANDSCAPES

Give me a field where the unmow'd grass grows."
—Walt Whitman

Proper, ongoing maintenance of water-wise landscapes and lawns helps to minimize water requirements and to ensure plant health and attractiveness. In addition to periodic water audits to assess landscape water-use efficiency, several basic maintenance principles can be applied with water-efficient lawns and landscapes. These practices, some of which vary according to region and climate, are described in the section "Water-Efficiency Measures for Landscape Maintenance" later in this chapter.

Conservation Policies and Regulations Related to Landscape Maintenance

Ordinances Requiring Periodic Landscape Water Audits

In California, all local jurisdictions are required to adopt a landscape water conservation ordinance to promote conservation of water used for residential and nonresidential landscapes. The state has created a model ordinance, California's Model Water Efficient Landscape Ordinance,[160, 161] which sets forth minimum requirements, including the provision that all landscaped areas that encompass more than one acre and that are supplied by a water utility are required to undergo a water audit at least every five years. The ordinance also specifies calculations for determining a landscape's maximum applied water allowance, estimated applied water use, and estimated total water use.

Water-Efficiency Measures for Landscape Maintenance

Water-efficiency measures related to turf and landscape maintenance practices include:[53, 130]

Repair Broken Irrigation Systems Promptly

Broken or improperly adjusted sprinkler heads, leaking hoses, and other damaged components of manual or automatic sprinkler systems should be repaired promptly to minimize water losses.

Maintain Turf Grass Efficiently

The following regular maintenance practices will help keep turf healthy and reduce its watering needs:

HELP GRASS DEVELOP DEEP ROOTS The roots of healthy turf grass are usually at least 4 to 6 inches deep. The deeper the roots, the more likely turf grass is able to withstand droughts and reduced irrigation. Stressing turf grass to help it develop deep roots is most effective during the spring growing season. During the summer, turf grass typically goes into dormancy, maintaining but not extending its root system. In the fall, turf grass often generates new root growth.[162]

SET MOWER BLADES HIGH   Mowing height plays an important role in determining the water requirements and appearance of turf. Optimal mowing height depends in part on grass species and local weather conditions. Grass should be cut at the maximum recommended height for its type, typically a minimum of 2 inches and as high as 4 inches. Keeping the blades of grass long helps turf develop deep roots and retain moisture, making the lawn more drought-resistant, and also helps minimize weed growth. Cutting grass too short can make it prone to weaker roots and browning. Mulching mowers are often preferred because they return grass clippings to the lawn, helping to fertilize the soil as they decompose.[53, 130] Mow grass before it needs more than 1 inch topped off; grass that has grown too high is more difficult to cut and can leave too thick a thatch on the lawn.[53, 130]

CUT GRASS WHEN IT IS DRY   How well grass is clipped influences its ability to retain water. Cut grass when it is dry to achieve uniform height and to avoid wet clippings, which stick to each other. The lawn-mower blade should be sharp; dull blades give grass a frayed appearance, and dull power mowers use more energy.

PRACTICE GRASS-CYCLING   Grass clippings should remain on the lawn if proper mowing techniques are followed. Grass clippings contain about 85% water and 5% nitrogen; leaving them on the lawn helps hold in moisture, reduces evaporation, and keeps grass cool. Clippings also help fertilize the lawn and can be used for mulch or compost material.[101]

AERATE TURF   Aerate lawns about once a year to help the soil retain moisture and absorb nutrients and air.

Fertilize Sparingly

Decrease the amount and frequency of fertilizer applications to save water and to reduce the landscape's reliance on chemicals. Avoid overapplying lawn fertilizer because grass that is too lush demands excessive amounts of water to maintain its appearance, a condition that invites fungal attacks.[163]

Make Use of Downspouts

Direct downspouts from home, garage, and building roofs to water lawns and gardens with nonedible crops, not driveways. Rain barrels placed under downspouts can be connected to drip or soaker hose systems.

Control Weeds

Weeds compete with turf and plants for water. Measures such as manual weeding and the use of mulches can minimize weed growth.[164]

Prune Sparingly

Plants, shrubs, and trees should be pruned only when necessary to curtail growth accelerations that would increase watering requirements.[78]

Practice Integrated Pest Management

Integrated pest management is a system of sustainable lawn and landscape management that relies on physical, mechanical, cultural, biological, and edu-

Let the rain kiss you. Let the rain beat upon your head with silver liquid drops. Let the rain sing you a lullaby."
—Langston Hughes, *April Rain Song*

cational steps to eliminate conditions that promote pest infestations. For example, small pest-killing worms such as nematodes can be used to kill root-eating, underground white grubs. Left uncontrolled, these grubs sicken or kill plants, causing replanting, increased irrigation requirements, and additional costs.

Water Savings, Benefits, and Costs From Landscape Maintenance

Water savings from landscape maintenance are largely indirect, except for measures involving the repair of broken or improperly adjusted irrigation system components. For example, a single improperly adjusted or cracked sprinkler head can lose several gallons of water a minute.

Water-wise and native landscapes typically require less time, money, and maintenance to stay healthy and attractive compared with conventional landscapes. Because water-wise landscaping emphasises reduced water use, reduced chemical use, and only practical or no turf areas, excessive plant growth and pests pose less of a problem. In summary, water-efficient lawns and landscapes typically require less work and money.

Implementation of Programs That Promote Landscape Maintenance

Programs that promote basic maintenance practices for water-wise landscapes can be facilitated by the following action on the part of the utility of other sponsoring agency:

Ongoing Public Education About Water-Wise Landscape Maintenance

Educating the public about outdoor water-use efficiency measures and natural and Xeriscape landscaping practices can be an ongoing process. Educational brochures, workshops, and community-based gardening programs that teach the concepts and practices associated with water-wise and natural landscaping are among the tools that can be used. Members of the local green industry—landscape professionals, garden centers, garden clubs, and municipal agencies—can be recruited to sponsor such projects.

3.9 WATER DECORATIONS AND FOUNTAINS

Water decorations such as fountains and constructed ponds, waterfalls, and streams are found in a variety of outdoor and indoor environments, such as public parks (see Figure 3.39), gardens, government buildings, office complexes, greenhouses, atriums, hotels and motels, amusement and water parks, zoos, cemeteries, shopping malls, and homes.

Many modern water decorations are designed to recirculate water, making demand less than if it were based solely on pumping rate and system configuration. Water consumption by a decorative feature operated with a *recirculating* water system can be estimated as the volume used for makeup (e.g., water lost to

Figure 3.39 Decorative fountains can use water efficiently with simple recirculation systems. (Photo courtesy of Amy Vickers & Associates, Inc.)

evaporation and splashing), maintenance (e.g., filter backwash and cleaning of pumps, hoses, and attachments), and leakage. During rainy periods (negative net evaporation), water may have to be removed from decorative features to avoid spillover.[165,166]

Water use by decorative features with *nonrecirculating* systems can be estimated roughly by multiplying the water pumping rate times the hours of operation. Adjustments should be made for operating conditions and the type of pump installed. (In rare cases, a separate meter may be installed to record actual water demand.) Fountains with water-level controller pumps use more water when evaporative losses are high, e.g., during hot, dry, and windy periods. Evaporative losses are greater in arid regions and during droughts, and this can increase demand, e.g., topping off ponds when water levels decrease.[165, 166]

Water use by simple decorations that are supplied by a hose connection without a pump can be estimated based on flow rate and hours of operation, with adjustments for leakage and pressure variations. The amount of water used by a water decoration with a pump can be estimated by determining pump size and output, usually measured in gallons per hour (gph) at a spray height (lift) of 1 foot, and making adjustments for the volume reused through recirculation. Depending on the type of pump, small fountains with lifts of 1 to 13 feet use 50 to 525 gph. Larger fountains with lifts of 15 to 23 feet use 750 to 4,200 gph.[165]

The use of decorations that feature moving water is sometimes criticized as an example of gross water waste, particularly during a drought or supply shortage. In some cases, this assessment is accurate and the water should be turned off, at least temporarily, especially if the feature is in a conspicuous location that makes it symbolic of a community's or utility's commitment (or lack thereof) to conservation. In other situations, efficient operation of water decorations can minimize waste and still allow people to be enchanted by the unique feelings that only flowing water evokes. There is no substitute for the soothing and restorative power of moving water, so one symbolic gesture need not sacrifice another. "Fountains are the magic that binds the world together," asserts Thelma Seear, founder of the Fountain Society of London.[167]

A pool is the eye of the garden in whose candid depths is mirrored its advancing grace."
—Louise Bebe Wilder

Conservation Policies and Regulations Related to Water Decorations and Fountains

Requirements for Separate Meters for Irrigation and Decorative Water Features Such as Fountains

Requiring a separate meter for irrigation systems and decorative water features can help conserve water by giving customers information about how much water they are using—as well as an appreciation of the money they could save by reducing flows or limiting hours of operation. Phoenix requires a separate meter for all outdoor water uses.[50]

Limitations or Prohibitions on Using Potable Water for Lakes, Fountains, and Other Decorative Features

Alternative water sources, such as reclaimed water or groundwater, are the only acceptable supplies for water decorations and lakes in some communities, e.g., San Francisco and the cities of Chandler, Mesa, and Phoenix, Arizona.[168] Other communities, such as Palo Alto, California, limit the use of potable water for decorative water features such as ponds, fountains, and certain landscaped areas.[169]

Water-Efficiency Measures for Water Decorations and Fountains

Water-efficiency measures applicable to decorative fountains, ponds, and waterfalls include:[165, 170–172]

- Shut off decorative features that are fed by continuously running water or replace them with a recirculating system.
- Recirculate alternative water sources that are used for decorative features, e.g., treated wastewater and groundwater, to minimize waste.
- Install meters for fountains and other decorative features to monitor water use, identify leaks, and control malfunctions early.

- Operate decorative water features for a limited number of hours and only while a facility is in use.
- Regularly check water-recirculation systems and water-level controller pumps (including pressure grouting, liners, seals, and drain valves) for cracks and leaks, damage, and other malfunctions that might inhibit the efficiency of the unit's water and energy use.
- Use lower pumping rates, smaller pumps, nozzles, and spray patterns, and pressure-reducing valves to reduce flows and evaporative losses yet retain the appearance of the decoration.
- Adjust the direction, pressure, and flow rate of fountains for proper jetting; make sure the fountain does not overspray water into the air (which would increase evaporative losses) or onto adjacent hardscapes.
- On windy or rainy days, avoid operating fountains and other outdoor water decorations that have spray features.
- Avoid or minimize splashing onto hardscapes by lowering the water level of ponds and fountains.
- Regularly check water decorations for leaks in tubing, pond liners, pumps, and connections.
- During a drought, it is usually prudent to shut off decorative water features. Even if the system is recirculating, operating a fountain during a water shortage might send the wrong message to the public.

Water Savings, Benefits, and Costs From Water Decorations and Fountains

A water-efficiency measure for an indoor decorative pool would be to cover it to reduce evaporative losses. For example, a 30-foot by 15-foot pool exposed to 78°F temperatures at 30% relative humidity loses about 3 inches of water depth a week, equivalent to about 1,500 gallons of water a week.[173] Operating the pool only 12 hours a day and covering it for the remaining 12 hours would save about 750 gallons of water a week, or 39,000 gallons a year. Based on a rate of $4 per thousand gallons of combined water and sewer service, the costs that could be saved with this measure would be $156. With a $65 purchase price for the pool cover, the payback period for this measure would be about five months.

$\sim$

1. Wayne B. Solley, Robert R. Pierce, and Howard A. Perlman, *Estimated Use of Water in the United States in 1995*, U.S. Geological Survey Circular 1200, U.S. Dept. of the Interior, U.S. Geological Survey, Reston, Va., 1998, p. 27.
2. Charles Fenyvesi, "His Whole World Is Grass: Lawn Guru Reed Funk Speaks to the Tough Little Cultivar Inside Us All," *U.S. News & World Report*, Oct. 28, 1996, p. 62.
3. Richard E. Bennett and Michael S. Hazinski, *Water-Efficient Landscape Guidelines*, American Water Works Association (AWWA), Denver, 1993, p. 1.
4. Personal communication, Jean Witherspoon, Water Conservation Officer, City of Albuquerque, N.M., Dec. 14, 2000.
5. Solley, *Estimated Use of Water in the United States in 1995*, p. 24.
6. Peter W. Mayer et al, *Residential End Uses of Water*, AWWA Research Foundation and AWWA, Denver, 1999, p. 86.
7. Mayer et al, *Residential End Uses of Water*, p. 114.

8. Vermont Water Conservation Study, prepared by Amy Vickers & Associates, Inc., Amherst, Mass., for the Vermont Dept. of Environmental Conservation, July 1997.

9. Final Report: Water Conservation Planning USA Case Studies Project, prepared by Amy Vickers & Associates, Amherst, Mass., for the Environment Agency, Demand Management Centre, Worthing, West Sussex, U.K., June 1996.

10. Nancy G. Scott, "Demand Management Strategies to Address Peak Day Demands," presented at the AWWA Conservation Workshop, Austin, Texas, February 1998.

11. Ken Gewertz, "The Course Suits Them to a Tee," *Harvard University Gazette*, vol. XCII, no. 35, July 9, 1998, p. 9.

12. Bruce F. Shank, "Recreational Turf Generates $350 Million in Irrigation," *Irrigation Journal*, February 1996, p. 22.

13. "New Golf Courses May Soon Be Forbidden to Use Groundwater," *U.S. Water News*, vol. 16, no. 2, February 1999.

14. Mary DeSena, "Irvine Ranch Water District Uses Rate Structures to Spur Conservation," *U.S. Water News*, vol. 15, no. 21, September 1998.

15. Andy Wasowski, with Sally Wasowski, *The Landscaping Revolution: Garden With Mother Nature, Not Against Her*, Contemporary Books, Chicago, 2000, p. 20.

16. Charles Fenyvesi, "His Whole World Is Grass," p. 61.

17. Thomas Farragher, "For Some Neighbors, It's a Turf War," *The Boston Globe*, Apr. 5, 1998, sect. B, p. 1.

18. National Gardening Assoc., *National Gardening Survey, 1991–1992*, National Gardening Assoc., Burlington, Vt., 1992, p. 11.

19. Herbert Muschamp, "Looking at the Lawn, and Below the Surface," *The New York Times*, New England edition, July 5, 1998, Arts & Leisure sect., p. 1.

20. F. Herbert Bormann et al, *Redesigning the American Lawn: A Search for Environmental Harmony*, Yale University Press, New Haven, Conn., 1993, p. 92.

21. Virginia Scott Jenkins, *The Lawn: A History of An American Obsession*, Smithsonian Institution Press, Washington, D.C., 1994.

22. Jenkins, *The Lawn*, p. 29.

23. Jenkins, *The Lawn*, p. 30.

24. Bormann, *Redesigning the American Lawn*, p. 22.

25. Sy Montgomery, "Lawns: An Un-American American Obsession," *The Boston Globe*, Aug. 25, 1997, sect. C, p. 1.

26. Jenkins, *The Lawn*, p. 31.

27. Jenkins, *The Lawn*, p. 184.

28. Sara Bonnett Stein, *Planting Noah's Garden: Further Adventures in Backyard Ecology*, Houghton Mifflin, Boston, 1997.

29. Jenkins, *The Lawn*, p. 187

30. Fox McCarthy, *Origins of Xeriscape*,™ Cobb County–Marietta Water Authority, Marietta, Ga., 1998.

31. Cooperative Extension Service, The University of Georgia College of Agricultural & Environmental Sciences, *Xeriscape™: A Guide to Developing a Water-Wise Landscape*, The University of Georgia College of Agricultural & Environmental Sciences, Athens, Ga., February 1992, p. 1.

32. Bret Rappaport, "From the President: Natural Landscaping Wins One," *Wild Ones® Journal*, March/April 1997, vol. 10, p. 3.

33. Patricia Leigh Brown, "House & Home: It Takes a Pioneer to Save a Prairie," *The New York Times*, New England edition, Sept. 10, 1998, p. D1.

34. Wasowski, *The Landscaping Revolution*, p. 126.

35. Wild Ones–Natural Landscapers, Ltd, *Wild Ones Journal*, Appleton, Wisc., 1997.

36. Northeastern Illinois Planning Commission, *Source Book on Natural Landscaping for Local Officials*, Northeastern Illinois Planning Commission, Chicago, May 1997.

37. "Drought Has North Carolina Residents Thinking Twice About Water Reuse," *U.S. Water News*, vol. 17, no. 8, August 2000, p. 21.

38. David Davis, as quoted by Cynthia Greenleaf in "Reclaimed Water Use Is Increasing in Irrigation Systems," *IBT Journal*, October/November 2000.

39. Memorandum of Understanding Regarding Urban Water Conservation in California, California Urban Water Conservation Council, Sacramento, Calif., amended Sept. 16, 1999, pp. 17, 28.

40. Bennett, *Water-Efficient Landscape Guidelines*, chapter 4.

41. Tom Ash, *Landscape Management for Water Savings: How to Profit From a Water Efficient Future*, Municipal Water District of Orange County, Calif., Fall 1998, p. 30.

42. Texas Agricultural Extension Service–Bexar County, Bexar County Master Gardeners, and Texas A&M University, San Antonio Evapo-Transpiration Pilot Study Report, prepared for the San Antonio Water System, San Antonio, Texas, 1998, p. 2.

43. Joseph M. Keyser, review of *The Lawn: A History of an American Obsession*, by Virginia Scott Jenkins, *Audubon Naturalist News*, December 1994, p. 20.

44. City of Albuquerque, Water Conservation Landscaping and Water Waste Ordinance, ordinance 18-1995, Albuquerque, N.M., 1995.

45. California Dept. of Water Resources, Model Water Efficient Landscape Ordinance, California Dept. of Water Resources, Sacramento, Calif., 1992.

46. Office of the Federal Environmental Executive, Guidance for Presidential Memorandum on Environmentally and Economically Beneficial Landscape Practices on Federal Landscaped Grounds, *Federal Register*, vol. 60, no. 154, Aug. 10, 1995, pp. 40837–40841.

47. Executive Order, "Greening The Government Through Leadership In Environmental Management," *The Weekly Compilation of Presidential Documents*, Apr. 22, 2000.

48. City of North Miami Beach, Ordinance No. 2000-9, an ordinance of the city council of North Miami Beach, Fla., amending Sections 24-115 through 24-125 of the Code of Ordinances of the City of North Miami Beach: Implementing and Requiring Additional Water Conservation Measures, Incorporating a Water Use Zone Table, Requiring Use of Xeriscape Plant Materials, and Amending Irrigation Requirements, Oct. 3, 2000.

49. State of California, Water Conservation in Landscaping Act, Assembly Bill 325, California Government Code Section 65591-65600, 1992.

50. The Bruce Company, Final Draft: Local Ordinances for Water Efficiency, prepared for the U.S. Environmental Protection Agency, Office of Policy Analysis, EPA Contract # 68-W2-0018, Subcontract # EPA 353-2, Work Assignment 24, Mar. 31, 1993, Appendix B.

51. North Marin Municipal Water District, Regulation 15: Water Conservation, North Marin Water District, Novato, Calif., May 1992.

52. Cooperative Extension Service, *Xeriscape™: A Guide to Developing a Water-Wise Landscape*, pp. 1–16.

53. Bennett, *Water-Efficient Landscape Guidelines*, chapter 5.

54. City of Albuquerque, "Xeriscape Basics," *The Complete How-To Guide to Xeriscaping*, prepared by Cooney, Watson & Associates, Inc., for the city of Albuquerque, N.M., undated, p. 4.

55. Virginia Polytechnic Institute and State University, Creating a Water-Wise Landscape, Publication No. 426-713, Blacksburg, Va., 1995.

56. T. Ching, "Gardening: Xeriscaping Helps When the Water Supply Is Low," *The New York Times*, July 1, 1990, p. 50.

57. Ash, *Landscape Management for Water Savings*, p. 6.

58. Cooperative Extension Service, *Xeriscape™: A Guide to Developing a Water-Wise Landscape*, p. 2.

59. Mitchell Zuckoff, "The Greening of Sydney," *The Boston Globe*, Sept. 5, 2000, pp. C1 and C3.

60. John Olaf Nelson, "Water Saved by Single Family Xeriscapes," presented at the AWWA Annual Conf., New York, June 22, 1994.

61. Fred Fuller, Tony Gregg, and James Curry, "Austin's Xeriscape It! Replaces Thirsty Landscapes," *Opflow*, AWWA, December 1995, p. 3.

62. "Conserving, Traditional Homes Compared: Landscaping Can Cut Use by 42%," *U.S. Water News*, April 1993, p. 9.

63. City of Austin, Texas, Xeriscaping: Sowing the Seeds for Reducing Water Consumption, prepared for the U.S. Bureau of Reclamation, Austin, Texas, May 1999.

64. Kyra Epstein, "Xeric Landscapes Not Saving Much Water, Phoenix Study Says," *U.S. Water News*, vol. 17, no.7, July 2000, p. 21.

65. Gary Paul Nabhan, *Cultures of Habitat: On Nature, Culture, and Story*, Counterpoint, Washington, D.C., 1997, p. 86.

66. San Antonio Water System, Watersaver Landscape Rebate Planning Guide, San Antonio, Texas, 1999.

67. Wasowski, *The Landscaping Revolution*, p. 26.

68. Wasowski, *The Landscaping Revolution*, p. 28.

69. Connie Ellefson, Tom Stephens, and Doug Welsh, "Practical Turf Areas," *Xeriscape Gardening: Water Conservation for the American Landscape*, Macmillan Publishing Co., New York, 1992, part 1(Xeriscape Landscaping), pp. 8–9.

70. L. R. Costello and K. S. Jones, *WUCOLS: Water Use Classification of Landscape Species (A Guide to the Water Needs of Landscape Plants)*, University of California Cooperative Extension, San Francisco and San Mateo County Office, revised Apr. 1, 1994.

71. Beth Hickenlooper, "Natural Florida Under Attack: Exotic Plants Are Taking Over the Landscape, Threatening More Than the Extinction of the State's Native Vegetation," *Streamlines*, produced by the St. Johns River Water Management District, Palatka, Fla., Summer 1998, vol. 8, p. 4.

72. United States Park Service, http://www.denix.osd.mil/denix/Public/ES-Programs/Conservation/Invasive/understand.html, Nov. 30, 2000.

73. Marin Municipal Water District, Ordinance 326: An Ordinance Revising Water Conservation Requirements, Section 11.60.030 (Requirements For All Services), Marin Municipal Water District, Corte Madera, Calif., Aug. 28, 1991.

74. City of Albuquerque, Dept. of Public Works, Water Conservation Office, http://www.ci.albuquerque.nm.us/waterconservation/program.html, Dec. 1, 2000.

75. Bret Rappaport, "May All Your Weeds Be Wildflowers: All About Weed Ordinances and Why They Are Applied to Natural Landscapes," *Wild Garden*, vol. 1, no. 1, 1998, pp. 32–36.

76. Bret Rappaport, "As Natural Landscaping Takes Root We Must Weed Out the Bad Laws: How Natural Landscaping and Leopold's Land Ethic Collide With Unenlightened Weed Laws and What Must Be Done About It," *The John Marshall Law Review*, vol. 26, Summer 1993. This article can also be accessed at http://www.epa.gov/glnpo/greenacres/weedlaws.

77. Ellefson, "Practical Turf Areas," *Xeriscape Gardening*, part 1 (Practical Turf Areas).

78. U.S. General Services Administration, *Water Management: A Comprehensive Approach for Facility Managers*, Office of Real Property Management and Safety, U.S. General Services Administration, Washington, D.C., prepared in collaboration with Enviro-Management & Research, Inc., Washington, D.C., 1994, pp. 3–45.

79. L. D. Leuthold and E. Mohr, Maintaining Good Lawns With Less Water, KSU Special Horticulture Report (Water Conservation Series), Cooperative Extension Service, Kansas State University, Manhattan, Kans., 1996.

80. Personal communication, Fox McCarthy, Water Conservation Coordinator, Cobb County–Marietta Water Authority, Marietta, Ga., October 1998.

81. "Home Landscapes Offer Great Opportunity for Water Conservation," *The Cross Section*, High Plains Underground Water Conservation District No. 1, Lubbock, Texas, March 1995, p. 3.

82. Ellefson, "Practical Turf Areas," *Xeriscape Gardening*, part 1 (Appropriate Plant Selection).

83. Stevie Daniels, guest ed., *Easy Lawns: Low Maintenance Native Grasses for Gardeners Everywhere*, Brooklyn Botanic Garden, Brooklyn, N.Y., 1999.

84. Cooperative Extension Service, *Xeriscape™: A Guide to Developing a Water-Wise Landscape*, p. 9.

85. Warren Schultz, *The Chemical-Free Lawn*, Rodale Press, Emmaus, Pa., 1989, pp. 16–22.

86. *Water-Wise Gardening For California*, Sunset Publishing Corp., 1998, p. 12.

87. Ellen Kraftsow, "Forum: Irrigation/Landscaping: Specifying Native and Non-invasive plants," posted at the WaterWiser Conf., <waterwiser-list@listserv.waterwiser.org>, Nov. 21, 1997.

88. Andy Solomon, Tim Ahern, and Matt Stout, "Clinton Issues Executive Order Designed to Combat Invasive Species," *U.S. Water News*, vol. 16, no. 6, June 1999, p. 9.

89. City of Albuquerque, "Xeriscape Basics," p. 7.

90. City of Albuquerque, Water Conservation Annual Report 1997, Albuquerque, N.M., p. 7.

91. Northeastern Illinois Planning Commission, *Source Book on Natural Landscaping for Local Officials*

92. City of Albuquerque, Start Your Journey Toward…The Xeri City, Albuquerque, N.M., 1998.

93. Bennett, *Water-Efficient Landscape Guidelines*, p. 57.

94. Bret Rappaport and J. Wolfe, "Green Development Makes Dollars and Sense: Innovative Development Pioneers Ecological and Cost-Saving Landscaping," *Professional Wildscaping*, October/November 1998, pp. 8-14.

95. Ted Shelton and B. Hamilton, *Landscaping for Water Conservation: A Guide For New Jersey*, Rutgers Cooperative Extension Service, New Jersey Agricultural Experiment Station, New Brunswick, N.J., 1992, p. 7.

96. "Benefits of Turfgrass," *Irrigation Journal*, October 1994.

97. J. F. Cigard, "X-SCAPE From the Ordinary," *Golf Course Management*, November 1995, p. 21.

98. Stevie Daniels, *The Wild Lawn Handbook: Alternatives to the Traditional Front Lawn*, Macmillan, New York, 1995.

99. Jenkins, *The Lawn*, p. 186.

100. Smaller American Lawns Today, Connecticut College, New London, Conn., http://www.conncoll.edu/ccrec/greennet/arbo/salt/impacts.html, Dec. 1, 2000.

101. Joseph M. Keyser, "Creating a Water-Wise Landscape," *Gazette Newspaper*, Gaithersburg, Md., July 18, 1997, p. C-20.

102. Norman H. Davis, "Maximizing the Installation of Automatic Rain Shutoff Devices," *Proc. Conserv96*, AWWA, Denver, 1995, p. 279.

103. Board of County Commissioners of Hillsborough County, Ordinance No. 94-12, An Emergency Ordinance Amending Hillsborough County Ordinance No. 91-27: Requiring Automatic Rain Sensor Devices or Switches on Automatic Irrigation Systems, Providing for Definitions, Providing for an Effective Date, Hillsborough County, Fla., Nov. 2, 1994.

104. Town of Cary, Town Ordinance Section 19-48, Cary, N.C., 1997.

105. "Conserve Regional Water Supplies With Efficient Landscape Water Use," *The Cross Section*, High Plains Underground Water Conservation District No. 1, Lubbock, Texas, July 1998, p. 2.

106. Greenleaf, "Reclaimed Water Use Is Increasing In Irrigation Systems," pp. 19–20, 36.

107. State of California, Graywater Systems for Single Family Residences Act of 1992, Assembly Bill 3518, 1992.

108. Marsha Prillwitz and L. Farwell, "California's Graywater Standards Are Finally Approved," *Water Conservation News*, California Dept. of Water Resources, Division of Planning & Local Assistance, Water Conservation Office, Sacramento, Calif., Summer 1994, p. 4.

109. Jennifer Platt, "Irrigation/Landscaping: Rain Sensor Ordinance," www.waterwiser.org, Aug. 3, 2000.

110. Doug F. Welsh, "Practical Turf Areas: The Controversial Xeriscape Guideline," *Turf News*, special issue, 1991, p. 47.

111. H. W. (Bill) Hoffman, "Rainwater Harvesting & Conservation and Reuse—Developing Sustainable Water Supplies Off the Grid in Texas," *Proc. Conserv99*, AWWA, Denver, 1999.

112. City of Albuquerque, *Rainwater Harvesting: Supply From the Sky*, City of Albuquerque Water Conservation Office, Albuquerque, N.M., 2000.

113. Wendy Price Todd and Gail Vittori, *Texas Guide to Rainwater Harvesting*, 2nd ed., Texas Water Development Board, Austin, Texas, 1997.

114. Mary DeSena, "New Guide Offers Tips on Rainwater Harvesting," *U.S. Water News*, May 1997, p. 15.

115. Ellefson, "Water Harvesting," *Xeriscape Gardening*, part 1 (Efficient Irrigation).

116. Ellefson, "Efficient Irrigation," *Xeriscape Gardening*, part 1 (Planning and Design).

117. Luke Frank and Doug Bennett, "Low Volume Irrigation Design and Installation Guide," Water Conservation Office, City of Albuquerque, N. M., Water Conservation Office, 2000, p.9.

118. Conservation Services, Water District No. 1 of Johnson County, "Definitions for the Sprinkler Evaluation Summary," Water District No. 1 of Johnson County, Merriam, Kans., 1998.

119. Personal communication, Marsha Prillwitz, Water Conservation Specialist, U.S. Bureau of Reclamation, Sacramento, Calif., October 1998.

120. Mary DeSena, "Denver Suburb Saves Water and Labor with State-of-the-Art Computerized Sprinkler System for Parks," *U.S. Water News*, October 1997, p. 15.

121. Joseph M. Keyser, "Water-Wise Irrigation," *Gazette Newspaper*, Gaithersburg, Md., Aug. 15, 1997, p. C-20.

122. "Association News: IA Water Management Committee Unveils BMPs," *IBT Journal*, October/November 2000, p.16.

123. Mary DeSena, "Texas Architect Specializes in Designs That Save Water," *U.S. Water News*, October 1996.

124. Shelley L. Grice, "The City of Toronto Trial Rain Barrel Installation Programme," presented at the AWWA Annual Conf., Toronto, June 1996.

125. R. Dodge Woodson, "Recycling Water for Irrigation," *Watering Systems for Lawn & Garden*, Storey Publishing, Pownal, Vt., 1996, chapter 4.

126. R. Gonzalez, "Water Conservation Pays Off for Eustis Grower," *Stream Lines*, St. Johns Water District, Fla., vol. 6, 1996, p. 2.

127. City of Austin, http://www.ci.austin.tx.us/watercon/efficient.htm, City of Austin Planning and Conservation Department, Austin, Texas, Dec. 3, 2000.

128. City of Austin, http://www.ci.austin.tx.us/watercon/rainwaterharvesting.htm, City of Austin Planning and Conservation Department, Austin, Texas, Dec. 3, 2000.

129. Cynthia Greenleaf, "The Golden Age of Irrigation," *Lawn & Landscape*, vol. 21, no. 10, October 2000, pp. 14–19.

130. New York City Department of Sanitation, Leave It on the Lawn, New York, June 1994.

131. D.B. Beck, "ET Scheduling Simplified: Stepping Up Runtimes," *Irrigation Journal*, October 1996, p. 14.

132. Irrigation Training and Research Center, *Landscape Water Management Principles, Version 1.01*, California Polytechnic State University, San Luis Obispo, Calif., October 1994, p. 7.

133. California Dept. of Water Resources, http://wwwdpla.water.ca.gov/urban/land/land.html, Dec. 2, 2000.

134. Peter H. Gleick, "The Power of Good Information: The California Irrigation Management Information System (CIMIS)," *Sustainable Use of Water: California Success Stories*, Pacific Institute, Oakland, Calif., January 1999, chapter 16 (pp. 179–185).

135. Personal communication, Tony Gregg, Water Conservation Manager, City of Austin, Texas, Oct. 5, 1998.

136. Roger Duncan and Randy J. Goss, Emergency and Peak Day Ordinance, Memorandum to mayor and council members, City of Austin, Texas, Aug. 12, 1998.

137. City of Austin, City Code Article II: Emergency and Peak Day Water Use Management, 81' Code, § 4-4-21, Ordinance 860703-K and Ordinance 970604-A, 1997.

138. Lloyd Hathcock, conference posting on www.waterwiser.org, Sept. 7, 2000.

139. Tom Ash, conference posting on www.waterwiser.org, Mar. 9, 2000.

140. T. E. Bilderback and M. A. Powell, Efficient Irrigation, publication no. AG-508-6, North Carolina Cooperative Extension Service, March 1996.

141. Ellefson, *Xeriscape Gardening*, p. 113.

142. Schultz, *The Chemical-Free Lawn*, p. 106.

143. Ellefson, "Philosophy for Efficient Irrigation," *Xeriscape Gardening*, part 1 (Efficient Irrigation).

144. Board of County Commissioners of Hillsborough County, Ordinance No. 00-10, An Emergency Ordinance Amending Hillsborough County Ordinance No. 91-27: Providing More Stringent Water Use Restrictions and Providing for an Effective Date, Hillsborough County, Fla., Mar. 17, 2000.

145. Evaluation of the MWD CII Survey Database, prepared by Hagler Bailly Services, Inc., San Francisco, for the Metropolitan Water District of Southern California, Los Angeles, Nov. 19, 1997, p. 6.

146. Personal communication, Nancy G. Scott, Conservation Manager, Water District No. 1, Johnson County, Kans., Nov. 3, 1998.

147. Dale Lessick, "Residential Landscape Water Efficiency Technology Utilizing New ET Controller Technology," AWWA Annual Conf., Denver, June 13, 2000.

148. Ed Craddock, "Monitoring Water Demand with CIMIS," *Water Conservation News*, California Dept. of Water Resources, Sacramento, Calif., January 1998, p. 3.

149. C. G. Gelinas and B. Brant, "A Systems Approach to Saving Water and Energy," presented at the 18th World Energy Engineering Congress, Atlanta, November 1995, p. 5.

150. Robert Ayers, "Sports Turf Irrigation: Using Water Rebates to Improve Irrigation Control," *Irrigation Journal*, June 1998, p. 10.

151. The Water Right Soil Probe, manufacturer's product brochure, Water Right, Costa Mesa, Calif., 2000.

152. Ash, *Landscape Management for Water Savings*, p. 24.

153. Ellen O'Brien, "Deep Division Takes Root Over Fertilizer Ban," *Boston Globe*, June 27, 1999, p. C-1.

154. Cooperative Extension Service, *Xeriscape™: A Guide To Developing A Water-Wise Landscape*, p. 14.

155. Gary L. Wade, Water Conserving Xeriscapes, Cooperative Extension Service, University of Georgia, Athens, Ga., Spring 1997.

156. Ash, *Landscape Management for Water Savings*, p. 28.

157. Shelton, *Landscaping for Water Conservation: A Guide For New Jersey*, pp. 9-10.

158. Ash, *Landscape Management for Water Savings*, p. 26.

159. Bruce Adams, "Xeriscape™ — The Key Answer for Urban Environmental Protection," *National Xeriscape News*, Summer 1990, p. 4.

160. State of California, Model Water Efficient Landscape Ordinance, Assembly Bill 325, Sacramento, Calif., 1993.

161. California Landscape Contractors Assn., A Guide to California's Model Water Efficient Landscape Ordinance, June 1992, p. 1.

162. S. Brauen and G. Stahnke, *Principles of Turfgrass Management: Water Use and the Healthy Lawn*, Seattle Public Utilities, Everett Public Works Department, and Tacoma City Water, Seattle, undated, p. 3.

163. Shelton, *Landscaping for Water Conservation: A Guide For New Jersey*, p. 8.

164. Cooperative Extension Service, *Xeriscape™: A Guide To Developing A Water-Wise Landscape*, p. 16.

165. Helen Nash and Eamonn Hughes, *Waterfalls, Fountains, Pools & Streams*, Sterling Publishing Co., Inc., New York, 1998, pp. 75–90.

166. Larry Calabro et al, *The Water Audit Guidebook*, Division of Water Supply Management, Rhode Island Department of Environmental Management, Providence, R.I., April 1996, p. 32.

167. Thelma Seear, quoted in "Fountain Fantasies, From Cascades to Curbs," by Julie V. Iovine, *The New York Times*, New England Edition, June 11, 1998, p. C-4.

168. The Bruce Company, "Final Draft: Local Ordinances For Water Efficiency," prepared for the U.S. Environmental Protection Agency, Office of Policy Analysis, EPA Contract #68-W2-0018, Subcontract #EPA 353-2, Work Assignment 24, Mar. 31, 1993, Appendix B.

169. The Bruce Company, "Final Draft: Local Ordinances For Water Efficiency," prepared for the U.S. Environmental Protection Agency, Office of Policy Analysis, EPA Contract #68-W2-0018, Subcontract #EPA 353-2, Work Assignment 24, Mar. 31, 1993, p. 11.

170. Calabro, *The Water Audit Guidebook*, Appendix E.

171. Bill Hoffman, Texas Water Development Board, Austin, Texas, quoted in "Design Makes Decorative Urban Fountains More Water-Efficient," by Ric Jensen, *The Cross Section*, Lubbock, Texas, November 1995, p. 2.

172. A Guide to Commercial/Industrial Water Conservation, prepared by Black & Veatch Consultants, Los Angeles, for Los Angeles Department of Water and Power, Los Angeles, 1991, p. 38.

173. Calabro, *The Water Audit Guidebook*, p. 48.

4

Industrial, Commercial, and Institutional Water Use and Efficiency Measures

"Genius is simply a fresh look at the obvious."
—Old Saying

THIS CHAPTER DESCRIBES industrial, commercial, and institutional (ICI) water use and presents water-efficiency measures that can be applied to the diverse processes, equipment, and products associated with ICI water use. Descriptions of the water-efficiency measures include potential water savings plus related benefits and costs, often presented through case studies.

PHOTO COURTESY OF AMY VICKERS & ASSOCIATES, INC.

Figure 4.1 Industrial water customers can be the largest-volume users served by public water supply systems. (Photo courtesy of Amy Vickers & Associates, Inc.)

ICI Water Use

Total commercial and industrial (excluding mining and thermoelectric) water use in the United States is estimated to average 9,590 million gallons per day (mgd) and 27,100 mgd, respectively, or a total of 36,690 mgd. Consumptive use of water for commercial and industrial purposes accounts for about 15% of total use, according to the U.S. Geological Survey's most recently reported (1995) survey of national water use. Of total commercial and industrial water use in the United States, 70% of commercial and 18% of industrial water demand is provided by public water supply sources; the balance is taken from self-supplied sources (groundwater and surface water, saline water, and reclaimed wastewater).[1]

For many public water supply systems, customers in the ICI water-use sector represent 20 to 40% of billed urban water demand. However, large-volume users often augment their supplies with nonmetered sources such as private wells, and augmentation with reclaimed water and saline water is increasing. Unlike residential water use, which is relatively stable except during times of drought or sharp rate increases, ICI water demand fluctuates more dramatically in response to economic conditions, changes in production, building occupancy, and weather patterns. In addition, ICI customers typically account for significantly more water use per site or account compared with the residential sector. As a result, potential water savings from conservation are considerably higher in the ICI sector on a per-customer basis. Sometimes, implementation of conservation measures by one or a small number of ICI customers, particularly industrial users, can have a significant impact on a local water system because those customers represent a major portion of the system's total demand (Figure 4.1).

Compared with residential water uses, ICI end uses are relatively complex. Many variables affect ICI water use, and facilities of the same type often have different water-use characteristics and potential efficiencies. Consequently, developing water conservation programs for ICI customers as a group is a challenge for water utilities, because the same types of ICI facilities may have appreciably different opportunities (and benefits and costs) for saving water. For example, two schools that are similar in terms of size, occupancy load, and climate can have significantly different volumes of water demand if one has a cooling tower and a cafeteria and the other has an outdated once-through cooling system and a swimming pool. These types of differences render it difficult to make blanket assumptions about the water-use characteristics and potential efficiencies of schools as a group, let alone all ICI customers. As a result, it is not easy to establish a simple standard for determining the water-use efficiency of a particular building without performing an on-site audit.[2]

Climate has a significant impact on ICI water use because seasonal and regional variations in temperature and rainfall affect facilities that use water for cooling and landscape irrigation.[3] Changes in the cost of water, such as increases in water rates or seasonal (peak-use) charges, influence some ICI customers. However, because water costs are often only a small part of an ICI water customer's operations budget, water-efficiency measures may not be a priority. Economic conditions can depress or elevate commercial and industrial activities and their associated water uses but usually have little or no impact on the water use of institutions (e.g., schools, hospitals, public buildings).

The water use of commercial facilities and institutions is often related to the populations they serve, such as the number of customers (hotels/motels, restaurants, retail and grocery stores, places of assembly, sports arenas), students (schools), visitors and patients (hospitals and health care facilities), and employees (office buildings).

There are several ways to estimate the efficiency of water use among ICI customer categories and subcategories, but an on-site water audit of each facility can produce the most accurate assessment. For industrial customers, changes in water use and water efficiency are a function of one or several relationships, depending on the type of industry or type of water use. For example, in a study of industrial water use by the Texas Water Development Board, water use by oil refineries was found to be *proportional* to production. Other types of industries reported a *linear* relationship between water use and production (e.g., a bottling operation), whereas others experience a *decreased unit consumption* of water for each increment of production.[4]

ICI Water Customers

Methods used to identify ICI water customers and their water-use characteristics vary by water utility. In addition, the customer classification and billing systems of many retail water suppliers are not user-friendly for water conservation managers who need to evaluate ICI water use and target programs to spe-

The three most populated states, California, Texas, and New York, account for 30 percent of all water withdrawn for public water supply uses in the United States.
—U. S. Geological Survey

cific customer subcategories. For example, some utilities categorize customers only by meter size. In such cases, most nonresidential customers are those that have 1- to 2-inch meters, although small businesses such as restaurants may operate with ½-inch meters (which can make it difficult to segment them from residential customers). The remaining nonresidential customers will likely have 3-inch meters, and a few large industrial users will have 4- to 12-inch meters. Multifamily residential properties are sometimes given a commercial customer classification if they share a meter with a retail operation or if they have larger meters (more than ¾-inch) than those typically used for single-family and small multifamily accounts. Other utilities identify customers by category, such as nonresidential, industrial, commercial, institutional, public, government, municipal (e.g., parks and municipal properties, which may include public housing), or some combination of categories, such as industrial and commercial.

Tracking Water Use by Standard Industrial Classification Codes

To better track water use by customer categories and subcategories, water utilities would be prudent to classify ICI customers by their meter sizes as well as their Standard Industrial Classification (SIC) or North American Industry Classification System (NAICS) codes. The four-digit SIC codes, developed by the U.S. Department of Commerce, classify a site into a group and characterize its activity. For example, the SIC code 5800 series represents "Eating and Drinking Places," and SIC code 5812 identifies a restaurant. The SIC code 8200 series represents "Educational Services," and SIC code 8211 identifies an elementary or secondary school.[5] Since the late 1990s, the SIC system has been replaced by the North American Industry Classification System (NAICS), which coordinates classifications in the United States, Canada, and Mexico. However, the drinking water profession has not integrated the new NAICS into general practice, and the use of SIC codes is still prevalent. The old SIC codes does do not correspond to the NAICS codes.

The amount of water used at each site with the same SIC code differs, of course, depending on variables such as number of employees and customers, product output, hours of operation, and so on. When supplemental data on these types of factors are collected, customers with the same SIC codes can be compared in terms of water-use efficiency, e.g., water use per employee, per customer, per patient, per student, or per inmate. Examples of annual and average-day water use by ICI customers in 37 SIC classifications, based on actual metered billing data for more than 5,000 ICI customers in Greater Vancouver, British Columbia,[6] are shown in Table 4.1.

INDUSTRIAL CUSTOMERS   Water users classified as industrial customers are typically involved in small- or large-scale product manufacturing and processing activities, such as those related to chemicals, food, beverage bottling, paper and allied products, steel, electronics and computers (e.g., microchips), metal finishing, petroleum refining, and transportation equipment (cars, trucks, trains, and airplanes).

Industrial customers typically use water for four primary functions: heat transfer (cooling and heating), materials transfer (industrial processing), washing, and as an ingredient. Among U.S. industrial customers, water for cooling

TABLE 4.1

Selected industrial, commercial, and institutional water uses from a survey of billing records for 5,000 ICI customers*

Customer Description	Average Daily Demand Per Connection gallons	SIC Code	Number of Connections Surveyed	Average Annual Demand Per Connection gallons
Beef cattle feedlots	1,088	211	12	397,203
Dairy farms	3,008	241	14	1,097,864
Veterinary services	347	742	7	126,703
Meat-packing plants	37,942	2011	12	13,848,814
Bottling plants	111,760	2086	3	40,792,304
Sawmills and planning mills	18,674	2421	70	6,816,043
Pulp mills	666,182	2611	1	243,156,470
Petroleum refining	136,288	2911	12	49,745,271
Cement production	4,291	3241	3	1,566,090
General warehousing and storage	1,931	4225	966	704,921
Airports/flying fields	53,213	4582	18	19,422,751
Stores and offices	2,437	5300	339	889,490
Grocery stores	7,490	5411	110	2,733,848
Stores and retail services	2,353	5535	646	858,937
Gasoline service stations	1,682	5541	245	614,007
Eating establishments	4,480	5812	452	1,635,141
Florists	6,277	5992	2	2,291,142
Hotels/motels/tourist courts	14,340	7011	232	5,234,109
Dry-cleaning plants	4,597	7216	8	1,678,066
Industrial laundries	60,347	7218	2	22,026,750
Funeral services/crematoriums	640	7261	6	233,641
Auto-repair shops	592	7539	29	216,052
Car washes	2,302	7542	24	840,068
Public golf courses	8,010	7992	73	2,923,594
Amusement parks	36,703	7996	6	13,396,481
Amusement and recreation facilities	5,919	7999	214	2,160,350
Dentist offices	363	8021	7	132,364
General medical and surgical facilities	31,110	8062	58	11,355,015
Hospitals	8,211	8069	14	2,996,915
Elementary and secondary schools	4,492	8211	370	1,639,623
Colleges/universities	83,553	8221	65	30,497,000
Vocational schools	4,882	8249	5	1,781,765
Day-care services for children	714	8351	18	260,692
Religious organizations	959	8661	394	350,171
Executive offices	3,289	9111	393	1,200,331
Prisons/correctional institutions	26,563	9223	4	9,695,612
Shopping centers/malls	7,083	9998	172	2,585,166

* Data obtained from ICI customers of the Greater Vancouver (B.C.) Regional District

Source: Adapted from Reference 6

(both for ambient-air comfort as well as for equipment and process cooling) and condensing operations has historically been the single largest component of water use, claiming more than 50% of total ICI water demand.[7] Service and manufacturing facilities often use large amounts of water for washing and process activities, whereas food-processing and beverage facilities consume large quantifies of water as part of product preparation. In a study of food-processing operations, Denver Water found water use to be divided by about 42% for washing and sanitation, 19% for cooling and heating, 14% for one-pass cooling, and 13% for processing; the remainder was used in restrooms and for other purposes.[8]

Computer and electronics manufacturers often consume large quantities of water for rinsing and cleaning circuit boards and silicon wafers, processes that require a high level of water purity. A study of computer and electronics manufacturers in California's Silicon Valley found the facilities surveyed to be using about 40% of their water for rinsing, 20% for cooling, 20% for fume scrubbers, 10% for water purification, and the balance for restrooms, landscaping, and other purposes.[9]

COMMERCIAL CUSTOMERS Water users classified as commercial or business customers typically provide or distribute a retail service or product. Examples include commercial businesses and retail stores, office buildings, restaurants, hotels and motels, laundries and laundromats, food stores, car washes, golf courses, amusement parks, and other places of commerce. The commercial customer classification should not (but may) include multifamily residences, agricultural users, or other types of nonresidential customers.

Commercial customers use water mainly for domestic purposes (e.g., sanitary plumbing fixtures), cooling and heating, and landscape irrigation. Cleaning and sanitation uses are also significant at hotels and motels. For example, a study of water use in office buildings in San Jose, California, found the buildings surveyed to be using about 40% of their water for restrooms, 28% for cooling and heating, 22% for landscape irrigation, and the remainder for kitchen use and other purposes.[10]

INSTITUTIONAL CUSTOMERS Water users classified as institutional customers, including those at governmental and public facilities, typically serve the public in some way whether they are publicly or privately owned or operated. Examples include municipal, county, state, and federal government buildings and facilities; schools and universities; hospitals and health care facilities; prisons; military installations; passenger terminals; sports arenas; and places of worship.

Institutional customers often use water chiefly for cooling and heating, domestic purposes, and landscape irrigation. Domestic, or restroom, water use often claims the major share of water demand at institutions (35 to 50%), although this may not be the case in facilities with efficient plumbing fixtures and appliances installed after nationwide implementation of the U.S. Energy Policy Act in the mid-1990s. Older facilities that have not been upgraded with modern cooling and heating equipment or that are poorly maintained often use water inefficiently and in large quantities; single-pass cooling systems and leaky steam and ventilation systems can also be sources of water waste and loss at such sites.

Except at hospitals and hotels, water demand for cleaning and sanitation is usually minor at institutions, although it is a component of almost all ICI customer water budgets.[11]

Sources of ICI Water Waste

Assessing the efficiency of ICI water use and waste is often difficult, given the diversity and complexity of how water is used in the nonresidential sector. On one hand, historical records of water demand per unit of product, if available, can provide useful information about water efficiency. On the other hand, because many ICI facilities produce a diverse mix of products, the only index available for production may be a dollar volume, which is not meaningful for comparisons of water use among similar facilities. When they exist, calculations of unit water consumption per employee, per floor area of plant, or per unit of plant production can be used in estimating the water use of a particular facility or group of ICI customers.

Historically, declining water rate structures and low water costs have benefited many businesses and industries but have resulted in little financial incentive to reduce water use. For some ICI customers, water costs constitute such a small portion of overall operating costs that reducing them is not a priority. Except during periods of drought and public attention to examples of excessive water use—e.g., the occasional television news image of an overactive sprinkler watering a sidewalk next to a corporate lawn or public park—the public is generally not very attuned to water waste by nonresidential users. Thus, incentives are often required to motivate ICI customers to adopt water-efficiency measures. Examples of such incentives include inclining water rates (which require customers to pay more per additional increment of water used rather than less, as

Study Summarizes ICI End Uses of Water, Savings from Conservation

A study of ICI water use and conservation, *Commercial and Institutional End Uses of Water* (2000), was conducted for the American Water Works Association Research Foundation (AWWARF). The study includes an analysis of a sample of ICI billing data for five California and Arizona water providers and presents key findings on potential water savings from conservation, water-use indicators (factors that influence water use), and gaps in data collected from ICI water audits.

- Potential water savings from conservation measures in the ICI sector range from 15 to 50%, with 15 to 35% being typical. Expect payback periods between one and four years and normally less than 2.5 years.
- Potable water is not needed for many ICI applications. Each ICI customer's water requirements should be examined to determine

if nonpotable water can be used or recycled on site or if using reclaimed effluent is feasible.
- Common water-demand indicators for ICI buildings and facilities include: number of water-using occupants (e.g., employees, visitors, guests, students, patients, prisoners) and frequency of water use, hours of operation, square footage, water and wastewater costs, number of restrooms and sanitary plumbing fixtures (type and year installed), number and type of water-using kitchen fixtures, presence of laundry facilities, presence of a swimming pool and athletic or health club facilities, type of cooling and heating systems (water- or air-based), climate (precipitation and temperature patterns), type of irrigation system (drip or overhead spray), and irrigable landscape area.
- Large water-using ICI facilities such as ware-

houses, correctional facilities, military bases, utility systems, and passenger terminals have been ignored by many water audit programs and thus have not typically received recommendations for conservation measures.
- Documentation of ICI audits and water saved through conservation is often lacking, and many evaluations of ICI conservation programs do not include specific information on generalizing water savings, program costs, and implementation considerations that could be of practical value to other ICI water users.
- Improved coordination and cooperation among water, wastewater, and energy utilities are needed to realize the water-efficiency potential in the ICI sector.[12]

is the case with declining rates), restrictions or prohibitions on certain types of inefficient use (e.g., single-pass cooling), stronger public sentiment and policies that demand more efficient use, and ICI customer awareness of the economic, environmental, and regulatory benefits of efficient water use.

Advances in ICI Water-Use Efficiency

In recent years, several policy initiatives and other factors have encouraged increased water-use efficiency in the ICI sector.

- *U.S. Clean Water Act.* The U.S. Clean Water Act[15] has prompted many industries and commercial water users to reduce their chemical requirements and waste loads, actions that have necessitated better pretreatment systems and more strategic use of chemical, water, and energy resources.
- *Pollution prevention laws and programs.* Pollution prevention laws and programs initiated by federal and state governments have indirectly helped to promote conservation and water reuse. Reuse and recycling of industrial wastewater often provide a pretreatment mechanism that enables large-volume water users to meet commercial wastewater discharge pollution requirements.
- *Energy conservation programs.* Energy conservation programs sponsored by electric and gas utilities, sometimes in cooperation with water utility conservation programs, have contributed to improved water efficiency at some ICI facilities.
- *National standards and federal programs for water- and energy-efficient heating and cooling equipment, plumbing fixtures, and appliances.* Federal water- and energy-efficiency requirements established in the 1990s for water-using equipment (e.g., heating and cooling systems, ice-makers, and drinking fountains), plumbing fixtures and appliances (e.g., toilets, urinals, faucets, showerheads, dishwashers, and clothes washers) have prompted improvements in energy and water efficiency among American consumers and businesses, as well as the federal government's more than 500,000 facilities worldwide. In response to the U.S. Energy Policy Act of 1992,[16] President Clinton in 1994 issued Executive Order 12902 *(Energy Efficiency and Water Conservation at Federal Facilities)*,[17] which requires federal agencies to conduct audits of water and energy efficiency and, where practicable, to purchase equipment that is within the top 25% of energy-efficient products (or is at least 10% more efficient than applicable national standards). Five years later, in 1999, the president signed Executive Order 13123 *(Greening the Government Through Efficient Energy Management)* because, "As a major consumer that spends $200 billion annually on products and services, the federal government can promote energy efficiency, water conservation, and the use of renewable energy products and help foster markets for emerging technologies."[18] Executive Order 13123 builds on Executive Order 12902 by requiring federal agencies to establish water conservation goals as well as to specify and purchase life-cycle, cost-effective ENERGY STAR® or other energy-efficient products and equipment to reduce greenhouse gas emissions by 35% (relative to 1985) per gross square foot of their facilities by 2010. ("Life-cycle" costs are the sum of the present value of capi-

tal, installation, operating, maintenance, and disposal costs over the lifetime of the project, product, or measure.)[18] Federal (and other) purchasers of energy- and water-efficient equipment and appliances can find useful technical guidance on resource-efficient products in *Buying Energy Efficient Products*,[19] a binder produced by the U.S. Department of Energy's Federal Energy Management Program, or online (see Chapter 6, *The Water Conservation Network*).

- *Improved water-cooling technologies and equipment.* Modern water-cooling technologies and equipment are almost all recycling systems that have largely eliminated new installations of inefficient, once-through (single-pass) cooling systems. Likewise, air-cooled compressors and vacuum pumps are replacing some older types of water-cooled equipment, although water-cooled equipment tends to be more energy-efficient than air-cooled equipment because it usually rejects heat more efficiently.[20]

- *Increased costs for water and sewer service.* The cost of water and sewer services is rising in many communities.[21] Increased rates and fees, either by necessity or used an incentive to promote conservation, are helping to encourage more ICI customers to optimize water use. In some communities, however, increasing rates are driving ICI customers to drill private wells to lower water costs. This strategy may result in lower ICI metered water use, even though the same amount or more water may be used because private well owners have less economic incentive to conserve.

- *Droughts and long-term water shortages.* Over the past 25 years, long-term water shortages and droughts in a number of U.S. regions and across the globe have forced many water providers and some businesses to reduce water use, although such changes are not always permanent once the crisis has passed. Droughts are drawing renewed attention because prolonged water shortages have been shown to cause serious economic and environmental losses in the United States. Droughts are estimated to cost the U.S. government more than $ 6 billion annually, a figure that does not include costs to the private sector. Losses in the agricultural and livestock sectors, for example, also affect wholesale and retail businesses—and ultimately consumers. To begin addressing these concerns in the United States, federal legislation, the National Drought Policy Act of 1998,[22] was passed, and the National Drought Policy Commission (NDPC) was established. In 2000, NDPC issued a major report, *Preparing for Drought in the 21st Century—Report of the National Drought Policy Commission*, recommending policies and programs to promote more coordinated local, state, and federal responses to future droughts in an effort to mitigate adverse costs.[23]

- *"Green" business practices.* Environmentally friendly, or green, practices are being adopted voluntarily by an increasing number of businesses and industries that recognize the economic, regulatory, and political benefits as well as the improved public image that such actions can generate.

- *Alternative water sources.* A number of industrial and commercial water uses do not require water of potable quality, e.g., certain cleaning, process, rinsing, cooling, heating, and irrigation applications. When potable water is not required, lower-cost and more resource-efficient alternative sources should be considered—for example, reclaimed municipal wastewater, on-site treated

The real wealth of the Nation lies in the resources of the earth— soil, water, forests, minerals, and wildlife. To utilize them for present needs while insuring their preservation for future generations requires a delicately balanced and continuing program, based on the most extensive research. Their administration is not properly, and cannot be, a matter of politics."

—Rachel Carson

process water, off-site treated process water, household graywater (untreated, used water from households, excluding that from toilets or other fixtures whose wastewater might have come into contact with human waste), and harvested rainwater.

In addition to these policy initiatives, several U.S. water utilities, federal and state agencies, businesses, and organizations have in recent years sponsored ICI water audits and research projects that have helped build the body of knowledge on water-use efficiency in the ICI sector. As the case studies and ICI water-efficiency measures described in this chapter attest, such efforts typically improve the financial bottom line for ICI water users who take the initiative to optimize their operations.

Types of ICI Water-Efficiency Measures

According to reports by water utility conservation programs, the most common conservation measures in the *industrial* sector are site-specific engineering modifications to water-using equipment and processes, such as optimization and recycling of cooling and process water, sequential reuse, improved control systems, and process modifications. Water savings from conservation actions in the *commercial* and *institutional* sectors are typically achieved by such measures as plumbing fixture replacement or retrofit (in particular, installing toilets and urinals with reduced flush volumes), improved flow control systems, more efficient landscape irrigation, automatic shutoff valves for hoses, and improved maintenance procedures. Facilities with access to reclaimed water typically use

EPA'S WAVE Program Saves Water and Reduces Pollution at Hotels and Schools

A U.S. Environmental Protection Agency program called Water Alliances for Voluntary Efficiency (WAVE) promotes water efficiency in commercial businesses and institutions, particularly hotels and motels, schools, and colleges and universities. The agency developed the WAVE program as part of its voluntary pollution prevention agenda to encourage the private sector to reduce water consumption while increasing efficiency, profitability, and competitiveness, according to John E. Flowers, WAVE program director. Water conservation is considered a pollution prevention effort because it reduces demands on the nation's water and wastewater infrastructure (which helps extend facility life and reduce or defer future capital expansion projects), lowers the amount of treatment chemicals required, and reduces the amount of energy required to heat, treat, and transport water and wastewater.

The WAVE program has a number of partners (hotels, motels, inns, and other commercial and institutional users) and supporters (water utilities, water service companies, manufacturers, and government agencies). These partners have agreed to audit water use in each of their U.S. properties and to improve water efficiency whenever doing so would be profitable (the criterion for profitability is a simple payback period of two years or less). For example, La Quinta Inns, a charter WAVE partner, has reduced its water use by about 20%—more than 1 billion gallons—and saved millions of dollars since 1995 when it developed an aggressive conservation program for its more than 300 inns in 28 states. Measures that hotels have implemented include installation of low-volume toilets, urinals, showerheads, and faucets. Columbia University in New York City has decreased its water use by about 25%, saving more than $1 million through multiple conservation measures that saved $200,000 a year in operating costs. The payback period on Columbia's water conservation measures was 1.8 years. The WAVE program has developed water-use analysis software, WAVE•Saver, which enables facility engineers to model water use and develop customized plans (and associated benefits and costs) for conservation measures that can be applied to guest room bathrooms, laundries, kitchens, housekeeping facilities, pools, cooling towers, and landscapes.[24] In a similar effort, the American Hotel and Motel Association, an organization representing a number of the 12,000 hotels and motels in the United States, has a "Good EarthKeeping" water conservation program. Participating members, including Disney-owned properties in Orlando, Florida, and Anaheim, California, place in-room cards offering guests the option of reusing sheets and towels to help save water and preserve other environmental resources. Holiday Inn Worldwide has launched a similar program at 360 of its 2,100 hotels. Experience has shown that only a few guests request daily laundering.[25]

it for cooling tower make-up water, landscape irrigation, and other nonpotable uses. Because of the variety and complexity of water uses among industrial and commercial customers who require ultrapure water (e.g., chip rinsing in plants that fabricate semiconductors), using reclaimed water is not always economical.[3, 28]

Potential Water Savings From ICI Water-Efficiency Measures

Case studies and water-efficiency audits of hundreds of ICI facilities have reported water savings from conservation measures to range from a low of 10% to a high of more than 90% of previous water use.[11, 29–31] Average potential demand reductions achievable from water-efficiency measures at ICI facilities are estimated to range from 15 to 50%, with 15 to 35% being typical. Payback periods are usually between one and four years, with the typical time less than 2.5 years.[12]

Several studies of large databases created from ICI water audits and calculations of actual or projected savings have documented water savings. For example, a study of water audits completed at 741 commercial sites in six states found that potential water savings from efficiency measures ranged from 20 to 26%, according to a report prepared by the U.S. Environmental Protection Agency and the California Department of Water Resources. The study evaluated 741 commercial customers classified in 22 categories and located in 12 large water service areas in the states of California, Florida, Minnesota, New York, Oregon, and Texas.[32] Average potential water savings from conservation measures at various types of commercial and institutional facilities have been estimated from on-site water audits, as shown in Figure 4.2.

A 1997 study of water-use audits conducted at 902 ICI facilities (hotels/motels, restaurants, office buildings, and industrial, educational, nursing, and other facilities) served by the Metropolitan Water District of Southern California estimated average potential water savings at the sites at 29%. Most of the opportunities to reduce water use were related to domestic plumbing fixtures, industrial processes, and landscape irrigation.[30] In terms of the cost-effectiveness of water-efficiency measures and related conservation program planning considerations, the study found the ICI sites surveyed to have the following characteristics:[28]

- At most of the sites, the greatest water savings (63%) were achieved through conservation measures related to domestic plumbing fixtures—specifically, the use of low-volume toilets, urinals, showerheads and faucets.
- Adjusting blow-down cycles in cooling equipment and recycling process water also offered significant potential water savings, particularly in the industrial sector.
- Cutting back irrigation schedules may be one of the most cost-effective efficiency measures for the sites surveyed.[33]
- Water use at most ICI facilities could be evaluated more cost-effectively if audits focused only on water-efficiency measures for domestic uses, particularly at commercial, governmental, and institutional sites. Facilities with complex production processes involving water (e.g., industrial sites) usually require a more sophisticated analysis to identify water-efficiency opportunities.[28]

"Green" Building Practices Grow

A number of agencies and professional organizations are dedicated to "green" building practices that promote water, energy, and resource efficiency as well as innovative and people-friendly approaches to architectural design. For example, the U.S. Environmental Protection Agency, in cooperation with the U.S. Department of Energy (DOE), sponsors the ENERGY STAR program, a group of initiatives to improve the energy (and often water) efficiency of equipment and buildings through technical assistance and product labeling. The ENERGY STAR Buildings Program involves more than 3,000 organizations (including large and small businesses, hospitals, schools, and universities) that are upgrading their cooling and heating equipment to reduce energy consumption by more than 25%. The ENERGY STAR program also sponsors an information hotline and provides assistance to individuals, businesses, and governmental and institutional buyers who want to purchase resource-efficient products. A number of government resources are available to assist federal agencies in designing, specifying, and purchasing energy- and water-efficient products, in particular, DOE's Federal Energy Management Program (FEMP). FEMP helps administer federal energy and water conservation regulations and Executive Orders through direct assistance, training, and software tools related to purchasing practices within the federal government.[26] Contact information for these resources can be found in Chapter 6, *The Water Conservation Network.*

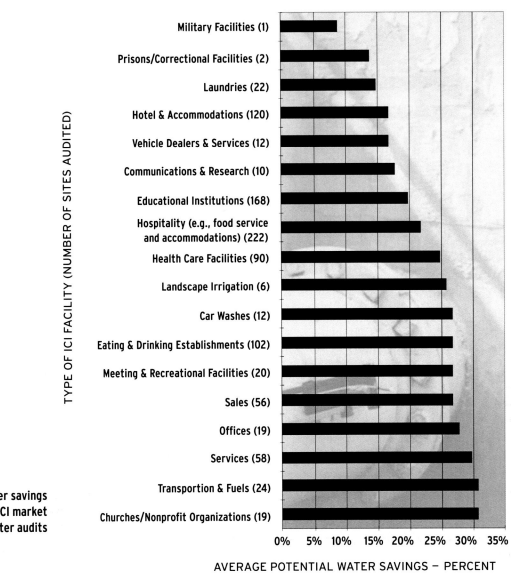

Figure 4.2 Potential water savings from conservation for major ICI market segments based on 741 site water audits

AVERAGE POTENTIAL WATER SAVINGS – PERCENT

Source: Adapted from Reference 32

Benefits and Costs of ICI Water Conservation

A number of benefits accrue to utilities and ICI water users who conserve water. Similarly, some costs and behavior modifications can be associated with water-efficiency measures.

Benefits

- Reduced operational costs for water and wastewater service
- Avoidance or minimization of water-capacity charges or limits, drought surcharges, and fines
- Reduced costs for energy to pump, heat, treat, and transfer water and wastewater
- Postponed increases in water, sewer, and energy rates

- Reduced chemical use and thus reduced treatment and disposal of aqueous hazardous wastes
- Reduced need for water softening and reverse osmosis filtration
- Lower pollution output (pollution prevention)
- Improved compliance with wastewater discharge permits
- Improved utilization of the capacity of existing equipment, appliances, pumps, tanks, and rinse baths
- Improved community status as an environmentally responsible, good neighbor

Costs

- Initial capital cost of water-efficiency devices ("hardware")
- Installation of water-efficiency devices (labor)
- Potential downtime during implementation of measures (e.g., renovations to existing equipment, processes, plumbing, and related connections)
- Some water-efficiency investments may reap only long-term financial returns (on the initial capital cost outlay) when only short-term paybacks are acceptable.
- Increased *concentrations* of chemicals and other pollutants per unit of wastewater discharge, even if the total *amount* of these pollutants does not increase (more efficient water use may affect ICI compliance with discharge permits in categories in which pollutants are measured on the basis of concentration rather than total volume)
- Initial employee resistance to changes in water-use practices (e.g., maintaining and cleaning a waterless urinal rather than a flush urinal)
- Adjustments to changes in operations, maintenance, and safety procedures

---

A U D I T

Basic Steps in an ICI Water Audit

The first step toward increased water-use efficiency at an ICI facility typically involves conducting a water audit and, subsequently, preparing a site water conservation plan. A successful ICI facility conservation program should be based on a sound water-use audit and a strategic plan to implement specific water-saving measures.

A water audit at an ICI site takes four to eight hours, plus follow-up analysis and paperwork back at the office. More or less time may be required, depending on the facility's size and the types and complexity of water use. For example, an audit of a small community college might require one to three days, whereas an audit of a large university could take a week or more. Similarly, a small factory might require one day of an auditor's time on site, but a large, complex industrial facility would call for more time. Additional audit time will be needed if the site has an irrigation system.

The cost of conducting an ICI water audit varies, depending on the level of expertise required. Some water utilities employ trained engineers and technicians who conduct audits for ICI customers. Consulting engineers and technicians who are trained to conduct audits charge $40 to $150 an hour, but costs vary because budgets for audits are often based on the site or the project.

Portland's ICI "BEST" Program Documents Water, Resource, and Cost Savings

The Energy Office of the city of Portland, Oregon, sponsors a free program, Businesses for an Environmentally Sustainable Tomorrow (BEST), offering technical support, assistance with applications for tax credits and other financial incentives, and related services to businesses that implement efficiency measures. The program's primary goal is to promote environmentally sustainable practices that help local businesses operate with greater efficiency and profitability, steps assumed to enhance local economic development and environmental protection. Fifty-five Portland-area ICI "BEST Business Award" winners have quantified the results of the measures they have taken to boost water and energy efficiency, reduce waste, and promote clean and efficient transportation. As of 2000, their combined annual savings total:[27]

- 857 million gallons of water
- $11.5 million in avoided costs
- 38.3 million kilowatt-hours of electricity
- 6.6 million therms of natural gas
- 687,000 gallons of gasoline
- 63,900 tons of solid waste
- 9.4 million miles of avoided transportation
- 98,000 tons of carbon dioxide emissions

The basic steps in conducting an audit and launching an effective water conservation program at an ICI facility are listed in this section.[34,35] A sample worksheet for use in conducting an ICI water-use efficiency survey is provided in Appendix G, *Sample Worksheet: Industrial/Commercial/Institutional Water Audit.*

1. **Obtain support from the ICI facility's owners, managers, and employees.** Management support is essential to ensure that the resources required to implement a conservation program—personnel, time, and money—are available. Boost this support by emphasizing the advantages of saving water plus the related benefits—for example, reduced operating costs for water, sewer, energy, and chemicals and public recognition as an environmentally friendly organization.

2. **Conduct an on-site inventory of water use.** A fundamental part of a water management plan is knowing where and how much water is used at the facility. Collect meter-reading records for all on-site meters. Do a walk-through survey of the facility with the plant manager or engineer to collect information on each water-using process, piece of equipment, fixture, and activity; specifically, record measured or estimated water use and flow rates. The end product of this survey should be a water "balance sheet" that identifies and quantifies water use at the facility.

3. **Calculate all water-related costs.** Using findings from the audit and data collected on the water balance sheet, prepare a summary of the volume and cost of water used at the site. Costs associated with water use include those for water and sewer service, energy costs (e.g., for pumping and heating volumes of water), chemical treatment costs (e.g., for cooling towers), and waste pretreatment. In cases in which excessive use or leaks have caused property damage, the cost of mitigating the damage should be included. Other costs to consider are future increases in the price of water and sewer service, chemicals, and energy.

   Base assessments of water-related costs on at least a two-year history at the site, because seasonal and business fluctuations reflected in metered water consumption can give a skewed picture of average water use. Knowing the true cost of water at the facility allows the value of investments in water-efficiency measures to be calculated more accurately.

4. **Identify and evaluate water-efficiency measures.** Identify all potentially feasible water-efficiency measures for each water-using activity. A detailed description of water-efficiency measures that are applicable to ICI customers, along with information about potential water savings and related benefits and costs, is provided in this and other chapters. Based on an analysis of water use and the potential water savings that could be achieved with each measure, determine the capital cost and related expenses associated with the measure. In addition, estimate avoided costs (benefits) associated with the measure (e.g., reduced water and sewer bills, reduced energy and chemical costs). Based on these data, estimate a simple payback period—the amount of time required for projected cost savings from the measure to equal the investment costs. The payback period can be calculated as follows:

$$Simple\ Payback\ Period\ (years)\ =\ \frac{Capital\ Costs\ (\$)}{Net\ Annual\ Savings\ (\$/year)}$$

Most ICI water users are willing to implement a water-efficiency measure whose simple payback period is two years or less. However, measures that require more time for payback can be good investments too. To estimate long-term paybacks, consider interest rates as well.

5. **Evaluate payback periods using life-cycle costing.** Life-cycle costing is a more accurate method for evaluating the cost-effectiveness of efficiency measures because instead of taking into account only the initial investment, it amortizes costs and benefits (e.g., avoided expenses such as reduced water and wastewater bills, reduced energy and chemical costs) over the life of the measure, including changes in interest rates. A measure that appears to be too expensive may be a cost-effective investment when its costs and benefits are amortized.

6. **Prepare and implement an action plan.** Prepare a written version of the ICI facility's water management plan. The plan should clearly state the program's goals, the way water is used, the water-efficiency measures to be implemented, projected water savings, benefits and costs associated with the efficiency measures, estimated payback periods, the schedule for implementing the measures, and the person responsible for the program. Once the plan is approved, it should be implemented promptly.

7. **Track and report progress.** Monitor results of the water-efficiency measures that were implemented to determine reductions in water use and related operational expenses. Keep employees informed about changes in the facility's water demand, perhaps by posting a water-use graph in the staff lunchroom or another visible location. Announce water savings in employee bulletins, corporate reports, publications of the facility's trade and professional organizations, and press releases to the media.

CAUTION: Before recommending or implementing an efficiency measure, conservation managers and ICI facility managers should verify that the measure can be implemented without any adverse health, safety, environmental, or regulatory impact. Water-efficiency measures for certain water uses and industries, such as but not limited to medical and food-processing facilities (including facilities where food is prepared or served), should be reviewed with appropriate local, state, and federal regulatory agencies and officials before being implemented. For example, state and local health codes often govern any changes to plumbing, building structures, cooling systems, or electrical equipment at hospitals, nursing homes, and other medical facilities. Likewise, the U.S. Department of Agriculture's Food Safety and Inspection Service is required to approve proposed changes to the processing of meat (which typically involves significant amounts of water for sanitation purposes) to ensure the changes comply with the facility's permit and other required conditions. Thus, it is a good rule of thumb to check all applicable health, safety, environmental, and other regulations that may apply to adjustments in water-using activities and equipment in ICI facilities.[36]

California ICI Conservation Response During Drought and Water Emergencies

According to a California Department of Water Resources (DWR) guidebook on managing an industrial conservation program during periods of drought, *Industrial/Commercial Drought Guidebook for Water Utilities*, a number of ICI customers have been surprisingly receptive to utility conservation programs in response to California's numerous droughts. For example, the industrial customers of East Bay Municipal Utility District, which serves Oakland, California, and some neighboring communities, once reduced their water use by 28% during a drought when only a 9% reduction had been projected. Experiences such as these may be valuable to other regions dealing with drought or other water emergencies. Industry's receptiveness to such a program depends largely on the marketing strategies used by the water utility, according to DWR.[37]

ICI Water-Efficiency Measures

This section describes water-efficiency measures—both technologies and practices—that are applicable to the water-using activities, processes, and equipment commonly found in ICI facilities. Because many of the measures applied in the ICI sector involve operational adjustments and engineering design changes that are unique to particular processes and facilities, specific conservation products are not always described. Information about organizations and vendors specializing in water-efficient ICI products are listed in Chapter 6, *The Water Conservation Network*.

The following information is included for the measures presented in this chapter:

- *Purpose.* The purpose of the water-efficiency measure is discussed, along with water use and operational characteristics of the ICI equipment, process, or activity.
- *Audit information to be collected.* The type of information that should be collected during an ICI water-use audit is outlined to help identify specific water-efficiency measures that might be implemented.
- *Conservation policies and regulations.* Examples of water conservation ordinances, regulations, and policies that apply to specific ICI water uses or facilities are presented.
- *Water-efficiency measures.* Water-efficiency measures are identified for each major type of ICI end use of water.
- *Water savings, benefits, and costs.* The potential water savings—as well as the water, sewer, and energy cost savings and other benefits—associated with ICI water-efficiency measures are often unique to a particular site because of the many variables associated with ICI water use. When sufficient data are not available, such information may be omitted. Some of the factors that affect ICI water use and potential water and costs savings from efficiency measures include: population (number of employees, occupants, students, patients, prisoners, and so on), type and number of products produced and processes used, and existing level of water-use efficiency.

When applicable, case studies are provided as examples of the potential water savings, benefits and costs, and program implementation considerations associated with water-efficiency measures.

4.1 METERING AND SUBMETERING

Technically an incentive, meters and meter reading are essential tools for ICI facilities to achieve efficient water use. By providing information about *how much* and *where* water is being used, meters help to monitor water use, identify waste, and pinpoint opportunities to save water during specific types of use. In general, all water used at ICI facilities—utility-supplied and private well water, billed and unbilled—should be metered with accurate, correctly sized meters that are read on a regular basis.

Three categories of meters—main meters, submeters, and flow meters (and similar temporary metering devices)—are commonly used at ICI facilities to measure water use and monitor efficiency.

MAIN METER   When an ICI customer receives public water supplies, the utility usually installs a main meter to measure total water inflows to the facility. For large-volume water users with multiple buildings on the premises, the utility often installs several meters. In such cases, the customer's water and sewer bill usually lists the readings recorded for each meter during a billing period.

The main meter is primarily for the utility's benefit (to measure water use and set charges), but ICI customers can benefit from monitoring main meter readings as well, particularly if the meter is read on a frequent (daily, weekly, or monthly) basis. ICI facilities that draw water from private on-site wells or other sources can also benefit from installing facility meters. Readings from the main meter can provide an understanding of baseline water demand as well as patterns of use (e.g., seasonal variations, differences in production activity). Furthermore, customers who check utility water meters themselves can help verify the accuracy of the meter and water and sewer bills. Reporting water-use information to facility employees is useful to increase awareness about conservation and to encourage personnel to identify and implement efficiency measures. In addition, regular reports of water-use data keep employees apprised of water savings and progress in achieving conservation goals.

SUBMETERS   Installing permanent submeters at ICI facilities that use a lot of water can have many benefits. Submeters can monitor specific (usually large-volume) water uses, such as those for cooling towers, irrigation, and other significant sources of demand. Because submeters help determine water uses and costs for specific equipment and processes, ICI customers can use their readings to assess water efficiency and to pinpoint opportunities to increase efficiency. Higher-than-expected water use registered by a submeter is a signal for the customer to track down the sources of potential inefficiencies. As conservation measures are implemented, ICI customers can use readings from a submeter to chart the results and to identify any fine-tuning needed to curb water use even further.

Another benefit to submetering is that it allows ICI facilities to compare the amount of water used with sewer discharges, information they might use to reduce sewage costs. Many water utilities base sewage bills on the amount of water metered, even though water lost to evaporation or used for irrigation and other consumptive uses is never discharged to the sewer system. If an ICI facility loses or consumes significant amounts of water through evaporation or other processes, it can use measurements of such "lost" water to support the case for a sewage bill adjustment.

For many of us, water simply flows from a faucet, and we think little about it beyond its immediate point of contact."

—Sandra Postel, *Last Oasis*

FLOW METERS AND TEMPORARY METERING DEVICES   A number of flow meters, totalizers, and similar types of portable measurement (e.g., data-logging) devices can be used permanently or temporarily to measure flow rates or volume uses for a specific site, piece of equipment, or process (e.g., rates of flow for a rinse process, autoclave, or utility faucet).

Figure 4.3 Positive displacement meters provide accurate readings of low volumes of water, such as those used in residential and small commercial applications (⅝- to 2-inch connections). They are less accurate for measuring continuous, high-volume flows.

Figure 4.4 Turbine meters provide reliable readings for high-volume water users, such as industrial, commercial, and large-volume irrigation customers.

Figure 4.5 Compound meters, which combine two meters in one, are installed at facilities that use both low- and high-volume flows.

(Photos 4.3 through 4.5 courtesy of JBS Associates, Inc.)

Types of Meters

The main meters and submeters used to measure water use at ICI sites are usually *cumulative* meters. Three types of cumulative meters are commonly used:

- *Positive displacement meters.* Positive displacement (PD) meters contain an oscillating piston or rotating disc that moves water in a rotary motion, and the meters translate measurements of volume into flow. Because displacement meters provide extremely accurate readings when measuring low volumes of water, they are often used for residential and small commercial applications. However, PD meters are not designed to operate continuously at high flows for long periods of time; they can become damaged and give inaccurate readings under such conditions. Displacement meters are usually installed in applications with ⅝- to 2-inch connections.[38, 39] A displacement meter is shown in Figure 4.3.

- *Turbine meters.* Turbine meters contain a multivaned rotor that spins as water flows through the meter; they register flow proportionally to the spin of the rotor. Turbine meters are best used to measure large-volume flows such as those required for irrigation and large-volume industrial or commercial applications; however, they can give accurate readings for some medium-volume flows.[38] If a turbine meter's rotor blades become coated or clogged with sediment, the meter can under-register flows. Turbine meters are usually installed in applications with 2- to 8-inch connections.[39, 40] A turbine meter is shown in Figure 4.4.

- *Compound meters.* Compound meters consist of two meters in one and are used at facilities that require both low and high flows. For example, water use at an industrial operation that requires high-volume flows during the day but only small quantities at night might be measured most accurately with a compound meter. Usually, the larger-diameter component of a compound meter is a turbine meter, and the smaller one is a displacement meter. The smaller meter records low-volume flows, and when the flow rates increase, the larger meter registers them. Compound meters record total metered volume either on a single register (dial) or on a separate register for each meter (in which case, reading both registers is required to determine total use). Compound meters are usually installed in large-volume industrial and commercial applications with 3- to 8-inch connections.[39, 40] A compound meter is shown in Figure 4.5.

Turbine and compound meters are the most common types of meters at large ICI facilities.[41] In addition, *ultrasonic* and *electronic* flow meters can be installed either inside or outside a pipe to measure water use for a specific process or piece of equipment. Ultrasonic and electronic flow meters can measure both instantaneous and cumulative flow volumes. For example, a flow meter can operate in conjunction with a meter to provide continuous readouts in gallons per minute as well as cumulative volume measurements. An example of an ultrasonic meter is shown in Figure 4.6.

Sizing and Reading Meters

Most meters at ICI sites are 1 to 2 inches in diameter; the rest are generally sized at 3 inches, except for a small number in the 4- to 12-inch range. Although

Figure 4.6 Ultrasonic meters can measure both instantaneous and cumulative flow volumes. (Photo courtesy of JBS Associates, Inc.)

meters are often sized to match the diameter of the water service line supplying the customer, this practice may not always result in accurate readings of water use because actual flows tend to be lower than the maximum flows pipes are designed to handle. Furthermore, as a facility's water use changes over time, a meter that was correctly sized for a specific purpose in the past may not be properly sized for current water use. Thus, records of metered water use are not always reliable.[42] For these reasons, a meter-sizing analysis is recommended as part of an on-site water-use efficiency evaluation. Testing with a portable master meter or other data-logging device can provide valuable information about meter-sizing accuracy and actual flows.

Proper meter sizing is extremely dependent on the types of flows and water demands at a facility, as well as variations in daily and seasonal flows. For example, a turbine meter sized for a building that was built for a water-intensive beverage bottling operation but was later renovated for use as an office building will probably not record all water use, because office water uses typically require lower flows than bottling operations. (This is particularly true for old buildings that are renovated with low-volume plumbing fixtures.) The Water and Sewer Department in Boston launched a meter-downsizing program in 1989 that resulted in 2,070 meters being downsized, some by as much as 50% (e.g., a 4-inch meter replaced by a 2-inch meter). After a one-time capital cost of about $700,000 to install correctly sized replacement meters, the improved accuracy of meter readings increased the department's net revenue by more than $5 million per year.[43]

Meters are read by recording the flows that have been registered. Two types of meter registers are common: dial registers and measurement units. Dial registers are found on either *straight-reading* or *round-reading* meters. A straight-reading dial looks like an automobile odometer and is usually measured in cubic feet (ft³); 1 ft³ equals 7.48 gallons. Water utilities usually bill in hundred cubic feet (ccf) but sometimes bill in gallon units (1 ccf equals 748 gallons). This type

Figure 4.7 The master meter for an ICI facility is sometimes located in a pit at a remote location on the property. (Photo courtesy of Amy Vickers & Associates, Inc.)

of dial has a rotating pointer that indicates the digit to be read; the pointer should be noted carefully or else the reading will be off by a factor of ten or more. A round-reading register is similar to an electric meter and has six separate dials to record units of flow. Meters that record flow with *measurement units* are usually calibrated in cubic feet or gallon units, which are printed on the meter dial. A unique serial number is affixed to or cast into the body of each meter.[44,45]

The value of submetering for ICI water users is applying the information gleaned to optimize water use and lower costs. Submeters should be read frequently if they are to yield beneficial information. In fact, many submeter readings are recorded on a daily basis.

Audit Information to Be Collected on Meters

Information that should be collected about meters during an ICI water audit includes:

- Location of utility-provided (main) meter(s) and customer-installed submeter(s) and flow meter(s) serving the site. The master meter(s) may or may not be easy to locate, as shown in Figure 4.7.
- Type of meters installed.
- Units of register used by each meter (gallons, cubic feet, and so on).
- Meter-reading frequency.

- Dates of installation, frequency of testing, and most recent calibration.
- Connection size of water pipe(s) serving the facility.
- Incoming water pressure at meter as pipe enters building.
- Flow rates and water-capacity requirements of connections (cooling towers, boilers, process lines, plumbing fixtures, appliances, and so on).
- Pressure settings, if a pressure-reducing valve is installed.
- Records of water use for all meters (for a minimum 3 years).
- All health, safety, operational, regulatory, administrative, and other requirements or policies that apply to the site.

Conservation Policies and Regulations Related to Metering

Some communities, utilities, and other water agencies have adopted rules to encourage water-use efficiency at large ICI facilities through the use of meters. Some examples of policies and regulations that are applicable to ICI meters are listed here.

- *Requirements for water audits and efficiency measures at federal facilities.* The U.S. Energy Policy Act of 1992[16] and federal Executive Order No. 13123, *Greening the Government Through Efficient Energy Management,* require every federal agency to conduct a comprehensive water audit of all its facilities and to implement cost-effective efficiency measures that have payback periods of ten years or less. Each federal agency must annually report on its progress in meeting water- and energy-efficiency goals to the U.S. Department of Energy and the Office of Management and Budget.
- *Separate meters for cooling towers and certain industrial processes required for sewer allowances.* Water utilities sometimes allow or require separate meters for the make-up lines to cooling towers and other industrial processes that involve consumptive water uses. A sewer allowance lets an ICI customer subtract from its wastewater bill the amount charged for water used but not returned to the sewer such as consumptive uses (e.g., bottling operation), once-through cooling water, and water lost to evaporation (e.g., cooling towers).[46] New York City, for example, has a sewer allowance for some industrial processes that consume water, although a sewer charge is assessed for metered flows that are less than 100%.[47]
- *Separate meters required for water lines attached to irrigation systems.* Water utilities sometimes require that separate meters be installed on water lines to irrigation systems, typically when outdoor water use is subject to different rates and charges than indoor use.[46]
- *Compliance With U.S. standards for meters.* In the United States, almost all meters are designed and tested according to standards set by the American Water Works Association (AWWA Standards 700-series for meters).

A *human brain is 80% water.*
—www.uselessfacts.net

Water-Efficiency Measures for Meters

Water-efficiency measures that might be implemented for meters at ICI facilities include:[48–50]

- Facility managers should regularly read all water meters on site. A suggested meter-reading schedule would be *monthly* for sites that use less than 1 million gallons of water per year (mgy), *weekly* for sites that use 1 to 7.5 mgy, and *daily* for sites with demand that exceeds 7.5 mgy. Keep logs indicating the date and time of readings as a regular maintenance procedure.

- Install submeters and record readings for large pieces of equipment or sub-processes, such as cooling tower make-up and blowdown, boiler make-up and blowdown, process water uses, irrigation, and other large-volume uses.
- Read meters when the facility is not in operation, such as evenings, to see if water is flowing at such times.
- Test and calibrate meters regularly to ensure their accuracy.
- Resize meters when flow rates change significantly as a result of the addition or removal of equipment or a change in process.
- Report water use and changes in use to employees on a regular basis.

Water Savings, Benefits, and Costs From Meters

Meters provide *indirect* water savings; they provide information that can be used to assess water use and to identify opportunities to reduce unnecessary water demand, leaks, and losses.

METERS   The cost of meters used at ICI facilities varies depending on the type and quantity purchased. Estimated prices for common sizes of meters are:

- Flow meters: $50 to $900
- 1- to 2-inch turbine: $175 to $450
- 1- to 2-inch compound: $400 to $800
- 3-inch turbine: $400 to $700
- 3-inch compound: $1,300
- 4-inch turbine: $600 to $1,200
- 4-inch compound: $1,800
- 6-inch turbine: $1,600 to $2,500
- 6-inch compound: $2,500

WATER-FLOW TESTS AND LEAK-DETECTION EQUIPMENT FOR AUDITS Several devices are useful for conducting water audits at ICI facilities. A pressure gauge and Pitot tube are often used to measure equipment water pressures and flows and to verify the accuracy of meters. A Pitot tube (or Pitot rod), shown in Figure 4.8, can determine flow or volume by measuring the velocity of water running through a pipe; it can also be used to test the accuracy of large meters. A water-flow test kit that includes a portable pressure gauge and Pitot tube kit costs $600 to $1,100, depending on the range of measurements required. A versatile water-flow test kit can measure a broad range of flows (e.g., 110 to 1,600 gpm at 40 to 120 pounds per square inch [psi] of pressure), although this capability may not be needed for all audits. Portable meter-testing devices cost $700 to $1,100. A variety of instruments are available for detecting leaks, from a simple industrial stethoscope or sonoscope to an electronic sensing device that measures leak vibrations and relative size. Stethoscopes and sonoscopes cost $15 to $50; more sophisticated electronic leak-detection devices cost $900 to $2,500.

Figure 4.8   A Pitot tube can be used to test meter accuracy as well as the flow of water through a pipe. (Photo courtesy of JBS Associates, Inc.)

> **Case Study** *Cooling Tower Submeter Helps Identify Water Losses From Broken Valve.* A broken valve that caused a constant overflow problem with a cooling tower at an ICI facility in Cambridge, Massachusetts, was promptly identified and repaired because the cooling tower was submetered and facility maintenance staff monitored its readings regularly. Without a submeter, the problem would likely have continued for months before being discovered, wasting water and money and possibly risking property damage.[51]

> **Case Study** *Canadian National Research Council Decreases Water Use by 20%.* A research facility of the Canadian National Research Council comprises more than 50 buildings, many of which contain laboratories and other facilities devoted to science and engineering research. Most of the water use at the facility is for equipment cooling, cooling towers, and domestic purposes. Each building is metered separately; meters are read and reconciled monthly. As part of the facility's efforts to reduce water waste, large discrepancies (those in excess of 20%) between metered demand and total water supplied are investigated if they persist for more than two or three months. Annual discrepancies of 13 to 20% were common before the facility initiated a water conservation program following a complete water audit of all 50 buildings in 1991. Among the conservation measures implemented were installation of closed-loop cooling systems, reuse of cooling tower water for process cooling whenever possible, and installation of low-volume toilets and showerheads in some of the buildings. One year after implementation of the measures, water use had declined by 20%, and water utility bills had decreased by about Can$100,000.[52]

4.2 CLEANING AND SANITATION

ICI facilities use water for cleaning and sanitation in multiple ways. This section describes cleaning and sanitation water uses in such categories as manual washing (products, surfaces, and so on), vehicle-washing (including automatic car-washing), steam sterilizers, and autoclaves.

Audit Information to Be Collected on Cleaning and Sanitation

Information that should be collected about cleaning and sanitation practices during an ICI facility water audit includes:

- Frequency of water use for cleaning activities.
- Areas, equipment, and appliances that are cleaned.
- Type of water-using cleaning equipment used.
- Cleaning and sterilization needs.
- All health, safety, operational, regulatory, administrative, and other requirements or policies that apply to the site.

Conservation Policies and Regulations Related to Cleaning and Sanitation

- *Requirements for water audits and efficiency measures at federal facilities.* Federal laws and executive orders pertaining to water and energy conservation requirements include: (1) The U.S. Energy Policy Act of 1992,[16] which established maximum water-use standards for plumbing fixtures (toilets, urinals, showerheads, and faucets) installed in both public and private facilities nationwide (see Chapter 2, *Residential and Domestic Water Use and Efficiency Measures*, Table 2.1, "Federal Maximum Water-Use Requirements for Toilets, Urinals, Showerheads, and Faucets"; (2) Executive Order 12902, *Energy Efficiency and Water Conservation at Federal Facilities,* which requires all federal agencies to conduct a comprehensive water and energy audit of their facilities and, where practicable, purchase equipment that is within the top 25% of energy-efficient products (or at least 10% more efficient than applicable national standards);[17] and (3) Executive Order 13123, *Greening the Government Through Efficient Energy Management,* which builds on Executive Order 12902 and requires federal agencies to establish water conservation goals and to specify and purchase life-cycle, cost-effective ENERGY STAR® or other energy-efficient products and equipment in order to reduce greenhouse gas emissions by 35% (relative to 1985) per gross square foot of their facilities by 2010.

• ***Shutoff valve required for hoses used to clean vehicles.*** Water-use restrictions in San Francisco and Goodyear, Arizona, require that hoses used to manually clean vehicles be equipped with shutoff valves that stop the flow of water when the hose is not in use.[53]

4.2.1 Manual Washing

Manual washing typically involves using water and hoses or cloths to clean a variety of items, including food (e.g., produce), tools, equipment, floors, counters, and other surfaces.

Water-Efficiency Measures for Manual Washing

Water efficiency measures that may be applicable to manual washing include:[54, 55]

• Floors and other surface areas should be swept before being cleaned with water unless applicable health codes and other regulations (e.g., for food, beverage, and medical facilities) require otherwise. This will save water as well as costs for labor, energy, and cleaning chemicals.
• When washing floors and other surface areas with a hose, use high-pressure, low-volume hoses with automatic shutoff valves to lower water use but boost the effectiveness of the spray for cleaning.
• Portable high-pressure pumps can lower water use for cleaning by as much as 40%.
• A variety of steam cleaners are available to clean heavily soiled items.
• Clean-in-place (CIP) systems should use high pressure and temperature to enhance cleaning if possible. CIP systems should also be designed to recirculate water internally. Continually running rinse streams and overflows should be avoided whenever possible.

Water Savings, Benefits, and Costs From Manual Washing

An example of a water-efficiency measure for cleaning would be to install an automatic shutoff valve with a reduced-flow nozzle on the hoses used to wash the sidewalks outside a shopping mall. If 5.0 gpm hoses used by maintenance personnel for a combined total of two hours a day were retrofitted to use an average of 2.0 gpm, the water savings that could be expected would be 360 gallons per day (gpd), or more than 131,000 gallons a year. Based on a combined water and sewer rate of $4 per thousand gallons, annual cost savings from this measure would be about $525. With an estimated cost of $40 for two reduced-volume automatic shutoff valves, the payback on this measure would be about one month. Automatic shutoff nozzles for spray hoses are available in variable spray patterns and cost $10 to $25.

4.2.2 Vehicle-Washing and Automatic Car Washes

In addition to commercial car wash operations, vehicle-washing is a regular maintenance practice at a variety of ICI facilities, including car dealerships, facilities with vehicle fleets, and truck operations. Some facilities have automated car wash systems, as shown in Figure 4.9; others rely on manual labor.

The amount of water used by car wash facilities depends primarily on the type of cleaning system used and whether its design includes reclamation. A study of three commercial automatic car washes in Phoenix found broad variations in the amount of water used per vehicle—28 to 63 gallons.[56] According to the International Carwash Association, water use by systems with no reclamation component averages 15 gallons per vehicle for self-service washes, 50 to 60 gallons per vehicle for in-bay (stationary) automatic washes, and 66 to 85 gallons per vehicle for conveyor washes. Car washes with reclaimed systems—which separate grit, oil, and grease from previously used wash and rinse water and then treat and filter it for reuse—can reduce water use by more than half.[57]

Other variables affecting water use by car wash facilities include the extent of manual prewashing, the number of spray nozzles used and their flow rates, line speed, leakage, and equipment maintenance. Water losses through evaporation and fine mists (carry-out losses) have been estimated to range from 3.0 to 7.5 gallons per vehicle, according to car wash industry sources.[56] The amount of water used at car wash facilities also depends on the size of the vehicles washed and vehicle-washing frequency, which can be affected by regional differences in cleaning needs (e.g., vehicles in regions where salt is applied to roads during the winter may require extra cleaning to remove salt residue and dirt buildup).

There are three types of car washes: automatic conveyor or "tunnel," in-bay automatic, and bay self-serve facilities. An automatic *conveyor car wash* operates by pulling a vehicle through a cleaning tunnel where it is subjected to a set of sprays, brushes, or strips of cloth (friction systems), high-pressure nozzles (frictionless systems), and air flows to wash, rinse, and dry it. This cleaning procedure is usually programmed with time- and motion-sensors that allow little human control over the amount of water used. Some automatic car washes employ line workers to manually prewash bumpers and tires with hoses and brushes before the vehicle enters the tunnel. Water uses along the conveyor line of automatic car washes include: pre-rinse (automated nozzles or manual sprays from a hand-

The primary constituents of concern to professional car wash operators are:

- *TSS (Total Suspended Solids)*
- *TDS (Total Dissolved Solids)*
- *oil and grease*
- *BOD (Biochemical Oxygen Demand or Biological Oxygen Demand)*
- *COD (Chemical Oxygen Demand)*
- *detergent*
- *lead*
- *zinc*
- *amounts of other priority metals*

Of these contaminants, the professional car wash operator introduces only the detergent."

—International Car Wash Association

Figure 4.9 Commercial automatic car washes use 50 to 85 gallons of water per vehicle washed, according to the International Carwash Association. (Photo courtesy of Jane Heller Ploeser)

held hose); wash and first rinse (includes detergent, automated brushes, and rinse water sprays); "rocker" panel brushes (rinse sprays on brushes that clean the vehicle's sides and undercarriage); wax and sealers (surface vehicle finishes, usually optional); final rinse; air blowers (to facilitate drying and remove water spots); and (sometimes) hand-drying with rags by workers. Car washes also have incidental (often small) water uses, such as those for food and drink facilities, restrooms, automotive services, and landscaping.[56]

At *in-bay automatic car washes*, located primarily at gas stations and coin-operated car washes, vehicles are parked in a bay where a machines moves back and forth over the car for cleaning. *Self-serve car washes* are usually coin-operated and allow the customer to control the amount of water used by a wand or hose (Figure 4.10).

Water-Efficiency Measures for Vehicle-Washing and Automatic Car Washes

Water-efficiency measures that may be applicable to vehicle-washing and automatic car washes include:[56–58]

- Install a recycling system that allows wash water to be reused; nonrecycled water may still be needed for the final rinse.

- Modify existing car washes to recycle as much water as possible by installing filters, storage tanks, and high-pressure pumping systems.
- Limit the number of spray nozzles and set flow rates at the minimum volume and pressure required.
- Ensure that the direction, arch, and timing of sprays on automatic car washes are properly set and that they shut off when no longer in contact with the vehicle. Take advantage of gravity to use the water most efficiently; place bigger nozzles on top and smaller nozzles on the sides.
- Install automatic shutoff valves on hoses or preset timers for self-serve car wash systems.
- Increase conveyor speed to reduce rinse cycles to no more than 40 seconds per vehicle.
- Sweep out self-service bays before washing them; use high-pressure wands instead of hoses.
- Minimize dripping by replacing or maintaining positive-cutoff solenoid valves at the control points for prewash, wash, hot wax, and rinse.
- Conduct regular checks for leakage and maintenance of all water-using equipment.

Water Savings, Benefits, and Costs From Car Washing

Case Study *Seattle Car Washes Reclaim Wash Water for Reuse.* The Grayline bus company in Seattle achieved a 93% reduction in water use by installing a reclaimed wash water system and reducing its use of freshwater to clean buses from 350 gallons per vehicle (gpv) to 25 gpv. These water savings are especially high because the company even uses reclaimed water for the final rinse (about 10 gallons). The reclamation system cost Grayline $85,000 to install. With a $42,400 rebate from Seattle Public Utilities' "Water Smart Technology" program and annual water and sewer cost savings of about $53,000, the payback

Figure 4.10 Self-serve car washes are usually coin-operated and use about 15 gallons of water per vehicle. (Photo courtesy of Amy Vickers & Associates, Inc.)

period for this conservation investment was less than one year. Another automatic (conveyor) car wash facility in Seattle installed a reclamation system that reduced its freshwater use from 70 to 85 gpv to 17 to 21 gpv, a 75% water savings, despite the facility's continued use of freshwater for the final rinse. Although the initial investment in the reclamation system was about $50,000, a rebate of about $20,000 from Seattle Public Utilities and annual water and sewer cost savings of about $13,000 made the payback period on this measure less than two years.[57, 59]

4.2.3 Steam Sterilizers

Steam sterilizers are used in medical and dental offices, hospitals, and nursing homes to clean and sterilize containers, instruments, surgical tools, and trays. Sterilizers use water to produce steam, cool steam, and, in some units, to create a vacuum to accelerate drying of the disinfected items. Some older sterilizers rely on a continuous flow of water to cool the steam once it is discharged—in some cases, 24 hours a day. The flow rates of steam sterilizers vary, but they typically range from 1.0 to 3.0 gpm and often continue operating even when the sterilizer is not being used. Newer steam sterilizers typically operate for preset wash cycles and use less water than continuously operating models.[60, 61]

Water-Efficiency Measures for Steam Sterilizers

Water-efficiency measures that may be applicable to steam sterilizers include:[60–62]

- Select new sterilizers that include water-efficiency features such as water recirculation and automatic shutoff devices (for preset runs and when the machine is not in use).
- Using water to cool the steam in sterilizers is not always necessary. In some cases, a small expansion tank can be used to collect the steam and let it cool to a satisfactory temperature before the condensate from the cooled steam is thrown away.
- Solenoid-operated valves may be installed on some sterilizers to shut off the continuous flow of water when the sterilizer is not in use, so long as this does not interfere with proper operation of the unit.
- If a sterilizer's operation depends on a continuous flow of water that cannot be discontinued (e.g., through retrofit or replacement), ask the unit's manufacturer or service contractor if the flow can be lowered to a minimum acceptable level.
- Uncontaminated steam condensate and noncontact cooling water from sterilizers may be reusable as make-up water for cooling towers, boilers, and other nonpotable uses.
- Check to see if sterilizers can be turned off when not in use (this may vary depending on such factors as the models in use and the facility's hours of operation).
- Make sure that staff follow consistent procedures for selecting sterilizer run times, e.g., not setting a 30-minute cycle if only a 10-minute cycle is required for a particular load.

Water Savings, Benefits, and Costs From Steam Sterilizers

Case Study *Hospital Saves Water by Recirculating Noncontact Sterilizer Cooling Water.* A water audit of the Norwood Hospital in Massachusetts determined that retrofitting the hospital's sterilizers with a system that collects, cools, pumps, and recirculates the cooling water could reduce water use. This measure has saved an estimated 4 million gallons annually, equivalent to 8% of the hospital's total water use. Although the hospital paid approximately $25,300 to purchase and install the system, annual cost savings of $27,500 made the payback on this measure just under one year.[63]

4.2.4 Autoclaves

Autoclaves are used to sterilize laboratory instruments and equipment and sometimes infectious waste in medical offices, hospitals, and health care facilities. Autoclaves are similar to sterilizers except that they use ethylene oxide as the sterilizing medium and a stream of pressurized water at high temperatures to draw off spent ethylene oxide. Like steam sterilizers, some autoclaves also use a continuous stream of water to create a vacuum to speed the drying process. The flow rate of an autoclave usually ranges from 0.5 to 2.0 gpm.[60, 62, 64]

Water-Efficiency Measures for Autoclaves

Water-efficiency measures that may be applicable to autoclaves include: [60, 62, 64, 65]

- Select new autoclaves that include water-efficiency features such as water recirculation and automatic shutoff devices (for preset runs and when the machine is not in use).
- If a large autoclave is routinely operated with small loads, replace or supplement it with a smaller unit that accommodates fewer items.
- Solenoid-operated valves may be installed on some autoclaves to shut off the continuous flow of water when the autoclave is not in use, so long as this does not disrupt the equipment's reliability or performance.
- When an autoclave's operation depends on a continuous flow of water that cannot be discontinued (e.g., through retrofit or replacement), ask the unit's manufacturer or service contractor if the flow can be lowered to a minimum acceptable level.
- Uncontaminated noncontact cooling water from autoclaves may be reusable for nonpotable purposes such as make-up water for cooling towers.
- Check to see if autoclaves can be turned off when not in use (this may vary depending on such factors as the models in use and the facility's hours of operation).
- Make sure that staff follow consistent procedures for selecting autoclave run times, e.g., not setting a 30-minute cycle if only a 10-minute cycle is required for a particular load.

Steam is an odorless, invisible gas consisting of vaporized water that is usually interspersed with minute droplets of water, which gives it a white, cloudy appearance.

Water Savings, Benefits, and Costs From Autoclaves

An example of a water-efficiency measure for an autoclave would be to operate the machine only when it contains a full load of items to be sterilized. If two autoclaves, each using 2.0 gpm for every 10-minute sterilization cycle, were operated five times a day with full loads instead of eight times a day with partial loads, about 120 gpd would be saved. Implementation of this measure at a medical office that operates the machines an average of 260 day per year would save 31,200 gallons of water per year (gpy). With no cost involved for implementation, this measure, along with a combined water and sewer service rate of $4 per thousand gallons, would save about $125 a year and provide instant payback.

4.3 PROCESS WATER USES

Process water in the commercial and industrial sectors is used primarily to clean products, to remove or transport ingredients, contaminants, or products, and to control pollution or dispose of waste. Some of the more common uses of process water are for washing and rinsing, materials transfer, photographic film and x-ray processing, and pulp, paper, and packaging production. The quantities of water used for processing vary according to use and are usually site-specific.

Audit Information to Be Collected on Process Water

Information that should be collected about process-water uses during an ICI facility water audit includes:

- Review facility production rates and determine or estimate total water use for each process-water end use by creating a diagram showing water going into the site and wastewater going out; include all water that is recycled and reused.
- Determine the hours of operation and actual pump and flow characteristics for all process-water uses.
- Review data from facility water and sewer meters and talk to operations staff about the source(s) of water used, including public and private (on-site wells, ponds) sources as well as water derived from reuse and recycling processes.
- Identify the water quality requirements (e.g., untreated, reclaimed, potable, or ultrapure) of each water-using process.
- Check the amount of wastewater being discharged and review records that might identify its chemical constituents.
- Identify all health, safety, operational, regulatory, administrative, and other requirements or policies that apply to the site.

Conservation Policies and Regulations Related to Process Water

- *Requirements for water audits and efficiency measures at federal facilities.* Federal laws and executive orders pertaining to water and energy conservation requirements are described under Section 4.2, "Cleaning and Sanitation."

4.3.1 Process Washing and Rinsing

Process washing and rinsing are water-intensive but necessary operations for a number of industries, particularly metal finishing shops and computer chip manufacturers. Water in a rinse bath, as shown in Figure 4.11, may be static, constantly flowing, or flowing in a countercurrent pattern. A static rinse bath is a tank filled with water and process chemicals. Products are dipped in the bath to remove contaminants and extraneous material, and the tank is regularly drained and refilled with freshwater for processes that require multiple rinses. Constant-overflow rinse baths, or running rinses, have water continuously flowing into the tank and an overflow connected to a discharge drain. Some constant-flow rinse baths are operated continually even though they are used only occasionally. Each rinse bath is usually an essential part of the manufacturing method and may involve delicate processes and chemical interactions. Thus, rinse baths should be carefully evaluated before water-efficiency modifications are made.[62, 67–69]

In the electronics and metal finishing industries, product components are often rinsed with ultrapure deionized water to remove the chemical residue accumulated during manufacture. Deionized water is produced from public or private water sources using treatment techniques such as filtration, ion exchange, reverse osmosis, carbon adsorption, or ultraviolet radiation. Because deionized water is relatively expensive to produce, reducing its use will also cut down on the cost of its production.[69] In some cases, deionized water can be treated and reused.[70]

Figure 4.11 Process washing and rinsing are often extremely water-intensive operations. (Photo courtesy of Denver Water)

Case Study *Improved Manufacture of Printed Circuit Boards Reduces Water Use.* The Merix Corporation's Forest Grove facility in Portland, Oregon, manufactures printed circuit boards (PCBs) for computers, a process that requires considerable water and energy. The Forest Grove plant implemented a number of conservation measures that reduced its water use by 12.6 mgy, saving $190,000 annually. Measures included adjusting the placement, frequency, and flow of process nozzles, valves, and floats used to wash PCBs after stripping and etching. The facility expanded its closed-loop chilled water system to additional process lines, began reusing filtered wastewater to rinse the sludge press, and installed a secondary reverse osmosis treatment system that is saving about 21,600 gallons of water a week. In addition, excess water around the building's foundation is now pumped and treated for reuse instead of being discharged to the sewer line, and energy-saving lighting, electrical switching, and programmable panels have been installed. Merix has also implemented similar measures at its Loveland, Colorado, site.[71]

Water-Efficiency Measures for Process Washing and Rinsing

Water-efficiency measures that may be applicable to industrial process washing and rinsing operations include:[11, 62, 67–69, 72–74]

- Identify all water-using processes and determine if less water could be used through process optimization, water reuse, more efficient technologies, and switching to alternative water sources. Apply water-efficiency technologies or modifications that are specifically geared toward a particular facility and process.
- Identify the most appropriate cleaning and rinsing process required. Potential options include switching to smaller tanks and sinks, converting from continuous-flow to intermittent-flow systems, using batch processing for equipment that processes items individually, and using measured amounts of water rather than continuous rinsing and cleaning streams whenever possible.
- Install in-flow meters, control valves, and sensors (e.g., electric-eye or level-float sensors) on equipment that uses freshwater to stop flows when a rinsing, washing, or filling process is completed; adjust flow rates to the minimum amount required. Use instruments that measure conductivity or total dissolved solids to monitor water quality and to control the quantity of water needed for rinses, electrically operated flows, and rinse-water feed valves.
- Install automatic timer-controlled shutoff valves for rinse flows wherever feasible, although in some cases manually operated valves may be preferable to automatic controls that allow unneeded flows.
- Use automatic washers that continuously recirculate wash and rinse water for items such as reusable containers.
- Use sequential rinsing when spent water from one process is reused as rinse water for another compatible process, e.g., using the rinse water from an acid bath for a caustic bath rinse.
- Treat rinse water from plating and metal finishing operations whenever feasible to recover metals and chemicals (for return to the plating bath) and rinse water (for return to the rinse system). Consider membrane systems and evapo-

rator/condenser systems as options to separate plating solutions and rinse water.

- Treat and reuse water from plating and metal finishing processes for certain cold water rinses. Improve the quality of the rinse water by reducing drag-out (the process solution separated from the plating bath by the product) through the use of air knives. Allow drag-out to drain into the plating tank sufficiently before the work is moved to the rinse tanks. Use of wetting agents in the plating bath can reduce drag-out by half because it reduces surface tension.

- For multitank operations, one option may be to use the first rinse tank as a static tank instead of a continuous-overflow tank in order to retain most of the drag-out in the first tank. This method can reduce the amount of water needed for additional rinses and for tank refilling. Another option for multi-tank operations may be to use countercurrent flow rinsing, a multitank rinse procedure in which water flows from tank to tank in the opposite direction from the process sequence. This protocol leaves the final tank with the freshest water and thus the cleanest rinse, allowing the preceding tanks to use less water from the subsequent tank(s). In some cases, using two countercurrent tanks instead of a single rinse tank has reduced water use by as much as 50%. Additional tanks, piping, and floor space may be required for setting up a counterflow system.

- Alternative rinse operations to improve the water-use efficiency, if compatible with the process, can include replacing rinse baths with a spray rinsing system that reuses spent rinse water and provides other water recovery processes.

- Use appropriate nozzles to direct rinse and cleaning sprays accurately. Spray rinses may be most effective with items that are flat, have small holes, or are cup-shaped.

- Avoid or minimize the use of water softening, reverse osmosis, and deionized water unless these processes are critical because they require additional backwash water, which is less reusable for other nonpotable needs. The amount of water required for reverse osmosis can be reduced by eliminating continuous rinses whenever feasible. Recycling deionized rinse water requires careful control of contaminated wastewater to avoid component failure, particularly in the electronics industry; treatment methods include many of the processes used to produce deionized water. Because the initial volumes of water in a rinse bath are likely to have the highest concentrations of contaminants, recycling only the less contaminated rinse water used later in the process may make more sense. Maintain the quality of deionized water by optimizing its use, eliminating some plenum flushes, and converting from continuous-flow to intermittent-flow systems.

- Reuse or recycle rinse water to the next wash whenever possible. Treatment options for wash water, if necessary, include dissolved air flotation and filtration.

- Water used for heat transfer purposes, such as cooling and heating water that is not chemically altered, can be pumped into holding tanks and used for another process.

- Avoid unnecessary dilution; use the maximum allowable contaminant concentrations in rinse tanks.

- Reduce rinse water in the solvent-degreasing process with tamper-proof conductivity meters to control make-up water for rinse tanks.

The Earth has music for those who listen."
—Shakespeare

- Recover, treat, and reuse filter backwash water.
- Install splashguards and drip trays. Install drain boards between process and rinse tanks to reroute drag-out back to the process tank.
- Repair leaks around process equipment.
- Reduce or eliminate trickle flows that continue to run after processing operations are finished.
- Extend the life of baths by inspecting all parts prior to plating; parts should be clean, dry, and free of rust and mill scale to minimize contamination. Wipe or prewash dirty parts using old solvent.
- Schedule wet process production so rinses occur for fewer hours during the day.
- Install pressure reducers if high-pressure incoming supply water is not needed. Low-pressure portable pumps may be an option for wash stations to reduce the total amount of water discharged.

Water Savings, Benefits, and Costs From Process Washing

A number of studies have investigated the water conservation opportunities and results achieved by commercial and industrial process washing and rinsing operations, particularly in the electroplating and electronic industries. For example, a study of water conservation measures implemented by ten electronics manufacturers in the Silicon Valley region of California identified significant water and cost savings achieved through water-use monitoring, recycling and reuse, equipment modification, improved landscape irrigation, and employee education. The companies involved in the study develop, test, manufacture, and market semiconductor chips, integrated circuits, and other electronic products. The amount of water saved per company ranged from 2 to 365 million gallons annually, and water use was typically reduced by 20 to 40%. Annual cost savings ranged from $28,000 to $153,000; paybacks on investments were typically less than one year.[69, 75]

Case Study *Chip Manufacturer Saves Water With Process Innovations and Reverse Osmosis.* Intel Corporation's microchip manufacturing facility in Rio Rancho, New Mexico, outside of Albuquerque is using about 4 mgd since implementing various water-efficiency innovations, far less than the 10 mgd originally projected. Furthermore, between 1995 and 1999, Intel's reductions in water use corresponded to a 70% increase in chip productivity. The water savings were achieved through installation of a high-recovery reverse osmosis system, improved chip washing and rinsing techniques, and water-efficient landscaping. Considerable amounts of ultrapure water are required to manufacture the computer wafers (chips) that are the brains of computers, cell phones, and other portable electronic devices. Intel's reverse osmosis system can suspend large amounts of silica in the water used in wafer production, thereby reducing the amount of purified water required. A pilot study of the system achieved an 85% recovery rate that yielded 1.0 gallon of purified water for every 1.2 gallons put through the system. Intel also saves approximately 757,000 gpd by reusing this water once it has gone through the manufacturing process for cooling tower make-up, exhaust scrubbers, and landscape irrigation. When a fluid-dynamics computer model of water used in Intel's wafer processing tanks showed that 50% of the flow was not rinsing chips, the company had a new wet bench designed, changing the shape and volume of the tank to optimize the amount of water used for rinsing. The redesigned wet bench not only saved water but also reduced the amount of chemicals and energy needed in process tanks. Intel now uses this new design at its other facilities worldwide. The Rio Rancho fabrication facility's 31 acres of grounds were upgraded with Xeriscape designs and plants and more efficient irrigation systems. These improvements reduced outdoor water use by about 60%.[76]

Case Study *Air Scrubbers Use Seawater Instead of Freshwater.* The Monsanto Company's NutraSweet Kelco plant in San Diego produces algin products used to stabilize, thicken, and suspend foods, pharmaceuticals, personal care products, paper and textiles, paints and coatings, oil field drilling fluids, and cement materials. As a by-product of algin production, volatile organic compounds (VOCs) are produced, and water-using packed-bed air scrubbers are used to control VOC emissions. Before implementation of water-efficiency measures, the air scrubbers used large quantities of freshwater. An engineering evaluation of the scrubbers led to major design changes allowing the use of salt water, an abundant water source in San Diego. The conversion was accomplished by installing high-quality corrosion-resistant copper/nickel alloy pipe to transfer seawater from the bay to the four scrubber units. Additionally, special strainers were included in the new lines to minimize fouling of the scrubbers by the corrosive saltwater. As a result of these measures, the plant's annual freshwater use declined by 150 mgy by the end of 1995; total water use declined by 20%, and reduced water and sewer costs saved more than $1 million.[77]

Case Study *Metal Finishing and Process Industries Conserve Rinse Water.* Two case studies of metal finishers in San Jose, California, illustrate the types of conservation measures and savings this type of industrial customer can achieve. Hi-Density Disc, a manufacturer of large magnetic memory discs for mainframe computers, began reusing its rinse water and implemented other process changes such as installing a new tank, piping, and a cartridge filter to reduce water waste. In addition, it instituted an aggressive training and monitoring program to ensure that its employees followed water-efficiency principles and procedures. Annual water savings from these efficiency measures totaled 2.3 million gallons, a 29% reduction from previous use. Annual cost savings were $200,000, and the payback period on the investment was less than one month. One adverse effect of the conservation measures for this company, however, was an increase in wastewater discharge violations because effluent contaminant concentrations increased. Another metal finisher, Dyna-Craft, installed air knives in its rinsing machinery to reduce the amount of rinse water needed. Dyna-Craft also installed flow restrictors in its deionized water rinse. Annual water savings from these measures totaled 13 million gallons, a 25% reduction from previous use. Annual cost savings were $129,000 a year, and the payback period on the company's water-efficiency investments was two months.[69, 75]

A good example is the best sermon."
—Benjamin Franklin

4.3.2 Materials Transfer

Water is used to transfer materials (e.g., edible produce but not computer chips) for such processes as rinsing, washing, and ingredient or product transport, as well as for pollution control and waste disposal. For example, a *fluming* operation transports fruits or vegetables from delivery trucks to processing lines. After a truck unloads large bins of produce onto platforms, water is released into the bins to transport the produce through a gate into channels that lead to sorting equipment.[69]

Water-Efficiency Measures for Materials Transfer

Water-efficiency measures that may be applicable to materials transfer include:[69, 76]

- Flume water may be reused through bins and channels, often without treatment.
- Lower the depth of water in bins and channels to reduce volumes.
- Use intermittent discharges of water for product transport instead of continuous flows.
- Filter or recycle process water for other purposes that don't require potable water.

Water Savings, Benefits, and Costs From Materials Transfer

Case Study *Chili Pepper Plant Removes Peels With Recycled Water.* Border Foods in New Mexico, one of the largest green chili and jalapeno pepper producers in the world, roasts and prepares for shipping about 1 million pounds of peppers a day. Between 1992 and 1995, Border Foods achieved water savings of 27% per pound of peppers prepared, dropping from 0.7 gallons of water per pound to 0.5 gallons per pound. The company accomplished these savings by straining out pepper peelings from process water and chlorinating the water for reuse in (nonfood contact) peel-removal flumes. Border Foods also recycles the 47 million gallons of wastewater it produces annually, using it to meet all the irrigation requirements of 100 acres of alfalfa and grass farms. (Total water use rose after 1995 because jalapeno pepper production increased by 300% and the peppers are canned in brine water).[76]

Case Study *Packing Company Uses Recycled Water for Product Fluming.* The Gangi Bros. Packing Company, a tomato processing and canning plant in Santa Clara, California, implemented water-efficiency measures in its fluming process for transporting tomatoes by replacing freshwater with previously used (but chlorinated) process water. At the company's fluming operation, trucks unload tomatoes in large bins (about 350 cubic feet in size) onto cannery platforms. At the platforms, water is released into the bins to carry the tomatoes to sorting equipment. Water for the fluming process is recirculated by means of special valves in the discharge bins and flume dump system.[75]

Case Study *Canadian Meat-Processing Plant to Reduce Water Use by 15%.* The meat-processing industry requires significant volumes of water for processing, refrigeration, and cleanup operations. The Gainers meat-processing facility in Edmonton, Alberta, processes and packages raw and smoked meat products. An energy and water audit of the facility identified five conservation measures estimated to achieve annual water savings of 211,200 cubic meters, about 15% of total water use. The water-efficiency measures included installing low-volume, fine-mist sprayers to wash and cool products and racks; installing high-pressure spray guns and nozzles; installing low-volume showerheads; and replacing or retrofitting washroom toilets, urinals, and faucets with new fixtures or related devices. The audit also recommended drilling a well to supply water for stock watering and summer cooling, an action that does not optimize water-use efficiency but saves money. Annual water and sewer cost savings from the efficiency measures were projected to be more than Can$250,000, with an estimated payback period of about eight months.[78]

4.3.3 Photographic Film and X-Ray Processing

Film processors are used in photographic film laboratories operated by commercial establishments, law enforcement agencies, schools, and other facilities, as well as for x-ray film development in hospitals, medical and dental offices, and other types of health care facilities.

Most large photo and x-ray processing operations use automatic film developing equipment, whereas smaller systems are often operated manually. Newer automatic machines are more efficient than older ones and produce less silver to be discharged into wastewater. Automatic film processors typically use a constant stream of water for a series of chemical reactions to develop, fix, harden, wash, and bleach film. Most of the water is used in the wash and rinse cycles, although the amount varies with the type of film or the particular process required for development. Film and x-ray processing machines use water at average flow rates of 2 to 4 gpm. An efficient photo processing system used at hospital and health care facilities can average 2.0 gpm or less, although some systems may be operated at higher flow rates. Although x-ray processors can be equipped with automatic shutoff (standby) switches to reduce or stop the flow of water when film is not being processed, some machines may not turn off as intended and may continue to draw water even while not processing film.[65, 79, 80]

Water-Efficiency Measures for Photographic Film and X-Ray Processing

Water-efficiency measures that may be applicable at photographic film and x-ray processing facilities include:[79–81]

- Upgrade equipment to newer, water-efficient models.
- Adjust the film processor's flow rate to the minimum required; this may require installation of a control valve in the water line supplying each unit. (Flow requirements may vary by machine, even among the same models produced by the same manufacturer.) Install a simple flow meter in the supply piping, and post a list of minimum acceptable flow rates near the processor as a guide for employees who operate it.
- Automatic water shutoffs with solenoid valves can be installed on some equipment to stop the flow of rinse and cooling water when the unit is not in use.

The German physicist Wilhelm Conrad Röntgen discovered X rays in 1895 by accident while studying cathode rays. The contrast between body parts in medical x-ray photographs is produced by the different scattering and absorption of X rays by bones and tissues.

—Encyclopædia Britannica

*T*he main source of pulp and paper is wood. Wood is debarked, chipped, and then processed into pulp. The pulp is then washed, screened, thickened by the removal of most water, and bleached. Paper manufacture involves beating the pulp, loading, introducing various additives, refining, and running the pulp into a paper machine.

Regularly check machines that are already equipped with such valves to make sure that the valve—and the developer—are turning off properly.

- Install pressure-reducing devices on water lines supplying equipment that does not need high pressure.
- If the unit is equipped with a squeegee, using the squeegee can reduce chemical carryover by as much as 95% and can lower the amount of water required in the wash cycle.
- Recycle rinse-bath effluent as make-up for the developer/fixer solution.

Water Savings, Benefits, and Costs from X-Ray Processing

An example of water savings that might be achieved with an x-ray processor in a medical office would be to reduce the flow of a continuously flowing unit from 4.0 gpm to 2.0 gpm (assuming such a measure is within acceptable operating procedures for the unit and film quality does not diminish) by adjusting the inlet valve (or installing a flow meter and adjustable valve) on the water line supplying the processor. For units that operate 12 hours a day, 260 days a year, estimated water savings would be approximately 374,400 gallons of water a year for each machine with such an adjustment. The flow meter and adjustable valve, if necessary, would cost about $175. Factoring in a combined cost of water and sewer service of $4 per thousand gallons, this measure would save about $1,500 a year in utility costs, generating an instant payback of about one month.

4.3.4 Pulp, Paper, and Packaging Production

The pulp and paper industry is one of the largest water-using industries in the United States. Factories have been estimated to use 15,000 to 60,000 gallons of water per ton of bleached pulp. Because of the intensity of water use in this industry, paper and packaging manufacturers who institute efficiency measures may have a competitive advantage over nonconserving facilities.[82]

Pulping, a common process in the paper industry, involves slurrying water and paper fibers to form a mixture containing 2 to 5% solids. The slurry or pulp is then dewatered through a series of steps, first on a rolling screen and then on continuously moving belts, to be used as an intermediate paper product in subsequent processes at the facility.[69]

Water-Efficiency Measures for Pulp, Paper, and Packaging Production

Water-efficiency measures that may be applied to pulp, paper, and packaging production include:[69, 82, 83]

- Recycling is the most effective water-efficiency measure in the pulp and paper industry, particularly recycling effluent from pulp mills and paper-production machines. The water and fibers recovered from the dewatering process during pulping can often be reused in subsequent pulping operations with little or no treatment, although recycling process water for paper production is more complicated. One of the challenges in using recycled water for paper production is the effect of "white," or process-contaminated, water on product quality and processing. The higher the quality of paper, the higher quality process water required. Thus, using reclaimed water to produce high-quality paper and packaging requires that the water be pretreated extensively to achieve an acceptable chemical balance and to reduce the concentrations of corrosive agents and scale-forming suspended solids.

- Other water-efficiency measures that may be effective in the paper and packaging industry are use of reclaimed water, water blending, partitioning of process or cooling water, and advanced treatment technologies.

Water Savings, Benefits and Costs From Paper Production

Case Study *California Paperboard Corporation Reduces Water Use by 72%.* The California Paperboard Corporation (CPC) in Santa Clara, California, recycles paper and cardboard into paperboard and corrugated medium at a production rate of 240 tons per day, employing 100 to 125 employees on three shifts. Recycling and reuse of process water and installation of a new clarifier to recycle effluent for use in processes that require high-quality water resulted in overall water savings of 1.3 mgd, representing a 72% reduction in water use. Conservation measures, implemented over a period of many years, had saved CPC an estimated $767,100 per year in water and recycling costs by 1990. The key steps CPC used to identify and implement water-efficiency measures were: (1) identify major water uses, (2) evaluate minimum water quality and quantity needs for processes, (3) evaluate the degradation of water quality that results from each process, and (4) evaluate the feasibility of recycling process effluent for use in the same or another process with little or no treatment.[69]

4.4 COMMERCIAL KITCHENS AND RESTAURANTS

Commercial and institutional kitchens use water primarily for food and drink preparation, dishwashing, ice machines, ice cream and frozen yogurt machines, garbage disposers, and scrapping troughs. These kitchens also use water for additional washing and sanitation activities (including laundry), plumbing fixtures in restrooms, cooling and heating systems, and landscape irrigation; often some water is lost through leaks. Commercial and institutional kitchens are typically found in restaurants, cafeterias, hospitals, hotels, office buildings, large commercial establishments, and educational and correctional institutions.[84–88]

Audit Information to Be Collected on Kitchens and Restaurants

Information that should be collected about kitchens and restaurants during an ICI water audit includes:

- Number and type of water-using appliances or pieces of equipment (dishwashers, garbage disposers, ice makers, faucets, food scrapping troughs, and so on).
- Average number of loads per day completed by each water-using appliance and piece of equipment.
- Average number of meals served per day.

- Amount of time faucets and other continuous-flow appliances are used each day.
- Pipe sizes and estimated flow rates of incoming water supply lines.
- Dripping faucets, puddles, and leaks.
- All health, safety, operational, regulatory, administrative, and other requirements or policies that apply to the site.

Conservation Policies and Regulations Related to Commercial Kitchen and Restaurants

- *Requirements for water audits and efficiency measures at federal facilities.* Federal laws and executive orders pertaining to water and energy conservation requirements are described under Section 4.2, "Cleaning and Sanitation."
- *Providing water to restaurant customers only on request.* Some communities have adopted the policy that restaurant customers receive glasses of water only if they request them.

4.4.1 Food and Drink Preparation

Water is used for a number of functions related to food and drink preparation, including cleaning and thawing ingredients, food preparation, filling of glasses and pots, and continuous-flow water troughs for food ladles and ice cream scoops.

Water-Efficiency Measures for Food and Drink Preparation

Water-efficiency measures that may be applicable to food and drink preparation include:[85-90]

- Kitchen faucets should use a maximum of 2.5 gpm at 80 psi (or 2.2 at 60 psi); if higher-volume flows are needed for utility sinks, install a fingertip control valve for aerated or full-flow options. Place a sign near the faucet instructing kitchen workers to use the aerated, lower flow for cleaning and rinsing.
- Install hands-free or foot-activated pedals on faucets.
- Presoak and wash items in basins of water instead of under running water unless otherwise required.
- Install automatic shutoff faucets for bar sinks.
- Reduce flows to the minimum required in wells and troughs for ice cream dippers and butter scoops.
- Turn off continuous flows used to clean drain trays, such as those installed at a coffee/milk/soda/beverage island, unless required by law.
- On-demand, point-of-use hot water dispensers can eliminate or reduce the need to run water at faucets that are slow to produce hot water. Choose a unit that does not require a constantly running recirculation pump.
- Promptly repair leaks and malfunctioning equipment, such as those in hot and cold water lines, steam traps, sterilizers, dishwashing equipment, hoses and faucets, and other water-using equipment and appliances.
- Reduce or eliminate the thawing of frozen food with water unless required by law; if the law requires that water be used for thawing, use the minimum flow needed. As much as possible, plan ahead and thaw food in the refrigerator.

There are several ways to reduce water use for thawing food, but applicable health codes must be checked before any measures are implemented. Many codes require that the water be constantly moving, often at a minimum temperature of not less than 70°F. If the code(s) or other applicable laws do not specify the flow rate for running water, the flow rate may be reduced if it poses no health hazard. If multiple sinks with flowing water are not being fully utilized, use the minimum number necessary.

- Avoid running water to melt ice in the sink strainers.
- Hoses used to wash down the kitchen area can be retrofitted with a throttling valve on the spigot to reduce water use; these valves should be checked regularly for leaks.
- Use full loads in sanitizers, sterilizers, dishwashers, and washing machines consistent with sound sanitary practices and infection control requirements.
- Recycle water wherever feasible and consistent with regulatory requirements. For example, use water from steam tables to wash down the cooking area, and reuse noncontact cooling water for water-cooled machinery such as milkshake machines, frozen yogurt machines, and refrigerators.
- As appliances or fixtures wear out, replace them with water-saving models.
- Serve water only when requested by customers.
- Provide signs at tables and in the kitchen urging water conservation.
- Take water only for drinking, filling of pots, and other necessary uses.
- Use the minimum amount of dishware, glassware, utensils, and cookware to reduce dishwashing loads.
- Report all leaks and water waste to management.

Water Savings, Benefits, and Costs From Food Preparation

Case Study *Commercial Kitchen Reduces Flows in Scrapper Trough.* The scrapper trough in the kitchen of a Boston office building used a constant 24 gpm flow rate for the 4 hours a day the kitchen was in operation. When a flow control device was installed to reduce the flow to 6 gpm (a flow reduction of 75%), water use decreased by more than 4,000 gpd. Water savings from the measure totaled 1.0 million gallons per year. With an investment of approximately $280 for the flow control device and annual net savings of $8,600, the payback period was less than two weeks.[51]

Water savings from efficiency measures implemented in kitchens and restaurants are achieved primarily from reduced flows for faucets and sprayers used for cleaning. The cost of low-volume, automatic shutoff nozzles and faucets for commercial kitchens ranges from $10 to $40. Simple faucet aerators cost $1 to $2 each.[91]

4.4.2 Commercial Dishwashers

Commercial dishwashers, including conveyor-type machines, are available in a variety of types, sizes, and flow rates. Water use by commercial dishwashers typically ranges from 2.5 to 8.0 gpm. Many commercial dishwashers are also equipped with prewash sprayers, which use an additional 1.8 to 6.0 gpm.[92, 93] Water use by dishwashers varies depending on size, hours of operation, and ef-

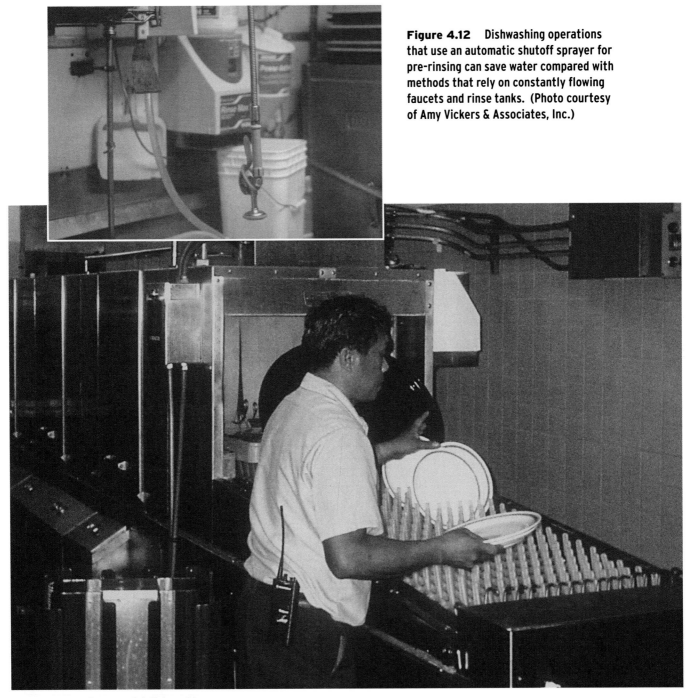

Figure 4.12 Dishwashing operations that use an automatic shutoff sprayer for pre-rinsing can save water compared with methods that rely on constantly flowing faucets and rinse tanks. (Photo courtesy of Amy Vickers & Associates, Inc.)

Figure 4.13 Commercial dishwashing operation using a conveyor belt. (Photo courtesy of Jane Heller Ploeser)

ficiency. For example, a large commercial dishwasher and prewash sprayer system operating at a combined flow rate of 9.0 gpm for eight hours a day, six days a week would use more than 1.3 mgy.

The commercial dishwashing process often starts with a prewash spray used to remove large food particles from dishes to a scrapping trough before the dishes enter the dishwasher, as shown in Figure 4.12. Sprayers are hand-held or automatic units that may or may not be coordinated to operate with the dishwasher. Automatic sprayers usually operate whenever the dishwasher is in operation and shut off automatically when the dishwasher turns off. Manual sprayers use 1.8 to 2.5 gpm, and automatic units use 3.0 to 6.0 gpm.[92, 93]

There are two types of automatic dishwashing machines—conveyor and spray. Dishes washed by machines using a *conveyor* system are loaded onto racks inside the machine or travel along a conveyor belt that passes through the machine, as shown in Figure 4.13. These dishwashers have several cycles of washing, rinsing, and sanitizing. *Spray* dishwashers operate with or without detergent or other cleaning solutions and use hot freshwater with or without a chemical sanitizing agent for the final rinse. Commercial dishwashers usually operate with a continuous flow of rinse water or release periodic feeds of water from the wash tank. Older machines sometimes discard water after each rinse step, whereas modern dishwashers recirculate water through the machine in a concurrent process that discharges water only after the final rinse.[93]

Water-Efficiency Measures for Commercial Dishwashers

Water-efficiency measures that may be applicable to commercial dishwashers and dishwashing operations include:[80, 85, 86, 92–95]

- Presoak utensils, dishes, and cooking vessels in basins of water or used washwater instead of running water to rinse them before they are cleaned in a dishwashing machine or conveyor system.
- Whenever possible, use simple tools (e.g., a brush) to scrape dishes and pots instead of using running water or prewash sprayers.
- Install spray rinses in kitchen sinks with a manually controlled ("dead man shutoff") valve to stop constant flows that are not required.
- Manual prewash sprayers are often more efficient than automatic sprayers; some automatic sprayers can be removed and replaced with a manual one. Operate sprayers only when dishware is present.
- Equip prewash sprayers with low-flow, high-pressure spray heads; use appropriate nozzles to accurately direct rinse and cleaning sprays.
- Operate scrapping troughs only during dishwashing operations. Actually, the scrapper system could probably be eliminated because discharging food waste to the sewer system is not necessary (see Section 4.4.3, "Commercial Food and Garbage Disposers and Scrapping Troughs," later in this chapter).
- Assess the water efficiency of the dishwashing system and its retrofit options. Consult with the equipment manufacturer or service contractor to experiment with a modest reduction (e.g., 10%) in the water flow rate to evaluate performance.
- Wash full loads only in rack-type machines.

- Operate conveyor dishwashers only when dishware is actually passing through the machine so that water flows only when needed for washing and rinsing. Install an electronic eye or motion sensor to detect the presence of dishes and adjust water use accordingly—e.g., automatically stop the flow of water after racks have passed though the machine.
- Install in-line temperature boosters for hot water to minimize losses of cold water.
- If allowable, reuse the final rinse water in the next wash cycle or for low-grade uses such as prewashing, garbage disposers, food scrappers, and flushing of trash troughs.
- Check the manufacturer's operating instructions to make sure the dishwashing system is using the minimum acceptable amount of water. Pressure or flow regulators may be an option to reduce flows to manufacturer specifications. Recommended pressure is typically 60 to 80 psi, but because this varies, pressure should be set to an appropriate value based on the requirements of the particular installation.
- Many older dishwashers and conveyor dishwashing machines are not water- or energy-efficient. Evaluate the costs and benefits of replacing equipment compared with retrofitting equipment and adjusting operations. New dishwashing systems should have automatic water controls and recycling systems. Check the water-use requirements and rinse water flow rates of new dishwashers under consideration. Many commercial machines use 2.8 to 8.0 gpm to clean and sanitize.
- Turn the dishwasher off when it is not in use.
- Check prewash sprayers regularly for leaks.
- Post signs asking employees and visitors to minimize their use of dishware, glassware, utensils, and cookware to reduce dishwashing loads.

Water Savings, Benefits, and Costs From Commercial Dishwashers

Case Study *Hospital Saves Water With Foot Pedal-Operated Spray Rinser.* The Milton Hospital in Milton, Massachusetts, installed a foot pedal-operated spray rinser on the pot-scrubbing sink in its kitchen. This efficiency measure resulted in water savings of 370,000 gpy. With a cost of $240 for purchase and installation of the spray rinser and annual water and sewer cost savings of $3,300, the payback period on this measure was less than one month.[96]

Case Study *Dishware Sensor Promises to Save Water for Boston Restaurant.* An audit of a large restaurant in Boston included a recommendation that the facility install a dishware-sensing gate in one of its dishwashers. The auditor estimated that this efficiency measure would save about 225,000 gpy. With a cost of $1,200 for purchase and installation of the sensor and estimated avoided costs of $2,700 per year from reduced hot water use, payback on this measure was projected to be about five months.[86]

4.4.3 Commercial Food and Garbage Disposers and Scrapping Troughs

Commercial restaurant and large kitchen *garbage disposers* can use surprisingly large quantities of water, with flow rates typically ranging from 3 to 8 gpm and even more if they are operated with a food scrapping trough.[84, 97] For example, a disposer operating at 5.0 gpm for eight hours a day, six days a week would use more than 745,000 gallons of water a year.

Garbage disposers operate by grinding solid food waste into small particles in a mixing chamber, where water is added to facilitate discharge down the sewer drain. Some grinders automatically receive a feed of water when waste is detected in the chamber; others require the faucet and grinder to be turned on manually. Often *scrapping troughs* or conveyor belts are used to carry food scraps and other waste to the disposer. Some scrapping systems, particularly older ones, rely on a constant water flow (3.0 to 5.0 gpm) in a trough to move the waste to the disposer. A conveyor system uses no water (but requires electricity) to move the waste to the grinder. Both systems can be controlled automatically or manually.[98]

Modernized commercial and institutional kitchens may use *garbage strainers* instead of garbage disposers because no regulation requires food waste to be discharged into the wastewater system. A garbage strainer consists of a strainer-type waste-collection basket that allows a recirculating stream of water to flow over food waste. Washing away soluble materials and small particles can reduce waste volumes by as much as 40%. Solid food particles are dumped into the trash or compost when the strainer is full or the load is completed. Strainers use about 2 gpm, less than half the amount of water used by disposers.[84]

Water-Efficiency Measures for Commercial Disposers

Water-efficiency measures that may be applicable to commercial food disposers include:[51, 84, 86, 98–100]

- In most instances, garbage disposers, scrapping troughs, and conveyors are unnecessary and can be eliminated. In addition to saving water, this measure would eliminate costs for disposer repair and replacement and employee time devoted to clogs and other malfunctions.
- Replace disposers with garbage strainers, which use less water and may be an alternative, more water-efficient waste collection system.
- The flow of water to disposers can be controlled by several methods. Electronic sensors that detect the amount of food waste in a disposer's grinding chamber can regulate flows. Solenoid valves can be installed to stop the flow of water when the disposer is turned off. Disposers already equipped with a solenoid valve should be checked periodically to ensure that the valve is not stuck in the open position. Some models have two water supply lines—one to the disposer bowl and one to the grinding chamber; both should be inspected.
- Use the minimum acceptable flow rate for water flowing through the disposer. Reduce the flow gradually to determine the disposer's minimum acceptable rate, or check with the manufacturer for recommendations.
- Adjust models with preset controls to reduce the amount of time the disposer is in operation as well as the volume of water used. Use timers with automatic

shutoff features to limit water flows while the disposer is not in use. Check the flow of water through the disposer to make sure it stops when the disposer is turned off. Be sure to check both water supply lines if the disposer has separate lines to the bowl and the grinding chamber.

- Reuse wastewater from the dishwasher in the mixing chamber of the disposer.
- Eliminate excess flows during periods of high water pressure by installing flow regulators on the disposer's water supply line(s).

Water Savings, Benefits, and Costs From Disposers

Case Study *Unnecessary Food Disposer and Cleaning Trough in Office Complex Kitchen Waste Water and Labor.* Some large kitchens use a combined scrapping trough and conveyor belt system, when cleaning could be accomplished just as easily without water. For example, a water audit of the main kitchen in the Pentagon in Washington, D.C., found that although dishwashing staff were manually removing plates and utensils from trays and placing them on a conveyor belt (involving no water use) for loading onto a dishwasher rack, they were removing food and paper wastes by shaking them off plates and trays into a constantly flowing scrapping trough that led to a disposer. Kitchen staff reported that the disposer regularly clogged (taking employee attention from their regular tasks) and needed about 30 minutes of constantly flowing water just to clear the drain. The auditor made two recommendations that would save water and employee time: placing garbage bins beside the conveyor belt, so that tray wastes could be emptied directly into the bins, and replacing the garbage disposer with a simple in-sink basket to collect waste.[99]

Figure 4.14 Ice machine. Depending on the type and model, icemakers use 20 to 90 gallons of water to produce 100 pounds of ice. (Photo courtesy of Amy Vickers & Associates, Inc.)

4.4.4 Icemakers

Icemakers typically use 20 to 90 gallons of water to produce 100 pounds of ice flakes or cubes, depending on the quality of the ice. Older and water-cooled ice cube machines use as much as 90 gallons—sometimes more—to produce the same quantity of ice. *Flake ice* machines require 15 to 20 gallons of water to produce 100 pounds of ice, and *ice cube makers* typically use 20 to 25 gallons per 100 pounds of ice. Making ice cubes is more water-intensive than making ice flakes because more than half of the water used in cube production drains off minerals and impurities to yield clear cubes. Cloudy ice flakes are accepted, so no bleed-off occurs in their production.[84, 101]

An estimated 1 million automatic icemakers are used in U.S. commercial facilities such as restaurants, kitchens, hotels and motels, hospitals, schools, and offices (Figure 4.14). Ice cube machines comprise more than 80% of icemaker sales. Three types of ice cube machines are available: ice-making head units, self-contained units, and remote condensing units. Ice-making head and self-contained units are either water- or air-cooled. Remote condensing units are air-cooled. Air-cooled machines use less water than water-cooled machines per unit of harvested ice, but they typically demand more energy than water-cooled units. The water and energy efficiency of ice cube makers varies by the ice harvest rate and by machine type and model; newer models tend to be more resource-efficient than older ones. Water use by icemakers—cube and flake—can often be reduced during both production and refrigeration.[101, 102]

Icemakers contain two major subsystems: a *water supply system* and a *refrigeration system*. The water system supplies the water to be frozen into cubes and flakes as well as the process water used in ice cube production to bleed off impurities during freezing. The refrigeration system includes either an air-cooled (involving no water use) or a water-cooled condenser; in water-cooled systems, the water either makes a single pass through the machine or is recirculated. Ice cubes are usually made in a batch process. Some icemakers recirculate water until it is frozen, whereas others use once-through flows to produce clear cubes. The clarity of an ice cube typically indicates its quality in terms of the presence or absence of minerals and other particles. Depending on the model and the method used to produce cubes, water and energy use for ice cube production varies widely.[84, 102]

Making ice flakes is nearly always more water-efficient than making cubes and is usually a continuous process. Generally less clear than cubes, flake ice tends to be thin, randomly shaped, and white or cloudy; it is broken and scraped into flakes, chips, or nuggets by an ice cutter. Machines that produce flake ice use no bleed-off to remove minerals and other particles, and only a small amount of water is lost in the production process.[84]

Water-Efficiency Measures for Icemakers

Water-efficiency measures that may be applicable to icemakers include:[84, 86, 101, 102, 104, 105]

- The useful life of an icemaker is about five years, so replacing an existing water-cooled model with a newer, more water-efficient air-cooled unit may be cost-effective. Because air-cooled models tend to be less energy-efficient than water-cooled machines, they may produce more heated air as exhaust and thus increase a facility's heat load (small facilities that are unable to remove this heated exhaust from the air may not be able to consider this option). Check the water- and energy-use specifications of available icemakers before making a purchase because their efficiency varies widely by manufacturer and model.
- If a water-cooled icemaker is used, make sure water in the cooling system is recirculated. If it is not a recirculating system, retrofit it to operate as a closed-loop system—either by tapping into another on-site, recirculating, chilled water system or by using a remote air-cooled condenser to cool the machine. (These adjustments are likely to be relatively inexpensive.)
- Use the minimum flow rate specified by the manufacturer for the cooling water in a water-cooled icemaker. The flow rate can usually be reduced sufficiently that the water becomes warm before being discharged.
- Use ice flake machines instead of ice cube machines whenever possible to take advantage of the fact that flake ice production involves much less bleed-off than cube production.
- Use softened water in ice cube makers to produce clear cubes and minimize bleed-off.
- To minimize waste, adjust ice machines to dispense ice only when it is needed.
- Collect spent cooling water from water-cooled machines in storage containers and reuse it for nonpotable purposes.

Icemaker Product and Efficiency Information Available

The Air-Conditioning and Refrigeration Institute (ARI), a trade organization of manufacturers of central air conditioning and refrigeration units, tests and sets standards for ice cube makers. Comprehensive, comparative data on the energy use, ice harvest rates, and costs of ARI-certified ice cube machines are published in its *Directory of Certified Automatic Ice-Cube Machines and Ice Storage Bins.*[103] The U.S. Department of Energy's (DOE's) Federal Energy Management Program produces a binder and on-line resource, *Buying Energy Efficient Products,* that provides purchasing recommendations on icemakers whose energy efficiency can be linked with water use.[104] The U.S. Environmental Protection Agency/DOE ENERGY STAR® Program is developing an ENERGY STAR labeling specification that will provide energy-use and efficiency information on icemakers.[102]

Water Savings, Benefits, and Costs from Icemakers

Case Study *Ice Company's Efficiency Measures Achieve Two-Year Payback.* An ice company in Denver produces cube and block ice year-round, with heaviest production occurring between April and October. Most of the company's water use is not for ice but for flushing and cleaning ice-making equipment between and during production runs and for cooling ice storage areas. Minimal structural modifications enabled the company to transfer water it would otherwise have discarded to the evaporative condensers that cool the storage area. The modifications consisted of installing a small vertical turbine pump, PVC pipe, and isolation valves from the pump to the condensers; the valves connect to a simple float-type water-level transmitter that triggers pump startup. Water savings from these measures were approximately 1.5 mgy, and annual reductions in water and sewer costs were about $3,250. With the cost of the structural modifications totaling $7,120, the payback period for this project was just over two years. Because of the conservation measures, the company was also able to defer payment on the cost of a new, larger tap from Denver Water for more than a year.[106]

Case Study *Restaurant Converts Water-Cooled Icemaker to Air-Cooled.* A restaurant in Austin, Texas, reduced its water use by 70% by converting a 400-pound water-cooled icemaker into a remote air-cooled unit. Conversion of the equipment involved retrofitting the piping of the water-cooled condenser and connecting it to a remote air-cooled condenser. With retrofitting costs of just under $600 and an equivalent amount in avoided water and sewer costs, the restaurant achieved a one-month payback period with this water-efficiency measure.[107]

4.4.5 Ice Cream and Frozen Yogurt Machines

Machines that make soft-serve ice cream and frozen yogurt are often standard equipment in ICI kitchens, cafeterias, and restaurants as well as in retail establishments that sell frozen desserts. These machines typically contain a refrigeration condenser that generates heat, and the condenser is cooled by a water-cooled or air-cooled system. Air-cooled systems use no water for cooling. Water use by water-cooled frozen yogurt and ice cream machines varies according to the unit but usually ranges from 2 to 3 gpm during operation. In many water-cooled units, the cooling water makes a single pass through the machine.[86, 89, 108, 109]

Water-Efficiency Measures for Ice Cream and Frozen Yogurt Machines

Water-efficiency measures that may be applicable to ice cream and frozen yogurt machines include:[86, 89, 108, 109]

- Replace water-cooled ice cream and frozen yogurt machines with air-cooled units that require no water for condenser cooling.
- Retrofit water-cooled machines by connecting them to the facility's existing chilled water system, if available, or by installing remote air-cooled condensers.
- Turn off the machine when it is not in use, e.g., during hours when food service is not available.

Water Savings, Benefits, and Costs From Ice Cream and Frozen Yogurt Machines

An effective way to save water in a facility with a water-cooled, soft-serve ice cream machine would be to replace the unit with an air-cooled machine. If a hospital cafeteria operated a 3.0 gpm water-cooled machine for an average of 10 hours a day, 365 days a year, the water savings from replacing it with an air-cooled unit would be 657,000 gpy. With a combined water and sewer rate of $4 per thousand gallons, the hospital would save about $2,630 per year in water and sewer costs. Based on a purchase price of $7,000 for a new air-cooled ice cream machine, the payback period for this measure would be 2.7 years.

4.5 LAUNDRIES AND LAUNDROMATS

Commercial and institutional laundry facilities include those that wash linens, uniforms, and other items for hotels and motels, hospitals, nursing homes, diaper services, and restaurants. Laundering facilities often consume large quantities of water for operations that include the wash and rinse cycles of washing machines, steam-heated dryers, steam-pressing equipment, and reclamation of dry cleaning solvent.

Conventional washer–extractor machines used by most laundry facilities operate with a rotating drum that agitates the laundry during wash and rinse cycles, then spins it at high speeds to extract the water. Washer–extractors and most other conventional large-scale washing machines use freshwater for each wash and rinse cycle; there is no internal recycling. The capacity of washer–extractors ranges from 25 to 400 dry pounds per load. They use 2.5 to 3.5 gallons of water per pound of laundry,[110, 111] the equivalent of 1,000 to 1,400 gallons of water per 400-pound load.

Water-efficient laundering equipment, such as continuous-batch washers and water reclamation systems, can reduce water use by as much as 70% at commercial and institutional facilities equipped with conventional washer–extractors. For example, a commercial laundry in the Boston area saved more than 25 mgy by installing a continuous-batch washer. The cost of the new laundry system was $1 million, but with a $500,000 reduction in annual water and operating costs, the new system paid for itself in less than two years.[54]

Laundromats, such as those found in apartment buildings, shopping centers, and dormitories, use coin-operated clothes washing machines. Conventional clothes washers used by laundromats are usually the same type of machines sold to residential customers except that laundromat washers are fitted with coin machines and usually have a slightly larger (16-pound) capacity compared with residential washers (14-pound capacity). Conventional washers currently installed in laundromats use 35 to 50 gallons of water per load, and they usually have shorter life cycles because of their high rate of use. Some laundromats have started to replace their conventional washers with more water- and energy-efficient front- and top-loading, horizontal-axis washing machines. Some newer machines offer high-speed spin options, which save additional energy and operating costs by extracting more water from laundry than conventional washers and thus reducing dryer use. (See Chapter 2, *Residential and Domestic Water*

*A*pproximately 15 million U.S. apartment units have access to a common area laundry room.
— U.S. Bureau of Census

Use and Efficiency Measures, Section 2.5, "Clothes Washers," for a more detailed description of commercial clothes washers).

An estimated 2 to 3 million commercial (16-pound capacity) washers are installed in the United States.[112] Approximately 200,000 to 300,000 of these commercial washers are replaced each year, most of them having had a useful life of 7 to 10 years. About 17% of commercial-size washers are used in laundromats; the balance are installed in multifamily dwellings.[112] According to estimates by the Coin Laundry Association, about 35,000 laundromats are in business in the United States, and each one has an average of 12 machines.[112]

Audit Information to Be Collected on Laundries and Laundromats

Information that should be collected about laundries and laundromats during an ICI water audit includes:

- Type of washer(s).
- Manufacturer, model number, and year of installation.
- Historical water-use records (for a minimum of three years).
- Average number of pounds of laundry washed per day (or per room or bed, depending on the nature of the facility).
- Average number of rooms and beds and percent occupancy (for hotels and motels, hospitals, dormitories, and similar facilities).
- Amount of detergent used for an average load of laundry.
- All health, safety, operational, regulatory, administrative, and other requirements or policies that apply to the site.

Conservation Policies and Regulations
Related to Laundries and Laundromats

- *Requirements for water audits and efficiency measures at federal facilities.* Federal laws and executive orders pertaining to water and energy conservation requirements are described under Section 4.2, "Cleaning and Sanitation."

Water-Efficiency Measures for Laundries and Laundromats

Water-efficiency measures that may be applicable to commercial laundries and laundromats include:[67, 94, 98, 110, 111, 113, 114]

- Operate laundry equipment with full loads only (weigh loads to make sure they are full-size).
- Reduce water levels, if possible, for partial loads.
- Replace or modify existing conventional laundry equipment (e.g., washer-extractors) to reduce water use. To assess potential water savings and costs involved in replacing equipment, collect and analyze information such as the amount of water the laundering operation uses, the laundering system's capacity (pounds per load), number of cycles or loads completed per day, hours of use, amount of water or wastewater (if any) that is recycled, amount of detergent and other chemicals used, and the estimated flow per cycle (number of gallons) for all laundering equipment, including steam dryers.

- Install a computer-controlled rinse water reclamation system. These systems can save as much as 25% of a wash load's water demand by diverting rinse water to a storage tank for later reuse as wash water.
- Install a wash and rinse water treatment and reclamation system. By recycling both wash and rinse water, these systems can reduce a laundry's water demand by about 50%. Although system design and water use vary by manufacturer, these systems typically treat laundry wastewater so it can be reused in the initial wash cycles of subsequent wash loads. The treatment processes incorporated into these systems include settling, dissolved air floatation, filtration, chemical feed, and carbon adsorption. Laundry recycling systems usually recycle all rinse water except that from the first rinse cycle; water from the first rinse is not recycled because it contains most of the solids, fats, oils, and greases removed from the soiled laundry.
- Install a continuous-batch washer, which can reduce water demand by about 60% compared with that of washer-extractors. Continuous-batch (or tunnel) washers operate with a countercurrent flow that reuses rinse water from all but the first rinse, and laundry automatically passes through a series of modules for each step in the wash cycle. Using only 1.2 to 2.0 gallons of freshwater per dry pound of laundry, continuous-batch washers are also more energy-, chemical-, and labor-efficient than washer–extractors. A disadvantage of these systems, however, is their high capital cost. Continuous-batch washers also require more careful scheduling of wash loads to minimize the need to reset equipment controls.
- Install an electrically generated ozone laundry system, which can reduce water use by about 10% compared with that of conventional laundering systems. The ozone acts as a cleaning agent and also reduces detergent use by 30 to 90%.
- Consult service personnel and the laundry's supplier of chemicals for the washer-extractors to ensure that equipment is operating at optimal efficiency. Adjustments to the chemical or washer program can reduce the number of wash and rinse steps, saving water as well as the amount of chemicals required for each wash. For example, a laundry in Boston that implemented this measure reduced water demand for each pound of laundry by 15%.[108]
- Avoid excessive backflushing of filters or softeners; backflush only when necessary.
- Place "save water" notices or table tents (standup note cards) in hotel and motel guest rooms, urging visitors to save water by minimizing the amount of linen that needs to be laundered. For example, the city of Santa Fe, New Mexico, and the Santa Fe Lodgers Association provide cards for guest rooms encouraging visitors to forego daily linen changes. The card states: "Help save water. Laundering linens uses lots of water! Sheets and towels are customarily changed daily. However, if you feel this is unnecessary, please leave this card on your pillow in the morning. Your towels will be straightened, the bed will be made, but the sheets will not be changed. If you wish fresh towels, place the used towels in the tub. Thank you for helping our community conserve water!"
- Replace conventional washing machines with high-efficiency, horizontal-axis machines, which can save as much as two thirds of the energy and water used

It's a crazy thing to demand fresh sheets and towels every day. No one does that at home."
—Patricia Griffin, president, Green Hotels Association

by conventional models. Optimize water efficiency by choosing a high-performance model that offers the following types of options:

— Water-level adjustments for partial loads.
— A mini-basket, or small tub, that fits over the agitator for washing very small loads.
— Pre-soaking options.
— Fast spin speeds to improve water extraction and reduce drying times.
— Suds-saver features.

Water Savings, Benefits, and Costs From Laundries and Laundromats

Case Study *Hotel Laundry Recycling System Saves $40,000 a Year.* The central laundry facility for seven Red Lion Hotels (now part of the Doubletree Hotel system) in the Portland, Oregon, area is saving more than $40,000 a year from reduced water, sewer, and gas bills after installing a wastewater recovery and recycling system. The laundry achieved these savings by replacing its twenty-year-old conventional, single-pass system with a pumped, closed-loop, three-phase microfiltration and water recycling system. The old system continually heated 52°F potable water to 150°F and then discharged it to the sewer line after a single use. The new system uses a microprocessor to recycle 110°F water through a mechanical shaker screen, a pressurized stainless steel strainer, and a submicron membrane filter that removes particulates as small as 0.5 microns. The filtered water is then heated to 150°F by an existing gas steam boiler and returned to the washers for reuse. As a result of these savings, Red Lion is planning similar improvements at other locations, and the company won the BEST Innovation Award from Portland's Energy Office in 1993. In addition to the cost savings achieved, the recycling system reduced carbon dioxide emissions by about 182 tons and is expected to extend the life of the facility's boiler equipment by 50%. The new system cost about $200,000, yielding a simple payback period of 4.1 years. In addition, the hotel now asks guests who are staying more than one night to agree not to have their sheets laundered every day.[115]

4.6 SWIMMING POOLS AND ZOOS

Swimming pools and pools used for zoo animal and fish habitats share many design, operation, and maintenance features. Water use by swimming pools and zoos varies depending on such factors as size, design, maintainance procedures, climate conditions, and water quality and treatment requirements.

Audit Information to Be Collected on Swimming Pools and Zoos

Information that should be collected about swimming pools and zoo pools during a water audit includes:

- Number and size of pool(s).
- Water-volume capacity and pumping or jetting rate.
- Number of hours per day and days per year of operation.
- Refilling rate and evaporative losses.
- Number of times filled per year.
- Type of water supply for pool(s) (e.g., continuously flowing, recirculating, or reused water).
- Requirements for heating and water treatment chemicals.
- Location and type of meter(s) location, frequency of meter readings, and historical use record (for at least the past three years).
- All health, safety, operational, regulatory, administrative, and other requirements or policies that apply to the site.

Some additional information should be collected for pools used as animal habitats at zoos:

- Number and type of animals present.
- Animal-cleaning and cage-cleaning requirements (e.g., frequency, duration, size of area).
- Number of hoses used, hose shutoff practices, and whether hose shutoff valves are used.
- Number, size, and type of watering troughs (continuously running or fill-and-dump style).
- Water filtration, reuse, and treatment systems.
- Age and condition of underground piping, including date of last on-site leak detection survey.
- Water use for cleaning and maintenance, landscape irrigation, restrooms, kitchens, cafeterias, heating and cooling, and other activities.

Conservation Policies and Regulations Related to Swimming Pools and Zoos

- ***Requirements for water audits and efficiency measures at federal facilities.*** Federal laws and executive orders pertaining to water and energy conservation requirements are described under Section 4.2, "Cleaning and Sanitation."
- ***Limits on refilling pools.*** Some communities limit the frequency of pool refilling, particularly during droughts. The city of Fresno, California, allows pools to be refilled only once every three years, with exceptions allowed for chemical contaminant buildup.[117]

Although manatees are excellent swimmers, the deepest that one has been observed diving is 33 feet. Typically, the large, gentle creatures feed no deeper than about ten feet below the surface of the water."
—www.uselessknowledge.com

- *Requirements for pool covers.* Marin Municipal Water District in California requires pool covers for all new outdoor swimming pools.[118]
- *Requirements for separate meters for irrigation systems and decorative water features.* Phoenix requires that outdoor water uses such as irrigation, fountains, and other water decorations be metered separately from indoor use.[53]
- *Restrictions on using potable water for lakes and fountains.* San Francisco and the Arizona cities of Chandler, Mesa, and Phoenix limit or prohibit the use of potable water to supply lakes and fountains.[53] Palo Alto, California, limits or prohibits the use of potable water for decorative water features such as ponds, fountains, and certain landscaped areas.[119]

4.6.1 Swimming Pools

Swimming pools are installed in a variety of settings, including school and athletic buildings, public recreational facilities, hotels and motels, gyms and health clubs, therapeutic health care facilities, water parks, multifamily residential properties, and private residences (Figure 4.15). More than 1,000 water parks are in operation in the United States,[120] and these facilities often have swimming pools combined with other recreational and decorative water features.

Pools are often drained and refilled more frequently than necessary.[121] Besides filling and refilling, water use by swimming pools includes replacement of losses caused by evaporation, splashing, filter backwashing, and leaks. Water is also used to dilute or remove contaminant buildup in pools.[122] An average uncovered outdoor pool loses about an inch of water a week during the summer because of evaporation,[121] and pools in extremely hot, dry climates lose even more. Indoor pools also lose water, but these losses vary according to the differential in water and ambient air temperatures. Inefficient water-use practices for pools also waste energy. For example, according to the U.S. Department of Energy, 70% of the energy losses from pools are associated with evaporation; adjustments to pool water temperatures can help control water and energy losses.[123]

Water-Efficiency Measures for Swimming Pools

Water-efficiency measures that may be applicable to swimming pools include:[121–125]

- Limit the frequency of pool refilling, taking into account water quality and treatment needs as well as other site-specific requirements.
- Cover the pool with an insulated cover when it is not in use to control heat losses and water lost to evaporation. Pool covers not only save water and reduce energy and chemical losses but also help prevent accidents when the pool is unattended.
- Lower the pool's water level to about 1 inch above the bottom of the tile lining the interior perimeter of the pool to reduce the amount of water that can be splashed out.
- Lower the pool temperature, if possible—particularly when the pool is not being used.

- Backwash pool filters only when necessary. If the backwash cycle is controlled by a timer, check and adjust the frequency and duration of the cycle to ensure optimal efficiency.
- Check the pool regularly for cracks and leaks (including pressure grouting, liners, and drain valves) and make repairs promptly.
- For indoor pools only, installing an in-space condensing unit to reclaim heat and water from the pool area may help reduce the amount of outside air ventilation, which increases evaporative losses.
- Keep pools and pool filters clean to minimize the frequency of filter backwashing. Several hundred gallons of water are used each time the water in a residential-size pool is backwashed through a sand filter.
- Where feasible, let filter backwash water run onto lawns and shrubs or into collection devices for reuse, provided chlorine levels are acceptable (chlorine concentrations of more than 3 milligrams per liter can damage plants).
- Investigate alternative treatment systems that might reduce water losses from filter backwashing.

Figure 4.15 Water must be added to swimming pools regularly to replenish losses caused by evaporation, splashing, and filter backwashing and to dilute contaminant buildup. Pool covers can help reduce such losses. (Photo courtesy of Pool Covers, Inc.)

Figure 4.16 Animal drinking water troughs do not need a constantly-running hose to be kept full, but they should be cleaned regularly and refilled with fresh water. (Photo courtesy of Amy Vickers & Associates, Inc.)

Water Savings, Benefits, and Costs From Swimming Pools

About 95% of pool water lost to evaporation can be saved through use of a pool cover.[121] A study of an athletic facility in Boston indicated that the evaporation and heat losses of a swimming pool normally kept at 84°F could be reduced by lowering the temperature to 80°F (the temperature recommended by the American Society of Heating Refrigeration and Air Conditioning Engineers). This small reduction in temperature was estimated to offer a combined annual savings of $2,350 in water and heating costs. Because implementation of the measure involved no cost, payback would occur immediately.[125]

4.6.2 Zoos

Zoos use water for multiple purposes, including animal and marine pools, water exhibits, animal feeding and care, cooling and heating, landscaping, visitor and employee eating and restroom facilities, and cleaning.

Zoos typically consume large volumes of water; in fact, a zoo can be one of the water utility's highest-volume customers. Measuring water use for various zoo functions and activities can be difficult because these facilities are often unmetered (particularly municipally owned zoos) or have a single meter for the entire facility. Newer facilities are more likely to have submeters that provide water-use data on specific activities or equipment. Zoos and marine facilities have extensive underground networks of pipes and connections to exhibits and animal care areas. Water audits at these facilities should include a careful analysis of the piping network so that a water balance analysis can be developed and unaccounted-for water and leakage can be estimated. This is imperative at older facilities, which have older (sometimes decrepit) pipes, valves, and connections and cracked pools that have been neglected and may be significant sources of water waste. Auditors should also investigate closed exhibit areas for connections that are leaking or are improperly shut off and still drawing water. (Figure 4.16)

Many zoos use water on a continuous, 24-hour basis to maintain animal habitats and pools; flows for these uses are often supplied by a single-pass system. Because zoos operate around the clock, changes in water system pressure may also affect their water use.[126] For example, an audit of the Philadelphia Zoo showed that the water flowing into a bird exhibit was discharging directly into a sewer line 24 hours a day. The audit also found that water use at the zoo increased 10% overnight, a phenomenon likely caused by pressure increases that boosted flows of continually running water to pools and animal habitats as well as leaks. Estimated water savings for about 15 specific water-efficiency measures at the Philadelphia Zoo equaled 34% of average daily use.[127]

A literature search and a series of interviews with managers at eight zoos and commercial amusement parks in the United States, Canada, and The Netherlands indicated that most of the facilities had initiated water conservation measures in response to costly water bills and local needs to save water. Many of the zoos reported high rates of unaccounted-for water assumed to be caused by leaks from pools and underground pipes. Almost all of the animal and marine pools at the facilities whose managers were interviewed use the "dump-and-fill" method for cleaning pools, though some had installed filtration systems to treat and recirculate pool water. Although many animal-keepers recognized the dump-and-fill method as wasteful, they reported a lack of reliable scientific guidance on satisfactory alternative water-treatment methods for pools not equipped with filtration systems (which is the case with many older pools and aquatic areas). Some animal-keepers felt strongly that pools should be kept as hygienic as possible, whereas others argued that animals in the wild—and in the zoo—regularly defecate in and drink from the same water sources without apparent adverse health effects. Although the U.S. Department of Agriculture has established water quality requirements for pools used as habitat for marine mammals in captivity, there are no water quality standards for pools used for nonmarine mammals at zoos. Without scientific guidelines, pool water quality and cleaning requirements, and thus pool water supply requirements, may be ambiguous.[126]

Water-Efficiency Measures for Zoos

Water-efficiency measures that may be applicable to zoos, aquariums, and other wildlife care facilities include:[126–128]

- Install meters at all major water-use areas; monitor use and investigate any flow increases that occur during hours when the zoo is open to visitors and when it is closed.
- Install submeters for all water uses that do not result in discharges to the sewer system (e.g., water used for irrigation and once-through cooling water). Apply for a sewer credit for these reduced wastewater flows. Conduct a leak detection survey of all pipes, valves, hydrants, and connections, including areas of

ADOPT A SPECIES is a special care and support program for endangered species and other wildlife conservation programs at the Smithsonian National Zoo in Washington, D.C. The ADOPT program helps care for more than 5,800 animals and plants at the zoo, and it also supports conservation programs that work to preserve and protect endangered species worldwide.
—Friends of the National Zoo

the facility that are closed. Regularly check for and repair all leaks both below-
and aboveground.

- Regularly check for and repair leaks and cracks in animal and marine pools
  as well as decorative fountains, waterfalls, and other water exhibits. Checks
  should include pressure grouting, liners, and drain valves.
- Limit the frequency of pool refilling, taking into account water quality and
  treatment needs as well as other requirements specific to the pool's use. Pools
  for animals, fish, and other special uses may have site-specific refilling requirements that should be investigated before any adjustments are made.
- As much as possible and as allowed by applicable codes and regulations, install water filtration, treatment, and recycling systems for all animal pools and
  habitats as well as decorative water features.
- Water from reuse systems consisting of conventional or constructed wetlands
  can have multiple applications at a zoo: cooling towers, irrigation, maintenance activities, environmental exhibits, and possibly ponds and pools.
- Reuse rainwater runoff and noncontact water collected in cisterns for nonpotable purposes such as cooling systems, irrigation, and maintenance activities.
- Install flow-control devices where feasible to reduce continuously flowing water, particularly during periods of rainfall and hours when the zoo is not open
  to visitors.
- Evaluate the design of existing and planned pools and ponds for depth and
  fill requirements.
- Water-based cooling systems should be recirculating systems; replace or retrofit water-cooled systems with air-cooled units where feasible.
- Install automatic-refill drinkers on animal drinking troughs instead of using
  continuously running hoses, making sure the water is kept clean.
- Remove animal wastes with shovels as much as possible before hosing down
  soiled areas.
- Use air blowers and vacuums instead of water hoses for cleanup functions that
  don't require water.
- Use high-pressure hoses with automatic shutoff valves for cleaning.
- Install pressure-reducing valves where feasible.
- Install flip valves that provide aerated and nonaerated flows on utility sinks
  in animal areas to reduce high-volume flows during cleaning and to minimize
  losses from splashing.

Water Savings, Benefits, and Costs From Zoos

Several zoos in the United Sates, Canada, and The Netherlands have implemented
innovative water-efficiency measures and creative exhibits that can serve as models for other zoos and marine parks considering similar actions.

Case Study *Audit of Denver Zoo Identifies Measures to Reduce Water Use by
60%.* Built in 1896, the Denver Zoo occupies about 76 acres that include active animal exhibits and support facilities. In a 1999 water audit, the
zoo's estimated use was about 383 mgy (it uses approximately the same amount
of water as the Los Angeles Zoo, though it is roughly half the size). A water balance analysis after a major leak had been repaired indicated that more than 90%
of the Denver Zoo's water use was for animals (primarily birds, mammals, and

primates), as shown in Figure 4.17. Prior to the audit, a leak amounting to about 30 mgy—more than 5% of total water demand at the zoo—was discovered to have occurred between 1992 and 1997. After this leak was repaired, a leak detection survey of the entire zoo was conducted. Additional leaks were discovered, including one flowing at a rate of about 3 gpm—1.6 mgy—near a valve underneath the flamingo pond. The audit identified a number of short- and long-term water conservation opportunities with the potential to reduce demand by as much as 229 mgy, a 60% reduction in water use with payback periods of six months to two years. Short-term measures included repairing leaks and hydrants, eliminating once-through water flows and recycling water where feasible, installing more low-volume showerheads and flushometer-valve toilets, and improving irrigation zones to better meet plant needs and eliminate runoff. Long-term measures included improving water exhibit recycling and filtering, using on-site groundwater sources more effectively, and using nonpotable reuse water from Denver Water's soon-to-be-completed reuse plant. The audit also found that one of the zoo's seven water meters was underregistering by about 6 million gallons per month.[128]

Case Study *Filtration System at Dutch Zoo Treats and Recirculates Wastewater.* The Noorder Dierenpark Emmen, a zoo in The Netherlands, has a central filtration system for wastewater treatment and recirculation to a series

Figure 4.17 Water use at the Denver Zoo-audit results

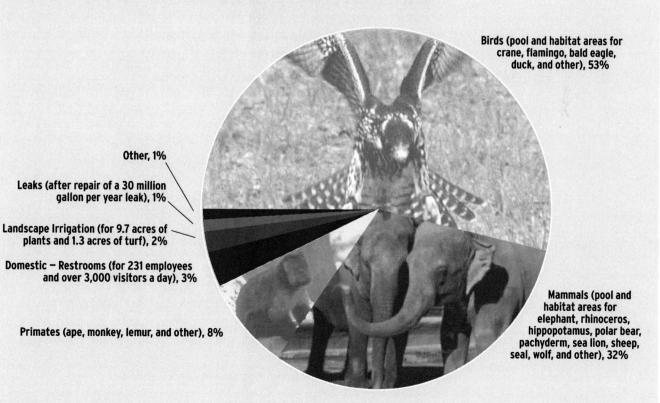

Water use at the Denver Zoo—audit results (383 million gallons in 1999)

Birds (pool and habitat areas for crane, flamingo, bald eagle, duck, and other), 53%

Other, 1%

Leaks (after repair of a 30 million gallon per year leak), 1%

Landscape Irrigation (for 9.7 acres of plants and 1.3 acres of turf), 2%

Domestic — Restrooms (for 231 employees and over 3,000 visitors a day), 3%

Primates (ape, monkey, lemur, and other), 8%

Mammals (pool and habitat areas for elephant, rhinoceros, hippopotamus, polar bear, pachyderm, sea lion, sheep, seal, wolf, and other), 32%

Source: Adapted from Reference 128

of ponds that constitute part of its exhibits. The zoo also collects rainwater from roofs and other sources to refill ponds and canals.[126]

Case Study *Wetlands Exhibit at Louisiana Zoo Provides Wastewater Treatment.* The Greater Baton Rouge Zoo in Louisiana includes a two-acre constructed marsh and wetlands system that supports aquatic and bird wildlife exhibits. The system also functions as a secondary treatment system for wastewater before it is discharged into a nearby bayou. As the bacteria in the wastewater feed on organic matter in the marsh, they decompose into carbon dioxide.[126]

Case Study *Phoenix Zoo Uses Shutoff Controls for Pools.* The Phoenix Zoo uses float controls and shutoff controls for pools that were once supplied with continuously running water. Zoo visitors and employees are educated about water conservation at various locations throughout the facility.[127]

Case Study *San Diego Wild Animal Park Irrigates Grazing Areas With Reclaimed Effluent and Well Water.* The San Diego Wild Animal Park has operated a water reclamation and reuse system since the facility's inception in 1972. With a capacity of 50,000 gpd, the system treats wastewater from animal exhibits, the petting zoo, and visitor and staff food service areas and restrooms. After the wastewater is disinfected, the reclaimed effluent is blended with well water to irrigate some 200 acres of forage areas servicing the park's East African exhibits, grazing areas for giraffe, rhinocerus, Cape buffalo, and other animals. The park has installed automatic-refill drinkers for animals instead of using continuously flowing hoses for watering troughs. The park also follows water-efficient landscape design and management practices, including the use of irrigation control and drip watering systems.[126]

Case Study *Conservation Measures at Oregon Zoo Reduce Water Use By 40%.* The Oregon Zoo in Portland, Oregon, reduced its water use by 40% from 1991 to 2000 after implementing a variety of conservation measures. Measures included more recycling of water in exhibits and improved irrigation practices. Submeters were installed to enable the zoo to receive sewer credits for water uses that involved no discharges to the wastewater system. By 2000 the zoo was saving about $250,000 a year from reduced water and sewer costs.[129]

4.7 COOLING SYSTEMS

Water use for cooling purposes represents a significant component of total nonresidential water demand in the United States; cooling systems are frequently the largest water users in ICI facilities. Cooling water is used to take away heat generated by building and process cooling systems, air and vacuum pumps, compressors, large commercial freezers and refrigerators, and ice machines.

Four common types of cooling systems involve the use of water:

- Once-through (or single-pass) cooling
- Cooling towers
- Evaporative coolers
- Equipment cooling

Audit Information to Be Collected on Cooling Systems

Information that should be collected about cooling systems during an ICI water audit is described for each type of system under its individual subsection.

Conservation Policies and Regulations Related to Cooling Systems

- *Requirements for water audits and efficiency measures at federal facilities.* Federal laws and executive orders pertaining to water and energy conservation requirements are described under Section 4.2, "Cleaning and Sanitation."
- *Prohibitions on single-pass cooling for most uses.* The use of single-pass cooling systems is prohibited in a number of cities and states, including New York City, Denver, Phoenix, and Hawaii.[117, 130] In Hawaii, for example, all newly constructed facilities that use potable water for cooling equipment operating at a rate greater than 1.0 gpm or for more than 10 hours within a 24-hour period must recirculate or reuse the cooling water.
- *Prohibitions on nonrecirculating evaporative coolers.* The city of Fresno, California, prohibits the operation of nonrecirculating (once-through) evaporative coolers.[131]
- *Provision of sewer bill credit for water used in cooling towers.* Some water and wastewater utilities, such as those in Seattle and New York City, offer customers a credit or billing adjustment for water used in cooling towers and lost to evaporation (i.e., not discharged to the sewer). Some utilities allow customers to use a "deduct meter" to measure water lost to evaporation, whereas others apply a formula or grant a sewer allowance to make adjustments. Nonmetered adjustments may be less accurate because evaporation rates vary according to such factors as efficiency of cooling tower design and maintenance, variability in cooling loads, and weather. These credits are similar to those allowed for irrigation, steam humidifiers, and other processes that consume water rather than returning it to the wastewater system.[132, 133]

4.7.1 Once-Through (Single-Pass) Cooling Systems

Once-through or single-pass cooling systems or processes are the most water-intensive cooling method. They are extremely inefficient because water is channeled through a piece of equipment or cooling system once and then discarded into the sewer drain, as shown in Figure 4.18, wasting water, energy, and money. Even with seemingly small flows, significant volumes of water are wasted by each piece of equipment or process that uses once-through flows. Once-through cooling systems are commonly used with the following types of equipment and processes: air conditioners and air conditioning systems, equipment cooling systems, refrigeration systems, condensers, air compressors, process tanks

Cooling system: apparatus employed to keep the temperature of a structure or device from exceeding limits imposed by needs of safety and efficiency. If overheated, the oil in a mechanical transmission loses its lubricating capacity, while the fluid in a hydraulic coupling or converter leaks under the pressure created. Cooling systems are employed in industrial plant machinery, nuclear reactors, automobiles, and many other types of machinery.

—Encyclopædia Britannica

Figure 4.18 Drainpipe for once-through cooling system (Photo courtesy of Denver Water)

and baths, CAT scanners, laboratory processes and equipment, film and x-ray processors, ice machines, degreasers, rectifiers, hydraulic presses and equipment, welding machines, vacuum pumps, and viscosity baths.[134-137]

Audit Information to Be Collected on Once-Through Cooling Systems

Information that should be collected about once-through cooling systems and once-through water-cooled equipment during an ICI water audit includes:

- Space (area), equipment, or process being cooled.
- Minimum requirements for cooling, including temperature, volume, and duration of flows (e.g., hours of use per day).
- Existence of meters, if any, on water-cooled equipment.
- Historical water-use records (for a minimum of three years).
- Known or estimated water use for cooling activities, expressed in gallons per hour.
- All health, safety, operational, regulatory, administrative, and other requirements or policies that apply to the site.

Water-Efficiency Measures for Once-Through Cooling Systems

Water-efficiency measures that may be applicable to once-through cooling systems include:[94, 134-139]

- Eliminate all single-pass cooling processes as soon as possible, unless the water is reused for another beneficial purpose. Facilities with substantial water demand for once-though cooling can often achieve short paybacks on investments in more water-efficient cooling systems.

- Replace water-cooled equipment, such as compressors, vacuum pumps, ice-makers, and ice cream and frozen yogurt machines, with air-cooled and energy-efficient models when equipment is upgraded.
- Some once-through cooling systems can be retrofitted into closed-loop systems that recycle water. Retrofitting typically consists of adding a (pipe) loop to return the discharge water back to the system inlet. Small equipment that includes a single-pass cooling system can sometimes be retrofitted by connecting it to an existing recirculating loop (e.g., the facility's chilled-water system).
- If feasible, install an automatic control device to operate the single-pass cooling unit only when it is needed, such as during operating hours only. There are several ways in which this might be accomplished, depending on the cooling needs, equipment, and configuration of the site. Install an automated shut-off valve to stop single-pass flows to compressor intercoolers and air dryers when the compressor is not running. Water-cooled equipment that is used only intermittently can be similarly equipped. Outdoor installations can be protected from freezing by adding a second electrically operated valve to drain water from the equipment when it is cold and not in use. Another option might be a temperature-controlled valve that adjusts the flow of water to maintain a certain temperature; only the volume of water that meets the required temperature is used.
- Monitor exit temperatures as water leaves each piece of cooling equipment. If water leaving identical pieces of equipment has different exit temperatures, investigate why (some of the equipment may be receiving higher-volume flows than needed). Determine the appropriate exit temperature and adjust the water circulation rate accordingly.
- Evaluate the feasibility of reusing single-pass water for another purpose, such as diverting it for compressors, vacuum pumps, and other equipment with water-cooled air condenser units (e.g., icemakers and ice cream and frozen yogurt machines), landscape irrigation, vehicle washing, and maintenance purposes. Some single-pass cooling systems can be connected to an existing cooling tower at the facility, allowing the water to be reused as make-up water, but the capacity of the cooling tower and its water quality requirements must be evaluated to determine the feasibility of this measure.

Water Savings, Benefits, and Costs From Once-Through Cooling Systems

Case Study *Ink Manufacturer Reduces Water Use by 80% by Replacing Single-Pass Cooling System.* A manufacturer of ink purchased a small, used cooling tower to replace a single-pass system that had cooled vats of pigment needed to make ink. Although the tower cost about $5,000 to purchase and install, it reduced the company's water use by nearly 80 percent. As a result, the company's water and sewer bills decreased by about $14,000 annually, yielding a payback period of less than five months.[134]

Case Study *Hospital Morgue Replaces Single-Pass Water-Cooled Refrigeration System With Air-Cooled Unit.* The Norwood Hospital in Massachusetts replaced the once-through water-cooling system for the refrigeration unit in the hospital's morgue with an air-cooled system, saving 2.1 mgy. Spending

$5,500 to purchase and install the recirculating system and saving $13,750 a year in water and sewer costs, the hospital achieved payback on this measure in about five months.[140] Some increase in energy use (and cost) is possible when a facility switches from a water-cooled to an air-cooled system. If increased energy costs were factored in, the payback period would be somewhat longer.

4.7.2 Cooling Towers

Cooling towers use significant amounts of water to operate air conditioning, process cooling, and refrigeration systems and equipment in the ICI water-use sector. Cooling towers use 90 to 95% less water than once-through cooling systems by using water over and over again. Even so, cooling towers, as shown in Figure 4.19, are often the largest single user of water in industrial plants, power generation facilities, large office buildings, manufacturing plants, hospitals, hotels, food processing plants, supermarkets, schools, and other facilities with large air conditioning or cooling requirements.[135, 141]

The basic function of a cooling tower is to use evaporation to lower the temperature of water that has been heated through the operation of a building, process, or piece of equipment, such as an air conditioning system. For example, as the temperature of the air inside a building is lowered by a water-cooled air conditioning system, the cooling water becomes warmer—a heat exchange occurs. Unlike the water from a single-pass cooling system, which is dumped once it has been warmed, the water from a cooling tower is returned to the tower for re-cooling, and the cycle is repeated. Re-cooling is accomplished by exposing a circulating stream of warmed water to a flow of air in the tower, causing the water to evaporate. As the warmed water evaporates, heat escapes and the remaining water is cooled. A loop from the cooling tower to the equipment being cooled allows this cycle to operate continuously. Several types of cooling towers are in use today, but they all operate on the same basic principles.[135, 141] The basic operation of a cooling tower is illustrated in Figure 4.20.

The capacity of a cooling tower or other cooling equipment is described in terms of *tons*, although in this context the term refers not to a unit of weight but to the rate at which the cooling tower can reject heat. One ton of cooling equals 12,000 British thermal units (Btus) per hour. The capacities of cooling towers at ICI facilities typically range from 50 to 1,000 tons or more, and large facilities may be equipped with several cooling towers.[135] The number of cooling towers in operation in the United States has been estimated at more than 350,000; about 50% of these are sized at 300 tons or smaller.[142]

Water Lost by Cooling Towers

Minimizing the amount of water lost by cooling towers is possible if their basic operating principles are understood. Cooling towers typically lose water in three ways: *evaporation*, *bleed-off*, and *drift and other losses*. These losses are replaced with *make-up* water.

Evaporation. Cooling towers operate by causing a portion of the warmed water to change from a liquid state to vapor, a process that cools the water left behind. The amount of evaporation that occurs depends on several factors, including

Figure 4.19
Cooling tower
(Photo courtesy of
Jane Heller Ploeser)

the length of time the cooling water remains in contact with the air, the temperature of the air and water, and wind. (Hot, dry, windy days can increase evaporation, and cool days with high humidity can decrease it.) Evaporative losses from cooling towers consume 1 to 3% of the circulating water. As the amount of evaporation increases, so does the cooling effect. Slowing the rate at which the water inside the cooling tower falls and increasing its surface area achieves more cooling. Placing media called "fill" or "decking" inside the tower increases the surface area in contact with air; high-pressure spray systems or water inlet basins located above the fill distribute the water. Cooling towers also contain a *mist* (or *drift*) *eliminator* that consists of a set of blades angled to remove water from the air stream. Mist eliminators are designed to minimize losses of water droplets in the air stream as it flows through the cooling tower. Evaporation in a cooling tower typically occurs at a rate of about 1% of the rate of recirculating water flow for every 10°F temperature drop, although this varies depending on the amount of cooling achieved and, to a lesser extent, weather conditions. In terms of water loss, this rate is equal to approximately 2.4 gpm per 100 tons of cooling.[135, 141] For example, a cooling tower that supplies 1,000 tons of cooling loses approximately 24 gpm (2.4 gpm/100 tons × 1,000 tons) to evaporation. If the cooling tower operates 24 hours a day, its evaporative losses would total about 34,500 gpd.

Bleed-off (or blowdown). Because water that evaporates from a cooling tower is pure vapor, dissolved and suspended solids normally present in the water are left behind in the cooling tower, where they become concentrated in the recirculating water. "Bleed-off" or "blowdown" involves releasing a small portion of the circulating water that contains high concentrations of these total dissolved solids (TDS) and replacing it with fresh make-up water. Without bleed-off, high TDS concentrations can seriously damage the cooling tower and process piping through scale buildup, corrosion, and biological growth (biofouling). Bleed-off water is released by draining it to a sanitary sewer or storm drain. The volume of bleed-off required depends on system requirements for the quality of make-up water. Blowdown is usually controlled by automatic devices that release bleed-off when the conductivity of the water reaches a preset value (high TDS). This is often accomplished using the "batch method," in which large volumes of water are discharged until the conductivity reaches a predetermined low value. Reducing the amount of water loss from bleed-off is usually the primary strategy for reducing water use by cooling towers[135, 141]

Drift and other losses. In addition to water lost through evaporation and not captured by a mist or drift eliminator, droplets of cooling tower water are also carried away by airflow in the form of mist, or *drift*. Drift contains suspended and dissolved solids and can be considered part of the cooling tower's bleed-off, but its release is not controlled. Although drift rates vary depending on the type of cooling tower, they are relatively low, typically ranging between 0.05 and 0.2% of the airflow rate. Drift and other losses are not generally considered critical to the water efficiency of a cooling tower if they do not exceed the appropriate bleed-off rate for the tower. In addition to drift, other types of losses include valve leaks and drawdown or draw-off for miscellaneous uses.[135, 141]

Optimizing the Water-Use Efficiency of Cooling Towers

The water-use efficiency of a cooling tower is primarily related to the quality of the water inside the tower. The cooling tower's water quality—TDS concentrations—determine how much water must be discharged for bleed-off and how much must be replaced with make-up water. Source water with high TDS concentrations increases concentrations in the tower's recirculating water. Maintaining water quality through satisfactory TDS concentrations in the cooling and make-up water is key to minimizing unnecessary water losses from cooling towers.

COOLING TOWER WATER QUALITY REQUIREMENTS Maintaining adequate water quality for a cooling tower includes controlling the rates of bleed-off and make-up water replacement, adding correct amounts of treatment chemicals, and applying other treatment techniques appropriately. The effective use of water treatment chemicals and other contaminant removal techniques plays an important role in the efficiency of water use in cooling towers.

Four major types of contamination are found in cooling tower systems: scale, corrosion, biological fouling, and foreign matter.

Scale. The result of mineral buildup, scale adheres as a film to all surfaces in contact with water. For example, waterborne minerals such as calcium carbonate, calcium sulfate, silica, and iron oxides adhere to the surface of cooling towers and form a film that builds up if not treated. Scale can inhibit the cooling capacity of the tower and piping by acting as an insulator. Orthophosphate is commonly used to control scale; other control techniques include high-quality make-up water that is low in scale-forming compounds, proper blowdowns, pH adjustments, and water softening chemicals. Proper treatment to minimize scale buildup maintains the cooling capacity of the tower and minimizes bleed-offs.

Corrosion. An electrochemical attack on metal surfaces in the tower, corrosion is caused by low pH (acidity), oxygen, galvanic action, and impingement (the wearing of metals by liquids, gases, or particles such as scale and dirt in the water). High concentrations of minerals in cooling water can increase conductivity and corrosion. Proper treatment of cooling tower water with corrosion inhibitors (e.g., polyphosphates) should eliminate the problem of corrosion and condition tower water to hold higher concentrations of minerals in solution, reducing bleed-offs.

Biological fouling. The growth of algae, bacteria, slime, or fungi in cooling towers promotes scaling and corrosion, reduces water pressure, and may threaten the health of people exposed to contaminated airborne droplets from the cooling tower system. For example, pathogens such as the bacterium that causes Legionnaires' disease (*Legionella pneumophila*) can grow in cooling towers if they are not controlled. (Scale, poorly treated cooling water, and other factors can also contribute to the growth of *Legionella* bacteria in cooling towers. Studies have shown that *Legionella pneumophila* was present in up to 60% of the cooling towers tested, though not necessarily at significant concentrations.) Chlorine and sometimes ozone are commonly used to control bacterial growth.[143]

Foreign matter. Dust, oil, and airborne pollution increase the turbidity of cooling water and impede its distribution through the system. If not removed, these contaminants can necessitate more frequent bleed-offs and increase the amount of make-up water needed. In addition, scale, slime, and other types of fouling can act as insulators, lowering the thermal efficiency and cooling capacity of the system and requiring more energy to generate the same amount of cooling.[135, 141, 144, 145]

MAKE-UP WATER REQUIREMENTS   Make-up water is the freshwater added to replace water that has been lost through evaporation and bleed-off (including drift). The volume of make-up water needed depends on bleed-off and evaporation rates. If evaporation is constant and little drift occurs, the amount of water required for make-up is largely a function of the volume of water lost through bleed-off. The relationship between evaporation (E), bleed-off (B) and make-up water (M) can be expressed as follows:[146]

$$M = E + B \qquad (1)$$

WATER LOST TO EVAPORATION   The amount of water lost to evaporation (E) can be determined by subtracting the amount of bleed-off from the amount of make-up water:[146]

$$E = M - B \qquad (2)$$

Because evaporation depends largely on how much cooling is needed, reducing the amount of water discharged as bleed-off (and thus the amount needed for make-up) is typically the focus of water-efficiency measures for cooling towers.

CONCENTRATION RATIOS (CYCLES OF CONCENTRATION)   The amount of bleed-off and make-up water required by a cooling tower is often expressed as the *concentration ratio*, or the *cycles of concentration*. This ratio indicates the number of times water is used in the tower before being released as bleed-off. The higher the concentration ratio (within limits), the lower the volume of bleed-off needed and the more water-efficient the cooling tower is. The relationship between the concentration ratio and the amount of water used by a cooling tower is shown in Figure 4.21.

Concentration ratios range from about 1.0 to 12. As a general rule, to increase cycles of concentration, decrease bleed-off; to decrease cycles of concentration, increase bleed-off. Operating a cooling tower at relatively high cycles of

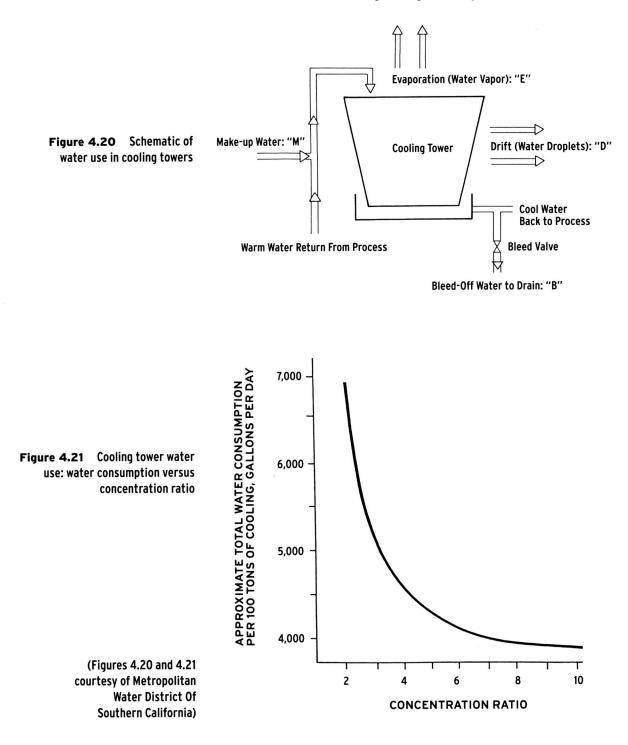

Figure 4.20 Schematic of water use in cooling towers

Figure 4.21 Cooling tower water use: water consumption versus concentration ratio

(Figures 4.20 and 4.21 courtesy of Metropolitan Water District Of Southern California)

concentration (with evaporation remaining constant) is generally more water-efficient than operating it at lower cycles. However, the relationship between the concentration ratio and the cooling tower's total water use is not a simple linear one, as illustrated in Figure 4.21. The most significant water savings can usually be achieved by increasing the concentration ratio if the tower has been operating at about 6 or less; incremental savings become less significant with operation at higher concentration ratios. Once high concentration ratios are achieved, about 90% of the tower's water consumption is for evaporation, which cannot be reduced. The concentration ratio is usually not increased above 10 because this saves only a small amount of water and increases the risk of scale or algal buildup.[141, 147, 148]

CALCULATING CONCENTRATION RATIOS   Concentration ratios for metered cooling towers can be calculated based on records of water use. Concentration ratios for unmetered cooling towers can be calculated based on TDS concentrations.

Metered cooling towers. If a facility meters the volume of make-up water and bleed-off, the relationships between the volume of make-up water (M), the volume of evaporation (E), the volume of bleed-off (including drift) (B), and the concentration ratio (CR) can be expressed by the following equation:[146]

$$CR = M/B \qquad (3)$$

By substitution,[146]

$$CR = (B + E)/B \qquad (4)$$

EXAMPLE   A facility with a metered 250-ton cooling tower uses 14,400 gallons for make-up and 5,760 gallons for bleed-off over one 24-hour period. The concentration ratio and volume of evaporation can be calculated as follows:

Concentration Ratio.
    According to Equation 3, $CR = M/B$.
    The facility's meter readings show that

$$M = 14,400 \text{ gallons and}$$
$$B = 5,760$$

Therefore,

$$CR = 14,400 \text{ gallons}/5,760 \text{gallons}$$
$$CR = 2.5$$

The concentration ratio was 2.5.

Evaporation.
According to Equation 2, $M = B + E$.
The facility's meter readings show that

$$M = 14{,}400 \text{ gallons and}$$
$$B = 5{,}760$$

Therefore,

$$14{,}400 \text{ gallons} = 5{,}760 \text{ gallons} + E$$
$$E = 14{,}400 \text{ gallons} - 5{,}760 \text{ gallons}$$
$$E = 8{,}640 \text{ gallons}$$

Evaporation was 8,640 gallons.

Unmetered cooling towers. For facilities that do not meter bleed-off and make-up water, the concentration ratio can be calculated based on the concentration of TDS or an individual dissolved constituent (e.g., calcium carbonate) in the bleed-off water (CB) and make-up water (CM). This approach is based on the fact that at equilibrium conditions, the mass of dissolved solids entering the cooling tower in make-up water is roughly equal to the mass leaving in the bleed-off water. The total mass of dissolved solids is equal to the concentration of the solids multiplied by the water volume in which it is dissolved. This can be expressed as follows:[146]

$$CM \times M = CB \times B$$

This equation can be rearranged as:[146]

$$CB/CM = M/B = CR \qquad (5)$$

EXAMPLE A facility with an unmetered 250-ton cooling tower measures TDS in the tower based on the conductivity of its make-up and bleed-off water. Over one 24-hour period, the TDS concentration in the bleed-off *(CB)* water is 1,400 and the TDS concentration in the make-up *(CM)* water is 550. The concentration ratio and volume of evaporation, bleed-off, and make-up can be estimated as follows:[146]

Concentration Ratio.
According to Equation 5, $CB/CM = CR$.
The facility's conductivity readings show that

$$CB = 1{,}400 \text{ and}$$
$$CM = 550$$

Therefore,

$$CR = 1{,}400/550$$
$$CR = 2.5$$

Evaporation.
As noted, the rate at which cooling towers lose water to evaporation is about 2.4 gpm per 100 tons of cooling.

TABLE 4.2

Water savings from increased concentration ratios in cooling towers*

Concentration Ratio Before Increasing Cycles	Concentration Ratio After Increasing Cycles											
	2	3	4	5	6	7	8	9	10	12	15	20
1.5	33%	50%	56%	58%	60%	61%	62%	63%	63%	64%	64%	65%
2		25%	33%	38%	40%	42%	43%	44%	44%	45%	46%	47%
3			11%	17%	20%	22%	24%	25%	26%	27%	29%	30%
4				6%	10%	13%	14%	16%	17%	18%	20%	21%
5					4%	7%	9%	10%	11%	13%	14%	16%
6						3%	5%	6%	7%	9%	11%	12%
7							2%	4%	5%	6%	8%	10%
8								2%	3%	5%	6%	8%
9									1%	3%	5%	6%
10										2%	4%	5%
12											2%	4%
15												2%

* Increases expressed as a percentage of tower's total water use

Source: Adapted from Reference 149

Therefore,

$$E = (2.4 \text{ gpm}/100 \text{ tons}) \times (250 \text{ tons}) \times (24 \text{ hr}) \times (60 \text{ min/hr})$$
$$E = 8,640 \text{ gallons}$$

Bleed-off.

$$B = E/(CR - 1) \qquad\qquad (6)$$

Therefore,

$$B = 8,640 \text{ gallons} /(2.5 - 1)$$
$$= 5,760 \text{ gallons}$$

Make-up.

Based on Equation 1 and assuming that drift is included in evaporation, *(M = E + B)*.

Therefore,

$$M = 8,640 \text{ gallons} + 5,760 \text{ gallons}$$
$$M = 14,400 \text{ gallons}$$

Saving water by increasing concentration ratios. Significant reductions in the amount of make-up water for cooling towers can be achieved by increasing the concentration ratio if the towers have been operating at a concentration ratio or 6 or less,[149] as shown in Table 4.2. For example, a cooling tower with a concentration ratio of 10 uses 44% less make-up water than a tower with a concentration ratio of 2.

The percentage of cooling tower water that can be conserved by increasing the concentration ratio can be calculated with the following equation:[150]

$$\text{Percent conserved} = \frac{CR_2 - CR_1}{CR_1 \, (CR_2 - 1)} \times 100\% \tag{7}$$

in which, CR_1 = concentration ratio before increasing cycles and CR_2 = concentration ratio after increasing cycles.

EXAMPLE   The concentration ratio for a cooling tower is increased from 2 *(CR_1)* to 6 *(CR_2)*. The percentage of water saved from this conservation measure is 40 percent, as shown in the following equation:

$$\text{Percent conserved} = \frac{6 - 2}{2 \, (6 - 1)} \times 100\%$$
$$= 4/10 \times 100\%$$
$$= 40\%$$

Audit Information to Be Collected on Cooling Towers

Information that should be collected about cooling towers during an ICI water audit includes:

- Number of cooling towers.
- Space (area), equipment, or process being cooled.
- Cooling load (capacity in tons) for each tower.
- Minimum requirements for cooling including temperature, volume, and duration of flows (e.g., hours of use per day).
- Existence of meters, if any, on cooling towers.
- Historical water-use records (for a minimum of three years).
- Meter readings for make-up water.
- Meter readings for bleed-off water.
- Evaporative and other losses.
- TDS concentrations in make-up and bleed-off water.
- Concentration ratios.
- All health, safety, operational, regulatory, administrative, and other requirements or policies that apply to the site.

Water-Efficiency Measures for Cooling Towers

In most cooling tower systems, the primary opportunity for conserving water is to reduce the amount of make-up water required to replace bleed-off. The bleed-off volume can be reduced through three types of conservation measures: improve system monitoring and operation, upgrade cooling water treatment (contaminant removal), and use alternative sources for make-up water.

Water-efficiency measures that may be applicable to cooling towers include:[11, 94, 137, 141, 144, 146, 149–151]

INSTALL METERS AND MONITOR WATER USE   Closely monitor cooling tower water use to help operators verify that the tower is performing within specified limits and to avoid water waste through unnecessary bleed-off and other losses. Record water use daily from flow meters installed on bleed-off and make-up lines. Meters that display current flow rates plus totalized flows are preferable. Keep a log of bleed-off and make-up volumes as well as TDS concentrations, evaporation volume, cooling load, and concentration ratio, and analyze these records on a regular basis. Utilities that offer a sewer bill credit for water lost to tower evaporation usually require a meter reading or a formula estimating these losses. Blank log sheets and instructions for recording the type of data needed to monitor cooling tower water use and efficiency are provided in Appendix G, *Sample Worksheet: Industrial-Commercial-Institutional Water-Use Efficiency Audit.*

REDUCE BLEED-OFF (INCREASE CONCENTRATION RATIOS) Reduce bleed-off by allowing higher concentrations of suspended and dissolved solids in the circulating water while maintaining cooling tower operation within satisfactory parameters. Adjust the physical or chemical treatment of circulating water to increase the cycles of concentration. For example, a potential goal might be to achieve at least 6 cycles of concentration or the maximum number of cycles achievable without scale formation. Increasing the concentration ratio to 10 or greater will yield only small additional water savings while increasing the potential for water quality problems.

OPERATE BLEED-OFF CONTINUOUSLY Cooling towers are usually bled off automatically in batches when the mineral concentration or conductivity reaches a certain level. Batch methods release bleed-off for a preset amount of time or until conductivity reaches a preset level. The batch method can result in wide fluctuations in bleed-off volumes if controls are improperly set, e.g., if they allow more bleed-off than necessary based on preset volume limits or conductivity values that are too low. Whenever possible, operate the cooling tower on a continuous basis to maintain conductivity at values that minimize water waste during bleed-off.

INSTALL CONDUCTIVITY CONTROLS Install or make better use of conductivity controllers and valves on cooling towers to help regulate bleed-off volumes. Some cooling towers release bleed-off automatically when TDS concentrations reach preset values, resulting in large batches of water being discharged until conductivity decreases to a pre-established low value. This practice can cause wide fluctuations in conductivity, often making average conductivity lower than optimal operating values. An alternative strategy is to operate bleed-off more continuously, maintaining conductivity closer to optimal TDS limits before bleed-off. This method prevents the discharge of bleed-off water before necessary and ensures more uniform water quality (which in turn reduces chemical treatment needs and keeps TDS concentrations from exceeding upper limits).

A control system may be operated by electricity, by mechanical means, by fluid pressure (liquid or gas), or by a combination of means."
—Encyclopædia Britannica

REQUIRE SERVICE CONTRACTORS OR VENDORS TO MAKE WATER EFFICIENCY A PRIORITY Inform cooling tower vendors and chemical treatment service contractors that water efficiency is a priority. Ask these service providers to justify the types and amounts of chemicals used to treat cooling tower water and to identify ways to reduce water use. A useful incentive for gaining a vendor's assistance in reducing cooling tower water use may be to prepare a performance-based contract specifying a predetermined minimum level of efficiency based on projections of annual water use, chemical consumption, and costs. Be aware that some vendors might resist optimizing cooling tower water-use efficiency because optimization would likely reduce chemical needs and sales.

EVALUATE OZONATION AND OTHER ALTERNATIVE WATER TREATMENT TECHNOLOGIES In addition to improving cooling tower management and conventional water treatment to boost cycles of concentration, cooling tower operators could consider several other water treatment strategies for saving water.

Ozonation. An ozonation system can sometimes be used to disinfect water and reduce bleed-off, but using ozone requires precautions to avoid human safety hazards and property damage. Ozone is a powerful biocide and oxidizer that kills viruses and bacteria and can control corrosion by oxidizing inorganic matter and soluble ions. It can also attack organic materials, such as wood and rubber, when not properly applied. Ozone must be produced on site because its useful life is less than one hour. Although ozonation can achieve concentration ratios of 10 and higher and can reduce or eliminate chemical treatment, it requires a large initial capital investment and a trained vendor, may present health and safety hazards, increases energy requirements, and can damage the cooling system if not used properly. Some cooling tower materials are not compatible with the use of ozonation.

Sulfuric acid. Adjusting the pH of cooling tower water with sulfuric acid can prevent scale by making scale-forming minerals more soluble. Adding sulfuric acid for this purpose can reduce cooling tower water use by 25% but may be hazardous to workers and may pose a threat to the cooling system if not carried out properly. Acid is added using a timer at points in the cooling tower system where the water is well mixed and moving rapidly. Workers must be fully trained to handle acids properly, and a lower pH may necessitate adding a corrosion inhibitor to avoid damaging the system.

Sidestream filtration. A sidestream filtration system, composed of a rapid sand filter or high-efficiency cartridge filter, can reduce bleed-off by reducing particulates in cooling tower water. Sidestream filtration can be particularly effective for cooling systems with high concentrations of dust, airborne contaminants, and cloudiness and for systems with narrow passages that are prone to clogging. This treatment method has a moderately high capital cost, increases energy requirements, and achieves limited removal of dissolved solids.

Recycling and reuse. Nonpotable water supplies, such as reject water from reverse osmosis systems, wastewater from once-through cooling systems, and reclaimed municipal wastewater, may be feasible alternative sources of make-up water. Alternative water sources may require pretreatment, however, which may increase energy and chemical costs as well as the potential for biofouling.

Magnets and electrostatic field generators. Magnets and electrostatic field generators have been reported to help remove scale and increase cooling tower cycles of concentration, but these claims have not been well substantiated and some people have challenged them as unreliable. Increased chemical and energy costs as well as the possibility of biofouling may be associated with this method.

INSTALL AN AUTOMATIC SHUTOFF CONTROL   Some cooling towers can be shut off when the facility is unoccupied, such as nights, weekends, and holidays.

Water Savings, Benefits, and Costs From Cooling Towers

Optimizing cooling tower water use can result in considerable water savings and savings in chemical treatment costs. For example, the annual cost to provide chemical treatment for cooling towers serving a medium-sized office building ranges from $5,000 to $10,000.[35] The cost of valves and controllers varies from less than $10 for simple, small sizes to several thousand dollars for large, complex types.

Case Study   *Beverage Plant Reduces Cooling Tower Make-up Water by 75%.* The 120-ton cooling tower at a beverage plant produced an excessive amount of bleed-off because make-up water was added at a constant rate of 4 gpm. Installation of a new valve for the make-up water and a conductivity controller reduced the flow of make-up water by 75%. Water savings from the measure totaled 1.6 mgy. With an investment of $3,500 to install the efficiency measures and annual net savings of $14,400, the payback period was about three months.[152]

4.7.3 Evaporative Coolers

Evaporative coolers, also know as swamp coolers or desert coolers, increase the humidity and lower the temperature of air drawn into a room or building. They are commonly used to cool commercial facilities (Figure 4.22) and for space-cooling in single-family and multifamily dwellings (Figure 4.23) in hot, arid regions such as the southwestern United States. Evaporative coolers are generally more energy-efficient than air-conditioning units, but they require water because they evaporate air over wet pads. In residential and other small areas, they are sometimes operated in combination with electric air conditioners because evaporative coolers can add an uncomfortable amount of moisture to the air. Compared with other cooling systems, evaporative coolers are a relatively old and inexpensive means of cooling.[153, 154]

Several types of evaporative coolers are available, but their operating principles are similar, as shown in Figure 4.24. Water is dripped onto porous pads, keeping the pads moist; as air passes over the pads, it is cooled and humidified. Water that doesn't evaporate trickles through the pads into a pan or tray, from which it is recirculated or discharged into the sewer line. Like cooling towers, evaporative coolers also accumulate scale and mineral deposits on the pads, and thus bleed-off is necessary to keep the pads functional.

Three types of evaporative coolers are common—*recirculating, nonrecirculating* (once-through), and a hybrid sometimes referred to as a *"dump pump."* Recirculating evaporative coolers are usually much smaller and use less water than once-through coolers and, if properly maintained, require only a small amount for bleed-off. Recirculating evaporative systems lower ambient air ("dry bulb") temperature by absorbing water vapor from recirculating water in the

Figure 4.22 Commercial evaporative cooler (Photo courtesy of Jane Heller Ploeser)

Figure 4.23 Residential evaporative cooler (Photo courtesy of Jane Heller Ploeser)

cooler. Once the recirculating water reaches saturation ("wet bulb") temperature, the temperature remains constant. Water is fed into a reservoir as needed to cool the air, and a pump recirculates the water from a pan to the top of pads covering the cooler's air inlet. Once-through evaporative coolers are relatively inexpensive to purchase and simpler to use than recirculating coolers, but they use far more water because water used for cooling and bleed-off is discharged directly to the sewer line. The "dump pump" cooler automatically empties and refills the water pan every few hours while the cooler is working. The capacity of evaporative coolers ranges from 750 cubic feet (of air) per minute (ft³/min) for small coolers to 20,000 ft³/min or more for large industrial coolers.[88, 137, 153, 155]

Recirculating evaporative coolers such as those used for households consume about 3 gallons of water for each hour of operation; nonrecirculating coolers with continuous bleed-off use about 10 gallons per hour.[155] The amount of bleed-off required by evaporative coolers varies according to model and site-specific conditions, but most small coolers lose less than a few gallons per hour for each 1,000 ft³/min of air flow.[153, 156] A study in Phoenix found that a typical home with an evaporative cooler used an average of 66 gpd during the 214-day cooling season. Households whose coolers had once-through bleed-off systems used nearly 50% more water than households whose coolers did not have once-through bleed-off systems.[154]

The city of Fresno, California, prohibits the use of nonrecirculating coolers. In 1998, the city began offering interest-free loans of up to $3,000 for the purchase of energy-efficient air coolers to an estimated 550 residents who were still operating once-through evaporative coolers installed before the end of the 1960s. Several manufacturers made these nonrecirculating units, including Carrier and York. In 1998, water use by the remaining 550 nonrecirculating evaporative coolers was estimated to total 328 mgy. Water use varies by the cooler's capacity: the 5-ton units were measured to use 14.1 gpm, the 3-ton units used 9.4 gpm, the 2-ton units used 6.4 gpm, and the 1-ton units used 3.1 gpm. The estimate assumed the units ran 8 hours a day, 150 days a year. In Fresno, summer encompasses May through September and includes with many days with temperatures well over 100°F.[131]

Audit Information to Be Collected on Evaporative Coolers

Information that should be collected about evaporative coolers during an ICI water audit includes:

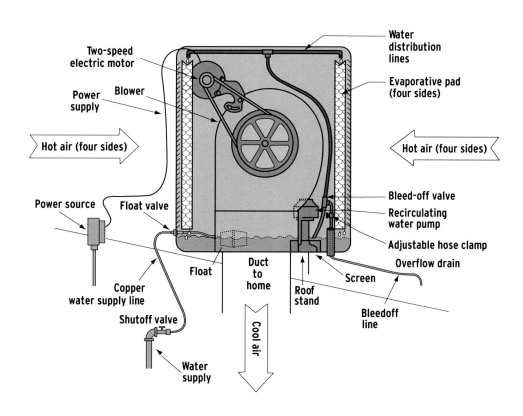

Figure 4.24 Typical operation of an evaporative cooler (Illustration courtesy of *Journal AWWA*. Reprinted from *Journal AWWA*, Vol. 90, No. 4, April 1998, by permission. Copyright © 1998, American Water Works Association)

- Type of cooler or condenser (recirculating or nonrecirculating).
- Existence of meters, if any, on evaporative coolers and condensers.
- Historical records of water used for make-up and bleed-off.
- Recirculation rate (measured in gallons per minute).
- Area cooled (measured in cubic feet).
- Average water use (measured in gallons) given in hours per day and total volume per year.
- All health, safety, operational, regulatory, administrative, and other requirements or policies that apply to the site.

Water-Efficiency Measures for Evaporative Coolers

Water-efficiency measures that may be applicable to evaporative coolers include:[94, 131, 137, 153–155, 157, 158]

- Discontinue the use of nonrecirculating and pumpless coolers and replace them with air-cooled units, if feasible. Recirculating evaporative coolers save water and increase thermal efficiency.
- If a nonrecirculating cooler cannot easily be replaced with an air-cooled unit or retrofitted with a recirculation system, divert bleed-off of acceptable quality and reuse it for nonpotable purposes such as washing vehicles and landscape irrigation.
- A typical evaporative cooler should not bleed off more than a few gallons of water per hour. If bleed-off volumes are higher than this, check for leaks, control or pump malfunctions, and worn or deteriorated pads.
- Before turning on the cooler's fan, run the water pump for a few minutes to saturate the pads and help the cooler run more efficiently.
- Replace worn or torn pads, at least annually, to remove mineral deposits and prevent microbiological growth, which impedes efficiency. The cleaner the pads, the more efficiently the cooler will operate.
- If feasible, shut off evaporative coolers when the building is unoccupied.
- At least yearly check for leaks and proper functioning of controls for recirculation pumps, reservoir levels, and bleed-off.
- Annually tune-up the cooler according to the manufacturer's specifications. Check for cracks (leaks) in the water pan, and clean debris; check for correct tension on fan belt (it should move about an inch when pressed by a finger); lightly oil bearings on the blower assembly; check the float valve adjustment and operation (a stuck valve will cause water to run constantly and make the pan overflow); make sure cooler pads are evenly saturated with water (if not, they could need replacing); and make sure the bleed-off valve on recirculating coolers is adjusted properly.
- When the cooling season ends, clean and protect the cooler to make sure it will operate during the next cooling season. Use vinegar to dissolve mineral buildup in the bottom of the pan; drain water from the pan; scrape out scale with a wire brush or putty knife; disconnect the water line to prevent freezing; inspect for cracks that could cause leaks; and cover the cooler to retain household heat.

Cool jazz: a style of jazz that emerged in the United States during the late 1940s. The term 'cool' derives from what journalists perceived as an understated or subdued feeling in the music of Miles Davis, The Modern Jazz Quartet, Gerry Mulligan, Lennie Tristano, and others."
    —Encyclopædia Britannica

Water Savings, Benefits, and Costs From Evaporative Coolers

Case Study *Metal Finishing Facility Reduces Water Use by Replacing Nonrecirculating Evaporative Cooler.* Because nonrecirculating evaporative water coolers use considerable amounts of water, replacing them often results in appreciable water and cost savings. For example, an electroplating and metal finishing operation in the Boston area replaced its industrial-size nonrecirculating evaporative cooler with an air-cooled unit, saving 370,000 gpy. Costs for the new equipment were $4,000; with annual water and sewer cost savings of $2,600, the payback on this measure was 1.5 years (excluding adjustments for changes in energy use).

4.7.4 Equipment Cooling Systems

Equipment cooling systems that rely on water, as shown in Figure 4.25, use either once-through or recirculating water to cool equipment, machinery, appliances, tools, and products in a variety of industrial facilities (Figure 4.26).

Audit Information to Be Collected on Equipment Cooling Systems

Information that should be collected about equipment cooling systems during an ICI water audit includes:

- Type of cooler or condenser (recirculating or nonrecirculating).
- Type of equipment or product being cooled with water.
- Existence of meters, if any, on coolers and condensers.
- Historical records of water used for make-up and bleed-off (for a minimum of three years).
- The recirculation or once-through flow rate (measured in gallons per minute).
- Average water use (measured in gallons) given in hours per day and total volume per year.
- All health, safety, operational, regulatory, administrative, and other requirements or policies that apply to the site.

Water-Efficiency Measures for Equipment Cooling Systems

Water-efficiency measures that may be applicable to equipment cooling include:[139, 159, 160]

- Eliminate once-though equipment cooling systems and replace them with air-cooled or closed-loop systems unless the water is being beneficially reused.
- Reuse contact and noncontact cooling water for boiler make-up water or other purposes if water quality and temperatures are acceptable.
- Recover steam condensate and recycle for boiler make-up water and other nonpotable uses.
- Reuse water used to immerse or otherwise cool hot or molten materials.
- Reuse reverse osmosis reject water (or concentrate) or other water used for single-pass purposes such as pump cooling.

Figure 4.25 Equipment cooling systems rely on once-through or recirculating water to cool a variety of machines, appliances, tools, and products. (Photo courtesy of Denver Water)

Figure 4.26 This small electronic parts factory used thousands of gallons of water a day for once-through cooling of equipment and ambient air. Installation of a water recirculation system for cooling was estimated to be able to reduce water use by 75%. (Photo courtesy of Amy Vickers & Associates, Inc.)

Water Savings, Benefits, and Costs From Equipment Cooling Systems

Case Study *Hospital Saves Water by Recirculating Cooling Water in Medical Air Compressors and Vacuum Pumps.* To save water and reduce operating costs, the Norwood Hospital in Massachusetts installed a recirculating seal and cooling-water system on four vacuum pumps and one medical compressor and removed one vacuum pump that was not needed. These efficiency measures achieved water savings of 8.5 mgy. Although purchase and installation of the recirculating system cost $19,500, annual water and sewer cost savings totaled $55,685, yielding a payback period of just over four months.[140]

4.8 HEATING SYSTEMS

Water used for heating systems and steam generation at modern ICI facilities is usually not a significant source of demand, although older and poorly maintained systems can be significant sources of water loss. Two common types of ICI heating and steam systems involve the use of water:

- Boilers and steam generators
- Humidifiers

Audit Information to Be Collected on Heating Systems

Information that should be collected about heating and steam-generation systems during an ICI water audit is described for each type of system under its individual subsection.

Conservation Policies and Regulations Related to Heating Systems

- *Requirements for water audits and efficiency measures at federal facilities.* Federal laws and executive orders pertaining to water and energy conservation requirements are described under Section 4.2, "Cleaning and Sanitation."

4.8.1 Boilers and Steam Generators

Boilers and steam generators are frequently used to heat large buildings and multiple-building facilities, such as college campuses, hospital compounds, and corporate office complexes, as shown in Figure 4.27. Boilers generate the steam or hot water that is sent to the facility's hydronic distribution system. At large complexes, the steam is often produced at a central plant that feeds an underground steam distribution network serving all or most of the complex's facilities. The distribution system includes traps, valves, insulation, and monitoring controls. Boiler systems use water at varying rates, depending on the size of the system, design characteristics, amount of steam used, amount of water not evaporated ("condensate return"), and the presence of leaks. Older boiler systems can be a source of significant and costly water losses caused by corroded or faulty steam traps and flange gaskets, worn valve seats and valve packing, long pipe runs, missing or deteriorated insulation, and leaking make-up and condensate recovery systems. The location of such leaks is sometimes visible outside a fa-

Over 45% of all the fuel burned by U.S. manufacturers is consumed to raise steam. A typical industrial facility can realize steam savings of 20% by improving its steam system. Simple approaches to improving energy performance include insulating steam and condensate return lines, stopping any steam leaks, and maintaining steam traps. Condensate return to the boiler is essential for energy efficiency."
—Office of Industrial Technologies, U.S. Department of Energy

Figure 4.27 Vent stack for a centralized low-pressure steam heating system at a state office and hospital complex in Waterbury, Vermont (Photo courtesy of Amy Vickers & Associates, Inc.)

cility during cold weather if the steam escapes aboveground over underlying steam lines and connections that have deteriorated.[161–164]

Several types of boiler and steam systems are available. The most common boiler design is the *fire tube boiler*, otherwise known as the *shell and tube* design. This design uses a gas- or oil-fired heater to direct heat to tubes and water in the shell to produce steam. Water in the boiler is chemically treated to inhibit corrosion and scale formation in the steam distribution system. Once the steam has been used—for heating, cooking, and other uses—it becomes condensate and is returned to the boiler for reuse, thereby reducing the need for boiler feedwater. This process itself is an efficiency measure that saves water and energy (the condensate is already hot). Some additional water must be added to replace lost steam, and small quantities of bleed-off (blowdown) are also required now and then to discharge accumulations of scale and other impurities. Some tube boiler systems that use water under high pressure are not equipped with condensate return systems and lose all the water used to generate stream, necessitating additional make-up water.[161, 163, 164]

Central steam plants serving entire building complexes are less commonly found in new construction; nowadays, high-efficiency hot-water boilers are more likely to serve individual buildings. Centralized controls are used for start/stop functions and to monitor temperature and operation of each building's boiler, but the heat and water losses associated with older centralized steam plants have been reduced significantly. The heating hydronic systems in newer buildings save large volumes of water because they are closed loops and because no losses can occur from underground distribution lines (because they have been eliminated). Separate boilers also allow unoccupied buildings to be shut down or operated with lower water and energy demands (e.g., certain university facilities that are not used during extended holidays). Another benefit of individual heating systems in each building is that they can be repaired more readily and cost-effectively. One reason centralized steam heating systems are in disrepair is that shutting them down for routine maintenance can mean shutting off heat and hot water to an entire complex and can create complications associated with repairing underground distribution lines (e.g., asbestos removal and confined-space entry procedures).[162]

Audit Information to Be Collected on Boilers and Steam Generators

Information that should be collected about boilers and steam generators during an ICI water audit includes:

- Number and type of boilers and steam generators.
- Location and length of steam lines and related heating system infrastructure.
- Existence of meters, if any, on boilers and steam generators.
- Historical records of water used for make-up and bleed-off (for a minimum of three years).
- Operating and steam pressures (measured in pounds per square inch).
- Line losses and frequency of system inspections, leak detection procedures, and repairs.
- Boiler capacity (measured in Btus per hour) and efficiency.

- All health, safety, operational, regulatory, administrative, and other requirements or policies that apply to the site.

Water-Efficiency Measures for Boilers and Steam Generators

Optimizing the water use of boilers and steam-generation systems will reduce energy and chemical costs as well as water costs. Boilers generally have small potential for water efficiency, but savings can be achieved when leaking steam traps and lines are repaired. Similarly, older boilers can be replaced with upgraded burner assemblies that are more water- and energy-efficient.

Water-efficiency measures that may be applicable to boilers and steam-generation systems include: [94, 137, 161–165]

- Regularly inspect the boiler, condensate system, and steam traps and lines for leaks and to ensure proper operation. Make repairs promptly. (Corroded and worn traps and lines allow steam to escape, wasting both water and energy.) Facility operations staff can repair many steam traps with replacement kits available from the system's manufacturer, although digging up and repairing or replacing leaking underground steam pipes can be expensive.
- If the system does not return steam condensate, consider recovering it for reuse as boiler make-up water by installing a condensate return system (closed loop). (Exceptions may include condensate collected from hospital steam autoclaves, sterilizers, and other equipment that may be contaminated.) This measure will optimize water use, reduce the pretreatment and energy requirements of boiler feedwater (returned warmed condensate needs less heating than incoming freshwater), and can reduce system operating costs by as much as 50 to 70%.
- Provide suitable insulation to steam and condensate piping and to the central storage tank to conserve heat and reduce steam requirements.
- Limit boiler bleed-off to the amount necessary to satisfy water quality requirements. Check continuous bleed-off systems regularly to make sure they are not discharging excessive amounts of water.
- Blowdown can be discharged through an expansion tank to allow it to cool and condense for later reuse. Avoid using cold water mixing valves to cool blowdown; if mixing valves are in use, check to make sure water is not flowing continuously. To save water, replace these valves with an expansion tank.
- Install automatic controls to discharge boiler blowdown, to treat boiler make-up water, and to shut off the unit when the building is unoccupied, if feasible.
- Consider separate or smaller individual heaters and boilers for domestic hot water needs, pools, and other equipment.
- Install flow meters on make-up and blowdown valves.

Water Savings, Benefits, and Costs From Heating Systems

Case Study *Steam Plant Saves Water by Improving Operations, Repairing Leaks, and Recycling Cooling Water.* Sandia National Laboratories in Albuquerque, New Mexico, employs more than 8,000 people, who work in 765 buildings comprising 5.4 million square feet. The facility designs components for nuclear weapons and conducts research on a range of topics, from solar cells to computers. Largely unmetered, the site was estimated to use about 400 mgy

In steam systems that have not been maintained for 3 to 5 years, between 15% to 30% of the installed steam traps may have failed—thus allowing live steam to escape into the condensate return system. In systems with a regularly scheduled maintenance program, leaking traps should account for less than 5% of the trap population. If your steam distribution system includes more than 500 traps, a steam trap survey will probably reveal significant steam losses."
—Office of Industrial Technologies,
U.S. Department of Energy

Example of savings from a steam trap repair: In a plant where the value of steam is $4.50 per thousand pounds ($/1,000 lbs), an inspection program indicates that a trap on a 150 psi steam line is stuck open. The trap orifice is ⅛ inch in diameter. The estimated steam loss is 75.8 lbs/hr. By repairing the failed trap, annual savings are:

$$Savings = 75.8 \text{ lbs/hr} \times 8,760 \text{ hrs/yr}$$
$$\times \$4.50/1,000 \text{ lbs}$$
$$= \$2,988/yr$$

—Office of Industrial Technologies, U.S. Department of Energy

in 1995 when it was first evaluated for opportunities to conserve water. By 1998, the site's water use had decreased to an estimated 324 mgy, a 19% reduction. (The goal by 2004 is 280 mgy, which would constitute a 30% savings.) Among the numerous water-efficiency measures implemented to achieve these savings were various practices at the on-site steam-generation plant, which went into service in 1949 and was found to be inefficient and leaking in 1995. By 1998, efficiency measures at the steam-generation plant had effected a number of changes: a synthetic resin was being used instead of a dealkalizer to lower pH and improve water quality; less frequent boiler blowdown was made possible by the water quality improvements (this measure alone was saving more than 8 mgy); water volumes required for pre-steam processing and blowdown had been reduced by 43%; repairs to leaking condensate return lines were saving energy and boosting steam recapture by more than 50%, the equivalent of more than 12 mgy; and once-through cooling water used for feedwater pump bearings, fan bearings, and conductivity meters was being reused as boiler make-up water.[166]

Case Study *Food Processing Facility Identifies Opportunities to Reuse Water.* A large food processing company with facilities throughout the United States conducted a water audit of its 22 boilers, determining that the boilers operated at pressures of 250 to 600 psi and generated 6.5 million pounds of steam per hour. In order to identify potential water-efficiency measures for the boilers, the audit team collected and analyzed information including water flow rates, temperature, water quality, theoretical versus actual system volumes, possible flow reductions, reuse opportunities, and potential operational modifications. During the audit process, a malfunctioning feedwater line was discovered to be losing considerable amounts of water. Based on these findings, identified water-efficiency measures included repairs as well as the development of specifications for automatic blowdown controls and proportional chemical injection equipment to eliminate excessive blowdown and water waste. After a demonstration study, these measures were estimated to have the potential to reduce water use and sewer discharges by more than 31 mgy. The $45,000 cost of equipment, consultant fees, and implementation was projected to be offset by annual costs savings of $186,000,[167] yielding a payback period of about three months.

Case Study *California State University Upgrades Inefficient Steam Heating System.* The heating system at the California State University in Hayward, California, was a high-pressure, high-temperature tube steam system that operated 24 hours a day and serviced the entire campus through an underground steam supply and condensate return system. When state air pollution regulations required the university to meet new, more stringent boiler emission standards, the university decommissioned its inefficient heating system and installed improvements projected to yield a $400,000 savings in annual operating costs. At a cost of $2.25 million, the university installed individual water- and energy-efficient boiler units in each building, as well as microprocessor-based controllers to optimize water temperatures and other features to improve water and energy efficiency. Accommodations were made for some peripheral steam heating requirements for campus science laboratories (e.g., sterilizers, water distillation equipment, and laboratory fume hoods) and laundry equipment. As a result of these measures, cost savings during the first year included nearly \$34,000 in natural gas costs, \$6,500 in costs for boiler make-up water, \$45,000 in chemical and other operating costs, and \$177,000 in salaries (only one engineer is required to oversee maintenance of the new heating system, whereas five were required previously). According to David Cowden, chief engineer at the university, "The rationale behind this boiler project was to modernize and make more energy-efficient one of the campus's largest energy consumers. This project and its ramifications were taken into consideration as part of the campus's facilities resource management strategy."[162]

4.8.2 Humidifiers

Humidifiers, which add moisture to the air, are available in several designs for use in residential and commercial applications. The *pan* humidifier uses a pan of water placed in the furnace air plenum; moisture is added to the air as the water in the pan evaporates from the heat of the furnace. Electric heaters are used with some types of pan units to increase evaporation. The *wetted media* humidifier has a wetted pad over which air passes to gather moisture. Water sprayers or a disc that rotates through a water reservoir are usually used to wet the pads. The evaporating water is atomized to a fine mist and released into the air by a spinning disc or cone. Some humidifiers have water reservoirs that bleed off water directly to the sewer line; others have a closed-loop system that uses much less water.[168, 169]

Audit Information to Be Collected on Humidifiers

Information that should be collected about humidifiers during an ICI water audit includes:

- Number, type, and location of humidifiers.
- Frequency of use (average number of hours per day, total hours per year)
- Check bleed-off controls and shutoff valves to verify proper operation.
- All health, safety, operational, regulatory, administrative, and other requirements or policies that apply to the site.

Water-Efficiency Measures for Humidifiers

Water-efficiency measures that may be applicable to humidifiers include:[168, 170]

- Use humidifiers only where and when needed.
- Check bleed-off controls and water supply shutoff valves to ensure proper operation, to identify leaks, and to avoid excessive bleed-off.
- Periodically check humidifiers to ensure that flow controls are operating correctly and that water is not being lost.
- Investigate the possibility of replacing old humidifier units with newer closed-loop systems that are more water- and energy-efficient.

Water Savings, Benefits, and Costs From Humidifiers

The potential for saving water used by humidifiers varies considerably, depending on the capacity, frequency of use, and efficiency of existing equipment.

Honeywell Saves 350,000 mgy by Improving Temperature and Humidity Control System. The Albuquerque, New Mexico, plant of the Honeywell Corporation, a manufacturer of heaters, humidifiers, water filtration products, thermostats, home security systems, and other products, reduced its water use from 8 mgy in 1994 to 1.4 mgy in 1998, an 82% savings. The 110,000-square foot assembly facility achieved this dramatic reduction in water use through implementation of efficiency measures in its manufacturing and assembly processes, landscaping, and other water uses. For example, installation of a more water-efficient humidifier system saved more than 350,000 gpy. During installation of the new equipment, a humidifier discharge pipe that was discovered to be discharging directly to the sewer was replaced with a closed-loop system.[168]

4.9 LEAKS AND WATER LOSSES

Leaks and related water losses at ICI facilities range from minuscule to staggering. They are often misperceived as "insignificant," particularly in relation to other water-using activities and equipment that require large volumes of flow (Figure 4.28). For example, consider the consequences of just one gallon of water wasted per minute: more than a thousand gallons a day, or 525,600 gallons a year. With a combined water and sewer rate of $4 per 1,000 gallons, this "small" flow alone would cost $2,100 annually. Leaks not only waste water and money but, in some circumstances, can also pose hazards to human safety and property (e.g., corrosion, accidents caused by slippery surfaces, and the introduction of unwanted water into an industrial process).

Buildings and facilities are much like water supply systems in that they require ongoing leak detection and repairs if they are to maintain an acceptable level of water-use efficiency. Leak detection and repair programs at ICI sites should extend to all water uses and connections, including meters, water distribution lines, piping, and connections for plumbing fixtures, appliances, landscape irrigation systems, and fire protection equipment.

Needed leak repairs are frequently bypassed until glaring water losses occur that require immediate action, as shown in Figure 4.29. Simple leaks such as dripping faucets are often ignored, despite the fact that just one lavatory faucet leak can waste hundreds of gallons of water a day and larger utility faucets can lose even more. Hidden and less obvious leaks, as well as open water lines and connections thought to have been closed off (e.g., those associated with old, deteriorated underground boiler steam-heating systems at large facilities) can lose thousands of gallons of water a day. Landscape maintenance contractors may or may not report irrigation system leaks, so it is up to the facility manager to find them (Figure 4.30). Repairing leaks saves water and limits the potential for unsafe conditions and property damage.[171, 172]

Visible leaks can sometimes be quantified with a premeasured bucket or plastic bag and a stopwatch. Some leaks are inaccessible or unsafe to measure, and their magnitude can only be estimated. The following guidelines can be used to estimate drips: one drip per second equals about 10 gpd; 5 drips per second (which amounts to a steady stream) equal at least 40 gpd.[173]

I was going to have an opening statement, but I decided I wanted a lot of attention so I decided to wait and leak it."

—Ronald Reagan, 40th U.S. President

Figure 4.28   This leaking water storage tank created a small lake.

Figure 4.29   Leak in hotel basement. The longer leaks are neglected, the more damage that results.

Figure 4.30   A leaking sprinkler head may or may not be reported by the person in charge of landscape maintenance, so it is up to the facility manager to find them.

(Photos 4.28 through 4.30 courtesy of JBS Associates, Inc.)

Figure 4.31 Some underground leaks eventually reach the surface and are obvious, others remain invisible. (Photo courtesy of JBS Associates, Inc.)

Nonvisible leaks, which are often responsible for the largest water losses, may be detectable only indirectly. For example, sudden, unexplainable increases in water use or building or equipment damage are clues that a significant leak or water loss problem is occurring. Leaks underlying grassy areas can be obvious if the turf above them is particularly green and thick compared with nearby patches that are receiving less water. In some cases, leaks bubble up and reach the surface, as shown in Figure 4.31. However, leaks that occur in sandy soil or locations where drainage is good may never be obvious to the eye, which is why periodic leak detection is necessary. Although underground leaks can be detected by several methods, sonic detectors, which pick up sound waves emanating from leaking pipes, can help auditors pinpoint where the leak originates.[171, 172]

Audit Information to Be Collected on Leaks

Information that should be collected about leaks during an ICI water audit includes:

- Frequency of leak detection and repairs for distribution lines, piping, connections, and water-using equipment and processes.
- Original and amended plumbing schematics for the facility, if they exist, for identifying and checking active connections and closed lines.
- Location and type of known leak (e.g., faucet, supply line to equipment).

- Size of leak in diameter (measured in inches) or area of hole (measured in square inches).
- Frequency of leak (slow drip, steady drip, constant stream) and estimated water losses.
- Building or facility water pressure.
- Presence of unsafe conditions or property damage caused by leakage.
- All health, safety, operational, regulatory, administrative, and other requirements or policies that apply to the site.

Conservation Policies and Regulations Related to Leaks

- *Requirements for water audits and efficiency measures at federal facilities.* Federal laws and executive orders pertaining to water and energy conservation requirements are described under Section 4.2, "Cleaning and Sanitation."

Water-Efficiency Measures for Leaks and Water Losses

Water efficiency measures that may be applicable to water leaks and losses include:[171, 172]

- Regularly check for visible and nonvisible leaks and water losses at all water-using connections, equipment, appliances, plumbing fixtures, hoses, and irrigation systems. Facilities and equipment that use high water pressures tend to have more leaks than those using lower pressures. Periodically use leak detection equipment to check for hidden leaks. Investigate lines and connections reported to be closed, including meter bypasses.
- Regularly check boilers and steam systems for leaks in steam traps, relief valves, and condensate return pumps and piping.
- Regularly inspect cooling systems for leaks in cooling towers, bleed-off and make-up connections and tanks, and related connections.
- Regularly check all water-using processes and equipment (e.g., rinse baths, x-ray machines, icemakers), plumbing fixtures (e.g., gravity-flush toilets, flapper valves, ballcock assemblies, and refill valves), and irrigation systems (piping, hoses, drip lines, sprinkler heads, and connections) for leakage; make repairs as needed.
- Post signs to inform employees, residents, and visitors about how to report leakage.

Water Savings, Benefits, and Costs From Leak Repair

Potential water savings from repairing leaks can be significant. For example, repairing a leak that is losing 1.5 gpm can recover 788,400 gallons of water a year. If the combined cost of water and sewer service is $4 per thousand gallons, repairing this leak would save more than $3,100 a year. With a cost of $50 for the repairs, this measure would yield a payback in less than one week.

WaterWiser Drip Calculator- Helps you measure and estimate water wasted due to leaks.
—www.waterwiser.org

4.10 MAINTENANCE PRACTICES FOR ICI WATER EFFICIENCY

This section highlights basic water-efficiency maintenance practices that should be standard operating procedure at ICI buildings and facilities. Many of the measures identified in this section are described in more detail in earlier sections of this chapter.

The ongoing performance of specific maintenance practices is critical to maintaining water efficiency at ICI sites. Regularly monitoring water use and maintaining the efficiency of water-using activities and equipment are necessary at new buildings and facilities as well as old ones.

Audit Information to Be Collected on ICI Maintenance Practices

Information that should be collected about water-efficiency maintenance practices during an ICI water audit includes:

- Utility bills showing water use and sewer discharge volumes and related charges for the past three years.
- Descriptions of any changes in water use and any water-efficiency measures implemented over the past three to five years.
- Frequency of meter readings (main meter and submeters) and staff analysis of water use.
- Frequency of leak detection and repair activities.
- Building or facility water pressure.
- Location of pressure-reducing valves and backflow-prevention devices.
- Building or facility occupancy.
- Any data on the facility's employee water conservation program, including provisions for following up suggestions for increased water efficiency.
- All health, safety, operational, regulatory, administrative, and other requirements or policies that apply to the site.

Conservation Policies and Regulations Related to ICI Maintenance Practices

- *Requirements for water audits and efficiency measures at federal facilities.* Federal laws and executive orders pertaining to water and energy conservation requirements are described under Section 4.2, "Cleaning and Sanitation."
- *Prohibitions on wasteful water use.* A number of communities and water utilities prohibit wasteful water use, which is usually defined as street runoff and overspray from irrigation systems, obvious leaks, and outdoor cleaning activities involving the use of hoses (e.g., cleaning sidewalks). For example, water-use restrictions in San Francisco and Goodyear, Arizona, prohibit the use of water hoses to clean driveways, sidewalks, and buildings.[53] Baseline water conservation ordinances tend to be enforced only during droughts, primarily because they require vigilant enforcement to be effective.
- *Required conservation plans in nonresidential developments.* New commercial and industrial developments are sometimes subject to water conservation and other energy and resource conservation plans or measures that are not required of existing facilities. For example, an ordinance established by

A little neglect may breed great mischief . . . for want of a nail the shoe was lost; for want of a shoe the horse was lost; and for want of a horse the rider was lost."
—Benjamin Franklin

the city of Tempe, Arizona, requires a water conservation plan for new non-residential developments.[174]

- *Notification of customers with high-volume water use.* The cities of Chandler and Peoria, Arizona, monitor customer water use and contact customers whose water use has substantially increased. Customers are contacted by letter or in person. Residential customers with increased use are offered a home water audit to help identify the reasons for the increased demand.[175]

Water-Efficiency Measures for ICI Maintenance Practices

Water-efficiency measures that may be incorporated into building and facility maintenance operations include:[172, 177, 178]

- Prepare a water-efficiency maintenance plan that includes checklists and schedules for tasks to be performed. Primary tasks should include at least regular meter readings, leak detection and repair, and education of employees about the importance of water conservation.
- Read and monitor water-use records for all meters and submeters at least monthly, and investigate the sources of increases or decreases in water use. Develop a water "balance sheet" (or schematic) of all water entry points and activities at the site—e.g., cooling and heating systems, process and rinse baths, plumbing fixtures, landscape irrigation, and other water-using connections.
- If the site has undergone a water audit, make sure that recommended measures have been implemented and that follow-up audits are conducted every one to three years to keep up with changes in the facility's water-use operations and activities and to identify technological improvements that may have become available.
- Regularly check all equipment, appliances, piping, steam lines and traps, solenoid valves, and related connections to identify leaks; make repairs promptly. Encourage employees to report leaks and water waste.
- Shut off the water supply to areas, rooms, equipment, and fixtures that are unused.
- Install a pressure-reducing valve, where appropriate, to reduce incoming flows, leaks, and wear and tear on equipment and plumbing.
- Maintain cooling and heating systems and other equipment that uses water on a regular treatment and cleaning schedule.
- Reduce loads on water-cooled air conditioning units by shutting them off when and where they are not needed.
- Recycle and reuse water wherever feasible.
- Use humidifiers only where and when needed. Adjust the level of humidification to a minimum acceptable level.
- To protect water lines from freezing, install shutoff valves where necessary rather than running water continuously.
- Maintain insulation on hot water pipes to minimize heat loss.
- When purchasing new water-using equipment, appliances, fixtures, and irrigation systems, choose state-of-the-art models in terms of water efficiency. Investigate local utility and state rebate and tax incentive programs that may help defray the cost of such purchases.

Office Complex Design Is in Tune with Maryland's "Smart Growth Initiative"

A historic 1925 Baltimore warehouse comprising 1.3 million square feet and covering 28 acres has been transformed into a giant office-building complex for up to 5,000 workers. The new $75 million Montgomery Park office complex is based on "green" design objectives that include energy and water efficiency, water recycling, and some recycled building materials. The complex includes such features as:

- Toilets that are flushed with rainwater stored in and pumped from underground tanks.
- A partial grass-and-shrub roof that is irrigated by rainwater and stormwater runoff.
- Ice-making at night (when energy rates are low) for use in cooling buildings during daytime.
- Use of recycled materials for office partitions, ceiling tile, resilient flooring, and carpeting.[176]

- View planned repairs or adjustments to water-using equipment, appliances, fixtures, and other processes as opportunities to improve water-use efficiency.
- Make sure that newly installed plumbing fixtures do not exceed the following maximum water-use rates: toilets—1.6 gallons per flush (gpf) (except prison toilets, which may be designed to use 3.5 gpf or 1.6 gpf); flush or waterless urinals—1.0 gpf; showerheads—2.2 gpm (at 60 psi) (excluding safety showers); faucets—2.2 gpm (at 60 psi); and metering faucets—0.25 gallons per cycle.
- Regularly check all plumbing fixtures, such as toilets, urinals, faucets, and showerheads, for leaks and malfunctions that contribute to water losses. If aerators in faucets and showerheads are removable, assess whether they need to be replaced or cleaned. Periodically check toilets and urinals retrofitted with devices that reduce water use to make sure they are properly adjusted and are still saving water.
- Install spring-loaded valves or timers on manually operated water outlets wherever practical.
- Evaluate hot water systems for water efficiency. Consider installing on-demand, point-of-use water heaters to minimize water losses caused by customers and employees running hot water taps while waiting for hot water.
- Minimize or eliminate water used for washdown (e.g., using hoses to clean sidewalks, tennis courts, pool decks, driveways, parking lots, and other hardscapes). Instead, use alternative cleaning methods that require little or no water, such as wet washrags and brooms. Dry extraction cleaning methods can be used for carpet cleaning instead of wet methods.
- When water is used for washdown, instruct clean-up crews to use less water for mopping. As much as possible, use high-pressure, low-volume streams of water with automatic shutoff valves. Mechanical floor scrubbers that recirculate water may be an alternative to wet-mopping.
- Minimize water use for landscape irrigation by employing water-efficient landscape design and maintenance methods. Check watering practices and irrigation schedules regularly to monitor the efficiency of landscape sprinkler systems.
- Maintain pools and decorative water features to reduce water waste (e.g., setting appropriate water temperatures and limiting losses to evaporation and splashing). Cover pools whenever possible.
- Wash trucks and vehicles only when necessary.
- Minimize water use for construction-related activities and fire-flow testing; consider reusing this water for purposes that do not require high water quality.
- Regularly inform employees about facility water use and progress in meeting water-efficiency goals (e.g., amount of water saved, reductions in water bills and facility operating costs) to help maintain awareness of a water conservation ethic.

Case Study *Maintenance Practices Improve Water Efficiency at Canadian Office Complex.* A water audit of the AGT Tower and McCauley office-building facility in Edmonton, Alberta, identified conservation measures for domestic (sanitary), process, and cooling uses with projected water savings of nearly 40%. The 34-floor office tower comprises 1 million square feet; 70% of the facility is devoted to office space, 20% to parking and general-use areas, and 10% to cafeteria and retail areas. Recommended measures included installation of 1.6 gpf toilets and waterless urinals; replacement of lavatory aerators; improved maintenance of hot water temperatures; installation of solenoid and shutoff valves in kitchen work areas; reduced cooling tower blowdown achieved through an improved filtration and treatment package; replacement of a once-through cooling system with a closed loop system; and replacement of water-cooled refrigerators, freezers, and ice machines with air-cooled models.[179]

Case Study   *Ten Federal Facilities in Canada Implement Conservation Measures for Cooling, Process, and Domestic Water Use.* As part of the Canadian government's Green Plan Code of Environmental Stewardship, Environment Canada completed audits of ten federal institutional facilities in the provinces of Quebec, Ontario, and British Columbia. Facilities included animal research centers, border-crossing stations, schools, offices, and the House of Commons in Ottawa. Building areas ranged from 780 to 75,220 square meters, and the number of people working at each site ranged from 9 to 3,300. Principal water uses at the facilities were for cooling, process, and domestic purposes. The audits found once-through cooling systems for air conditioning units or refrigerator/freezer cooling systems at many of the facilities. Process cooling uses included humidification, dishwashers, cage washers, heating system make-up, area washing, floor drain flushing, and laboratory use. Plumbing fixtures in employee and public washrooms accounted for most of the water used for domestic purposes.

The audit identified numerous opportunities for conservation at the ten facilities. For example, replacing the once-through cooling systems with closed-loop units was feasible at many of the facilities. At nine sites, reducing domestic water use involved preventing the self-flushing urinals from operating continuously 24 hours a day. Retrofitting many of the lavatory sinks with aerators or similar devices was possible. Two facilities were eligible for water utility rebates because their humidification water was not discharged into the sewer system. Opportunities for reducing water use and costs at other sites included stopping the continuous flow of water to a drain flushing system and replacing a flow meter that was registering water use of more than ten times actual use. Potential water savings from these and other measures were significant, averaging 34 to 97% of the previous year's demand. Cooling water had the greatest potential for reduction, with projected savings ranging from 4 to 59%. Potential reductions in process and domestic water uses were projected at 1 to 37% and 3 to 26%, respectively. Total savings in water and sewer costs at all the facilities were estimated at Can$354,000, based on the previous year's total water bill of Can$784,000. Estimated payback periods for investments in the recommended conservation measures ranged from 0.2 to 3.2 years.[180]

If you had enough water to fill one million goldfish bowls, you could fill an entire stadium."
—www.uselessfacts.net

Case Study   *Canadian Prison's Conservation Program Serves as Model for Other Federal Facilities.* The Warkworth Institution in Brighton, Ontario, Canada, is a federally owned, medium-security correctional facility encompassing more than 40 buildings. The facility operates its own water filtration and wastewater treatment plants. After a water audit and conservation study costing Can$50,000 identified a 20 to 40% difference between measured water supply and estimated demand, leaks totaling approximately 120,000 liters per day were located. Conservation measures implemented as a result included system leak detection and repair; toilet, sink, and showerhead retrofits; installation of timers and solenoid valves on once-through cooling systems; and installation of automatic shutoff valves on outdoor spraying devices. Water and wastewater reductions achieved by the measures have saved Warkworth more than Can$150,000 in avoided capital costs that otherwise would have been required to expand the capacities of the water and wastewater plants. The facility's ongoing conservation program includes staff education, daily monitoring of flows, routine inspection and repair of the supply system, installation of water-efficient plumbing devices, and periodic evaluation of the program. In addition, the Warkworth audit and conservation program has provided a database and methodology used by Correctional Services Canada at 31 other major prison facilities. By November 1993, water savings from conservation measures undertaken at these other facilities totaled more than 1 million liters per day, saving the federal government an estimated Can$1,000 a day.[181]

1. Wayne B. Solley, Robert R. Pierce, and Howard A. Perlman, *Estimated Use of Water in the United States in 1995*, U.S. Geological Survey Circular 1200, U.S Department of the Interior, U.S. Geological Survey, Reston, Va., 1998, pp. 28, 40.
2. Benedykt Dziegielewski, Jack C. Kiefer, and Eva M. Opitz, "Analysis of Commercial and Institutional Water Demands," presented at the American Water Works Assoc. (AWWA) Annual Conf., Chicago, June 22, 1999.
3. J. Douglas Kobrick, "Nonresidential Water Conservation Programs and Examples," *Proc. Conserv93: The New Water Agenda*, AWWA, Denver, 1993, p. 465.
4. Pequod Associates, Inc., Texas Industrial Water Use Efficiency Study. Final Report, Texas Water Development Board, Austin, Texas, October 1993.
5. California Urban Water Conservation Council, The CII ULFT Savings Study: Final Report, prepared by Hagler Bailly Services, Inc., San Francisco, for the California Urban Water Conservation Council, Sacramento, Calif., Aug. 5, 1997, pp. 2-5.
6. Regional Water Demand by Sector, Greater Vancouver Regional District, Policy and Planning Department, Regional Utility Planning, Burnaby, B.C., September 1999, Table 19-Regional Significant End Uses (1997).
7. California Department of Water Resources, *Water Efficiency Guide for Business Managers and Facility Engineers*, California Dept. of Water Resources, Sacramento, Calif., October 1994, p. 2.
8. Denver Board of Water Commissioners, Nonresidential Water Audit Program: Summary Report, prepared by Black & Veatch, Aurora, Colo., for the Denver Board of Water Commissioners, Denver, July 1991, pp. 3-15.
9. City of San Jose, *Water Conservation Guide for Computer and Electronics Manufacturers*, City of San Jose Environmental Services Department, San Jose, Calif., 1992.
10. City of San Jose, *Water Conservation Guide for Office Buildings and Commercial Establishments*, City of San Jose Environmental Services Department, San Jose, Calif., 1992.
11. Jane Heller Ploeser, Charles W. Pike, and J. Douglas Kobrick, "Nonresidential Water Conservation: A Good Investment," *Journal AWWA*, vol. 84, no. 10, 1992, p. 65.
12. Benedykt Dziegielewski et al, *Commercial and Institutional End Uses of Water*, AWWA Research Foundation, Denver, 2000.
13. Traci Watson, "Ski Areas Set Conservation Guidelines: Pledge Takes a Hit From Those Who Call It 'Greenwash,'" *USA Today*, June 14, 2000, p. 3.
14. Michael Janofsky, "Environment Groups' Ratings Rile Ski Industry," *The New York Times*, New England edition, Dec. 3, 2000, p. 30.
15. *U.S. Clean Water Act*, U.S. Code 33, sect. 1251-1377.
16. *Energy Policy Act of 1992*, Public Law 102-486, 106 Stat. 2776, 102d Congress, Oct. 24, 1992.
17. Executive Order, *Energy Efficiency and Water Conservation at Federal Facilities*, Executive Order 12902, Office of the President (William J. Clinton), Washington, D.C., Mar. 8, 1994.

18. Executive Order, *Greening the Government Through Efficient Energy Management,* Executive Order 13123, Office of the President (William J. Clinton), Washington, D.C., June 3, 1999.

19. Federal Energy Management Program, *Buying Energy Efficient Products,* U.S. Dept. of Energy, Office of Energy Efficiency and Renewable Energy, Washington, D.C., 1997, 2000.

20. Margaret Suozzo et al, "High-Performing HVAC Systems," *Guide to Energy-Efficient Commercial Equipment,* 2nd ed., American Council for an Energy-Efficient Economy, Washington, D.C., 2000, chap. 3, pp. 3-1 to 3-34.

21. Raftelis Financial Consulting, *2000 Water and Wastewater Rate Survey,* Raftelis Financial Consulting, Charlotte, N.C., 2000.

22. *National Drought Policy Act of 1998,* Public Law 105-199, 105th Congress, Washington, D.C., July 16, 1998.

23. National Drought Policy Commission, *Preparing for Drought in the 21st Century—Report of the National Drought Policy Commission,* U.S. Dept. of Agriculture, Washington, D.C., May 16, 2000.

24. U.S. Environmental Protection Agency, Office of Water, Water Alliances For Voluntary Efficiency (WAVE), http://www.epa.gov/owm/faqw.htm, Dec. 18, 2000.

25. "Hotel/Motels Conserve Water by Offering Guests Option to Re-use Towels and Sheets," reprinted from *U.S. Water News* in *The Cross Section,* Lubbock, Texas, October 1996, p. 4.

26. Suozzo et al, *Guide to Energy-Efficient Commercial Equipment,* app. VI: Additional Resources.

27. City of Portland Energy Office, Businesses for an Environmentally Sustainable Tomorrow (BEST) Program Documented Annual Results, City of Portland, Ore., April 2000.

28. Metropolitan Water District of Southern California, Evaluation of the MWD CII Survey Database, prepared by Hagler Bailly Services, Inc., San Francisco, for the Metropolitan Water District of Southern California, Los Angeles, Nov. 19, 1997, p. S-1.

29. Sandra Postel, "Industrial Recycling," *Last Oasis,* W.W. Norton & Co., New York, 1992, rev. ed., 1997, chap. 21.

30. Jon G. Sweeten and Ben Chaput, "Identifying the Conservation Opportunities in the Commercial, Industrial, and Institutional Sector," presented at the AWWA Annual Conf., Atlanta, June 17, 1997.

31. Massachusetts Water Resources Authority, MWRA Honors Spalding Sports Worldwide for Water Conservation, news release, Boston, Mass., Sept. 27, 1991.

32. Final Report: Study of Potential Water Efficiency Improvements in Commercial Businesses, U.S. Environmental Protection Agency with the California Dept. of Water Resources, Sacramento, Calif. (Grant No. CX 823643-01-0), April 1997, p. 9.

33. Metropolitan Water District of Southern California, Evaluation of the MWD CII Survey Database, p. 6.

34. Office of the State Engineer of New Mexico, "How to Create a Successful Water Conservation Program," *A Water Conservation Guide for Commercial, Institutional and Industrial Users,* prepared by Schultz Communications, Albuquerque, N.M., for the State Engineer of New Mexico, Santa Fe, N.M., July 1999, sec. 2.

35. Massachusetts Water Resources Authority, *A Guide to Water Management: The MWRA Program for Industrial, Commercial and Institutional Water Use,* prepared in collaboration with Douglas Kobrick of Black & Veatch, Massachusetts Water Resources Authority, Boston, June 1995, p. 9.

36. California Department of Water Resources, *Water Efficiency Guide for Business Managers and Facility Engineers,* p. 5.

37. California Department of Water Resources, *Industrial/Commercial Drought Guidebook for Water Utilities,* California Dept. of Water Resources, Sacramento, Calif., June 1991.

38. *Water Meters—Selection, Installation, Testing, and Maintenance,* AWWA Manual M6, 4th ed., AWWA, Denver, 1999, pp. 6-23, 29-32.

39. Harry Von Huben, technical ed., *Water Distribution Operator Training Handbook,* 2nd ed., AWWA, Denver, 1999, chap. 13, pp. 140-154.

40. Virginia Porter, "Metering and Demand Management: A Critical Link," presented at Conserv99—Water Efficiency: Making Cents in the Next Century, Monterey, Calif., Feb. 1, 1999.

41. JBS Associates, Inc., *Water Conservation Issues: The Water Audit (Unaccounted-for Water, Leak Detection, Meter Application and Sizing),* workbook from University of Wisconsin-Madison seminar, February 1997, p. 19.

42. Personal communication, James B. Smith, JBS Associates, Inc., June 12, 1998.

43. James Liston and Steve Gilham, "Data-Logging Water Meters to Reduce Capital Costs and Increase Accountability," presented at the AWWA Annual Conf., Chicago, June 21, 1999.

44. Massachusetts Water Resources Authority, *A Guide to Water Management,* p. 40.

45. California Department of Water Resources, *Water Efficiency Guide,* p. 79.

46. American Water Works Assoc., *Helping Businesses Manage Water Use,* AWWA, Denver, 1993, p. 17.

47. Warren Liebold, "Fed Regs for Utility Rebates?" WaterWiser Conf.<waterwiser-list@listserv.water-wiser.org>, Apr. 4, 1997.

48. Massachusetts Water Resources Authority, *A Guide to Water Management,* p. 15.

49. U.S. General Services Administration, *Water Management,* Office of Real Property Management and Safety, U.S. General Services Admin., Washington, D.C., prepared in collaboration with Enviro-Management & Research, Inc.,1994, pp. 2-6.

50. California Department of Water Resources, *Water Efficiency Guide,* p. 22.

51. Massachusetts Water Resources Authority, *A Guide to Water Management*, p. 30.
52. Environment Canada, *Water Audit Case Studies*, 2nd ed., Conservation and Protection, Environment Canada, Hull, Que., November 1993.
53. The Bruce Company, Final Draft: Local Ordinances for Water Efficiency, prepared for the U.S. Environmental Protection Agency, Office of Policy Analysis, EPA Contract # 68-W2-0018, Subcontract # EPA 353-2, Work Assignment 24, Mar. 31, 1993, app. B.
54. Massachusetts Water Resources Authority, *A Guide to Water Management*, p. 33.
55. Black & Veatch, *A Guide to Commercial/Industrial Water Conservation*, prepared for the Los Angeles Dept. of Water and Power, Los Angeles, 1991, p. 35
56. J. Douglas Kobrick, Jane Heller Ploeser, and John Corbin, "Water Uses and Conservation Opportunities in Automatic Car Washes: A City of Phoenix Study," *Proc. AWWA Annual Conf.*, AWWA, Denver, 1997.
57. Chris Brown, "Water Conservation in the Professional Car Wash Industry," presented at the AWWA Annual Conf., Denver, June 12, 2000.
58. Car Wash Facilities, Massachusetts Water Resources Authority, Boston, undated.
59. Personal communication, Philip Paschke, Water Smart Technology Program Manager, Seattle Public Utilities, Seattle, Oct. 11, 2000.
60. Office of the State Engineer of New Mexico, *Water Conservation Guide*, p. 74.
61. Black & Veatch, *A Guide to Commercial/Industrial Water Conservation*, p. 33.
62. Irwin B. Margiloff, "The Variety of Types of ICI Sites," *Proc. Conserv99-Water Efficiency: Making Cents in the Next Century*, AWWA, Denver, 1999.
63. Massachusetts Water Resources Authority, Hospital Cost Reduction Case Study: Norwood Hospital, http://www.mwra.state.ma.us/html/bullet1.htm, May 16, 2000.
64. Black & Veatch, *A Guide to Commercial/Industrial Water Conservation*, p. 34.
65. Los Angeles Department of Water and Power, Water Conservation Report: Hospital of the Good Samaritan, prepared by Black & Veatch for the Los Angeles Dept. of Water and Power, Los Angeles, Feb. 7, 1991.
66. Mark D. Wilson, "Water Conservation for Hospitals and Health Care Facilities," *Proc. Conserv93: The New Water Agenda*, AWWA, Denver, 1993.
67. California Department of Water Resources, *Water Efficiency Guide*, p. 36.
68. Black & Veatch, *A Guide to Commercial/Industrial Water Conservation*, p. 28.
69. Brown and Caldwell, *Case Studies of Industrial Water Conservation in the San Jose Area*, prepared by Brown and Caldwell, Pleasant Hill, Calif., for the City of \, Calif., and the California Dept. of Water Resources, Sacramento, Calif., February 1990.
70. Office of the State Engineer of New Mexico, *Water Conservation Guide*, p. 28.
71. City of Portland Energy Office, BEST Results: Merix's Conservation Merits BEST Award, press release issued by the City of Portland, Ore., 2000.
72. Office of the State Engineer of New Mexico, *Water Conservation Guide*, pp. 28, 70-73.
73. University of Missouri Extension, Pollution Solution: Waste Reduction Solutions for Business, Web site of the Office of Waste Management, www.orion.org/~owm/metal.htm#op, June 1999.
74. City of Albuquerque, *How to Save Water at Work: The City of Albuquerque Institutional/Commercial/Industrial Water Conservation Manual*, August 1997, pp. 24-25.
75. Mark Manzione, Barbara Jordan, and William O. Maddaus, "California Industries Cut Water Use," *Journal AWWA*, vol. 83, no. 10, 1991, p. 55.
76. Office of the State Engineer of New Mexico, "Case Studies," *Water Conservation Guide*, sec. 7, pp. 77-104.
77. World Business Council for Sustainable Development, "Case 7: Reduction in Fresh Water Usage in San Diego, Monsanto," *Industry, Fresh Water and Sustainable Development*, April 1998, p. 30.
78. Magna IV Engineering Ltd., Gainers Meat Processing Plant, Energy Audit Results, prepared for Edmonton Power and Edmonton Public Works, Edmonton, Alta., February 1995.
79. Office of the State Engineer of New Mexico, *Water Conservation Guide*, p. 75.
80. U.S. General Services Administration, *Water Management*, pp. 3-27.
81. California Department of Water Resources, *Water Efficiency Guide*, pp. 39, 41.
82. Industrial Water Conservation References of Paper and Packaging Manufacturers, prepared by Brown and Caldwell for the California Dept. of Water Resources, Sacramento, Calif., and the Metropolitan Water District of Southern California, Los Angeles, 1989.
83. T. Nandy, S. N. Kaul, and S. Shastry, "Paper Industry Effluent Recycling," *World Water and Environmental Engineering*, vol. 22, June 1999, pp. 14-15.
84. Office of the State Engineer of New Mexico, *Water Conservation Guide*, p. 39.
85. California Department of Water Resources, *Water Efficiency Guide*, p. 40.
86. Massachusetts Water Resources Authority, Water Efficiency & Management for Restaurants, Massachusetts Water Resources Authority, Boston, Apr. 25, 1994.
87. Black & Veatch, *A Guide to Commercial/Industrial Water Conservation*, p. 10.
88. Denver Board of Water Commissioners, Nonresidential Water Audit Program, pp. 2-9.
89. Office of the State Engineer of New Mexico, *Water Conservation Guide*, p. 40.

90. Los Angeles Department of Water and Power, Water Conservation Report: Little Joe's Restaurant, prepared by Black & Veatch for the Los Angeles Dept. of Water and Power, Los Angeles, Feb. 7, 1991, p. 8.

91. Metropolitan Water District of Southern California, Evaluation of the MWD CII Survey Database, p. 28.

92. Office of the State Engineer of New Mexico, *Water Conservation Guide*, p. 38.

93. Black & Veatch, *A Guide to Commercial/Industrial Water Conservation*, p. 11.

94. Larry Calabro et al, *The Water Audit Guidebook*, Rhode Island Dept. of Environmental Management, Div. of Water Supply Management, Providence, R.I., April 1996, app. E, unpaginated.

95. Massachusetts Water Resources Authority, *A Guide to Water Management*, p. 29.

96. Massachusetts Water Resources Authority, Water Efficiency & Management for Hospitals, Massachusetts Water Resources Authority, Boston, Apr. 18, 1994.

97. In-Sink-Erator, *Disposer Digest*, In-Sink-Erator, a division of Emerson Electric Co., Rept. C190 92 D-06, Racine, Wisc., 1992.

98. Black & Veatch, *A Guide to Commercial/Industrial Water Conservation*, p. 13.

99. Pacific Northwest National Laboratory, *Energy Efficient/Environmentally Sensitive DoD Showcase Facility: The Pentagon, A National Landmark*, prepared by Rocky Mountain Institute, Snowmass, Colo., for Pacific Northwest National Laboratory, Richland, Wash., 1995, p. 89.

100. California Department of Water Resources, *Water Efficiency Guide*, p. 41.

101. Black & Veatch, A Guide to Commercial/Industrial Water Conservation, p. 16.

102. Suozzo et al, "Other Energy-Using Equipment," *Guide to Energy-Efficient Commercial Equipment*, chap. 5, pp. 5-11 to 5-13.

103. Air-Conditioning and Refrigeration Institute, *Directory of Certified Automatic Commercial Ice-Cube Machines and Ice Storage Bins*, Air-Conditioning and Refrigeration Institute, Arlington, Va., 2000.

104. Federal Energy Management Program, *Commercial Ice-Maker Efficiency Recommendation*, <www.eren.doe.gov/gov/femp/procurement/icemkr.html, U.S. Dept. of Energy, Washington, D.C., 2000.

105. Massachusetts Water Resources Authority, *A Guide to Water Management*, p. 31.

106. M. Clifford Bjorgum and Edwin L. Hernandez, "Denver Water Nonresidential Case Studies," *Proc. Conserv93: The New Water Agenda*, AWWA, Denver, 1993, p. 543.

107. Beauford Anderson, "Commercial and Industrial Program Case Studies," *Proc. Conserv93: The New Water Agenda*, AWWA, Denver, 1993, p. 485.

108. Massachusetts Water Resources Authority, *A Guide to Water Management*, p. 32.

109. Black & Veatch, *A Guide to Commercial/Industrial Water Conservation*, p. 18.

110. Office of the State Engineer of New Mexico, *Water Conservation Guide*, p. 41.

111. Black & Veatch, *A Guide to Commercial/Industrial Water Conservation*, p. 30.

112. Commercial, Family-Sized Washers: An Initiative Description of the Consortium for Energy Efficiency, Consortium for Energy Efficiency, Boston, 1998, pp. 4-7.

113. U.S. Department of Energy, <http://www.eren.doe.gov/buildings/consumer_information/clotheswashers/clotips.html, Feb. 11, 1998.

114. Pacific Northwest National Laboratory, *Water Resource Management*, prepared by Pacific Northwest National Laboratory, Richland, Wash., for the U.S. Department of Energy's Federal Energy Management Program, Seattle, August 1997, p. 2.14.

115. City of Portland Energy Office, "Red Lion: 'Greener' Ways to Whiter Laundry," City of Portland, Ore., undated.

116. Kathryn Tong, "An Inn on the Green: Adopting Custom Widespread in Europe and Asia, US Hotels Want Their Guests to Reuse Linen and Save Water, Other Costs," *The Boston Globe*, Jul. 29, 2000, pp. C1-C2.

117. The Bruce Company, Final Draft: Local Ordinances for Water Efficiency, p. 12.

118. Marin Municipal Water District, Ordinance 326: An Ordinance Revising Water Conservation Requirements, sec. 11.60.030 (Requirements For All Services), Marin Municipal Water District, Corte Madera, Calif., Aug. 28, 1991.

119. The Bruce Company, Final Draft: Local Ordinances for Water Efficiency, p. 11.

120. Beth Wade, "Making a Splash in Local Recreation," *American City & County*, vol. 113, no. 10, 1998, p. 20.

121. California Department of Water Resources, "Swimming Pool Tips Translate to Savings," *Water Conservation News*, Water Conservation Office, Div., of Planning & Local Assistance, California Dept. of Water Resources, Sacramento, Calif., October 1998, p. 7.

122. Black & Veatch, *A Guide to Commercial/Industrial Water Conservation*, p. 39.

123. Pacific Northwest National Laboratory, *Water Resource Management*, p. 2.15.

124. City of Albuquerque, How to Save Water at Home: A Step-by-Step Manual for the Do-It-Yourselfer, Water Conservation Office, City of Albuquerque, N.M., undated, p. 73.

125. Massachusetts Water Resources Authority, Water Efficiency & Management in Schools, Colleges & Athletic Facilities, Massachusetts Water Resources Authority, Boston, Sept. 2, 1994.

126. Cleveland Metroparks Zoo, Final Report: Water Conservation Opportunities at the Cleveland Metroparks Zoo, prepared by Amy Vickers & Associates, Inc., Boston, for the Cleveland Metroparks Zoo, Cleveland, Ohio, March 1994.

127. W. G. Richards et al, "Conserving Water at America's First Zoo," *Proc. Conserv93: The New Water Agenda*, AWWA, Denver, 1993, p. 565.

128. Robert Nagle, "Water Survey of the Denver Zoo and Opportunities Identified," *Proc. AWWA Annual Conf.*, AWWA, Denver, 2000.

129. Teri Liberator, "Think BIG: Business, Industry & Government Water Conservation Program," presented to the International Facilities' Managers Assoc., May 24, 2000.

130. State of Hawaii Plumbing Code, sec. 1101(e).

131. Personal communication, Dave D. Todd, Supervisor of Water Conservation, City of Fresno, Calif., June 9, 1998.

132. Robert Hatton, "Credit for Cooling Tower Use," waterwiserlist@listserv.waterwiser.org, Aug. 16, 2000.

133. Warren Liebold, "Credit for Cooling Tower Use," waterwiserlist@listserv.waterwiser.org, Aug. 16, 2000.

134. Columbia-Willamette Water Conservation Coalition and City of Portland, Bureau of Water Works, Cooling Water Efficiency Guidebook, Water Conservation Program, Bureau of Water Works, City of Portland, Ore., 2000, pp. 6-11.

135. Office of the State Engineer of New Mexico, "Water Conservation Guidelines for Cooling and Heating," *Water Conservation Guide*, sec. 5, pp. 59-68.

136. Massachusetts Water Resources Authority, *A Guide to Water Management*, p. 23.

137. U.S. General Services Administration, *Water Management*, pp. 3-34.

138. City of Portland Energy Office, BEST Results: Saving Water, Recycling Saves Tek Millions, City of Portland, Ore., 1998.

139. California Department of Water Resources, *Water Efficiency Guide*, p. 33.

140. Massachusetts Water Resources Authority, Reducing Costs in Hospitals: A Case Study of Norwood Hospital, Massachusetts Water Resources Authority, Boston, February 1996.

141. Columbia-Willamette Water Conservation Coalition and City of Portland, Bureau of Water Works, *Cooling Water Efficiency Guidebook*, pp. 12-23.

142. W. Osborne, cited by Mike Henley, "Cooling Market Remains Stable With Few New Developments," *Industrial Water Treatment*, January/February 1995, p. 14.

143. Nelson Yarlott, "Cooling Towers Provide Happy Home for *Legionella*," *Opflow*, vol. 26, no. 10, 2000, pp. 3, 14.

144. Puckorius & Associates, Inc., *Water Conservation for Cooling Water Systems Seminar*, workbook prepared by Puckorius & Associates, Evergreen, Colo., for the East Bay Municipal Utilities District, Oakland, Calif., Jul. 27, 2000, unpaginated.

145. Douglas J. Kobrick and Mark D. Wilson, "Uses of Water and Water Conservation Opportunities for Cooling Towers," Black & Veatch, Los Angeles, 1993, unpaginated.

146. Black & Veatch, *A Guide to Water Conservation for Cooling Towers*, prepared for the Los Angeles Dept. of Water & Power, Los Angeles, December 1991, pp. 3-11.

147. Puckorius & Associates, Inc., *Water Conservation for Cooling Water Systems Seminar*, pp. 73-86.

148. Black & Veatch, "Cooling Tower Function and Operation," *Water Conservation for Cooling Towers*, prepared for the Metropolitan Water District of Southern California, Los Angeles, 1993, unpaginated.

149. Massachusetts Water Resources Authority, *A Guide to Water Management*, pp. 23-28.

150. Black & Veatch, *A Guide to Water Conservation for Cooling Towers*, pp. 16-18.

151. California Department of Water Resources, *Water Efficiency Guide*, p. 35.

152. Massachusetts Water Resources Authority, *A Guide to Water Management*, p. 27.

153. Office of the State Engineer of New Mexico, "Water Conservation Guidelines for Cooling and Heating," *Water Conservation Guide*, sec. 5, pp. 66-67.

154. Martin M. Karpiscak et al, "Evaporative Cooler Water Use in Phoenix, *Journal AWWA*, vol. 90, no. 4, 1998, p. 121.

155. City of Albuquerque, How to Save Water at Home: A Step-By-Step Manual for the Do-It-Yourselfer, pp. 40-41.

156. Brian C. Wilson, *Water Conservation and Quantification of Water Demands in Subdivisions: A Guidance Manual for Public Officials and Developers*, Office of the State Engineer of New Mexico, Santa Fe, N.M., May 1996, app. B, pp. 1-2.

157. Pacific Northwest National Laboratory, *Water Resource Management*, p. 2.12.

158. Black & Veatch, *A Guide to Commercial/Industrial Water Conservation*, p. 23.

159. City of Portland Energy Office, BEST Results: Elf Atochem Captures Impressive Water Savings, City of Portland, Ore., 1998.

160. Black & Veatch, *A Guide to Commercial/Industrial Water Conservation*, p. 22.

161. Office of the State Engineer of New Mexico, *Water Conservation Guide*, p. 68.

162. David C. Cowden, "Save Money, Energy & Water With Multiple Boilers," *PM Engineer*, vol. 4, no. 1, January/February 1998, pp. 52-55.

163. Massachusetts Water Resources Authority, *A Guide to Water Management*, p. 28.

164. Black & Veatch, *A Guide to Commercial/Industrial Water Conservation*, p. 25.

165. California Department of Water Resources, *Water Efficiency Guide*, p. 31.

166. Office of the State Engineer of New Mexico, "Case Studies in Commercial, Institutional, and Industrial Water Conservation," *Water Conservation Guide*, sec.7, pp. 80-82.

167. A. Owens, "Water Conservation and Reuse Programs Can Be Self-Supporting," presented at WATERTECH '92, Houston, Texas, Nov. 11, 1992.

168. Office of the State Engineer of New Mexico, *Water Conservation Guide*, p. 94.

169. Black & Veatch, *A Guide to Commercial/Industrial Water Conservation*, p. 24.

170. Black & Veatch, *A Guide to Water Conservation for Cooling Towers*, p. 24.

171. Massachusetts Water Resources Authority, *A Guide to Water Management*, p. 36.

172. California Department of Water Resources, *Water Efficiency Guide*, p. 42.

173. *Water Audits and Leak Detection*, AWWA Manual M36, AWWA, Denver, 1998.

174. Arizona Municipal Water Users Association, Summary of Water Conservation Activities Implemented by AMWUA Member Cities, Phoenix, January 1993, p. 2.

175. Arizona Municipal Water Users Association, Summary of Water Conservation Activities, p. 6.

176. Charles Belfoure, "From Warehouse to Giant Office Building: Baltimore Renovation Will Feature 'Green' Design Practices," *The New York Times*, New England ed., Oct. 22, 2000, Real Estate sec., p. 34.

177. Office of the State Engineer of New Mexico, *Water Conservation Guide*.

178. Massachusetts Water Resources Authority, *A Guide to Water Management*, p. 34.

179. Reid Crowther & Partners Ltd., AGT Building Water Audit, prepared for A.G.T. Real Estate, Edmonton, Alta., June 1994.

180. Proctor & Redfern Ltd., Water Audits of Ten Federal Government Facilities, prepared by Proctor & Redfern Ltd., Don Mills, Ont., for the Water Planning & Management Branch, Engineering & Development Div., Environment Canada, Hull, Que., May 22, 1992.

181. Environment Canada, *Water Audit Case Studies*, p. 8.

5

Agricultural Water Use and Efficiency Measures

There is no substitute for water.

THIS CHAPTER describes water use for agricultural irrigation and presents water-efficiency measures that can optimize on-farm water use. Descriptions of the water-efficiency measures include potential water savings plus related benefits and costs, including impact on crop yields. Case studies are sometimes used to illustrate relative benefits and costs.

Agricultural Irrigation Water Use

Globally, two thirds of the water withdrawn from rivers, lakes, and aquifers is used for irrigation systems to grow crops. In developing counties, as much as 90% may be used for agricultural purposes.* Approximately 83% of the world's cropland is watered only by rain. The other 17%, or 630 million acres, which is irrigated, accounts for 35 to 40% of the global harvest, representing nearly three times the productivity of rainfed land.[1-3]

In the United States, irrigated agriculture remains the dominant user of freshwater.[4] Total freshwater withdrawals for irrigation for agricultural and horticultural purposes (including golf courses) are estimated to average 134 billion gallons per day (bgd), or 39% of total freshwater withdrawals, according to the most recent U.S. Geological Survey of national water use. Of total irrigation withdrawals in the United States, 63% are from surface water sources, 37% are from groundwater sources, and just a fraction of 1% are from reclaimed water. Of the 134 bgd withdrawn for irrigation purposes, 61% goes to consumptive uses, 20% becomes return flow to surface water and groundwater supplies, and 19% is lost in conveyance.[5]

The practice of irrigation dates back 6,000 years to the Sumerians, members of one of the earliest known civilizations in Mesopotamia. Through the ages, irrigation has transformed many sunny and fertile but arid regions of the world into useful, crop-producing lands. For 2,000 years, Sumerian farmers produced wheat and barley with irrigation water diverted from the Euphrates River.[6] The great food-producing regions of California's Central Valley, the Great Plains of the western United States, northern China, Egypt, and northwest India are just a few dramatic examples of the power of irrigation to coax life out of dry, sun-baked soil.

Many factors affect agricultural water use, including the price of water, water availability and allocations, climate, crop water requirements, soil, type of irrigation system used, the irrigator's ability to control the application of water, and physical characteristics of the farm. Major factors affecting water loss include temperature, wind, and humidity. In the future, the effects of climate change on agriculture—some beneficial, some damaging—may influence water use by this sector.

Defining Agricultural Beneficial Water-Use Efficiency

Agricultural irrigation efficiency is defined many ways, often emphasizing the efficiency of different elements of the irrigation process. Simply put, it can be characterized as crop yield per unit of water use. Inversely, this relationship can be expressed as the amount of water needed to produce a unit of crop yield. More complex definitions of agricultural irrigation water-use efficiency consider factors that affect yield, such as rainfed or dryland farming practices, fertility, crop variety, pest control, soil moisture at planting, planting density, row spacing, and harvest date. Irrigation efficiency can be measured at various lev-

Perhaps one of the greatest challenges for irrigated agriculture is the fact that many irrigation projects have a deficit of irrigation water, while simultaneously having other amounts of irrigation water going to unreasonable or non-beneficial uses."

—Charles M. Burt, Director, Irrigation Training and Research Center, California Polytechnic State University, San Luis Obispo, California

---

* Water used for livestock purposes (dairies, feedlots, fish farms) and other farm applications represents a very small portion of total agricultural demand and is not considered here.

Declining Ogallala Aquifer Threatens Farming on the U.S. High Plains

The Ogallala Aquifer, North America's largest underground water supply and the source of about 20% of all irrigation water pumped in the United States, continues its seemingly irrevocable decline after years of overpumping. The Ogallala lies under the U.S. High Plains, which encompass nearly 210,000 square miles of prime arable land in parts of Texas, Oklahoma, Kansas, Nebraska, Colorado, and New Mexico. This highly productive agricultural region includes some 10.4 million acres that are irrigated with water derived primarily from the Ogallala. But more than 60 years of intensive pumping by farmers and ranchers on the High Plains has resulted in dramatic decreases in well yields and is now threatening the viability of many farming operations and ultimately the entire economy of this vital region.[7] Although depletion of the Ogallala is most pronounced in Texas and least serious in Nebraska, individual farms throughout the region have been forced to abandon irrigation because of lack of available water. Unlike renewable aquifers, the Ogallala is considered nonrechargeable because it is overlain primarily by rock that is impervious to percolation of rainwater. The amount of recharge that occurs in certain areas is so small (about 1 inch per year) in comparison with the rate of withdrawal that it cannot delay the aquifer's decline. Essentially, the water being pumped out is not being replaced. Droughts in the early 1990s caused water levels to decline at the steepest rate since the early 1980s.[8] More recently, those declines have slowed somewhat. In 2000, the Ogallala Formation was reported to contain 106 million acre-feet (acre-ft) of water; this amount is expected to decline to 84 million acre-ft by 2020 and to 61 million acre-ft by 2050.[9] Although some water districts, such as the High Plains Underground Water Conservation District No. 1 in Lubbock, Texas, are implementing aggressive water conservation programs to mitigate depletion, others are not. If depletion is allowed to continue, the Ogallala at some point may no longer contain sufficient water to satisfy future agricultural irrigation needs.

els—for a farm, an irrigation project or network, or an entire river basin.[10] This chapter focuses on measures designed to improve on-farm irrigation efficiency.

Efficient use of agricultural irrigation water is defined here as the reduction of on-farm water use through improved irrigation technologies and efficient water-management practices. The efficiency of on-farm water use, before and after conservation measures are implemented, is always less than 100% because some portion of the water applied to a field is unavailable to crops because of farm and weather conditions (e.g., evaporation) that cannot be completely overcome. Expressed as an equation, on-farm irrigation efficiency (IE) is often defined simply as the ratio of applied irrigation water used beneficially to produce a crop to total applied water, expressed as a percentage:[11]

$$IE = \frac{Volume\ of\ Irrigation\ Water\ Beneficially\ Used}{Volume\ of\ Irrigation\ Water\ Applied} \times 100$$

Beneficially used water is the amount of irrigation water that satisfies a portion or all of the following plant and soil needs: evapotranspiration (ET), leaching requirements, and moisture stored in the soil for use by crops. The ET represents water lost to the atmosphere by evaporation from the soil surface and by transpiration from plants. The leaching requirement is the amount of water required to flush enough accumulated salts downward out of the crop root zone to maintain full crop productivity.[12] For on-farm purposes, water not used beneficially by a crop may be considered inefficiently used or wasted. However, this "lost" water may be beneficially reused on another nearby field or farm.

Not All Farm Water "Waste" Is Lost

Measuring on-farm irrigation efficiencies is different from measuring other agricultural water-use efficiencies. Water "wasted" or "lost" on one farm may be reused on a nearby farm or field that is hydrologically connected to the land originally irrigated. These differences can be important for decision-makers who

Irrigated U.S. agricultural acreage by irrigation method-percent

Microirrigation (Drip), 4%

Surface (Gravity), 50%

Sprinkler, 46%

Source: Adapted from Reference 14

Figure 5.1 The majority of U.S. agricultural irrigation depends on surface and sprinkler systems, with only a small portion utilizing highly-efficient microirrigation methods.

formulate water allocation and transfer policies, because traditional measurements of agricultural irrigation water-use efficiency have been challenged in recent years for ignoring the role of return flows—irrigation runoff and seepage—that reenter the water supply. Keller and Keller have proposed the concept of "effective efficiency" (E_e) for water resource decision-making:

$$E_e = U_{ci} / U_e$$

in which U_{ci} is the irrigation water consumed by crops, and U_e is the effective use of water (or the effective inflow minus the effective outflow). According to Keller and Keller, the concept of E_e "takes into account both the quantity and quality of the water delivered from and returned to a basin's water supply when estimating the total freshwater input for each use cycle."[13]

Efficiency of Agricultural Irrigation Technologies

There are three basic types of irrigation technology: surface (gravity) irrigation, sprinkler irrigation, and microirrigation. Worldwide, approximately 85 to 90% of irrigation systems are surface systems, 10 to 15% are sprinklers, and drip systems (a form of microirrigation) make up 1%.[1] Farmers in the United States most commonly use surface irrigation (50%), although sprinkler (46%) and drip (4%) irrigation are becoming more popular,[14] as shown in Figure 5.1.

Potential on-farm irrigation efficiencies typically range from 40 to 85% for gravity systems, from 60 to 98% for sprinkler systems, and from 80 to 95% for microirrigation,[14–17] as shown in Table 5.1. To achieve potential on-farm efficiency for each irrigation system, appropriate system selection and design and proper management are critical.

The efficiency of agricultural irrigation in the United States has improved since the late 1960s. For example, the total area of U.S. irrigated cropland has increased by approximately 30% since 1969, but field-irrigation application rates decreased by about 15% between 1968 and 1998.[4]

Factors That Influence On-Farm Irrigation Efficiency

On-farm irrigation efficiency is influenced not only by the type of irrigation system used but also by several other factors including the irrigator's ability to control the application of water, the physical characteristics of the farm, and the irrigation requirements of individual crops.

APPLICATION OF WATER   A farmer's ability to control the application of irrigation water is influenced by the following factors:

- *Distribution uniformity.* Distribution uniformity (DU) is a measure of the variation in the amount of water applied to the soil surface throughout an irrigation area and in the amount of water that infiltrates into the soil across a field. Thus it is the primary indicator of an irrigation system's efficiency.

TABLE 5.1

Field application water-use efficiencies of agricultural irrigation systems

Irrigation System	Potential On-Farm Efficiency[*] *percent*
Gravity (Surface)	
Improved gravity[†]	75–85
Furrow	55–70
Flood	40–50
Sprinklers	
Low energy precision application (LEPA)[‡]	90–98
Center pivot[§]	70–85
Sideroll	60–80
Solid set	65–80
Hand-move	60–65
Big gun	60–65
Microirrigation	
Drip	80–95

[*] Efficiencies shown assume appropriate irrigation system selection, correct irrigation design, and proper management.

[†] Includes tailwater recovery, precision land leveling, and surge flow systems

[‡] LEPA application efficiencies in the 95 to 98% range are possible when surface runoff and deep percolation are negligible.

[§] Includes high- and low-pressure center pivot

Sources: References 14–17, and 88

Expressed as a percentage, DU is calculated by dividing the average depth of infiltration in the quarter of the field where the smallest amount of infiltration occurs by the average depth of total infiltration. The DU concept can be applied to all irrigation systems and should be comparable if measured correctly. Natural rainfall has a DU of 100%, but irrigation systems cannot achieve a perfect DU so irrigators must compensate for underirrigation of any section of a field by applying additional water to attain full coverage.[11] Although irrigation systems have demonstrated a range of DUs, 80% appears to be a reasonable and attainable target on average. As irrigation design and technology advance, DUs up to 90% may be achievable in the future.[18]

- *Evaporation.* Evaporation and water losses vary according to type of irrigation system. Open ditches and flooded fields, as shown in Figure 5.2, experience evaporative losses ranging from 10 to 40%. The efficiency of sprinkler irrigation systems is particularly affected by evaporation because these systems spray water high up into the air, creating droplets that either evaporate quickly or drift away with the wind. Evaporative and drift losses from sprinkler systems can be as high as 50%.[19]

- *Salinity buildup.* Dissolved salts are present in all river water and groundwater. Because plants extract almost pure water from the soil, salts remain in the root zone. If salinity buildup is beyond a crop's salt-tolerance threshold, it can damage the soil to the point of adversely affecting the crop's yield and reducing the land's productivity. According to international water resources expert Sandra Postel, one in five units of irrigated farmland worldwide suffers from salt buildup. In the United States, 23% of irrigated farmland has been damaged by salt.[20] For example, in the Central Valley of California—America's premier fruit and vegetable basket—heavy irrigation over several decades has caused high salt concentrations in shallow groundwater aquifers. As a result, the water quality and productivity of some 2.5 million acres in the region are now at risk.[21] To prevent excessive accumulations of salt in the soil, some incremental amount of water beyond that required for crop ET is needed to pass through the root zone. Davidoff et al have suggested that a leaching requirement of 5% with a DU of 80% may be sufficient to achieve an irrigation efficiency of 80%.[11]

FARM CONDITIONS AND CHARACTERISTICS   The influence of farm conditions and characteristics on the ability of farmers to control the efficiency of their water use is significant, even when the most efficient irrigation technologies are used. These conditions and characteristics include:

- *Water*—availability, reliability of the supply, quantity, quality, method of delivery, evaporation rate, amount of conjunctive use or reuse of deep percolated and runoff water.
- *Economics*—cost of water, crop values, farm and irrigation system capital investments, energy costs, maintenance costs, labor requirements and availability.
- *Crop*—type, water requirements.
- *Climate and weather*—rainfall, temperature, wind, sunlight.
- *Soil*—type, texture, water-holding capacity, drainage characteristics, salinity, variability of types within a field.

- *Field*—size, topography (including slope).
- *Regulatory requirements*—water allocation permit conditions.

CROP IRRIGATION REQUIREMENTS   The water requirements of crops are an essential consideration in the selection of irrigation technology and the adoption of on-farm water-management practices to improve water-use efficiency. Factors that influence a crop's water needs include:

- *Crop characteristics*— type, root depth, stage of development.
- *Crop growth characteristics*—tolerance for moisture depletion.
- *Reference ET*—the ET rate of a reference crop (e.g., pasture grass).
- *Crop coefficient*—the relationship of the ET rate of a particular crop to the reference ET.

These factors are discussed in greater detail in Section 5.3, "Irrigation Scheduling," later in this chapter.

Figure 5.2   High evaporative losses occur when solid-set furrow irrigation patterns leave an entire field exposed to evaporation. Measured water losses in such fields have been as high as 40%. (Photo courtesy of High Plains Underground Water Conservation District No. 1, Lubbock, Texas)

Agricultural Irrigation Systems: How They Work

An understanding of the design and operation of the three types of irrigation methods can elucidate their applicability, potential water-use efficiencies, and advantages and disadvantages.

Conventional flood and furrow surface systems, used since irrigation began thousands of years ago, typically have irrigation efficiencies of 40 to 70%, but improvements such as tailwater recovery and surge-flow valves can boost surface system efficiencies up to 85%. Most other sprinkler technologies are more efficient than gravity systems because they distribute water more evenly, reducing percolation and runoff. Drip systems, a type of microirrigation, use small tubes to emit water directly into the plant root zone, minimizing evaporation and eliminating runoff and deep percolation. When properly managed, drip systems achieve efficiencies as high as 95%.[1, 14] Despite the high efficiencies that are achievable with microirrigation systems, they serve only a tiny portion of total irrigated area in the United States. However, their use is more widespread in countries such as Cyprus, Israel, and Jordan.[25]

Surface (Gravity) Irrigation

Surface or gravity systems are the oldest, most common irrigation method; in fact, until the twentieth century, they were the only irrigation method used. As diesel pumps and electricity became available in rural areas, pressurized irrigation systems came into use. In the United States, half of total irrigated farmland is still watered by surface methods.[14] Conventional surface methods typically have the lowest water-use efficiencies of any irrigation system, ranging from 40 to 70% for most systems.[14] Surface methods include flood and furrow irrigation and are sometimes considered to include subirrigation (or seepage) systems. Surface irrigation typically involves pumping water to the upper end of a field via a ditch or pipe so that enough head is created to allow water to flow by gravity across the field's surface. Flood irrigation involves flooding the entire surface of the field, starting at the top and moving downward and laterally, so there is enough water to reach the bottom of the field and to soak into the root zone there. Furrow irrigation entails pumping water to the top of the field and then channeling it along shallow furrows or trenches between parallel crop rows running down the field.

Gravity irrigation techniques are often favored over other methods because they are typically the least expensive to install and involve lower pumping costs (if any) per unit of water, even though they are usually the least efficient. With the application of advanced surface technologies and management practices, however, efficiencies of 85% can be obtained.[26]

INEFFICIENCIES OF SURFACE SYSTEMS   Three principal water-use inefficiencies are associated with conventional flood and furrow surface systems. The first is lack of uniform water absorption across the field or along the furrows. Because surface irrigation works on the principle of gravity, soil at the upper end of the field absorbs a considerable amount of water before the flow reaches the lower end, preventing soil along the entire length of the furrow or field from having an equal opportunity to retain water. Farmers often must apply excessive amounts of water at the upper end of the field to ensure that crops at the lower end receive sufficient water. As a result, water is not absorbed uniformly. This phenomenon often creates a second inefficiency—excessive runoff. Once water reaches the bottom of the furrow, excess water runs off at the tail end of the field, creating tailwater playas or pools of water that cause deep percolation beyond the crop root zone at the lower end of the field. The third problem with gravity methods is water losses caused by deep percolation and evaporation, as shown in Figure 5.3.

The water efficiency of surface irrigation systems can be improved primarily through better distribution of water along furrows and across fields. Four of the most effective strategies to increase the efficiency of gravity systems are furrow diking, surge flow valves, tailwater reuse, and laser leveling, all described later in this chapter under the section "Agricultural Water-Efficiency Measures."

Sprinkler Irrigation

In the United States, approximately 46% of total irrigated farmland is watered by sprinkler methods. Both conventional and state-of-the-art sprinkler irrigation systems are generally more water- and labor-efficient than gravity methods. Water-use efficiencies of sprinkler irrigation systems range from 60 to 98%.[14] Sprinkler irrigation systems discharge water through the air from sprinkler heads or spray nozzles mounted on pressurized distribution pipes (laterals). Most sprinkler systems depend on pumps to distribute water and to operate sprinkler heads. In some locations where the elevation of the water source is high enough above the irrigated area, gravity may provide the pressure needed to operate the system. The amount and rate of water application vary according to the particular system used.

Sprinkler systems can be classified into three types, based on how the laterals are operated:

- *Fixed sprinklers* are permanently installed and require sufficient lateral piping and sprinkler heads to cover an entire field. Laterals are buried or placed on the

Fields irrigated by gravity-flow systems are generally rectangular, with water runs typically ranging from one-eighth to one-half mile in length. Gravity systems are best suited to medium- and fine-textured soils with higher moisture-holding capacities; field slope should be minimal and fairly uniform to permit controlled advance of water. The predominance of gravity systems in arid regions of the West reflects early project development on broad, flat alluvial plains.

—Economic Research Service, U.S. Department of Agriculture

Figure 5.3 Open-ditch irrigation with siphon tubes, a common method of gravity irrigation, supplies water to fields by siphoning it from a ditch. Water losses caused by deep percolation and evaporation from these open, unlined ditches range from 10 to 30% per 1,000 feet in the High Plains region of Texas. In this region, about 5,000 gallons of water per foot of ditch are lost during a typical 2,000-hour irrigation season. (Photo courtesy of High Plains Underground Water Conservation District No. 1, Lubbock, Texas)

field's surface. Most fixed sprinklers have small sprinklers spaced 30 to 80 feet apart; large "gun" or hydraulic-type sprinklers are spaced 100 to 160 feet apart.[27]

- *Periodically moving* sprinklers are similar to fixed systems except that they consist only of enough laterals and sprinklers to irrigate a portion (or set) of the field at a time. To irrigate the entire field, the laterals and sprinklers must periodically be moved from one set to another. *Hand-move* sprinklers use portable laterals that are supplied with water from movable or buried mains. Laterals for hand-move sprinklers are typically made of aluminum tubing that is easily coupled and uncoupled, although labor requirements for these sprinklers can be high. *End-tow* lateral sprinklers are similar to the hand-move type except that their pipe sections are rigidly coupled and usually must be towed from set to set by a tractor. *Sideroll* laterals are also rigidly coupled, but a large wheel supports each section of pipe. The lateral line serves as an axle for the wheels and can be rotated from set to set. Sideroll systems can be moved mechanically by an engine placed at the center of the lateral or by an outside power source placed at the end of the line.[27]

- *Continuously moving* sprinklers apply water to the field as they move. A *center pivot* irrigator, the most common moving sprinkler system, requires an underground pipeline to transport water to the point of application. These systems, which usually rotate around a groundwater well, help to eliminate losses from deep percolation and evaporation by eliminating the use of open, unlined ditches. Center pivot sprinklers have a lateral that is fixed at one end (the pivot point), where it connects to the water supply; the other end of the lateral is rotated to irrigate a large circular area. Water is pumped into the pipe at the center of the field, and as the pipeline rotates, sprinkler nozzles mounted on the pipeline distribute water under pressure to the field. This basic design has been adapted into both high-pressure (45 to 100 pounds per square inch [psi]) and low-pressure (15 to 45 psi) systems. The *traveler* system uses a big gun sprinkler, moves in a straight line, and is supplied with high-pressure water by a flexible hose.

- *Lateral-move* (or linear-move) sprinklers are self-propelled and combine the structure of the center pivot system with a water-feed system similar to that of the traveler, except that it operates at lower pressures.[14]

Compared with gravity systems, sprinkler irrigation systems distribute water more evenly and give irrigators more control over the irrigation schedule and the amount of water applied. In these ways, sprinkler systems help to reduce runoff and percolation below the crop root zone. However, they require significantly higher capital outlays and energy than gravity systems. Although the center pivot design is commonly used in many irrigated areas of the United States,[14] newer and more efficient sprinkler systems include the *low energy precision application (LEPA)* center pivot system, which delivers water near plant roots through drag hoses and drag socks. When used with furrow dikes, the LEPA system has the potential to achieve irrigation efficiencies up to about 95%, possibly 98%, as reported in the 15-county High Plains Underground Water Conservation District No. 1 service area in Texas.[28]

INEFFICIENCIES OF SPRINKLER SYSTEMS Sprinkler systems, like other irrigation technologies, cannot apply water with perfect efficiency. Continuously moving systems generally apply water more uniformly than periodically moving and fixed systems because the traveling speed of continuously moving systems limits the amount of water applied. However, the amount of water applied is not the sole determinant of uniformity of application. Generally, distribution uniformity is enhanced by uniform conditions—i.e., uniform wind conditions, uniform spray patterns, correct type and placement of sprinklers, and so on. But water-use inefficiencies associated with sprinkler systems include losses caused by evaporation and wind drift, often as a result of water being discharged in small droplets at high angles and great heights. More water is typically lost from sprinkler systems on hot, dry days than on cool, cloudy, and humid days. Sprinkler irrigation efficiencies are also reduced by nonuniform application of water, often caused by improper sprinkler selection, unmatched spacing and operating pressures, manufacturing variations in components, and clogged and enlarged nozzles.

The efficiency of sprinkler irrigation can be improved primarily by using LEPA center pivot systems, typically the most water- and energy-efficient sprinkler systems available. For a more detailed description of LEPA systems, see Section 5.6, "Low Energy Precision Application," later in this chapter.

Sprinkler irrigation systems have the highest acreage concentrations in the Pacific Northwest and Northern Plains, and they are also used extensively for supplemental irrigation and specialty-crop irrigation in Eastern States.

—Economic Research Service, U.S. Department of Agriculture

Microirrigation

About 4%, or approximately 3 million acres, of U.S. farmland is irrigated by microirrigation. Because microirrigation systems water only a small portion of the soil, they can achieve the highest irrigation efficiencies, including efficiencies up to about 95%.[14] Drip irrigation, the most commonly used type of microirrigation, is the frequent application of small quantities of water at low pressure on or below the soil surface around the plant root zone. Microirrigation systems apply water in drops, tiny streams, or miniature spray patterns; the water is delivered through emitters or applicators from plastic tubing placed next to the root zone.

Three basic types of microirrigation systems are available:

- *Drip* (or *trickle*) irrigation uses tubing and emitters to water plants close to the root zone and is the most widely used microirrigation system by crop type. *Subsurface drip irrigation* uses drip systems with tubing and emitters that are buried below the soil surface.
- *Bubbler irrigation* releases small streams of water to form pools on the soil surface, such as the area around trees. Bubbler system water outlets and discharge rates are larger than those of drip or subsurface systems.
- *Microspray* (or *mist)* irrigation, used primarily for orchard and citrus crops, consists of miniature sprinklers that apply water as a small spray or mist.

In addition to its potential for high water-use efficiency, microirrigation offers several other advantages including increased yields, enhanced water penetration into problem soils, reduced weed growth on unwatered areas, adaptability for use in uneven terrain, ability to be automated, and reduced farm operation and maintenance costs. For many farmers, higher yields are the primary benefit of microirrigation. Because microirrigation generally requires higher capital costs (about $500 to $1,000 per acre) than other irrigation systems, it may be most cost-effective on high-value crops such as citrus and deciduous fruits, nuts, vineyard grapes, and certain landscaping plants. Drip irrigation, which was introduced into the United States in the 1970s, is becoming more widespread in Texas, Florida, and California and is frequently used for high-value crops such as fruits and vegetables in areas with sandy soils, uneven terrain, and high water costs.[29] In some circumstances, it has also proved effective in irrigating sugar cane and cotton, both relatively thirsty, widely cultivated crops.[30]

Despite the larger capital outlays required for microirrigation systems, a relatively new, low-cost drip irrigation system designed for use on small farms in developing countries is gaining attention. Developed by International Development Enterprises, a nonprofit organization based in Lakewood, Colorado, these low-cost drip systems with moveable dripper lines and other features reduce costs to about $100 per acre, a reduction of up to 90%.[31] A simple foot pump, called the treadle pump, which costs $35, and a $5 drip and sprinkler bucket kit for gardens offer poor farms an opportunity to access water and to irrigate food crops efficiently.[1]

DISADVANTAGES OF MICROIRRIGATION SYSTEMS   Some disadvantages of microirrigation include the need for a reliable, sometimes continuous, water supply; the need for site-specific designs that suit crops and local soil and climate conditions; and the need for filtration to avoid emitter clogging, which can sometimes impede water discharge and application uniformity. Once a subsurface drip system is installed, it is difficult to rotate crops that have different spacing requirements. In addition, disposing of old drip tapes, lines, and components adds to solid waste disposal burdens and can be an environmental issue.

Sources of Agricultural Water Waste

Inefficient irrigation technology and practices, as well as the institutionally protected status—political, legal, and economic—of agricultural water use throughout many parts of the world have created the false perception among some farmers and landowners that water resources exist unconstrained and practically free for the taking. In particular, governmental subsidies for irrigation water distort market water prices by hiding the true cost of water delivery, creating a strong disincentive for efficient water use. This situation contributes to water shortages and conflicts over allocations, both of which are becoming commonplace in a number of regions and countries with growing populations, including many prime growing regions in the western United States.[32]

Inefficient use of water for agricultural irrigation also contributes to other adverse environmental effects such as soil waterlogging and erosion, silting, salinity, water contamination, groundwater overpumping, plant diseases, waterborne human diseases, and wildlife habitat degradation. In some cases, these problems have rendered otherwise productive land exhausted, depleted of nutrients, and ultimately useless. "Worldwide, an estimated 150 million hectares [371 million acres]—nearly two thirds of the world's total irrigated area—needs some form of upgrading to remain in good working order,"[33] notes Sandra Postel, director of the Global Water Policy Project, based in Amherst, Massachusetts, and author of *Last Oasis*[34] and *Pillar of Sand*.[35] "The biggest gains for the foreseeable future," Postel adds, "will come from irrigating crops more efficiently."[36]

Advances in Agricultural Water-Use Efficiency

Estimates indicate that potential water savings from improved agricultural water management and irrigation systems can be as much as 50%.[1] Improvements can be achieved through the use of more efficient irrigation technology, such as drip and LEPA systems, as well as on-farm water-management practices including water measurement (metering), soil-moisture monitoring, improved irrigation scheduling, tailwater reuse, conservation tillage, canal and conveyance system lining and management, laser leveling, and limited-irrigation, dryland farming. In some cases, better irrigation management practices, not necessarily new technology, are the key to increased water-use efficiency and reduced drainage on farms. Finally, incentives—educational, financial, and regulatory—can play a role in encouraging farmers and irrigators to use water more efficiently.[40,41] Example options for improving the productivity of agricultural irrigation water are listed in Table 5.2.

Innovative agricultural programs sponsored by regional, state, and federal water suppliers and agencies, as well as conservation incentives, are discussed in the following sections.

For the last half-century, agriculture's principal challenge has been raising land productivity — getting more crops out of each hectare of land. As we move into the twenty-first century, the new frontier is boosting water productivity—getting more benefit from every liter of water devoted to crop production."

—Sandra Postel,
Pillar of Sand

TABLE 5.2

Options for improving agricultural on-farm irrigation efficiency and crop productivity

Category	Options
Institutional	Conservation coordinator
	Conservation plan and program
	Policies for efficient on-farm water use and penalties for inefficient use
Educational	On-farm water audits
	Field and workshop training programs
	Training materials, workbooks, and software
	Newsletters and periodicals
	Internet information networks and listservs
Financial	Conservation-oriented pricing
	Water marketing
	Low-interest loans
	Grants and rebates for purchase of more efficient irrigation equipment and tools
Managerial	On-farm water measurement (metering)
	Soil moisture monitoring
	Irrigation scheduling
	Evapotranspiration rates and other data from weather station networks
	Tailwater reuse
	Conservation tillage
	Canal and conveyance system lining and management
	Limited irrigation/dryland farming
	Deficit irrigation
Technical	Laser-graded land leveling to allow more uniform application of water
	Furrow diking to promote soil infiltration and minimize runoff
	Low energy precision application (LEPA) to reduce water losses from evaporation and wind drift
	Surge irrigation to spread irrigation applications uniformly
	Drip irrigation to reduce water losses from evaporation, increase crop yields, and reduce chemical and energy use
Agronomic	Enhanced precipitation capture (rainwater harvesting)
	Reduced evaporation through improved use of crop residues, conservation tillage, and plant spacing
	Sequencing crops to optimize yields, given soil and water salinity conditions
	Selection of native and drought-tolerant crops to match climate conditions and water quality
	Breeding of water-efficient crop varieties

Sources: Adapted from References 40 and 41

Innovative Agricultural Conservation Programs

The potential for agricultural water-use efficiency has increased significantly in recent years, thanks to improved irrigation technologies and innovative on-farm water-management practices developed in response to water shortages, competition for limited supplies, increasing costs, and other factors. In the United States, several agricultural water suppliers stand out for their exemplary on-farm water conservation programs and results; one of these is the High Plains Underground Water Conservation District No. 1 in Lubbock, Texas. For many years, the High Plains Water District has sponsored pioneering on-farm research and pilot projects, working with farmers who draw water from the Ogallala Aquifer, a vast but diminishing underground source of water that irrigates many farms in the breadbasket region of the American Midwest. *The Cross Section*, a monthly publication produced by the water district, provides information about the value of efficient agricultural water-management practices and technology as well as practical guidance about their implementation.

USE OF RECYCLED WATER FOR AGRICULTURAL IRRIGATION   The use of recycled and reclaimed water for agricultural irrigation is gaining momentum in the United States and other countries. Some California farmers use secondary-treated wastewater on fodder and fiber crops and tertiary-treated water on fruit and vegetable crops. For example, walnut farms in Visalia, California,

---

Pricing Agricultural Water: Incentives and Disincentives for Conservation

The relationship between the cost of agricultural water and the efficiency of its use has attracted growing interest in recent years. Increasing the unit cost of water has proved to be a strong incentive for some urban water users to conserve, but so far pricing has not been a very effective tool with farmers. There are several reasons for this, including the complexities of how agricultural water rights have been established and how water is allocated to farms, particularly in the western United States. Using pricing as a conservation incentive in the agricultural sector is not always a simple task. In some cases, farmers have long-standing contracts to purchase a specific volume of water at a fixed price; if they don't use all the water, they risk losing their rights to it in the future (the "use it or lose it" principle) because they have not put their allotment to beneficial use. Regional water districts do not always recoup the true cost of water delivery through the rates they charge their agricultural irrigation customers. Furthermore, many irrigation systems are not metered, compounding the challenge of charging for water based on use.[37]

Water authorities and elected officials who establish water pricing structures must strike a balance between achieving demand reductions through pricing strategies, such as tiered (inclining or inverted) rates that charge more per additional unit of water used, with the need to ensure that all growers have affordable access to supplies. An example of tiered pricing would be to charge one rate for up to 80% of a contract's total allocation, a second, higher rate if the irrigator uses 80 to 90% of the allocation, and a third, even higher, rate for use of more than 90% of the allocation.[38, 39]

Studies of U.S. irrigators have shown that demand for water is usually price-inelastic—meaning that price is not a significant factor in how much water irrigators use, assuming that the amount is within reasonable bounds for agricultural water use. The primary reason for this is that the cost of water usually constitutes only a small part of the cost of growing crops. The value of crops, not water prices, typically dictates the economics of crop production, although this varies to some degree. For agricultural water users who pump their own supplies, using water efficiently—in terms of crop yield and energy requirements (for pumping) per unit of water applied—has long been a smart business practice.[38] Water costs as a percentage of total production costs varied significantly among 13 crops studied in the Tulare Lake Region of California. For example, average water costs for dry onions, almonds, pistachios, processing tomatoes, and wine grapes comprised less than 10% of the farmers' total costs for those crops; water costs for alfalfa hay, barley, dry beans, wheat, cotton, sugar beets, and safflower constituted 11 to 19% of total costs; and water costs for irrigated pastures accounted for as much as 36% of total costs.[39]

In California, the Colorado River Basin, and some other water-short regions, new approaches to pricing and allocating irrigation water are gaining ground. In addition to tiered pricing strategies, new allocation approaches include water marketing—which enables farmers to purchase, sell, and trade water based on their irrigation needs—and water banking, which enables one farmer to "deposit" unused water in a bank for another farmer to rent at a price that is profitable for the depositor. Chile and Mexico, in particular, are promoting water marketing.[37]

rely on treated wastewater supplied via percolation ponds for some of their irrigation supplies.[42] The city of Santa Rosa, California, has embarked on a major project called "The Geysers," which will use treated wastewater to irrigate grapes, pasture, and other crops for half of the year. During the other six months, an average of 11 million gallons per day of water not needed for irrigation will be used to recharge aquifers underlying The Geysers geothermal field in the Mayacamas Mountains; the geothermal field produces steam used in the process of generating electricity.[43]

CALIFORNIA'S EFFICIENT WATER MANAGEMENT PRACTICES At a statewide level, the California Department of Water Resources (DWR), which sponsors the California Irrigation Management Information System (CIMIS) and numerous other on-farm programs and publications, has also helped to advance understanding about the value of efficient agricultural irrigation and the tools necessary for farmers to put such ideas into practice. In response to state legislation, DWR and the California Urban Water Conservation Council, along with others, developed 17 voluntary Efficient Water Management Practices (EWMPs) for agricultural water suppliers (as outlined in Appendix H, *Efficient Water Management Practices for Agricultural Water Suppliers in California*) for the more than 30 agricultural water agencies that have signed California's 1996 Agricultural Memorandum of Understanding. These agencies provide water for about 3 million acres of irrigated farmland.[44]

Federal Focus on Agricultural Water Conservation

Nationally, the U.S. Bureau of Reclamation has in recent years concentrated more on building water efficiency than dams, a departure from the past. The bureau's new focus reflects goals such as reducing the high capital and energy costs associated with development of new water supplies and minimizing the negative environmental impact of diverting instream flows. In the western states, the bureau has initiated several conservation programs that address agricultural water use. In 1997, the bureau established the voluntary Water Conservation Field Services Program (WCFSP) to provide water districts and farmers with technical assistance and funding to help them improve their water-use efficiency. The WCFSP also sponsors local demonstration projects on innovative and effective on-farm conservation measures, such as improved water measurement, appropriate use of automation and telemetry, new approaches to minimizing canal and ditch seepage, and on-farm irrigation-management methods.[45]

Incentives for Agricultural Water Conservation

Educational, economic, and policy or regulatory incentives are often effective in encouraging farmers to adopt efficient irrigation technologies and on-farm water-management practices. Some incentives that water suppliers can use to promote conservation in the agricultural sector are described in this section.

Educational Incentives

Educational incentives in the form of public information about conservation as well as direct technical assistance can give farmers and irrigators useful information explaining why and how improving water-use efficiency is beneficial.[46]

DISSEMINATE INFORMATION ABOUT THE BENEFITS OF CONSERVATION Farmers and irrigators need specific information about the financial and environmental benefits of water conservation. Conservation information can be provided in a variety of formats including newsletters, other printed materials, workshops, and videos tailored to specific conservation needs and measures. Such materials tend to be most effective when they focus on how improving irrigation efficiency benefits farmers, particularly through economic benefits.

PRESENT ON-FARM DEMONSTRATIONS A farmer's decision to invest in a more efficient irrigation system can be complex. Among the many factors to be considered are potential water savings, investment costs and financing options, cost-effectiveness and payback period, and changes in labor requirements, field operations, crop yields, and chemigation or herbigation needs. On-farm demonstrations of efficient irrigation equipment, scheduling techniques, and management practices offer area farmers working information on conservation options that they can evaluate themselves. For example, the Texas High Plains Underground Water Conservation District No. 1 regularly sponsors field demonstration days at local farms to demonstrate efficiency technologies and practices (including water-use monitoring tools and efficiency assessment methods) and to allow irrigation equipment manufacturers to offer information about their products.[47]

PROVIDE DIRECT TECHNICAL ASSISTANCE TO FARMERS Direct technical assistance offering farm-specific evaluations and suggestions for improving the water-use efficiency of irrigation systems and farm practices gives farmers customized information about conservation benefits and costs. This type of assistance can be provided by water conservation specialists employed by water supply districts and agencies as well as consultants. Direct technical assistance usually includes information about weather, soil moisture-holding capacity, crop ET, other crop characteristics, irrigation scheduling, water-use planning, suggested approaches to water-management problems, and financial incentives available to help fund water-efficiency improvements.

Economic Incentives

The strongest incentives for water-use efficiency in the agricultural sector have often been economic—for example, charging the true cost of water delivery, establishing conservation-oriented pricing structures, and providing financial assistance to help farmers implement conservation measures.

CHARGE THE TRUE COST OF WATER DELIVERY Agricultural water allocation and use, particularly in many irrigated areas in the western United States, often follow historical allotment practices and permits rather than market prices. The cost of water from federal irrigation projects is often subsidized by the government (taxpayers), reducing incentives for efficient water use. When the price of water reflects its true cost, the charges include all supplier costs, such

The most cost-effective means for expanding or getting more benefit from [a] developed supply is usually demand reduction and increasing water use efficiency."
—Jack Keller, professor emeritus of Agricultural and Irrigation Engineering, Utah State University, Logan, Utah

as wholesale water purchases, the cost of energy (for pumping and distribution) and chemicals, and the capital, maintenance, and labor expenses associated with water delivery.[46]

Shifting to a pricing strategy that charges the true (unsubsidized) cost of water can serve as a strong financial incentive for farmers to implement conservation measures. Unsubsidized prices also help distribute water costs more equitably and provide a context in which farmers receive realistic feedback about actual water use. Farmers with greater awareness of their water use are likely to learn more about water waste and the actual water needs of crops.[46]

ADOPT CONSERVATION-ORIENTED WATER RATE STRUCTURES   As in other water-use sectors, adoption of conservation-oriented pricing structures for agricultural users sends a strong signal about the value of water: the more you use, the more it's going to cost. Many farmers have historically paid relatively low prices for irrigation water, often at a flat rate. Implementation of alternative tiered or block rate pricing structures often drives such irrigators to apply water more efficiently as they seek ways to contain costs. The degree of response to a new pricing strategy depends to a large extent on the significance of the increase compared with previous prices and on the overall additional cost to the farmer. Tiered rate structures are typically designed to increase the price of water for each incremental block of demand. The design of such structures should factor in leaching requirements, groundwater availability, and crop, soil, climatic, and other conditions specific to a particular area or region. In some cases, water districts use the additional funds collected from conservation pricing strategies to help improve the efficiency of district delivery facilities and for loan programs to help farmers invest in improved irrigation systems.[48] Tiered pricing can also be crop-based, but water districts are sometimes reluctant to influence farmers' decisions about crops through water prices.

PROVIDE FINANCIAL INCENTIVES AND ASSISTANCE   In addition to charging the true cost of water delivery and establishing conservation-oriented pricing structures, water suppliers sometimes offer other economic incentives that irrigators can accept voluntarily. Some water and energy utilities use financial assistance in the form of rebates, grants, equipment giveaways, and low-cost loans to induce farmers to adopt conservation measures. For case studies presenting examples of these programs, see the sidebars entitled "Farm-Efficiency Program Saves Water and Energy" and "Loan Programs Help Irrigators Buy Water Conservation Equipment."

Policy and Regulatory Incentives

Several types of policy and regulatory incentives for agricultural water conservation can also help induce farmers to adopt conservation measures.

ALLOW CHANGES OR FLEXIBILITY IN THE CONTRACT YEAR   Irrigation water suppliers who provide service on the basis of a fixed water year may foster a "use it or lose it" philosophy among farmers, creating a disincentive for conservation. Greater flexibility in the contract year, correlated with the water-use characteristics of crops, can promote more efficient use.

INCREASE THE FLEXIBILITY OF WATER-DELIVERY SCHEDULES Water deliveries to farmers are often limited by problems of access and conveyance and storage system capacity; some water suppliers cannot provide reliable, arranged-demand water delivery. Water-use inefficiencies can be exacerbated when farmers do not receive water when they need it. Operational and delivery system improvements can help farmers improve irrigation efficiencies, although such options may require capital expenditures by the water supplier if significant engineering work is required.

PROMOTE CONJUNCTIVE USE OF GROUNDWATER AND SURFACE WATER SUPPLIES Conjunctive water use involves the operation of a groundwater basin in coordination with a surface water storage system to maximize available supplies. During seasons or years with above-average surface supplies, the groundwater basin is recharged with surface water so that stored water can be withdrawn in dry years when surface supplies are below normal. Although some groundwater recharge occurs through seepage from canals, overapplication of irrigation water, and other sources, unplanned losses should not be considered conjunctive use. To be effective, conjunctive-use programs require adequate recharge and extraction capabilities as well as the equipment and budget to maintain pumps in standby condition.

FACILITATE VOLUNTARY TRANSFERS OF WATER AMONG SUPPLIERS To promote maximum use of available supplies and discourage a "use it or lose it" philosophy, water suppliers can establish internal pooling arrangements through which customers can sell or transfer excess water to others who need it. Suppliers can facilitate such arrangements by removing unnecessary barriers to the voluntary transfer, exchange, or marketing of conserved water.

ADOPT PERFORMANCE GOALS Conservation programs that are driven by goals and monitored for effectiveness are likely to be more effective than less formal programs. Performance goals to achieve water savings can be established for system losses, irrigation efficiency, reduced seepage, improved drainage management, and other agricultural water-management practices.

FACILITATE VOLUNTARY RETIREMENT OF LAND (FROM IRRIGATION) THAT IS NOT ECONOMICALLY FEASIBLE TO FARM Water suppliers can facilitate alternative beneficial uses of water previously used on land that has been retired from irrigation.

ENCOURAGE THE USE OF RECYCLED WATER Use of recycled water that meets applicable health, environmental, and related standards and legal requirements should be encouraged to promote more sustainable use.

Loan Programs Help Irrigators Buy Water Conservation Equipment

Some water suppliers and government agencies offer low-interest loans to farmers who want to purchase improved irrigation systems to optimize water use. For example, the California State Water Resources Control Board, in cooperation with federal agencies, has implemented such a program to serve California farmers,[50] and the High Plains Underground Water Conservation District No. 1 sponsors a similar program in Texas.

Benefits and Costs of Agricultural Water Conservation

In addition to saving water, improved agricultural irrigation efficiency can result in further benefits as well as some costs to farmers, irrigation districts, and the environment. Thus, selection and application of efficiency measures are complex decisions that should take into account the environmental and economic effects of efficient irrigation technologies and water-management practices, particularly as they influence crop production.[26, 34]

Benefits

- Reduced water purchases and costs
- Increased or stabilized available groundwater supplies, well yield, and pumping reliability
- Increased crop productivity (yields)
- Lower energy costs from reduced groundwater pumping
- Reduced runoff and reduced soil erosion, salinity, waterlogging, and nutrient depletion
- Decreased leaching of plant nutrients
- Lower pesticide, herbicide, and fertilizer costs
- Reduced wear and tear on farm equipment such as pumps, filters, irrigation lines, and other water-handling equipment
- Reduced labor costs

Mobile Laboratories Allow Agricultural Field Evaluations

Some water suppliers send technical specialists to work directly with agricultural water users who want to adopt water conservation measures. Some states and a number of water districts have mobile laboratories staffed by trained specialists who conduct field evaluations that measure the efficiency of on-farm irrigation systems, as shown in Figure 5.4. For example, the U.S. Bureau of Reclamation's Water Conservation Field Services Program has funded on-farm irrigation system evaluations in California's Central Valley and other western water districts. With mobile labs, technical staff members can evaluate irrigation system design, maintenance, efficiency (e.g., distribution uniformity), and operations costs. On-site data collection takes three to five hours, after which the staff person prepares a report back at the office and schedules a meeting with the farmer to review the evaluation's findings. Specific recommendations include measures to improve on-farm water management so irrigators can reduce water applications, save energy, improve yields, and resolve drainage and soil erosion problems. The cost per evaluation is about $500 to $750.[51]

Figure 5.4 On-farm testing with a mobile, mini field laboratory can help farmers evaluate the efficiency and distribution uniformity of their irrigation systems. (Photo courtesy of High Plains Underground Water Conservation District No. 1, Lubbock, Texas)

Key Elements of a Successful Agricultural Water Conservation Program

Agricultural water conservation planners who help farmers implement water-efficient irrigation technologies and management practices can boost the effectiveness of their programs through comprehensive outreach strategies designed to gain farmer awareness and acceptance of the program and ultimately participation in it—i.e., adoption of efficiency measures. Based on case studies of successful agricultural conservation programs conducted by the Rocky Mountain Institute,[46] the following outreach approaches have proved to be effective:

- **Create a positive attitude.** The manner in which irrigators are approached about participating in a conservation program is an important component of success. Rather than declaring, "You are doing something wrong," planners are more likely to convince farmers to adopt conservation measures with observations such as: "These new irrigation techniques might work better for you, and here are some reasons why," or "These improved irrigation technologies can save you money and also increase crop yields."

- **Simplify.** A conservation program doesn't have to solve every problem at once. Launching a program that is too big too soon or that fails to give irrigators clear information invites problems and damages future efforts. Expanding an existing program at some later date is always possible.

- **Specify.** Customizing conservation programs to meet the needs of individual farmers is more useful to them than simply disseminating generic information and guidelines about ways to save water on the farm.

- **Demonstrate.** On-farm workshops and demonstrations of conservation technologies and practices are particularly convincing because farmers can see the measures at work. Although statistical information is useful for presenting the results and benefits of efficiency measures, field-testing and demonstrations are critical and often convincing approaches.

- **Use economic arguments.** Farmers are most likely to adopt conservation measures when they understand how the measures will improve the farm's bottom line—e.g., reduced water requirements, lower pumping costs, and increased crop yields. As expressed by A. Wayne Wyatt, former manager of the High Plains Underground Water Conservation District No. 1 in Lubbock, Texas, "The nerve to the hip pocket is mighty sensitive."[46]

- **Contact leading farmers.** Many agricultural communities have farmers who set the standard for farming practices in the region. Working with these leaders first and persuading them to adopt more efficient technologies and practices can enable them to become examples or mentors who convince other farmers to do the same.

- **Build trust in the field.** Conservation program field representatives must be respected in the community they serve if they are to gain farmers' confidence and convince them to accept advice about efficiency practices. Achieving this goal may require training individuals from the community in order to reinforce the local connection.

- Reduced competition for limited supplies, particularly between urban and agricultural use sectors
- Improved water and environmental quality as a result of fewer diversions and reduced agricultural chemical requirements
- Reduced pollution from energy combustion by-products and chemical use

Costs

- Capital outlays for purchasing and installing new equipment
- Increased or different on-farm irrigation-management tasks (e.g., new irrigation technologies, irrigation scheduling changes, and improved on-farm water-management practices that may require retraining farm workers)
- Possible short-term delays in achieving water savings, crop yield increases, and other goals because of the learning curve required to maximize the benefits of conservation measures
- Possible increased soil salinity if irrigation is not managed properly
- Increased irrigation maintenance requirements for some drip systems
- Possible jeopardy of future water allocations under "use it or lose it" water rights policies in some regions unless a new agreement can be reached

Basic Steps in an Agricultural Water Audit

On-farm water audits can help agricultural irrigators better understand their water use as well as the many benefits they can reap by irrigating more efficiently. Some water districts sponsor mobile laboratories that allow agricultural conservation engineers and technicians to provide technical assistance directly on farms. Another effective outreach device is conducting on-farm demonstrations of efficient irrigation systems and practices; farmers who observe such demonstrations may decide to adopt water conservation measures because "seeing is believing."

The basic steps for conducting an audit of agricultural irrigation water use are outlined here.

1. **Explain purpose of audit.** Explain the purpose of conducting the water audit to the irrigator (e.g., to identify ways to save water and energy, boost crop yields, lower farm chemical needs, save money, reduce environmental burdens, and comply with conservation guidelines or policies).

2. **Determine water use.** If the irrigation system is metered, review on-farm water use records as well as crop yields and farm costs.

3. **Identify on-farm conservation measures that have already been implemented.** Assess the results from prior conservation measures that may have been implemented, considering measure installation or application, changes in technology since the measure was applied, and any changes in irrigation system maintenance that may have occurred.

4. **Review irrigation system type, layout, and current irrigation schedule.** Review irrigation system type and design, installation (including upgrades), maintenance practices, irrigation scheduling program, and weather network used.

5. **Evaluate irrigation system efficiency. Perform irrigation system field tests to determine irrigation efficiency.** Measure irrigation system application rate and distribution uniformity. Measure pressure and flow rates in the field. Check the operation of pumps, filters, and emitters or sprinklers. Advance times for surface irrigation systems should be measured at several locations throughout the field. Measure all potential variables affecting the amount of water received by crops across a particular field.

6. **Review crop types, water and energy costs, and other irrigation-related matters.** Review crop selection and crop yields with existing irrigation system(s)and discuss potential improvements with more efficient irrigation systems, including the associated benefits, costs, and installation considerations. Determine effective rainfall, leaching needs, ET, and irrigation water requirements throughout the growing season. Evaluate the energy efficiency of the irrigation system's design and operation, including pumping.

7. **Conduct a water quality test to determine total dissolved solids and the leaching fraction.** Test parameters should include pH, electrical conductivity, nitrate concentrations, and hardness and iron for microirrigation systems.

8. **Identify all appropriate conservation measures for the farm's irriga-**

The complexity of water demands requires that we understand our water sources and water destinations. It is only with a good water balance in hand that we can make good long-term decisions on overall water conservation and management plans."
—Charles M. Burt, Professor and Director, Irrigation Training and Research Center, California Polytechnic State University, San Luis Obispo, California

tion systems, including technology-based and practice-based measures. Typical recommendations may include: replace worn nozzles in sprinklers, use pressure regulators where needed, use media filters for drip irrigation, optimize flow rates and rate of water advance in surface systems, modify irrigation timing and application rates, and install and manage runoff recovery systems for fields.

9. **Give the irrigator a written evaluation that includes observations and recommendations on benefits and costs of recommended measures, irrigation system design, operation, and maintenance.** Estimate capital, installation, and operations costs for each measure as well as the reduced costs and changes in crop yield that are likely to result. Determine the payback period for the investments in recommended measures. In addition to identifying all technological and management conservation measures that would be suitable for the irrigator, provide site-specific irrigation scheduling recommendations, including guidance on how to use recommended software and weather network resources to optimize irrigations. Provide written materials about other available technical assistance, demonstration projects, equipment loans, financial loans, and grant programs that promote agricultural water efficiency.

10. **Plan follow-up visit.** Plan a follow-up visit to review the conservation measures implemented, along with their results, and to identify additional measures that may be appropriate.

Training Programs in Agricultural Irrigation Management and Evaluation

A number of water districts, universities, agencies, and other organizations offer training classes, workshops, courses, and seminars in agricultural irrigation management and technology. Such programs teach skills to irrigation specialists and water conservation program managers as well as farmers. For example, the Irrigation Association based in Falls Church, Virginia, and the Irrigation Training and Research Center of the California Polytechnic State University in San Luis Obispo offer training and certification programs that address agricultural irrigation methods, water delivery system operation, irrigation auditing, irrigation scheduling, and related subjects.

Agricultural Water-Efficiency Measures

This section describes water-efficiency measures—on-farm water-management practices and irrigation technologies—that are applicable to agricultural water use. When appropriate, case studies are provided as examples of the measures as well as the water savings and related benefits and costs they can achieve. The following types of information are provided for each measure:

- *Purpose.* The water-efficient irrigation technology or on-farm water-management practice is described, along with related background information.
- *Water savings, benefits, and costs.* The potential water savings that can be expected from implementation of the measure are discussed, along with associated benefits and costs. In discussions of measures for which only limited data are available, case study examples are sometimes presented in lieu of data. The water savings and related benefits and costs associated with many agricultural water-efficiency measures are extremely site-specific because of the variables in on-farm water use, crop types, growing conditions, and other factors. In some cases, agricultural water-use efficiency is measured by increased crop yields.

5.1 MEASUREMENT OF ON-FARM WATER USE

Accurate measurement of agricultural irrigation water use is essential to determining the efficiency of irrigation technology and on-farm water-management practices. Without some form of measurement, the volume and efficiency of water use cannot be reliably ascertained. Water-efficiency benefits can be derived from the installation and correct sizing and reading of on-farm meters.

Agricultural water supply as well as on-farm irrigation uses can be measured by a variety of devices, including meters, flumes, weirs, electric pump meters, and engine-hour meters. Irrigation meters, often referred to as flow meters, provide the most accurate method of on-farm water measurement. Available in a range of sizes, configurations, and capacities, on-farm flow meters can measure flows from groundwater or surface water sources and can track water from delivery to application in the field. Agricultural meters can be read manually or automatically via remote instrumentation. In general, irrigation meters should register both the *flow rate* and the *total amount* of water applied. An example of a portable agricultural flow meter is provided in Figure 5.5.

The frequency of meter maintenance, repair, and replacement vary according to the particular meter installed and its level of use. Meter accuracy should generally be within about 3% of the true flow rate, although some water districts accept measurements from devices that are less accurate. To ensure accurate meter readings over the life of the meter, agricultural meter selection and ongoing maintenance practices should include:

- Correct meter sizing relative to flow requirements
- Proper meter installation
- Regular meter testing to determine accuracy
- Regular meter maintenance and calibration
- Meter repair or replacement, when necessary

Even when on-farm water use is monitored and quantified with meters, the measurements may not always be recorded accurately. Burt, Clemmens, and Solomon have identified some typical problems that inhibit accurate measurement:[52]

- Inaccurate water measurement device at the source of supply
- No continuous recording of flows, which may vary with time
- Undocumented or poorly documented splitting of flows in irrigation canals
- Poor record-keeping
- Inadequate rainfall records
- Rainfall not separated from irrigation water use

Water Savings, Benefits, and Costs From On-Farm Water Measurement

Water Savings

Water savings derived from accurate measurement of irrigation are indirect in that they provide information that can be used to plan more efficient water

Figure 5.5 Portable flow meters, such as this polysonic meter, can measure how much water is being delivered to farms and irrigation systems. (Photo courtesy of High Plains Underground Water Conservation District No. 1, Lubbock, Texas)

use. For example, farmers can use meter records to calculate the efficiency of an irrigation system compared with past performance, projected performance, expected crop yields per unit of water applied, and other types of irrigation systems. With this information, opportunities to increase system efficiencies can be more readily identified. Similarly, the effectiveness of water pricing strategies that encourage efficient use depends on accurate measurements of water supplied to users. Meter readings of agricultural water deliveries can also help water managers identify the amount of water lost to leaks in conveyance systems; otherwise, these leaks would not be detectable.

Case Study *Meters Help Citrus Growers Reduce Water Flows and Costs.* The Orange Cove Irrigation System, a 28,000-acre agricultural district in California's San Joaquin Valley, supplies water to 500 (mostly citrus) producers in parts of Fresno and Tulare counties. In 1997, after more than 20 years of delivering unmetered water to producers through leaky concrete pipes that allowed water losses of 10 to 14% (from leaks, uncontrolled flows, excessive evaporation, and percolation), the water district installed a new distribution system to increase water-use efficiency, among other goals. The new distribution system comprises 116 miles of piping, 750 flow meters, 750 butterfly valves, and 750 gate valves. Now irrigators can gain access to the system simply by opening a valve (in the past, they had to notify the district in advance when they wanted water to be delivered). Meters used for the project were custom-designed with few moving parts, high corrosion resistance, a water-lubricated, ceramic bearing that is constantly flushed, and a special locking device for the totalizer on each meter. As a result of these improvements, at least one farmer has reduced water costs by 10% without sacrificing any of his citrus crop yield.[53]

Energy Savings

The increased water-use efficiency and decreased system losses associated with meters can reduce the cost of water deliveries and the cost of energy used for pumping. Irrigators who use a pumping plant (engine, gear head, and pump) that is worn out or improperly sized may pay much higher fuel costs than those with properly working equipment. They may also be wasting water by pumping more than is needed. As noted by A. Wayne Wyatt, former manager of the High Plains Underground Water Conservation District in Texas, "Some irrigators may run out of money before they run out of water if they do not become more efficient in the production and distribution of irrigation water. Many irrigators are using pumping plants that are worn out or incorrectly sized for the amount of water they are pumping or the depth from which the water must be lifted. This means they are paying significantly higher fuel costs than they should for each gallon of water pumped. These extra costs, coupled with water lost during irrigation system application (sometimes as much as 40%), will likely result in many farmers having to abandon irrigation."[54]

An energy-use efficiency test should be conducted before any work is done on a pump or pumping plant. The test should measure the yield of the well in volume per minute, the pumping water level, the operating pressure of the delivery system, and the amount of fuel required to produce a unit of water. For example, turbine pumps should be about 75% efficient; electric, vertical hollow-shaft motors should be about 90% efficient; and submersible motors should be approximately

Good water management requires water measurement."
—Marsha Prillwitz, environmental specialist, California Department of Water Resources

80% efficient, according to the Texas High Plains Underground Water Conservation District No. 1. Sources for pumping plant efficiency evaluations may include pump dealers, fuel suppliers, extension services, or water supply districts.[54]

Cost Savings

The cost of each installed flow meter ranges from 200 to $1,750, depending on the size and type of the meter and related installation requirements. Irrigators can obtain assistance with identifying, purchasing, and maintaining agricultural meters from irrigation equipment manufacturers and representatives, water management specialists, and consultants.

5.2 SOIL MOISTURE MONITORING

Soil moisture is the fundamental (and sometimes only) piece of empirical data from which farmers determine crop irrigation requirements, and collecting this information is usually simple and inexpensive. Farmers who know the amount of moisture stored in the soil in their fields—and who use this information in conjunction with weather data and crop ET requirements to schedule irrigations precisely—can help their crops reach optimal yields while using water more efficiently.

The oldest method of measuring soil moisture is the "look and feel" approach, which involves comparing soil samples taken by hand with tables or pictures indicating the moisture characteristics of different soil textures. With practice, adept farmers can produce estimates that are within 5% of actual moisture content. Most irrigators only need to be familiar with the soils and textures of their own fields.[55] Another advantage to this method is that farmers can rapidly test soil moisture at desired locations.

For most farmers, the most precise readings of soil moisture content are collected from soil moisture monitors. A number of monitoring devices and techniques are available to measure the amount of moisture in soil at any given time or depth. Soil moisture monitoring devices can be classified into two general categories: (1) portable monitoring instruments and techniques that do not require extensive field preparation and (2) permanent, or relatively permanent, monitoring installations that take measurements at fixed locations. The three moisture sensors that are most commonly used for irrigation scheduling are gypsum blocks, tensiometers, and neutron probes.

Soil moisture monitoring conducted on a regional basis can give farmers information to help them determine the amount of water they need to apply to avoid over- or underirrigating. For example, an annual preplanting soil moisture survey to determine general soil moisture availability and deficit trends across a 15-county service area is conducted by the Texas High Plains Underground Water Conservation District No. 1 and the US Department of Agriculture's (USDA's) Natural Resources Conservation Service (NRCS). Personnel from the water district and NRCS test soil moisture conditions at approximately 300 semipermanent monitoring sites during the region's preplanting period. Data collected are used to construct maps illustrating the moisture available for plant use within the soil of a 5-foot root zone as well as the amount of water needed to bring the soil to field

*W*ater in the soil resides within soil pores in close association with soil particles. The largest pores transport water to fill smaller pores. After irrigation, the large pores drain due to gravity and water is held by the attraction of small pores and soil particles. Soils with small pores (clayey soils) will hold more water per unit volume than soils with large pores (sandy soils)."

—Terry L. Prichard,
Water Management Specialist,
University of California-Davis

capacity. The maps and results of the preplanting soil moisture survey are provided to producers and local news media prior to the preplanting irrigation season.[56]

Permanent, Fixed-Location Instruments

Four major, fixed-location moisture-monitoring devices are available; of these, gypsum blocks and tensiometers are the most common. Some moisture-sensing devices are connected to computer-controlled irrigation systems that automatically apply water only when it is needed, but these devices are not commonly used.

Gypsum Blocks

Gypsum blocks are widely considered the most practical, most flexible, and least expensive devices available to monitor soil moisture for agricultural purposes. Gypsum blocks rely on the simple principle of electrical resistance—the wetter the gypsum block (and therefore the soil), the lower the resistance. The method involves burying blocks of gypsum or polymer-coated gypsum in root-zone soil at strategic locations throughout the field; the blocks assume the same moisture content as the surrounding soil. The blocks are made by casting an inch-long cylinder of gypsum around two stainless steel electrodes with lead wires connected to a stake at the ground's surface; the wires are coded to indicate the depth at which they are buried. Gypsum blocks have also been used successfully to determine the extent of lateral movement under drip irrigation. Measurement of the flow of electrical resistance through the soil (as measured by a resistance meter), typically expressed in centibars or kilopascals, is translated into a moisture-content reading, which can be used to determine crop irrigation needs. Newer meters give digital readings of the percentage of water-holding capacity in the soil, whereas older meters rely on needle and dial readings.[57-59]

Gypsum blocks are typically installed after crop emergence in sets of three for every 40 acres of irrigated land; they are buried at 1-foot intervals at a depth of 3 to 4 feet. Gypsum blocks work most effectively when used with less water-sensitive crops, such as cotton, grain sorghum, and other small grains. They tend to give inaccurate readings when used with crops (such as rice) that require saturated soil and are therefore not recommended for those applications. They also do not work well with saline soils. Although gypsum blocks are an inexpensive way to determine soil moisture content, their accuracy may vary slightly because of differences in each block's electrical characteristics. New blocks are usually required for each season because gypsum deteriorates.

Granular-Matrix Sensor Blocks

This type of moisture-resistant block, made of a sand–ceramic mixture, may provide greater accuracy than gypsum blocks for measuring soil moisture content greater than 25%. In some instances, it may also be more appropriate than gypsum blocks for scheduling irrigations.[58]

After a complete wetting and time is allowed for the soil to de-water the large pores, a typical soil will have about 50% of the pore space as water and 50% air. This is a condition generally called field capacity or the full point."

—Terry L. Prichard,
Water Management Specialist,
University of California-Davis

Figure 5.6 Devices used to monitor soil moisture include a neutron moisture meter, tensiometers, and gypsum blocks or resistance meters. Monitoring soil moisture helps farmers determine when and how much water to apply to fields, minimizing overirrigation. (Photo courtesy of High Plains Underground Water Conservation District No. 1, Lubbock, Texas)

Heat Dissipation Blocks

Similar to gypsum blocks, heat dissipation blocks are made of ceramic materials that convert heat loss to soil moisture. Heat dissipation blocks are more durable than gypsum blocks, but they are more expensive.[60]

Tensiometers

Tensiometers, among the oldest and most commonly used devices on the market, measure soil moisture tension by quantifying the amount of water a plant can draw from the soil. A tensiometer consists of a plastic water-filled tube with a porous ceramic cup and a vacuum gauge attached to the other end. The tensiometer and the porous cup are installed in the soil at the depth where readings are desired; the soil moisture is measured by the negative pressure that registers on the vacuum gauge as water is pulled through the porous tip while the soil dries. Tensiometers are usually 12, 24, or 36 inches in length and can measure soil moisture at depths of 1, 2, or 3 feet, respectively, for every 40 acres of land. Their key advantage is that they give moisture readings directly; their disadvantage is that the range of operating conditions under which they can work is limited. Most accurate in sandy soils with high moisture content and in clay soils with lower moisture content, tensiometers are easy to install, read, and maintain, and they are also reusable.[7, 58, 60]

Several commonly used moisture-monitoring devices are shown in Figure 5.6.

Portable Instruments and Techniques

Soil Feel and Appearance

The oldest and perhaps still most commonly used method of monitoring soil moisture is the simple feel and appearance method, in which handfuls or small amounts of soil are collected from each foot of depth where moisture needs to be measured (typically the plant root zone). Soil moisture is detected by manipulating the hand and fingers to observe soil wetting and color patterns on the hand. Experienced observers can estimate soil moisture to within 5% of its actual value. Soil moisture guides can help irrigators learn to use this technique to judge soil moisture available for crops.[55]

Neutron Moisture Meter

Neutron moisture meters are among the most accurate moisture-sensing devices because they are not affected by temperature or pressure and only slightly by the chemical composition of the soil and other factors. Neutron moisture meters consist of a probe containing a source of "fast neutrons" (a radioactive material that emits neutrons at a speed of about 6,000 miles per second). Moisture is measured by the slowdown of the neutrons as they strike water molecules in the soil. Because of the hazards associated with using low-level radioactive material and the high cost of the equipment, neutron probes are usually not practical for farmers without the assistance of specially trained, licensed technicians.[61] Water suppliers such as the High Plains Water District use neutron moisture meters to conduct preplanting soil moisture surveys for agricultural producers. Survey information helps farmers to bring the soil in their 5-foot root zone to field capacity without over- or underirrigating.[62]

Gravimetric Moisture Monitoring

The gravimetric technique for monitoring soil moisture involves the collection of core soil samples to be analyzed in a laboratory. Soil samples are weighed, dried by heating, and reweighed to determine the percentage of moisture by weight. Carried out properly, this is one of the most accurate and reliable techniques for soil analysis. However, removing the soil sample from the field for measurement at a later time makes it difficult to relate the measurement to current irrigation needs because soil moisture content changes from the point of sample collection to analysis.[60]

Infrared Thermometry

Infrared thermometry uses a device that measures plant canopy temperature, ambient temperature, and relative humidity to determine crop stress and irrigation requirements. The device is easy to use and can cover large acreages quickly, but it requires a full canopy of plant materials (limiting its use early in the growing season) and can produce reading errors as a result of cloud cover, wind, pests, or disease.[60]

Pressure Bomb

This method gauges moisture by measuring plant pressure. The target stress point for a particular plant must be determined to establish a reference for subsequent tests. The usefulness of this measure depends on the time of day and stage of growth of the crop.[60] It is used for scheduling cotton irrigation in California's San Joaquin Valley.

Resistance Probes

Resistance probes measure ionic, or salt and fertilizer, concentrations in soil to indicate the watering requirements of crops. Although resistance probes are typically used by home gardeners, some attempts have been made to apply them to agricultural irrigation. However, they can register large measurement errors when fertilizer is added to or leached from a field.[60]

Capacitance Probes and Meters

Capacitance probes and meters measure the dielectric constant of the water in soil to determine its volumetric content. Capacitance probes provide instantaneous readings and can be used with most soils; their biggest disadvantage is that they require a pilot hole for hard, tight soils. Capacitance meters measure soil moisture using two electrodes (inserted into the soil) separated by a dielectric sensor. In a test, some dielectric sensors showed better correlations with soil moisture measurements than others, suggesting that farmers who want to use these sensors to schedule irrigations should make sure the instruments are properly calibrated before taking readings.[58, 60]

Water Savings, Benefits, and Costs From Soil Moisture Monitoring

Water Savings

Devices and techniques that monitor soil moisture do not provide direct water savings, but they make improved water-use efficiency possible. For example, the benefit of using gypsum blocks, a particularly effective moisture monitoring device, was once summed up by Wes Robbins, formerly of the Ogallala Water Management Office in Burlington, Colorado: "Irrigating without gypsum blocks is like driving a car without a gas gauge. You can do it, but you put gas in a lot more often than you need to."[46]

Crop Yields

A study of dozens of California farmers who for more than ten years have used gypsum blocks to plan irrigations showed that these farmers reduced the amount of water used to irrigate alfalfa and cotton crops by 6 to 58%. With a number of the fields tested, the farmers also increased crop values by $25 to $125 per acre and achieved energy costs savings of $1 to $100 per acre.[63]

Costs

With the exception of the no-cost but labor-intensive "look and feel" method, monitoring on-farm soil moisture for a growing season can cost from several hundred dollars for simple readings to several thousand dollars for highly accurate readings. To save money on soil moisture readings (with reduced accuracy for specific fields), irrigators can often take advantage of regional soil moisture readings available from extension services and other agricultural support organizations. For example, the Texas High Plains Water District regularly publishes moisture surveys for farmers in its district.

Selection of a cost-effective moisture-sensing device depends on such considerations as the acreage to be covered and the comparative cost of the method per acre. Estimated costs for soil moisture monitors include:

- Gypsum blocks: $5 to $15 per block (depending on length of lead wires); meter for gypsum blocks: $200
- Heat dissipation blocks: $30 to $50 per block; meter for heat dissipation blocks: $150 to $600
- Tensiometers: $50 to $75
- Neutron probes: $3,500 to $4,500; automated permanent installation: $12,000
- Gravimetric measurement techniques: $25 to $100 per sample
- Infrared thermometers: $2,500 to $5,000
- Pressure bombs: $1,100 to $2,500
- Resistance probes: $10 to $175 each
- Hand-held resistance meters: $150 to $250
- Capacitance probes: $500

5.3 AGRICULTURAL IRRIGATION SCHEDULING

Irrigation scheduling is used to plan precisely *when* and *how much* water to apply to crops—ideally, no more and no less than needed to ensure optimal growth. By customizing irrigation schedules, farmers can maximize crop growth potential and at the same time maximize water-use efficiency.

Determining irrigation water requirements requires an hourly or daily measurement or estimate of the rate of crop water use. Crop ET, or crop consumptive use, is the amount of water plants use for transpiration plus the amount evaporated from the adjacent soil surface. Crop ET is influenced by several factors, including plant temperature, air temperature, solar radiation, wind, humidity, and water availability in the soil.[64]

Soil Moisture Monitoring

Devices that monitor soil moisture measure the amount of water available for uptake by crop roots and the amount that must be replaced (by irrigation, rainfall, or both) for healthy growth. Soil moisture monitoring devices include gypsum blocks, tensiometers, neutron probes, and other techniques (see Section 5.2, "Soil Moisture Monitoring," earlier in this chapter). The amount of soil moisture that is depleted through ET and the amount that must be replenished are affected by current weather conditions—primarily crop ET and rainfall—as measured by a weather monitoring device, typically a weather station. Depending on the type of monitoring device used, soil moisture readings can be recorded manually from the instrument itself or accessed via electronic sensors connected to weather stations or other radio telemetry systems. Many computer programs for irrigation scheduling use soil moisture measurements to

Timing is everything."
—Old Saying

update scheduling methods based on computations of the balance of soil and water.[65]

Plant Moisture and Stress Monitoring

Measurements of plant water use can also be used to schedule irrigations, but these methods are less common. One method uses a crop water stress index, determined with measurements from an infrared gun, to correlate measurements of plant canopy, ambient air temperature, solar radiation, and relative humidity to help determine irrigation requirements. Other techniques involve the use of calibrated evaporation pans and atmometers placed at the height of the plant canopy to measure available moisture.[55]

Irrigation Guides

Irrigation guides available from agricultural water districts typically provide climatic data from local weather stations (e.g., crop ET, soil water-holding capacity) for a number of crops to help farmers plan and evaluate irrigations. The guides are usually produced on a weekly, monthly, or seasonal basis, but to use them reliably, farmers must make adjustments for rainfall events and for specific farm and crop conditions that differ from conditions across an entire farming region. Irrigation guides may instruct farmers on how to determine irrigation efficiency, and they are sometimes used to establish or justify farmers' water allocations.

Evapotranspiration and Weather Monitoring

Weather monitoring for the purpose of scheduling irrigation involves the collection of climatic data for a particular area—preferably the field to be irrigated, for greatest accuracy—in order to establish crop irrigation requirements relative to available soil moisture and overall crop water needs. Weather data collected typically include temperature, rainfall, humidity, and crop ET.

Factors that affect crop ET include crop type, density, health, and stage of growth; size of cultivated area; available soil moisture; and related climatic and environmental variables. Several types of ET rates can be determined: peak, daily or weekly, long-term, and aggregate. Peak ET rates are used to design irrigation system capacities; daily and weekly rates are used to determine irrigation schedules; long-term average ET and average rainfall help determine net crop irrigation requirements; and aggregate irrigation requirements for individual farms or areas are useful in managing supply allocations and delivery system operations.

Climatologic methods for determining ET for a given crop first require determining the potential, or reference, ET (ET_0). The ET_0 represents the maximum rate of water use under ideal growing conditions for a healthy plant with full canopy development. Crop coefficients (K_c) relate the actual rate of crop water use, or crop ET (ET_c), to the ET_0, according to the following equation:[66]

$$ET_c = K_c \times ET_0$$

Weather stations or networks of stations often collect weather and ET data for transmission to irrigators through one or several mediums including recorded (sometimes daily) telephone messages, on-line and satellite information services, newsletters, newspapers, radio, and television. Irrigators can access many weather stations for ET and irrigation-scheduling advisories via computer modem, using weather-retrieval programs that download data directly to a regional or on-farm irrigation-scheduling program that controls irrigation applications.

Automated Weather Networks

Increasingly, irrigators of large acreages are accessing real-time weather station data from the Internet and using computerized irrigation programs to automatically update irrigation schedules. More than 1,200 stationary, automated weather stations are in operation in the United States and Canada; this figure does not include the U.S. National Weather Service's Cooperative Station Network or its Automated Surface Observation Stations located near airports to serve aviation forecasting needs.

Although weather services can help irrigators plan more efficient irrigation, farmers need to be careful in applying weather data to a particular farm. Readings from weather stations usually cover a fixed region, but they cannot specify conditions at a particular site other than where the reading is taken, and on-farm microclimates can significantly influence the accuracy of irrigation scheduling.[68] Because individual farms may have unique microclimates with conditions that differ somewhat from weather data retrieved from a regional network, irrigation schedules may need to be adjusted accordingly (e.g., using measurements of soil or plant moisture or both). The more closely the weather data used in irrigation scheduling represent actual conditions on a farm, the more precise the schedule is likely to be.

As weather stations—and the number of irrigators who rely on them—have multiplied, agricultural managers and engineers have started to address the need for practices and standards to ensure that weather stations produce accurate, reliable data. The engineering practices "Measurement and Reporting Practices for Automatic Agricultural Weather Stations," developed by the Irrigation Management Committee of the American Society of Agricultural Engineers, are an early step toward creation of standardized guidelines for agricultural weather-sensing equipment, calibration and maintenance of weather station instruments, and collection and analysis of weather data.[69]

California's Computerized Weather Station Network

Several agencies and states maintain computerized weather networks that collect data from strategically placed weather stations and make the data available to irrigators. For example, the California DWR, along with other agencies, maintains the California Irrigation Management Information System (CIMIS). CIMIS consists of more than 100 computerized weather stations located throughout the state in agricultural areas as well as irrigated urban areas such as parks and golf courses, as shown in Figure 5.7. Each station is equipped with a microcomputer that collects climatological data such as hourly solar radiation, wind speed, air and soil temperature, relative humidity, and rainfall. Information

THE MAGICAL CONTROL OF RAIN: *Sometimes, when a drought has lasted a long time, people drop the usual hocus-pocus of imitative magic altogether, and being far too angry to waste their breath in prayer they seek by threats and curses or even downright physical force to extort the waters of heaven from the supernatural being who has, so to say, cut them off at the main."*
—Sir James George Frazer, *The Golden Bough* (1922)

Figure 5.7 Automated weather stations provide crop water-use data that help farmers plan efficient irrigation schedules. Accurate irrigation schedules not only conserve water but also help control pests, reduce soil erosion, and decrease farm chemical requirements. (Photo courtesy of California Department of Water Resources)

is transmitted to a central computer in Sacramento, California, where it is checked for accuracy. CIMIS data are accessible for free; users simply log on to CIMIS via the Internet or connect directly to the CIMIS system with a personal computer and high-speed modem. Among the more than 2,500 CIMIS users who access the system directly are growers, irrigation consultants, and water agencies as well as pesticide applicators, farm product suppliers, engineers, weather forecasters, golf course managers, and universities. CIMIS provides information directly to farm advisors, conservation and irrigation services, newspapers, and radio stations and also disseminates data via telephone recordings.[71]

Online U.S. and Canadian Weather Networks

Irrigators in virtually every U.S. state and region and every Canadian province can access pertinent weather station data via the Internet. In addition to the CIMIS network, a few examples of other weather networks are the Soil Climate

Analysis Network (administered by the USDA's NRCS), the U.S. Bureau of Reclamation's Pacific Northwest Cooperative Agricultural Weather Network, the Michigan State University Agricultural Weather Station, the Arizona Meteorological Network, Texas Mesonet, the Florida Automated Weather Network, Vermont Mesonet, and the Agriculture and Agri-Food Canada Lethbridge Research Centre Weather Station Network.

Irrigation-Scheduling Software Programs

More and more irrigators are relying on computer software programs and personal computers to control and monitor applications of water to crops. Some programs develop irrigation schedules based on soil moisture and climatic data that must be entered manually, whereas others automatically generate schedules based on data downloaded via modem from soil moisture sensors and weather stations. Irrigation-scheduling software programs are sometimes linked directly to an irrigation system's flow-control valve so that water applications can be continually adjusted to weather and soil conditions. Software programs that read water meters are sometimes used in conjunction with irrigation scheduling programs to record field and total on-farm water use, allowing more accurate tracking of application flow rates and related costs.[68]

Software programs for scheduling agricultural irrigation are available from a number of sources, including government agencies, local institutions (often universities), and private firms. One well-known irrigation-scheduling program—the *SCS Scheduler*—is available from the U.S. government.

Developed by Michigan State University engineers for the USDA's NRCS (formerly known as the Soil Conservation Service), *SCS Scheduler* has been used across the United States and is applicable to most climates. The program can be useful to individual farmers, large-scale irrigation system operators, and irrigation districts for on-farm irrigation scheduling as well as regional analysis of irrigation water use.[72] The *SCS Scheduler* uses on-farm characteristics and local, real-time climate data to:

- Determine daily and monthly crop ET.
- Maintain daily records of water content in the root zone throughout the growing season.
- Adjust for soil moisture changes since the last measurement.
- Predict the rate of soil moisture change.
- Determine seasonal irrigation requirements.
- Indicate groundwater conditions related to irrigation water management.

The *SCS Scheduler* is flexible in that it works with any soil and can be applied to a large number of crops; it can also be updated at any time either manually or from local computerized weather networks. The program can account for discrepancies in actual versus *SCS Scheduler* predictions of soil moisture so that future irrigations can address in situ conditions by incorporating crop coefficient curves. The program can also generate "what if" scenarios and end-of-year reports on how much water was over- or underapplied. An additional feature

*R*ecent extreme climatic variations have demonstrated that water-resource managers must develop their management systems in a context that assumes a wide range of possible climatic conditions, including the potential for significant and long-lasting departures from historically normal conditions."
—U.S. Geological Survey, *Strategic Directions for the Water Resources Division, 1998–2008*

of the *SCS Scheduler* is its ability to format data for graphic output, such as displays of crop ET curves and soil moisture status.[73, 74]

Water Savings, Benefits, and Costs From Agricultural Irrigation Scheduling

Water Savings

Water savings achieved through improved irrigation scheduling result primarily from better-timed applications and more precise identification of the amount of water needed by crops. As with other conservation measures, the amount of water that can be saved through improved irrigation scheduling depends on the efficiency of the existing irrigation system and the management practices on a particular farm. When carefully applied, irrigation scheduling has been shown to save water, energy, labor, and fertilizer and to improve crop yields and quality. Farmers who use the U.S. Bureau of Reclamation's AgriMet Northwest Irrigation Network serving the Pacific Northwest typically achieve estimated water savings of 15 to 20%.[75]

In addition to minimizing water waste, one of the primary economic advantages of irrigation scheduling is maximizing crop yield per unit of water used. Irrigation scheduling can also help to ensure more efficient timing for applying fertilizers and other agricultural chemicals as well as for scheduling labor, maintenance, and other farm activities.

Crop Yields

In a 1995 survey of 55 growers representing 134,000 acres of irrigated agricultural land in California, the cooperative extension service at the University of California, Berkeley, found that an 8% increase in average annual crop yields could be attributed to use of the CIMIS weather information network. A 13% reduction in average volumes of applied water was also attributed to CIMIS data. The annual value of these water reductions and increased yields is estimated at $14.7 million.[76]

Energy Savings

According to a 20-year study of irrigation-scheduling equipment and techniques conducted by the USDA's Agricultural Research Service, two commercial, sprinkler-irrigated farms in Colorado and Oregon (encompassing a total of 15,000 acres) achieved average annual water savings of 30% from improved irrigation-scheduling practices. In addition to saving water, the farms also reduced water pumping and energy requirements and lowered labor and fertilizer costs. The Oregon research site reduced water applications from its center pivot irrigation system by 30 to 50% and decreased its irrigation staff from 20 people to 10 by installing irrigation monitoring and control technology. The Colorado farm increased its corn yield by 25 bushels per acre in addition to its water savings.[77]

Costs

The cost of improving agricultural irrigation schedules varies, depending on the grower's needs and existing tools and practices. In many agricultural regions,

Some irrigators may run out of money before they run out of water if they do not become more efficient in the production and distribution of irrigation water."
—A. Wayne Wyatt, former manager, High Plains Underground Water Conservation District No. 1, Lubbock, Texas

weather and ET data may be available for free or at a small charge from state or regional weather stations. Large farms may install private weather stations or access data from other stations.

Computerized irrigation scheduling requires a personal computer and irrigation-scheduling software. Government- and university-sponsored irrigation-scheduling software, such as *SCS Scheduler*, is usually available at a nominal charge. More and more television weather channels provide baseline weather data for farmers, and such data are often available on the Internet as well. Customized software and other application programs and support are available from irrigation consultants for a fee.

Figure 5.8   Laser (or precision) land leveling equipment grades fields to minimize variations in field contour. Laser-leveled fields allow efficient applications of irrigation water and high distribution uniformity. (Photo courtesy of High Plains Underground Water Conservation District No. 1, Lubbock, Texas)

5.4 LASER LEVELING

Laser leveling, or precision leveling, involves the use of laser-controlled land-grading equipment to minimize variations in field contour. A laser beam is used to raise and lower the plane that levels the land. Laser leveling of fields removes the high and low spots that cause farmers to overwater some areas while ensuring that all areas receive enough water. By facilitating the uniform application of water across a field, precise land leveling increases distribution uniformity and water-use efficiency. Under certain conditions, laser leveling can achieve irrigation efficiencies up to 85%. Widely used in parts of Arizona, Texas, and the lower Colorado River region,[78] land leveling must be maintained approximately every two to five years.[26] A laser-leveling unit is shown in Figure 5.8.

Laser leveling is a key tool in the practice of level-basin irrigation. Not to be confused with the historic use of basin irrigation—synonymous with wild flooding or flood irrigation—level-basin irrigation by modern definition is the ap-

TABLE 5.3

Water use and crop yields for wheat, alfalfa, and cotton before and after conversion from conventional land grading to laser-graded level basins*

	Water Use			Crop Yields		
Crop	Before[†], *inches*	After[‡], *inches*	Difference After Conversion to Laser Leveling, *percent*	Before[†]	After[‡]	Difference After Conversion to Laser Leveling, *percent*
Wheat	47	32	-32	2.7 tons/acre	3.3 tons/acre	22
Alfalfa	123	93	-24	1.4 tons/acre	1.6 tons/acre	14
Cotton (lint)	66	53	-20	189 lb/acre	212 lb/acre	12

* Conversion was part of a Wellton-Mohawk Valley (Arizona) on-farm irrigation improvement program.

† Before improvements, land was graded with conventional equipment, and most surface irrigated fields had some slope.

‡ After improvements, nearly all land was converted to laser-graded level basins. Some yield increases may be due in part to improved irrigation scheduling. Improvements made on 47,640 acres out of approximately 59,300 acres irrigated.

lb = pound

Sources: Adapted from References 78 and 79

plication of a uniform depth of water to a level field by means of rapid flooding.[78]

Farmers in Arizona's Wellton-Mohawk Valley, a large growing area for alfalfa, cotton, and wheat, installed laser-graded level basins after having used conventional land-leveling techniques (with some improvements in irrigation scheduling). A study of the conversion found a 20 to 32% reduction in water use and a 12 to 21% increase in crop yields, as shown in Table 5.3.[79]

Water Savings, Benefits, and Costs From Laser Leveling

Water Savings

The efficiency of level-basin irrigation has been reported to be as high as 85%, although some studies conducted in the 1990s reported that the practice is not always economical unless the cost of water is high. Also, "farmers tend to make conversions without doing their homework—making basins too long on high-intake soils or making large cuts and fills without proper soil surveys," notes Albert (Bert) J. Clemmens, director and research hydraulic engineer at the USDA Agricultural Research Service's Water Conservation Laboratory in Phoenix. "We have experienced many cases where farmers convert to level basins and don't change the way they irrigate, resulting in gross over application."[78]

Between 1962 and 1998, the rice-growing industry reduced its applied water use by 38%, from 8.9 acre-ft/acre to 5.5 acre-ft/acre, partly as a result of laser leveling. With the use of laser beams as benchmarks, rice fields are scraped and filled so that they impound water at a consistent, shallow depth across the field. The precision-graded fields impound water more efficiently and also help reduce the need for herbicides. Other practices that have reduced the amount of water required for growing rice include switching from sandy, loamy soils through which water percolates quickly to heavy clay soils with low permeability and installing recirculation systems to collect and redistribute water among growers.

Costs

The cost of laser leveling varies, depending on the size and condition of the field as well as grading costs. A study of California rice-growers found that those who use laser-leveling techniques spend about $40 per acre every two to three years for precision grading.[80]

5.5 FURROW DIKING

Furrow diking conserves water by trapping irrigation water or rainwater that would otherwise be lost to runoff. Furrow dikes are mounds of soil mechanically installed at intervals across a furrow to form small water storage basins, as shown in Figure 5.9. Rain or irrigation water is trapped and stored in the basins, as shown in Figure 5.10, allowing it to soak uniformly into the root zone. The longer the infiltration time, the more soils with low permeability will benefit.[81] Developed in the early 1930s by researchers in the U.S. Great Plains region, furrow diking is also referred to as basin tillage, reservoir tillage, row diking, ridge ties, basin listing, dammer diking, furrow damming, and furrow blocking. Furrow dikes are used mainly in areas that receive rainfall during the irrigation season; they are not common in California or Arizona, for example.

Furrow diking can be extremely effective when used in conjunction with plant-residue management, alternate-row irrigation, and irrigation systems such as LEPA center pivot sprinklers.[82] With a LEPA system, water is applied directly to furrows by drop lines that have drag hoses or socks attached, as shown in Figure 5.11. The drag hoses or socks wet a narrow band of soil in furrows; the furrow dikes hold water in the furrows until it infiltrates the soil, allowing more uniform infiltration across the field.[83]

Furrow dikes should be established or reestablished as soon after harvest as possible so they can capture moisture during the fallow season and reduce the need for irrigation before crops are planted. In arid regions, dikes should be in place prior to periods of normal and high rainfall (Figure 5.12).[84] The USDA's Agricultural Research Service has developed the Limited Irrigation Dryland (LID) system to make use of furrow dikes in areas where irrigation water is limited. The LID system applies irrigation water to all furrows, which are diked for the length of the field, causing water to accumulate in each basin and spill into the next basin through the upper half of the field. The lower half of the field is then irrigated by tailwater, watered by rainfall, or both.[17]

Furrow-dikers are available in two basic designs: the raising shovel paddle and the tripping shovel. Dikers vary considerably in terms of size of dike created, basin volume capacity, diking interval, operating speed, and ability to form functional dikes in a range of soil textures. A plow-out attachment may be needed if diking is to be used in every furrow, and hydraulically lifted sweeps are required to run in front of the tractor wheels to plow out existing dikes. Irrigators who are purchasing a furrow-diker should make sure the equipment is of sturdy construction, has low maintenance requirements, attaches easily to other farm equipment to combine field operations, is capable of high-speed operation, and has the capacity to construct a furrow dike large enough to hold runoff during intense thunderstorms.[84]

If you haven't put in furrow dikes and deep-chiseled your land, don't pray for rain because you aren't ready for it!"
—Charles Huffman, farmer from Lockney, Texas

Figure 5.9 A furrow-diker creates dikes to trap irrigation water or rainwater that would otherwise be lost to runoff.

Figure 5.10 Furrow dikes hold precipitation in the furrows until it seeps into the ground, providing more uniform infiltration across the field.

Figure 5.11 A center pivot system with drag hose and drag sock is used in conjunction with furrow dikes to irrigate cotton.

(Photos 5.9 through 5.12 courtesy of High Plains Underground Water Conservation District No. 1, Lubbock, Texas)

In regions where precipitation is unpredictable, it is important to keep furrow dikes in place as long as possible. For example, in the Texas High Plains, it is particularly important from June through August when the region receives most of its annual rainfall.

Water Savings, Benefits, and Costs From Furrow Diking

Water Savings

Furrow diking can typically achieve water efficiencies of 55 to 70%, depending on what type of irrigation system is used.[17]

Crop Yields

Research in the Texas High Plains region has shown that 1 inch of precipitation saved from runoff can increase crop yields significantly when the water is stored in the soil through the use of furrow dikes and plant residues.[81] For example, water savings from furrow diking in Lubbock, Texas, was associated with cotton yields of 250 to 300 pounds of lint per acre compared with yields of 150 to 175 pounds per acre on farms without furrow dikes and plant residues. In addition, plant-residue management and furrow dikes in this area have returned as much as $60 per acre in additional produce in dry years.[85]

Costs

The initial investment for furrow dikers ranges from $150 to $250 per row. In many cases, farmers can recover this cost during the first year as a result of reduced irrigation and pumping costs plus increased crop yields.[86]

Figure 5.12   Empty furrow dikes

Figure 5.13 High-pressure, center pivot irrigation systems used in the 1960s and 1970s had nozzles attached to the main line and lost high volumes of water to wind drift and evaporation.

Figure 5.14 A low energy precision application (LEPA) center pivot sprinkler equipped with drag hoses and drag socks can achieve water application efficiencies of 95%.

5.6 LOW ENERGY PRECISION APPLICATION (LEPA)

The major advance in efficient sprinkler technology is the LEPA sprinkler. An adaptation of the center pivot and lateral-move sprinkler systems, LEPA technology is a major improvement over the high-pressure, center pivot systems of the past, as shown in Figure 5.13. Compared with conventional sprinkler systems, LEPA sprinklers apply water closer to the ground, in larger droplets, and with greater distribution uniformity. As a result, water losses from evaporation and wind drift are minimized, and deep percolation, tailwater runoff, and under-watering are reduced. Because they operate at low pressures, LEPA systems also require less energy and incur lower costs. When properly applied, LEPA sprinklers can achieve application efficiencies as high as 95 to 98%; the highest efficiencies occur when LEPA systems are used in conjunction with furrow dikes, drag hoses, and drag socks,[17, 87]as shown in Figure 5.14, and when surface runoff and deep percolation are negligible.[88]

LEPA sprinklers operate on a center pivot and distribute water to plants through drop tubes that extend 8 to 18 inches down from the sprinkler arm directly to the furrow, as shown in Figure 5.15. The drop tubes emit water at low pressure (about 10 to 20 psi compared with 30 to 90 psi for conventional sprinklers) either just above or below the crop canopy, as shown in Figure 5.16. A typical LEPA system consists of four basic parts that are adapted to the main pipeline of an existing center pivot sprinkler system: nozzles, drop lines (or drop tubes), attachments, and pressure regulators. The height of the nozzles and drop lines—

Figure 5.15 Drag hoses and drag socks on LEPA systems deliver water directly to the furrow and can achieve application efficiencies of about 95 to 98% when used in conjunction with furrow dikes.

Figure 5.16 A center pivot LEPA nozzle irrigates wheat

(Figures 5.13 through 5.16 courtesy of High Plains Underground Water Conservation District No. 1, Lubbock, Texas)

Figure 5.17 Full drop-line pivots. Center pivot sprinkler systems without drag hoses and/or drag socks have an irrigation application efficiency of about 90%.

Figure 5.18 Partial drop-line center pivot systems discharge water about 4 feet above the ground and have an application efficiency of about 80% (the remaining 20% of the water is lost to evaporation).

(Figures 5.17 and 5.18 courtesy of High Plains Underground Water Conservation District No. 1, Lubbock, Texas)

that is, their distance from the plants—affects irrigation efficiency, as shown for full drop-line pivots in Figure 5.17 and for partial drop-line pivots in Figure 5.18.

Furrow diking is an important factor in achieving maximum efficiency with a LEPA system, particularly when less permeable soils are irrigated. The microbasins created by the small dams across furrows reduce runoff by capturing irrigation water and rainwater for additional soil infiltration and crop use. Gypsum blocks and other devices for monitoring soil moisture are also critical to determining irrigation water needs and preventing over- or under-irrigation.[89, 90] Farmers who replace older irrigation systems with LEPA sprinklers need to adjust their operation and management practices so they do not continue to use excess water and allow it to be wasted as runoff. As water losses decrease, the number of irrigation runs required to wet the soil will decrease as well.[91]

The LEPA concept was developed in the early 1980s by agricultural engineers at Texas A&M University in an effort to eliminate evaporative water losses from sprays extending high in the air. Such losses were common in Texas, sometimes amounting to more than 90% of the water intended for application to crops.

Since its introduction, LEPA technology has been transformed into a number of commercial products that are now installed on hundreds of center pivot systems in Texas.[90]

Although LEPA technology has been used primarily in the Texas High Plains where it was developed, it can also benefit other pump-irrigated regions across the United States. More than 40 California growers are now using modified versions of LEPA called *linear-move irrigation systems,* or LIS.[92] A demonstration project using LIS to irrigate carrots in California's Imperial Valley during the 1998-99 growing season showed that LIS technology used 50% less water than the conventional sprinkler and furrow method of irrigation, although crop yields from the LIS field were slightly lower.[93]

Compared with conventional center pivot systems, LEPA systems have numerous advantages and few disadvantages. Benefits include efficiency and uniformity of application; decreased wetting of foliage and, in turn, reduced evaporation and potential disease problems; lower energy costs; and ease of use for chemigation and positioning of pivot-tower wheel tracks.[14]

The primary drawback of LEPA systems is higher initial costs for purchase and installation, although these costs are usually offset by paybacks achieved in water savings, reduced pumping and energy costs, more efficient use of farm chemicals, and increased crop yields.[90] The high efficiency and uniformity possible with LEPA sprinklers can be offset by surface runoff caused by insufficient tillage; runoff of more than 50% of LEPA system applications has been reported. Basin and reservoir tillage are common methods of managing runoff from LEPA systems. Basin tillage involves the construction of dams or dikes in furrows to create surface storage; reservoir tillage involves the use of a subsoiler or chisel shank that forms pits with small dikes within the soil.[88]

Water Savings, Benefits, and Costs From LEPA

Water Savings

Farmers who use LEPA sprinklers for irrigation in the Texas High Plains have reduced their water use by 20 to 40%. They have also reduced fuel costs by 35 to 50% and labor costs by as much as 75%.[87] According to the Texas High Plains Underground Water Conservation District No. 1, a field in which a LEPA system applied 8.8 inches of water per acre on cotton or 19 inches of water per acre on corn would have the same crop yield that could be obtained by applying 14 inches of water on cotton or 30 inches of water on corn through furrow irrigation. The energy savings from avoided pumping would amount to about $21 per acre for cotton and $44 per acre for corn, although these savings would vary according to the depth of the farmer's well.[95]

Crop Yields

Increased crop yields are another benefit associated with the use of LEPA systems. A 1,400-acre Texas farm that upgraded from furrow irrigation to a LEPA system with drag socks doubled its cotton yield from one bale per acre to two without increasing water use.[87] Two alfalfa farmers who replaced their sideroll irrigation systems with LEPA sprinklers and soil moisture monitoring (using

> ### 'Smart' Variable-Flow Nozzle May Boost Center Pivot System Efficiency
>
> A variable-flow nozzle developed by agricultural engineers David Kincaid and Bradley King (with the Agricultural Research Service of the U.S. Department of Agriculture) may significantly increase the water-use efficiency of center pivot irrigation systems. Conventional sprinkler nozzles apply water in uniform amounts—the variable-flow nozzle allows for adjustments in flow rate accomplished by inserting a pin into the nozzle. An electromagnetic device that can adjust nozzle flow from a remote computer controls the pin. The nozzle will work in conjunction with a field map that includes information such as variations in soil and crops within different field grids. A computer program can use these data to create a field-specific irrigation schedule that is water-efficient and that minimizes the use of farm fertilizers, herbicides, and pesticides. Although the variable-flow nozzle has not yet been widely tested, estimates indicate the new technology has the potential to reduce water use by center pivot irrigation systems by 30%.[94]

buried gypsum blocks) achieved water savings of 47%, electricity reductions of 30%, and crop yield increases of nearly one third, resulting in a 150% increase in water productivity.[96]

Costs

The cost of converting an existing partial-drop, center pivot irrigation system to a LEPA system is $6,500 to $8,500. A new partial-drop, center pivot system in Texas costs $36,000 to $40,000 per quarter section (160 acres), and a full LEPA system costs $40,000 to $45,000.[86] The payback—in reduced water use, improved crop yields, and energy savings—on the cost of a LEPA system occurs in two to seven years, depending on whether a partial system retrofit or a total conversion is implemented.[34]

5.7 SURGE VALVES

Surge valves improve the water efficiency of conventional furrow irrigation by releasing intermittent surges or pulses of water during a series of on–off periods when furrows or field borders are watered for predetermined amounts of time. Once the surface of the furrows is wet, the irrigation time can be reduced according to the rate at which water infiltrates the soil. The first surge seals the soil, allowing the next application to advance more quickly and uniformly down the furrow. As a result, water is distributed more uniformly, and losses from evaporation, deep percolation, and tailwater runoff can be reduced. Surge valves are controlled by a timer or by changing water-pressure releases that occur at preestablished intervals and alternate applications between two furrows.[97]

Used with furrow irrigation systems, surge valves require the use of above- or underground pipelines to transport water to the point of application, as shown in Figure 5.19. The pipelines help to minimize losses from deep percolation and evaporation by eliminating the use of open, unlined ditches.[98] Two principal types of surge valves are available: bladder and mechanical. Surge valves can be used with level gated pipe, sloped gated pipe, concrete-lined ditches, and border strips. Border strip irrigation offers the greatest potential for saving water with surge valves because this type of irrigation provides full-field flooding.

Surge cycles correspond to the length of time required to complete an on–off cycle and may vary from 30 minutes to several hours, depending on soil characteristics, furrow length, furrow stream size, and other factors. Because surge irrigation typically has high flow rates, cycle times must be set carefully to avoid water waste. Once the water reaches the end of the furrow, the flow is often applied continuously at a lower rate until the desired amount of water is applied.[99]

Surge irrigation works in many but not all soils. It works best with light, loose soils and is less effective with heavier soils or after soil has become compacted later in the growing season. For coarse-textured soils, long furrows, large furrows, and abundant crop residues, the size of furrow streams should be relatively large and cycles times should be relatively long. Fine-textured soils and short, small, clean furrows require smaller furrow streams and shorter cycle times. Surge irrigation may not improve yields when used on short, level furrows where irrigation is already relatively efficient.[100]

Monitoring soil moisture (with devices such as gypsum blocks or resistance meters) to determine crop water needs is an important tool in establishing on–off cycles for surge irrigation. Too long an on-time would simulate continuous-flow irrigation and could cause excess deep percolation. The off-time for each cycle must also be long enough to allow the furrow to become dewatered before the next surge is released.[101]

The newer generation of surge valves allows irrigators to adjust the valve controller for individual farm characteristics—such as soil type, moisture content, slope, furrow size, infiltration rate, and compaction—using a computer program. Programmable controllers can be modified at any time during irrigation to reduce tailwater or to extend opportunities for deeper penetration of water. For example, a surge valve installed in the center of a gated pipe can direct water to half of the pipe for a set time and then automatically switch to the other half. On-cycles can be repeated or extended for either side as necessary to deliver an appropriate amount of water to the end of each row.[99]

Figure 5.19 Surge irrigation delivers water in time-controlled releases. A surge valve, used correctly in conjunction with a furrow irrigation system, can eliminate irrigation tailwater losses, minimize deep percolation losses, and reduce the amount of time water in the furrow is subject to evaporation. Adding surge valves to conventional furrow irrigation systems has achieved water savings of 10 to 40%. (Photo courtesy of High Plains Underground Water Conservation District No. 1, Lubbock, Texas)

Water Savings, Benefits, and Costs From Surge Valves

Water Savings

Surge irrigation, in combination with the reduction or elimination of deep percolation and tailwater losses, can achieve average water savings of 10 to 40% and can sometimes achieve savings as high as 50% compared with conventional

Figure 5.20 Corn yields have increased in response to the use of surge irrigation. (Photo courtesy of Amy Vickers & Associates, Inc.)

furrow irrigation.[97,102-104] However, because surge irrigation reduces the amount of water applied, soil moisture must be closely monitored to ensure that the field is not significantly underwatered.

A demonstration study of surge irrigation technology used by 41 farmers in the Lower Gunnison Basin of Colorado showed that the surge systems reduced deep percolation of irrigation water and reduced applications by 40 to 50%. Participating farmers used the surge systems to irrigate corn, alfalfa, beans, vegetables, pasture, and fruit tree crops in orchards.

Crop Yields

Surge irrigation has been shown to increase fertilizer application efficiency and crop yields through "fertigation" (the practice of adding liquid fertilizer to irrigation water). A study conducted by the Colorado State University Cooperative Extension Service found that farmers in Colorado's Grand Valley achieved 12% increases in corn yields with the use of surge fertigation compared with conventional irrigation and fertilizer treatment. In addition, the farmers benefited from increases in residual nitrogen in the soil (Figure 5.20) and from enhanced hay yields and other crop yields.[105, 106]

Salt Loading Reductions

Surge irrigation has been credited with being instrumental in lowering salt loadings under the Colorado River Salinity Control Program, which is funded by state and federal agencies. The goal of the program at its inception was to reduce the 9 million tons of salt the Colorado River annually carries past Hoover Dam. Various conservation measures, including surge valves, have been promoted to achieve this goal. Greater use of surge irrigation has helped to reduce the deep percolation that was causing water to pick up salts from ancient dried-up seabeds in the Mancos Shale Formation of the Lower Gunnison Basin. By 1998, program participants had removed more than 700,000 tons of salt since the program began in the late 1970s.[107]

Energy and Pumping Savings

As part of an agricultural water conservation program, in the early 1990s the California Pacific Gas & Electric (PG&E) utility conducted a performance study of 50 surge valves in California's San Joaquin Valley. The study found that the surge irrigation systems required an average of 45% less watering time than continuous-flow surface irrigation systems, resulting in combined water and energy savings of about 38%. Energy savings from the surge valves totaled more than 600,000 kilowatt-hours (kWh), or about 17,719 kWh per valve. The PG&E program gave irrigators a direct rebate of $450 per surge valve installed, and the utility avoided energy-production costs of approximately 2.5 times the cost of the rebates.[99]

Costs

Depending on the size of the valves and controllers required, the initial investment for surge irrigation systems ranges from $1,000 to $1,500 per valve,[86] with most valves expected to cover about 80 acres. On a per-acre basis, the cost of adding a surge system ranges from approximately $12 per acre for fields with gated pipe already in place to $50 per acre for fields without gated pipe and associated equipment.[104] Labor costs can be reduced somewhat by adding additional pipe to allow more sets to be irrigated before the pipe and valve must be moved.[102] According to findings from farmers using surge valves in the Texas High Plains Underground Water Conservation District No. 1, the cost of the valve can often be recovered within two years through savings in energy and pumping costs alone.[97]

5.8 DRIP IRRIGATION

As described earlier in this chapter, drip irrigation is a form of microirrigation involving the slow, frequent application of water through a network of small-diameter porous or perforated pipes placed either directly on top of or below the soil surface surrounding plant roots. The use of drip irrigation avoids runoff and minimizes or eliminates deep percolation and evaporation. Because of the precise application rates of drip systems, application volumes are significantly less than those of conventional furrow, flood, or sprinkler systems. Drip systems can be operated manually or can easily be automated with the use of controllers or timers and soil moisture sensors. Drip systems have the potential to achieve application efficiencies of up to 95%.[14, 16]

Drip irrigation has some unique benefits compared with other irrigation systems. For example, because drip systems wet smaller areas, soil waterlogging and related water losses are minimized, weed growth is inhibited, smaller amounts of farm chemicals are needed, salt accumulation is reduced, and associated labor costs are lowered. Because runoff is reduced, fertile topsoil is better protected. Drip systems have also been shown to increase crop yield and quality.

Although drip systems typically must run longer to meet crop water needs, they use much less water. For example, a cotton field irrigated by sprinklers designed to apply 5.0 gallons per minute and spaced at 30 × 50 inches will use about 0.32 inches of water per hour and require a run time of 6.3 hours for a 2-

Microirrigation is the most common method of irrigation for citrus in Florida. Typically, citrus trees are irrigated with drip systems or microsprinklers on stake assemblies."
—Brian J. Boman,
Associate Professor of
Agricultural Engineering,
University of Florida

inch application. In contrast, a field irrigated by a drip tape designed to apply 24 gallons per hour per 100 feet will use about 0.12 inches of water per hour and require a run time of 16.6 hours for a 2-inch application. However, because drip systems deliver water directly to plant roots, the crop would not need 2 inches of water with a drip system.[108]

> Research and experience have shown that insects can substantially increase the costs of operating and maintaining microirrigation systems in Florida. One of the biggest challenges is caused by ants that enter the system when it is not in use, and then end up clogging emitters when the system is pressurized."
>
> —Brian J. Boman,
> Associate Professor of
> Agricultural Engineering,
> University of Florida

Drip irrigation was perfected by agricultural irrigation researchers in Israel, where water supplies for growing crops are limited. Because of its water-use efficiency and crop yields, drip irrigation has enabled Israel to achieve what is "widely perceived as an agricultural miracle" according to water resources expert Sandra Postel. About half of Israel's agricultural land is irrigated by drip systems, and efficiency improvements have reduced water use per irrigated area by one third while crop yields have increased.

Although drip irrigation systems currently represent only about 4% of U.S. agricultural irrigation systems,[14] the technology is gaining popularity throughout the United States, particularly in Arizona, California, and Texas, and particularly for row crops such as cotton, corn, grapes, citrus, tomatoes, peppers, asparagus, soybeans, melons, strawberries, and sugar cane.[109, 110] The capital cost for upgrading from a conventional irrigation system to a drip system is an initial impediment for some farmers, but drip irrigation can be very cost-effective. The cost of installing a drip system is declining as a result of recent technological advances; in addition, fields irrigated by drip systems typically achieve higher crop yields and incur lower costs for water, fertilizers, and other crop chemicals.

A basic drip irrigation system includes five major components: a delivery system to distribute water to the field, feeder tubes and drip tape (connected to the main by submains or laterals), filters (sand, disk, or screen), pressure regulators (spring or valve), and valves or gauges (hand-operated, hydraulic, or electrical). Drip tubing comes in three basic types: single-walled, double-walled, and soaker hoses. Usually consisting of inner and outer chambers that distribute water evenly over a range of conditions, drip tubing is typically made of black polyethylene plastic with emitter holes at preset intervals of 8 to 24 inches. Because the tubing is flattened on a roll, it is often called "drip tape." Flow rates depend on the tape's diameter and wall thickness, as well as the space between emitters. Tape diameters usually range from 10 to 35 millimeters (about 0.4 to 1.4 inches); large-diameter tapes allow for lateral lengths of 400 to 800 meters (about 1,310 to 2,625 feet).[109] Drip lines can be placed on the soil surface, as shown in Figure 5.21, or buried, as shown in Figure 5.22.

To perform efficiently, a drip system generally requires a substantial investment in new equipment as well as an ongoing commitment to system maintenance, which may cost more than maintaining the irrigation system it replaced. Drip irrigation and microsprinklers can be particularly effective for uneven terrain, young trees and vines, and shallow-rooted crops grown on sandy soils. However, drip irrigation has some disadvantages, including: higher initial costs, although these may be offset by reduced operating costs and increased income from higher yields; clogging of drip tubes; increased maintenance requirements caused by tubing leaks and clogs; increased susceptibility to rodent and insect damage, which can cause clogs or leaks; and potential salt buildup caused by improper system design, scheduling, or maintenance.

Figure 5.21 Surface drip irrigation lines, placed on the ground next to plants, deliver water in slow, frequent applications. (Photo courtesy of Sandra Postel)

Figure 5.22 Buried drip irrigation lines deliver water directly to plant roots, eliminating soil surface evaporation and runoff. (Photo courtesy of High Plains Underground Water Conservation District No. 1, Lubbock, Texas)

Proper design, installation, and operation of a drip irrigation system should take into account the following factors:

- *Water.* Water used by drip irrigation systems must be filtered to remove sand and other organic particles that can clog the tubing's tiny emitters and orifices. Screen or disc filters can be used for well water or municipally supplied water; sand filters are used for surface water sources. Filters are usually installed in a series to facilitate automatic self-cleaning.[111] Portable "drip trailers" are sometimes used to reduce the in-place equipment costs associated with drip irrigation systems. The trailers are equipped with an engine, pump, filters, fertilizer injector, and other pipes and connections needed to transfer water from underground pipelines into the drip tape.
- *Crop type.* Drip irrigation is appropriate for many crops, but the specific irrigation practices and the amount of water required vary with each type of crop.

Drip Irrigation Under Plastic Mulch
Saves Water and Increases Melon Production in Texas

Growers in the Lower Rio Grande Valley of Texas first adopted "drip under plastic" in 1986, and now the technique is used for more than 95% of all melon production in the state. The technique involves the use of thin-wall drip tape and plastic mulch, both of which are discarded after one or two seasons. The plastic mulch increases soil and plant moisture retention, which in most years causes melons to ripen quickly and allows an early harvest when prices are highest. Compared with furrow irrigation, "drip under plastic" is more water-efficient, requires less fertilizer, and produces better crop yields. Improvements in water efficiency and crop yields attained with melons grown in Starr County, Texas,[114] are shown in Table 5.4. In some areas, "drip under plastic" is being amplified with water harvesting techniques. Depressions in soil beds are covered with plastic mulch, and holes are punched in each depression to allow rainfall to infiltrate directly into the bed. This technique for capturing rainwater allows growers to take advantage of early spring rains, and in Winter Garden, Texas,[109] it has reduced irrigation needs by one or two applications.

Drip irrigation can be used for virtually all vegetable and orchard crops, as well as cotton and sugar cane. However, it is usually not practical for closely spaced crops like rice, wheat, and corn—crops that account for much of the world's irrigated area.

- *Soil and topography.* Different types of emitters are used for various soil conditions. Drip emitters are the most common for general soil conditions. When the land slope is moderate to steep, tubing should be placed perpendicular to the slope to ensure more uniform pressure. Pressure irregularities can also be minimized with pressure regulators and pressure-compensating emitters.

- *Irrigation scheduling.* Optimal water-use efficiency with drip systems requires irrigation scheduling. Schedules should be based on actual soil moisture conditions, as determined by soil moisture monitoring devices.

- *Plastic mulches.* Drip systems can be particularly effective when used in conjunction with plastic mulches. Opaque plastic mulch is spread over the soil surface to trap heat from the sun and accelerate the rate of soil warming, increasing the likelihood of an early harvest. According to Guy Fipps, assistant professor and agriculture extension specialist with Texas A & M University, the use of drip irrigation under plastic mulch in vegetable production "has increased dramatically in Texas because most vegetables have responded favorably to the technique." The primary reason for drip irrigation's popularity, according to Fipps, is the "quicker to market" benefit of faster seed germination and plant growth associated with the combination of drip irrigation and plastic mulch.[112]

- *Drip system installation requirements.* Drip irrigation tubing is typically installed by means of specialized equipment that plows the tubing into the soil at a minimum of 6 to 12 inches beneath the surface. The length of drip tape required depends on factors such as field shape and slope, flow rate, tape size, and the acceptable losses caused by friction in the tape. Drip tape thickness is measured in "mil" units, or one thousandth of an inch. Tape thickness ranges from 4 to 25 mils. Row crops in heavy soils require thicker (e.g., 15-mil) tape, whereas 4-mil tape can be used for single-season crops. Drip tubes are pressurized, usually at 10 to 25 psi, depending on the pressure requirements of the particular tape installed.

- *Drip system options.* Variations in drip irrigation products can help to improve performance and lower costs. For example, strip tubing is a light, thin material that can be used to replace older, hard-walled tubes with inserted emitters. Some strip tubing products include turbulent-flow emitters that provide extremely uniform flows and are more resistant to plugging than older, laminar-flow or orifice-type drip products. Strip tubing is available in thin-wall or thick-wall products. Thin-wall strips (4 to 8 mils in thickness) are lower-cost products often used for leased ground, single-season production, or rotating crops. Thick-wall strips (about 15 mils) can be buried deeper (10 to 18 inches) and can be removed at the end of the growing season for reuse.[111]

• ***Drip system maintenance and repair.*** With proper maintenance, thick-wall drip tape should last up to ten years. Drip system maintenance requirements include flushing lines about four times a year, depending on soil conditions and amount of use. Flushing the lines with acid and other chemicals cleans out deposits from hard water, roots, algae, and rock particles. Irrigators must be careful to flush drip lines with freshwater after chemical applications to ensure that the chemicals are removed. Animals and insects often damage drip lines, but repairs usually consist of splicing new tape into the line. Because drip tape can be buried near the soil surface, leaking water usually comes to the surface and forms a puddle, indicating the location of the problem in the line. Use of drip tape for a single growing season can minimize maintenance requirements.[113]

Water Savings, Benefits, and Costs From Drip Irrigation

Water Savings

Drip irrigation systems can achieve application efficiencies as high as 95%.[17,28] The water savings that can be achieved by installing drip irrigation vary, depending on the type of crop grown and the type of irrigation system used previously.

TABLE 5.4

Melon production with furrow irrigation compared with drip tape and plastic mulch*

Production Characteristics	Furrow Irrigation	Drip Tape With Plastic Mulch	Difference in Drip Compared With Furrow, *Percent*
Rainfall—inches	2.6	2.6	0
Irrigation water applied—inches	13.1	4.4	−66
Number of irrigations	7	8	14
Nitrogen—pounds	158	61	−61
Yield—boxes per acre	300	500	67
Nitrogen use efficiency —boxes/pound	1.9	8.2	332
Water use efficiency—boxes/inch	19.1	71.8	276

* Data from Starr County, Texas

Source: Adapted from Reference 114

In the United States, the earliest recorded practice of applying small volumes of water to the root zone of plants dates back to World War I.

Case Study *Cotton yields increase with conversion from furrow to drip irrigation.* Cotton yields from a farm in Lubbock County, Texas, increased from 1.01 bales per acre in 1997 to 2.22 bales per acre in 1998, when the farm converted from furrow to drip irrigation. Drip systems in two cotton fields (a 62-acre site and a 108-acre site) with five different varieties of cotton use 3 gallons of water per acre per minute, or about 0.18 inches of water per acre a day. Cotton rows on the 170 acres are spaced 40 inches apart; the drip lines are buried 13 inches deep beneath the crop and spaced 80 inches apart. "Converting to drip irrigation allowed us to achieve application efficiencies of nearly 100%," said grower Walter Heinrich. Heinrich noted that his overall operational costs had declined, and even though he uses more electricity to run a booster pump, the crop "yield far outweighs the cost." Heinrich's son Russell noted the benefit of decreased labor. "It was difficult to furrow-irrigate," he said, "because we were always putting in a lot of hours. But with drip irrigation, the labor input has been greatly reduced."[115]

Case Study *Drip system drops water requirements for chili farm.* A Columbus, New Mexico, farmer who each year grows 1,000 acres of chilies reported that the chili fields irrigated by drip systems use only 15 to 20% of the amount of water needed on the fields watered by conventional, siphon-tube ditch irrigation. In addition, the fields irrigated by drip systems produced 12 tons of chilies per acre compared with 6 to 9 tons for fields with nondrip irrigation. Because of these results, the farmer is in the process of installing drip irrigation in his other fields.

Case Study *Study documents lower watering needs for cotton with subsurface drip irrigation.* A ten-year study of subsurface drip irrigation of cotton crops at a 3-acre experimental plot at the USDA's Cotton Research Station in Shafter, California, found that the amount of water required for drip systems is only 24 inches per acre compared with 42 inches per acre for furrow irrigation systems.[117]

Case Study *Drip systems boost crop production in Israel.* A study of the production of potatoes, apples, and bananas in Israel showed a 60% reduction in water demand when growers used drip irrigation compared with the conventional irrigation practices used in 1970. Drip irrigation of avocados and cotton achieved a 30% reduction in water demand.[118]

Case Study *Water savings increase corn growth with drip in Kansas study.* A three-year study of corn grown with subsurface drip irrigation in Colby, Kansas, found a water demand reduction of approximately 25% compared with previous irrigation requirements. Corn grown with the drip system produced higher yields per unit of water use compared with that grown with furrow irrigation.[119]

Crop Yields

Drip-under-plastic irrigation produced a 60% higher yield of melons (cantaloupe and honeydew) than furrow irrigation in a side-by-side evaluation of the two methods conducted by the Texas Agricultural Extension Service. The higher production rate was attained with about 33% of the water and 50% of the fertilizer required by the furrow-irrigated field. The large water savings and higher crop yields were attributed to the efficiency of drip irrigation and the elimination of tailwater and overirrigation. The higher cost of the drip-under-plastic system was paid back primarily from the "quicker-to-market" benefit achieved through faster seed germination and crop growth.[112]

Costs

The cost of drip irrigation ranges from $850 to $1,000 per acre,[86] depending on the type of drip tape used, tape spacing, the filtration system required, and the automation system installed. Capital costs for drip systems are higher than those for sprinkler systems because drip systems require large quantities of pipes, tubes, filters, emitters, and related devices. Routine maintenance costs can also be higher, although not in all cases. The cost of drip irrigation is expected to decline as the technology becomes more widely used and competition among drip system manufacturers intensifies. The higher initial costs of drip systems are often offset by lower water costs, improved crop yields, and reduced chemical needs.

An inexpensive drip system designed for small farms in developing countries and pioneered by International Development Enterprises, a nonprofit organization based in Colorado, costs only about $100 per acre.[31]

5.9 TAILWATER REUSE

Tailwater reuse involves capturing field runoff in pits dug at the end of gravity-irrigated rows in low-lying areas of a field or farm and reapplying the water at the top of the field or on an adjacent field. Tailwater runoff occurs when the soil in irrigated rows becomes saturated, causing water to travel down the drainage ditches and resulting in water losses from evaporation and deep percolation. Prolonged runoff in drainage ditches often leads to waterlogging of the field, as shown in Figure 5.23, particularly near the lower end of the furrows where tailwater collects in small reservoirs or playas. This situation can reduce crop yields and require land to be removed from production.

Components of a typical tailwater reuse system include a drainage ditch, a tailwater reservoir, and a pump and pipeline to collect the tailwater at the end of the field and return it for reapplication, as shown in Figure 5.24. The tailwater collects in the drainage ditch and is carried to the tailwater reservoir for temporary storage. The pump transfers the water from the reservoir through a pipeline back to the same or a nearby field for reuse. Tailwater reuse is typically practiced only with gravity irrigation systems because under normal circumstances sprinkler and microirrigation systems should not cause tailwater runoff. The following factors should be considered in assessing whether tailwater reuse would be a beneficial water-management practice.

- Tailwater reuse is primarily effective with soils that have high water-holding capacity (the water-intake rates of sandy or porous soils limit runoff).
- In areas where soils contain high concentrations of salt, irrigators often avoid recirculating runoff water to prevent further salt buildup.
- Tailwater reuse can also spread weed seeds, diseases, and chemicals (e.g., herbicides, pesticides, and fertilizers) to other farms.

Figure 5.23   Tailwater waste depletes groundwater supplies, does not benefit crop yields, wastes fuel expended for unnecessary pumping, and can cause accidents. Allowing tailwater to escape from the property on which it is produced is a violation of state law in Texas.

Figure 5.24   A typical tailwater reuse system consists of a drainage ditch, a tailwater reservoir or lake, a pump, and a pipeline. Tailwater that collects in the drainage ditch is transferred to the lake, where it is stored temporarily and pumped out later for reapplication to the field.

(Figures 5.23 and 5.24 courtesy of High Plains Underground Water Conservation District No. 1, Lubbock, Texas)

In many areas of California and Arizona, tailwater reuse is encouraged because it allows farmers to use higher irrigation flow rates, which can improve DU by reducing differences in the amount of time soils at the top and bottom of a field have for water uptake. Although tailwater is typically used on the same field (tailwater return) or an adjacent field, it can be reused effectively at the district level if it contains no troublesome constituents.

In Texas, tailwater runoff is subject to rules governing water waste. According to Texas state law, water waste as it pertains to irrigation tailwater is defined as "willfully or negligently causing, suffering, or permitting underground water to escape into any river, creek, natural watercourse, depression, lake, reservoir, drain, sewer, street, highway, road or road ditch, or onto any land other than that of the owner of the well; or groundwater pumped for irrigation that escapes as irrigation tailwater onto land other than that of the owner of the well unless permission has been granted by the occupant of the land receiving the discharge."[120]

A survey of tailwater occurrences in the Texas High Plains Water District found a common thread: producer use of furrow irrigation to irrigate the corners of fields where center pivots could not reach. Because furrow irrigation of field corners is only about 60% efficient and invariably causes tailwater runoff, it may make more sense for farmers to sacrifice cultivating those areas than to pay fines for causing tailwater runoff. To alert farmers to this problem before a fine is levied, the water district documents incidents of tailwater runoff with photographs, written reports, and notifications to the landowners and irrigators. Chronic incidents of tailwater runoff may be subject to lawsuits by the district, with maximum fines of $500 for each incident and six months in the county jail.[120]

Even on sandy soil, surface residues left by conservation tillage are essential to improved rainfall infiltration. They reduce raindrop impact energy, prevent surface sealing, and slow runoff to allow more of the rain to get into the soil. Surface residues help irrigation infiltration too."

—Jim Hook, professor of soil and water management, College of Agriculture and Environmental Sciences, University of Georgia at Tifton

Water Savings, Benefits, and Costs From Tailwater Reuse

Water Savings

By recirculating field runoff, tailwater reuse pits can achieve water savings of 10 to 30% compared with conventional gravity systems, depending on field topography and soil characteristics.[17] The type and extent of drainage ditch modification and tailwater recirculation to the top of the field determine the amount of water a tailwater reuse system can save. Irrigators should also consider the use of technologies such as surge valves to minimize or eliminate tailwater problems altogether. Tailwater recirculation systems provide the best results on fields that have been laser-leveled because the depth of water on those fields is carefully managed.[121]

Costs

Installing a tailwater reuse system typically requires purchasing one or more pumps and installing a pipeline, preferably with a surge valve. Periodic maintenance tasks include removal of silt that accumulates in the tailwater pits. Reusing tailwater runoff typically reduces electricity costs for pumping, helping to defray the cost of the reuse system. Depending on the cost of water and electricity, the payback on investing in a tailwater reuse system can be less than a year to more than ten years.[122]

Figure 5.25   Residues from terminated wheat reduce soil moisture losses and help protect cotton plants from wind-blown sand.

(Figures 5.25 through 5.27 courtesy of High Plains Underground Water Conservation District No. 1, Lubbock, Texas)

Weed Control Is Critical With Conservation Tillage

Effective conservation tillage practices must include weed control. Uncontrolled weeds can take as much as 5 millimeters of water per day from soil, reducing the moisture available for crops and even lowering crop yields. Weeds also compete with crops for sunlight, space, and vital nutrients, further jeopardizing crop vitality and yield. Cropland managed under dryland conditions is especially vulnerable if weeds take water stored in the soil at planting time. Crop rotations, hand-weeding, effective tillage practices, and herbicides are options for controlling weeds.[126]

5.10 CONSERVATION TILLAGE

Conservation tillage involves leaving crop residue, or stubble, in fields to hold moisture received during winter months, helping to conserve soil and retain soil moisture. Conservation tillage requires at least 30% of the soil surface to be covered with crop stubble until preparation for the final seedbed begins. The plant stubble holds in moisture by reducing wind and water erosion, trapping water that would otherwise be lost to evaporation,[123, 124] as shown in Figure 5.25. The stubble also serves as a food source for migrating waterfowl. Used over a number of years, conservation tillage builds up organic matter in the soil and boosts fertility, helping to reduce future fertilizer needs.[123]

Conservation tillage techniques include minimum tillage, mulch tillage, ridge tillage, and no-till. Conservation tillage is often practiced with dryland farming, a system of producing crops in semi-arid regions (usually with less than 20 inches of annual rainfall) without irrigation. Dryland farming practiced with conservation tillage helps farmers rebuild soil moisture by leaving the land fallow (unplanted) or mulched in alternate years (summer fallowing).

Sowing a crop in plant residue left on the soil surface from the previous year is relatively simple. The practice also helps producers take advantage of multiple-cropping programs—for example, planting wheat in the fall as a "nurse crop" for cotton that will be planted in the spring. The cotton is sown in the killed wheat, and the wheat residue helps eliminate wind erosion and evaporation of soil moisture. Multiple-cropping practices also give the cotton a stronger start, increasing the likelihood of a healthier crop, as shown in Figure 5.26.[123]

Conservation tillage can help reduce pollution of nearby waterways by reducing runoff and nonpoint source pollution, such as farm chemicals attached to soil particles; reductions of 80 to 90% have been reported. Although conservation tillage is often credited with improving agricultural efficiency in the Great Plains, it may also be linked with reduced streamflows and lower reservoir levels, according to a computer modeling study at Kansas State University. In some cases, the effects of conservation tillage on water yields can be substantial, particularly in areas with large moisture deficits, because this practice can hold back much of a cropland's potential runoff.[125]

Figure 5.26   Healthy cotton plant

Water Savings, Benefits, and Costs From Conservation Tillage

Water Savings

The amount of water that can be saved through conservation tillage is not well documented. In general, the practice allows more water to be stored in the crop root zone and helps to reduce wind erosion and soil compaction from rainfall. This can help reduce irrigation needs for the next year's crop, especially during planting season.[123]

Crop Yields

Conservation tillage practices in the Texas High Plains have helped to increase cotton crop yields. For example, studies at the Agricultural Complex for Advanced Research and Extension Systems in Lamesa, Texas, showed that irrigated cotton planted in terminated wheat yielded 11% more cotton, increasing the net return by 20%. Similarly, experiments with dryland farming (Figure 5.27) have achieved lint increases of up to 32% and net returns of up to 75% compared with those achieved through conventional cotton-growing practices.[123]

Costs

The costs associated with conservation tillage are not well documented. The increased likelihood of weed growth associated with conservation tillage can increase farm management and herbicide costs. At the same time, over a number of years, conservation tillage practices can build up organic matter in soil that increases the soil's fertility; this, in turn, may reduce fertilizer needs and costs.

Figure 5.27   Dryland farming depends on rainfall and moisture stored in the soil to grow crops. Dryland farming practices incorporate conservation tillage and other techniques.

Figure 5.28 Canal lining helps to reduce water losses caused by seepage. Lining conveyance systems can also reduce on-farm water losses and eliminate weed growth and other obstructions to water flow. However, not all seepage is true loss, so lining should be planned carefully to avoid threatening plants, trees, and wildlife habitats that otherwise would not survive. (Photo courtesy of California Department of Water Resources)

5.11 CANAL AND CONVEYANCE SYSTEM LINING AND MANAGEMENT

Open, unlined canals and conveyance systems can lose large volumes of water through evaporation and seepage. Such losses vary with soil type, climate, and other factors, but conveyance systems constructed of earthen ditches have been reported to lose as much as 30% of their water from seepage and evaporation. Canal lining is illustrated in Figure 5.28.

Lining canals and conveyance systems can reduce water losses, allowing more water to reach the farms for which it is intended. Lining materials include concrete, bentonite clay, and newer pour-in-place plastics and textile membranes

The Downside of Canal Lining: Farmer Against Farmer—and Environmentalists

For several years, two groups of farmers in California's Tulare Irrigation District (TID) have been at odds and are engaged in a court battle over the TID's attempts to line a 10-mile stretch of earthen canal with cement. The project is designed to stop water from seeping into the ground on its way to farms in southern Tulare County, but lining this portion of the canal would destroy more than 200 mature oak trees. Landowners along the canal—most of them farmers who are joined by environmentalists—claim the project would inhibit aquifer recharge, lower the area's water table by an estimated 12 to 40 feet, and jeopardize their farms. They also argue that such water losses would kill most vegetation along the canal, spoil its tranquil riverlike setting, and force farmers along the canal to find new sources of water for their orchards and fields. The TID argues that it has a right to all the water in the canal, claiming that farmers along the canal do not have a right to the water—and do not pay for its use—whereas farmers served by the district do pay for the water they use. At least one farmer with walnut trees along the canal claims he has a signed contract from 1892 allowing him to use canal water, but the TID claims those rights have lapsed as a result of disuse. The canal, constructed in the 1870s, is a historic waterway. As of early 2001, the conflict had yet to be settled in court.[128]

such as fiberglass fabric or polyurethane dipped in a thermal-setting plastic. Water losses can also be reduced by installing underground plastic pipe to convey water and by removing flow obstructions such as weed growth on earth canals.[48]

Several management techniques can also reduce operational water losses associated with delivering water through ditches, canals, and conveyance systems. Irrigation districts that operate canals with automation can reduce spills and other losses by delivering water to farmers only on demand. Computer hardware and software programs are available to optimize canal automation and water delivery scheduling for farmers served by irrigation districts.[48]

Water Savings, Benefits, and Costs From Canal and Conveyance System Lining

Water Savings

A study of canal lining in dry climates indicates that a well-operated, lined conveyance system can reduce network losses to less than 5 to 10%.[127]

Costs

The scope of lining and managing canal and conveyance systems varies significantly, and lining projects can require large capital investments.

In certain situations, lining canal and conveyance systems can involve disadvantages that might be considered costs. In regions where irrigation water comes from both surface water and groundwater sources, seepage from unlined canals can recharge downstream groundwater wells that provide a vital source of supply for other irrigators. In such areas, canal lining may be counterproductive or a source of conflict. Irrigators should also evaluate other potential environmental effects before implementing this measure. Some plants, trees, and wildlife habitats near unlined canals may depend on seepage for survival; canal lining can shunt their water lifeline.[48]

In most irrigation systems, particularly those with long conveyance lengths, a disproportionate amount of water is lost as seepage in canals and never reaches the farmlands. For example, 40% of the water diverted from the Indus basin in Pakistan is lost in conveyance."

—World Commission on Dams, *Dams and Development: A New Framework for Decision-Making*

~

1. Sandra Postel, "Growing More Food With Less Water," *Scientific American,* vol. 284, no. 2, February 2001, pp. 46-51.
2. Sandra Postel, *Pillar of Sand: Can The Irrigation Miracle Last?* W.W. Norton & Company, New York, 1999, p. 112.
3. Sandra Postel, *Last Oasis,* W.W. Norton & Company, New York, rev. ed., 1997, p. 49.
4. U.S. Department of Agriculture, Economic Research Service, "Irrigation and Water Use: Overview," http://www.ers.usda.gov/Briefing/wateruse/overview.htm#this%20research, Jan. 4, 2001.
5. Wayne B. Solley, Robert R. Pierce, and Howard A. Perlman, *Estimated Use of Water in the United States in 1995,* U.S. Geological Survey Circular 1200, U.S Department of the Interior, U.S. Geological Survey, Reston, Va., 1998, pp. 11, 32.
6. Postel, *Pillar of Sand,* "History Speaks," chap. 1, pp. 13-39.
7. David E. Kromm and Stephen E. White, Conserving Water in the High Plains, Dept. of Geography, Kansas State University, Manhattan, Kans., 1990.
8. "Texans Draft Ogallala Plan," *U.S. Water News,* vol. 12, no. 3, September 1995.
9. "Llano Estacado Regional Water Plan Overview Presented During September 26 Public Hearing," *The Cross Section,* High Plains Underground Water Conservation District No. 1, Lubbock, Texas, vol. 46, no. 10, October 2000, p. 1.
10. Terry A. Howell, "Irrigation's Roles in Enhancing Water Use Efficiency," *Proc. of the Fourth Decennial National Irrigation Symposium,* Phoenix, Nov. 14-16, 2000, pp. 66-88.

11. B. Davidoff et al, "Optimum On-Farm Irrigation Efficiency for Sustainable Agriculture," North American Water and Environment Congress, American Society of Civil Engineers, 1996.

12. Policy Statement on Efficient Water Management for Conservation by Agricultural Suppliers, State Water Conservation Coalition Agricultural Conservation Task Force, Sacramento, Calif., March 1994.

13. Andrew A. Keller and Jack Keller, "Effective Efficiency: A Water Use Efficiency Concept for Allocating Freshwater Resources," Discussion Paper 22, Center for Economic Policy Studies, Winrock International, Arlington, Va., 1995, pp. 5-6.

14. United States Department of Agriculture, Economic Research Service, "Irrigation and Water Use: Questions and Answers: What Are the Available Irrigation Technologies and their Relative Advantages?" http://www.ers.usda.gov/Briefing/wateruse/Questions/qa5.htm, Jan. 4, 2001.

15. Postel, *Pillar of Sand*, p. 187.

16. "Irrigation Efficiency: System Upgrade Can Help Reduce Water Losses," *The Cross Section*, High Plains Underground Water Conservation District No. 1, Lubbock, Texas, vol. 44, no. 8, August 1998, p. 1.

17. D. H. Negri and J. J. Hanchar, *Water Conservation Through Irrigation Technology*, Agriculture Information Bulletin No. 576, U.S. Dept. of Agriculture, Economic Research Service, Washington, D.C., November 1989.

18. California Department of Water Resources, "Urban, Agricultural, and Environmental Water Use," *California Water Plan Update*, Bulletin 160-98, California Dept. of Water Resources, Sacramento, Calif., November 1998, chap. 4, pp. 4-19.

19. "Producers Can Save Water by Reducing Furrow Irrigation Losses," *The Cross Section*, High Plains Underground Water Conservation District No. 1, Lubbock, Texas, vol. 44, no. 2, 1998.

20. Postel, *Pillar of Sand*, pp. 92-93.

21. Postel, *Pillar of Sand*, pp. 100-101.

22. Peter H. Gleick, *Water: The Potential Consequences of Climate Variability and Change for the Water Resources of the United States*, prepared by the Pacific Institute for Studies in Development, Environment, and Security, Oakland, Calif., for the U.S. Dept. of the Interior through the U.S. Geological Survey, September 2000, pp. 1-5.

23. Gleick, *Water*, p. 1.

24. Gleick, *Water*, p. 9.

25. Postel, *Last Oasis*, p. 105.

26. Willem Van Tuijl, Improving Water Use in Agriculture: Experiences in the Middle East and North Africa, Technical Paper No. 201, The World Bank, Washington, D.C., 1993.

27. Natural Resources Conservation Service, "Irrigation Systems and Management," *National Engineering Handbook*, 210-vi-NEH, U.S. Dept. of Agriculture, Washington, D.C., August 1996 draft, p. 30.

28. "Surge Valves, Center Pivots, Drip Tape Improve Irrigation Efficiencies," *The Cross Section*, High Plains Underground Water Conservation District No. 1, Lubbock, Texas, vol. 44, no. 8, August 1998, p. 3.

29. National Research Council, *A New Era for Irrigation*, National Academy of Sciences, National Academy Press, Washington, D.C., 1996, p. 62.

30. Postel, *Pillar of Sand*, p. 176.

31. P. Polak, B. Nanes, and D. Adhikari, "A Low-Cost Drip Irrigation System for Small Farmers in Developing Countries," *Journal of the American Water Resources Assoc.*, vol. 33, no. 1, February 1997, p. 119.

32. Postel, *Last Oasis*, pp. 166-171.

33. Postel, *Last Oasis*, p. 53.

34. Postel, *Last Oasis*.

35. Postel, *Pillar of Sand*.

36. Postel, *Last Oasis*, p. 58.

37. Postel, *Pillar of Sand*, pp. 235-242.

38. California Department of Water Resources, *California Water Plan Update*, pp. 4-22.

39. California Department of Water Resources, "Appendix 4A: Urban and Agricultural Water Pricing," *California Water Plan Update*, pp. 5-6.

40. J. S. Wallace and C. H. Batchelor, "Managing Water Resources for Crop Production," *Philosophical Transactions of the Royal Society of London: Biological Sciences*, 1997, vol. 352, pp. 937-947.

41. Postel, *Pillar of Sand*, p. 172.

42. Megan Fidell and Arlene K. Wong, "Using Recycled Water for Agricultural Irrigation: City of Visalia and City of Santa Rosa," *Sustainable Use of Water: California Success Stories*, Pacific Institute for Studies in Development, Environment, and Security, Oakland, Calif., 1999, chap. 13, pp.141-143.

43. Kyra Epstein, "Reclaimed Water to Be Used for Recharge at Geothermal Electric Plant," *U.S. Water News*, vol. 17, no. 12, December 2000, p. 7.

44. California Department of Water Resources, *California Water Plan Update*, pp. 4-20, 5-21.

45. U.S. Bureau of Reclamation, Water Conservation Field Services Program, http://www.uc.usbr.gov/pro-gact/waterconsv/wcfsp_int.html, Aug. 16, 2000.

46. Colin Laird and Jim Dyer, "Feedback and Irrigation Efficiency," *Water Efficiency Implementation Report #4*, Rocky Mountain Institute, Snowmass, Colo., 1992.

47. "Hockley and Lynn County Drip Irrigation Field Days Scheduled for August," *The Cross Section*, High Plains Underground Water Conservation District No. 1, Lubbock, Texas, vol. 41, no. 8, August 1995, p. 1.

48. Agricultural Water Conservation Section, California Department of Water Resources, "Agricultural Efficient Water Management Practices That Stretch California's Water Supply," California Dept. of Water Resources, Sacramento, Calif., August 1995.

49. Richard Pinkham and Jim Dyer, "Linking Water and Energy Savings in Irrigation," *Water Efficiency Implementation Report #5*, Rocky Mountain Institute, Snowmass, Colo., 1993.

50. Division of Planning and Local Assistance, California Department of Water Resources, Loan Application for Water Conservation Project Construction, California Dept. of Water Resources, Sacramento, Calif., March 1998.

51. T. Slavin and G. Townsend, "On-Farm Irrigation System Evaluation Programs in California's Central Valley," presented at the Annual Conf. of the Irrigation Assoc., Nashville, Tenn., November 2-4, 1997.

52. C.M. Burt, A. J. Clemmens, and K.H. Solomon, "Identification and Quantification of Efficiency and Uniformity Components," *Proc. of the American Society of Civil Engineers Water Resources Division Specialty Conference*, San Antonio, Texas, Aug. 14-18, 1995.

53. "Irrigation District Reduces Waste by Improving Flow Control," *Irrigation Business & Technology*, August 1997.

54. J. Funck, "Poor Pumping Plant Efficiency Contributes to High Irrigation Costs; Maintaining Efficient Equipment Helps Reduce Energy and Water Waste," *The Cross Section*, High Plains Underground Water Conservation District No. 1, Lubbock, Texas, vol. 40, no.10, October 1995, p. 3.

55. L. Hardy, C. Gustafson, and D. Nelson, "Agricultural Water Supply and Conservation Issues in Northeast States," presented at the American Society of Civil Engineers Water Resources Planning and Management Division's Conf. on Integrated Water Resources Planning for the 21st Century, Boston, May 7-11, 1995.

56. G. Crenwelge, "Area Receives Above-Average Precipitation Following Soil Moisture Survey, "*The Cross Section*, vol. 44, no. 2, February 1998, p. 1.

57. Richard Mead, "Soil Moisture Instrumentation: Sensors & Strategies for the 21st Century," *Irrigation Journal*, September/October 1998, pp. 8-11.

58. B. Hanson and D. Peters, "Update on Moisture Sensors," *Irrigation Business & Technology*, vol. 5, no. 6, Expo Issue 1997, p. 43.

59. Lynn Moseley, "Cooperative Program Helps Producers Track Soil Moisture Conditions," *The Cross Section*, High Plains Underground Water Conservation District No. 1, Lubbock, Texas, vol. 43, no. 5, May 1997, p. 4.

60. T. Weems, "Survey of Moisture Measurement Instruments," *Irrigation Business & Technology*, January/February 1991.

61. M. Risinger and K. Carver, Neutron Moisture Meters, High Plains Underground Water Conservation District No. 1, Lubbock, Texas, August 1987.

62. "Soil Moisture: A Barometer of Next Year's Crop Yield," *The Cross Section*, High Plains Underground Water Conservation District No. 1, Lubbock, Texas, vol. 39, no. 12, December 1993, p. 3.

63. G. Richardson, "New Technology Cuts Farm Water Waste From the Ground Up," *U.S. Water News*, April 1992.

64. Natural Resources Conservation Service, "Irrigation Guide," part 652, *National Engineering Handbook*, p. 4-1.

65. Natural Resources Conservation Service, "Irrigation Guide," part 652, *National Engineering Handbook*, pp. 9-25.

66. Marvin E. Jensen and Richard G. Allen, "Evolution of Practical ET Estimating Methods," *Proc. of the Fourth Decennial National Irrigation Symposium*, Phoenix, Nov. 14-16, 2000, pp. 52-65.

67. R. L. Elliott et al, "The Role of Automated Weather Networks in Providing Evapotranspiration Estimates," *Proc.of the Fourth Decennial National Irrigation Symposium*, Phoenix, Nov. 14-6, 2000, p. 243.

68. S. Pleban, "Irrigation Software: Farming in the 21st Century," *Irrigation Business & Technology*, January/February 1995, p. 17.

69. R. E. Yoder, T. W. Ley, and R. L. Elliott, "Measurement and Reporting Practices for Automatic Agricultural Weather Stations," *Proc. of the Fourth Decennial National Irrigation Symposium*, Phoenix, Nov. 14-16, 2000, pp. 260-265.

70. Gary Hoffner, "Demonstrating Technology's Role in Irrigation Efficiency," *Irrigation Business & Technology*, January/February 1995.

71. California Irrigation Management Information System, California Department of Water Resources, http://www.dpla.water.ca.gov/cgi-bin/cimis/cimis/hq/main.pl, July 27, 2000.

72. Natural Resources Conservation Service, U.S. Department of Agriculture, "SCS SCHEDULER," http://www.wcc.nrcs.usda.gov/water/quality/common/h2oqual.html, Oct. 6, 1997.

73. Natural Resources Conservation Service, U.S. Department of Agriculture, "Irrigation Guide," part 652, *National Engineering Handbook*, pp. 9-28.

74. V. F. Bralts, W. Shayya, and R. von Bernuth, "Irrigation Management and Water Resources Planning Using the SCS Scheduler," presented at the American Society of Civil Engineers Water Resources Planning and Management Division's Conf. on Integrated Water Resources Planning for the 21st Century, Boston, May 7-11, 1995.

75. Postel, *Pillar of Sand*, p. 181.

76. California Department of Water Resources, Fifteen Years of Growth and a Promising Future: The California Irrigation Management Information System, California Dept. of Water Resources, Sacramento, Calif., December 1997, p. 2.

77. F. Frank, "Researchers Save Agriculture Millions," *Irrigation Business & Technology*, January/February 1995.

78. Albert J. Clemmens, "Level-Basin Irrigation Systems: Adoption, Practices, and the Resulting Performance," *Proc. of the Fourth Decennial National Irrigation Symposium*, Phoenix, Nov. 14-16, 2000, pp. 273-282.

79. V. M. Bathurst, Wellton-Mohawk On-Farm Irrigation Improvement Program Post Evaluation Report, Soil Conservation Service, U.S. Dept. of Agriculture, Phoenix.

80. "Rice Growers Use Lasers, Manage Soils to Cut Water 38%," *Water Conservation News*, Water Conservation Office, California Dept. of Water Resources, Sacramento, Calif., July 1998, p. 1.

81. "Furrow Dikes, Crop Residues Help Conserve Ground Water," *The Cross Section*, High Plains Underground Water Conservation District No. 1, Lubbock, Texas, vol. 45, no. 1, January 1999, p. 4.

82. Furrow Diking in Texas, Publication No. B-1539, Texas Agricultural Extension Service, College Station, Texas, March 1986.

83. "Drag Socks, Furrow Dikes Help Area Producers Reduce Water Losses," *The Cross Section*, High Plains Underground Water Conservation District No. 1, Lubbock, Texas, vol. 41, no. 6, June 1995, p. 4.

84. "Lockney Producer Seizes Opportunities to Capture Precipitation," *The Cross Section*, High Plains Underground Water Conservation District No. 1, Lubbock, Texas, vol. 39, no.12, December 1993, p. 1.

85. "Furrow Dikes and Plant Residues Capture Precipitation on Field," *The Cross Section*, High Plains Underground Water Conservation District No. 1, Lubbock, Texas, vol. 41, no.1, January 1995.

86. Personal communication, Carmon McCain, Information/Education Director, High Plains Underground Water Conservation District No. 1, Lubbock, Texas, Oct. 28, 1998.

87. Lynn Moseley, "Irrigation Application Efficiency Pays Off for Lubbock County Producer," *The Cross Section*, High Plains Underground Water Conservation District No. 1, Lubbock, Texas, vol. 44, no. 9, September 1998, p. 1.

88. A.D. Schneider, G. Buchleiter, and D.C. Kincaid, "LEPA Irrigation Developments," *Proc. of the Fourth Decennial National Irrigation Symposium*, Phoenix, Nov. 14-16, 2000, pp. 89-96.

89. S. M. Masud and R. D. Lacewell, Energy, Water, and Economic Savings of Improved Production Systems on the Texas High Plains, Technical article 25155 of the Texas Agricultural Experiment Station, published in the *American Journal of Alternative Agriculture*, vol. 5, no. 2, 1990.

90. Leon New and Guy Fipps, LEPA Conversion and Management, Publication No. B-1691, Texas Agricultural Extension Service, College Station, Texas, October 1990.

91. Ken Carver, "Pump Plant Efficiency Affects Design and Performance of Center Pivots," *The Cross Section*, High Plains Underground Water Conservation District No. 1, Lubbock, Texas, vol. 39, no.11, November 1993, p. 1.

92. Fawzi Karajeh et al, "Linear Irrigation System on the Move in California," *Proc. Conserv99*, American Water Works Assoc., Denver, 1999.

93. R. J. Panowicz, C. J. Phene, and L. Bensel, "Linear-Move Irrigation System Improved Water Use Efficiency of Carrots in California's Imperial Valley," *Proc. of the Fourth Decennial National Irrigation Symposium*, Phoenix, Nov. 14-16, 2000.

94. Mary DeSena, "USDA Researchers Develop 'Smart' Sprinkler Nozzle," *U.S. Water News*, vol. 16, no.1, January 1999, p. 21.

95. "Pipelines Stop Water Losses Associated With Irrigation From Open Ditches," *The Cross Section*, High Plains Underground Water Conservation District No. 1, Lubbock, Texas, vol. 41, no. 1, January 1995, p. 3.

96. "Irrigation System Upgrade Provides Producers With Substantial Water, Fuel Savings," *The Cross Section*, High Plains Underground Water Conservation District No. 1, Lubbock, Texas, vol. 36, no. 12, December 1990.

97. "Surge Valves Help Furrow Irrigators Improve Application Efficiencies," *The Cross Section*, High Plains Underground Water Conservation District No. 1, Lubbock, Texas, vol. 40, no.6, June 1994, p. 1.

98. Ken Carver and Becca Williams, Agricultural Water Conservation Equipment Low Interest Pilot Loan Program Establishment, Guidelines, Loan and Water Conserved, High Plains Underground Water Conservation District No. 1, Lubbock, Texas, 1992, p. 17.

99. J. A. Belt, "Surge Offers Hope for Surface Irrigation Efficiency," *Irrigation Business & Technology*, March 1993.

100. Conserving Water in Irrigated Agriculture, Texas Water Development Board, Austin, Texas, January 1988.

101. J. C. Henggeler, J. M. Sweeten, and C. W. Keese, "Surge Flow Irrigation," Publication No. L-2220, Texas Agricultural Extension Service, College Station, Texas, August 1986.

102. "Surge Valves, LEPA Systems Help Farmers Stop Tailwater Waste," *The Cross Section*, High Plains Underground Water Conservation District No. 1, Lubbock, Texas, vol. 40, no. 8, August 1994.

103. R. C. Bartholomay, "Surge Irrigation Works," *The Waterline*, Colorado State University Cooperative Extension, Fort Collins, Colo., no. 61, April 1993.

104. V. Moody, "The Benefits of Surge," *Irrigation Business & Technology*, March 1993.

105. D. F. Champion and R. C. Bartholomay, "Fertigation Through Surge Valves," *Service in Action*, Colorado State University Cooperative Extension, Fort Collins, Colo., no. 508, 1992.

106. R. C. Bartholomay, Note to Certain Area Farmers, Colorado State University Cooperative Extension, Fort Collins, Colo., June 2, 1992.

107. U.S. Bureau of Reclamation, Colorado River Basin Salinity Control Program, http://dataweb.usbr.gov/html/crwq.html#general, Feb. 5, 2001.

108. Edward Norum, "Drip Irrigation Run Times," *Irrigation Business & Technology*, vol. VIII, no. 2, January/February 2000, pp. 31-32.

109. B. R. Hanson, G. Fipps, and E. C. Martin, "Drip Irrigation of Row Crops: What Is the State of the Art?" *Proc. of the Fourth Decennial National Irrigation Symposium*, Phoenix, Nov. 14-16, 2000, pp. 391-400.

110. S. R. Evett et al, "Automatic Drip Irrigation of Corn and Soybean," *Proc. of the Fourth Decennial National Irrigation Symposium*, Phoenix, Nov. 14-16, 2000, pp. 401-408.

111. "Drip Irrigation: A Measured Approach to Farming," *Irrigation Business & Technology*, March 1992.

112. G. Fipps, "Melons Demonstrate Drip Under Plastic Efficiency," *Irrigation Journal*, November/December 1993, p. 8.

113. T. Daniel, "Producers Ask Questions About Drip," *The Cross Section*, High Plains Underground Water Conservation District No. 1, Lubbock, Texas, vol. 40, no.10, October 1994, p. 2.

114. Adapted from G. Fipps and E. Perez, "Microirrigation of Melons Under Plastic Mulch in the Lower Rio Grande Valley of Texas," *Proc. of the Fifth International Microirrigation Congress*, American Society of Agricultural Engineers, Orlando, Fla., 1995.

115. Lynn Moseley, "Drip Irrigation Helps Lubbock County Producers Increase Cotton Yield, "*The Cross Section*, High Plains Underground Water Conservation District No. 1, Lubbock, Texas, vol. 44, no. 12, December 1998, pp. 1-2.

116. Mary DeSena, "Drip Irrigation Moving Into Mainstream Farming," *U.S. Water News*, 15, August 1998, p. 21.

117. "Irrigation by Subsurface Drip Proves Cost Effective," *Water Conservation News*, California Dept. of Water Resources, Sacramento, Calif., July 1991.

118. M. Xie, U. Kuffner, and G. Le Moigne, User Water Efficiently: Technological Options, Technical Paper No. 205, The World Bank, Washington, D.C., 1993, p. 21.

119. F. R. Lamm et al, "Drip Irrigation for Corn: A Promising Prospect," *Irrigation Business & Technology*, March 1992.

120. "Area Residents Becoming Less Tolerant of Irrigation Tailwater Waste," *The Cross Section*, High Plains Underground Water Conservation District No. 1, Lubbock, Texas, vol. 40, no.10, October 1995.

121. Peter H. Gleick, "Improving Water Quality Through Reducing the Use of Herbicides on Rice: An Effective Collaboration Between Growers and Public Agencies," in *Sustainable Use of Water: California Success Stories*, Pacific Institute for Studies in Development, Environment, and Security, Oakland, Calif., 1999, chap. 17, pp. 191-193

122. "Cost-Effective Farm Management Practices Available to Stop Tailwater Waste," *The Cross Section*, High Plains Underground Water Conservation District No. 1, Lubbock, Texas, vol. 40, no. 8, August 1994, p. 1.

123. Lynn Moseley, "Conservation Tillage Can Help Hold Winter Precipitation on Farmland," *The Cross Section*, High Plains Underground Water Conservation District No. 1, Lubbock, Texas, vol. 42, no. 10, October 1996, p. 4.

124. Jim Hook, "Drought Management Essential in Southeast," *Irrigation Journal*, vol. 50, no. 2, March/April 2000, p. 27.

125. "Computer Model Shows Reduced Streamflows," *U.S. Water News*, September 1994.

126. M. B. Kirkham, "Water Conservation Practices," *Irrigation Business & Technology*, vol. VIII, no. 4, August/September 2000, pp. 17-21, 30.

127. Harald D. Frederiksen, Drought Planning and Water Efficiency Implications in Water Resources Management, Technical Paper No. 185, The World Bank, Washington, D.C., 1992.

128. "Canal Lining Project Pits Farmer Against Farmer in California," *U.S. Water News*, vol. 17, no. 12, December 2000, p. 21.

The Water Conservation Network

"Access to knowledge is the superb, the supreme act of truly great civilizations."
—Toni Morrison

THIS CHAPTER IDENTIFIES organizations, government agencies, publications, directories of manufacturers, and Internet resources related to water conservation. This listing is not inclusive and does not imply any endorsement, recommendation, or criticism of any person, organization, agency, publication, company, manufacturer, service, or product.

6

6.1 ORGANIZATIONS

Water Conservation
- California Urban Water Conservation Council, http://www.cuwcc.org
- WaterShare, U.S. Bureau of Reclamation's Virtual Water Conservation Center, http://www.watershare.usbr.gov or http://208.186.132.85
- Water Wiser, National Water Efficiency Clearinghouse, http://www.waterwiser.org

Water
- American Water Works Association, http://www.awwa.org
- American Water Works Research Foundation, http://www.awwarf.com
- American Water Resources Association, http://www.awra.org/
- Association of Metropolitan Water Agencies, http://www.amwa-water.org
- California Department of Water Resources, http://www.dwr.water.ca.gov
- Delaware River Basin Commission, http://www.state.nj.us/drbc
- National Association of Water Companies, http://www.nawc.org
- National Drinking Water Clearinghouse, http://www.estd.wvu.edu/ndwc/ndwc_homepage.html
- National Rural Water Association, http://www.nrwa.org
- National Small Flows Clearinghouse, http://www.estd.wvu.edu/nsfc/NSFC_homepage.html
- National Water Center, http://nationalwatercenter.org
- National Watershed Network, http://www.ctic.purdue.edu/watershed/US_watersheds_8digit.html
- Soil and Water Conservation Society, http://www.swcs.org
- Texas Waternet, http://twri.tamu.edu
- The World's Water, http://www.worldwater.org
- Universities Water Information Network, http://www.uwin.siu.edu
- Water Environment Federation, http://www.wef.org
- Water Quality Association, http://www.wqa.org
- Water Resources of the United States, http://water.usgs.gov

Drought
- National Drought Mitigation Center, http://enso.unl.edu/ndmc
- National Drought Policy Commission, http://www.fsa.usda.gov/drought
- Western Drought Coordination Council, http://enso.unl.edu/wdcc

Climate Change
- Climate Ark, http://www.climateark.org
- Global Change, http://www.globalchange.org

Rivers and Dams

- American Rivers, http://www.amrivers.org
- International Rivers Network, http://www.irn.org/
- United States Society on Dams, http://www2.privatei.com/~uscold/
- World Commission on Dams, http://www.dams.org

Education

- Georgia Water Wise Council, http://www.griffin.peachnet.edu/waterwise/wwc.htm
- Learning to Be Water Wise & Energy Efficient, http://www.getwise.org
- Renew America, http://solstice.crest.org/sustainable/renew_america
- Water Education Foundation, http://www.water-ed.org
- Water Science For Schools, http://wwwga.usgs.gov/edu
- Water Use It Wisely, http://www.wateruseitwisely.com

Codes and Standards

- American National Standards Institute, http://www.ansi.org
- American Society of Plumbing Engineers, http://www.aspe.org
- Appliance Standards Awareness Project, http://www.standardsASAP.org
- Association of Home Appliance Manufacturers, http://www.aham.org
- Building Officials Code Administrators International, http://www.bocai.org
- Council of American Building Officials, http://www.icbo.org
- Green Seal Standards, http://www.greenseal.org/standard.htm
- International Association of Plumbing & Mechanical Officials, http://www.iapmo.org
- National Institute of Standards and Technology, http://www.nist.gov
- NSF International, http://www.nsf.org
- Standards Council of Canada, http://www.scc.ca
- Underwriters Laboratories, http://www.ul.com
- Uniform Building Code, http://www.bicsi.org/bcodes/sld014.htm
- Uniform Plumbing Code, http://www.iapmo.org

Appliances and Plumbing Fixtures

- American Society of Plumbing Engineers, http://www.aspe.org
- Association of Home Appliance Manufacturers, http://www.aham.org
- Consortium for Energy Efficiency, http://www.CEEforMT.org
- Green Seal, http://www.greenseal.org/
- Laundry Rooms Save Water, http://www.laundrywise.com
- Multi-Housing Laundry Association, http://www.mhla.com
- National Association of Plumbing Heating Cooling Contractors, http://www.naphcc.org
- National Kitchen & Bath Association, http://www.nkba.org
- Plumbing Manufacturers Institute, http://www.pmihome.org
- Restrooms of the Future, http://www.restrooms.org

Landscape

Design and Maintenance

- American Society of Landscape Architects, http://www.asla.org
- Clean Air Lawn Care, http://www.aqmd.gov/monthly/garden.html
- Georgia Water Wise Council, http://www.griffin.peachnet.edu/waterwise/wwc.htm
- Irrigation Association, http://www.irrigation.org
- Professional Lawn Care Association of America, http://www.plcaa.org
- Smaller American Lawns Today,
  http://www.conncoll.edu/ccrec/greennet/arbo/salt/salt.html
- Smart Gardening, http://www.smartgardening.com
- Xeriscape™, http://www.xeriscape.org

Native Plants and Ecological Restoration

- American Association of Botanical Gardens & Arboreta, http://www.aabga.org
- Atlas of Relations Between Climatic Parameters and Distributions of Important Trees and Shrubs in North America (U.S.G.S),
  http://greenwood.cr.usgs.gov/ pub/ppapers/p1650-a
- Butterfly WebSite, http://www.mgfx.com/butterfly
- Center for Plant Conservation, http://www.mobot.org/CPC/welcome.html
- Evergreen Foundation, http://www.evergreen.ca
- Flora of North America, http://hua.huh.harvard.edu/FNA
- Greatplains.org, http://greatplains.org
- Green Landscaping With Native Plants, http://www.epa.gov/greenacres/
- Lady Bird Johnson Wildflower Center, (formerly the National Wildflower Research Center), http://www.wildflower.org
- National Plants Database (USDA), http://plants.usda.gov
- Native Plant Conservation Initiative, http://www.nfwf.org/rfp_2001.html#npci
- Native Plant Organizations in North America,
  http://www.wildflower.org/links.html
- Native Plants Forum, http://www.gardenweb.com/forums/natives/
- Organic Mulches,
  http://www.ext.vt.edu/departments/envirohort/factsheets2/landsmaint/jul93pr4.html
- Plant Conservation Alliance, http://www.nps.gov/plants
- Society for Ecological Restoration, http://www.ser.org
- Wildland Invasive Species Program, http://tncweeds.ucdavis.edu
- Wild Ones-Natural Landscapers, Ltd., http://www.for-wild.org
- WindStar Wildlife Institute, http://www.windstar.org

Rainwater Harvesting and Cisterns

- American Rainwater Catchment Systems Association,
  http://www.nku.edu/~biosci/arcsa/arcsa.html
- Center for Maximum Potential Building Systems, http://www.cmpbs.org
- Tree People, http://www.treepeople.org

Industrial, Commercial, and Institutional

- American Society of Heating, Refrigeration and Air-Conditioning Engineers, http://www.ashrae.org
- BEST: Businesses for an Environmentally Sustainable Tomorrow (City of Portland Energy Office, Oregon),
  http://www.ci.portland.or.us/energy/bestmain.html
- Buildings That Save Water Project,
  http://www.cranfield.ac.uk/sims/water/recyclingintro.htm
- Business For Social Responsibility, http://www.bsr.org
- Cooling Tower Institute, http://www.cti.org
- Ecology Building Society, http://www.ecology.co.uk
- Environmental Building and Design, http://www.lib.msu.edu/link/envbldg.htm
- Evaporative Coolers, http://www.ci.phoenix.az.us/WATER/evapcool.html
- Green Hotels Association, http://www.greenhotels.com
- High-Efficiency Commercial Air Conditioning and Heat Pump Initiative,
  http://www.ceeformt.org/com/hecac/hecac-main.php3
- National Spa & Pool Institute, http://www.nspi.org
- Office of Industrial Technologies: Petroleum (U.S. DOE),
  http://www.oit.doe.gov/petroleum
- Office of Industrial Technologies: Steel (U.S. DOE), http://www.oit.doe.gov/steel
- Ski Area Citizen's Coalition, http://www.skiareacitizens.com
- Steam Challenge Program (U.S. DOE),
  http://www.oit.doe.gov/bestpractices/steam
- U.S. Green Building Council, http://www.usgbc.org
- Waste Minimization/Pollution Prevention Resource Directory (U.S. EPA),
  http://www.epa.gov/owm/genwave.htm
- Water Alliances for Voluntary Efficiency (WAVE) Program (U.S. EPA),
  http://www.epa.gov/owm/faqw.htm

Agricultural

- American Society of Agricultural Engineers, 616/429-0300,
  http://www.asae.org
- Food and Agriculture Organization of the United Nations, http://apps.fao.org
- Food and Development Policy/Food First, http://www.foodfirst.org
- High Plains Underground Water Conservation District No. 1, Lubbock, Texas, http://www.hpwd.com
- International Development Enterprises, http://www.ideorg.org
- Irrigation Association, http://www.irrigation.org

Weather Stations

- Agriculture and Agri-Food Canada Lethbridge Research Centre Weather Station Network (Alberta), http://res2.agr.ca/lethbridge/weather/webwthr.htm
- AgriMet, http://mac1.pn.usbr.gov/agrimet/index.html
- Arizona Meterological Network, AZMET, http://ag.arizona.edu/azmet/
- Automated Weather Network, http://fawn.ifas.ufl.edu/

- California Irrigation Management Information System (CIMIS), http://www.dpla.water.ca.gov/cgi-bin/cimis/cimis/hq/main.pl
- GCIP Insitu Data Source Module, Atmospheric Data Links, State/Local Network Links, http://www.joss.ucar.edu/gcip/state_nets.html
- Massachusetts Department of Environmental Management Rainfall Program, http://www.state.ma.us/dem/programs/rainfall/index.htm
- Michigan State University Agricultural Weather Office Hourly Automated Weather Station Data, http://www.agweather.geo.msu.edu/AWO/Current/Automated/hourly.html
- National Weather Service, www.srh.noaa.gov
- National Weather Service: Interactive Weather Information Network, http://weather.gov
- North Dakota Agricultural Weather Network, http://www.ext.nodak.edu/weather/ndawn/
- NWS BVT Vermont Mesonet, http://www.nws.noaa.gov/er/btv//html/mesonethome.html
- Public Agricultural Weather System (Washington State University), PAWS, http://frost.prosser.wsu.edu
- Soil Climate Analysis Network (SCAN), http://www.wcc.nrcs.usda.gov/scan
- Texas Mesonet , http://www.met.tamu.edu/texnet/mesonet.html

Water Recycling and Reuse
- National Onsite Wastewater Recycling Association, http://www.nowra.org
- Water Recycling and Reuse: Environmental Benefits, http://www.epa.gov/region9/water/recycling/index.html
- WateReuse Association, http://www.webcom.com/h2o

Energy Efficiency
- American Council for an Energy-Efficient Economy, http://www.aceee.org
- Consortium for Energy Efficiency, http://www.CEEforMT.org
- Environmental and Energy Study Institute, http://www.eesi.org
- Northeast Energy Efficiency Partnerships, http://www.neep.org
- Rocky Mountain Institute, http://www.rmi.org
- Solstice, http://solstice.crest.org

6.2 GOVERNMENT AGENCIES AND PROGRAMS

Federal

Army Corps of Engineers

- Army Corps of Engineers Homepage, http://www.usace.army.mil

Department of Agriculture

- Agricultural Research Service, Natural Resources and Sustainable Agricultural Systems, http://www.nps.ars.usda.gov/programs/nrsas.htm
- Economic Research Service, http://www.econ.ag.gov/
- National Agricultural Library, Water Quality Information Center, http://www.nal.usda.gov/wqic

Department of Energy

- Energy Efficiency and Renewable Energy Network, http://www.eren.doe.gov/EE/buildings.html
- Federal Energy Management Program, http://www.eren.doe.gov/femp
- Lawrence Berkeley National Laboratory, http://eande.lbl.gov/CBS/femp/femp.html
- National Renewable Energy Laboratory, http://www.nrel.gov

Department of the Interior

- Bureau of Reclamation, http://www.usbr.gov
- Bureau of Reclamation, WaterShare, http://208.186.132.85
- Environmental Protection Agency
  - Office of Water, http://www.epa.gov/watrhome
  - Water Alliance for Voluntary Efficiency (WAVE Program), http://www.epa.gov/OWM/genwave.htm

U.S. Geological Survey

- U.S.G.S. Homepage, http://www.usgs.gov
- U.S.G.S. Water Use in the United States, http://water.usgs.gov/public/watuse

State, Regional, and Municipal Water Conservation Programs

- Albuquerque, New Mexico: http://www.cabq.gov/waterconservation
- Arizona Municipal Water Users Association, http://www.amwua.org
- Austin, Texas, http://www.ci.austin.tx.us/watercon
- Brainerd Public Utilities, Minnesota, http://www.bpu.org/conserve.htm
- California Department of Water Resources, http://www.dwr.water.ca.gov
- Cary, North Carolina, http://www.townofcary.org/depts/pwdept/wcp.htm
- Central Utah Project, http://www.cuwcd.com/cupca
- Chicago Department of Water, Illinois, http://www.ci.chi.il.us/Water/Conservation.html

- Colorado Office of Water Conservation, http://cwcb.state.co.us/owc/Officewc.htm
- Delaware River Basin Commission, http://www.state.nj.us/drbc/drbc.htm
- Denver Water, Colorado, http://www.water.denver.co.gov/indexmain.html
- Easton Utilities Water Department, Maryland, http://www.eastonutilities.com/water/wconspro.html
- Florida Water Wise Council, http://www.urdls.com/fwwc/index.htm
- Georgia Water Wise Council, http://www.griffin.peachnet.edu/waterwise/wwc.htm
- Hillsborough County, Florida, http://www.hillsboroughcounty.org/soilwater/water.html
- Houston, Texas, http://www.ci.houston.tx.us/pwe/utilities/conservation
- Imperial Irrigation District, California, http://www.iid.com/water
- Las Vegas Valley Water District, Nevada, http://www.lvvwd.com
- Los Angeles Department of Water and Power, California, http://www.ladwp.com/water/conserv
- Marin Municipal Water District, California, http://www.marinwater.org/waterconservation.html
- Montana Water, http://water.montana.edu
- New Mexico Water Conservation Program, http://www.ose.state.nm.us/water-info/conservation/index.html
- New York City, New York, http://www.ci.nyc.ny.us/html/dep
- North Carolina Division of Pollution Prevention and Environmental Assistance, http://www.p2pays.org
- Phoenix Water Department, Arizona, http://www.ci.phoenix.az.us/WATER
- Pollution Prevention Coalition of Palm Beach County, Florida, http://p2.ces.fau.edu
- Portland, Oregon, http://www.water.ci.portland.or.us/siteindx.htm#conservation
- San Diego, California, http://www.ci.san-diego.ca.us/water/conservation/index.shtml
- Seattle Public Utilities, Washington, http://www.ci.seattle.wa.us/util/RESCONS
- Southwest Florida Water Management District, http://www.dep.state.fl.us/swfwmd/xeris/swfxeris.html
- Southwestern Water Conservation District, Colorado, http://www.waterinfo.org
- St. Louis County Water Company, Missouri, http://www.slcwater.com/othinfo/conserve.htm
- Susquehanna River Basin Commission, http://www.srbc.net
- Texas Water Development Board, http://www.twdb.state.tx.us
- Texas Water Resources Institute, http://twri.tamu.edu
- Virginia Beach, Virginia, http://www.virginia-beach.va.us/dept/putility
- Virginia Conservation Reference Source, http://www.virginiaconservation.org
- Western States Water Council, http://www.westgov.org/wswc

6.3 INTERNATIONAL ORGANIZATIONS AND AGENCIES

Canada

- Canadian Water and Wastewater Association, http://www.cwwa.ca
- Canadian Water Resources Association, http://www.cwra.org
- Greater Vancouver Regional District, British Columbia, Canada, http://www.gvrd.bc.ca/services/water
- Environment Canada, http://www.ec.gc.ca/water/en/manage/effic/e_weff.htm
- Toronto, Ontario, Canada, http://www.city.toronto.on.ca/water
- Western Canada Water and Wastewater Association, http://www.wcwwa.ca
- Winnipeg, Manitoba, Canada, http://www.mbnet.mb.ca/wpgwater

United Kingdom

- Environment Agency, National Water Demand Management Centre, http://www.environment-agency.gov.uk/envinfo/nwdmc
- Office of Water Services, http://www.ofwat.gov.uk
- Water UK, http://www.water.org.uk

Other

- Global Water Partnership, http://www.gwp.sida.se/gwp/gwp/welc.html
- International Irrigation Management Institute, http://www.cgiar.org/iwmi
- International Water Resources Association, http://www.iwra.siu.edu
- Stockholm International Water Institute, http://www.siwi.org
- World Bank: Water, http://wbln0018.worldbank.org/egfar/gfsc.nsf

6.4 PUBLICATIONS

- *Conservation News, California* Department of Water Resources, Sacramento, California
- *The Cross Section,* High Plains Underground Water Conservation District No. 1, Lubbock, Texas
- *Demand Management Bulletin,* National Water Demand Management Centre, Environment Agency, United Kingdom
- *FEMP Bulletin,* U.S. Department of Energy, Federal Energy Management Program, Washington, D.C.
- *Irrigation Business & Technology,* Falls Church, Virginia
- *Irrigation Journal,* Chicago, Illinois
- *Journal AWWA,* American Water Works Association, Denver, Colorado
- *Pipeline,* West Virginia University, Morgantown, West Virginia
- *Small Flows Quarterly,* West Virginia University, Morgantown, West Virginia
- *U.S. Water News,* Halstead, Kansas

6.5 DIRECTORIES FOR WATER-EFFICIENT PRODUCTS

Appliances and Plumbing Fixtures
- American Supply Association, http://www.asa.net/asa.asp
- Appliance.com, http://www.appliance.com
- Consumer Reports, http://www.ConsumerReports.org
- MasterPlumber.com, http://www.masterplumber.com
- Plumbing Manufacturers Institute, http://www.pmihome.org
- PlumbingSupply.com, http://www.PlumbingSupply.com
- PlumbingWeb.com, http://www.plumbingweb.com
- PlumbNet, http://www.PlumbNet.com
- Terry Love's Consumer Toilet Reports, http://www.terrylove.com/crtoilet.htm
- Toiletology 101, http://www.toiletology.com/index.shtml
- TumbleWash, http://www.tumblewash.com/
- World of Composting Toilets, http://www.compostingtoilet.org

Landscape and Irrigation Products
- Green Net, http://www.greenindustry.com
- Irrigation Association, http://63.72.168.122/ia/products.cfm
- IrrigationJournal.com, http://www.irrigationjournal.com
- National Gardening Association, http://www.garden.org/buyersguide
- Open Here, http://www.openhere.com/hag/gardening/plants/wildflowers
- Turfgrass Producers International, http://www.lawninstitute.com

Industrial, Commercial, and Institutional Equipment
- Flow Control Network, http://www.flowcontrolnetwork.com
- Green Builder, http://www.greenbuilder.com/sourcebook
- PM Engineer, http://bnp.com/listrental/pme_list.html
- USA BlueBook, 800/548-1234, http://www.usabluebook.com
- Water Online, http://www.wateronline.com

Agricultural and Irrigation Equipment
- Green Net, http://www.greenindustry.com
- Irrigation Association, http://63.72.168.122/ia/products.cfm
- IrrigationJournal.com, http://www.irrigationjournal.com

Appendices

APPENDIX A

Contents of a comprehensive water conservation plan, according to the U.S. Environmental Protection Agency's Water Conservation Plan Guidelines*

1. SPECIFY CONSERVATION PLANNING GOALS

- ☐ List of conservation planning goals and their relationship to supply-side planning
- ☐ Description of community involvement in the goals-development process

2. DEVELOP A WATER SYSTEM PROFILE

- ☐ Inventory of existing facilities, production characteristics, and water use
- ☐ Overview of conditions that might affect the water system and conservation planning

3. PREPARE A DEMAND FORECAST

- ☐ Forecast of anticipated water demand for future time periods
- ☐ Adjustments to demand based on known and measurable factors
- ☐ Discussion of uncertainties and "what if" (sensitivity) analysis

4. DESCRIBE PLANNED FACILITIES

- ☐ Improvements planned for the water system over a reasonable planning horizon
- ☐ Estimates of the total, annualized, and unit cost (per gallon) of planned supply-side improvements and additions
- ☐ Preliminary forecast of total installed water capacity over the planning period based on anticipated improvements and additions

5. IDENTIFY AND EVALUATE CONSERVATION MEASURES

- ☐ Review of conservation measures that have been implemented or that are planned for implementation
- ☐ Discussion of legal or other barriers to implementing recommended measures
- ☐ Identification of measures for further analysis

6. ANALYZE BENEFITS AND COSTS

- ☐ Estimates of total implementation costs and anticipated water savings
- ☐ Cost-effectiveness assessment for recommended conservation measures
- ☐ Comparison of implementation costs with avoided supply-side costs

7. SELECT CONSERVATION MEASURES

- ☐ Selection criteria for choosing conservation measures
- ☐ Identification of selected measures
- ☐ Explanation of why recommended measures will not be implemented
- ☐ Strategy and timetable for implementing conservation measures

8. INTEGRATE RESOURCES AND MODIFY FORECASTS

- ☐ Modification of water demand and supply capacity forecasts to reflect anticipated effects of conservation
- ☐ Discussion of the effects of conservation on planned water purchases, improvements, and additions
- ☐ Discussion of the effects of planned conservation measures on water utility revenues

9. PRESENT IMPLEMENTATION AND EVALUATION STRATEGY

- ☐ Approaches for implementing and evaluating the conservation plan
- ☐ Certification of the conservation plan by the system's governing body

---

* For the Intermediate Plan and Advanced Plan Guidelines (the Basic Plan Guidelines for small systems are simplified). See the source document for guidance on the scope of analysis and level of detail associated with each planning step shown; these vary by the size of the population served by a water system.

Source: U.S. Environmental Protection Agency, Water Conservation Plan Guidelines *(EPA-832-D-98-001), U.S. EPA, Washington, D.C., August 1998, Table 2-2, p. 41.*

Basic elements of a water integrated resource plan

These elements reflect a comprehensive planning approach that could be implemented by very large water systems. Not all water systems can or should invest the same level of resources in their planning processes. Elements of the outline can be adapted to particular needs and circumstances.

PRELIMINARIES

LETTER OF TRANSMITTAL AND ACKNOWLEDGMENTS

☐ To the agency for which planning report was prepared

☐ List of individuals and agencies who helped develop the plan

EXECUTIVE SUMMARY

☐ Should highlight findings, conclusions, and recommendations

☐ Should be specific, orderly, and concise

☐ May refer to specific sections of the report

☐ Clearly states requests for agency actions

TABLE OF CONTENTS

☐ Major headings and subheadings, including appendixes

☐ List of tables

☐ List of figures

NEED, SCOPE, AND OBJECTIVES OF THE PLAN

☐ Origins of the plan, including statutory and regulatory mandates

☐ Time frame of the plan

☐ What the plan does and does not cover

☐ Objectives of the plan (e.g., reliable service, minimal environmental impact, low costs and reasonable rates, load management, drought management, and long-term conservation and wise use)

☐ How study will be used in and adapted to future management and regulatory decision-making

GENERAL AND HISTORICAL BACKGROUND

☐ Location of system and nearby systems

☐ Geography, hydrology, meteorology, geology, surface water and groundwater, and so on

☐ Soil characteristics and subsurface conditions

☐ Demographics (past, present, and future population characteristics)

☐ Employment (industry, commercial, service, government)

☐ Residential, industrial, commercial, recreational, agricultural, and institutional development and redevelopment

☐ Land use (present and future, including land use in detail in the vicinity of existing and proposed water supply facilities)

☐ Drainage, water pollution control, and flood control management

☐ Wastewater facilities

STATEMENT OF CONDITIONS

DESCRIPTION OF WATER DELIVERY SYSTEM

☐ Map of service territory, including location of nearby systems

☐ Detail of location, age, cost, and physical condition of source of supply and pumping facilities, transmission facilities, treatment facilities, storage facilities, fire hydrants, and administrative offices and all other physical plant

DESCRIPTION OF RATE STRUCTURE

☐ Rate history, including regulatory proceedings

☐ Current rate structure including fees

☐ Metering and billing practices

☐ Ancillary services and rates charged

WATER QUALITY ISSUES

☐ Record of certification by state drinking water agency

☐ Record of water quality and compliance with water quality regulations

☐ Existing contamination issues and potential solutions

☐ Potential contamination issues and potential solutions

☐ Existing and planned water quality monitoring

WATER QUANTITY ISSUES

☐ Historical supply and reasons for variations

☐ Water supply forecasts (for utility and region)

☐ Description of drought probabilities and occurrence

☐ Historical demand and reasons for variations

☐ Description of average and peak demand patterns

☐ Water demand forecasts (short- and long-term by water-use sector)

☐ Potential for conservation and load management to affect demand

☐ Estimates of price elasticities for water demand by water-use sector

ANTICIPATED INFRASTRUCTURE NEEDS

☐ Replacements

☐ Improvements

☐ Additions to capacity to meet growth in demand

DESCRIPTION AND PRESCREENING OF ALTERNATIVES TO MEET INFRASTRUCTURE NEEDS

☐ Includes both structural (new supply) and nonstructural (conservation) options

☐ Technical feasibility of each alternative

☐ Benefits and costs of each alternative

☐ Economic, environmental, societal, and regulatory considerations

☐ Potential barriers

☐ Prescreening of alternatives for effectiveness and feasibility

EVALUATION OF ALTERNATIVES

ANALYSIS OF ALTERNATIVES

☐ Selection of most promising options for fashioning an effective, flexible, and responsive plan based on prescreening

☐ Integration of supply methods, methods for controlling and moderating demand

☐ Construction of scenarios pitting selected options against possible economic, environmental, societal, and regulatory circumstances

☐ Evaluation of economic and technical success of each mix of options under the circumstances of the various scenarios

☐ Analysis of uncertainties associated with each course of action

☐ Screening to eliminate unfeasible alternatives

SELECTION OF ALTERNATIVES FOR THE PLAN

☐ Ranking of alternatives according to incremental costs

☐ Further testing of each alternative for cost-effectiveness from various viewpoints (including rate-payers, utilities, and society)

☐ Reevaluation of alternatives considering economic, environmental, societal, and regulatory factors

☐ Development of rules for selecting the alternatives that optimize the plan's objectives

☐ Selection of the optimal course of action for implementation

IMPACT ANALYSIS OF SELECTED ALTERNATIVES

☐ Economic impact analysis (e.g., societal and rate-payer costs)

☐ Environmental impact analysis (e.g., irreversible effects)

☐ Societal and cultural impact analysis (e.g., consumer satisfaction)

☐ Regulatory impact analysis (e.g., regulatory costs)

DROUGHT CONTINGENCY AND EMERGENCY MANAGEMENT PLAN

☐ Identification of priority uses consistent with appropriate public policies

☐ Sources of emergency water supplies and diversions

☐ Potential use of pressure reduction

☐ Plans for public education and voluntary use reduction

☐ Plans for water-use bans, restrictions, and rationing

☐ Plans for pricing and penalties for excess use

☐ Coordination with other utilities and local authorities

COORDINATION AND CONSISTENCY

☐ Coordination of long-term plan with drought contingency and emergency management plan

☐ Relationship of the plan to nearby water utilities

☐ Regional economic, environmental, and societal effects

☐ Economic development and land-use policy issues

☐ Consistency of the plan with federal, state, regional, and river basin plans and water resource policies

IMPLEMENTATION

PLANNED IMPLEMENTATION

☐ Timetables and organization charts

☐ Anticipated milestones

☐ Regulatory filings and anticipated decisions

☐ Monitoring and ongoing evaluation

☐ Coordination with other planning processes

☐ Flexibility of plan in meeting changing conditions

ADMINISTRATION AND FINANCING

☐ Administrative and associated costs

☐ Financing methods

☐ Cost allocation

☐ Short-term and long-term effects on rates

PUBLIC PARTICIPATION

☐ Public information and education

☐ Opportunities for public comment

☐ Identification of likely participants in planning proceedings

Best management practices (BMPs) for urban water conservation in California*

Best Management Practice	Water Savings Assumptions†		
		Pre-1980 Construction	Post-1980 Construction
1. Water survey programs for single-family residential and multifamily residential customers	Low-flow showerhead retrofit	7.2 gpcd	2.9 gpcd
	Toilet retrofit (5-year life)	1.3 gpcd	0.0 gpcd
	Leak repair	0.5 gpcd	0.5 gpcd
	Landscape survey (outdoor use reduction)	10%	10%
2. Residential plumbing retrofit	Low-flow showerhead retrofit	7.2 gpcd	2.9 gpcd
	Toilet retrofit (5-year life)	1.3 gpcd	0.0 gpcd
3. System water audits, leak detection, and repair	Assume unaccounted-for water losses will constitute no more than 10% of the total volume of water entering the water supplier's system.		
4. Metering with commodity rates for all new connections and retrofit of existing connections	Assume meter retrofits will result in a 20% reduction in demand by retrofitted accounts.		
5. Large landscape conservation programs and incentives	Assume landscape surveys will result in a 15% reduction in demand for landscape water use by surveyed accounts.		
6. High-efficiency washing machine rebate programs	Assume an interim estimate of 5,100 gallons annually per replacement of a low-efficiency clothes washer with a high-efficiency washer. Signatory water suppliers may use an estimate exceeding 5,100 gallons or may select a lower estimate so long as it is no lower than 4,600.		
7. Public information programs	Not quantified		
8. School education programs	Not quantified		
9. Conservation programs for commercial, industrial, and institutional accounts	Assume commercial water reductions from best management practices such as interior and landscape water surveys, plumbing codes, and other factors, but exclude ultralow-flush toilet replacement. Also assume a reduction in gallons per employee per day in year 2000 use occurring from 1980 forward.		
10. Wholesale agency assistance programs	Not quantified		
11. Conservation pricing	Not quantified		
12. Conservation coordinator	Not quantified		
13. Water waste prohibition	Not quantified		
14. Residential ultralow-flush toilet replacement programs‡	See Exhibit 6 of the Memorandum of Understanding for methods of estimating water savings by low-volume toilets based on household size, number of toilets per household, and mix of pre-1980 and post-1980 toilets.		

* Applies to the 260-plus signatories (retail and wholesale water suppliers, public advocacy organizations, and other interested groups) to the Memorandum of Understanding Regarding Urban Water Conservation in California, as amended Sept. 16, 1999.

† Memorandum of Understanding notes that the estimates of reliable water savings shown may be refined in the future as more and better data are collected.

‡ For replacement of high-water-use toilets with low-volume fixtures using 1.6 gallons or less

gpcd = gallons per capita per day

Source: Adapted from endnote 15 in Chapter 1 (Memorandum of Understanding Regarding Urban Water Conservation in California, California Urban Water Conservation Council, Sacramento, Calif., amended Sept. 16, 1999).

APPENDIX D

Water and sewer rates, costs, and savings by volume of use

This table can be used to calculate water and sewer costs and potential savings from conservation based on volume of use and flow reduction. The rates shown do not include other charges or fixed fees that may be added to water and sewer bills.

| Gallons | Rate per 1,000 gallons | | | | | | | | | | | | | | | | | | |
| | $1.00 | $1.50 | $2.00 | $2.50 | $3.00 | $3.50 | $4.00 | $4.50 | $5.00 | $5.50 | $6.00 | $6.50 | $7.00 | $7.50 | $8.00 | $8.50 | $9.00 | $9.50 | $10.00 |
	Cost per volume of use																		
1,000	$1	$1.50	$2.00	$2.50	$3.00	$3.50	$4.00	$4.50	$5.00	$5.50	$6.00	$6.50	$7.00	$7.50	$8.00	$8.50	$9.00	$9.50	$10.00
2,000	$2	$3	$4	$5	$6	$7	$8	$9	$10	$11	$12	$13	$14	$15	$16	$17	$18	$19	$20
3,000	$3	$5	$6	$8	$9	$11	$12	$14	$15	$17	$18	$20	$21	$23	$24	$26	$27	$29	$30
4,000	$4	$6	$8	$10	$12	$14	$16	$18	$20	$22	$24	$26	$28	$30	$32	$34	$36	$38	$40
5,000	$5	$8	$10	$13	$15	$18	$20	$23	$25	$28	$30	$33	$35	$38	$40	$43	$45	$48	$50
6,000	$6	$9	$12	$15	$18	$21	$24	$27	$30	$33	$36	$39	$42	$45	$48	$51	$54	$57	$60
7,000	$7	$11	$14	$18	$21	$25	$28	$32	$35	$39	$42	$46	$49	$53	$56	$60	$63	$67	$70
8,000	$8	$12	$16	$20	$24	$28	$32	$36	$40	$44	$48	$52	$56	$60	$64	$68	$72	$76	$80
9,000	$9	$14	$18	$23	$27	$32	$36	$41	$45	$50	$54	$59	$63	$68	$72	$77	$81	$86	$90
10,000	$10	$15	$20	$25	$30	$35	$40	$45	$50	$55	$60	$65	$70	$75	$80	$85	$90	$95	$100
20,000	$20	$30	$40	$50	$60	$70	$80	$90	$100	$110	$120	$130	$140	$150	$160	$170	$180	$190	$200
30,000	$30	$45	$60	$75	$90	$105	$120	$135	$150	$165	$180	$195	$210	$225	$240	$255	$270	$285	$300
40,000	$40	$60	$80	$100	$120	$140	$160	$180	$200	$220	$240	$260	$280	$300	$320	$340	$360	$380	$400
50,000	$50	$75	$100	$125	$150	$175	$200	$225	$250	$275	$300	$325	$350	$375	$400	$425	$450	$475	$500
60,000	$60	$90	$120	$150	$180	$210	$240	$270	$300	$330	$360	$390	$420	$450	$480	$510	$540	$570	$600
70,000	$70	$105	$140	$175	$210	$245	$280	$315	$350	$385	$420	$455	$490	$525	$560	$595	$630	$665	$700
80,000	$80	$120	$160	$200	$240	$280	$320	$360	$400	$440	$480	$520	$560	$600	$640	$680	$720	$760	$800
90,000	$90	$135	$180	$225	$270	$315	$360	$405	$450	$495	$540	$585	$630	$675	$720	$765	$810	$855	$900
100,000	$100	$150	$200	$250	$300	$350	$400	$450	$500	$550	$600	$650	$700	$750	$800	$850	$900	$950	$1,000
200,000	$200	$300	$400	$500	$600	$700	$800	$900	$1,000	$1,100	$1,200	$1,300	$1,400	$1,500	$1,600	$1,700	$1,800	$1,900	$2,000
300,000	$300	$450	$600	$750	$900	$1,050	$1,200	$1,350	$1,500	$1,650	$1,800	$1,950	$2,100	$2,250	$2,400	$2,550	$2,700	$2,850	$3,000
400,000	$400	$600	$800	$1,000	$1,200	$1,400	$1,600	$1,800	$2,000	$2,200	$2,400	$2,600	$2,800	$3,000	$3,200	$3,400	$3,600	$3,800	$4,000
500,000	$500	$750	$1,000	$1,250	$1,500	$1,750	$2,000	$2,250	$2,500	$2,750	$3,000	$3,250	$3,500	$3,750	$4,000	$4,250	$4,500	$4,750	$5,000
600,000	$600	$900	$1,200	$1,500	$1,800	$2,100	$2,400	$2,700	$3,000	$3,300	$3,600	$3,900	$4,200	$4,500	$4,800	$5,100	$5,400	$5,700	$6,000
700,000	$700	$1,050	$1,400	$1,750	$2,100	$2,450	$2,800	$3,150	$3,500	$3,850	$4,200	$4,550	$4,900	$5,250	$5,600	$5,950	$6,300	$6,650	$7,000
800,000	$800	$1,200	$1,600	$2,000	$2,400	$2,800	$3,200	$3,600	$4,000	$4,400	$4,800	$5,200	$5,600	$6,000	$6,400	$6,800	$7,200	$7,600	$8,000
900,000	$900	$1,350	$1,800	$2,250	$2,700	$3,150	$3,600	$4,050	$4,500	$4,950	$5,400	$5,850	$6,300	$6,750	$7,200	$7,650	$8,100	$8,550	$9,000
1,000,000	$1,000	$1,500	$2,000	$2,500	$3,000	$3,500	$4,000	$4,500	$5,000	$5,500	$6,000	$6,500	$7,000	$7,500	$8,000	$8,500	$9,000	$9,500	$10,000

Sample worksheet: Residential (indoor) water audit

AUDIT COMPLETED BY (NAME):   DATE:

GENERAL INFORMATION

Customer/Account Name: Account No.

Address:

Telephone No.   E-mail address:

Type of dwelling *(check one)*:   ☐ Single-family detached   ☐ Single-family other   ☐ Multifamily   ☐ Other

Meter *(check one)*:   ☐ Separate   ☐ Master   Age of dwelling *(years)*:

No. of occupants: Adults   Children   Total no. occupants   No. months dwelling occupied/year

INDOOR RESIDENTIAL WATER-USE INVENTORY

Item (Describe for each)	No. 1	No. 2	No. 3	No. 4	No. 5
TOILETS					
Gallons per flush (gpf)					
Year toilet installed					
Retrofit device installed? (yes/no, bag/dam)					
Year retrofit device installed					
Leak detected? (yes/no, dye test/other)					
Leak source (flapper, ballcock, overflow tube, other)					
Leak repaired? (yes/no, describe)					
SHOWERS					
Gallons per minute (gpm), full flow/typical flow					
Retrofit device installed? (yes/no, year)					
Leak detected at showerhead? (yes/no)					
Leak detected at tub diverter? (yes/no)					
Leak repaired? (yes/no, provided-describe)					
FAUCETS					
Gallons per minute (gpm), full flow/typical flow					
Bathroom/Lavatory					
Kitchen					
Retrofit device installed? (yes/no, year)					
Bathroom/Lavatory					
Kitchen					
Garbage disposal present? (yes/no)					
Leak detected? (yes/no)					
Bathroom/Lavatory					
Kitchen					
Leak repaired? (yes/no, provided-describe)					

CLOTHES WASHER

Washing machine present? ☐ Yes ☐ No *(If "no," skip to next item).*   Year clothes washer installed:

No. loads per week: Typical size of load: ☐ Small   ☐ Medium   ☐ Large

Gallons per wash load (gpl):   ☐ Small load ☐ Medium load   ☐ Large load

Leak detected at washer or hose connections?   ☐ Yes ☐ No   Leak repaired? ☐ Yes ☐ No

DISHWASHER

Dishwasher present?   ☐ Yes ☐ No *(If "no," skip to next item).*   Year dishwasher installed:

No. loads per week: Typical size of load: ☐ Small   ☐ Medium   ☐ Large

Gallons per wash load (gpl):   ☐ Small load ☐ Medium load   ☐ Large load

Leak detected at washer or hose connections?   ☐ Yes ☐ No   Leak repaired? ☐ Yes ☐ No

WATER FILTER/REVERSE OSMOSIS (RO) PURIFIER

Water filter/RO purifier present?   ☐ Yes   ☐ No *(If "no," skip to next item).*   Shutoff switch? ☐ Yes ☐ No

Leak detected? ☐ Yes ☐ No   Leak repaired? ☐ Yes ☐ No

WATER SOFTENER

Water softener present?   ☐ Yes ☐ No *(If "no," skip to next item).*   Shutoff switch? ☐ Yes ☐ No

Type: Auto-regenerating? ☐ Yes ☐ No   Portable exchange?   ☐ Yes ☐ No

Leak detected?   ☐ Yes ☐ No   Leak repaired? ☐ Yes ☐ No

EVAPORATIVE COOLER

Evaporative cooler present? ☐ Yes ☐ No *(If "no," skip to next item).*   Year installed:

Type (check one):   ☐ Recirculating   ☐ Noncirculating ("once through")

Leak detected?   ☐ Yes ☐ No   Leak repaired? ☐ Yes ☐ No

SPA/JACUZZI

Spa/Jacuzzi present?   ☐ Yes ☐ No *(If "no," skip to next item).*   Year installed:

Type (check one):   ☐ Indoor ☐ Outdoor   Covered? ☐ Yes ☐ No

Capacity (gallons):   Frequency of refill *(no. times):*   day/week/month (circle one)

Leak detected?   ☐ Yes ☐ No   Leak repaired? ☐ Yes ☐ No

OTHER

Other:

Amount of water used (gallons and frequency):

Leak detected?   ☐ Yes ☐ No   Leak repaired? ☐ Yes ☐ No

Additional comments:

RECOMMENDED RESIDENTIAL WATER-EFFICIENCY MEASURES

Item (Describe for each)	No. 1	No. 2	No. 3	No. 4	No. 5
Toilets					
Showers					
Faucets					
Bathroom/lavatory					
Kitchen					
Garbage disposal					
Clothes washer					
Dishwasher					
Water filter/RO purifier					
Water softener					
Evaporative cooler					
Spa/Jacuzzi					
Other					

POTENTIAL WATER SAVINGS FROM RESIDENTIAL EFFICIENCY MEASURES

Water-Efficiency Measure	Current Water Use (A)	Potential Water Savings From Efficiency Measures (B)	Estimated Future Water Use With Conservation (A – B)	Estimated Future Water Use With Conservation (B/A)	Projected Life of Measure
	Average Gallons Per Day (gpd)			Percent	Years
Total					

POTENTIAL BENEFITS AND COSTS FROM RESIDENTIAL EFFICIENCY MEASURES

Water-Efficiency Measure	Water and Sewer Savings		Other Savings	Annual Costs	Capital Cost	Payback Period
	Gallons/Year	$/Year	$/Year	$/Year	$	Years
Total						

APPENDIX F

Sample worksheet: Landscape and irrigation water audit

AUDIT COMPLETED BY (NAME):   **DATE:**

GENERAL INFORMATION

Customer/Account Name: Account No.

Address:

Customer contact person: Telephone No.   Fax No.   E-mail address:

Customer Type *(check one):* ☐ Residential ☐ Golf/Sports Field ☐ Industrial/Commercial/Institutional ☐ Other

Meter *(check one):* ☐ Separate ☐ Master   System pressure:

Is recycled water currently used on site? ☐ Yes ☐ No   If yes, describe and give amount used *(e.g., gallons per year):*

Pool, pond, fountain, waterfall on site? ☐ Yes ☐ No   Is pool covered when not in use? ☐ Yes ☐ No

LANDSCAPE AND IRRIGATION WATER-USE INVENTORY

IRRIGATION SYSTEM

Type: ☐ Hose ☐ Sprinkler   ☐ Drip   ☐ Rain catchment/cistern   ☐ Other (describe)

Location: ☐ In-ground   ☐ Aboveground

Irrigation controller: ☐ Manual   ☐ Automatic   No. of valves: Rain shutoff valve? ☐ Yes ☐ No

Frequency of use: Avg. no. days per week: Avg. no. minutes per irrigation cycle:

Irrigation time: ☐ Morning   ☐ Afternoon   ☐ Evening   Hours:

Irrigation months *(circle all that apply):* Jan Feb Mar Apr May Jun Jul Aug Sep Oct Nov Dec

Irrigation water use/cycle *(gal):*   Beginning meter reading   Ending reading   Total cycle water use

Irrigation water use/time *(gal):*   Avg. Day: Avg. Week: Avg. Month: Avg. Year:

Irrigation water use/area *(%):*   Lawn: Other landscape: Plant beds/garden: Leaks: Other:

Irrigation runoff: ☐ Yes ☐ No   If yes, describe:

Leaks: ☐ Yes ☐ No   If yes, describe:

Controller schedule reset: ☐ Weekly ☐ Monthly ☐ Season ☐ Yearly ☐ Never

Controller schedule set by: ☐ Homeowner/Site Manager ☐ Maintenance Contractor

LANDSCAPE AREA

Total lot size *(sq ft):*   Lot area irrigated *(sq ft):*   Lot area irrigated *(%):*

Shaded area (low, medium, high):   Irrigated area that is sloped *(sq ft):*

Irrigated area that is turf *(sq ft):*   Irrigated area that is nonturf *(sq ft):*

Irrigated area that is turf *(%):*   Irrigated area that is sloped *(%):*

TURF GRASS AND PLANTS

Grass type: ☐ Cool-season   ☐ Warm-season   Mix: cool (%)   warm (%)

Irrigated nonturf area (describe):

Grass mow height (in.):   Excess thatch: ☐ Yes ☐ No   Dry spots: ☐ Yes ☐ No

Watering zones/valves: Separated by plant/turf watering needs? ☐ Yes ☐ No

SOIL

Soil type: ☐ Clay ☐ Loam ☐ Sandy loam   ☐ Mix *(describe):*

Condition: Nutrient level: ☐ good ☐ poor   Root depth *(in.):*   Moisture depth *(in.):*

Compaction: ☐ Light ☐ Medium ☐ Heavy   Sufficient mulch around plants? ☐ Yes ☐ No

WATER FEATURES

Fountains, ponds, and waterfalls	
Rainwater harvesting/cisterns	
Pool	
Other	
Additional comments:	

LANDSCAPE AND IRRIGATION SYSTEM INSPECTION DATA (DESCRIBE CONDITION)

Item	Valve/ Zone 1	Valve/ Zone 2	Valve/ Zone 3	Valve/ Zone 4	Valve/ Zone 5	Valve/ Zone 6	Valve/ Zone 7	Valve/ Zone 8	Valve/ Zone 9	Valve/ Zone 10
OPERATION										
Normal run time										
Gallons per minute (gpm)										
Square footage (sq ft)										
Shade (low, medium, high)										
PLANTS										
Type: warm-season grass, cool-season grass, ground-cover, mix, ornamental plants, trees, vegetables, mulch, native plants, drought-tolerant plants										
Valves not operated according to plant water needs										
Valves not operated according to sun exposure										
Area overwatered										
Area underwatered (dry spots)										
Excess thatch buildup										
Mulch needed										
Sloped area										
Runoff										
Ponding										
SYSTEM TYPE: ROTOR, SPRAY, BUBBLER, DRIP										
Head inventory										
Rotor										
Impact										
Stream rotor										
Soaker										
Bubbler										
Full head										
Three-quarter head										
Half head										
Side spray head										
Quarter head										

Item	Valve/ Zone 1	Valve/ Zone 2	Valve/ Zone 3	Valve/ Zone 4	Valve/ Zone 5	Valve/ Zone 6	Valve/ Zone 7	Valve/ Zone 8	Valve/ Zone 9	Valve/ Zone 10
SPRINKLER PROBLEMS										
Broken head										
Broken pipe										
Broken seal										
Broken valve										
Head clogged										
Head too high or too low										
Head stuck or tilted										
Incorrect pressure (low or high)										
Radius long or short										
Spray blocked or misdirected										
DRIP PROBLEMS										
Pinched or broken tubing										
Emitters separated from tubing										
Emitters spaced incorrectly										
Clogged/missing/ broken emitters										

ADDITIONAL COMMENTS

RECOMMENDED LANDSCAPE AND IRRIGATION WATER-EFFICIENCY MEASURES

Water-Efficiency Measure	Description

RECOMMENDED IRRIGATION SCHEDULE (SPECIFY MONTH):

Zone	No. Heads/ Type	Current Controller (Clock-Timer) Setting				Recommended Controller (Clock-Timer) Setting			
		Run Time minutes	Rate gpm	Application Rate* inches per watering	Frequency (Every _____ days)	Run Time minutes	Rate gpm	Application Rate* inches per watering	Frequency (Every _____ days)
1									
2									
3									
4									
5									
6									
7									
8									
9									
10									

* Amount of water applied

POTENTIAL WATER SAVINGS FROM LANDSCAPE AND IRRIGATION EFFICIENCY MEASURES

Water-Efficiency Measure	Current Water Use (A)	Potential Water Savings From Efficiency Measures (B)	Estimated Future Outdoor Water Use With Conservation (A – B)	Estimated Future Outdoor Water Use With Conservation (B/A)	Projected Life of Measure
	Average Gallons Per Day (gpd)			*Percent*	*Years*
Total					

POTENTIAL BENEFITS AND COSTS FROM LANDSCAPE AND IRRIGATION EFFICIENCY MEASURES

Water-Efficiency Measure	Water Savings		Other Savings	Annual Costs	Capital Cost	Payback Period
	Gallons/Year	*$/Year*	*$/Year*	*$/Year*	*$*	*Years*
Total						

APPENDIX G

Sample worksheet: Industrial/commercial/institutional water audit

AUDIT COMPLETED BY (NAME):   DATE:

GENERAL INFORMATION

Customer/Account Name: Account No.

Address:

Facility contact person: Telephone No.   Fax No.   E-mail address:

Product(s) or service(s):

SIC category(ies):

Facility dimensions (for each building) in sq ft: No. floors   Width   Height   Age of facility (years)

Avg. no. of occupants (employees and nonemployees):   Female   Male   Total

Avg. no. days facility occupied/year   Avg. no. hours occupied/day: Weekdays   Weekends   Holidays

Is recycled water currently used on site? ☐ Yes ☐ No   If yes, describe and give amount used (e.g., gallons per year):

Building wastewater is: ☐ Treated on site ☐ Connected to municipal/off-site system ☐ Other (describe)

METER INFORMATION

	Meter No. 1 ID No.	Meter No. 2 ID No.	Meter No. 3 ID No.	Meter No. 4 ID No.	Meter No. 5 ID No.
Meter location					
Meter type					
Reading frequency					
Units of register					
Multiplier (if any)					
Meter size					
Connection size					
Meter installation date					
Testing frequency					
Last service (date)					
Last test/calibration (dates)					

Item (Describe for each)	Location (building, floor)	Type and No. of Units	Average Flow Rate or Water Use Per Unit (e.g., gallons per use, per minute, etc.)	Average No. Uses Per Unit Per Day	Average Water Use Per Day (365-day average)
BATHROOMS/LAVATORIES					
Drinking water fountains					
Women's					
Toilets					
Showerheads					
Sinks (faucets)					
Whirlpool					
Other					
Men's					
Toilets					
Urinals					
Showerheads					
Sinks (faucets)					
Whirlpool					
Other					
CLEANING AND SANITATION					
Manual washing					
Vehicle washing					
Steam sterilizers					
Autoclaves					
Mop sink					
Laboratory					
Other					
PROCESS WATER USES					
Process water and rinsing					
Materials transfer					
Film and x-ray processing					
Pulp, paper, and packaging					
KITCHENS AND RESTAURANTS					
Food and drink preparation					
Dishwashers					
Icemakers					
Ice cream/yogurt machines					
Garbage disposers					
Scrapping troughs					
Washdown hoses					
Other					

Item (Describe for each)	Location (building, floor)	Type and No. of Units	Average Flow Rate or Water Use Per Unit (e.g., gallons per use, per minute, etc.)	Average No. Uses Per Unit Per Day	Average Water Use Per Day (365-day average)
LAUNDRIES AND LAUNDROMATS					
Washing machines					
Other					
SWIMMING POOLS AND ZOOS					
Swimming pools					
Fountains, ponds, and waterfalls					
Rainwater harvesting/cisterns					
Zoos					
Other					
COOLING SYSTEMS					
Once-through cooling					
Cooling towers					
Evaporative coolers					
Equipment cooling					
Other					
HEATING SYSTEMS					
Boilers/steam generators					
Humidifiers					
Other					
LEAKS AND LOSSES					
Leaks					
Malfunctions					
Other					
MISCELLANEOUS					
Additional comments:					

RECOMMENDED EFFICIENCY MEASURES

Water-Efficiency Measure (itemize)	Description

POTENTIAL WATER SAVINGS FROM ICI EFFICIENCY MEASURES

Water-Efficiency Measure	Current Water Use (A)	Potential Water Savings From Efficiency Measures (B)	Estimated Future Water Use With Conservation (A – B)	Estimated Future Water Use With Conservation (B/A)	Projected Life of Measure
	Average Gallons Per Day (gpd)			*Percent*	*Years*
Total					

POTENTIAL BENEFITS AND COSTS FROM ICI EFFICIENCY MEASURES

Water-Efficiency Measure	Water Savings Gallons/Year	$/Year	Other Savings $/Year	Annual Costs $/Year	Capital Cost $	Payback Period Years
Total						

SAMPLE WORKSHEET: COOLING TOWER LOG SHEET "A"   *(For data collection with cooling towers that use make-up and bleed-off meters)*

Cooling Tower _____   Capacity (tons) _____   Location _____
Meter Units _____

Date	Make-up Meter Reading	Make-up Water Use, *M*	Bleed-off Meter Reading	Bleed-off Water Use, *B*	Evaporation, *E = M - B*	Concentration, Ratio, *CR = M/B*	Comments

SAMPLE WORKSHEET: COOLING TOWER LOG SHEET "B"   *(For data collection with cooling towers that use a conductivity meter or other method of measuring concentrations of dissolved solids in make-up and bleed-off water)*

Cooling Tower _____   Capacity (tons) _____   Location _____
Parameter Measures _____   Units _____

Date	Make-up Concentration	Bleed-off Concentration, *CB*	Concentration Ratio, *CR = CB/CM*	Cooling Load, 100's of tons	Minutes per day *(min/day)*	Evaporation, gpd, where *E = 2.4 × (load) × (min/day)*	Bleed-off, gpd, where *B = E/(CR - 1)*	Make-up, gpd, where *M = B + E*	Comments

gpd = gallons per day

Efficient water management practices (EWMPs) for agricultural water suppliers in California*

LIST A: GENERALLY APPLICABLE EWMPS

- ☐ Prepare and adopt a water management plan.
- ☐ Designate a water conservation coordinator.
- ☐ Support the availability of water management services to water users.
- ☐ Improve communication and cooperation among water suppliers, water users, and other agencies.
- ☐ Evaluate the need, if any, for changes in institutional policies to which the water supplier is subject.
- ☐ Evaluate and improve the efficiency of water supplier's pumps.

LIST B: CONDITIONALLY APPLICABLE EWMPS

- ☐ Facilitate alternative land use.
- ☐ Facilitate using available recycled water that otherwise would not be used beneficially, meets all health and safety criteria, and does not cause harm to crops or soils.
- ☐ Facilitate the financing of capital improvements for on-farm irrigation systems.
- ☐ Facilitate voluntary water transfers that do not unreasonably affect the water user, water supplier, the environment, or third parties.
- ☐ Line ditches and canals or install conveyance pipes.
- ☐ Increase flexibility in water ordering by, and delivery to, water users within operational limits.
- ☐ Construct and operate water supplier spill and tailwater recovery systems.
- ☐ Optimize conjunctive use of surface water and groundwater.
- ☐ Automate canal structures.

LIST C: OTHER EWMPS

- ☐ Report water-use measurements.
- ☐ Implement pricing or other incentives.

* Applies to signatories to the Memorandum of Understanding Regarding Efficient Water Management Practices by Agricultural Water Suppliers in California, Nov. 13, 1996.

Source: California Department of Water Resources, "Urban, Agricultural, and Environmental Water Use" (per the Memorandum of Understanding Regarding Efficient Water Management Practices by Agricultural Water Suppliers in California, Nov. 13, 1996), California Water Plan Update, Bulletin 160-98, November 1998, chap. 4, pp. 20–21.

Glossary

A

absorption assimilation of molecules or other substances into the physical structure of a liquid or solid with chemical reaction.

acre-foot (acre-ft) a uniform volume of water that will cover one acre (43,560 square feet) to a depth of 1 foot (often averaged to 326,000 gallons).

adaptive plants plants that are not indigenous to an area but that easily adapt to the climate and thus require little or no supplemental irrigation once established.

adjusted water budget a quantity of water that is used to maintain a landscape and that is based on area and evapotranspiration rate; adjusted to reflect an efficiency standard.

adsorption physical adhesion of molecules or colloids to the surfaces of solids without chemical reaction.

aerator see *faucet aerator*.

aerobic treatment a biological treatment technique used to oxidize and remove soluble or fine materials.

agricultural drainage (1) the process of directing excess water away from root zones by natural or artificial means, such as a system of pipes and drains placed belowground; also called *subsurface drainage*. (2) the water drained away from irrigated farmland.

algae simple, chiefly aquatic organisms containing chlorophyll and ranging in size from microscopic forms to giant seaweed. Under favorable conditions, they grow in colonies, producing mats and similar masses.

alkalinity a measure of the capacity of water to neutralize strong acid. Total alkalinity (also called "M" alkalinity) reacts with acid as the pH of a water sample is reduced to the methyl orange endpoint—about pH 4.2. "P" alkalinity, which exists above pH 8.2, reacts with acid as the pH of a sample is reduced to 8.2.

allowable depletion the total available water that can be removed from soil before irrigation is required, measured as a percentage.

American National Standards Institute (ANSI) an association of individuals and organizations involved in developing voluntary consensus standards for a wide range of products including plumbing fixtures (e.g., toilets or "water closets"), urinals, showerheads, and faucets.

American Society of Mechanical Engineers (ASME) a professional organization whose Codes and Standards Committee helps to write and publishes ANSI standards.

American Water Works Association (AWWA) a professional organization serving the drinking water supply profession, primarily in North America.

American Water Works Association Research Foundation (AWWARF) a nongovernmental organization that sponsors research for the drinking water supply profession.

anion a negatively charged ion formed when an atom acquires one or more extra electrons.

anti-drain device a device that prevents water from being lost from an irrigation lateral through the lowest sprinkler heads after irrigation stops.

anti-drain valve a valve, located under the sprinkler head, that holds water in the system to minimize drainage from the lowest sprinklers.

application rate the rate of water delivery to a given area, usually expressed in inches per hour for sprinkler irrigation and in gallons for drip irrigation.

applied water water applied by irrigation, usually expressed as a depth of water in inches or feet.

applied water demand the amount of water withdrawn from a supply source to meet customer demand; the quantity of water delivered to the intake of a city water system or factory, the farm head gate, or a marsh or wetland (either directly or through incidental drainage flows). Applied water demand includes water that returns to groundwater supplies, streams, and other sources that can be reused.

appropriation the amount of water a user has the legal right to withdraw from a water source.

aquifer a geologic formation of permeable rock, gravel, or sand that stores and transmits water to wells and springs.

arid a climate characterized by less than 10 inches of annual rainfall; a climate or region in which precipitation is so deficient in quantity or occurs so infrequently that intensive agricultural production is impossible without irrigation.

arranged-demand water delivery a period of water availability arranged between the water supplier and the user; the rate and duration of water applied during irrigation is controlled by the user.

artificial recharge the intentional addition of water to an aquifer by injection or infiltration (e.g., directing surface water onto spreading basins).

audit (end-use) a systematic accounting of water uses by end users (e.g., residential, landscape, commercial, industrial, institutional, or agricultural customers), usually conducted to identify potential opportunities for water-use reduction through efficiency measures or improvements.

audit (system) a systematic accounting of water throughout the production, transmission, and distribution facilities of a water supply system.

automatic controller a mechanical or solid-state irrigation timer, capable of operating valve stations to set the days and length of time of water applications.

available soil moisture see *available water-holding capacity*.

available supply the maximum amount of reliable water supply, including surface and groundwater sources and purchases under secure contracts.

available water-holding capacity (AWHC)   the amount of moisture plants can store in the root zone, usually expressed as a depth of water in inches or feet; the difference in soil moisture content between the *field capacity* and the *permanent wilting point*. Also referred to as *available soil moisture*.

average annual runoff   the average amount of annual runoff calculated for a selected period of record for a specific area that represents average hydrologic conditions.

average-day demand   a water system's average daily use based on total annual water production divided by 365.

average-year demand   water demand under average hydrologic conditions for a 365-day period.

average-year water supply   the average amount of water available annually through a water system.

avoided cost   the savings achieved by undertaking a given activity such as implementing a water-efficiency measure; can be used to establish the least-cost means of achieving a specified goal.

AWWA   see *American Water Works Association*.

AWWARF   see *American Water Works Association Research Foundation*.

B

backflow prevention device   a safety device used to prevent contamination or pollution of a potable water supply line from the reverse flow of water.

bacteria   single-cell microorganisms that reproduce by fission or by spores, identified by their shapes: coccus (spherical), bacillus (rod-shaped), and spirillum (spiral-shaped).

baseline   an established value or trend used for comparison when conditions are altered, as in the introduction of water-efficiency measures; also the historical water use of a water supply system's customers, either in total or for a selected sample.

beneficial use   the use of water resources to benefit people or nature; irrigation water that satisfies some or all of the following needs or conditions—evapotranspiration, leaching, water stored in the soil for use by crops, or special cultural practices; usually expressed as a depth of water in inches or feet.

benefit-cost ratio   benefits and costs measured in terms of money are expressed as a ratio, with benefits divided by costs.

best management practice (BMP)   a conservation measure or system of business procedures that is beneficial, empirically proven, cost-effective, and widely accepted in the professional community; also an urban water conservation measure that member agencies of the California Urban Water Conservation Council agree to implement under the Memorandum of Understanding Regarding Urban Water Conservation in California.

biochemical oxygen demand (BOD)   the oxygen required by bacteria to oxidize soluble organic matter under controlled test conditions.

biological treatment   treatment processes that remove contaminants through bacterial or biochemical action.

bleed-off   the release of built-up solids and contaminants in a cooling tower or boiler by removing a portion of the recirculating water that carries dissolved solids.

block   a quantity of water for which a per-unit price (or billing rate) is established.

blowdown   see *bleed-off*.

bluegrass   or *Kentucky bluegrass*, a variety of cool-season turf grass of the genus *Poa*. Commercial turf grass mixes are usually a blend of varieties.

BMP   see *best management practice*.

bubbler   a type of sprinkler head that delivers a large volume of water to a level area where the water slowly infiltrates the soil. Because the flow rate of bubblers is large relative to the area to which the water is delivered, they are used to irrigate shrubs and trees.

budget (water-use)   an accounting of total water use or projected water use for a given activity, facility, or location.

building footprint   the area covered by a building (calculated with the dimensions of its foundation), as represented in a two-dimensional plan.

C

cablegation   an irrigation method in which water pressure pushes a plug through gated pipe to regulate the flow of water from the gates and to distribute it to the field sequentially, several gates at a time. Watering time is controlled by the rate at which the plug moves though the pipeline.

California Irrigation Management Information System (CIMIS)   a network of California weather stations electronically connected to a mainframe computer that downloads the weather data of individual stations and calculates their evapotranspiration values for use in scheduling irrigations.

Canadian Standards Association (CSA): a Canadian code-setting body that establishes performance and water-use standards for plumbing fixtures and other products.

canvass   a conservation program method of distributing plumbing fixture retrofit kits throughout a water service or geographical area.

catch-can test   a measurement of precipitation from a landscape sprinkler system, determined by collecting water in graduated containers placed at evenly spaced intervals throughout an irrigated area.

cation   a positively charged ion resulting from dissociation of molecules in solution.

ccf   a unit of measure equal to 100 cubic feet of water or 748 gallons.

center pivot sprinkler system   an irrigation system consisting of a pipe lateral, elevated on wheels, that rotates on a fixed pivot point as it applies water to the land.

central irrigation control   a computerized system that programs irrigation system controllers from a central location, using personal computers and radio waves or hard wiring to send program information to controllers in the field.

check valve   a device that prevents drainage of water from the low points of an irrigation circuit after irrigation stops.

chemigation   the injection of agricultural chemicals or fertilizer into irrigation water for distribution to the field.

cistern a tank or collection system to capture and store rainwater.

closed basin a basin whose topography prevents surface outflow of water and thus is considered hydrologically closed.

commercial landscape a landscape adjacent to a facility used for commercial purposes, such as a retail center, office building, or office park.

community water system according the U.S. Safe Drinking Water Act, a drinking water conveyance system serving at least 15 service connections used by year-round residents or regularly serving at least 25 year-round residents.

concentration (1) the amount of a specified substance dissolved in a unit volume of solution. (2) the process of increasing the dissolved solids per unit volume of solution, usually by evaporation of the liquid.

condensate (1) water obtained by evaporation and subsequent condensation; water that is used in a boiler or steamer and that has not been lost to evaporation. (2) the product from a distillation water treatment process.

conductivity the ability to conduct heat, electricity, or sound; electrical conductivity is typically expressed in micromhos/cm.

confined aquifer a water-containing subsurface stratum bounded above and below by a formation of impermeable, or relatively impermeable, soil or rock; also known as an artesian aquifer.

conjunctive use operation of a groundwater basin in coordination with a surface water storage and conveyance system (an example would be storing water for later use by intentionally recharging the groundwater basin with surface water during periods of above-average supply).

conservation (1) the act of conserving; preservation from loss, injury, decay, or waste. (2) the protection of rivers, forests, and other natural resources. See also *water conservation*.

conservation pricing water rate structures that encourage consumers to reduce water use.

conservation tillage any tillage and planting system that leaves at least 30% of the soil surface covered by residue after planting. Conservation tillage maintains a ground cover with less soil disturbance than traditional cultivation, thereby reducing soil loss and energy use while maintaining crop yields and quality. Conservation tillage techniques include minimum tillage, mulch tillage, ridge tillage, and no-till.

consumptive use water use that permanently withdraws water from its source; water that is no longer available because it has evaporated, been transpired by plants, incorporated into products or crops, consumed by people or livestock, or otherwise removed from the immediate water environment.

contaminant any foreign constituent present in another substance (e.g., anything in water that is not H_2O).

conveyance loss water lost in transit between the point of withdrawal and the point of delivery—e.g., water lost from a pipe, canal, conduit, or ditch by leakage or evaporation. Generally, water lost during conveyance is not available for further use; an exception would be leakage from an irrigation ditch that percolates to a groundwater source.

cooling tower equipment that uses water to regulate air temperature in a facility, either by rejecting heat from air-conditioning systems or by cooling hot equipment.

cool-season turf grass turf grass that usually is not damaged by sub-freezing temperatures and does not lose its color unless average ambient temperatures drop below 32°F (0°C) for an extended period. Cool-season grass experiences the most growth during the cool weather of spring and fall and grows less during the heat of summer. Cool-season grasses prefer shady, cool areas and are optimally suited for northern climates where temperatures range from 60 to 75°F. Cool-season turf grasses include bluegrass, Kentucky bluegrass, perennial rye grass, red fescue, and tall fescue.

coring the mechanical cultivation of turf grass using hollow tines to remove cores of turf for the purpose of improving soil texture and increasing air and water circulation.

corrugations small furrows, usually 2 to 4 feet apart, formed to guide water across a field.

cost-beneficial when the benefits are equal to or greater than the cost.

cost-effectiveness the comparison of total benefits with total costs; costs are usually expressed in dollars, but benefits can be expressed in other units of measure (e.g., a quantity of water).

crop coefficient (K_c) a factor used to adjust reference evapotranspiration and to calculate the water requirements of a given plant species.

crop root zone the layer of soil that plant roots occupy and from which they extract water and nutrients; usually expressed as depth in inches or feet.

crop water requirement (CWR) the amount of water required to grow a specific crop, usually expressed as a depth of water in inches or feet.

cultivar a variety of plant produced only under cultivation.

cultural practices irrigation water used for farming practices as opposed to that consumed by evapotranspiration or leaching; usually expressed as a depth of water in inches or feet. Cultural practices include soil reclamation, climate control, crop quality, and weed germination.

customer class a group of customers (e.g., residential, commercial, industrial, institutional, wholesale) defined by similar water-use patterns and costs of service.

cutoff control valve a faucet or showerhead retrofit device that enables the user to shut off water flow (e.g., while shampooing) and restart it at the previous temperature.

cycles of concentration the number of times water is used in a cooling tower before it is discharged as bleed-off.

D

declining (or decreasing) block rate a pricing structure in which the amount charged per unit of water (i.e., dollars per 1,000 gallons) decreases as customer water consumption increases.

dedicated metering metering water service for a single type of use (e.g., landscape irrigation).

deduct meter a separate meter for connections to irrigation systems or other consumptive water uses, such as cooling towers. Because irrigation water and most cooling water are consumed rather than returned to the wastewater system, the volumes recorded by a deduct meter are subject only to water charges, not wastewater charges.

deep percolation   the movement or percolation of water through the ground and beyond the lower limit of the root zone of plants into an aquifer; the amount of water below the plant root zone that is unavailable for evapotranspiration; usually expressed as a depth of water in inches or feet.

demand forecast   a projection of systemwide future water demand or of future demand by a specific customer class.

demand management   water-efficiency measures, practices, or incentives implemented by water utilities to reduce or change the pattern of customer water demand.

demand management alternatives   water management programs—such as water conservation, water rationing during drought, or rate incentive programs—that reduce water demand.

demineralization   the removal of dissolved minerals and inorganic constituents from water.

demographic   having to do with human population or socioeconomic conditions.

dependable supply   the annual average quantity of water that can be delivered during a drought period.

depletion   the water consumed within a service area and thus no longer available as a source of supply; the withdrawal of water from a stream or groundwater aquifer at a rate that exceeds the rate of replenishment; in relation to irrigation or municipal water uses, depletion is the diversion at the head gate or wellhead minus the flow returned to the same stream or groundwater aquifer.

depot   a facility that serves as a distribution center where customers can pick up conservation materials such as plumbing fixture retrofit kits; depots could include water utility customer service offices and public facilities such as malls, post offices, and fire departments.

depth of water   the depth of a volume of water spread over a given area, usually expressed in inches, feet, acre-inches per acre, or acre-feet per acre.

depth to water   the depth of the water table below the surface of the earth.

desalination   a process that converts seawater or brackish water to freshwater, or to a condition that renders it more usable, through removal of mineral salts and other dissolved solids; also called *desalting*.

diatoms   microscopic algae characterized by brown pigmentation and cell walls of silica.

disinfection   the process of removing or inactivating pathogenic organisms by physical or chemical means.

displacement device   see *toilet displacement device*.

distribution facility   the pipes and storage facilities used to distribute drinking water to end users.

distribution uniformity (DU)   a measure of the variation in the amount of water applied to the soil surface throughout an irrigated area, expressed as a percent.

diversion   an alteration in the natural course of a stream for the purpose of water supply, usually causing some of the water to leave the natural channel. In some states, diversion may involve consumptive use directly from a stream; in other states, diversion may include taking water through a canal, pipe, or other conduit.

domestic water use   in this book, water used by sanitary plumbing fixtures (toilets, urinals, faucets, and showerheads) and appliances (clothes washers and dishwashers) in nonresidential settings such as industrial, commercial, and institutional properties; in other contexts, sometimes synonymous with *residential water use*, or water used for household purposes, such as drinking, food preparation, bathing, washing clothes and dishes, flushing toilets, and watering lawns and gardens.

drainage basin   the area of land from which water drains into a river; also called *catchment area*, *watershed*, or *river basin*.

drainline   the sewer pipe that carries wastewater from toilets and other drain connections inside a building; sometimes used to refer to the sewer pipe located outside the building and connected to the sewer main.

drip irrigation   a type of microirrigation system that operates at low pressure and delivers water in slow, small drips to individual plants or groups of plants through a network of plastic conduits and emitters; also called *trickle irrigation*.

drought   an extended period of below-normal precipitation that can result in water supply shortages, increased water demand, or both.

drought condition   the hydrologic conditions during a defined drought period in which rainfall and runoff are much less than average.

drought-year supply   the average annual supply of a water system during a defined drought period.

dryland farming   a type of farming practiced in semiarid regions (usually with less than 20 inches of annual rainfall) and relying solely on precipitation and water stored in the soil during periods when crops are not produced. Dryland farming incorporates water-efficiency practices such as minimum tillage, summer fallowing, planting of drought-resistant crops, and use of mulches to minimize evaporation.

dual and multiple programming   the use of an irrigation controller to meet varying water requirements of plants or turf (or hydrozones) by scheduling multiple start times that stagger the frequency and duration of irrigation cycles.

dual-distribution system   a water distribution system that uses one set of pipes to distribute potable water and a separate set to distribute water of lesser quality (e.g., nonpotable reclaimed water).

dual-flush adapter   a toilet retrofit device designed to use a lower volume of water (partial flush) to flush a toilet bowl containing liquid-only wastes and a higher volume (full flush) to remove solid wastes.

dual-flush toilet   a toilet designed to use a lower volume of water (partial flush) to flush a toilet bowl containing liquid-only wastes and a higher volume (full flush) to remove solid wastes.

E

early closure device   a toilet flapper valve that closes early to reduce the amount of water required to flush a toilet bowl.

ecosystem   a system of interacting physical and biological components, including the flora, fauna, and geophysical environment.

effective precipitation   the total amount of rainfall minus the volume lost to evapotranspiration, leaching, or both during a given time period; rainfall absorbed by soil and available to plants or turf when needed; expressed as a depth of water in inches, feet, acre-inches, or acre-feet.

efficiency   (1) the state or quality of being efficient; competency in performance. (2) the ability to accomplish a job with a minimum expenditure of time and effort.

efficient   (1) performing or producing effectively with a minimum of waste, expense, or unnecessary effort; competent. (2) satisfactory and economical to use.

efficient water management practice (EWMP)   an agricultural water conservation measure as adopted under the Memorandum of Understanding Regarding Urban Water Conservation in California.

effluent   water, wastewater, or other liquid that is flowing outward (e.g., a stream flowing out of a body of water, water or wastewater leaving the treatment plant, a discharge of liquid waste from a factory). Effluent can be in its natural state or partially or completely treated.

emitter   a control on an irrigation lateral line that regulates the discharge of water; a drip irrigation system fitting that delivers water to plants at a predictable rate, usually measured in gallons per hour.

end use   fixtures, appliances, equipment, and activities that use water.

end user   a consumer of water (e.g., a residential, commercial, industrial, or agricultural water customer).

Energy Policy Act of 1992 (EPAct)   a federal law that established maximum allowable water-use requirements for toilets, urinals, showerheads, and faucets manufactured, sold, or installed in the United States.

environment   the sum of all external influences and conditions affecting the life and development of an organism or ecological community; total social and cultural conditions.

EPAct   see *Energy Policy Act of 1992.*

escalation rate   a percentage used to adjust a forecast of expenditures to account for the increasing value of a product or service over time (apart from the discount rate and the effects of inflation).

established landscape   a landscape whose plants have developed roots that are growing into the soil adjacent to the root ball.

ET   see *evapotranspiration.*

ET adjustment factor   a factor, usually 0.8, used to adjust reference evapotranspiration (ET_o) to account for plant factors and irrigation efficiency.

evaporation   the process by which water or other liquids change from liquid to vapor.

evapotranspiration (ET)   water lost from the surface of soils and plants through evaporation and transpiration, respectively.

evapotranspiration (ET) rate   the quantity of water transpired from plant tissues and evaporated from the surface of surrounding soil, expressed as a depth of water in inches or feet. The ET rate is affected by temperature, solar radiation, humidity, wind, and soil moisture.

evapotranspiration of applied water (ETAW)   the portion of plant evapotranspiration provided by irrigation, expressed as a depth of water in inches or feet.

exotic species   a nonnative plant or animal introduced from another geographic area.

F

fallowed land   agricultural land left unseeded during a growing season.

faucet aerator   a screenlike device that screws onto or is enclosed in a faucet and that reduces flows by adding air to the water.

faucet flow control   a replacement faucet end or insert located behind the faucet screen to reduce flow volumes through the faucet.

faucet restrictor   a device that is inserted into a faucet behind the particle trap screen and that forces water through a small orifice in order to reduce flow volumes.

field capacity   the depth of water retained in soil after irrigation or rainfall, expressed as a depth of water in inches or feet.

filtered wastewater   oxidized, coagulated, clarified wastewater that has been passed through natural, undisturbed soils or filter media, such as sand or diatomaceous earth, so that its turbidity does not exceed an average operating turbidity of 2 turbidity units and does not exceed 5 turbidity units more than 5 percent of the time during any 24-hour period.

filtration   the process of separating suspended solids from a liquid by passing the liquid through a porous substance.

fixed charge   the portion of a water bill that does not vary with water use.

fixed costs   costs associated with water service that do not vary with the amount of water produced or sold to customers.

flat rate   a fee structure in which the price of water per unit is constant, regardless of consumption.

flood irrigation   a surface irrigation system by which water is applied to the entire surface of the soil, covering it with a sheet of water; referred to as *controlled flooding* when water is impounded or the flow is directed by border dikes, ridges, or ditches.

floodplain   land bordering a stream and subject to flooding.

flow rate   the amount of water transmitted, such as through a pipe, fixture, appliance, or irrigation system; often measured in gallons per minute, hour, or cycle.

flow restrictors   washerlike disks that fit inside faucets or showerheads to restrict water flow.

flushometer-tank toilet   see *pressurized-tank toilet.*

flushometer-valve toilet   a tankless toilet with the flush valve attached to a pressurized water supply pipe. When activated, the connecting pipe supplies water to the toilet at a flow rate necessary to flush waste into the sewer. Also known as a *flushometer toilet.*

freshwater   water having a relatively low mineral content, usually less than 500 to 1,000 milligrams of total dissolved solids per liter of liquid; generally, more than 500 milligrams of dissolved solids per liter is undesirable for drinking and many industrial uses.

fungi   as applied to water, plants without chlorophyll or vascular systems; includes single-cell forms (e.g., yeasts) and higher forms (e.g., molds).

furrow   a long, narrow, shallow trench made by a plow; a small ditch or channel.

furrow diking   installation of mounds of soil in the small depressions of furrows to retain rainfall and irrigation water for use by crops.

furrow irrigation   surface irrigation in which water is applied at the high end of a field so it flows down the slope of the land through furrows between the rows of crops.

G

gated-pipe irrigation   an irrigation system that applies water to crops through a series of openings in a pipe placed at the upper end of a field. Gates are used to control the amount of water that flows from end openings to furrows.

gpc   gallons per cycle.

gpcd   gallons per capita per day.

gpd   gallons per day.

gpf   gallons per flush.

gph   gallons per hour.

gphd   gallons per household per day.

gpl   gallons per (wash) load.

gpm   gallons per minute.

gpy   gallons per year.

grading   the process of establishing desired landscape gradients; landscape contours designed to facilitate a site's uses and to allow adequate storm drainage.

grading plan   a drawn-to-scale plan of the landscape gradient and elevation designed for a particular area; uses contour lines or numeric notation of elevations.

gravity-flush toilet   a toilet with a rubber stopper (flapper valve) that releases water from the toilet tank, after which gravity forces the contents of the toilet bowl through a trapway for discharge into the wastewater system.

graywater   untreated, used water from a household or small commercial establishment (excluding that from toilets or other fixtures and appliances whose wastewater might have come into contact with human waste); used for nonpotable purposes, such as irrigation and industrial purposes. Specific local laws and policies governing the use of graywater may define the term in slightly different ways.

green industry   the interests, trades, professions, disciplines, and stakeholders concerned with landscape and irrigation design, installation, management, and research.

groundwater   water beneath the earth's surface; specifically, that portion of subsurface water in the saturated zone, where all pore spaces in the alluvium, soil, or rock are filled with water.

groundwater overdraft   the long-term withdrawal of groundwater at a rate that exceeds the amount of natural and artificial replenishment, resulting in a lowering of the groundwater level.

groundwater recharge   replenishment of a groundwater supply through natural conditions (e.g., percolation) or artificial means (e.g., injection).

groundwater storage capacity   the spaces or voids contained in a given volume of soil and rock deposits.

groundwater table   (1) the upper surface of a body of unconfined groundwater. (2) the depth below the ground of such a water surface.

gypsum block   a device buried in the soil and used to measure soil moisture.

H

hardness   the concentration of calcium, magnesium, and other salts in water.

hardpan   a layer of nearly impermeable soil beneath more permeable soil, formed by natural chemical cementing of the soil particles.

hardscape   landscaped areas covered by nonliving materials, such as concrete, brick, rocks, or lumber.

hardware   plumbing fixture retrofit devices and other technology or equipment that can be installed.

head ditch   the water supply ditch at the head end of an irrigated field.

head radius   the radius of the circular arc pattern of an overhead irrigation sprinkler, nozzle, or sprayer.

high-value crops   crops with a limited number of producers and demand or with high per-acre production costs and value (e.g., certain fruit and vegetable crops, ornamental plants, greenhouse crops, spices, and low-volume crops such as artichokes).

high-water-use landscape   a landscape comprising plants, turf, and other features whose irrigation requirements are 50 to 80% of the reference evapotranspiration required to maintain optimal appearance.

historic basis   historical water use on which water allotments are based.

horticultural practices   activities to maintain plants and landscapes, such as fertilization, mowing, and thatch control.

hydraulic balance   an accounting of all water inflow to, water outflow from, and changes in water storage within a hydrologic unit over a specified period of time.

hydrozone   a portion of a landscaped area comprising plants with similar water requirements; a portion of a landscaped area with specific irrigation requirements; a group of plants with similar water requirements served by one irrigation valve. Also referred to as *water zone* or *watering zone.*

I

impact head   a type of single-stream rotor using a lever driven by its impact on the stream of water to rotate a nozzle in a full circle or arc. Impact heads generate large-radius irrigation areas and relatively low precipitation rates but do not match application rates for arc patterns of less than a full circle.

inclining block (or increasing block) rate   a pricing structure in which the amount charged per unit of water (i.e., dollars per 1,000 gallons) increases as customer water consumption increases.

incremental cost   the additional cost associated with adding an increment of capacity to a water supply.

infiltration rate   the rate at which water permeates soil, expressed as a depth of water per unit of time in inches per hour or feet per day. The infiltration rate changes with time, both during and between irrigations.

infrared canopy monitor   a sensor that determines plant stress by measuring plant canopy temperatures.

inputs   items used to operate a farm (e.g., fertilizers, pesticides, seed, fuel, and animal feed and drugs).

instream flow   water in rivers and streams that maintains stream quality, aquatic life, and navigation, as well as providing opportunities for recreation, fishing, aesthetics, and scenic enjoyment.

instream flow requirement   generally, flow required in a stream to maintain desired instream benefits, such as water quality, fish propagation, hydroelectric power production, and recreation.

instream use   water that is used, but not withdrawn, from a surface water source for purposes such as hydroelectric power generation, navigation, water-quality improvement, fish and wildlife maintenance, recreation, and aesthetic enjoyment; sometimes called nonwithdrawal use or in-channel use.

integrated resource planning   an open, participatory planning process emphasizing least-cost principles and balanced consideration of supply and demand management options for meeting water needs.

invasive plant   a nonindigenous plant that invades landscapes and other types of vegetation, including that in wetlands and forests. Invasive plants replace native plant species and often form exotic monocultures (where nothing else grows). Aggressive invasive plants reduce the amount of light, water, nutrients, and space available to native species; alter hydrologic patterns, soil chemistry, moisture-holding capacity, and erodibility; and, in some cases, change fire regimens. Some exotic (nonnative) plants are capable of hybridizing with native plant relatives, resulting in unnatural changes to the native plant's genetic makeup; some harbor pathogens that can affect both native and nonnative plants; and some contain toxins that may be lethal to certain animals.

investor-owned utility   a privately owned utility usually regulated by a state public utility commission.

ion   an atom carrying an electrical charge that is either positive (cation) or negative (anion).

ion exchange   a chemical reaction involving the interchange of ions between a solution and an insoluble medium (usually a resin); used in water softening, the process allows undesired ions of a given charge to be absorbed from solution into the ion-permeable resin, and ions in the solution are replaced by desirable ions of similar charge from the absorbent.

irrecoverable losses   water lost to a salt sink or by evaporation from a conveyance system, such as a drainage canal.

irrigated acreage   land area that is irrigated; equivalent to total irrigated crop acreage minus the amount of acreage that yielded more than one crop in a year.

irrigation   the application of water to soil to meet the water needs of crops, turf, shrubbery, gardens, or wildlife food and habitat not satisfied by rainfall.

irrigation audit   an on-site evaluation of an irrigation system to assess its water-use efficiency as measured by *distribution uniformity*, irrigation schedule, and other factors.

irrigation circuit   a group of irrigation system components, such as heads, emitters, and pipes, that are controlled and operated simultaneously by a remote control valve; the area controlled by an irrigation circuit.

irrigation controller   a mechanical or electronic clock programmed to operate remote-control irrigation system valves at specified times.

irrigation cycle   a scheduled application of water by an irrigation circuit with a defined start time and duration. Schedules may include multiple cycles, separated by specified time intervals, to allow infiltration of applied water and to minimize water waste.

irrigation efficiency   the ratio of irrigation water consumed by evapotranspiration to the total amount applied to a field or farm; the efficiency of irrigation water application and use, determined by calculating the amount of water *beneficially* applied divided by the *total* volume applied, expressed as a percentage, decimal, or ratio. Irrigation efficiency can be determined for single or multiple irrigations systems and for farm, district, or basin applications. Higher irrigation efficiencies can be expected from well-designed, well-maintained systems.

irrigation frequency   the time interval between irrigations.

irrigation plan   a two-dimensional, drawn-to-scale plan illustrating the layout of an irrigation system's components and related specifications. Irrigation pipes, heads, and schedules should be specified.

irrigation return flow   applied water that is not transpired, evaporated, or infiltrated into a groundwater basin but that returns to a surface water source.

irrigation scheduling   use of an automated timetable for applying irrigation water in order to match watering schedules to plant needs and optimize outdoor water use.

irrigation timer   a device that can be manually programmed to regulate when and how much water a landscape receives.

irrigation water requirement   a measure of the water required in addition to precipitation to obtain desired crop yield under normal field conditions.

irrigation zone   see *hydrozone*.

K

kilowatt-hour (kWh)   a unit of electric power equivalent to the energy provided by one thousand watts acting for one hour.

L

land leveling   the practice of moving earth on irrigated fields to improve surface slope and smoothness in order to facilitate water application. Land leveling, which can include laser leveling, can produce uniform slopes in the direction of irrigation streams and may enhance salinity control by improving the uniformity of surface irrigation.

landscape area   the combination of irrigated and nonirrigated turf and plant areas, natural undeveloped areas, and decorative water features comprising a landscape; excludes building footprints and hardscapes (e.g., driveways and parking lots) unless otherwise noted.

landscape coefficient   a factor used to modify reference evapotranspiration and to calculate water requirements for a hydrozone.

landscape irrigation audit   see *irrigation audit*.

landscape water requirements   a measure of the supplemental water required to maintain the optimum health and appearance of landscape plants and decorative water features.

laser land leveling   precision leveling of cultivated fields to improve irrigation efficiency; also called *precision field leveling*.

lateral the water delivery pipeline that supplies water to an irrigation nozzle or emitter.

leaching the removal or flushing of salts from the soil by water moving through the soil.

leaching requirement the theoretical amount of irrigation water that must pass downward through soil beyond the plant root zone to maintain soil salinity within acceptable levels for sustained crop growth; expressed as a depth of water in inches, feet, acre-inches per acre, or acre-feet per acre. The leaching requirement is dependent on crop tolerance for salinity, salinity of the irrigation water, and annual evapotranspiration.

leak detection methods for identifying water leakage from pipes, plumbing fixtures, and fittings.

level basin a level area of land surrounded by earthen dikes that retain applied irrigation water until it infiltrates the soil.

lifeline rate a minimum, sometimes subsidized, rate for an adequate amount of water to meet basic human needs.

limited irrigation an irrigation schedule incorporating planned water deficits for drought-tolerant crops or crops in stages of growth that can tolerate less water.

limited tillage see *minimum tillage*.

limited turf areas turf grass limited to a prescribed portion of a landscaped area.

looped pooling the process of assigning one water allocation to a group of metered accounts in a looped system (a set of meters serving the same irrigation main). Total consumption for all accounts is compared with the water allocation.

low energy precision application (LEPA) a center-pivot agricultural irrigation system that applies water directly onto or near the soil by distributing it at low pressure from an overhead lateral pipeline through drop tubes and orifice-controlled emitters.

low-volume faucet a faucet that uses no more than 2.5 gallons per minute at 80 pounds of pressure per square inch; also referred to as *low-flow faucet*.

low-volume showerhead a showerhead that uses no more than 2.5 gallons per minute at 80 pounds of pressure per square inch; also referred to as *low-flow showerhead*.

low-volume toilet (water closet) a toilet that uses no more than 1.6 gallons per flush; also referred to as *low-flow toilet*.

low-volume urinal a urinal that uses no more than 1.0 gallons per flush; also referred to as *low-flow urinal*.

low-water-use landscape use of plants (often native species) that are appropriate to an area's climate and growing conditions. See *Xeriscape*.

low-water-use plants plants that require less than 30% of reference evapotranspiration to maintain optimum health and appearance.

M

main the pressurized water delivery pipeline that delivers water from the supply system to the customer's service lines.

management efficiency the portion of irrigation water beneficially applied through scheduling, maintenance, and repair of irrigation systems; expressed as a percentage or decimal fraction of total irrigation water applied.

marginal-cost pricing a rate design method in which prices reflect the costs associated with producing the next increment of supply.

market penetration the extent to which a water-efficiency measure is actually implemented by targeted water users.

master meter a large meter located upstream of other smaller meters and used for water accounting, billing purposes, or both.

matched precipitation rate an equal rate of water delivery from sprinkler heads with varying arc patterns within an irrigation circuit. Matched precipitation rates are central to achieving uniform distribution of irrigation water.

maximum water allowance the maximum amount of water that may be applied to an irrigated area.

medium-water-use plants plants that require 30 to 50% of reference evapotranspiration to maintain optimum health and appearance.

megawatt one million watts; a measure of power plant output.

membrane a barrier, usually thin, that permits the passage of particles only up to a certain size or of a special nature.

meter an instrument that measures water use; often installed by a water utility to measure end uses, such as uses by a household, building, facility, or irrigation system.

mgd million gallons per day.

mgy million gallons per year.

microclimate the climate conditions of a specific habitat or place in a small, limited area.

microirrigation an irrigation system with small, closely spaced outlets (either emitters or small sprinkler heads) that frequently apply small amounts of water at low pressure either above or below the soil surface. Microirrigation includes several methods, including bubbler, drip or trickle, mist or spray, and subsurface.

microorganism a microscopic organism observable only through a microscope.

mineral a naturally occurring inorganic substance having a definite chemical composition and structure.

minimum tillage a practice that minimizes soil water loss and soil erosion by retaining crop residuals. Also referred to as *limited tillage*.

moisture stress a condition of physiological stress in a plant caused by a lack of water.

MOU Memorandum of Understanding.

mulch a protective covering (e.g., usually leaves, bark, straw, or other organic materials) placed around plants to minimize weed growth, reduce evaporation of moisture from the soil surface, and maintain uniform temperatures around plant roots.

multiple start times an irrigation schedule involving more than one irrigation cycle per circuit in a given day.

N

native landscape   a landscape whose turf and plants are indigenous to the area.

native plants   plants that are indigenous to an area and thus require little or no supplemental irrigation after becoming established.

natural flow   the flow of a stream under natural rather than regulated conditions; unaffected by diversions, storage, imports, exports, return flows, or changes in use caused by modifications in land use.

natural landscape   a landscape designed to reflect the character and spirit of nature by arrangement of plants in a context that simulates their arrangement in nature; may consist exclusively of native plants or incorporate a small number of nonnative exotic and ornamental plants.

net benefits   the numerical difference between total benefits and total costs. See also *cost-effectiveness*.

net depletion   total water consumed by irrigation or other uses in an area; equal to water withdrawn minus return flow.

net present value   the present value of benefits minus the present value of costs.

net water demand   the amount of water needed to meet all requirements in a water service area; includes consumptive use, evapotranspiration of applied water (ETAW), irrecoverable losses from the distribution system, and outflow leaving the service area but does not include water reused within a service area. Also called *net water use*.

neutron probe   an instrument that measures soil moisture content by emitting "fast neutrons" from a radioactive source placed in the soil.

nonconsumptive use   water withdrawn for use but not consumed and thus returned to the source.

nonfunctional landscape   a landscape designed for aesthetics rather than to support a practical use or activity.

nonresidential water use   water use by industrial, commercial, institutional, public, and agricultural users.

no-tillage agriculture   a practice that reduces soil water loss and erosion by not tilling the soil.

O

operating pressure   the water pressure required to operate a water supply system, plumbing fixture, appliance, or other piece of water-using equipment, usually measured in pounds per square inch.

orifice   an opening through which a fluid can pass.

overdraft   see *groundwater overdraft*.

overspray   the application of water from a sprinkler system beyond the areas intended for irrigation, usually nonlandscaped areas such as sidewalks, pavements, and structures.

oxidation   a chemical reaction in which a molecule, atom, or ion loses electrons to an oxidant.

ozonation   the process of applying ozone to a liquid for disinfection.

P

pathogens   disease-producing microorganisms (e.g., bacteria, viruses, fungi, and protozoa).

peak demand (water)   the highest total water use experienced by a water supply system, measured on an hourly, daily, monthly, or annual basis.

peak load (power)   the maximum electrical energy used in a stated period of time, usually computed over an interval of one hour during the day, week, month, or year.

per capita residential use   residential water use divided by the total population served.

per capita use   the amount of water used by one person during a standard period of time; in relation to water use, expressed in gallons per capita per day.

percolation   the downward movement of water through soil or alluvium to a groundwater table.

perennial yield   the maximum annual quantity of water that can be withdrawn from a groundwater basin over a long period of time (during which water supply conditions approximate average conditions) without causing groundwater overdraft. Also called *sustained yield*.

permeability   the capability of soil or other geologic formations to transmit water.

plan view   a representation of a landscape on a two-dimensional surface; a bird's-eye view.

plant water requirement   the amount of irrigation water needed to replace moisture depleted from the soil around plant roots as a result of evapotranspiration.

playa   a depression in a basin with a relatively impervious surface that lacks an outlet for water runoff and that inhibits infiltration.

point source   a specific site from which waste or polluted water is discharged into a body of water, when the source can be identified.

pollutant   a contaminant at a concentration high enough to endanger an aquatic environment or public health.

polymer   a group of water-absorbing compounds; a chain of organic molecules produced by joining primary units called *monomers*. Polymers are used as soil amendments in landscaping applications to increase water-holding capacity.

polyphosphate   molecularly dehydrated orthophosphate; used as a corrosion inhibitor.

potable water   water suitable for drinking.

pounds per square inch (psi)   a standard measure of water pressure.

practical turf areas   turf areas that serve a functional purpose and require supplemental irrigation.

precipitate   an insoluble product of an aqueous chemical reaction, usually a crystalline compound that grows in size to become settleable.

precipitation rate (irrigation)   the amount of water applied in a specific unit of time during landscape or agricultural irrigation.

preirrigation   irrigation of an area prior to planting a crop to increase water availability in the soil.

present value future expenditures expressed in current dollars by adjusting for a discount rate that accounts for financing costs.

pressure-compensating emitter a drip irrigation emitter designed to deliver water at a consistent flow rate under a range of operating pressures.

pressure loss loss in water pressure caused by friction of water against the inner walls of pipe or system components.

pressure reducer a component designed to reduce water pressure, sometimes used in water supply system pipe or irrigation lines.

pressure regulator a device used to limit water pressure.

pressurized-tank toilet a toilet that flushes by using pressure from the waterline entering a pressurized plastic vessel inside the tank; also known as a *flushometer-tank toilet*.

price elasticity of demand a measure of the responsiveness of customer water use to changes in the price of water; measured by the percentage change in use divided by the percentage change in price.

pricing signals rate structures that encourage water conservation.

prior appropriation a water law doctrine under which users who can demonstrate earlier use of a particular water source are given rights that take precedence over all future users of the source.

project yield the water supply attributed to all features of a water supply project, including integrated operation of units that could be operated individually.

public trust doctrine a judicial doctrine under which the state holds its navigable waters and underlying beds in trust for the public and is required or authorized to protect the public interest in regard to such water sources. All water rights issued by the state are subject to the overriding interest of the public and the exercise of the public trust by state administrative agencies.

R

rain sensor (or rain-sensing device or rain shutoff device) a sensor system that automatically adjusts the schedule for or shuts off an irrigation system before or during rainfall.

rain switch a switch on an irrigation system used to prevent irrigations during (and sometimes after) precipitation.

rationing mandatory water-use restrictions, usually imposed during a drought or other emergency water conditions.

recharge the addition of water to the groundwater supply by natural (precipitation) or artificial (infiltration or pumping) means.

reclaimed water (or reclaimed wastewater) treated, recycled wastewater of a quality suitable for nonpotable applications, such as landscape irrigation, decorative water features, and nonfood crops; also described as *treated sewage effluent*.

recycled water (1) a type of reuse water usually run repeatedly through a closed system. (2) sometimes used to refer to reclaimed water.

reference evapotranspiration (ET_0) the evapotranspiration of a broad expanse of adequately watered cool-season grass 4 to 6 inches in height. Reference evapotranspiration is used as a standard measurement for determining maximum water allowances for plants so that regional differences in climate can be accommodated.

remote operation of controllers operation of an irrigation controller with a remote, hand-held electronic device consisting of a receiver located at the controller and a transmitter that is carried in the field.

Residential End Use Study (REUS) the *Residential End Uses of Water* study published by the American Water Works Association Research Foundation.

residential water use water use in homes (e.g., for drinking, food preparation, bathing, washing clothes and dishes, flushing toilets, and watering lawns and gardens).

retrofit to change, alter, or adjust plumbing fixtures or other equipment or appliances to save water or make them operate more efficiently.

return flow water that reaches a surface water or groundwater source after being released from its point of use; thus it becomes available for further use.

REUS see *Residential End Use Study.*

reuse (1) the additional use of previously used water; see also *recycled water.* (2) the beneficial use of treated wastewater; see also *reclaimed water.*

revenue-producing water water that is metered and sold.

reverse osmosis a pressure-driven membrane separation process that removes ions, salts, and other dissolved solids and nonvolatile organics from water.

riparian located on the banks of a stream or other body of water.

riparian rights a water law doctrine under which authorization to use water from a stream is based on ownership of the property adjacent to the stream.

runoff surface water from irrigation or precipitation that is not absorbed by the soil or landscape to which it is applied and thus flows from the area.

S

Safe Drinking Water Act (SDWA) federal drinking water quality legislation administered by the U.S. Environmental Protection Agency through state primacy agencies.

safe yield the maximum amount of surface water or groundwater that can be withdrawn from a source over time without compromising its quality or its ability to continue providing that same amount of water; the amount of water that can be reliably withdrawn from a groundwater source because it does not exceed the source's recharge rate.

saline water slightly saline water contains 1,000 to 3,000 milligrams per liter (m/L) of dissolved solids; moderately saline water contains 3,000 to 10,000 mg/L; and highly saline water contains 10,000 to 35,000 mg/L.

salinity the concentration of mineral salts dissolved in water, measured by weight (total dissolved solids), electrical conductivity, or osmotic pressure.

salt balance the condition that occurs when the amount of salts added to the soil through irrigation and the amount removed by leaching are equal (i.e., no net gain or net loss of salt in the crop root zone).

salt water intrusion (or saline water intrusion) the movement of salt water into a body of freshwater, either surface water or groundwater.

scale   precipitate that forms on surfaces in contact with water as a result of a chemical or physical change.

seasonal application efficiency   the sum of the evapotranspiration of applied water and the leaching requirement divided by total applied water; expressed as a percentage.

seasonal rate   a pricing structure in which the amount charged per unit of water varies by season; higher rates are usually charged during the peak-demand season (usually the summer months).

secondary treatment   with regard to sewage, the biological process of reducing suspended, colloidal, and dissolved organic matter in effluent from primary treatment systems; usually carried out through the use of trickling filters or by the activated sludge process.

sediment   soil or mineral material transported by water and deposited in streams or other bodies of water.

seepage   the gradual movement of a fluid into, through, or from a porous medium.

self-closing faucet   a faucet that automatically shuts off water flow after a designated amount of time, usually seconds.

semiarid climate   a climate characterized by 10 to 20 inches of annual rainfall.

service area or territory   the geographic area served by a water utility's distribution system.

sideroll sprinkler system   a sprinkler irrigation system in which the pipe lateral forms an axle allowing the system to be rolled to the next irrigation area within the field. Water is not applied when the system is being moved.

sidestream filtration system   a rapid-sand or high-efficiency cartridge that draws water from a cooling tower basin, filters out particulates, and returns the filtered water to the cooling tower, enabling the system to operate more efficiently while using less water.

simple payback period   the length of time, usually in months or years, over which the cost savings associated with a conservation measure must accrue to equal the cost of implementing the measure.

simple water budget   a water budget that is the product of reference evapotranspiration, irrigated area, and a conversion factor.

siphonic-jet urinal   a urinal that automatically flushes when the water flowing continuously into its tank reaches a preset level.

skip-row planting   a method of reducing crop water requirements by leaving one or more unplanted strips between planted rows.

softening   the removal of hardness (calcium and magnesium ions) from water.

soil amendment   the addition of organic and inorganic materials to soil to improve its texture, nutrient load, moisture-holding capacity, and infiltration rate.

soil moisture deficit   the amount of water required to saturate the plant root zone at the time of irrigation, expressed as a depth of water in inches or feet.

soil moisture replacement   the amount of water applied to replace a portion or all of the soil moisture deficit, expressed as a depth of water in inches or feet.

soil moisture sensor (or soil moisture sensing device)   a sensing device placed in the plant root zone to measure the amount of water in the soil. Soil moisture sensors are often used to determine the amount of irrigation water required by plants (usually agricultural crops) and to develop an appropriate irrigation schedule.

soil moisture tension   negative pressure of soil water relative to atmospheric pressure.

soil tensiometer   see *tensiometer.*

soil texture   the classification of soil based on its percentage of sand, silt, and clay.

soils report   a report by a soils engineer indicating soil type(s) and depth, uniformity, infiltration rates, and pH for a given site.

source meter   a water meter that records the total volume of water withdrawn from a surface water or groundwater source, the total volume purchased from a wholesale supplier, or the total flow into a facility (e.g., for water treatment).

spray head (or sprinkler head)   a sprinkler irrigation system nozzle that is installed on a riser and that delivers water in a fixed pattern.

spray irrigation   sprinkler irrigation using spray heads that are mounted on fixed or pop-up risers and that have relatively high precipitation rates.

sprinkler irrigation   overhead delivery of water to land through nozzles (sprinkler heads) mounted on a pressurized pipe that is either stationary or mobile. Nozzles include bubblers, sprinkler spray heads, stream rotors, and impact heads. Precipitation rates vary depending on system layout, type of head used, and water pressure.

standard industrial classification (SIC) codes   four-digit codes established by the U.S. Office of Management and Budget and used to classify nonresidential facilities (e.g., industrial, commercial, and institutional) by the type of activity for which they are used.

station   an irrigation area served by one valve or by a set of valves that operate simultaneously, as programmed by an irrigation controller.

streamflow   the rate of water flow past a specified point in a channel.

stream rotors   sprinkler irrigation heads that deliver rotating streams of water in arcs or full circles at relatively low precipitation rates. Stream rotors use gear mechanisms and water pressure to generate a single stream or multiple streams. Multiple stream rotors can match precipitation from varying arc patterns.

subirrigation   application of water to the plant root zone by raising the water table.

submeter   a water meter that records water use by a specific process, by a building within a larger facility, or by a unit within a larger service connection (such as apartments in a multifamily building).

subsidence   lowering of the land surface as a result of changes occurring in the underlying earth, such as reduced groundwater levels caused by overdraft.

subsurface irrigation   the application of water below the soil surface, generally with a buried drip irrigation system.

sulfuric acid treatment   a chemical process that lowers the pH in cooling tower water by converting a portion of the calcium bicarbonate to the more soluble calcium sulfate; controls scale or mineral buildup and allows the cooling tower to operate more efficiently.

supplemental irrigation   the application of water to a landscape to supplement natural precipitation.

surcharge   a special charge included on a water bill to recover costs associated with a particular activity or use or to convey a message about water prices to customers.

surface irrigation   the application of water to land by surface flow; also called *gravity irrigation*.

surface water supply   water supplied from a stream, lake, or reservoir.

surge flow   a surface (gravity) irrigation method through which water is applied to crops intermittently.

surplus water   developed water supplies in excess of contract entitlement or apportioned water.

T

tailwater   applied irrigation water that runs off the lower end of a field. Tailwater is not necessarily lost because it can be collected and reused on the same or an adjacent field.

tailwater recovery system   a system used to collect, store, and reuse irrigation water and other runoff; the runoff is collected in a tailwater pit.

tall fescue   a hybridized cool-season turf grass characterized by deeper root systems and greater drought tolerance than bluegrass.

tariff   the schedule of a utility's rates and charges; rate for marginal cost of water.

tensiometer   a device for measuring water pressure (moisture) in the soil.

thatch   the buildup of organic material at the base of turf grass blades. Thatch repels water and reduces infiltration capacity.

toilet dam   a flexible rectangular device placed across the bottom of a toilet tank to reduce the amount of water used per flush.

toilet displacement device   a toilet retrofit device (e.g., a dam, bag, or bottle) designed to displace water in the toilet tank in order to reduce the volume required for flushing.

toilet flapper   the valve that controls flushing in a gravity-tank toilet.

total dissolved solids (TDS)   a quantitative measure of the dissolved minerals remaining in water after evaporation has occurred; usually expressed in milligrams per liter. See also *salinity*.

transfer (conveyance of a water right)   the passing or conveyance of title to a water right; a permanent assignment as opposed to a temporary lease or disposal of water.

transpiration   the transfer of water vapor from plants to air, a process involving absorption of water through the plant's root system and evaporation from wet plant cells to the atmosphere.

trapway   the outlet of a toilet where the waste exits to the drainline.

turbidity   a suspension of fine particles that obscures light rays and requires many days for sedimentation because of the small size of the particles.

turf (or turf grass)   hybridized grass that forms a dense growth of blades and roots when regularly mowed; a surface layer of earth containing mowed grass with its roots.

U

ultralow-volume toilet   see *low-volume toilet*.

unaccounted-for water   water that does not go through meters (e.g., water lost from leaks or theft) and thus cannot be accounted for by the utility.

underirrigation   the difference between the amount of water stored in a plant root zone during irrigation (soil moisture replacement) and the amount needed to refill the root zone to field capacity (soil moisture deficit); expressed as a depth of water in inches or feet.

uniform rate   a pricing structure in which the price per unit of water is constant, regardless of the amount used.

unmetered water   water delivered but not measured for accounting and billing purposes.

V

variable charge   the portion of a water bill that varies with water use; also known as a *commodity charge*.

variable cost   water utility costs that vary with the amount of water produced or sold.

W

warm-season turf grass   turf grass that grows vigorously during warm summer months and that generally loses its green color and is dormant during winter if the average temperature drops below about 50°F. Some turf grass may die if exposed to subfreezing temperatures for extended periods. Warm-season turf grasses include: Bermuda grass, buffalo grass, St. Augustine grass, and zoysia grass.

wastewater   the used water, liquid waste, or drainage from homes, businesses, industries, and institutions in a community.

water allowance   see *water budget*.

water audit   an on-site survey and assessment of water-using hardware, fixtures, equipment, landscaping, irrigation systems, and management practices to determine the efficiency of water use and to develop recommendations for improving indoor and outdoor water-use efficiency. Also referred to as a *water-use survey*.

water balance diagram   a diagram that tracks water flow through a building or facility, showing total inflows and total outflows (consumption, irrigation, evaporation, and leaks and losses).

water banking   the storage of unused water for future use; the process of adding unused water allocations to future allocations.

water budget   (1) the amount of water required to maintain plants in a landscape. (2) a method of establishing water-efficiency standards by prescribing limits on water applications to irrigated landscapes.

water conservation   (1) any beneficial reduction in water loss, waste, or use. (2) reduction in water use accomplished by implementation of water conservation or water-efficiency measures. (3) improved water management practices that reduce or enhance the beneficial use of water.

water conservation incentive   a policy or regulation, rate strategy, or public education campaign designed to promote customer awareness about the value of reducing water use and to motivate consumers to adopt specific water conservation measures.

water conservation measure   an action, behavioral change, device, technology, or improved design or process implemented to reduce water loss, waste, or use.

water efficiency   (1) accomplishment of a function, task, process, or result with the minimal amount of water feasible. (2) an indicator of the relationship between the amount of water required for a particular purpose and the quantity of water used or delivered.

water-efficiency measure   a specific tool (device or technology) or practice (behavioral change) that results in more efficient water use and thus reduces water demand. The value and cost-effectiveness of a water-efficiency measure must be evaluated in relation to its effects on the use and cost of other natural resources (e.g., energy or chemicals); also called *water conservation measure*.

water-efficiency standard   a value or criterion establishing maximum or acceptable levels or conditions of water use.

water-efficient landscape   a landscape that minimizes water requirements through appropriate design, installation, and management.

water feature   a pool, fountain, water sculpture, waterfall, constructed pond or lake, canal, channel, or other decorative feature that uses water as part of its design composition.

water harvesting   the capture and use of runoff from rainfall and other precipitation (e.g., the collection of rainwater in cisterns).

water-holding capacity   the volume of water that a specific soil can hold.

water pressure   the average flowing pressure of moving water.

water quality   the chemical, physical, and biological characteristics of water, usually characterized in regard to the water's suitability for a particular purpose or use.

water reclamation   the treatment of wastewater to make it reusable, usually for nonpotable purposes; includes water recycling.

water recycling   the treatment of urban wastewater to a level rendering it suitable for a specific, direct, beneficial use.

water right   under the riparian system, a legally protected right to take possession of water occurring in a natural waterway and to divert that water for beneficial use; under the prior appropriation system, a property or legal claim to withdraw a specified amount of water in a specified time frame for a beneficial use.

water saver   a term applied to toilets that use 3.5 gallons per flush, not to be confused with low-volume toilets, which use a maximum of 1.6 gallons per flush.

watershed   the regional area of land from which all precipitation and runoff drain into a single water source, such as a reservoir or stream; also called *drainage basin* or *river basin*.

water system   a series of interconnected conveyance facilities owned and operated by a drinking water supplier; some utilities operate multiple water systems.

water table   (1) in an unconfined aquifer, the top of the saturated zone. (2) the level at which a well penetrates the top of an unconfined aquifer.

water use   in a restrictive sense, water that is actually used for a specific purpose (end use) or by a particular customer group, such as residential, industrial, or agricultural users; in a broader sense, water use ;pertains to human interaction with and influence on the hydrologic cycle and includes elements such as water withdrawal and delivery, consumptive use, wastewater release, wastewater reuse, return flows, and instream uses.

water-use efficiency   the water-use requirements of a particular device, fixture, appliance, process, piece of equipment, or activity—usually compared with its optimal (minimum) water-use requirements; marketable crop production per unit of water consumed through evapotranspiration.

water-use survey   see *water audit*.

water year   a continuous 12-month period for which hydrologic records are compiled and summarized.

watt-hour (Wh)   a unit of electrical energy equal to one watt of power steadily supplied to, or taken from, an electrical circuit for one hour.

weather adjustment   water demand, revenues, or other variables adjusted to approximate those of a "normal" weather year; also known as weather normalization.

weather station   a facility or location where meteorological data are gathered, recorded, and released; one of a network of observation posts where meteorological data are recorded.

weed   any undesirable or troublesome plant, especially one that grows profusely where it is not wanted.

wholesale water   water purchased or sold for the purpose of resale.

withdrawal   water diverted or withdrawn from a surface water or groundwater source.

X

Xeriscape™   a trademarked term denoting landscaping that involves the selection, placement, and care of low-water-use and native ground cover, turf, plants, shrubs, and trees. Xeriscape landscaping is based on seven principles: proper planning and design, soil analysis and improvement, practical turf areas, appropriate plant selection, efficient irrigation, mulching, and appropriate maintenance.

Acknowledgments

A number of sources were consulted in the compilation of this glossary. Those depended on primarily include: *The Drinking Water Dictionary*, James M. Symons, Lee C. Bradley Jr., and Theodore C. Cleveland, eds., American Water Works Assoc., Denver, 2000; *California Water Plan Update, Bulletin 160-98*, California Dept. of Water Resources, Sacramento, Calif., November 1998; *Estimated Use of Water in the United States in 1995*, Wayne B. Solley, Robert R. Pierce, and Howard A. Perlman, U.S. Geological Survey Circular 1200, U.S. Dept. of the Interior, U.S. Geological Survey, Reston, Va., 1998; *Water Conservation Plan Guidelines*, U.S. Environmental Protection Agency, (EPA-832-D-98-001), Washington, D.C., August 1998; *Soil, Plant & Water Relationships*, Charles M. Burt, Irrigation Training and Research Center, California Polytechnic State University, San Luis Obispo, Calif., 1992; *Effective Use of Water in Irrigated Agriculture, Report No. 113*, Council for Agricultural Science and Technology, Ames, Iowa, June 1988.

Conversion Factors

VOLUME OF WATER

1 gallon (gal)	=	0.833 Imperial gal
	=	0.1337 ft³
	=	4.951 × 10⁻³ yd³
	=	3.785 L
	=	.003785 m³
1 Imperial gallon	=	1.201 gal
	=	0.16054 ft³
	=	4.546 L
1 cubic foot (ft³)	=	1,728 in.³
	=	7.481 gal
	=	0.03704 yd³
	=	2.832 × 10⁴ cm³
	=	28.32 L
	=	0.02832 m³
1 liter (L)	=	0.2642 gal
	=	61.02 in.³
	=	0.03531 ft³
	=	1,000 cm³
	=	1 × 10⁻³ m³
1 cubic meter (m³)	=	264.2 gal
	=	35.32 ft³
	=	1.307 yd³
	=	1 × 10⁶ cm³
	=	1,000 L
1 acre-foot (acre-ft)	=	325,851 gal
	=	43,560 ft³
	=	1,234 m³
1 inch of rain	=	5.610 gal/yd²
	=	2.715 × 10⁴ gal/acre
1 million gallons (mg)	=	3.069 acre-ft

FLOW RATES OF WATER

1 gallon per minute (gpm)	=	3.785 L/min
	=	1.44 x10⁻³ mgd
	=	2.23 × 10⁻³ cfs
	=	4.42 × 10⁻³ acre-ft/day
1 million gallons per day (mgd)		
	=	3,785 m³/day
	=	694 gpm
	=	1.55 cfs
	=	3.069 acre-ft/day
1 cubic foot per second (cfs)		
	=	2,447 m³/day
	=	449 gpm
	=	0.646 mgd
	=	1.98 acre-ft/day
1 acre-foot per day (acre-ft/day)		
	=	1,233.48 m³/day
	=	226 gpm
	=	0.326 mgd
	=	0.504 cfs

AREA

1 acre (a)	=	0.40469 hectare (ha)
1 ha	=	2.4710 a
1 inch of rain	=	17.4 mg per square mile
	=	27,200 gals per acre

LENGTH

1 inch (in)	=	25.4 millimeters (mm)
	=	2.54 centimeters (cm)
1 mm	=	0.03937 in
	=	0.1 cm
1 foot (ft)	=	0.3048 meters (m)
1 m	=	3.2808 ft
1 mile (mi)	=	1.6093 kilometers (km)
1 km	=	0.6214 mi

WEIGHT OF WATER

1 gallon	=	8.34 lb
1 Imperial gallon	=	10.0 lb
1 cubic inch	=	0.0361 lb
1 cubic foot	=	62.4 lb
1 cubic meter	=	1 tonne

ENERGY

1 British thermal unit (Btu)		
	=	2.93 × 10⁴/kWh
1 kilowatt-hour (kWh)	=	3,412 Btu
1 therm	=	10⁵ Btu

PRESSURE

1 pound per square inch (psi)		
	=	0.06895 bar
	=	6.8948 kilopascals (kPa)
1 bar	=	14.5034 psi
	=	100 kPa
1 kPa	=	0.14505 psi
	=	0.01 bar

CONCENTRATION

1 parts per million (ppm)	=	1 milligram per liter (mg/L)

TEMPERATURE

degrees Celsius or Centigrade (°C)

$$°C = (°F - 32) \times 5/9$$

degrees Fahrenheit (°F) $= 32 + (°C \times 1.8)$

Index

Sumerians, 330
Surface (gravity) irrigation, 332. *See also* Irrigation, agricultural
    how they work, 336-337
    inefficiencies of, 337-339
    systems, 336-337
        flood, 333 (Table 5.1), 336-337
        furrow, 333 (Table 5.1), 336-337
        improved, 333 (Table 5.1), gravity 337
Surface runoff, 371, 373
Surge valves, 374-377
Swamp coolers. *See* Evaporative coolers
Swimming pools, 141, 143, 154, 179, 234, 258, 282, 281-288
    pool covers, 282, 283

T

Tailwater reuse, 383-385
Tailwater runoff, 370, 374, 383, 385
Tampa, Florida, 33-34, 36 (Table 2.5)
Tensiometers, 354, 355, 356, 359
Texas, 141, 173 (Table 3.1), 174, 187, 207, 231, 239, 331
    Austin, 162, 163, 164, 177, 187, 202, 205, 207, 276
        Xeriscape program, 162
    Corpus Christi, 183
    Lubbock, 331, 343, 349, 369, 382
    Texas Water Development Board, 231
Toilets, 18 (Table 2.1), 24-75, 236, 238, 239, 251, 252, 265, 280, 287, 317, 319-321
    alternative designs, 30-32
    automatic flushing sensors, 30
    ballcock, 28, 29, 35, 43, 58, 66, 67, 68, 71, 72, 73, 75
    blowout-jet, 39
    blowout-valve, 39
    composting, 24, 41, 47, 48, 48-49, 50, 51, 52, 53, 54, 55
    costs, 30, 35, 39-40
    dams, 56, 57, 58, 60
    diaphragm retrofit kits, 56, 58, 59
    displacement devices (bottles, bags, and bladders), 23, 56, 56-58, 65
    dual-flush, 29
    dual-flush adapters, 56, 59, 60, 67
    early closure devices, 56, 65-67
    electromechanical, 50 (Table 2.7)
    electromechanical hydraulic, 25 (Table 2.2), 27 (Table 2.4), 31, 40, 51 (Table 2.8)
    flapper valves, 29, 43, 47, 64, 68, 69, 70, 75
    flapperless, 31
    flow rates, 25, 31
    flushometer, 30, 60
    flushometer-tank (pressurized), 25 (Table 2.2), 27 (Table 2.4), 30, 31, 40, 43, 44, 46, 50 (Table 2.7), 51 (Table 2.8), 64
    flushometer-valve, 26 (Table 2.3), 27 (Table 2.4), 30, 31, 36, 37-38, 39, 40, 46, 51 (Table 2.8), 56, 58, 59, 62, 64, 67, 68, 70, 76
    frequency of use, 25 (Table 2.2), 25-27, 27 (Table 2.4), 64, 50 (Table 2.7), 51 (Table 2.8)
    gravity-tank, 25 (Table 2.2), 26 (Table 2.3), 27 (Table 2.4), 28, 28-29, 30, 31, 34-35, 38, 39, 40, 41, 42, 43, 46, 50 (Table 2.7), 51 (Table 2.8), 56, 57, 58, 59, 62, 63, 64, 65, 67, 68, 70, 74, 75
    high-volume, 20, 24, 25, 26, 27, 29, 32, 33, 34, 36, 37, 38, 39, 41, 42, 46, 56, 57, 58, 59, 60, 63, 67
    incinerator, 47, 49, 51, 52, 53, 54, 55
    installation, 27, 45-47
    leak detection dye tablets, 21, 23, 56, 70, 72, 73, 95
    leak repair, 67-76
    leakage, 21, 25, 29, 31, 47, 49, 58, 67-71
    low-volume, 24, 25, 27-47

performance, 24, 32-36
principles for operation, 28, 29, 30
pump-assisted, 32
rebate and replacement programs, 41, 42-45, 54
retrofit devices, 56-67
sensor-activated, 81, 105
siphon-jet, 39
siphonic, 31
types, 27-28
ultra-efficient, 27
water use and savings, 25-27, 25 (Table 2.2), 27 (Table 2.4), 36 (Table 2.5), 37 (Table 2.6), 51 (Table 2.8)
water-saver, 25, 27, 49
waterless, 24, 47-56
Tomatoes, 343
Total dissolved solids (TDS), 253, 260, 293
Training programs for conservation, 211, 239
    agricultural irrigation, 342 (Table 5.2), 351
Turf. *See* Turf grass
Turf grass, 242, 287 (Figure 4.17), 316
    area, 178-181
    colors, 171
    cool-season, 171, 173, 175, 180, 184, 204, 210
    curbside, 183
    dormancy, 171, 172, 184, 203, 219
    drought tolerances, 168, 173 (Table 3.1)
    drought-resistant, 168, 170, 171, 187
    functional, 157, 160, 170, 179, 180
    high-water, 143, 170, 177, 203
    low-water, 157, 163, 166, 167, 169, 170-179, 180, 185
    maintenance, 218-219
    medians, 170, 179
    narrow strips, 160, 170, 179, 183
    native, 172. *See also* Native plants
    nonfunctional, 160, 170, 172, 180
    tolerance, 172, 180
    United States, 171
    warm-season, 171-172
    watering needs, 201, 209, 218
    zones, 171

U

U.S. Bureau of Reclamation, 344, 348, 363, 364, 401
U.S. Clean Water Act, 236
U.S. Department of Agriculture, 243, 272, 285, 373, 401
    Economic Research Service, 337, 339
    Fish and Wildlife Service, 164
    Water Conservation Laboratory, 366
U.S. Department of Energy, 40, 237, 239, 249, 275, 282, 309, 311, 312, 401
    Federal Energy Management Program, 45, 237
U.S. Department of Housing and Urban Development, 17, 26, 128
U.S. Department of Interior, 401
U.S. Energy Policy Act of 1992, 17, 18 (Table 2.1), 20, 24, 40, 41, 63, 76, 84, 86, 95, 96, 102, 104, 112, 113, 236, 249, 251, 405 (Appendix A)
U.S. Environmental Protection Agency, 2, 181, 238, 239, 275, 280. *See also* Water Alliances for Voluntary Efficiency (WAVE)
U.S. General Accounting Office, 17
U.S. Geological Survey (USGS), 12, 15, 140, 230, 330, 336, 363, 401-404
U.S. National Weather Service, 400
    Automated Surface Observation Stations, 361
    Cooperative Station Network, 361
U.S. Safe Drinking Water Act, 4
Uniform Building Code (UBC), 43
Uniform Plumbing Code (UPC), 43
United Kingdom, 13, 31, 403
United States, 236, 238, 272, 280, 306, 401-402

Executive Orders, 236, 249, 251, 252
federal laws, 18 (Table 2.1), 19, 24, 40, 41, 84, 89, 95, 104, 112, 116-117, 251
Urinals, 18 (Table 2.1), 76-87, 236, 238, 239, 252, 265, 320, 321
    automatic flushing sensors, 30, 83
    blow-out valve, 81
    composting, 76, 78, 80, 81, 82, 83, 84, 85, 86, 87
    costs, 83
    flow rate, 76, 77, 82, 84
    flushometer, 77, 80, 84, 86
    flushometer-valve, 77
    frequency of use, 77 (Table 2.10)
    high-volume, 77, 80, 82, 83, 85, 86
    installation, 86
    leakage, 81-87
    low-volume, 76, 77
    performance, 81
    rebate and replacement programs, 84, 85-87
    repair, 81
    retrofit devices, 80-81
    sensor-activated, 81
    siphonic, 77, 81
    types, 76
    water use and savings, 76-77, 77 (Table 2.10)
    waterless, 76, 78-80

V

Vacuum pumps, 237, 258, 288, 290, 291, 309
Vehicle-washing and automatic car washes, 253-256

W

Walden Pond, 50
Washington
    Seattle, 142 (Figure 3.2), 211, 255-256, 289
    Wastewater, 149, 150, 184, 223
Wastewater, 13, 20, 38, 44, 45, 50, 51, 61, 65, 72, 73, 82, 93, 94, 96, 110, 111, 121, 130, 230, 235, 237, 238, 240, 241, 243, 249, 258, 260, 261, 263, 264, 265, 273, 274, 278, 279, 280, 285, 287, 288, 289, 302, 322, 343, 344
Water
    bills, 22, 44, 72, 74, 151, 161, 163, 184, 186, 204, 206, 210, 218, 242, 243, 245, 251, 280, 285, 318, 320
    costs, 141, 143, 146, 150, 151, 154, 170, 181, 211, 235-236, 340, 343, 346, 353, 383, 409 (Appendix D)
    education, 33
    nonpotable, 19, 149, 184, 235, 239, 256, 257, 261, 275, 286, 287, 302, 306, 307
    potable, 19, 149, 150, 179, 184, 187, 188, 222, 235, 237, 258, 264, 280, 282, 289
    reclaimed, 149, 150, 179, 222, 230, 235, 237, 238, 239, 253, 255, 258, 267, 288, 302, 330, 343
    recycling, 202, 236, 237, 238, 239, 254, 258, 261, 262, 266, 267, 272, 277, 279, 280, 286, 287, 288, 302, 311, 319, 344
    reuse, 19, 149-150, 236, 238, 251, 253, 259, 260, 261, 262, 264, 266, 267, 269, 272, 274, 275, 279, 280, 283, 286, 287, 288, 290, 291, 302, 306, 307, 310, 311, 312, 319, 331, 334, 337, 341, 342 (Table 5.2), 381, 383-385
    seawater, 263
    stormwater, 151, 161, 164, 201, 319
    sustainable, 150, 236, 241, 347
Water Alliances for Voluntary Efficiency (WAVE) program, 238
Water and sewer rates, costs, and savings by volume of use (Appendix D), 409
Water audit, 11, 322
    agricultural, basic steps in, 350

DISCLAIMER

THIS HANDBOOK IS DESIGNED to provide information on water use, water-efficiency measures, and conservation. It is sold with the understanding that the publisher and author are not engaged in rendering engineering, technical, legal, or other professional services. If engineering or other assistance is required, the services of a competent professional should be sought.

It is not the purpose of this handbook to reprint all the information that is otherwise available, but rather to complement, amplify, and supplement other texts and information materials. You are urged to read all available material on water use, water-efficiency measures, and conservation, learn as much as possible, and tailor the information to their individual needs.

Every effort has been made to make this handbook as complete and accurate as possible. However, there *may be mistakes,* both typographical and in content. Although the information in this handbook is believed to accurately represent the current state of the art, neither the author, nor WaterPlow Press, nor any of their employees or representatives, makes any warranty, express or implied, with respect to the accuracy, effectiveness, or usefulness of any information, method, product, or material in this handbook, nor assumes any liability or responsibility for the use of any information, methods, products, or materials disclosed herein, or for losses or damages arising from such use. Therefore, this text should be used only as a general guide and not as the ultimate source of water use and conservation information. Furthermore, this handbook contains information that is current only up to the printing date.

The author and WaterPlow Press shall have neither liability nor responsibility to any person or entity with respect to any errors, omissions, or loss or damage caused, or alleged to have been caused, directly or indirectly, by the information contained in this handbook.

The mention or omission of any person, entity, corporation, organization, agency, publication, or trade name for products, services, or businesses does not represent or imply an approval, endorsement, or criticism.